SUBSCRIPTION NOTICE

This Wiley product is updated on a periodic basis with supplements to reflect important changes in the subject matter. If you purchased this product directly from John Wiley & Sons, Inc., we have already recorded your subscription for this update service.

If, however, you purchased this product from a bookstore and wish to receive (1) the current update at no additional charge, and (2) future updates and revised or related volumes billed separately with a 30-day examination review, please send your name, company name (if applicable), address, and the title of the product to:

Supplement Department
John Wiley & Sons, Inc.
One Wiley Drive
Somerset, NJ 08875
1-800-225-5945

HAZARDOUS SUBSTANCES IN BUILDINGS: LIABILITY, LITIGATION, AND ABATEMENT

C. JAYE BERGER, Esquire

Wiley Law Publications

JOHN WILEY & SONS, INC.

New York • Chichester • Brisbane • Toronto • Singapore

Library of Congress Cataloging-in-Publication Data

Berger, C. Jaye.
    Hazardous substances in buildings : liability, litigation, and
abatement / by C. Jaye Berger.
       p.   cm. — (Environmental law library)
    Includes bibliographical references.
    ISBN 0-471-52777-7 (cloth) : $105.00 (est.)
    1. Liability for hazardous substances pollution damages—United
States. 2. Hazardous substances—Law and legislation—United
States. 3. Asbestos—Law and legislation—United States.
4. Asbestos in building—United States. 5. Actions and defenses—
United States. I. Title. II. Series.
KF1299.H39B47   1992
343.73′0783631791—dc20
[347.303783631791]   91-24760
                                       CIP
                                       Rev.

Printed in the United States of America

10 9 8 7 6 5 4 3 2 1

To the memory of my husband, John A. Ackermann,
and my parents, Aaron M. Berger, Esq. and Marcia Berger.

PREFACE

When I was first asked to write a book about environmental law, I thought about all that had already been written and I realized that no one had yet written a comprehensive guide to all the key environmental issues pertaining to buildings. Much of what has been written is focused on hazardous waste sites and landfill in noncity areas.

Almost every week we hear about new and proposed laws. In New York City, we have experienced a couple of emergency situations in which occupants of residential homes and bystanders were faced with exposure to asbestos after steam pipes exploded. We hear about insurance policy exclusions for environmental issues. Renovations in office buildings raise many environmental concerns because hazardous substances may be stirred up. Those who own, manage, live or work in buildings need more information about these issues and advice on how to handle them in a way that will prevent or minimize health risks and property damage.

I set about the task of writing a comprehensive guide to dealing with hazardous substances in buildings in order to fill this void. All the key areas that anyone who owns or manages a building or a home needs to know about are discussed.

As an attorney, I have written about the legal and contractual aspects of these issues. I have called upon top-notch nonlawyer experts to write chapters about the areas they work in and know best. All of these people have hands-on experience in these areas.

I have written the book to be readable by lawyers and nonlawyers alike. Although new lawsuits are constantly being commenced and decided and laws are being proposed, the hard core of information in this book will continue to hold true for a long time to come. New events, legislative amendments, and decisions will appear in Supplements issued annually.

The more you know, the better you can plan to avoid property damage, health risks, and litigation. This book will be of use to you in whatever aspect of environmental issues you are involved.

New York City　　　　　　　　　　　　　　　　　　C. JAYE BERGER, ESQ.
December 1991

ACKNOWLEDGMENTS

I would like to give special thanks to several people who made this book possible, particularly Kenneth Gesser, my publisher, for inviting me to write the book, and Mark Dennison, my editor, and all the contributing authors. Special thanks to Hal Marcus, Hal Marcus Public Relations, for his encouragement and feedback, and to Michael O. Laddin and Jane Whitehouse, Entek Environmental & Technical Services, Inc., for their comments on Chapter 3. Finally, thanks to my secretary, Stephanie A. Thomas, for decoding my manuscript.

ABOUT THE AUTHOR

C. Jaye Berger is the founder of Law Offices C. Jaye Berger, located in New York City. Ms. Berger is the author of numerous articles and books and is widely quoted in newspapers and magazines on environmental and building construction law. She is a frequent lecturer on these subjects across the United States. Her clients include owners, developers, property managers, architects, contractors, and interior designers. She is admitted to practice in state and federal courts in New York, Michigan, and Massachusetts. She attended Syracuse Law School and Cornell Law School.

SUMMARY CONTENTS

Introduction		xxiii
Chapter 1	Federal Statutes	1
Chapter 2	State and Local Statutes	51
Chapter 3	Identification of Hazardous Substances Martin R. Bennett Law Associates, Inc.	65
Chapter 4	Sick Building Syndrome Hal Finkelstein Empire Testing & Balancing, Inc.	101
Chapter 5	Plaintiffs and Defendants	133
Chapter 6	Theories Used in Cost Recovery and Other Environmental Litigation	195
Chapter 7	Defenses to Liability	247
Chapter 8	Environmental Hazards and the Market Value of Real Property Harindra de Silva, Mark H. Egland, and Michael F. Koehn Analysis Group, Inc.	273
Chapter 9	Contracts of Sale	309
Chapter 10	Liabilities Insurance for Hazardous Substances in Buildings Henry Nozko, Jr. United Coastal Insurance Company	317
Chapter 11	Environmental Audits, Management Plans, and Contracts	339
Chapter 12	Emergency Situations Brent Kynoch Asbestos Abatement Services, Inc.	357
Chapter 13	Contracts with Contractors	391
Chapter 14	Asbestos Abatement and Management: A Case Study Laura J. Kuhman	403
Environmental Statutes		421
Table of Cases		423
Index		441

DETAILED CONTENTS

Introduction

Chapter 1   Federal Statutes

§ 1.1   Introduction
§ 1.2   History of CERCLA and SARA
§ 1.3   —Overview of CERCLA
§ 1.4   State Cost Recovery
§ 1.5   Elements of a CERCLA Claim
§ 1.6   —CERCLA Defendants
§ 1.7   —Owner or Operator—Defined
§ 1.8   —Facility—Defined
§ 1.9   —Hazardous Substances Under CERCLA
§ 1.10   —Nature of CERCLA Liability
§ 1.11   —Disposal—Defined
§ 1.12   —Release or Threatened Release—Defined
§ 1.13   —Consistency with National Contingency Plan
§ 1.14   —Removal Versus Remedial Actions
§ 1.15   —Building Material Exception
§ 1.16   —Injunctive Relief Under CERCLA
§ 1.17   —*De Minimis* Settlement
§ 1.18   —Notice Requirement
§ 1.19   —Superliens
§ 1.20   Asbestos Hazard Emergency Response Act (AHERA)
§ 1.21   Resource Conservation and Recovery Act (RCRA)
§ 1.22   Toxic Substances Control Act (TSCA)
§ 1.23   Clean Air Act and National Emission Standards for Hazardous Air Pollutants (NESHAP)
§ 1.24   Occupational Safety and Health Administration Act (OSHA)
§ 1.25   Penalties
§ 1.26   —CERCLA Penalty Provisions
§ 1.27   —RCRA Penalty Provisions
§ 1.28   —NESHAP Penalty Provisions
§ 1.29   —TSCA Penalty Provisions
§ 1.30   —Other Environmental Penalty Provisions
§ 1.31   —State and Local Penalty Provisions

§ 1.32   Proposed Legislation
§ 1.33   Notification
§ 1.34   Underground Storage Tanks
§ 1.35   Indoor Air Pollution and Sick Building Syndrome

Chapter 2   State and Local Statutes

§ 2.1   Introduction
§ 2.2   New Jersey's Environmental Cleanup Responsibility Act (ECRA)
§ 2.3   Minnesota Environmental Response and Liability Act (MERLA)
§ 2.4   Virginia
§ 2.5   Washington, DC
§ 2.6   Mandatory Inspection for Asbestos Before Issuance of a Building Permit
§ 2.7   Co-operative and Condominium Apartments
§ 2.8   California
§ 2.9   Pennsylvania
§ 2.10   Training, Certification, and Licensing
§ 2.11   —New York
§ 2.12   —Massachusetts
§ 2.13   —Virginia
§ 2.14   Colorado
§ 2.15   Tobacco Smoke

Chapter 3   Identification of Hazardous Substances
Martin R. Bennett
Law Associates, Inc.

§ 3.1   Introduction
§ 3.2   Getting Started
§ 3.3   Hiring a Consultant
§ 3.4   Identification and Evaluation of Hazardous Substances
§ 3.5   Sampling Methodology and Analysis
§ 3.6   Comparison to Standards
§ 3.7   Asbestos—Generally
§ 3.8   —Asbestos: Uses
§ 3.9   —Asbestos: Health Effects
§ 3.10   —Asbestos: Evaluation and Analysis
§ 3.11   —Asbestos: Remedial Alternatives
§ 3.12   —Asbestos: Regulations
§ 3.13   —Asbestos: Summary
§ 3.14   Lead: Generally

§ 3.15   —Lead: Health Effects
§ 3.16   —Lead: Evaluation
§ 3.17   —Lead: Standards
§ 3.18   —Lead: Remedial Alternatives
§ 3.19   —Lead: Summary
§ 3.20   Radon: Generally
§ 3.21   —Radon: Sources and Locations
§ 3.22   —Radon: Health Effects
§ 3.23   —Radon: Evaluation and Standards
§ 3.24   —Radon: Remedial Alternatives
§ 3.25   Polychlorinated Biphenyls (PCBs): Generally
§ 3.26   —PCBs: Regulations
§ 3.27   —PCBs: Health Effects
§ 3.28   —PCBs: Evaluation and Remedial Alternatives
§ 3.29   —PCBs: Summary
§ 3.30   Formaldehyde: Generally
§ 3.31   —Formaldehyde: Sources
§ 3.32   —Formaldehyde: Health Effects
§ 3.33   —Formaldehyde: Identification and Evaluation
§ 3.34   —Formaldehyde: Standards
§ 3.35   —Formaldehyde: Remedial Actions

APPENDIXES
3A   U.S. Environmental Protection Agency Regional Offices
3B   EPA Asbestos Ban and Phase-Down Rule Timetable
3C   Common Asbestos-Containing Materials in Buildings
3D   Comparison of Advantages and Disadvantages of Analysis
            Methods for Lead-Base Paint
3E   Blood Lead Level—Standards for Intervention
3F   Radon Risk Evaluation Chart
3G   EPA Transformer Classifications
3H   Comparison of Common Methodologies for Detection of
            Formaldehyde

Chapter 4   Sick Building Syndrome
            Hal Finkelstein
            Empire Testing & Balancing, Inc.

§ 4.1   Defining Sick Building Syndrome
§ 4.2   Identifying Sick Building Syndrome Complaints
§ 4.3   Performing a Background Assessment
§ 4.4   Building Reviews
§ 4.5   Complaint Documentation

§ 4.6   Interpreting the Data Collected: Guidelines
§ 4.7   —Proper Sampling Procedures
§ 4.8   —Interpretation of Results
§ 4.9   —Chemical Inventory
§ 4.10   —Contaminant Sources
§ 4.11   Quantitative Analysis
§ 4.12   Expert Selection
§ 4.13   The Role of an Expert Before Trial
§ 4.14   —Educating the Client
§ 4.15   —Analyzing and Testing
§ 4.16   —Interrogatories
§ 4.17   —Depositions
§ 4.18   —Budgets
§ 4.19   —Checklist for Expert's Report
§ 4.20   Experts' Fees
§ 4.21   Conclusion

APPENDIXES
4A   Expert Witness Referral Groups
4B   Project Time Account
4C   Agreement and Rate Schedule

Chapter 5   Plaintiffs and Defendants

§ 5.1   Introduction
§ 5.2   Class Actions
§ 5.3   States, Municipalities, and Schools
§ 5.4   Manufacturers
§ 5.5   Commercial Building Owners
§ 5.6   —CERCLA Liability
§ 5.7   —Landlords
§ 5.8   —Tenants
§ 5.9   Sellers of Property
§ 5.10   Buyers
§ 5.11   Homeowners
§ 5.12   Real Estate Brokers
§ 5.13   Developers as Defendants
§ 5.14   Corporate Shareholders, Officers, Directors, and Managers as Defendants
§ 5.15   —Corporate Dissolution
§ 5.16   Successors-in-Interest
§ 5.17   Subsidiary Corporations and Piercing the Corporate Veil
§ 5.18   Lenders

§ 5.19   Appraisers
§ 5.20   Property Managers
§ 5.21   Employers
§ 5.22   Employees
§ 5.23   Contractors
§ 5.24   Consultants, Architects, Engineers, and Designers
§ 5.25   Attorneys

Chapter 6   Theories Used in Cost Recovery and Other Environmental
              Litigation

§ 6.1   Introduction: Basis for Liability
§ 6.2   How Courts Handle Claims
§ 6.3   Pendent Jurisdiction
§ 6.4   Types of Damages
§ 6.5   Suits under the Comprehensive Environmental Response,
           Compensation, and Liability Act (CERCLA)
§ 6.6   —Building Materials Exception
§ 6.7   —New or Useful Product Exception
§ 6.8   Petroleum Exclusion
§ 6.9   Strict Liability
§ 6.10   —Duty to Warn
§ 6.11   —Economic Loss
§ 6.12   Enhanced Risk of Cancer and Impairment of Quality of Life
§ 6.13   Breach of Warranty
§ 6.14   —Covenant of Quiet Enjoyment and Warranty of Habitability
§ 6.15   Indemnification and Restitution
§ 6.16   Fraud
§ 6.17   Negligence
§ 6.18   Breach of Contract
§ 6.19   Securities Law Violations
§ 6.20   Racketeer Influenced and Corrupt Organization Act (RICO)
           Violations
§ 6.21   Market Share, Conspiracy, and Other Alternate Theories of
           Liability
§ 6.22   Rescission and "As Is" Clauses
§ 6.23   Public Nuisance
§ 6.24   Private Nuisance
§ 6.25   Injunctions
§ 6.26   Tax Assessment Reduction
§ 6.27   Contribution
§ 6.28   Punitive Damages
§ 6.29   Attorney Fees

Chapter 7   Defenses to Liability

§ 7.1   Introduction
§ 7.2   Statute of Limitations
§ 7.3   Privity of Contract
§ 7.4   Bankruptcy
§ 7.5   —Automatic Stay
§ 7.6   —Abandonment
§ 7.7   —Dischargeability
§ 7.8   Product Identification and Causation
§ 7.9   Asbestos Is Not Dangerous
§ 7.10   State-of-the Art Defense
§ 7.11   CERCLA's Third-Party Defense
§ 7.12   SARA's Innocent Landowner or Due Diligence Defense
§ 7.13   —Checklist for Innocent Landowner Defense
§ 7.14   Estoppel
§ 7.15   Assumption of Risk
§ 7.16   Contributory Negligence
§ 7.17   Unclean Hands
§ 7.18   *Caveat Emptor*
§ 7.19   Disclaimers
§ 7.20   Damage Control

Chapter 8   Environmental Hazards and the Market Value of Real Property

Harindra de Silva, Mark H. Egland, and Michael F. Koehn
Analysis Group, Inc.
Los Angeles, California

§ 8.1   Introduction
§ 8.2   Market Value of Property—The Appraiser and Economist
§ 8.3   A Framework to Estimate Market Value Reduction
§ 8.4   —A Real Estate Valuation Model
§ 8.5   —Cash Flows
§ 8.6   —Value of Debt
§ 8.7   —Estimating the Change in Market Value
§ 8.8   Regulations and Market Value
§ 8.9   Evaluating the Impact of Asbestos on Market Value
§ 8.10   —Scope of Government Regulations Relating to Asbestos
§ 8.11   —Cost Implications of Regulations
§ 8.12   —Media Response to Asbestos in Buildings
§ 8.13   —Lender and Investor Response
§ 8.14   Building Occupant Response

§ 8.15   —Response to the Presence of Asbestos
§ 8.16   —Response to Abatement Activity
§ 8.17   —Stigma of Abated Building
§ 8.18   Estimation of Impact of Asbestos on Market Value
§ 8.19   Market Value of Residential Property
§ 8.20   Actual Market Response—Transaction Prices
§ 8.21   —Impact of Environmental Hazards on Market Value
§ 8.22   Property Taxes and Market Value
§ 8.23   —Filing for Reassessment
§ 8.24   Investing in Buildings Containing Hazardous Materials
§ 8.25   Conclusion

Chapter 9   **Contracts of Sale**

§ 9.1   Buyer's and Seller's Considerations
§ 9.2   Landlord's and Tenant's Considerations
§ 9.3   Lender's Considerations

Chapter 10   **Liabilities Insurance for Hazardous Substances in Buildings**
              Henry Nozko, Jr.
              President, United Coastal Insurance Company

§ 10.1   Introduction
§ 10.2   Market Cycle
§ 10.3   Liability and Litigation Issues
§ 10.4   What Types of Coverages Are Needed?
§ 10.5   Building Owner
§ 10.6   —Insurance for Asbestos Left in Place
§ 10.7   Professional Liability
§ 10.8   Environmental Impairment Liability Insurance
§ 10.9   Storage and Treatment
§ 10.10   How to Evaluate the Insurer and Its Coverage
§ 10.11   Policy Terms and Conditions
§ 10.12   Claims Made, Sunset Clauses, True Occurrence
§ 10.13   Minimizing Building Owners' Loss Exposure

Chapter 11   **Environmental Audits, Management Plans, and Contracts**

§ 11.1   Generally
§ 11.2   Checklist for Environmental Audit
§ 11.3   What to Look For in a Consultant
§ 11.4   What Is Involved in an Audit
§ 11.5   Contracts with Environmental Consultants
§ 11.6   Recordkeeping

§ 11.7   Locating an Attorney

§ 11.8   Anatomy of an Asbestos Survey in a Commercial Building or
            Retail Complex

§ 11.9   Operations and Maintenance (O&M) Plans

§ 11.10   —EPA O&M Guidelines

§ 11.11   Areas to Discuss with Consultant

Chapter 12 Emergency Situations
            Brent Kynoch
            President, Asbestos Abatement Services, Inc.

§ 12.1   Introduction

§ 12.2   Prior Planning

§ 12.3   Establishment of an Operations and Maintenance (O&M) Plan

§ 12.4   —Survey

§ 12.5   —Training

§ 12.6   —Notification

§ 12.7   —Labeling

§ 12.8   —O&M Manual

§ 12.9   Name an Environmental Coordinator

§ 12.10   Emergency Procedures Manual

§ 12.11   —Asbestos Emergency Checklist

§ 12.12   Phone Tree and Emergency Contacts

§ 12.13   When an Accident Occurs

§ 12.14   Execution of Plan

§ 12.15   Locating the Problem

§ 12.16   Isolating the Area

§ 12.17   Cleanup of Environmental Contamination

§ 12.18   Notifications

§ 12.19   —Regulatory Notification

§ 12.20   —Occupants' Notification

§ 12.21   —Neighbors'/Public Notification

§ 12.22   —Insurance Companies' Notification

§ 12.23   —Attorneys' Notification

§ 12.24   —Others

§ 12.25   Handling Regulatory Agencies

§ 12.26   —Making Contact

§ 12.27   —Acknowledging Possible Violations

§ 12.28   —Establishing Ongoing Communications for Remediation
            Efforts

§ 12.29   —Working within "Intent" of Regulations

§ 12.30   —Agreeing on Objectives

§ 12.31   Handling Public Relations/Media
§ 12.32   —Developing Message Points
§ 12.33   —Selecting a Spokesperson
§ 12.34   —Honesty
§ 12.35   Conclusion

Chapter 13   Contracts with Contractors

§ 13.1   Introduction
§ 13.2   Selecting a Contractor
§ 13.3   Site Conditions
§ 13.4   Contract Documents
§ 13.5   Compliance with Laws
§ 13.6   Payment
§ 13.7   Observation of Work
§ 13.8   Title to Waste Materials
§ 13.9   Time
§ 13.10   Subcontractors
§ 13.11   Licenses and Permits
§ 13.12   Final Acceptance
§ 13.13   Standard of Care
§ 13.14   Damages for Delays
§ 13.15   Indemnification
§ 13.16   Confidentiality
§ 13.17   Dispute Resolution
§ 13.18   —Arbitration
§ 13.19   —Mediation
§ 13.20   —Rent-a-Judge
§ 13.21   Insurance and Bonding
§ 13.22   Notification and Recordkeeping
§ 13.23   Applicable State Law

Chapter 14   Asbestos Abatement and Management: A Case Study
Laura J. Kuhman
Building Supervisor

§ 14.1   What Is a Facility Manager?
§ 14.2   Facility and Contractor Philosophy
§ 14.3   Certified Asbestos Training
§ 14.4   Identifying the Asbestos Problem
§ 14.5   An Asbestos Removal Project
§ 14.6   Asbestos Handling Policy
§ 14.7   Communication

§ **14.8** Prequalification of Contractors
§ **14.9** Specifications for Contingency Planning
§ **14.10** The Bid Process
§ **14.11** Conclusion of Project

Environmental Statutes

Table of Cases

Index

INTRODUCTION

At work or at home, most of us spend a large part of our day inside buildings. In most office buildings, we are enclosed in a structure that contains a variety of chemicals and substances, some of which may be hazardous to our health. There may be hazardous materials or hazardous byproducts of the manufacturing process at industrial sites. We may be exposed to potentially harmful substances in our homes because of the furniture we own, the location of our residence, or the building materials used in its construction.

Certain substances are clearly toxic and have been acknowledged as such in federal, state, and local legislation. Others, such as tobacco smoke, are arguably toxic and have been regulated only at the local level in some areas. Asbestos, which has been identified as a hazardous substance, has received—and will continue to receive in the future—a tremendous amount of attention.

There may be organisms, bacteria, and viruses that can breed and spread throughout a building within the ventilation systems. This problem may be exacerbated by "tight" or "sick" building syndrome: a building may be designed and constructed to be so airtight and energy-efficient that clean air flow is restricted and toxic chemicals and bacteria remain trapped in the building. Indoor air is recycled and not replenished with sufficient amounts of outdoor air.

Indoor air pollution can arise from: asbestos, formaldehyde foam insulation, or particle board materials; fiberglass duct lining; radon from granite building materials; pentachlorophenol from logs; polychlorinated biphenyls (PCBs) from electrical transformers; and diisocyanate insulation—to name just a few potentially hazardous products.

Asbestos fibers may be released from materials that were once commonly sprayed or applied onto ceilings, beams, and other structural building parts for purposes of fireproofing, insulation, soundproofing, and pipe and boiler insulation. Renovation work can cause asbestos to be disturbed, and the fibers released into the air where they may be inhaled. The renovation process can introduce more hazardous substances into buildings than were already there.

The choice between asbestos removal versus asbestos encapsulation remains controversial. As we will see, there appears to be a growing trend in favor of more operations and maintenance (O&M) programs, rather than removal. Removal can increase the exposure of building occupants to airborne asbestos fibers, and the process of dislodging asbestos products may create an airborne asbestos problem where none previously existed. Asbestos exposure may be above preabatement levels a number of months after completion of even a well-conducted removal. In addition, asbestos-removal workers, without proper equipment, may be exposed to high levels of fibers, and illegal dumping of asbestos products can create health problems.

Some U.S. government-sponsored studies have been consistent with international studies that describe the risks from asbestos in buildings as generally not significant. In a 1987 Environmental Protection Agency (EPA) survey of 49 government buildings, including 37 in which asbestos material was seriously damaged, average airborne levels ranged from 0.00059 to 0.00073 fiber per cubic centimeter of air (f/cc), or about 15 times lower than the reoccupancy level of 0.01 f/cc required after removing asbestos.[1]

An EPA study required by the Asbestos Hazard Emergency Response Act of 1986 (AHERA) concluded that approximately 733,000 (20 percent) of the 3.6 million public and commercial buildings surveyed contained friable asbestos-containing material (ACM). About 5 percent of the buildings had sprayed-on or troweled-on asbestos-containing surface material such as acoustical ceiling plaster, and 16 percent contained thermal asbestos insulation located on pipes, boilers, tanks, and ducts. Approximately 501,000 buildings (14.1 percent of those surveyed) contained damaged ACM and about 317,000 buildings (9 percent) contained at least some "significantly damaged" material.[2]

The EPA did not recommend any particular abatement action, but did estimate that an AHERA-type[3] program would cost approximately $51 billion. The EPA suggested, as many others have argued, that the mere presence of asbestos in a building does not create a health risk to the building's occupants. The danger occurs when fibers are released into the air as materials deteriorate or become damaged or distributed.

New York City's Department of Environmental Protection (DEP) did a survey and found that approximately 500,000 buildings contained some form of ACM. The DEP reported that 87 percent of the ACM had some damage, 68 percent was in fair condition, and 16 percent was in poor condition. It also concluded that asbestos in a building did not necessarily constitute a health risk unless the fibers were airborne.

---

[1] *Asbestos in Buildings; When Further Study Is the Wisest Course,* Legal Times, Sept. 12, 1988, at 21.

[2] U.S. Environmental Protection Agency, Study of Asbestos-Containing Materials in Public Buildings, Feb. 1988.

[3] See § 1.20.

However, the DEP recommended the following five-part program:

Inspection and assessment to locate ACM and determine its condition;
Training of service workers;
Development of operations and maintenance (O&M) programs for worker protection;
Surveillance of asbestos;
Development of remediation results and management plans.

This is an AHERA-type approach that is being discussed more and more at all levels of government.[4] For tall office buildings, the DEP estimated that initiating such a program would cost $168,000 per building, and the annual cost of the O&M plan would be approximately $50,000. Larger office and residential buildings would have abatement costs of $20 to $30 per foot or more.

Apart from asbestos, buildings may have many other substances that require inspection and periodic monitoring, even if these are not currently mandated by law. The presence of certain toxic substances in buildings can create unusually difficult emergency situations that only special expertise can bring under control. Advance planning is essential, to minimize personal injury and property damage.

Certain hazardous substances are governed by the federal law referred to as CERCLA.[5] Other substances are not covered by CERCLA, but are covered in state and local laws.[6] Still other substances may create health problems and indoor air pollution but are not regulated. Although indoor air pollution is being widely discussed, there is still little actual legislation or regulation governing this area. Many bills and laws have been proposed, but none have been enacted. In the absence of such statutes, legal remedies have been found using common-law theories.

Faced with all these hazardous substances and a plethora of federal, state, and local laws governing certain hazardous substances, most building owners do not know what to do and when to do it. Commercial building owners, lenders, tenants, employees, homeowners, and all others who come in contact with hazardous substances need to understand the laws and their own rights and risks in the area. This book demystifies the issues, clarifies

---

[4] City of New York, Dept. of Environmental Protection, Final Report on the Assessment of the Public's Risk of Exposure to In-Place Asbestos, Dec. 1, 1988.

[5] Comprehensive Environmental Response, Compensation, and Liability Act of 1980, 42 U.S.C. §§ 9601–9675 (1980) (hereinafter, "CERCLA").

[6] See ch. 2.

the legal ramifications, and recommends methods for dealing with these issues in order to avoid or mitigate legal problems.

A building owner faced with an asbestos problem, for example, will have to comply with EPA regulations and guidelines concerning notice, removal, and disposal. Federal and state Occupational Safety and Health Administration (OSHA) regulations will have to be met.[7] Any disposal will be governed by the Resource Conservation and Recovery Act (RCRA).[8] There may also be state laws concerning the licensing of the removal contractors. Right-to-know laws may require an employer to follow certain planning, labeling, training, and disclosure provisions with respect to hazardous chemicals in the workplace.[9] Anyone involved with hazardous substances must understand which laws apply and how they will affect him or her.

In the 1970s, there was a rash of suits claiming personal injury from asbestos. Property damage suits pertaining to removal of asbestos and cost recovery began in the 1980s and will continue for the foreseeable future. We will see lawsuits concerning a variety of other toxic substances in the coming years; sick building syndrome cases in particular can be expected. Many different legal theories have been used in these lawsuits. Both the plaintiffs' allegations and the defenses[10] are explained in this book.

The cases cover a broad spectrum of the law, from products liability and statutory violations to tort and contract, landlord and tenant, securities, and bankruptcy law. Most lawsuits utilize a number of legal theories. Each of the theories used in such suits will be discussed. Damages range from personal injury to property damage and simply fear of illness because of exposure.

Much of what has been written in the past about environmental hazards has dealt with hazardous substances that were buried in containers and seeped into the ground, air, and water. This book is intended to be a guide through the maze of laws and legal theories in the environmental area, but its sole focus is on buildings. It touches on all the major areas that need to be considered when purchasing, selling, leasing, or financing a commercial or industrial building or a residential home or apartment.

Even for persons who do not personally believe that substances, such as asbestos, are truly dangerous, there is a need to understand these substances and to manage and maintain buildings to avoid health risks, property damage, and potential litigation. This book covers all the key issues and the various hazardous substances that can cause problems.

Building owners or property managers need to know what the law requires, how to set up systems to comply, and what factors to consider

---

[7] See § 1.24.

[8] See § 1.21.

[9] See § 2.10.

[10] See ch. 6.

before purchasing a building in which there may be hazardous substances. Those who are damaged as a result of hazardous substances should understand how to handle the situation, whom to call, when to retain legal counsel, their legal rights, who the potential defendants are, what legal theories apply, and what the possible damages are. Expert consultants, contractors, and attorneys may have to be retained. One needs to know where to find and how to select such individuals, and what terms should be contained in their contracts. This book guides you through the entire process.

CHAPTER 1
FEDERAL STATUTES

§ 1.1   Introduction
§ 1.2   History of CERCLA and SARA
§ 1.3   —Overview of CERCLA
§ 1.4   State Cost Recovery
§ 1.5   Elements of a CERCLA Claim
§ 1.6   —CERCLA Defendants
§ 1.7   —Owner or Operator—Defined
§ 1.8   —Facility—Defined
§ 1.9   —Hazardous Substances Under CERCLA
§ 1.10   —Nature of CERCLA Liability
§ 1.11   —Disposal—Defined
§ 1.12   —Release or Threatened Release—Defined
§ 1.13   —Consistency with National Contingency Plan
§ 1.14   —Removal versus Remedial Actions
§ 1.15   —Building Material Exception
§ 1.16   —Injunctive Relief Under CERCLA
§ 1.17   —*De Minimis* Settlement
§ 1.18   —Notice Requirement
§ 1.19   —Superliens
§ 1.20   Asbestos Hazard Emergency Response Act (AHERA)
§ 1.21   Resource Conservation and Recovery Act (RCRA)
§ 1.22   Toxic Substances Control Act (TSCA)
§ 1.23   Clean Air Act and National Emission Standards for Hazardous Air
         Pollutants (NESHAP)
§ 1.24   Occupational Safety and Health Administration Act (OSHA)
§ 1.25   Penalties
§ 1.26   —CERCLA Penalty Provisions
§ 1.27   —RCRA Penalty Provisions
§ 1.28   —NESHAP Penalty Provisions
§ 1.29   —TSCA Penalty Provisions

1

§ 1.30 —Other Environmental Penalty Provisions

§ 1.31 —State and Local Penalty Provisions

§ 1.32 Proposed Legislation

§ 1.33 Notification

§ 1.34 Underground Storage Tanks

§ 1.35 Indoor Air Pollution and Sick Building Syndrome

§ 1.1 Introduction

The Comprehensive Environmental Response, Compensation, and Liability Act of 1980 (CERCLA)[1] is generally not applicable to routine asbestos abatement in buildings, but it may be applicable to a variety of other situations encountered in buildings, particularly situations found in industrial facilities. In addition, much of the reasoning used by the courts in analyzing CERCLA cases, and the overall environmental policies surrounding that reasoning, may be applicable to other situations that involve hazardous substances but do not fall within the statute.

This chapter gives an overview of the CERCLA statute and the other key statutes that may apply to problematic environmental situations in a building.

CERCLA, a federal statute, has been used extensively in cases involving hazardous waste that has been dumped on land or on landfill and has the potential to wind up in water, soil, or buildings. Often, hazardous substances originate in a building, such as an industrial plant, and then leak into soil and water. CERCLA is the main statute that has been used to recover cleanup costs and damages caused by such conditions.

Section 104 of the law, added in 1986,[2] prohibits the federal government from conducting Superfund cleanup actions involving indoor contamination from part of the structure of a building. CERCLA and its 1986 Amendments are commonly referred to as the Superfund statute.

Thus, as the law currently stands, *in situ* asbestos is not covered by CERCLA, nor is petroleum; however, hundreds of other hazardous substances are covered by the statute. The asbestos exclusion may be changed in the future. However, until then, plaintiffs suffering property damages from *in situ* asbestos, particularly enormous removal costs, must instead rely on common-law legal theories, which are discussed in **Chapter 6.**

The CERCLA statute is rather lengthy and complex. Its amendments have made it even more complex. It is discussed here in detail, because (1) many situations involve a particular substance in a building, and CERCLA

---

[1] 42 U.S.C. §§ 9601–9675 (1980) (hereinafter, "CERCLA").

[2] Superfund Amendments and Reauthorization Act of 1986, 42 U.S.C. §§ 9601–9675 (Supp. IV 1986), Pub. L. No. 99–499, 100 Stat. 1613 (1986) (hereinafter, "SARA").

may apply, and (2) many plaintiffs attempt to utilize the statute, along with common-law theories, in their lawsuits. CERCLA is most likely to be useful where hazardous substances are being disposed of in an industrial-type building. In addition, some of the legal precedents and policies that have developed may have broad application to non-CERCLA environmental lawsuits. CERCLA has not been held to apply to private causes of action to voluntarily remove asbestos from a commercial building, although it has been argued in many recent lawsuits that it should apply.

§ 1.2   History of CERCLA and SARA

After many years of dumping of hazardous waste by generators, haulers, and disposers, Congress passed CERCLA on December 11, 1980, to facilitate the cleanup of hazardous waste discharges.[3] CERCLA has been applied "primarily to the cleanup of leaking inactive or abandoned sites and to emergency responses to spills."[4] It covers, among other installations, old factory sites, smelters, scrap yards, and electric transformers. Congress sought through CERCLA to cover some of the costs resulting from past disposal practices by holding all responsible parties, as well as some "innocent" parties who were not directly responsible, liable for cleanup costs.[5]

Opponents of CERCLA have criticized it for being too strict, particularly because of the imposition of liability on innocent, successor owners of contaminated sites. In addition, the Bankruptcy Code may allow some guilty parties to escape actual liability.[6] One member of Congress said in 1980 that CERCLA's epitaph would one day read: "Noble of purpose but notorious in operation."[7] Thus, CERCLA was amended by the Superfund Amendments and Reauthorization Act of 1986 (SARA),[8] in which Congress attempted to clarify CERCLA and address some of its inadequacies.

Under common law, an owner of contaminated land, or land containing any other nuisance, is exempt from liability if the owner can prove that he

---

[3] 42 U.S.C. §§ 9601–9675 (1980); *see also* Retirement Community Developers, Inc. v. Merine, 713 F. Supp. 153 (D. Md. 1989).

[4] State of New York v. Shore Realty Corp, 759 F.2d 1032, 1040 (2d Cir. 1985) (quoting Anderson, Mandelker, & Tarlock, Environmental Protection: Law and Policy 568 (1984)).

[5] 42 U.S.C. § 9607(a), CERCLA § 107(a); *see* State of New York v. Shore Realty Corp., 759 F.2d 1032, 1040 (2d Cir. 1985).

[6] Bankruptcy Reform Act of 1978, 11 U.S.C. §§ 101–151, 136, 326 (1982), amended by Bankruptcy Amendments and Federal Judgeship Act of 1984, Pub. L. No. 98-353, 98 Stat. 333 (1984). See § **7.4**.

[7] H.R. Rep. No. 1016, 96th Cong., 2d Sess., pt. 2, at 65 (statements of Representative Dannemeyer), *reprinted in* 1980 U.S. Code Cong. & Admin. News 6141, 6142.

[8] SARA, *supra* note 2.

or she had no knowledge of the contamination during the period of owner-ship. If a purchaser has knowledge of a nuisance upon purchasing the prop-erty, the common law imposes liability on the purchaser (the successor landowner). Liability would exist for the purchaser if the condition was discovered after the purchase was made and the purchaser failed to abate it, or if the purchase price was substantially reduced because of the contami-nation or nuisance.[9] This concept has been codified into *Restatement (Second) of Torts,* Section 839, which states that the possessor of land is liable for an "abatable, artificial condition on the land" if he or she knows or should have known that it is there and fails to correct the condition in a reasonable fashion.[10]

CERCLA is contrary to the common law in that it imposes liability for cleanup on successor landowners, regardless of their fault or knowledge of the nuisance, and offers only a limited defense to innocent successor landowners who had no way of knowing that there was contamination on the property. The only defense to liability, under CERCLA, is if the release of the hazardous substance was solely due to an act of God, war, or an act or omission of a third party who acted with reasonable care in abating the contamination.[11]

Although CERCLA does not expressly authorize apportionment of li-ability, the courts have interpreted the statutes as imposing joint and sev-eral liability on all "responsible parties."[12] This means that a potentially responsible party (PRP) who may technically be responsible for less than 1 percent of the total contamination may be held liable for the entire cost of cleanup.

---

[9] Mott, *Liability for Cleanup of Inactive Hazardous Waste Disposal Sites,* 14 Nat. Re-sources Law. 379, 414 n.220 (1982) (citing, e.g., Tennessee Coal, Iron & Railroad Co. v. Hortiline [sic], 244 Ala. 116, 11 So.2d 833, 837–38 (1943); Glenn v. Crescent Coal Co., 145 Ky. 137, 140 S.W. 43, 44 (1911); Department of Environmental Protection v. Exxon Corp., 151 N.J. Super. 464, 376 A.2d 1339 (Ch. Div. 1977).

[10] Restatement (Second) of Torts § 839 (1979) states in full:

A possessor of land is subject to liability for a nuisance caused while he is in possession by an abatable artificial condition on the land, if the nuisance is otherwise actionable, and

(a) the possessor knows or should know of the condition and the nuisance or unreasonable risk of nuisance involved, and

(b) he knows or should know that it exists without the consent of those affected by it, and

(c) he has failed after a reasonable opportunity to take reasonable steps to abate the condition or to protect the affected persons against it.

[11] 42 U.S.C. § 9607(b). The SARA amendments offer only a slightly more extensive defense.

[12] United States v. Chem-Dyne Corp., 572 F. Supp. 802 (S.D. Ohio 1983); United States v. Wade, 577 F. Supp. 1326 (E.D. Pa. 1983).

The burden is on defendants to demonstrate that the harm is divisible.[13] The harshness of the joint and several liability was mitigated somewhat by the SARA amendments, which provided for *de minimis* settlements for defendants who the EPA believes are responsible for only a small portion of the harm[14] and allowed contribution.[15]

The statute authorizes response actions by the federal government, as well as private causes of action.[16] Response actions may be initiated by the federal government when:

1. There is a "release" or substantial threat of a release[17] of a "hazardous substance"[18] into the environment;[19]

2. In the event of a release or threat of release of any "pollutant or contaminant" into the environment which may pose an imminent and substantial danger to the public health and welfare.[20]

The federal government may undertake response actions to abate or clean up releases or threatened releases and recover the costs of such actions from responsible parties. The federal government may also issue administrative orders or obtain judicial relief requiring the responsible party to abate any imminent and substantial endangerment to public health or the environment. The response action may be a short-term and temporary removal action or a more permanent remedial action. Both types of response action must be consistent with the National Contingency Plan (NCP) (see § **1.13**).

The EPA's response actions may be funded by the Superfund if the responsible parties do not take action to eliminate the contamination. The Superfund allowance was $8.5 billion for the five-year period beginning on October 17, 1986.[21] The state in which a release occurs must assure payment of 10 percent of the cost and assume responsibility for future maintenance of the response action.[22] The government may then sue to recover these response costs from the responsible parties.[23]

---

[13] O'Neil v. Picillo, 883 F.2d 176 (1st Cir. 1989); United States v. Chem-Dyne Corp., 572 F. Supp. at 809–11.

[14] 42 U.S.C. § 9622(g).

[15] 42 U.S.C. § 9613(f)(1).

[16] 42 U.S.C. § 9607.

[17] 42 U.S.C. § 9601(22).

[18] 42 U.S.C. § 9601(14).

[19] 42 U.S.C. § 9604(a).

[20] 42 U.S.C. § 9601(33).

[21] 42 U.S.C. §§ 9611, 9631.

[22] 42 U.S.C. § 9604(c)(3). The state must also assure the availability of a permitted hazardous waste disposal facility that can accept hazardous substances from response actions.

[23] 42 U.S.C. § 9607.

The statute was passed in the last days of the Carter Administration and did not have the benefit of careful review by a committee. Thus, it has drawn some criticism for its inartful drafting and ambiguities.[24]

CERCLA does not preempt state law,[25] but it precludes recovering compensation for the same removal costs, damages, or claims under both CERCLA and state (or other federal) laws.[26]

SARA included two important provisions designed to alleviate the unfair imposition of liability on innocent landowners and to plug the bankruptcy loopholes.[27] One provision eliminated liability for innocent landowners who can prove that they did not know about the contamination and undertook "appropriate" investigation of possible sources of contamination on the property before purchasing it.[28] This is called the "due diligence" defense. Congress also passed a "federal lien" provision.[29] In addition, states may not require contributions to any fund whose purpose is to pay compensation for claims that may be compensated under CERCLA.[30]

As noted generally throughout this chapter, the Superfund law applies to properties listed as "priority sites." The government may:

1. Clean up a site and recover costs from the potentially responsible parties (PRPs); or
2. Notify the PRPs that the site must be cleaned up and allow them to either (i) clean it up, or (ii) allow the government to do it with the understanding that they will be sued for costs later on.

§ 1.3 —Overview of CERCLA

The major provisions of CERCLA are as follows:

- Section 9601 contains the definitions that relate to the Act. Of particular importance are the definitions of facility,[31] hazardous substances,[32] owner or operator, release, and contractual relationship.[33]

---

[24] Grad, *A Legislative History of the Comprehensive Environmental Response, Compensation and Liability ("Superfund") Act of 1980,* 8 Colum. J. Envt'l. L. 1 (1982).

[25] 42 U.S.C. § 9607(a)(4)(A).

[26] 42 U.S.C. § 9614(b).

[27] SARA, *supra* note 2.

[28] 42 U.S.C. § 9601(35).

[29] 42 U.S.C. § 9607(1). Superfund liens apply more to sites than building structures and will not be discussed.

[30] 42 U.S.C. § 9614(c).

[31] 42 U.S.C. § 9601(9).

[32] 42 U.S.C. § 9601(14).

[33] 42 U.S.C. § 9601(20)(A).

- Section 9602 bestows on the Administrator of the Environmental Protection Agency (EPA) the authority and obligation to promulgate regulations designating what will be considered a hazardous substance and what level of release must be reported.
- Section 9603 contains the requirements with respect to reporting the existence of a release of hazardous substances. An amendment added a penalty for failure to notify, and recordkeeping requirements.
- Section 9604 establishes the parameters and procedures of the governmental response to the hazardous waste disposal site problem. Among other provisions, this section gives the President the authority to act in response to the release of hazardous substances; puts certain limits on expenditures from the fund created by the Act; and provides for cooperation between the federal government and state and local governmental authorities.
- Section 9605 requires that the President prepare a National Contingency Plan (NCP) for the removal of hazardous substances and calls for the EPA to devise a comprehensive scheme for addressing the problem of hazardous waste disposal sites. Further, this section directs the EPA to establish priorities and to reflect those priorities in a national list of priority cleanup sites.
- Section 9606 provides for abatement actions brought by the government in cases involving an imminent and substantial endangerment to public health and welfare, and sets forth penalties for violations. The EPA is directed to establish guidelines for the application and use of the procedures in this section.
- Section 9607 assigns liability for the release of hazardous wastes. The reach of the liability is extremely broad. Liable parties include owners of vessels, owners of the site at the time of dumping, present owners of the site, anyone who by contract or agreement arranged for the disposal or transportation of hazardous wastes to the site, and any person who accepted hazardous wastes for disposal at the site.
- Section 9607(a)(4)(A)–(D) makes the liable parties responsible for:
  1. All costs of removal or remedial action that are incurred by the U. S. Government or a state or an Indian tribe and are not inconsistent with the National Contingency Plan (NCP);
  2. Any other necessary costs of response that are incurred by any other person and are consistent with the NCP;
  3. Damages for injury to or loss of natural resources;
  4. Costs of any health assessment study carried out under Section 9604(i).
- Section 9607(b) contains the defenses to liability, which are limited to acts of God, acts of war, and acts of a third party if the defendant can show that he or she exercised due care and took reasonable precautions

against foreseeable acts of third parties. (SARA made a significant amendment to this section; see **Chapter 7**.) The remainder of the section concerns determinations of the amount of damages that can be recovered from liable parties.

- Section 9608 provides that parties who are engaged in transporting hazardous waste materials must produce a bond ensuring their financial responsibility for any damages that may occur.

- Section 9609 provides civil penalties against any parties who do not comply with the requirements of the Act.

- Section 9610 protects employees who report the existence of a hazardous waste disposal site. This section essentially protects "whistleblowers" from adverse employment actions that may arise from their reporting.

- Sections 9611 and 9612 control the use of the Superfund. Section 9611 spells out the authorized uses of the $8.5 billion appropriation for the five-year period beginning on October 17, 1986.

- Section 9612 establishes the procedures for making claims against the fund.

- Section 9613 describes jurisdiction and venue. (A SARA amendment added contribution and settlement provisions as well as a statute of limitations for actions for recovery of costs.)

- Section 9619 addresses the liability of response action contractors and their indemnification.

- Section 9622 contains the provisions for settlement.

- Section 9659 discusses citizens' suits.

§ 1.4   State Cost Recovery

States may recover the costs of removal or of remedial actions that are not inconsistent with the NCP and were taken in response to releases or threatened releases.[34] These costs may result from emergency responses, studies, investigations, samples, cleanup, litigation expenses, and interest.[35] Actions to recover response costs are not limited to facilities listed on the National Priorities List (NPL).[36] States or political subdivisions may enter into contracts or cooperative agreements with EPA whereby both may take action on a cost-sharing basis.[37]

---

[34] 42 U.S.C. § 9607(a)(4)(A). The burden is on the defendant to show that the costs were inconsistent with the NCP. United States v. Northeastern Pharmaceutical and Chemical Co., Inc., 597 F. Supp. 823 (W.D. Mo. 1984), *aff'd in part, rev'd in part and remanded*, 810 F.2d 726, 747–48 (8th Cir. 1986), *cert. denied*, 484 U.S. 848 (1987).

[35] *Id.*

[36] Wickland Oil Terminals v. Asarco, Inc., 792 F.2d 887, 892 (9th Cir. 1986).

[37] 42 U.S.C. § 9601(c), (d).

The statute imposes strict liability, i.e., liability regardless of fault. Defendants are jointly and severally liable.[38] Defendants may include: the owner or operator of the facility at the time of disposal; the current facility owner and operator; and transporters and others who arranged for the transportation of the hazardous substances to the facility.[39]

An action for response costs may be commenced at any time after such costs have been incurred, so long as it is not beyond the statute of limitations set forth in CERCLA.[40] The state does not need to wait until the cleanup is complete before beginning a lawsuit.

The court may grant a declaratory judgment as to liability for future response costs.[41] The state may also use this declaratory judgment for bringing subsequent actions.[42] States often incur only preliminary response costs, such as those for investigation and monitoring, and then seek a declaratory judgment to hold the defendant liable for any of the state's past and future response costs that are consistent with the NCP. If a state incurs such costs before getting a declaratory judgment and they are found to be inconsistent with the NCP, the state may not be able to recover its costs.

The federal courts have exclusive jurisdiction over CERCLA actions. To the extent that complaints include common-law theories of recovery, the federal courts must exercise pendent jurisdiction over state claims.

Consequently, states will generally undertake their own abatement measures and then sue to recover their costs.[43] Unlike the federal government, states cannot get injunctive relief under CERCLA to compel a defendant to perform a remedial action.[44]

States have broad authority to recover damages for natural resources injured by releases of hazardous substances in order to "restore, replace or acquire the equivalent of such natural resources."[45] These damages are intended to compensate for injuries that remain after response actions are complete.

Therefore, recovery is not available until there has been an actual injury to or destruction or loss of public natural resources. For this reason, states often couple CERCLA claims with common-law public nuisance theories when they begin lawsuits. This allows the courts to grant both monetary damages and equitable relief mandating mitigation of the hazardous substance.

---

[38] State of New York v. Shore Realty Corp., 759 F.2d 1032 (2d Cir. 1985); United States v. Stringfellow, 661 F. Supp. 1053 (C.D. Cal. 1987).

[39] 42 U.S.C. § 9607(a).

[40] 42 U.S.C. § 9613(q)(2).

[41] Id.

[42] 42 U.S.C. §§ 9607(a), 9613(g)(2).

[43] 42 U.S.C. § 9607(a).

[44] State of New York v. Shore Realty Corp., 759 F.2d 1032 (2d Cir. 1985). However, in this case, an injunction was granted on the state's public nuisance claim.

[45] 42 U.S.C. § 9607(f)(1).

Some writers have argued that the SARA amendment in Section 9621(e)(2) makes injunctive relief available to states. It provides, in part: "A State may enforce any Federal or State standard, requirement, criteria, or limitation to which the remedial action is required to conform under this chapter in the United States district court for the district in which the facility is located."[46] This section appears to enforce compliance once a remedial action has begun, but it is not clear whether it allows injunctive relief requiring a defendant to begin remedial action when the defendant has not been ordered to do so in a federal action under Section 9606.

§ 1.5 Elements of a CERCLA Claim

For a person to state a private claim under CERCLA, a plaintiff must allege that:

1. The waste disposal site is a facility[47] within the meaning of Section 9601(9);
2. A release or threatened release of a hazardous substance from the facility has occurred;[48] and
3. The release or threatened release has caused the plaintiff to incur response costs that are consistent with the NCP.[49]

§ 1.6 —CERCLA Defendants

To be a defendant in a CERCLA lawsuit, the party must fall within one of the following four classes of persons:

(1) the owner and operator of a vessel or a facility;

(2) any person who at the time of disposal of any hazardous substance owned or operated any facility at which such hazardous substances were disposed of;[50]

(3) any person who by contract, agreement, or otherwise,[51] arranged for disposal or treatment, or arranged with a transporter for transport for

---

[46] Under § 9621(e)(2), the state also has authority to promulgate and impose more stringent state standards upon remedial actions.

[47] Facility is defined broadly to include any property at which hazardous substances have come to be located. 42 U.S.C. § 9601(9).

[48] 42 U.S.C. § 9607(a)(4).

[49] 42 U.S.C. § 9607(a)(4) and (a)(4)(B). *See* State of New York v. Shore Realty Corp., 759 F.2d at 1043.

[50] 42 U.S.C. § 9607(a)(1)-(2).

[51] 42 U.S.C. § 9607(a)(3). The phrase "or otherwise" has not really been defined and thus leaves wide latitude for interpretation.

disposal or treatment, of hazardous substances owned or possessed by such person, by any other party or entity, at any facility or incineration vessel owned or operated by another party or entity and containing such hazardous substances; and

(4) any person who accepts or accepted any hazardous substances for transport to disposal or treatment facilities, incineration vessels or sites selected by such person from which there is a release, or a threatened release which causes the incurrence of response costs, of a hazardous substance.[52]

The language of the statute is disjunctive. Therefore, defendants who attempt to prove that they are not persons whom the statute covers must prove that they do not fit within *any* of the four defined categories. Moreover, in an effort to find liability wherever possible, the courts have interpreted the statutory categories of liable parties quite broadly. Thus, when defendants argue that they are not persons whom the Act was designed to cover, they are not likely to prevail if they are associated with or profited from the use, transport, or production of the hazardous substance.

A "person" can include "an individual, firm, corporation, association, partnership, consortium, joint venture, commercial entity,[53] United States Government, State, municipality, commission, political subdivision of a State, or an interstate body."[54] As will be discussed in **Chapter 5**, it can also include employees, officers, directors, majority shareholders, and subsidiary corporations.

These parties are known as "potentially responsible parties" (PRPs). They are strictly liable to the EPA for injunctive relief requiring cleanup[55] and to any "person," including the EPA, and state and local governments, for the cost of cleanup of contaminated property.[56] Liability also applies retroactively to contamination caused before the effective date of CERCLA.[57]

All PRPs face absolute, strict liability under the statute. For owners of facilities (the first category), this can be problematic when the present owner was not the one who created and profited from the facility's waste disposal. In addition, the concept of who is an "owner" has been expanded to include a lessee/sublessor.[58]

---

[52] 42 U.S.C. § 9607(a)(4). *See also* Retirement Community Developers, Inc. v. Merine, 713 F. Supp. at 155–56.

[53] The phrase "commercial entity" has not been defined or distinguished from the list of other specific forms of business.

[54] 42 U.S.C. § 9601(21).

[55] 42 U.S.C. § 9606(a).

[56] 42 U.S.C. § 9607.

[57] United States v. Northeastern Pharmaceutical and Chemical Co., Inc., 810 F.2d at 734.

[58] United States v. South Carolina Recycl. & Disp., Inc., 653 F. Supp. 984 (D.S.C. 1984), *aff'd in part, vacated in part, sub nom.* United States v. Monsanto Co., 858 F.2d 160 (4th Cir. 1988), *cert. denied,* 109 S. Ct. 3156 (1989).

PRPs in the second category—prior owners—are liable if they owned the facility at the time of the disposal. Thus, a prior owner who purchased the facility *after* the hazardous substance was disposed of and who is not a present owner may not be liable. Such an owner may also not be liable if the hazardous substance was stored or deposited at the facility, rather than disposed of.

However, owners can be drawn back into liability and be without a defense if they have had *actual knowledge* of a release or threatened release of a hazardous substance and have transferred the property without disclosing it.[59] There may be ongoing liability for the disposal of a hazardous substance, such as asbestos, even after it has been removed, if it has not been properly disposed of.

The government is supposed to identify all PRPs but, as a practical matter, the PRPs must find one another. Because they are all jointly and severally responsible, it is in their interest to find other PRPs. Some PRPs even hire special consultants to track down other PRPs, in an effort to spread the liability. The 1986 Superfund amendments (SARA) now provide a right of contribution that allows PRPs to sue other PRPs for their share.[60] SARA also helps toward this goal by having the government give a "nonbinding allocation of responsibility" opinion, which encourages settlements.

§ 1.7   —Owner or Operator—Defined

The courts have interpreted the terms "owner" and "operator" very broadly, in order to find liability. A party who controls property, by title, lease, or otherwise, may be liable even if the party did not contribute directly or indirectly to the contamination.[61]

Thus, the following individuals have been deemed owners and operators: a present owner of a site who did not contribute to the contamination;[62] a company that held title for only one hour before transferring it;[63] an owner/lessor whose lessee caused contamination;[64] a lessee whose sublessee caused the contamination;[65] corporate officers who were stockholders and had responsibility for disposal of hazardous substances at the contaminated

---

[59] 42 U.S.C. § 9601(35)(c).

[60] 42 U.S.C. § 9613(f).

[61] State of New York v. Shore Realty Corp., 759 F.2d 1032 (2d Cir. 1985); United States v. Cauffman, 21 Envtl. L. Rep. (Envtl. L. Inst.) 2167 (C.D. Col. 1984).

[62] State of New York v. Shore Realty Corp., *supra* note 60.

[63] United States v. Carolawn Co., 14 Envtl. L. Rep. (Envtl. L. Inst.) 20,698, 21 Env't Rep. Cas. (BNA) 2125 (D.S.C. 1984).

[64] United States v. Argent Corp., 21 Env't Rep. Cas. (BNA) 1354 (D.N.M. 1984).

[65] United States v. Carolawn Co., *supra* note 62.

property;[66] and lenders who foreclosed on property and held title for four years.[67]

One court has interpreted "owner and operator" literally, requiring that a defendant be both an owner and operator, but this has not been held generally.[68] The statute has been interpreted by courts to apply to owners who are not operators and to operators who are not owners.

A lender who merely holds a security interest on a property is excluded from the definitions if "[he] without participating in the management . . . holds indicia of ownership primarily to protect his security interest. . . ."[69] This is discussed in greater detail in **Chapter 5**.

Partners in a partnership that is an "owner or operator" of a facility may face personal liability. This liability may extend to members of a limited partnership.[70]

State and local governments are exempt from the definition when they involuntarily acquire control of hazardous waste sites.[71]

§ 1.8   —Facility—Defined

CERCLA defines "facility" as "any building, structure, installation, equipment, pipe or pipeline (including any pipe into a sewer or publicly owned treatment works), well, pit, pond, lagoon, impound, ditch, landfill, storage container, motor vehicle, rolling stock or aircraft or . . . any site or area where a hazardous substance has been deposited, stored, disposed of, or placed, or otherwise come to be located . . . .".[72]

The term "facility" has been broadly interpreted by the courts to include "almost every place a hazardous substance could find its way into."[73] The terms "facility" and "release or threatened release" have been so broadly defined that seemingly anything will satisfy these first two requirements.

---

[66] United States v. Northeastern Pharmaceutical and Chemical Co., Inc., 597 F. Supp. 823 (W.D. Mo. 1984), aff'd in part, rev'd in part and remanded, 810 F.2d 726 (8th Cir. 1986), cert. denied, 484 U.S. 848 (1987); United States v. Mirabile, 23 Env't. Rep. Cas. (BNA) 1511 (E.D. Pa. 1985).

[67] United States v. Maryland Bank and Trust Co., 632 F. Supp. 573 (D. Md. 1986). However, in United States v. Mirabile, supra note 65, no CERCLA liability was found where former mortgagees foreclosed on property and resold it four months later.

[68] United States v. Maryland Bank and Trust Co., 632 F. Supp. at 578.

[69] 42 U.S.C. § 9601(20)(A).

[70] Idaho v. Howmet Turbine Component Co., 814 F.2d 1376 (9th Cir. 1987), aff'd, 882 F.2d 392 (9th Cir. 1989).

[71] 42 U.S.C. § 9601(20)(D).

[72] 42 U.S.C. § 9601(9).

[73] T&E Industries v. Safety Light Corp., 680 F. Supp. 696, 708 (D.N.J. 1988).

For example, horse stables,[74] roadbeds,[75] dragstrips for automobile racing[76] and trailer parks[77] have all qualified as "facilities."[78] Even the air within a facility may be included in CERCLA. However, the term excludes "any consumer product in consumer use."[79] No court has yet used this provision to prevent buildings contaminated with asbestos-containing materials (ACMs) from being considered facilities under CERCLA. One court has held that ACMs installed within a building, such as thermal system insulation, do not fall under this exclusion.[80]

§ 1.9   —Hazardous Substances Under CERCLA

CERCLA requires liable parties to remediate "hazardous substances." The definition of this term is quite complex because it refers to numerous other environmental statutes in which hundreds of substances are listed.[81] A plaintiff must show that the waste meets the definition of hazardous under any of the statutes listed in Section 9601(14) of CERCLA, or that it constitutes "any element, compound, mixture, solution, or substance designated" under Section 9602 of CERCLA. Because the definition is so broad, litigation rarely focuses on whether a substance is considered hazardous under CERCLA. Asbestos is prominent on the list. One major exception, however, is petroleum.[82] This is significant because leaks from underground storage tanks are not uncommon.

Liability exists regardless of the amount of hazardous substance present.[83] In *City of New York v. Exxon Corp.,* the company was found

---

[74] *See* United States v. Bliss, 667 F. Supp. 1298, 1305 (E.D. Mo. 1987) (horse stables and paths were a "facility" where dust-suppressants sprayed on them contained hazardous substances).

[75] United States v. Ward, 618 F. Supp. 884, 895–96 (E.D.N.C. 1985) (roadbeds sprayed with hazardous substances were a "facility").

[76] New York v. General Electric Co., 592 F. Supp. 291, 297 (N.D.N.Y. 1984) (dragstrip where hazardous substances were sprayed was a "facility").

[77] United States v. Metate Asbestos Corp., 584 F. Supp. 1143, 1148 (D. Ariz. 1984) (trailer park where hazardous substances were placed was a "facility").

[78] In United States v. Conservation Chemical Co., 619 F. Supp. 162, 185 (W.D. Mo. 1985), for example, the court held that "every place where hazardous substances come to be located" qualifies as a "facility."

[79] 42 U.S.C. § 9601(a). This will be discussed in § 6.7 *infra.*

[80] United States v. Fleet Factors Corp., 901 F.2d 1550, *reh'q denied, en banc,* 911 F.2d 742 (11th Cir. 1990).

[81] 53 Fed. Reg. 27,268 (1988).

[82] 42 U.S.C. § 9601(14).

[83] United States v. Carolawn Co., 21 Env't Rep. Cas. (BNA) 2124 (D.S.C. 1984).

liable for dumping waste into a landfill that contained only trace amounts of cadmium, chromium, and lead.[84]

§ 1.10 —Nature of CERCLA Liability

A PRP may be sued for:

1. Costs of removal or remediation, such as reimbursement for money spent to remediate a facility;[85]
2. Any other necessary costs consistent with the NCP;[86]
3. An order from the EPA requiring abatement of the hazardous substance if there is "imminent and substantial endangerment";[87]
4. Damages to natural resources;[88]
5. Costs of any health assessment carried out under Section 9604(i).[89]

§ 1.11 —Disposal—Defined

The definition of disposal is very important in determining whether CERCLA governs a spill of a hazardous substance, such as a PCB-containing fluid, onto a floor in a building.

The definition of "disposal," for the purposes of CERCLA, is set forth in the Solid Waste Disposal Act:

the discharge, deposit, injection, dumping, spilling, leaking, or placing of any solid waste or hazardous waste into or on any land or water so that such solid waste or hazardous waste or any constituent thereof may enter the environment or be emitted into the air or discharged into any waters, including ground waters.[90]

Although such a spill is not "into or on any land or water," several courts have found that the placement of hazardous substances inside an enclosed building may constitute disposal of such waste into or on any land and thus may satisfy the CERCLA definition.

---

[84] N.Y.L.J., Aug. 8, 1990, at 1, col. 4.

[85] 42 U.S.C. § 9607.

[86] 42 U.S.C. § 9607(a)(4)(B).

[87] 42 U.S.C. § 9606.

[88] 42 U.S.C. § 9607(a)(4)(C).

[89] 42 U.S.C. § 9607(a)(4)(D).

[90] 42 U.S.C. § 9603(3) (incorporated at 42 U.S.C. § 9601(29)).

In one case, a disposal was found when the floors and fixtures of a warehouse facility were covered with a layer of dust contaminated by lead, as a result of the operations of the prior tenant.[91] The court found that Congress intended the term "land" to encompass buildings and other types of real estate.[92] A disposal was found in a manufacturing plant that had stored drums containing PCBs when they spilled and contaminated the floor and roof of the plant.[93]

Liability attaches to a party who has taken an affirmative act to dispose of a hazardous substance. The party is considered to have "dumped" waste on the site, as opposed to conveying a useful substance for a useful purpose.[94] The sale of contaminated soil for transport to a landfill constitutes a statutory disposal for which the seller may be liable.[95] However, the mere sale of a hazardous substance for use in the wood-treatment process is not arranging for disposal or treatment of a hazardous substance, even when process runoff containing that substance has been placed at the site.[96]

In *United States v. Westinghouse Electric Corp.*,[97] the court found that a defendant who sold a product that contained PCBs for use in manufacturing did not engage in a disposal and hence was not liable for the costs related to the cleanup of the contaminated effluent deposited in a landfill. The court found it significant that plaintiff did not allege that defendant made the sale of the substance in order to dispose of its own wastes or manufacturing by-products.[98]

If the transaction involves the sale of a new, useful product containing a hazardous substance, as opposed to the sale of a substance merely to "get rid of it," a claim under CERCLA may not be made. One defendant had sold the plaintiff equipment that contained PCB oil. The court found that, because the equipment was nonleaking and usable when sold and the hazardous substance was enclosed when sold, the sale was not an affirmative act to dispose of waste in some manner by dumping the waste on the site.[99]

---

[91] BCW Associates Ltd. v. Occidental Chemical Corp., 1988 U.S. Dist. LEXIS 11,275 (E.D. Pa. Sept. 29, 1988).

[92] *Id.* at 45.

[93] Emhart Industries, Inc. v. Duracell Int'l., Inc., 665 F. Supp. 549, 555 (M.D. Tenn. 1987); *see also* Amland Properties Corp. v. Aluminum Company of America, 711 F. Supp. 784 (D.N.J. 1989).

[94] Prudential Ins. Co. of America v. U.S. Gypsum, 711 F. Supp. 1244, 1253 (D.N.J. 1989), *cert. denied*, 110 S. Ct. 1113, 107 L. Ed. 1020 (1990).

[95] Jersey City Redevelopment Authority v. PPG Industries, 655 F. Supp. 1257, 1261–1262 (D.C.N.J. 1987), *aff'd*, 1988 U.S. App. LEXIS 18,998 (3d Cir. 1988).

[96] Edward Hines Lumber Co. v. Vulcan Materials Co., 685 F. Supp. 651, 654 (N.D. Ill. 1988), *aff'd*, 861 F.2d 155 (7th Cir. 1988).

[97] 22 Env't. Rep. Cas. (BNA) 1230 (S.D. Ind. 1983).

[98] *Id.* at 1233.

[99] C. Greene Equipment Corp. v. Electron Corp., 697 F. Supp. 983 (N.D. Ill. 1988).

The transfer of asbestos-containing products is a sale of a substance for use in the construction of a building and is not considered an arrangement for disposal of a hazardous substance.[100]

§ 1.12   —Release or Threatened Release—Defined

In order to establish CERCLA liability, a plaintiff must demonstrate that the disposal of the hazardous substances resulted in "a release or a threatened release" into the environment.

The term "release" is defined by CERCLA as:

> any spilling, leaking, pumping, pouring, emitting, emptying, discharging, injecting, escaping, leaching, dumping, or disposing into the environment (including the abandonment or discarding of barrels, containers, and other closed receptacles containing any hazardous substance or pollutant or contaminant).[101]

The courts have given broad definitions to these terms. The courts have found a threat of release where there was evidence of the presence of hazardous substances in drums and tanks at the facility, and the unwillingness of any party to assert control over the substances.[102] However, the definition of "release" excludes any release that results in exposure to persons solely within a workplace, with respect to a claim that such persons may assert against the employers of such persons.[103]

The test for "threatened releases" is similarly broad, requiring only that the regulating agency have a "reasonable belief" that a release of a hazardous substance might occur.

A threatened release has been found when corroding and deteriorating tanks were present, when expertise in handling hazardous waste was lacking, and when the facility failed to obtain a license.[104] The presence of PCBs in concrete flooring may also constitute a threatened release.[105] When dust contaminated with lead was found on goods being shipped to customers and on shoes and clothing of workers leaving a warehouse, the condition was construed as a threatened release.[106]

---

[100] Prudential Ins. Co. of America v. U.S. Gypsum, 711 F. Supp. at 1254.

[101] 42 U.S.C. § 9601(22).

[102] United States v. Northernaire Plating Co., 670 F. Supp. 742 (W.D. Mich. 1987), aff'd, 889 F.2d 1497 (6th Cir. 1989), cert. denied, 110 S. Ct. 1527 (1990).

[103] 42 U.S.C. § 9601(22)(A).

[105] State of New York v. Shore Realty Corp., 759 F.2d at 1045.

[105] Amland Properties Corp. v. Aluminum Company of America, 711 F. Supp. at 793.

[106] BCW Associates Ltd. v. Occidental Chemical Corp., 1988 U.S. Dist. LEXIS 11,275 at 44.

A release into the air of a building or structure, if it does not reach the outside air directly or via a ventilation system, is not subject to the EPA reporting regulations.[107] Building owners, arguing that cost recovery for asbestos abatement falls within CERCLA, may try to claim that the ventilation and exhaust systems required by building codes make the release of asbestos into the ambient air unavoidable. Thus far, such claims have not been accepted by the courts.

The EPA has the right of access to property if it determines there could be a release or threatened release of hazardous substances from the property, or if it has probable cause to believe that hazardous wastes have been stored there.[108]

§ 1.13 —Consistency with National Contingency Plan

In private cost recovery actions, response costs incurred must be consistent with the National Contingency Plan (NCP), and this element must also be established in a CERCLA plaintiff's case. The federal or state government may recover response costs that are not inconsistent with the NCP.[109] Cleanup occurs first; then the government assesses liability.

The NCP is a detailed set of regulations[110] required by CERCLA to effectuate the powers created by the statute for response actions. Pursuant to the National Priorities List (NPL),[111] the NCP prioritizes sites of known or threatened releases for response actions.[112]

In determining what sites should be cleaned up and in what order, the EPA must balance many factors. These include:

1. The degree of harm or threatened harm to human health and welfare;
2. The burden on the responsible parties;
3. The technology available to accomplish adequate cleanup and to return the site to a condition in which it no longer poses a threat to health and welfare;
4. The political climate of the area in which the site is located.[113]

---

[107] 50 Fed. Reg. 13,462 (1988).

[108] United States v. Long, 687 F. Supp. 343 (S.D. Ohio 1987); National-Standard Co. v. Adamkus, 685 F. Supp. 1040 (N.D. Ill. 1988), aff'd, 881 F.2d 352 (7th Cir. 1989).

[109] 42 U.S.C. § 9607(a)(4)(A).

[110] 40 C.F.R. § 300.1-16.41 (1988).

[111] 42 U.S.C. § 9605(a); 40 C.F.R. § 300 app. B (1988).

[112] 42 U.S.C. § 9604(a)(1).

[113] See U.S. Environmental Protection Agency, Office of Solid Waste and Emergency Response, Superfund's Remedial Response Program Pub. No. HW-4 (rev. ed. 1983).

§ 1.14   —Removal versus Remedial Actions

Costs incurred in responding to releases or threatened releases of hazardous waste are divided by CERCLA into two categories. The first are removal actions, which are defined as:

> the cleanup or removal of released hazardous substances from the environment, such actions as may be necessary taken in the event of the threat of release of hazardous substances into the environment, such actions as may be necessary to monitor, assess, and evaluate the release or threat of release . . . . The term includes, in addition, without being limited to, security fencing or other measures to limit access . . . .[114]

Although these costs may constitute the bulk of a claim, they are distinct from damages.

Removal actions are to be taken in response to an immediate threat to the public welfare or to the environment and are primarily intended for short-term abatement of toxic waste hazards.[115] Initial monitoring, surveying, sampling, and assessment of threatened releases are included, even if there are no subsequent recoverable response costs.[116] Temporary evacuation and housing of threatened individuals may also be included.[117]

All other responses are termed remedial actions and are defined as:

> those actions consistent with permanent remedy taken instead of or in addition to removal actions in the event of a release or threatened release . . . to prevent or minimize the release of hazardous substances so that they do not migrate to cause substantial danger to present or future public health or welfare or the environment. The term includes . . . neutralization, cleanup of released hazardous substances or contaminated materials.[118]

Remedial actions are generally long-term or permanent remedies.[119]

The distinction between these two types of actions is important because removal actions need only comply with the relatively simple NCP requirements.[120] Remedial actions, on the other hand, must comply with the more detailed procedural and substantive provisions of the NCP.[121]

---

[114] 42 U.S.C. § 9601(23).

[115] Piccolini v. Samon's Wrecking, 686 F. Supp. 1063, 1068 (M.D. Pa. 1988).

[116] Amland Properties Corp. v. Aluminum Company of America, 711 F. Supp. at 795.

[117] 42 U.S.C. § 9601(23).

[118] T&E Industries v. Safety Light Corp., 680 F. Supp. at 706.

[119] *Id.* Costs such as permanent relocation of a business must be approved by the President to be categorized as reimbursable response costs.

[120] 40 C.F.R. § 300.65 (1988).

[121] 40 C.F.R. § 300.68 (1988).

To be consistent with the NCP, private parties must address all the alternatives outlined in Section 300.68(f) of the Code of Federal Regulations and must comply with all other provisions of Section 300.68(e)–(i). There must be an opportunity for public comment, which must be consistent with Section 300.67(d).[122]

A remedial action is consistent with the NCP if the party:

(A) Provides for appropriate site investigation and analysis of remedial alternatives as required under § 300.68;

(B) Complies with the provisions of paragraphs (e) through (i) of § 300.68;

(C) Selects a cost-effective response; and

(D) Provides an opportunity for appropriate public comment concerning the selection of a remedial action consistent with paragraph (d) of § 300.67 unless compliance with the . . . appropriate State and local requirements . . . provides a substantially equivalent opportunity for public involvement in the choice of remedy.[123]

The requirements of the NCP must be adhered to, unless the party seeking recovery explains why a specific requirement is not appropriate to the specific site and problem.

Section 300.68(e)(2) lists factors that are to be assessed for private party actions, as appropriate, in determining what type of remedial action will be considered. These factors are:

(1) population at risk;

(2) routes of exposure;

(3) amount, concentration, and form of hazardous substances;

(4) hydrogeological factors, such as soil permeability;

(5) current and potential groundwater use;

(6) climate;

(7) extent to which source can be adequately identified;

(8) whether substances at the site may be reused or recycled;

(9) likelihood of future releases if substances remain on-site;

(10) extent to which barriers contain the substances;

(11) extent of migration of substances;

(12) extent to which federal environmental and public health requirements are applicable to site;

(13) extent to which contamination levels exceed federal requirements;

---

[122] 50 Fed. Reg. 47,934 (1985).

[123] 40 C.F.R. § 300.71(a)(2)(ii) (1988). Amland Properties Corp. v. Aluminum Company of America, 686 F. Supp. at 797–98.

(14) air, land, water, and/or food chain contamination;

(15) ability of the responsible party to implement remedy until the threat is permanently abated;

(16) for fund-financed responses, the availability of other appropriate enforcement mechanisms; and

(17) other appropriate matters may be considered.[124]

A plaintiff must affirmatively prove, as a prerequisite to establishing a cause of action under CERCLA, that actual costs of response consistent with the NCP have been incurred. Failure to allege that the plaintiff has (1) actually incurred costs that are (2) necessary, and (3) consistent with the NCP will be fatal to the cause of action, which can be dismissed as not yet ripe for review. Claims for response costs, which may have been viable had they been brought later, may be dismissed as premature if the costs alleged have not yet been incurred or if the site, although hazardous, has not yet been placed on the NPL.

The statutory maximum that may be spent on a Section 9604 response action under SARA is $2 million or the expenses incurred after 12 months have elapsed from the date of initial response, whichever occurs first.[125] Therefore, a Superfund defendant who is asked to restore response costs for a site cleaned up under Section 9604 could contest all expenditures over $2 million. With limited exceptions, the EPA is not authorized to spend more than $2 million cleaning up a site under Section 9604.[126] If it did so, the EPA would be exceeding the scope of its statutory authority. The government would be acting inequitably if it sought restitution for funds it was not authorized to spend.[127]

§ 1.15   —Building Material Exception

Through SARA, Congress added the following language to the CERCLA section entitled "Response authorities":

(3) Limitation on response

The President shall not provide for a removal or remedial action under this section in response to a release or threat of release—

---

[124] 40 C.F.R. § 300.68(e)(2) (1988).

[125] 42 U.S.C. § 9604(c)(1)(C) (Supp. IV 1986). Under the original Act, the maximum was $1 million and 6 months. See 42 U.S.C. § 9604(c)(3) (1982).

[126] 42 U.S.C. § 9604(b).

[127] SARA allows the EPA Administrator to exceed the limits if it would be appropriate and consistent with permanent cleanup. See H.R. Rep. No. 253, 99th Cong., 2d Sess., pt. 1, reprinted in 1986 U.S. Code Cong. & Admin. News 2839.

(B) from products which are part of the structure of, and result in exposure within, residential buildings or business or community structures . . . .[128]

The very next section states an exception to this prohibition:

(4) Exception to limitations

Notwithstanding paragraph (3) of this section, to the extent authorized by this section, the President may respond to any release or threat of release if in the President's discretion, it constitutes a public health or environmental emergency and no other person with the authority and capability to respond to the emergency will do so in a timely manner.[129]

The language of Section 9604(a)(3) would appear to limit only responses by the President to releases that are part of building structures. However, the legislative history and subsequent interpretation by the courts indicate that Congress intended for private persons to be limited also in responding to such releases. This limitation is of particular importance in the area of cost recovery actions for the removal of asbestos in buildings.

The language of Section 9604(a)(3) originated in Section 112(b) of Senate Bill S. 51 in 1985. The report accompanying that bill stated the following:

Scope of Program

Summary

This section amends section 104 (response authorities) to clarify that the President should give primary attention to releases which may present a public health threat and that the President has the discretion to decide when responsible parties are authorized to conduct response in lieu of Fund-financed response. It also makes more explicit the fact that certain circumstances which may present genuine threats to human health, welfare or the environment are not within the scope of CERCLA.

Discussion

*   *   *

CERCLA response authorities are extremely broad, but there are nevertheless situations, some of which may be life-threatening, which are not within the law's scope. The Agency has encountered some difficulties, primarily political, in restraining CERCLA responses to the scope of the law. For this reason, S. 51 proposes to make more explicit certain areas which the law does not cover. Specifically, S. 51 makes more clear the exclusion from remedial or removal action of a release or a threat of a release:

*   *   *

---

[128] 42 U.S.C. § 9604(a)(3)(B).
[129] 42 U.S.C. § 9604(a)(4).

—from products which are part of the structure of, and result in exposure within a facility . . .

* * *

The Environmental Protection Agency has received requests to take removal or remedial action in situations where the contamination was from building materials used in the structure and was creating an indoor hazard. This section would clarify that such situations are not subject to remedial or removal action.[130]

CERCLA provides that response costs are not recoverable unless they are "consistent with the national contingency plan."[131]

The NCP states under the heading "Other party responses:"

(2) For purposes of cost recovery under § 107 of CERCLA . . . a response action will be consistent with the NCP . . . if the person taking the response action:

(i) Where the action is a removal action, acts in circumstances warranting removal and implements removal action consistent with § 300.65.[132]

Section 300.65 governs federal removal actions. Therefore, to conduct a removal action consistent with the NCP, a private party must follow the same rules that apply to government removal actions. Because the government clearly is not authorized (absent presidential approval) to remove hazardous substances that are part of the structure of a building, it follows that private parties generally cannot act consistent with the NCP and conduct such removal actions absent presidential approval. To state it differently, because private parties must conduct removal actions in a manner consistent with federal removal actions, private parties generally cannot conduct removal actions involving hazardous substances that are part of a building structure, absent presidential support.[133]

One court that analyzed this issue found that the financial consequences of imposing liability for removal of all asbestos in buildings would be "inestimable" and "astronomical."[134]

Since CERCLA applies not only to owners of facilities but also to generators and transporters of hazardous substances, plaintiff's interpretation of CERCLA could extend strict liability coverage to all individuals and businesses

---

[130] S. Rep. No. 11, 99th Cong., 1st Sess. 15–17 (1985); *see also* Retirement Community Developers, Inc. v. Merine, 713 F. Supp. at 156.

[131] 42 U.S.C. § 9607(a)(4)(B).

[132] 40 C.F.R. § 300.71(a)(2).

[133] 42 U.S.C. § 9607(a)(3) and (a)(4)(B) and 40 C.F.R. § 300.71(a)(2).

[134] Retirement Community Developers, Inc. v. Merine, 713 F. Supp. at 158.

who manufactured, delivered, and installed asbestos over the past seventy or more years. Were this the case, CERCLA could conceivably hold liable for removal or remedial costs all persons who presently own houses or buildings with asbestos in them, all persons who ever installed asbestos, all person who transported or delivered asbestos, and all manufacturers of asbestos. If Congress intended such a result, it could have said so clearly and specifically. To the contrary, the legislative history of SARA indicates that Congress specifically intended that CERCLA generally not apply to this type of action, although it is recognized that Congress' expression of intent could well have been more direct. The Court will not impose such broad liability with such far reaching consequences until Congress clearly shows its intent to dictate such a result.[135]

Thus, absent some Congressional action, it appears unlikely that typical asbestos abatement actions will be covered by CERCLA.

§ 1.16   —Injunctive Relief Under CERCLA

CERCLA empowers the President of the United States, through the Attorney General, in certain limited and exigent circumstances, to seek injunctive relief.[136] However, private parties may not invoke injunctive relief. They are limited to recovering response costs that are consistent with the NCP.[137]

Injunctive relief may not be provided for in the statutes, but courts always have inherent power to fashion appropriate remedies, including injunctive relief, unless they are expressly precluded from doing so by Congress. Injunctive relief granted by a court might include compelling defendants to comply with their obligations or to reimburse the plaintiff for "necessary costs."[138]

§ 1.17   —De Minimis Settlement

A party may qualify for a *de minimis* settlement with the EPA for a minor portion of the property's cleanup costs rather than be subject to litigation if, *inter alia,* (1) the amount of contamination contributed by the party and its toxic or hazardous effects are minimal, or (2) the party did not manage hazardous substances at the property and did not contribute

---

[135] *Id.*

[136] 42 U.S.C. § 9606(a).

[137] T&E Industries v. Safety Light Corp., 680 F. Supp. at 704. *See also* 42 U.S.C. § 9607(a)(2)(B).

[138] T&E Industries v. Safety Light Corp., 680 F. Supp. at 705.

to the contamination through any act or omission.[139] The second qualification would not apply if the party purchased the property with actual
or constructive knowledge that it was used for or contained hazardous
substances.

§ 1.18   —Notice Requirement

CERCLA requires potential claimants against the Superfund to send a demand letter to all potential parties. Initiation of an action is permitted if,
after 60 days, there is no response to this demand letter.[140]

The EPA has stated that a demand letter should detail the location of the
site, the presence of the hazardous substance that was released or threatens
to be released, the dates and types of response activity undertaken at the
site, the prior notice or notices given to the recipient of the demand letter
regarding response activities, the total response cost, a general statement
that the recipient is a responsible party under the Act, and a demand for
payment.[141]

The demand letter serves as a means by which the plaintiff can control
the scope of litigation. Additional defendants may be admitted to the case
only if the plaintiff wants them in and has served them with proper notice.
The claimant, having incurred expenses on cleanup, should be able to recover the response costs quickly.

Cases interpreting the notice requirement hold that courts may overlook
the notice requirement in situations where the plaintiff has substantially
complied with the provisions.[142] These courts have been willing to overlook
the strict formalities required by the statute and have followed the EPA
guidelines, which provide that the PRP must receive a 60-day notice in
some form.[143] Thus, waiver of the requirement demands a balancing of the
equities of all parties concerned and ultimately depends on a finding that
the PRP had 60 days' notice, in some form, which was sufficiently detailed
to constitute the functional equivalent of a demand letter. In the absence of
such notice, the plaintiff will not have met the jurisdictional prerequisites
for suit, and the court can properly dismiss the action.

---

[139] 42 U.S.C. § 9622(g).

[140] 42 U.S.C. § 9612 (1982). This can be used as a procedural defense by claiming lack of
jurisdiction due to failure to comply with the demand letter requirement.

[141] Bulk Distribution Centers, Inc. v. Monsanto Co., 589 F. Supp. 1437, 1449 n. 25 (S.D.
Fla. 1984).

[142] See United States v. Allied Chemical Corp., 587 F. Supp. 1205, 1208 (N.D. Cal. 1984);
see also Mola Dev. Corp. v. United States, 22 Env't Rep. Cas. (BNA) 1443, 1445 (C.D.
Cal. 1985).

[143] Id.

§ 1.19 —Superliens

A number of states, including Arkansas,[144] Connecticut,[145] Massachusetts,[146] New Hampshire,[147] New Jersey [148] and Tennessee[149] have enacted superlien provisions,[150] and others have considered enacting a superlien bill.[151] A superlien gives the state a "first-priority lien against property subject to a cleanup,"[152] regardless of any security interests filed prior to the state's lien. In most cases, the cost of cleanup exceeds the value of the property, so mortgage liens are effectively erased.[153]

Superliens are established, in part, to offset CERCLA's requirement of state contribution (minimum 10 percent) to the cleanup costs within its borders.[154] A superlien permits a state to recover part of the cost from the sale of the cleaned property, but it does so at the expense of any other lien holder. States that have a superlien provision have implemented it in an effort to shift the burden onto another party. This financial burden is just another hazard to lending that must be considered by banks before lending funds.

Even without superliens, if a bankruptcy petition is filed, states may be successful in recovering cleanup costs as administrative expenses. In *Lancaster v. Tennessee (In re Wall Tube & Metal Products Co.),*[155] the Sixth Circuit held it proper that "the response costs incurred by Tennessee and recoverable under CERCLA be deemed an administrative expense."[156]

In reversing the district court's affirmance of the bankruptcy court's decision, Judge Keith relied on the Supreme Court's rationale in *Ohio v. Kovacs*[157] and *Midlantic National Bank v. New Jersey Department of*

---

[144] Ark. Stat. Ann. §§ 8-7-417, -514, -516 (Michie 1987 & Supp. 1989).

[145] Conn. Gen. Stat. Ann. § 22a-452a (West Supp. 1990).

[146] Mass. Gen. Laws Ann. ch. 21E, § 13 (West Supp. 1990).

[147] N.H. Rev. Stat. Ann. § 147-B:10-b (Equity Supp. 1989).

[148] N.J. Stat. Ann. § 58:10-23.11f(f) (West Supp. 1989).

[149] Tenn. Code Ann. § 68-46-209 (Michie Supp. 1989).

[150] *See* Cohen, *Hazardous Waste: A Threat to the Lender's Environment,* 19 U.C.C. L.J. 99, 115–23 (1986) (reviewing 11 state superlien statutes).

[151] *Attorney General Proposes State Liens for Those Who Cannot Repay Cleanup Costs,* 18 Env't Rep. (BNA) 1936 (Dec. 18, 1987).

[152] Dean, *How Hazardous Waste Statutes Influence Real Estate Transactions,* 18 Env't Rep. (BNA) 933, 935 (July 31, 1987).

[153] *Id.*

[154] *See* 42 U.S.C. § 9604(c)(3)(C)(ii) (1982 and Supp. V 1987).

[155] 831 F.2d 118 (6th Cir. 1987) (hereinafter, "Wall Tube"). This is discussed in greater detail in **Chapter 7.**

[156] *Id.* at 123.

[157] 469 U.S. 274 (1985).

Environmental Protection.[158] Based on his reading of *Kovacs,* Judge Keith determined that the bankruptcy trustee had a duty to "'comply with the environmental laws of the State.'"[159]

Citing *Midlantic,* he found that "the efforts of the trustee to marshal and distribute the assets of the estate must yield to governmental interest in public health and safety." As might be expected, these rulings have caused great concern among creditors. In addition, the legal community has used this conflict between bankruptcy and environmental law to their clients' best advantage.

§ 1.20   Asbestos Hazard Emergency Response Act (AHERA)

The Asbestos Hazard Emergency Response Act (AHERA),[160] enacted in 1986, requires the EPA to establish a program that gives schools precise guidance in dealing with asbestos and prescribes a certification regimen for asbestos inspections and contractors. AHERA also calls for the inspection of school buildings for asbestos materials, the implementation of management plans for dealing with any potential hazards found, submission of the management plans to state authorities, and disposal. The plans were to be submitted by May 9, 1989, and the schools were then required to begin to implement any abatement actions called for in the plans.[161]

All public and private schools must have inspections conducted by accredited inspectors to determine the location, extent, and condition of all known or suspected asbestos-containing material (ACM). The local educational authority (LEA) must conduct air testing, to aid in determining whether any type of response action is required, but no specific level of airborne asbestos is mandated as a basis for triggering abatement action.

Routine visual inspections by the LEA's staff are required, as are periodic, more substantive re-inspections. The results of the inspections and air samples, as well as the management plans, must be made available to service workers, teachers, and parents.

In a 1988 case, former manufacturers of asbestos products challenged the school rule promulgated by the EPA under AHERA, because it did not provide the specific guidance for asbestos control that AHERA requires.[162]

---

[158] 474 U.S. 494 (1986).

[159] Wall Tube, 831 F.2d at 122 (quoting Ohio v. Kovacs, 469 U.S. at 285).

[160] 20 U.S.C. § 3601 et seq.

[161] It is likely that the federal aid program for asbestos abatement in the schools will be reauthorized for five years. Asbestos Abatement Report, Oct. 19, 1990, at 1.

[162] Safe Buildings Alliance v. EPA, 846 F.2d 79 (D.C. Cir. 1988), *cert. denied,* 488 U.S. 942 (1988).

The court found the EPA's listing of acceptable responses, which left the choice of which response to implement to the schools, sufficiently responsive to the statute. Thus, except under extreme circumstances, repair is always an acceptable response for "damaged" asbestos building material. AHERA is "neutral" on the issue of the desirability of removal.

A five-day training course is required for certification of contractors. The same contractors who recommend which response action should be taken can also do the work—some say this may lead to more expensive removal projects than are necessary.

Numerous attempts have been made at the federal, state, and local levels to extend AHERA-type programs to all buildings. So far, none has passed, but it is probably only a matter of time until one is enacted. (See § 1.32.)

§ 1.21   Resource Conservation and Recovery Act (RCRA)

The Resource Conservation and Recovery Act (RCRA)[163] regulates the disposal of hazardous wastes on land, and tracks them from "cradle to grave." RCRA allows equitable relief, such as injunctions, against handling, storage, transport, and disposal of hazardous waste. Its remedies are somewhat different from CERCLA's, which are mainly compensatory.

To establish liability under RCRA, a defendant must show: (1) the defendants are "persons" who; (2) "contributed to" the "past or present handling, storage, treatment, transportation or disposal" of a "hazardous waste;" and (3) the hazardous substance "may present an imminent and substantial endangerment to health or the environment."[164]

The term "person" includes both individuals and corporations and does not exclude corporate officers and employees.[165] Corporate officers and major shareholders may be liable if they have "ultimate authority to control" the proper handling of the hazardous substance.[166] Thus, RCRA liability may arise even for a person who does not control or have charge of the overall operation.

"Handling," which has not been defined in the Act, can subject a person to liability. In *State of Vermont v. Staco Inc.,* handling was found where a mercury thermometer plant's protective procedures were inadequate to

---

[163] 42 U.S.C. § 6901 et seq.

[164] 42 U.S.C. § 6972(a)(1)(B).

[165] 42 U.S.C. § 6903(15).

[166] United States v. Northeastern Pharmaceutical and Chemical Co., Inc., 810 F.2d at 745. *See also* State of Vermont v. Staco, Inc., 684 F. Supp. 822 (D. Vt. 1988), *modified,* 1989 WL 225428 (D. Vt.), 31 Env't Rep. Cas. (BNA) 1814 (D. Vt. Apr. 20, 1989).

prevent employees from becoming carriers of mercury.[167] The mercury had been carried by the workers into their homes, on their bodies and their clothing.

The phrase "contributed to" can be stretched considerably to find liability. In some cases where the court did not find CERCLA liability for arranging for disposal of hazardous substances, it found RCRA liability based on this clause.[168]

Once it has been determined that a material is "waste," as opposed to recycled material or material used in a process but never actually discarded, one must decide whether it is hazardous waste. The first step is to search for it among the hundreds of substances listed in the statutes and regulations as hazardous wastes.[169] The next step is to determine whether the waste is ignitable, corrosive, toxic, or reactive. Any waste generated from the treatment, storage, or disposal of hazardous waste is also hazardous waste. This is the so-called "derived from" rule.

After waste is determined to be hazardous, an elaborate set of requirements becomes effective. These requirements will only be summarized here. One must:

1. Obtain an EPA identification number;
2. Make sure that the waste is properly packaged and labeled;
3. Prepare a manifest;[170]
4. Make sure that the waste is delivered to authorized transporters or management facilities.

If waste is accumulated at a facility for more than 90 days, a "temporary storage and disposal facility" permit must be obtained.[171] A 1984 RCRA amendment provides that the EPA cannot grant such a permit unless the facility has taken corrective action with respect to prior releases of hazardous waste at the same facility.

The manifest system allows the hazardous waste to be tracked from the generator to the transporter to the hazardous waste disposal facility, not

---

[167] State of Vermont v. Staco, Inc., 684 F. Supp. at 836.

[168] United States v. Northeastern Pharmaceutical and Chemical Co., Inc., 810 F.2d at 745. *See also* United States v. Aceto Agricultural Chemicals Corp., 872 F.2d 1373 (8th Cir. 1989).

[169] Although the EPA has classified asbestos as a hazardous substance governed by the National Emission Standards for Hazardous Air Pollutants (NESHAP) and CERCLA, it has not declared the removed ACM to be a "hazardous" waste governed by RCRA. Instead, asbestos disposal and transport are regulated by NESHAPS, CERCLA, federal transportation regulations, and state and local laws.

[170] 40 C.F.R. § 262 (1989).

[171] 42 U.S.C. § 6925.

unlike a relay race in which a baton is passed.[172] A manifest must describe the waste, detailing the total quantity, type, and number of containers. Generators must retain for three years, records of any test results, waste analyses, and manifests.[173] Transporters must also retain copies of manifests for three years.

Underground storage tanks, another topic of the 1984 RCRA amendments,[174] are broadly defined to include any tank that is at least 10 percent underground, with some exceptions. If a facility has underground storage tanks, the government must be notified and the necessary interim steps taken. New tanks must be properly constructed and protected from corrosion. They must be tested to ensure that they are not leaking.

RCRA imposes penalties for violations of compliance orders,[175] "knowing" transportation of hazardous waste to unlicensed facilities, disposal without permits, and false statements on permit applications.[176]

The EPA has determined that "[w]astes containing asbestos are not hazardous wastes under the Resource Conservation and Recovery Act."[177] Disposal of asbestos waste, therefore, is regulated under the nonhazardous waste regulations promulgated pursuant to RCRA.[178] These regulations pertain to facility siting and the general operation of solid waste disposal facilities.

Additional requirements for asbestos disposal facilities are imposed, however, by the asbestos NESHAP, discussed in § 1.23. These requirements are designed to prevent asbestos emissions into the ambient air and to prevent public asbestos exposure.[179] Therefore, a building owner or asbestos abatement contractor must take care that asbestos waste is sent only to an "approved" or licensed asbestos disposal site.

The EPA can require, by administrative order, monitoring, testing, analysis, and reporting of any site that it believes presents a substantial hazard.[180] Thus, the EPA can use its authority under RCRA to investigate inactive hazardous waste sites outside the RCRA net.

---

[172] 42 U.S.C. § 6922(a)(5).

[173] 40 C.F.R. § 262.40 (1989).

[174] Solid Waste Disposal Act, 42 U.S.C. § 6901, as amended by RCRA, 42 U.S.C. § 6991.

[175] 42 U.S.C. § 6925.

[176] 42 U.S.C. § 6928. Civil penalties can be up to $25,000 per day and criminal penalties can be up to $50,000 per day. Individuals may be fined $25,000 per day and receive 5 years' imprisonment. Corporate offenders may be fined up to $1 million.

[177] U.S. Environmental Protection Agency, Asbestos Waste Management Guidance 7 (May 1985). State waste disposal regulations may be more restrictive than federal regulations. Therefore, some states may list asbestos as a hazardous waste.

[178] 40 C.F.R. § 257.1–.4 (1988).

[179] See generally 40 C.F.R. § 61.156 (1988).

[180] 42 U.S.C. § 6984.

On March 5, 1990, the EPA promulgated amendments to its regulations under RCRA.[181] These amendments are known as the Hazardous Waste Management System; Identification and Listing of Hazardous Waste; and Toxicity Characteristics Revisions. They expand the number of substances regulated as "hazardous wastes." Twenty-five organic chemicals have been added; their presence determines toxicity under RCRA's toxicity characteristics provision. As a result of the Toxicity Characteristics Revisions, an additional 15,000 to 17,000 facilities will be considered waste-generating facilities under the purview of RCRA.[182]

§ 1.22   Toxic Substances Control Act (TSCA)

The Toxic Substances Control Act (TSCA),[183] passed in 1976, provides a data base of knowledge about existing chemicals and new chemicals that may be hazardous.

TSCA requires that anyone who manufactures, imports, or processes asbestos and other chemicals must keep prescribed records about them, to enable the EPA to decide whether certain chemicals should be controlled.

On July 6, 1989, the EPA announced the promulgation of new regulations under Section 6 of TSCA, which bans the manufacture, import, and processing of asbestos products in three stages over a six-year period. Among the asbestos products banned were felt products such as roofing and floor felt, pipeline wrap, and vinyl asbestos floor tile.[184]

The EPA may require any company that manufactures, distributes, or disposes of a chemical substance that may present an unreasonable risk of injury to be chemically tested. There are also reporting and record-keeping requirements.[185] The government may commence a civil action to seize an "imminently hazardous chemical substance or mixture."[186]

The EPA may request preliminary assessment information, such as where a chemical is manufactured, the quantity manufactured, estimates of worker exposure, customer uses, and trade names. Violations in the form of monetary fines may be issued for incorrect information.

Most importantly, manufacturers, processors, or distributors of chemicals must inform the EPA if they have notice that the chemical poses a substantial risk of injury to health or the environment. This rule applies to

---

[181] 42 U.S.C. § 6901 et seq.

[182] 55 Fed. Reg. 11,855 (1990).

[183] 15 U.S.C. § 2601 et seq. *See also* Fabricant, *TSCA Liability in Court: Is Ignorance Bliss or Will a Strict Liability Standard Be the Result?*, 6 J. Contemp. L. & Pol'y 297 (1990).

[184] EPA Environmental News, July 6, 1989.

[185] 15 U.S.C. § 2607.

[186] 15 U.S.C. § 2606(a)(1)(A).

all persons engaged in the manufacture, processing, or distribution of a chemical, including the officers and employees of the company.

TSCA requires that all schools be inspected to determine the presence and quantity of ACM in school facilities. Regulations require the cleanup of asbestos-contaminated schools. The Act also regulates the storage and disposal of PCBs.

On January 11, 1990, the National Federation of Federal Employees filed a petition under Section 21 of TSCA requesting that the EPA regulate 4-phenylcyclohexene found in carpeting.[187] Although the petition was denied, the EPA has asked carpet companies to test their products voluntarily for total chemical emissions, to reduce the public's exposure to chemical emissions from new carpet and carpet installation materials.[188]

§ 1.23   Clean Air Act and National Emission Standards for Hazardous Air Pollutants (NESHAP)

The Clean Air Act, enacted in 1970 and was amended in 1990. The Act prohibits the emission of hazardous air pollutants in violation of EPA standards and prescribes, under the National Ambient Air Quality Standards (NAAQS), maximum concentration levels for certain pollutants.

The new Clean Air Act uses a two-phase approach.[189] The first phase establishes controls based on the maximum available control technology (MACT). The second phase deals with any remaining risk after application of MACT. The Act lists nearly 200 substances for which the EPA is to establish emission standards. Included are methanol (used as a solvent, antifreeze, and cleaner), methyl chloroform (used to clean metal and electronic parts, and to manufacture pesticides and process tiles), and toluene (used in medicines, dyes, and detergents).

The EPA can add a substance to the list if it finds evidence that the substance causes or is reasonably anticipated to cause cancer, reproductive dysfunction, or other health problems.

The EPA is required to establish emission standards for (1) major sources—those emitting 10 metric tons per year of any single hazardous air pollutant or 25 metric tons per year of any combination of hazardous air pollutants—and (2) area sources—those which the EPA judges should be controlled, based on aggregate emissions of hazardous air pollutants in a particular area. This would make the Act applicable for the first time to small businesses concentrated in an urban area, such as dry cleaners, bakeries, and auto refinishing shops.

---

[187] Indoor Pollution News, May 17, 1990, at 1.

[188] Indoor Air Review, March 1991, at 3.

[189] The Clean Air Act Amendments (CAA) of 1990, Pub. L. No. 101-549, 21 Env't Rep. (BNA) 1631 (1991) (Database BNA-ER).

The Act calls for periodic monitoring,[190] reporting, and appropriate civil penalties.[191] There is no statutory maximum dollar assessment per violation.

The National Emission Standards for Hazardous Air Pollutants (NESHAP)[192] are nationally uniform standards for notification of work to be done and work practices for specific hazardous pollutants. Currently, there are standards for asbestos, benzene, beryllium, coke-oven emissions, inorganic arsenic, mercury, radionuclides, and vinyl chloride.

In 1973, the EPA designated asbestos as a hazardous air pollutant under NESHAP and established standards that prohibited the use of sprayed-on asbestos fireproofing and insulation materials containing more than 1 percent asbestos. These regulations are designed to prevent the emission of asbestos to the outside air.[193]

The asbestos NESHAP imposes notification and work practice requirements on "owners and operators" of demolition or renovation projects involving asbestos.[194] Although the terms "owner" and "operator" are not defined in the NESHAP, EPA's interpretation is that an owner or operator of a facility who purchases the services of an outside contractor is considered to be the owner or operator of a renovation or demolition under this regulation.[195] That interpretation was upheld in *United States v. Geppert Brothers.*[196]

The regulations also require prior notification and reporting to EPA and removal of asbestos materials before any demolition or renovation involving more than 260 linear feet of asbestos pipe or more than 160 square feet of asbestos surfacing material.[197] The removed asbestos must be disposed of in specially designated disposal sites.[198] The NESHAP standard, which was extended in 1978 to ban all spraying of asbestos materials for any

---

[190] *Id.* § 504.

[191] *Id.* § 113(a),(d).

[192] 42 U.S.C. § 7401 et seq. (1982); 40 C.F.R. § 61.01(a) (1988).

[193] OSHA establishes workplace standards for worker protection inside the buildings. This is discussed in § 1.24.

[194] 40 C.F.R. §§ 61.145–61.147. The asbestos NESHAP was amended to include a definition of nonfriable ACM as "material containing more than 1 percent asbestos by area that cannot be crumbled, pulverized or reduced to powder by hand pressure." 40 C.F.R. pt. 61 (Nov. 20, 1990). Fed. Reg. Category I nonfriable ACM which, under normal conditions, does not have to be removed prior to demolition, includes resilient floor covering, roofing products, gaskets, and packings.

[195] *See* 49 Fed. Reg. 13,659 (1984).

[196] 638 F. Supp. 996 (E.D. Pa. 1986).

[197] 38 Fed. Reg. 8,826 (1973); 40 C.F.R. §§ 61.145–61.160 (1990).

[198] *Id.* If the asbestos content of material is less than 10 percent, as determined by a method other than point counting by polarized light microscopy (PLM), the asbestos content must be verified by point counting using PLM. 40 C.F.R. § 61.141.

purpose, did not contain any numerical threshold and EPA has not set any action response standard.[199]

However, a federal court in West Virginia has found that the government may not act to enforce federal asbestos regulations under NESHAP in cases where the amount of asbestos *actually removed* is less than the minimum amount that triggers NESHAP requirements.[200] Thus, the notification and work-practice requirements did not apply merely because the government believed the project *eventually* would involve more than the minimum amount of asbestos.

Under this standard, "renovation" is defined as "altering in any way one or more facility components."[201] Wrecking or taking out any load-supporting structural members of a facility is excluded from the definition of "renovation" and classified as "demolition."[202] The term "facility" includes any industrial, institutional, or commercial structure, installation, or building, except apartment buildings with no more than four units.[203]

The EPA has set forth the general framework and minimum standards, but the Act is implemented through state plans, which must be approved by the federal government.[204]

In reviewing a permit application, the EPA will look at the total air quality and will negotiate with one or more plants to allow a "bubble": the pollutants may come from one or more smoke stacks, as long as the total level of pollution does not increase. The procedure is somewhat analogous to buying air rights for construction.

Civil and criminal penalties are applicable to building owners and contractors if friable asbestos is inadvertently released during renovation or demolition, even if the owner had no actual knowledge.[205]

The Clean Air Act provides the EPA with several administrative and judicial options for enforcement.[206] Violators may be subject to civil penalties of up to $25,000 per day.[207] In addition, criminal penalties of up to $25,000 per day, or up to two years of imprisonment, or both, may be assessed for

---

[199] 43 Fed. Reg. 26,372 (1978). Asbestos-containing floor tile and roofing materials are exempt. They must only be removed if they are in poor condition and friable, prior to renovation or demolition. Asbestos Abatement Report, Dec. 10, 1990, p. 1.

[200] United States v. Fiber Free Co. No. A-89-0624 (D.W. Va. 1990); Asbestos Abatement Report, Oct. 15, 1990 at 3.

[201] 40 C.F.R. § 61.141 (1988).

[202] *Id.*

[203] *Id.*

[204] 42 U.S.C. § 7410.

[205] United States v. Geppert Brothers, 638 F. Supp. 996 (E.D. Pa. 1986).

[206] *See* 42 U.S.C. § 7413 (1990).

[207] 42 U.S.C. § 7413(b).

knowing violations.[208] Penalties may be doubled for subsequent criminal convictions.

A recent EPA memorandum implied that nonfriable ACM would not have to be removed prior to demolition if it was in good condition. (The asbestos NESHAP requires removal of friable asbestos materials from buildings that are being renovated or demolished.) Nonfriable materials include flooring and roofing materials that may be broken up and may release fibers as a building is torn down.[209]

§ 1.24   Occupational Safety and Health Administration Act (OSHA)

The Occupational Safety and Health Administration Act (OSHA), through the National Institute for Occupational Safety and Health, promulgates standards for asbestos in the workplace.[210] On June 20, 1986, OSHA passed regulations pertaining to occupational exposure to asbestos, based on a determination that "employees exposed to asbestos face a significant risk to their health, and that these final standards will substantially reduce that risk."[211] However, the regulations only apply to the employer/employee relationship, not to building owners in their capacity as owners. The regulations are for the safety of abatement contractors and employees[212] and proscribe acceptable levels of airborne asbestos and the conduct of renovation, encapsulation, and abatement work.

OSHA has promulgated both a construction standard and a general industry standard; these standards apply to all workplaces in all industries.[213] The general workplace standard obligates commercial employers to maintain workplaces free of asbestos hazards; the construction standard applies to construction work and asbestos-related activities, including demolition, renovation, repair, and remediation.

Under OSHA regulations, the federal limit for workers' exposure to airborne asbestos is 0.2 fibers per cubic centimeter of air (f/cc) average exposure over an eight-hour, time-weighted workday. The exposure limit over a 30-minute period is 1.0 f/cc.[214]

---

[208] 42 U.S.C. § 7413(c) and (c)(2).

[209] Asbestos Abatement Report, Apr. 30, 1990, at 7.

[210] 29 C.F.R. § 1910.1001 (1987).

[211] 51 Fed. Reg. 22,612 et seq. (1986).

[212] 29 C.F.R. at § 1926.58.

[213] 29 C.F.R. pts. 1910.1001 and 1926.58 (as amended by 53 Fed. Reg. 35,610, 35,625, and 35,627 (1988).

[214] Indoor Pollution News, Nov. 30, 1989, at 4.

Building owners who are employers are obligated to comply with the general industry standard. OSHA applies to "office employees in buildings where asbestos products has [sic] been installed and to employees who work in the vicinity of asbestos abatement and renovation activities."[215] The asbestos NESHAP applies to "owners or operators" of a demolition or renovation.[216] Although the terms "owner" and "operator" are not defined in the NESHAP, the EPA's interpretation is that the owner or operator of a facility who purchases the services of an outside contractor is considered to be the owner or operator of a renovation or demolition under the regulation.[217] Building owners do not incur obligations under the OSHA asbestos standard if the occupants of the building are not employed by the owner.[218]

The regulations require owner-employers to perform initial and periodic asbestos exposure monitoring of employees who are or may be reasonably expected to be exposed to airborne concentrations of asbestos above the action level.[219] This monitoring is in addition to any common-law duty the owner may have and to any local laws.

Every employer subject to the general industry standard is required to conduct initial air monitoring to determine exposure levels for employees who are or may reasonably be expected to be exposed to airborne asbestos concentrations exceeding prescribed levels.[220] Periodic monitoring may be required.[221]

The OSHA Hazardous Communications Standard (HAZCOM) requires companies to have material safety data sheets for "hazardous chemicals."[222] Under HAZCOM, all employers must provide certain information and training to workers who might be exposed to "hazardous substances" under normal conditions of use or in a "foreseeable emergency."[223] The HAZCOM standards differ from the OSHA Asbestos Rules in that the OSHA standards contain an action level threshold (0.1 f/cc), while HAZCOM has no threshold. If building workers have been exposed to asbestos in their normal work, then HAZCOM applies and the employers must satisfy added obligations for training, preparation and dissemination of material safety data sheets, and more specific warnings.

---

[215] 51 Fed. Reg. 22,677 (1986).

[216] 40 C.F.R. § 61.141 (1988).

[217] 49 Fed. Reg. 13,659 (1984).

[218] *Id.* at 22,678.

[219] *See generally* 29 C.F.R. § 1910.1001(d), (j)(5), (l), § 1926.58(f), (k)(3), (m) (1987).

[220] 29 C.F.R. § 1910.1001(d)(2)(i) (1988) (as amended by 53 Fed. Reg. 35,610 and 35,626 (1988)).

[221] 29 C.F.R. § 1910.1001(d)(3).

[222] 52 Fed. Reg. 31,877 (1988).

[223] *Id.*

Under OSHA, supervisors on large-scale, asbestos-related operations must be designated "competent persons" who have completed EPA-sponsored courses. There are specific engineering and work-practice controls to reduce exposure to asbestos, but no training or certification requirements are mandated for nonsupervisory personnel on job sites.[224]

An employer's failure to comply with OSHA's asbestos standards can result in a variety of civil and criminal penalties. Any employer cited for a "serious" violation will be assessed a civil penalty up to $7,000 per violation.[225] The same penalty may be imposed for violations that are not determined to be serious,[226] or for failure to correct a violation.[227] Willful or repeated violations can subject an employer to a more stringent $10,000 civil penalty.[228] Willful violations that cause an employee's death are punishable by a criminal fine of up to $10,000, imprisonment for up to six months, or both.[229] Criminal penalties can be doubled for subsequent convictions.[230]

Responding to a two-year-old court order, OSHA has proposed a new rule that would require building owners to keep records concerning asbestos materials in their buildings and to notify workers about potential asbestos hazards. Among other provisions, the rule would:

1. Lower OSHA's permissible exposure limit for asbestos from 0.2 f/cc to 0.1 f/cc;

2. Require contractors to provide OSHA with 10 days' advance notice before beginning asbestos abatement, renovation projects, or demolition projects involving asbestos;

3. Require employers other than the building owner who plan work that would affect asbestos, or who gain knowledge about asbestos materials in the building, to notify the building owner (contractors working in a building would be required to inform the building owner of any asbestos materials encountered during the course of their work, and the building owners would be required to pass this information on to their employees and to other employers in the building);

4. Building owners would be required to keep written records of all information they obtain through the OSHA notification scheme, or

---

[224] 55 Fed. Reg. 29,712 (1990); *see also* Asbestos Abatement Report, Mar. 19, 1990, at 4.

[225] 29 U.S.C. § 666(b) (1990).

[226] *See* 29 U.S.C. § 666(c) (1990).

[227] A penalty of $7,000 per day may be assessed as long as the failure or violation continues. 29 U.S.C. § 666(d).

[228] 29 U.S.C. § 666(a).

[229] *See* 29 U.S.C. § 666(e).

[230] *Id.*

through any other means, about the presence, location, and quantity of asbestos materials in their buildings, and to transfer these records to successive owners when a building changes ownership;

5. A "competent person" would have to be present during small-scale asbestos jobs.[231]

§ 1.25   Penalties

Violators of environmental statutes can face severe penalties and possible imprisonment.

The United States Department of Justice (DOJ) has actively prosecuted environmental crimes since approximately 1982. From 1983 through January 1990, the DOJ has had 606 indictments resulting in 461 guilty pleas and convictions.[232] These pleas and convictions resulted in over $26 million in fines and approximately 286 years in jail terms.[233] However, of the 286 years in prison sentences, only 104 years' actual confinement has resulted.[234] Consequently, the average guilty defendant spent barely six months in prison,[235] a situation that raises questions about whether substantial criminal penalties are being imposed as often as the public may believe.

§ 1.26   —CERCLA Penalty Provisions

Violations of CERCLA Section 9603 reporting requirements can result in civil penalties of up to $20,000 for single violations.

Potential criminal sanctions for violating the reporting requirements include imprisonment of up to three years (five years, for a second or subsequent conviction) and fines under title 18 of the United States Code.[236]

Felony penalties can be levied on a "person in charge" who fails to notify the EPA "as soon as [he or she] has knowledge" of a violation or who knowingly submits false or misleading information.[237]

---

[231] 55 Fed. Reg. 29,712 (1990).

[232] Interoffice memorandum from Peggy Hutchins to Joseph G. Block, Chief, Environmental Crimes Section, U. S. Dept. of Justice (Jan. 26, 1990).

[233] *Id.*

[234] *Id.*

[235] Fromm, *Commanding Respect: Criminal Sanctions for Environmental Crimes,* 21 St. Mary's L.J. 771, 821, 822–23 (1990). Harris et al., *Criminal Liability for Violations of Federal Hazardous Waste Law & The "Knowledge" Of Corporations and Their Executives,* 23 Wake Forest L. Rev. 203 (1988).

[236] 42 U.S.C. § 9603(b) (1982 and Supp. V 1987).

[237] 42 U.S.C. § 9603(b)(3).

Section 9603(b)(3) of CERCLA requires the person "in charge" of a facility to notify the appropriate agency of the release as soon as he or she has such knowledge.

The statute does not define the term "in charge." At least one court has held that the term "in charge" extends to two persons of relatively low rank.[238] The defendant in *United States v. Carr* was a maintenance foreman at an army installation. He instructed several workers to dispose of cans of waste paint in a pit that was filled with water. When the workers noted that some of the paint cans were leaking and told Carr that they believed dumping into ponds was illegal, he continued to permit the disposal. Two weeks later, Carr ordered one of the workers to cover up the pit with earth. On appeal, the Second Circuit upheld Carr's conviction, equating the term "in charge" with "responsible." The court further found that the person "in charge" must have had some supervisory control over the facility but need not have been the sole person in charge of the facility.[239]

Section 9603(c) of CERCLA also provides for criminal sanctions. Certain persons were required to notify the EPA, within 180 days after the enactment of CERCLA, of the existence of facilities that had been used for the treatment, storage, or disposal of hazardous substances.[240]

CERCLA also provides for felony sanctions for any person who knowingly destroys, mutilates, erases, disposes of, conceals or otherwise renders unavailable or unreadable, or falsifies any records to be provided to the EPA.[241] Section 9603(d)(2) most often arises in connection with Superfund sites. When the EPA finds it necessary to obtain information from potentially responsible parties (PRPs) who may be connected with a specific site, it will ordinarily send out what is known as a "Section 104(e) letter" requesting records and documents. Criminal penalties can arise if the company destroys records after receiving a request from the EPA.

Conviction under this provision could result in imprisonment for up to three years and/or a fine in accordance with the provisions of title 18.[242] CERCLA also provides for criminal sanctions if a person "knowingly gives or causes to be given any false information as a part of any such claim" against the Superfund.[243] A person convicted under this section can be fined in accordance with the provisions of title 18 or imprisoned for up to three years, or both.[244]

---

[238] United States v. Carr, 880 F.2d 1550, 1554 (2d Cir. 1989).

[239] *Id.* at 1555.

[240] 42 U.S.C. § 9603(c) (1982).

[241] 42 U.S.C. § 9603(d)(2) (Supp. V 1987).

[242] 42 U.S.C. § 9603(d)(2) (1982 and Supp. V 1987).

[243] 42 U.S.C. § 9612(b)(1) (Supp. V 1987).

[244] *Id.*

The Emergency Planning and Community Right-to-Know Act of 1986 (EPCRA), one of the SARA amendments to CERCLA, contains criminal sanctions for a knowing and willful failure to report a release of a reportable quantity of certain chemicals identified under EPCRA.[245] A violation of this provision could result in a fine of up to $25,000 and imprisonment for up to two years.[246]

The final notable penalty provision of CERCLA, Section 9609(d), allows the President to award up to $10,000 to any individual who provides information leading to the arrest and conviction of any person for any criminal penalty under CERCLA. This has become known as CERCLA's "bounty hunter" provision.[247]

The majority of convictions under CERCLA stem from the failure to report a release. *United States v. Carr,*[248] previously noted, and *United States v. Greer*[249] involved failure to report a release under CERCLA. Recently, a felony conviction for a release of asbestos under CERCLA was obtained. In *United States v. Derecktor,* the company pled guilty to failure to report a release of asbestos that occurred during ship repair operations— a violation of CERCLA.[250] The company was fined $600,000 for the CERCLA violation and accompanying violations of the Clean Air Act and the Clean Water Act.[251]

§ 1.27   —RCRA Penalty Provisions

Civil penalties can be levied for failure to provide information requested by the EPA.[252] RCRA also imposes criminal penalties on any person who:

(1) knowingly transports or causes to be transported any hazardous waste to a facility which does not have a permit;[253]

(2) knowingly treats, stores, or disposes of any hazardous waste without a permit, or in knowing violation of any material condition or requirement of such permit, or is "in knowing violation of any material condition or requirement of any applicable interim status regulations or standards;[254]

---

[245] 42 U.S.C. §§ 11001–11050 (Supp. V 1987); 42 U.S.C. § 11045(b)(4).

[246] 42 U.S.C. § 11045(b)(4).

[247] 42 U.S.C. § 9609(d) (Supp. V 1987).

[248] 880 F.2d 1550, 1554 (2d Cir. 1989).

[249] 850 F.2d 1447, 1453 (11th Cir. 1988).

[250] 17 Env't Rep. (BNA) 1540, 1541 (1987).

[251] *Id.*

[252] United States v. Charles George Trucking Co., 624 F. Supp. 1185 (D. Mass. 1986), *aff'd,* 823 F.2d 685 (1st Cir. 1987).

[253] 42 U.S.C. § 6928(d)(1) (Supp. V 1987).

[254] 42 U.S.C. § 6928(d)(2)(A)–(C).

(3) knowingly omits material information or makes any false statement or representation in any application, record or other document filed, maintained or used for compliance purposes;[255]

(4) knowingly generates, treats, stores, exports, or disposes of hazardous waste and knowingly destroys, alters, conceals, or fails to file any record or other document required under the Act;[256]

(5) knowingly transports hazardous waste or causes hazardous waste to be transported without a manifest;[257]

(6) knowingly exports a hazardous waste to another country without its consent or in violation of an agreement between the United States and the government of the receiving country;[258]

(7) knowingly treats, stores, disposes of, or otherwise handles any used oil in knowing violation of a permit or "any material condition or requirement" of any applicable regulations or standards established under RCRA.[259]

A conviction under the foregoing provisions is a felony punishable by a fine of up to $50,000 per day, per violation, and imprisonment for two to five years.[260] A second conviction could result in the doubling of penalties with respect to both the fine and imprisonment.[261]

RCRA imposes more stringent felony sanctions upon any person who knowingly "transports, treats, stores, disposes of, or exports" any RCRA-listed or identified hazardous waste in violation of the above-delineated provisions, if the person "knows at the time that he thereby places another person in imminent danger of death or serious bodily injury."[262] This section is commonly referred to as the "knowing endangerment" provision. A violation of Section 6928(e) could subject the offender to a fine of up to $250,000 or imprisonment for up to 15 years, or both.[263] If the offender is an organization, fines can be as much as $1 million upon conviction.[264]

---

[255] 42 U.S.C. § 6928(d)(3).

[256] 42 U.S.C. § 6928(d)(4).

[257] 42 U.S.C. § 6928(d)(5).

[258] 42 U.S.C. § 6928(d)(6).

[259] 42 U.S.C. § 6928(d)(7).

[260] 42 U.S.C. § 6928(d).

[261] Id.

[262] 42 U.S.C. § 6928(e).

[263] Id.

[264] Id. Section 6928(f) of RCRA enumerates the special rules that relate to the knowing endangerment section. In particular, an organization is defined as "a legal entity, other than a government, established, or organized for any purpose, and such term includes a corporation, company, association, firm, partnership, joint stock company, foundation, institution, trust, society, union, or any other association of persons." 42 U.S.C. § 6928(f)(5). The special rules also address a person's state of mind, the level of knowledge required, affirmative defenses, the applicability of general criminal defenses, and the term "serious bodily injury." 42 U.S.C. § 6928(f)(1)–(4), (6).

There are felony penalties for "knowing" violations,[265] which include omitting material information or making false material statements or representations in reports and other filings.[266]

§ 1.28 —NESHAP Penalty Provisions

Violations of these regulations are punishable with civil penalties of as much as $25,000 per day, per violation. For a knowing violation, criminal fines in the same amounts can be levied, plus imprisonment for up to two years.[267] There can also be injunctions to prevent further violations of emission standards.

§ 1.29 —TSCA Penalty Provisions

Under TSCA, it may be a misdemeanor to knowingly or willfully violate any of the Act's provisions or the regulations promulgated pursuant to the Act.[268] Specifically, a person commits a violation if he or she knowingly or willfully violates regulations promulgated pursuant to Section 2603 (testing of chemical substances and mixtures), Section 2604 (premarket manufacturing and processing notices), or Section 2605 (the regulation of "hazardous chemical substances and mixtures" which may present an unreasonable risk of injury to the public health or the environment).[269] Criminal penalties also accrue for violations of subchapter II of the Act (asbestos hazards).[270]

It is a misdemeanor under TSCA to fail or refuse to: establish or maintain records; submit reports, notices, or other information; or permit access to or copying of records as required by the Act.[271] Additionally, a person can commit a misdemeanor by failing or refusing to permit entry or inspection as required by the Act.[272] Finally, it is a misdemeanor to use for commercial purposes a chemical substance or mixture which a person "knew or had reason to know was manufactured, processed, or distributed in commerce in violation of section 2604 or 2605" or of an order issued under sections

---

[265] United States v. Protex Industries, 874 F.2d 740, 742 (10th Cir. 1989).

[266] 42 U.S.C. § 6928(d) (Supp V 1987).

[267] Clean Air Act, 42 U.S.C. § 7413(c).

[268] 15 U.S.C. § 2615(b) (1988).

[269] 15 U.S.C. §§ 2603–2605.

[270] 15 U.S.C. § 2615(b) (1988).

[271] 15 U.S.C. § 2614(3) (1988).

[272] *Id.*

2604 and 2605 of TSCA.[273] Conviction under Section 2615(b) of TSCA could result in a fine of up to $25,000 per day, per violation, and/or imprisonment for up to one year.[274]

§ 1.30   —Other Environmental Penalty Provisions

Violators of any environmental law can be subject to alternative fines under title 18[275] of the United States Code, which provides for fines of up to $250,000 for an individual found guilty of a felony and fines of up to $500,000 for a corporation found guilty of a felony.[276] This is in addition to the fines in individual statutes.

A felony is committed when two or more persons conspire to commit an offense against the United States or any agency of the United States, and one or more of the persons commits an act to effect the object of the conspiracy. Violations of this statute are often alleged where two or more persons have conspired to violate environmental laws, such as the illegal disposal of hazardous wastes. Punishment for a conviction under this statute can result in imposition of a fine of up to $10,000 and/or imprisonment for up to five years. However, if the offense that is the object of the conspiracy is punishable as a misdemeanor, then the punishment for the conspiracy cannot exceed the punishment for the misdemeanor.

Another statute frequently used in connection with environmental crimes relates to the making of false statements. This statute makes it a felony to "knowingly and willfully" falsify, conceal, or cover up by any trick, scheme, or device, a material fact; to make any false, fictitious, or fraudulent statements or representations; or to make or use any "false writing or document knowing the same to contain any false, fictitious, or fraudulent statement or entry."[277] Because the statute applies to any matter

---

[273] 15 U.S.C. §§ 2614(2), 2615.

[274] 15 U.S.C. § 2615(b).

[275] See 18 U.S.C. § 3571 (1988) (applicable fines for defendants found guilty of offenses); see also § 3551 (authorized sentences). This section of title 18 states that a defendant who has been found guilty of an offense described in any Federal statute shall be sentenced in accordance with this chapter. 18 U.S.C. § 3551(a). It covers both individuals and organizations. 18 U.S.C. § 3551(b)–(c).

[276] 18 U.S.C. § 3571(b)–(c) (1988); see also § 3551. Note that this statute also permits a fine of twice the gross gain or gross loss, if any person derives a pecuniary gain from the offense or if the offense results in a pecuniary loss to a person other than the defendant. Id. § 3571(d). Under this provision, prosecutors are allegedly seeking the bulk of the penalties against Exxon in the Exxon Valdez incident. The prosecutors are purportedly trying to recover twice the economic loss caused to others. Another Political Prosecution?, Wall St. J., Mar. 5, 1990, at A10, col. 1.

[277] 42 U.S.C. § 1001 (1988).

within the jurisdiction of any department or agency of the United States, it would be useful where the environmental statute violated did not contain criminal provisions for making false statements to an agency.[278]

Recently, the number of prosecutions for environmental crimes seems to be greater than in the past. One individual was convicted on charges of knowing endangerment under the federal Clean Water Act for allegedly scooping nitric acid and nickel wastes out of vats and pouring them down a sink.[279]

It has been reported that, in fiscal 1989, federal courts handed out prison terms totaling about 37 years and fines of $11.1 million for environmental crimes, compared with less than two years of sentences and $198,000 in fines five years earlier.[280] Prison terms are more likely now because former misdemeanors have become felonies.

§ 1.31 —State and Local Penalty Provisions

State and local laws also have penalty provisions. For example, a New York City ordinance, Section 16-117.1 of the New York City Administrative Code, requires that asbestos materials be wet down, sealed, labeled, and separated from other waste when removed. An offense is punishable by a fine of not less than $500 and not more than $25,000 and/or imprisonment not to exceed one year.

When one guilty plea to criminal charges brought under this section was entered, the corporation was required to pay a $2,500 fine and place an ad in a metropolitan realty trade publication, urging compliance with the law.[281]

§ 1.32 Proposed Legislation

Environmental legislation is constantly being proposed. A major proposal of interest is Senator Howard Metzenbaum's (D.-Ohio) bill, S.1340, which would extend the federal regulatory framework of AHERA to federal and commercial buildings and would mandate that states adopt training and accreditation programs for all consultants, contractors, and workers performing asbestos abatement in public and commercial buildings.

---

[278] See also 18 U.S.C. §§ 1341, 1343 (1988) (mail fraud and wire fraud); 18 U.S.C. § 2 (1988) (aiding and abetting).

[279] Wall St. J., Sept. 10, 1990, at 1.

[280] Id.

[281] N.Y.L.J., Jan. 6, 1988, at 1, col. 4.

The amendment differs from AHERA in that it does not require inspections and implementation of management plans for asbestos. However, many states already comply with AHERA guidelines in their training and accreditation requirements for work in nonschool buildings. It has been estimated that the Metzenbaum proposal would cost between $50 and $150 billion.[282]

In 1988 the United States Senate's Committee on Environment and Public Works recommended to the full Senate the passage of a bill (S. 1629) known as the Indoor Air Quality Act of 1988. The bill was not enacted in 1988 but was reintroduced in substantially identical form as the Indoor Air Quality Act of 1991.[283] Representative Joseph P. Kennedy (D.-Mass.) has introduced a bill also known as the Indoor Air Quality Act of 1991[284] which has not yet been enacted. Both bills are discussed in greater detail in § 1.35.

The New York City Council has been trying for some time to pass legislation requiring the managers and owners of more than 800,000 city-owned and private buildings to inspect for damaged asbestos and take corrective action. One- and two-family homes would be exempt from abatement requirements, but sellers would have to inspect and disclose findings to buyers. The bill has gone through a number of revisions.

In its latest form, three different deadlines would be allowed for compliance, depending on the type of building.[285] The first group of buildings—including tall office buildings (over eight stories), hospitals, hotels, apartment buildings with elevators, postsecondary schools, and utility plants—would have six-and-a-half years to comply with all inspection, planning, and abatement requirements. Other buildings would have an additional three to six years.

Civil penalties for failure to comply could be up to $10,000 per violation, per day.

Building managers and owners would be required to employ city-accredited professionals and workers to repair and remove friable asbestos.

New York City's accreditation requirements for professionals and workers in the asbestos industry are more stringent than federal standards in AHERA. Training for custodians and building maintenance workers would be provided.

---

[282] Federal Building Asbestos Hazard Abatement Act of 1987, S. 981, reintroduced in substantially identical form in the 100th Congress as S. 2300. *See also Asbestos in Buildings: When Further Study Is the Wisest Course,* Legal Times, Sept. 12, 1988, at 21.

[283] S. 455, 102nd Cong., 1st Sess., (1991).

[284] H.R. 1066, 102d Cong., 1st Sess. (1991).

[285] Admin. Code of the City of New York, Proposed Intro. No. 1164-A.

§ 1.33   Notification

CERCLA[286] and TSCA[287] both require disclosure whenever there is potentially dangerous contamination. The Superfund requires two levels of reporting:

1. Any person in charge of a vessel or facility from which there is a release of a hazardous substance in reportable quantities into the environment must notify the EPA's National Response Center immediately upon learning of the release.[288]
2. The owner and operator of a vessel or facility from which a hazardous substance is released must notify potentially injured parties.[289]

The National Response Center must be notified whenever there is a "release" of a reportable quantity of any hazardous substance, or a "continuous" release, except for "federally-permitted releases."[290]

Before filing a lawsuit, a plaintiff must give the EPA, the state Department of Health Services, and all alleged violators a 60-day notice.[291]

Owners must publish a notice in local newspapers serving the affected area. Failure to notify the government of a discharge or release is a crime and may be punished by a fine of up to $10,000, imprisonment for up to one year, or both.

TSCA requires immediate notification by "any person" who obtains information of a "substantial risk."[292] This classification includes employees within a company's reporting chain.[293]

Beginning in July 1988, about 30,000 facilities were required to give an annual report on environmental releases of hundreds of toxic chemicals to the EPA and the states.[294] Furthermore, under SARA, no information is kept confidential except the "specific chemical identity" of a hazardous substance if the information is a "trade secret."[295]

The asbestos NESHAP imposes notification requirements as an audit tool, to allow regulatory agencies to inspect projects for compliance with

---

[286] 42 U.S.C. § 9603.

[287] 42 U.S.C. § 2607(e).

[288] 42 U.S.C. § 9603(a).

[289] 42 U.S.C. § 9611(a).

[290] 42 U.S.C. §§ 9602 and 9603(a), (f); 40 C.F.R. pt. 302 (1989).

[291] 42 U.S.C. § 9659. *See also* Reaves, *Causes of Action in Hazardous Waste Litigation,* California Lawyer, August 1989, at 65.

[292] 42 U.S.C. § 2607(e).

[293] 43 Fed. Reg. 11,110 (1978).

[294] 42 U.S.C. § 11023.

[295] 42 U.S.C. § 11042.

required work-practice standards.[296] Owners or operators of renovation projects regulated under the NESHAP[297] must notify the EPA in writing "[a]s early as possible before renovation begins."[298] The written notice must include the name and address of the owner or operator, the location and a description of the facility, an estimate of the quantity of friable asbestos present, scheduled start and completion dates, the nature of the operation, a description of the procedures to be used to comply with the regulations, and the name and location of the disposal site where the asbestos waste will be deposited.[299]

Notification requirements for demolition are similar to requirements for renovations. A demolition that involves at least 80 linear meters or 15 square meters of friable asbestos is subject to all requirements of the standard,[300] and written notification to the EPA must be postmarked at least 10 days before demolition begins.[301] Demolitions involving less than 80 linear meters or 15 square meters of friable asbestos are subject to only some of the requirements.[302] The notification need not include an explanation of the nature of the planned demolition, the procedures to be used to comply with the regulations, or an identification of the disposal site.[303]

In California, if owners of public or commercial buildings constructed prior to 1979 know that the building has asbestos-containing materials, they must provide to all employees working within the building a written notice concerning specified matters relating to asbestos.[304]

The Emergency Planning and Community Right-to-Know Act of 1986 (EPCRA) requires owners and operators of all facilities that use "hazardous" chemicals and "extremely hazardous chemicals"[305] to report their use to (1) the local fire department, (2) the local Emergency Planning Committee, and (3) the State Emergency Response Commission.[306]

---

[296] *See* Memorandum from Edward Reich and Michael S. Alushin to Air and Waste Mgmt. Div. Directors 4, 15 (Apr. 6, 1984) (asbestos strategy document).

[297] Renovation activities are regulated under the asbestos NESHAP if at least 80 linear meters of friable asbestos on pipes or at least 15 square meters of friable asbestos on other facility components will be stripped or removed. 40 C.F.R. § 61.145 (1990).

[298] 40 C.F.R. § 61.146(a), (b)(4).

[299] 40 C.F.R. § 61.146(c).

[300] 40 C.F.R. § 61.145(a).

[301] 40 C.F.R. § 61.146(b)(1).

[302] 40 C.F.R. § 61.145(b).

[303] 40 C.F.R. §§ 61.145(b), 61.146(b)(2), (c).

[304] Cal. Health & Safety Code, § 25910.

[305] 40 C.F.R. pt. 355 (1989).

[306] EPCRA was enacted as Title III of SARA, 42 U.S.C. §§ 11001–11050.

The facility owner or operator must submit copies of material safety data sheets (MSDS) or lists of any MSDS chemicals in the facility that are in excess of threshold amounts.

The facility must notify the State Emergency Response Commission if it is subject to EPCRA and if the total of extremely hazardous substances is in excess of threshold planning quantities (TPQs). Qualifying facilities must provide immediate reports of unexpected "releases" or "extremely hazardous substances," even if notice under CERCLA Section 9603(a) is not required.

§ 1.34   Underground Storage Tanks

Underground storage tanks (UST) have only recently become subject to stringent EPA regulations.[307] The regulations require tank registration, tank construction standards, leak detection devices, and assurance of financial responsibility by the owner or operator.

Leaks must be reported to a government regulatory agency, which will require a cleanup. Existing tanks may have to be retrofitted, unless they are closed or removed pursuant to strict requirements.

New York is one of the first states to require stricter standards for above-ground tanks of more than 1,100 gallons.[308] The standards affect most apartment buildings, co-operative apartments, and condominiums. A 1985 regulation required registration of such tanks. Now the registered owners must comply with standards such as color-coded fill ports, gauges, and safety valves to prevent overflow. Owners must provide a secondary means of liquid-tight containment, such as a basement floor with a drain. Florida now has underground storage tank (UST) regulations, which became effective in 1990.[309] There are regulations in many other states.

§ 1.35   Indoor Air Pollution and
Sick Building Syndrome

Indoor air pollution can occur as a result of statutorily defined "hazardous substances" or the accumulation of unacceptable levels of various pollutants—gases, vapors, radon, and bacteria—because of inadequate fresh-air ventilation. Pollution can also be caused by asbestos; formaldehyde used in building materials, wall fabrics, and pressed wood furniture; plasticizers

---

[307] 42 U.S.C. §§ 6991–6991(i); 40 C.F.R. pt. 280, effective Dec. 22, 1988. *See also* 53 Fed. Reg. 37,082 (1988).

[308] N.Y. Times, Aug. 26, 1990, at 3, col. 1.

[309] Fla. A.C. Rule 17-761; *see also* N.J. Stat. Ann. 58:10A-21 et seq. (1990).

in rugs; paint; tobacco smoke; and microbes in the ventilation system. Copy machines generate ozone. These pollutants accumulate because buildings are designed with sealed windows and insulated walls to be "tight" so as not to allow heat to escape. When the building occupants suffer illnesses such as eye irritation, nausea, headaches, heart problems, and cancer, it is called "sick building syndrome" (SBS) and may provide a basis for litigation.

Despite the potential for illness, there are currently no federal, state, or local legislative guidelines setting forth standards for conduct. Therefore, the law in this area is developing case-by-case in the courts, which are using the common-law theories discussed in **Chapter 7**. As is discussed in **Chapter 6**, few cases in this area have actually gone to trial as of this writing.

The American Society of Heating, Refrigerating, and Air-conditioning Engineers (ASHRAE) has issued a new Standard 62-1989 in which it recommends that HVAC (heating, ventilating, and air-conditioning) systems be designed to deliver at least 15 cubic feet per minute per person (cfm/p) of outdoor air in mechanically ventilated buildings. The standard applies to hotel lobbies and certain retail shops. Higher minimum rates are recommended for most buildings, such as 20 cfm/p for office buildings.

This standard is not presently a legal requirement; however, if it is adopted by national model and local building codes, it will be. Two indoor air quality bills have been proposed in Congress.

The Indoor Air Quality Act of 1991[310] introduced by Representative Joseph P. Kennedy (D.-Mass.), proposes that any pubic or commercial building granted a permit for construction or for significant renovation must have an HVAC system designed to provide a minimum of 20 cfm/p of outdoor air to all occupied space and a minimum of 60 cfm/p of outdoor air per smoking occupant where smoking is permitted. New buildings would be required to comply with ASHRAE's Standard 62-1989. Exhaust air from a room where smoking is permitted could not be returned to the general ventilation system.[311] OSHA would have the power to fine and imprison offenders, and the Department of Labor would have the authority to set workplace standards for indoor air pollutants.

The proposed Act requires that products bear labels warning of potential contaminant effects and prohibits the importation of unlabeled products.

A similar bill has been introduced in the Senate by Senator George Mitchell (D.-Maine).[312] This bill also addresses ventilation rates but is less specific than the House bill, and it asks the EPA to evaluate existing standards. The EPA, in coordination with other federal agencies, would then

---

[310] H.R. 1066, 102d Cong., 1st Sess. (1991).

[311] H.R. 1066, Sec. 15(a). New Hampshire, Maine, and Washington have imposed operating standards for state office buildings only. Asbestos Abatement Report, Nov. 12, 1990, at 6.

[312] S. 455, 102d Cong., 1st Sess. (1991).

make recommendations concerning the establishment of ventilation standards to protect the health of the public and of workers. The Senate bill does not create any new authorities to regulate indoor air pollution. It requires the EPA to develop a "national response plan" to direct existing authorities to identify contaminants of concern and specify actions to reduce exposures.

Under the bill, the authority of the National Institute for Occupational Safety and Health would be expanded to include assessments of sick buildings.

Both the Mitchell and Kennedy bills would provide funding for research on indoor air contaminants and new buildings technologies; create a federal Office of Indoor Air Quality (IAQ); set up a grant system for states to develop IAQ programs and establish health advisories for hazardous indoor air pollutants; and require nationwide assessment of indoor air quality in buildings owned by local educational agencies and day-care facilities.

The EPA would be required to issue a building ventilation standard to be enforced by OSHA. New buildings would have to comply with ASHRAE requirements.[313]

In an unusual move, the State of Washington's Department of General Administration has issued design requirements for its new buildings, in response to sick building issues.[314] The requirements include an air distribution system that will ensure a consistent volume of circulating air after the building is occupied; direct digital controls of temperature and humidity; and ventilation systems that operate at full capacity during the 90-day "flush-out period" and for an additional 90 days after employees move in. Furniture and carpets must be tested for contaminants.

---

[313] ASHRAE Standard 62-1989, a voluntary standard for architects, engineers, and building owners and operators, prescribes minimum ventilation rates for various settings, such as offices, stores, meeting rooms, and other types of rooms.

[314] Washington State, Dept. of General Administration, East Campus Plus Program, Indoor Air Quality Specifications for Washington State Natural Resources Building and Labor and Industries Building, Dec. 1989.

CHAPTER 2

STATE AND LOCAL STATUTES

§ 2.1   Introduction
§ 2.2   New Jersey's Environmental Cleanup Responsibility Act (ECRA)
§ 2.3   Minnesota Environmental Response and Liability Act (MERLA)
§ 2.4   Virginia
§ 2.5   Washington, DC
§ 2.6   Mandatory Inspection for Asbestos Before Issuance of a Building Permit
§ 2.7   Co-operative and Condominium Apartments
§ 2.8   California
§ 2.9   Pennsylvania
§ 2.10   Training, Certification, and Licensing
§ 2.11   —New York
§ 2.12   —Massachusetts
§ 2.13   —Virginia
§ 2.14   Colorado
§ 2.15   Tobacco Smoke

§ 2.1   Introduction

Federal law does not currently require asbestos abatement in public and commercial buildings;[1] however, many states regulate asbestos in some types of commercial facilities. Almost every state has some form of hazardous waste laws and regulations that cover many hazardous substances, of which asbestos is only one. In a 1989 report, all states except Arkansas, South Carolina, and Wyoming had such statutes.[2]

---

[1] Marcotte, *Toxic Blackacre: Unprecedented Liability for Landowner,* 73 A.B.A.J. 66, 68 (1987).

[2] Morissette and Hourcle, *State Environmental Laws Redefine Substantial and Meaningful Involvement,* A.F.L. Rev., 137–144 (1989).

Many states allow their governor or another state official to select the remedy; Colorado is an example. In Montana and North Carolina, this authority is in the state's CERCLA statute. In New York, Texas, and West Virginia, the statutes require the regulatory agency to develop or approve the remedial action plan.[3]

Most states have some form of contractor licensing or certification program and require training for workers who do any type of repair work involving asbestos. These laws address requirements for abating asbestos in public buildings, performance standards for abatement projects, and public education concerning asbestos-related health risks.

§ 2.2 New Jersey's Environmental Cleanup Responsibility Act (ECRA)

A number of states have passed statutes designed to isolate and secure the assets of responsible parties, regardless of bankruptcy.[4] One of the leading states in aggressive environmental legislation is New Jersey. The New Jersey legislature has passed two hazardous waste statutes aimed at rectifying some of the problems perceived in CERCLA.

The Spill Compensation and Control Act[5] created for the government a statutory, priority lien on the responsible party's assets that supersedes all other claims or liens on the assets. Lenders who try to shirk responsibility for the illegal activities of the site owners are punishable. The statute also created a tax on all hazardous substances transported into the state.[6]

The Environmental Cleanup Responsibility Act (ECRA)[7] sets forth detailed requirements for the transfer of land, to protect buyers who

---

[3] *Id.* at 140.

[4] *See, e.g.,* Environmental Cleanup Responsibility Act (ECRA), N.J. Stat. Ann. §§ 13:1K-6 to -13 (West Supp. 1988); Mass. Gen. Stat. Ann. ch. 21E, § 13 (West 1983); N.H. Rev. Stat. Ann. § 147-B:10 (1983); Ohio Rev. Code Ann. § 3734.22 (Anderson 1988); Tenn. Code Ann. § 68-46-209 (1987).

Bankruptcy Reform Act of 1978, 11 U.S.C. §§ 101 et seq., 362 (1982), amended by Pub. L. No. 99-554, 100 Stat. 3124 (1986). *See* Lockett, *Environmental Liability Enforcement and the Bankruptcy Act of 1978: A Study of H.R. 2767, the "Superlien" Provision,* 19 Real Prop. Prob. and Tr. J. 859, 861 (1984); Moore, *Bankruptcy Stays Thwarting Cleanups,* Legal Times, May 9, 1983, at 1, col. 1; *see also infra* notes 39–45 and accompanying text.

[5] N.J. Stat. Ann. § 58:10-23, 11f(f) (West 1982 and Supp. 1988).

[6] *Id.* § 58:10-23.11h(b) (West Supp. 1988).

[7] N.J. Stat. Ann. §§ 13:1K-6 to -13 (West Supp. 1988). *See also* Wagner, *Liability for Hazardous Waste Cleanup: An Examination of New Jersey's Approach,* 13 Harv. Envtl. L. Rev. 245–311 (1989).

unknowingly purchase contaminated property. Other states, such as Connecticut,[8] have followed New Jersey's example.

ECRA extends to owners and operators of "industrial establishments," which are defined by the Standard Industrial Classification (SIC)[9] codes. These numbers are assigned according to the principal products manufactured or major services furnished.

The statute is triggered upon "closing, terminating or transferring operations." It includes sales, leases, or changes in control of the owner. It does not apply to corporate reorganizations that do not substantially affect the ownership of the industrial establishment. All owners and operators of industrial establishments must notify the Department of Environmental Protection, submit a detailed description of site operations and management of hazardous wastes, and clean up any contamination before the property is transferred.

ECRA applies if there is:

1. A pending transaction;
2. A transfer of an industrial establishment and it falls within a specific Standard Industrial Classification (SIC) enumerated in the Act;
3. A property that contains hazardous substances or wastes as defined in the Act.

There are exemptions for establishments already subject to closure and postclosure requirements under the Resource Conservation and Recovery Act and for producers or distributors of agricultural commodities. This is designed to exempt hazardous waste treatment, storage, and disposal facilities and does not exempt typical industrial operations that handle hazardous substances.

There is a two-part application, which must be filed in order to sell, transfer, or close property. One part requires a General Information Submission (GIS) concerning the intent to close, sell, or transfer the facility and the past use of the facility.[10] The second part, the Site Evaluation Submission (SES), must be filed with the New Jersey Department of Environmental Protection (NJDEP) no more than 45 days after the notice of closure, sale, or transfer has been made public.[11]

The GIS must be filed with the NJDEP within five days of the execution of any agreement of sale or option to purchase.[12] It requires general

---

[8] *See supra* note 1; Connecticut Transfer Act, Pub. Act No. 85-568.

[9] N.J. Rev. Stat. § 13:1K-9 (1983). *See also* Wagner, *supra* note 7.

[10] N.J. Rev. Stat. 26B-3.2(b) (1988).

[11] *Id.* § 26B-3.2(c) (1988).

[12] N.J. Admin. Code tit. 7, § 26B-3.2 (1988).

information about the owners and operators of the site, including a description of all past operators, a list of all environmental permits held, and a list of all governmental enforcement actions.

Within 30 days after the GIS has been submitted, the SES, a more specific submission, must be filed. It requires an in-depth survey of all hazardous waste substances on-site, a detailed site map of hazardous waste storage and management locations, descriptions of any known spill or discharge of hazardous substances, any remedial actions undertaken, and a detailed description of all current and past operations and processes occurring at the site. The SES must also include a detailed sampling plan to determine the presence and quantity of any contamination on-site.

After the GIS and SES applications, NJDEP personnel inspect the site to verify the information submitted.[13] Next, a Negative Declaration or cleanup plan is submitted.[14] The Negative Declaration, an affidavit signed by an authorized officer or management official, must contain a description of the cleanup actions taken at the site and any sampling results that can substantiate the affidavit.[15]

The Negative Declaration or a cleanup plan[16] should be submitted to the state for review and approval prior to the transaction, along with general and specific information about the site and financial security guaranteeing the complete performance to ensure the cleanup.[17] Notice to the state must be submitted 60 days before the date of the contemplated transfer.

A cleanup schedule must use the most practical method of cleaning up the site and include time schedules for implementation and itemized cost estimates.[18]

The fact that a prior owner caused the discharge is not a defense to ECRA.

Implementation of the cleanup plan can be deferred if the transfer of the industrial establishment results in the new owners' having essentially the same operations on-site as the prior owner. They must prove that the site poses no threat to the public health and safety and must obtain a deferral certification from NJDEP.[19] In some cases, NJDEP will allow a transaction to proceed pursuant to an Administrative Consent Order (ACO), even before the GIS and SES are completed or the cleanup plan is submitted.[20]

---

[13] Id. § 26B-3.5 (1988).

[14] Id. § 13:1k-9(b)(2).

[15] Id. § 7:26B-5.2.

[16] Id. § 26B-5.1 to 5.8.

[17] Id. § 26B-6.1 to 6.7.

[18] Id. § 7:26B-5.3.

[19] Id. § 13:1k-11(b).

[20] Id. § 7:26B-7.1.

If the transferor does not satisfy the ECRA requirements, the real estate transaction may be voided for noncompliance.[21] The transferor can be strictly liable for all cleanup costs, and the transferee may recover damages.[22] There are fines of up to $25,000 per offense for falsifying information or failing to comply with the statute's requirements.[23]

A significant feature of ECRA is the government's first-priority lien for the cost of cleanup, which is paramount to all other liens on all assets of a responsible party.[24] ECRA applies to all owners, not merely those involved in the ECRA process. Because the Act includes all petroleum products, facilities that have fuel oil tanks for heating purposes are covered. Facilities that store such commercial products as cleaning fluids, degreasers, and lubricating oils on-site are subject to ECRA unless they are present in *de minimis* quantities.[25]

The lien eliminates the bankruptcy loophole for responsible parties and encourages creditors of those operating hazardous waste sites to take precautions so that their debtors are not paying back loans at the public's expense. An amendment has limited the extent of the lien by permitting attachment of only the "dirty" assets of the responsible party and placing the lien behind all prior liens on the "clean" property.[26] This amendment may allow the owner to escape liability by removing assets from the "dirty" property to other properties.

A company that owns both contaminated and uncontaminated property can use the contaminated property as collateral in financing operations or investments on the clean property. If the contamination is discovered and a lien is imposed by the state, the company will lose only the contaminated property. If the company goes bankrupt, the liens of secured creditors attaching prior to the government's lien for cleanup costs take priority over the government's claim. Little may be left after secured creditors are paid.[27]

The applications for transfers or sales of land may take many months to be processed.[28] This process endeavors to ensure that purchasers are buying clean property.

---

[21] N.J. Stat. Ann. § 13:1K-13 (West Supp. 1988).

[22] *Id.*

[23] *Id.* §§ 13:1K-13(c) and 26B-9.3(a).

[24] *Id.* § 58:10-23.11f(f).

[25] N.J. Admin. Code tit. 7, § 26B-1.1.

[26] *Id.* § 58-10-23.11f(f) (West Supp. 1988).

[27] This makes subsidiary corporations attractive. They can purchase, sell, or own the "dirty" assets and keep them separate from the parent company's assets.

[28] *ECRA: Environmental Gridlock,* N.J.L.J., Nov. 6, 1986, at 4, col. 1.

§ 2.3   Minnesota Environmental Response and Liability Act (MERLA)

This statute, enacted in 1983, contains some noteworthy provisions. Any person responsible for the release of a hazardous substance may be strictly liable, jointly and severally, for all economic damages and all damages for death, personal injury, or disease resulting from the release. Economic damages include destruction of real or personal property, loss of use of such property, and loss of past or future income from such injury.[29] Damages for death, personal injury, or disease include medical, rehabilitation, and burial expenses, loss of past or future income, and damages for pain and suffering.[30]

MERLA reduces a plaintiff's burden of establishing causation in order to reach a jury. The court may not direct a verdict against the plaintiff on the issue of causation if the plaintiff's evidence is sufficient to enable a reasonable person to find that:

1. The defendant is responsible for the release;
2. The plaintiff was exposed to a hazardous substance;
3. The release could reasonably have resulted in plaintiff's exposure;
4. The death, injury, or disease suffered by the plaintiff is caused or was significantly contributed to by exposure to the hazardous substance.[31]

Evidence to a "reasonable medical certainty" that exposure caused or significantly contributed to the plaintiff's injury is not required in order to submit the case to a jury.[32]

§ 2.4   Virginia

Virginia has an aggressive program to abate asbestos. Since July 1, 1989, an asbestos inspection has been required as a condition of obtaining or renewing a license for a hospital[33] or child-care center.[34]

The license of a hospital or child-care center will be issued or renewed only if: (1) no asbestos was detected; (2) asbestos was detected and response

---

[29] Minn. Stat. Ann. § 115B.05(a)(1)–(3) (West Supp. 1985).

[30] *Id.*

[31] *Id.* § 115B.07(a)–(d).

[32] *Id.*

[33] Va. Code Ann. § 32.1-126.1 (Supp. 1987).

[34] *Id.* § 63.1-198.01.

actions to abate any risk to human health are complete; or (3) asbestos was detected and response actions to abate any risk to human health will be conducted in accordance with an approved schedule and plan.[35]

A similar asbestos inspection and abatement program is required in order to make a public offering of a condominium, if the building was substantially completed prior to July 1, 1978.[36]

Another of Virginia's asbestos abatement requirements could have an impact on almost all buildings built prior to 1978. With very few exceptions, an asbestos inspection is required to obtain the building permit necessary to renovate or demolish a building.[37] Exceptions to this requirement are limited to:

> single-family dwellings, residential housing with four or fewer units, farm buildings, buildings with less than 3,500 square feet and buildings with no central heating system, or to public utilities required by law to give notification to the Commonwealth of Virginia and to the United States Environmental Protection Agency prior to removing asbestos in connection with the renovation or demolition of a building.[38]

Thus, although owners of commercial buildings in Virginia are not all required to inspect for and abate asbestos, any renovation requiring a building permit will require them to do so.

The Virginia Department of General Services has developed standards that govern any of the statutorily required asbestos inspections mentioned above.[39] These standards enumerate the areas of a building that must be inspected and describe sampling requirements. They also include guidance for developing an asbestos management plan.[40]

§ 2.5 Washington, DC

Washington, DC, has a bill pending before its Council which, if passed, would create one of the most stringent radon testing and abatement programs in the country.[41] The bill would mandate radon testing of many rental housing units, government offices, and schools. If high levels of radon

---

[35] *Id.* §§ 32.1-126.1, 63.1-198.01.

[36] *Id.* § 55-79.94(A)(5).

[37] *Id.* § 36-99.7(A).

[38] *Id.* § 36-99.7(B).

[39] *See generally* 5 Va. Regs., Reg. 1219-54 (Jan. 30, 1989) (asbestos survey standards for buildings other than school buildings).

[40] *Id.*

[41] Indoor Safe Air Act, Bill 8-163.

are found, abatement would be required.[42] Among the buildings excluded from the bill would be those with four or fewer units, those rented to diplomats by foreign governments, and most buildings constructed after 1975.

As part of the closing of a sale of a building, the seller would have to provide a certificate of testing. If the radon level is not acceptable, abatement would have to occur prior to closing.

§ 2.6   Mandatory Inspection for Asbestos Before Issuance of a Building Permit

A number of states and cities, including Virginia[43] and New York City,[44] require inspections and removal of friable asbestos prior to the issuance of a permit for renovation, modification, or demolition of a building.

The Virginia statute provides:

> Asbestos inspection in buildings to be renovated or demolished: exceptions.—A. After January 1, 1988, a local building department shall not issue a building permit allowing a building built prior to 1978 to be renovated or demolished until the local building department receives a statement from the owner or his agent that the building has been inspected for asbestos as defined in § 2.1-256.12 . . . and that either (i) no asbestos was detected or (ii) asbestos was detected and any potential risk to human health arising therefrom was abated.[45]

The New York City law requires, among other things, that the presence and condition of asbestos be ascertained by a certified asbestos inspector before any building alteration, renovation, or demolition is performed. If any work involves disturbing asbestos, an asbestos inspection report and plan must be filed and approved by the City, that the abatement be done by certified abatement contractors who follow prescribed procedures, and the work be certified as completed by a certified asbestos consultant. Asbestos must be removed or encapsulated if such work will cause asbestos to become airborne. All asbestos abatement activities must be conducted in accordance with approved safety procedures by people who have received

---

[42] The EPA only has guidelines to assist homeowners in making informed decisions about radon.

[43] Va. Code Ann. § 36-99.7 (Supp. 1987).

[44] Local Law No. 76 of 1985 and No. 80 of 1986, N.Y.C. Administrative Code §§ 24-146.1 and 27-198.1. A court rejected a suit by owners claiming that Local Law No. 76 was an unconstitutional taking of property because it required them to expend funds for abatement to correct the City's error in approving the use of asbestos prior to 1971. Kaufman v. City of New York, 891 F.2d 446 (2d Cir. 1989), *cert. denied,* 110 S. Ct. 2561 (1990).

[45] Va. Code Ann. § 36-99.7 (Supp. 1987).

appropriate training and certification. The law does not require that building owners remove asbestos that is undisturbed or will not be disturbed by alteration or demolition. The City must be notified about the disposal of all ACM waste.

The statute exempts "single-family dwellings, residential housing with four or fewer units, farm buildings, buildings with less than 3,500 square feet and buildings with no central heating system" and certain public utilities.[46]

§ 2.7 Co-operative and Condominium Apartments

Co-ops and condominiums are a common type of dwelling, especially in cities. As with other buildings, they may contain asbestos installed during the period before the building was converted to co-operative or condominium ownership. In New York City, sponsors of any residential building undergoing co-op or condominium conversion must disclose in a report by a qualified asbestos inspector whether asbestos is present and, if so, its condition and the recommendations adopted for dealing with it.[47]

No remediation is required. Originally, the regulations required remediation, but that provision was struck down by the courts.[48] On a practical level, sponsors generally arrange and pay for remediation because they would probably find difficulty selling units otherwise.

§ 2.8 California

California's Hazardous Substance Act is much like CERCLA. It even defines "liable person" to have the same meaning as under CERCLA.[49]

One interesting provision is that the California Department of Health Services is required to preliminarily allocate responsibility among the potentially responsible parties. A party allocated more than 50 percent of the responsibility can demand that the share be arbitrated.[50] The decision will be based on the party's responsibility for the presence of the waste.

With the enactment of Chapter 1302, an owner of nonresidential real property has a duty to give notice prior to the sale of the property, if the

---

[46] Id. § 36-99.7(B).

[47] 13 N.Y.C.R.R. §§ 18.7(aa), 20.7(z), 21.7(z), and 24.7(aa). The regulations were upheld in In The Matter of Council for Owner Occupied Housing v. Abrams, 125 A.2d 10, 511 N.Y.S.2d 966 (3d Dept. 1987).

[48] Matter of Council for Owner Occupied Housing v. Abrams, supra note 47.

[49] Cal. Health & Safety Code § 25310.

[50] Id. §§ 25356.1(d), 25356.3(a) and (c).

owner knows or has reason to know that a hazardous substance has been released on or beneath the property.[51] Failure to provide this notice will subject the violator to actual damages and any other remedies available by law. An owner who has actual knowledge of a hazardous condition and knowingly and willfully fails to give written notice to the buyer will be liable for civil penalties.[52]

A lessee or renter of real property who knows or has reasonable cause to know that a hazardous substance is present on or beneath the real property must give written notice to the owner upon the discovery of the presence or suspected presence of the hazardous substance.[53] Failure to provide notice gives the owner the option of voiding the leasehold or the rental agreement.

Since January 1, 1989, owners and tenants of certain buildings that were constructed before 1979 and are known to contain asbestos are subject to disclosure requirements.[54] An owner must provide written notice regarding asbestos to all employees working in the building and to other owners with whom he or she is in privity of contract. The statute covers all public and commercial buildings, except school buildings, apartment buildings containing fewer than 10 units, and residential dwellings.

The term "owner" includes lessees, sublessees, and agents of the owner, such as building managers. "Employees" include people under contract to perform services in a building on other than a "casual or incidental basis." Security guards and maintenance personnel may be included.

The notice, which must be provided to each individual employee and repeated each year, must contain information such as: a description of any studies; where the ACM is located; procedures or handling instructions for asbestos; results of any monitoring or air sampling; and an assessment of health risks to employees from exposure.

A warning notice must be posted when contracting work is being done in an area where ACM may be disturbed. Failure to give notice is not deemed to be a breach of any covenant under the lease. Fines of up to $1,000 or imprisonment for up to one year may be imposed for violations.

§ 2.9   Pennsylvania

A seller is required to give notice of any hazardous waste disposed of on the property sold.[55]

---

[51] *Id.* § 25359.7(a).

[52] *Id.* § 25359.7(a) (the civil penalty may be up to $5,000 for each violation).

[53] *Id.* § 25359.7(b).

[54] *Id.* §§ 25915–25924.

[55] 35 Pa. Cons. Stat. Ann. § 6018.405 (Purdon Supp. 1989).

§ 2.10   Training, Certification, and Licensing

The EPA's asbestos contractor's certification program applies only to schools regulated under AHERA. However, states are establishing a trend of requiring licensure or certification for asbestos contractors and workers in many other types of facilities. Most states have enacted fairly comprehensive programs requiring contractor training,[56] certification, and licensing, with inspection requirements, air monitoring, and operation and maintenance programs.

Recently, the Senate adopted an amendment by Senator Howard Metzenbaum (S. 1340) which would extend the training and accreditation requirements established under AHERA to public and commercial buildings. Workers and managers involved in asbestos abatement projects in public and commercial buildings would be required to undergo training and be certified in courses approved by the EPA or by a state that has EPA approval to establish its own training and certification program for abatement workers.[57]

Currently, abatement workers and managers—asbestos inspectors and management planners, abatement project designers, abatement supervisors and workers—must meet the EPA's minimum accreditation requirements for working in schools.

Under the AHERA program, states are to establish their own training and accreditation programs and to approve courses that abatement personnel could take to receive state certification. Most states have training and licensing requirements for abatement workers, but not all of the state programs have EPA approval to grant AHERA accreditation.

§ 2.11   —New York

New York State requires contractors involved in the removal of ACM to be licensed, and their workers must be certified.[58] The State Department of Labor has issued regulations detailing the requirements.[59] A contractor must ensure that workers are certified, but building owners may be liable if the contractor fails to do so.

The New York State Department of Health has promulgated regulations defining the requirements for asbestos worker training courses.[60]

---

[56] N.Y. Lab. Law §§ 901, 902 (1988); N.J. Stat. Ann. § 34:5A-32 et seq. (1988); Md. Envtl. Code Ann. § 6-401 et seq. (1987).

[57] Asbestos Abatement Report, Mar. 19, 1990, at 3.

[58] N.Y. Labor Law §§ 900–911, effective June 1, 1987.

[59] 12 N.Y.C.R.R. 800.3, effective July 28, 1987.

[60] 10 N.Y.C.R.R. 73, effective Sept. 3, 1987, as amended Dec. 9, 1988.

§ 2.12   —Massachusetts

Massachusetts has comprehensive guidelines for licensure, certification, and training of individuals doing asbestos abatement work. These regulations were recently upheld and found not to be preempted by OSHA standards.[61] OSHA does not require either certification or licensure.

§ 2.13   —Virginia

In Virginia, it is unlawful for anyone without an asbestos license as an inspector, supervisor, contractor, management planner, or project designer to contract for compensation to carry out an asbestos project or develop a management plan.[62] An individual working on an asbestos project must have an asbestos worker's license.[63] To be licensed, the individual must have successfully completed a training course approved by the Virginia Department of Commerce.[64]

There is an exemption when an emergency "results from a sudden unexpected event that is not a planned renovation or demolition."[65] Written notice to the Department of Commerce is required and the project cannot begin until the exemption from licensure has been approved.[66]

Employers who wish to have their own employees conduct an asbestos project on premises they own or have leased may obtain an exemption from licensure if they provide training to their employees comparable to the approved course.[67]

Asbestos contractors must maintain detailed records describing asbestos projects. The names and license numbers of supervisors and workers involved, the amount of asbestos removed, procedures used to comply with federal and state regulations, and the name and address of the disposal site must be included, along with disposal site receipts.[68] These records must be maintained for at least 30 years and, upon request, must be made available to the Department of Labor and Industry.[69] A list of

---

[61] Associated Industries of Massachusetts v. Snow, 717 F. Supp. 951 (D. Mass. 1989), *aff'd in part, rev'd in part*, 898 F.2d 274 (1st Cir. 1990).

[62] Va. Code Ann. § 54.1-503.

[63] *Id.* § 54.1-504.

[64] 5 Va. Regs., Reg. 1434-43 (1989).

[65] Va. Code Ann. § 54.1-512(A).

[66] 5 Va. Regs., Reg. 1444-45, § 10.1 (1989).

[67] *Id.* Reg. 1445, § 10.3.

[68] Va. Code Ann. § 54.1-507.

[69] *Id.* § 54.1-507(B).

supervisors and workers on a particular asbestos project, along with their current license numbers and expiration dates, must be maintained at the job site.[70]

§ 2.14   Colorado

On July 1, 1987, Colorado enacted an asbestos law that empowered the Colorado Air Quality Control Commission to promulgate rules and regulations for implementing the bill with regard to any building, facility, or property which any member of the general public may enter, and performance standards for abatement.

The Colorado Department of Health may issue violations and cease and desist orders. It may also file an action in the district court of the county where the violation is alleged to have occurred and request the court to order the person to comply.[71]

§ 2.15   Tobacco Smoke

Some states and local municipalities have begun to enact legislation restricting tobacco smoke in indoor areas. As of January 1, 1990, New York City has one of the most restrictive smoking laws in the country. Smoking is prohibited in indoor areas open to the public, such as auditoriums, elevators, gymnasiums, classrooms, and ticketing and boarding areas in public transportation terminals.[72] Smoking is restricted to areas designated by the owner, operator, or manager in public buildings, educational and vocational institutions, and hospitals.

Smoking in the workplace is also restricted. Employers, as defined in the Act, must provide nonsmokers with a smoke-free work area and an employer must use its best efforts to comply with an employee's request for a smoke-free work area. The constitutionality of the law was challenged and upheld.[73]

As of October 1989, 43 states and the District of Columbia had enacted restrictions against smoking in at least one public place. At least 26 states have enacted comprehensive clean indoor air acts.[74]

Interestingly, employers, administrators, managers, owners, or operators who fail to comply with the law are liable only under the law's enforcement

---

[70] 5 Va. Regs., Reg. 1424, § 3.2 (1989).

[71] Colo. Rev. Stat. § 25-7-501 et seq.

[72] Pub. Health Law, § 1399-n et seq.

[73] Fagan v. Axelrod, 550 N.Y.S.2d 552 (Sup. Ct. 1990).

[74] *Id.* at 557.

provisions, which include injunctions and fines of up to $100. There does not appear to be any private right of action under the statute, but it also does not restrict the use of any theories of liability under which any person may be liable for exposure to smoke.

The country's strictest antismoking legislation was passed in San Luis Obispo, California, on August 2, 1990.[75] City ordinance 1172 prohibits all smoking in bars, restaurants, offices, and most other indoor areas open to the public. There may be fines of up to $500 for repeated noncompliance.

---

[75] Indoor Pollution News, Aug. 9, 1990, at 2.

CHAPTER 3

IDENTIFICATION OF HAZARDOUS SUBSTANCES

Martin R. Bennett
Law Associates, Inc.

§ 3.1   **Introduction**

§ 3.2   **Getting Started**

§ 3.3   **Hiring a Consultant**

§ 3.4   **Identification and Evaluation of Hazardous Substances**

§ 3.5   **Sampling Methodology and Analysis**

§ 3.6   **Comparison to Standards**

§ 3.7   **Asbestos—Generally**

§ 3.8   **—Asbestos: Uses**

§ 3.9   **—Asbestos: Health Effects**

§ 3.10   **—Asbestos: Evaluation and Analysis**

§ 3.11   **—Asbestos: Remedial Alternatives**

§ 3.12   **—Asbestos: Regulations**

§ 3.13   **—Asbestos: Summary**

§ 3.14   **Lead: Generally**

§ 3.15   **—Lead: Health Effects**

§ 3.16   **—Lead: Evaluation**

§ 3.17   **—Lead: Standards**

§ 3.18   **—Lead: Remedial Alternatives**

§ 3.19   **—Lead: Summary**

§ 3.20   **Radon: Generally**

§ 3.21   **—Radon: Sources and Locations**

§ 3.22   **—Radon: Health Effects**

§ 3.23   **—Radon: Evaluation and Standards**

§ 3.24   **—Radon: Remedial Alternatives**

§ 3.25   **Polychlorinated Biphenyls (PCBs): Generally**

§ 3.26   **—PCBs: Regulations**

§ 3.27   —PCBs: Health Effects

§ 3.28   —PCBs: Evaluation and Remedial Alternatives

§ 3.29   —PCBs: Summary

§ 3.30   Formaldehyde: Generally

§ 3.31   —Formaldehyde: Sources

§ 3.32   —Formaldehyde: Health Effects

§ 3.33   —Formaldehyde: Identification and Evaluation

§ 3.34   —Formaldehyde: Standards

§ 3.35   —Formaldehyde: Remedial Actions

APPENDIXES

3A   U.S. Environmental Protection Agency Regional
         Offices

3B   EPA Asbestos Ban and Phase-Down Rule Timetable

3C   Common Asbestos-Containing Materials in Buildings

3D   Comparison of Advantages and Disadvantages of
         Analysis Methods for Lead-Base Paint

3E   Blood Lead Level—Standards for Intervention

3F   Radon Risk Evaluation Chart

3G   EPA Transformer Classifications

3H   Comparison of Common Methodologies for Detection of
         Formaldehyde

§ 3.1   Introduction

To begin the process of identifying the potential hazards that may exist in a given building, it is useful to follow a recognized scientific methodology. This includes careful definition of the purpose and scope of an investigation, to ensure its success. Adherence to a defined project scope should enable the formation of precise and accurate conclusions. The branch of environmental science that addresses health hazards in occupational settings is industrial hygiene. The three objectives of an industrial hygiene investigation are recognition, evaluation, and control. These are readily adapted to the identification of both health and environmental hazards in buildings.

To fully understand the current focus on hazardous substances in buildings, it is essential to recognize the life-style changes that have taken place and are responsible for the shift in emphasis from outdoor pollution to indoor pollution. The shift is due primarily to a change that occurred over the past 100 years: most people now spend the majority of their lives indoors. Also contributing to the emphasis on identification of hazardous substances indoors is a combination of an increasing number of synthetic products used in the construction and furnishing of buildings and increased energy conservation measures. It has been estimated that Americans, especially those residing in urban environments, spend nearly 90 percent[1] of their lives in some type of building. For these reasons, the additional emphasis now placed on the pollution of indoor environments is no surprise.

The way we view buildings has also changed dramatically. The buildings of yesterday were looked upon as safe, secure places for either residence or work, as well as financial investments. Today, a sophisticated home buyer cannot look at a home as just a sound structure; a company cannot look at an office as just a convenient and secure workplace; and an investor cannot look at a company as just a profitable business. In each instance, a building is involved, and buildings have unique "minienvironments." These minienvironments accommodate people but are often host to substances that may harm building occupants and consequently may carry considerable liability for the building owner.

A plethora of substances has been identified by toxicologists and others in the medical community as posing a health risk to humans exposed to them; 700 substances are named and at least partially regulated under the Comprehensive Environmental Response, Compensation, and Liability Act of 1980 (CERCLA). Five of these substances have received considerable media attention—asbestos, lead, radon, polychlorinated biphenyls (PCBs), and formaldehyde. Each is addressed individually in this chapter. There are many other potential hazards in buildings, but limiting the discussion to these five hazardous substances will illustrate the investigative process that is necessary to identify hazardous materials within a building. Among the less common and often least regulated hazards are bacteria, ozone, carbon monoxide, and glass fibers.

It is important to understand that the presence of asbestos, lead, radon, PCBs, and formaldehyde in buildings is not uncommon. The use of these materials may at one time have been mandated by building codes. Only a small fraction of even the most recently constructed buildings will not contain at least one of these problem substances. Sellers of buildings in today's market face disclosure laws, and lending institutions approached for financing of a purchase routinely require surveys that will reveal the presence of any environmental hazards.

§ 3.2   Getting Started

With hazardous substances now a ubiquitous problem in contemporary building environments, assessing the liability associated with any hazard that may exist in a building becomes inevitable and prudent. The first step

---

[1] Burge and Hoyer, *Indoor Air Quality,* 5 Appl. Occupational Envtl. Hygiene (Feb. 1990).

in the process is to recognize the problem. Completion of this first goal usually requires a joint effort between the building staff and a qualified environmental consultant who specializes in buildings and facilities. The building staff provides valuable information on the history of the building and property, access to all building spaces, and insight into the operation of the building and the practices employed in handling hazardous material. The environmental consultant brings to the site a trained eye, knowledge of current laws and regulations, and the necessary sampling apparatus to detect the presence of hazardous materials.

To be an effective partner in identifying hazardous materials, the building owner's representative may require some outside environmental training. In-house personnel will find numerous resources available throughout the country, for both awareness seminars and certification programs related to the various hazards. A good start can be made by contacting the continuing education department at a local university or the regional office of the Environmental Protection Agency (EPA) for a list of offerings and dates. (See **Appendix 3A.**)

In addition to training, a wise building owner will have a reference library. Applicable regulations and laws that address building hazards should be filed chronologically and organized by hazard type. The EPA, the Occupational Safety and Health Administration (OSHA), and the National Institute for Occupational Safety and Health (NIOSH)—all federal agencies—produce numerous guidance documents designed to assist building owners.

Who should be trained and what documents should be read? The answer will depend greatly on the size of the particular organization and the number of buildings involved. For most situations, a single individual should be selected, at least initially, to research the various subjects and attend seminars. A likely candidate would be in-house legal counsel or someone who has a technical background, such as an engineer, and who can assess the relative magnitude and impact of a potential hazard. The training effort should emphasize a "big picture" approach. The targeted result should be attaining the knowledge necessary to evaluate and hire a consulting firm.

§ 3.3   Hiring a Consultant

Regardless of its in-house capabilities, if a business is not in the environmental field, an independent consultant who can fully evaluate the presence of hazardous substances within or surrounding a building is generally a necessity. If hiring a consulting firm seems a burdensome or unnecessary expense, it is important to remember that ignorance of the law is no excuse for failure to meet environmental obligations. An ever growing number of building owners now face fines and possible criminal prosecution for their shortsightedness. In many cases, an evaluation by an independent, qualified, environmental consultant will be required by a lender or potential buyer of a property.

A properly chosen consultant will provide the expertise and experience necessary to identify hazardous substances and to implement the industrial hygiene goals of evaluation and control. In the initial consultant selection process, emphasis should be placed on firms that have a wide range of expertise and experience because potential problems at a building could be complex and may go undetected by a firm that has too narrow a specialty. Résumés of all key personnel should be carefully reviewed. A college degree in the specific field of expertise or in related sciences should be a minimum qualification. Depending on the scope of the project, personnel in the following disciplines may be required: engineering, environmental studies, geology, hydrology, industrial hygiene, and toxicology. Professional certification in these areas is also desirable.

Extensive continuing education course work is essential because many of the current environmental issues postdate areas of specialization or curricula offered by colleges. In addition to the formal training of a firm's staff, the experience of the firm in conducting similar projects is an important consideration. Firms that specialize in assessments of large, complex, industrial properties may not be a cost-effective choice for a residential property evaluation, and companies with residential experience may not have the resources required to perform a complex multidisciplinary assessment. A firm's references should be checked; the lowest-priced consultant may often not be the best choice.

§ 3.4   Identification and Evaluation of Hazardous Substances

Attempts made by building owners to conduct a preliminary assessment of potential hazards with in-house personnel may be a reasonable approach, provided that (1) those conducting the investigation are appropriately trained, possess a basic understanding of hazardous substances, and are able to recognize the emitting sources of these hazards, and (2) no previous complaints suggest that an imminent hazard exists in the building.

Identification and evaluation of the potential hazards in a building are most effectively managed as a joint effort between the building owner or property management staff and an environmental consultant. Much of the existing documentation on the building and its history can be assembled by the building owner prior to any involvement with a consultant. Among the important documents to be assembled are: the original construction specifications and blueprints; a history of building ownership and usage; current hazardous material documentation, including chemical inventory, discharge permits, waste disposal manifests, and material storage locations;

and adjoining property owners and uses. All of this documentation will be necessary for a thorough assessment by the consultant, and any preliminary investigation conducted by the building owner will assist in this research.

A poll of the people who work in the building and a thorough review of all construction specifications can provide many clues on the types of hazardous substances that may be present. Building engineers, plumbers, electricians, and maintenance staff are good sources for this information. These people are most familiar with the infrastructure of a building and would know the construction materials used originally and in any renovations. This group often comprises the largest contingent of users and storers of chemicals and solvents in a building. Preliminary investigative efforts conducted by an owner, though usually not sufficient by themselves, can reduce the amount of investigation time (and consequently, the fee) required by a consultant.

The pitfall with most in-house investigations is that they typically end following the completion of the identification phase. It is imperative to understand that the act of identifying possible hazards is a step in the right direction, but it does not account for sources that are inaccessible nor for those that may not have been observed. Most importantly, such limited efforts are only one-dimensional. They fail to address either the evaluation or control of the hazards present.

An environmental consultant is best qualified to refine the identification or recognition phase begun by the building owner and to evaluate the effect of any hazardous substances on the property or the building's occupants. Using specialized training in environmental assessment, the consultant may recognize additional hazardous substances overlooked by or unknown to the building owner. The consultant may also begin the evaluation phase of the investigation by selecting the appropriate sampling techniques required to determine the presence or absence of a hazardous material and the concentration or quantity of a particular substance.

§ 3.5   Sampling Methodology and Analysis

A preliminary survey of a building performed by a consultant will identify areas of potential concern and will provide basic information on the types of hazards present. In this phase of an assessment, it is prudent for the building owner and consultant to discuss the type and number of samples necessary to confirm the presence of the suspected hazards. Because sampling and analysis of hazardous materials may be both costly and time-consuming, the scope of this evaluation phase should be clearly defined prior to developing a sampling scheme.

The technical issues of environmental sampling may be beyond the knowledge of most building owners; still, an educational discussion with the consultant is important to ensure that a proper evaluation is performed within the scope and cost constraints of the project. Numerous sampling and analytical techniques may be used to evaluate the presence of a particular substance. The existing environment and the relative concentration of the pollutant will dictate which is most appropriate. Methods employed in industrial settings, where a particular substance is used in manufacturing, will vary greatly from those used in a private residence for determining whether that same substance is found in construction materials. The sensitivity of an analytical method is also important, to ensure the testing is appropriate for comparison to applicable OSHA and EPA requirements.

§ 3.6   Comparison to Standards

After the proper samples have been collected and analysis has been completed, the results must be compared to the standards that define hazardous substances and the allowable limits of these substances. When the sample results are received, the consultant will complete the evaluation phase of the investigation by identifying the hazardous substances and prioritizing the hazards according to the applicable standards.

Hazardous material standards may be separated into various categories. They are usually classified by agency (EPA, OSHA, NIOSH), by jurisdiction (federal, state, county, municipal), by setting (schools, public buildings, residences, private sector, general industry, construction industry), and by sample type (personnel, ambient, indoor). State and federal standards are the most widely enforced, but they may be superseded by more stringent local regulations. It is essential to understand which regulations apply to a given situation and to differentiate among regulations, recommendations, and industry standards. Adoption of the most stringent standard will usually provide the maximum shield against legal liability, but this solution may not be prudent or cost-effective in a given situation. Some building owners may choose to comply with only the regulations applicable to their building and location. Others may choose to comply with the most stringent regulation for a particular substance (a commercial building owner may follow the asbestos regulations established for school buildings) or to go beyond the current requirements in anticipation of more stringent regulations in the future.

If measured levels are found to exceed the appropriate standard, then control measures should be implemented as soon as possible. Regulations often address specific deadlines for compliance but may allow several options for control of a hazard and compliance with the regulations. The compliance options generally fall into three broad areas: removal, engineering controls, and administrative controls. The most desirable control option is generally to eliminate the hazardous substance entirely, either by removing it from the building (asbestos abatement) or by substituting a less hazardous material for the material of concern (replacing PCB-containing transformers with transformers that do not contain PCB). Eliminating the hazard entirely, which is generally the most desirable control option, may not be the most feasible or cost-effective control.

A variety of engineering control options may be available to control the hazardous substance within the limits set by the regulations. These control options include ventilation techniques, isolation of the hazard, or enclosure of the hazardous substance. Administrative controls may also be used to manage a hazardous material by ensuring that it does not present an exposure hazard to personnel. Other options would include an operations and maintenance program, worker training, and the use of protective equipment.

A decision on which of the control options to select and how to comply with hazardous material regulations should be made by the building owner only after careful consideration of the current regulations, the degree of hazard posed by the substance, the compliance options and costs, and the various legal and liability issues.

§ 3.7   Asbestos—Generally

Asbestos is probably the most common of the hazardous substances found today in buildings. The origins of this naturally occurring mineral have been traced back 2000 years: the Greeks first used it in the wicks of temple lamps. Amazed at the fiber's resistance to burning, the Greeks called it *asbesta,* meaning inextinguishable. Today, the term asbestos refers to a group of naturally occurring fibrous minerals comprised predominantly of magnesium (Mg) and silica (Si). Six distinct types of asbestos are, by virtue of their fibrous nature, currently regulated under federal law: chrysotile, amosite, crocidolite, anthophyllite, tremolite, and actinolite. In general, these minerals differ very little in their chemical composition but are commonly distinguishable by their morphology (shape) and color. The most common types of asbestos are chrysotile (mined in Canada and the U.S.S.R., and comprising 97 percent of all asbestos used in the United States) and amosite (an acronym for Asbestos Mines of South Africa; comprising approximately 2 percent of all asbestos used).

§ 3.8   —Asbestos: Uses

Commercial use of asbestos first became widespread in the United States in the late 1800s, concurrently with the industrial revolution. Asbestos was first used in factories as an insulator for steam pipes and boilers, which were the primary source of power at that time. Because asbestos was in great abundance and was available at a low cost, the demand for the mineral grew dramatically. Usage first peaked in the 1940s, when asbestos was used extensively in the shipbuilding industry.

In the 1950s, numerous other marketable properties of asbestos were discovered and exploited, including its high tensile strength, flexibility, and resistance to chemical and frictional wear. The mineral was deemed the "Miracle Product of the 20th Century," and Underwriters Laboratories Inc. (UL) gave asbestos its approval. Suddenly, asbestos was being used in over 3000 building products, including textiles, cementitious shingles, paper products, roofing felts, caulks and adhesives, vinyl flooring, wall coverings, and paints and coatings. The use of asbestos was often specified in building and construction codes. The asbestos industry realized its greatest sales volume in spray-applied fireproofing. Sales growth was steady until 1973, when it peaked at over 900,000 short tons used annually.[2] In that year, the EPA issued its first ban of asbestos, restricting its use in spray-applied applications, specifically fireproofing. Asbestos continued to be used in sprayed-on applications of decorative and acoustical ceiling finishes. The EPA responded with additional bans in 1975 and 1978, effectively limiting the use of asbestos in buildings.[3]

Banned from many commercial and building uses today, asbestos is still widely present in a variety of products, including brakepads, roofing felts, and asbestos cement pipes. These products, as well as many others, will continue to be used for several years despite the EPA's Asbestos Ban and Phase Out Rule, issued in July 1989.[4] The rule took effect in 1990, but the enactment of its three phases will not be complete until 1997. (See **Appendix 3B.**)

§ 3.9   —Asbestos: Health Effects

The health concerns related to asbestos stem directly from its fibrous form and minute size. By definition, an asbestos fiber must be longer than 5 microns and must have a length-to-width ratio of 3:1 or greater. Because of their minute size, asbestos fibers released from a source may remain airborne for hours, with even the slightest of air movement. Once airborne, the fibers enter the body through inhalation. The mechanism of disease is manifested in the lungs. Diseases caused by asbestos exposure include

---

[2] Zurer, *Asbestos: The Fiber That's Panicking America,* 63 Chem. and Engrg. News (Mar. 4, 1985).

[3] U.S. Environmental Protection Agency (EPA), National Emission Standards for Hazardous Air Pollutants (NESHAP, 40 C.F.R. § 61.01(a) (1988).

[4] *Id.*

asbestosis (a scarring of the lungs), *mesothelioma* (a rare cancer of the pleural lining), and *lung cancer,* the most common of the three diseases. Although not nearly as common or well documented, according to current medical research the ingestion of asbestos may result in tumors.[5] This occurrence is thought to result from drinking water that has been contaminated during passage through the asbestos cement water pipes common in most cities.[6] Considerable debate continues as to the concentration of asbestos and the fiber size required to initiate disease, but research has proven that asbestos is one of the most carcinogenic substances known[7] and that, as exposure increases, so does the risk of contracting an asbestos-related disease. Most health professionals, as well as the EPA, believe that no safe level of airborne asbestos exists.[8] Although asbestos is a recognized hazard, it is prudent to remember that asbestos is only a hazard if it is respirable or ingested and that the mere presence of asbestos-containing materials (ACM) does not in itself constitute a hazard.

§ 3.10 —Asbestos: Evaluation and Analysis

Asbestos found in buildings is generally in one of three broad categories: surfacing materials, thermal systems insulation (TSI), and miscellaneous materials (See **Appendix 3C**). For a building owner, evaluation of asbestos should begin with a thorough survey of the structure, and collection of representative samples of all suspect materials by qualified individuals. The precise identification of asbestos in these samples can only be accomplished by a qualified laboratory using the technique of polarized light microscopy (PLM) coupled with dispersion staining. In this technique, asbestos minerals are identified by the observance of various optical properties unique to each mineral. An estimate of their relative percentage in the material is also made. An asbestos-containing material (ACM) is defined by the EPA as having greater than 1 percent asbestos by weight.[9]

After the ACMs have been identified, a hazard assessment will be made for each material in each location. The variables that must be addressed in this hazard assessment include physical condition (whether the material is damaged), location (whether the material is accessible to building

---

[5] Kanarek, *Asbestos in Drinking Water and Cancer Incidence in the San Francisco Area,* 112 A.J. Epidemiology 54 (1980).

[6] *Id.*

[7] EPA and National Institute for Occupational Safety and Health (NIOSH), A Guide to Respiratory Protection for the Asbestos Abatement Industry, Sept. 1988, at 1.

[8] NIOSH, Workplace Exposure to Asbestos, Pub. No. 81-103, Apr. 1980, at 3.

[9] 55 Fed. Reg. 48,415, § 6.1-141 (1990).

occupants or in an area likely to be distributed through vibration, abrasion, air erosion, or water damage), and friability (a measure of a material's ability to be crushed or pulverized by hand pressure). The compilation of these variables will enable the consultant to prioritize each ACM according to the existing or potential hazard it poses within a building.

Although generally not recommended as part of an initial building survey, the collection and analysis of air samples for asbestos may be performed to aid in the evaluation of the overall hazard posed by the asbestos. As an assessment tool, this technique may or may not provide useful information, depending on the number and location of samples collected, the frequency of sampling, the volume of air collected, and the analytical method chosen. Perhaps the worst drawback to air sampling is that a single sample, like a snapshot, is indicative of only the conditions existing at that time and in that location. For this reason, an air sample cannot accurately predict future disturbances or deterioration of the asbestos.

The analytical method selected for the evaluation of air samples is, as mentioned, a decisive factor in the usefulness of the data collected. There are two EPA-approved methods for airborne fiber analysis, and both involve the microscopic examination of a filter on which airborne fibers have been collected. The two methods differ in their ability to detect asbestos fibers and the level of quantification. The most common and least expensive method, phase contrast microscopy (PCM), is unable to resolve very small fibers and, most importantly, is unable to distinguish asbestos fibers from other fibrous materials. In this technique, the counting of fibers is based solely on their length and width. By definition, a fiber is any particle that is at least 5 microns in length and has a length-to-width ratio of at least 3:1.

This methodology, although specified in federal and state regulations,[10] is most suitable for the evaluation of asbestos release episodes that are a direct result of working with or disturbing previously identified ACM. The method is not suitable for the evaluation of asbestos levels in most buildings nor for the determination of personal exposure to airborne asbestos.

For these applications, as well as any others that require the definitive identification and quantification of airborne asbestos levels, transmission electron microscopy (TEM) should be utilized. Only through this method can low-level exposures typical of ambient settings, both indoors and outdoors, be accurately measured. TEM enables the identification of asbestos fibers by their optical properties and chemical composition. Because this analysis is routinely performed at a magnification of $20,000\times$, even the smallest fibrils can be seen and counted.

---

[10] Occupational Safety and Health Administration (OSHA), OSHA Reference Method, 29 C.F.R. § 1926.58 app. A.

Following the completion of the hazard assessment, a remedial action should be selected for each homogeneous ACM.

§ 3.11   —Asbestos: Remedial Alternatives

The alternatives for asbestos remediation include operations and maintenance (O&M) programs, enclosure, encapsulation, and removal. Each of these alternatives should be evaluated based on its appropriateness and compatibility with present and future concerns regarding the ACM found to be present.

An O&M program is a procedural document and responsibility matrix in which the principal objective is to minimize the exposure of all building occupants to asbestos fibers by managing the material and its disturbance. A complete O&M program includes work practices to:

1. Maintain ACMs in good condition;
2. Ensure the proper cleanup of asbestos fibers previously released;
3. Prevent further release of asbestos fibers;
4. Monitor the condition of all ACMs.

The elements of a successful program include notification, surveillance, work-practice controls, recordkeeping, worker protection, and training. An O&M program is a commonly selected remedial action for asbestos, primarily because of its low initial cost. It is important to implement an O&M program during the completion of all other remedial actions. An implemented O&M program acts as a building owner's first shield against liability by serving as a response action to the hazard detected.

Enclosure and encapsulation can be effective solutions for dealing with ACM, under certain building conditions. Enclosure consists of constructing a barrier around ACM to limit accessibility and disturbance of the material. Encapsulation is accomplished by spraying or painting a sealant over the ACM to minimize the release of asbestos fibers into the air. The effectiveness of these actions is based on their reduction of exposure by placing a barrier between the asbestos and the building environment. Their main drawback is that the asbestos remains in place and therefore requires periodic reinspection under an O&M plan and continued avoidance of activities that might otherwise disturb the ACM. The cost is often comparable to removal over the long term, when the expense of implementing an O&M program is included in the estimates. The future removal of encapsulated or enclosed materials will usually result in a higher end cost, because of the added difficulty involved in the abatement process.

Where ACM has sustained significant damage or is difficult to manage successfully in-place, removal may be the most advantageous solution.

Under the EPA's National Emission Standards for Hazardous Air Pollutants (NESHAP) regulation,[11] building owners are required to remove asbestos under two conditions:

1. When a renovation project will disturb more than 160 square feet of surfacing or miscellaneous material or more than 260 linear feet of thermal system insulation;
2. When asbestos could become airborne prior to demolition.

The removal process is strictly regulated under federal OSHA regulations,[12] as well as many state and local laws. Within OSHA regulations for the construction industry, the complex removal process is described, including the requirements for air filtration, hygiene facilities, engineering controls, work practices, and respiratory protection. In general, building owners should thoroughly consider each of the previously mentioned alternatives prior to a decision to remove undisturbed and undamaged ACM. Improper removal can result in an increased exposure level for all building occupants as well as a severe fine against the owner. Under the NESHAP regulation, removal becomes the only viable business alternative for many building owners who are faced with either renovating their buildings to accommodate new tenants (and being forced to comply with the requirements of removal) or competing in a real estate market where a building with ACM is difficult to sell or lease.

§ 3.12 —Asbestos: Regulations

The federal regulations governing exposure to asbestos rely on the collection and analysis of air samples taken from the breathing zone of people who work with or around ACM. These limits are measured in units of fibers per cubic centimeter (f/cc) of air. The limits are based on the "generic analyte" of fibers as opposed to the specific analysis of asbestos. Therefore, the specified analytical methodology is phase contrast microscopy (PCM). Although nonspecific for asbestos, this method was developed and designed to evaluate worker exposure in asbestos mining, manufacturing, and removal occupations. In these settings, an ability to distinguish among fiber types was unnecessary; it was assumed that the majority of fibers generated would be asbestos. The results were thought to be biased toward the high side, thus providing conservative measurement. Unfortunately, this logic is not appropriate when evaluating

---

[11] 40 C.F.R. 61, subpart M (1988).
[12] 29 C.F.R. 1926 (1988).

asbestos exposure in building environments; the asbestos is often combined with other fibrous materials and is present in much lower concentrations than in an industrial setting.

Regardless of its limitations, the PCM methodology remains specified by regulations and is the basis for determining compliance with the law. The PCM methodology is widely available, can be performed quickly, is relatively inexpensive, and has established quality control programs to address variability.

Currently, three federal OSHA limits govern asbestos exposure:[13] the permissible exposure limit (PEL), the action limit, and the excursion limit. These limits, as defined in both the General Industry and Construction Industry Standards on asbestos, are based on a time-weighted average (TWA) over an eight-hour workday. The PEL is currently set at 0.2 f/cc; if the limit is exceeded, respiratory protection must be used to reduce a worker's exposure below the PEL. In addition to establishing exposure limits, OSHA regulations require medical monitoring, respirator fit testing, protective clothing, and training for workers handling asbestos. The action level requires an employer to take certain steps to reduce exposure, if a worker's exposure exceeds 0.1 f/cc for 30 days or more in a single calendar year. OSHA has recently set a third standard, an excursion limit of 1 f/cc measured over a 30-minute period.[14] Unlike the other two limits, the excursion limit addresses the hazard related to short-term exposures typically experienced by trades, engineering, maintenance, and custodial staff in a building.

Although these limits appear low, they actually may offer very little protection against the liability associated with asbestos exposure. Building owners should not construe these limits as being "safe"; they represent a compromise between technical feasibility and current analytical sensitivity. The current PEL, 0.2 f/cc, translates into an allowable exposure of a worker to *2 million* asbestos fibers per day. Liability-conscious owners should consider adopting the more conservative "industry standard" of 0.01 asbestos structures per cubic centimeter, determined by TEM to be an acceptable upper level for both personnel and area samples.

As a clearance criterion set to aid in the evaluation of completed abatement activities, the TEM standard should always be considered to supersede PCM. The most widely used and accepted protocol compares the asbestos levels inside a remediated work area to that of outside air. If there is no statistical difference between the two, then the space is judged acceptable for reoccupancy.[15]

---

[13] OSHA, Asbestos, Tremolite, Anthophyllite, and Actinolite, 29 C.F.R. § 1926.58.

[14] EPA, Managing Asbestos in Place, A Building Owner's Guide to Operations and Maintenance Programs for Asbestos-Containing Materials, Pub. No. 20T-2003, July 1990.

[15] EPA, Guidelines for Conducting the AHERA TEM Clearance Test, To Determine Completion of an Asbestos Abatement Project (EPA 560/5-89-001, May 1989) app. H.

In October 1987, the EPA issued final regulations to carry out the Asbestos Hazard Emergency Response Act of 1986 (AHERA). The AHERA regulations, which deal with public and private elementary and secondary school buildings, require schools to conduct inspections, develop comprehensive asbestos management plans, and select asbestos response actions to deal with asbestos hazards.[16] Although not a requirement in the commercial market, AHERA is considered the highest regulatory standard of care that currently exists.

§ 3.13   —Asbestos: Summary

The presence of ACM is widespread in buildings throughout the United States. The regulations governing the work practices and allowable exposures for asbestos are extensive, but there are no laws that specifically require the removal or remediation of asbestos in commercial buildings unless the material will be disturbed in renovation or demolition activities. However, the devaluation of real estate in today's market and the liability associated with owning, managing, or occupying a building containing asbestos should be a strong enough force to trigger owners to thoroughly evaluate and remediate any hazard in their buildings.

§ 3.14   Lead: Generally

The hazards of lead were first recognized by the ancient Romans.[17] For the past 100 years, however, these hazards have been largely overlooked and unregulated in this country, except in industrial settings. Lead, like asbestos, has been widely used in buildings. Other uses of lead, a naturally occurring metal found and mined in great abundance all over the world, date back to the earliest records of human history. Some of the first applications of lead were in the manufacture of weapons, tools, utensils, and storage containers. In the Middle Ages, it was even added to foods as a sweetener.

The chemical symbol for lead, Pb, is derived from the Latin word *plumb*. Literally thousands of lead compounds exist, but only a few are typically encountered as hazards in buildings: lead carbonate (commonly known as white lead), lead chromate (commonly known as red lead), and lead acetate. Metallic lead is used for lining tanks, piping, and other equipment where pliability and corrosion resistance are required. The most common sources

---

[16] *Id.*

[17] Chisolm, Toxicology of Exposure to Lead-Based Paint, John F. Kennedy Institute.

of these compounds in residential and commercial properties are lead-based paint and lead solder.

Red and white lead pigments have been found on buildings that date back more than 5000 years. Manufactured by essentially the same process until the 1950s, white lead was added to and has been a mainstay of house paints since the 13th century.[18] Apart from its use as a pigment, lead was added to paints for a variety of functional reasons, including aesthetics and durability. Over the years, the use of lead-based paints grew; they were considered the best and the most expensive type of paint available. The use of lead in paints was eventually banned in the United States in 1977.

Some statistics may help in fully comprehending the extent of the lead hazard in buildings. In 1978, the U.S. government banned the use of lead as an additive in paints used for residential purposes. Lead-based paints were almost exclusively used in American homes constructed prior to that year.[19] Fifty-two percent of the nation's 80 million housing units are estimated to contain potentially hazardous levels of lead-based paint.[20] Lead plumbing solder, which was used on copper water pipes and is a typical material in all but the newest of buildings, was not banned until 1987.[21] The implications are staggering. Liability-conscious building owners should carefully note the dates of the bans and take appropriate action if their buildings have painted surfaces (especially if in poor condition), lead pipes, or copper plumbing systems.

§ 3.15   —Lead: Health Effects

Lead enters the body by either inhalation or ingestion. Inhalation of lead dust and fumes takes place primarily during the removal of old paint, often during renovation activities. Ingestion can take place via drinking lead-containing water and eating lead-based paint chips (a serious problem with young children). As water passes through piping made of lead or joined with lead solder, minute quantities of lead may be released and then ingested with the potable water. Lead was once used as a lining in various water coolers located in schools and commercial buildings. These uses of lead were banned by the EPA in 1988.[22]

Concern over lead has been well documented. A classical study in 1839 by French physician Tanquerel des Planches[23] clearly linked lead poisoning

---

[18] *Id.*

[19] *Reporting on Lead Paint Guidelines,* 73 A. Paint & Coatings J. 12 (June 12, 1989).

[20] *Id.*

[21] Safe Drinking Water Act and Amendment, 40 C.F.R. § 141.11.

[22] Lead Contamination Control Act of 1988.

[23] Tanquerel des Planches, Traité des Maladies de Plomb, ou Saturnines (1839).

to the occupational use of lead-based paints. As a result, the manufacture of white lead was banned in Germany and Scandinavia over 100 years ago.[24] The substance was judged far too dangerous for workers to produce. The first case of lead poisoning in a child was diagnosed in this country in 1914,[25] but not until the 1950s was paint-related lead poisoning in children recognized as a serious public health problem.[26] Research since that time has shown that children (especially those under the age of six) are most susceptible to the effects of lead poisoning.[27]

The health effects related to lead exposure are many, and there are no established "safe levels."[28] Because lead accumulates in the body following exposure, lead poisoning may be the result of a single large dose or, more commonly, small or low-level exposures over time. The brain and nervous system are particularly susceptible to damage, as are the kidneys, digestive system, and reproductive system. In children, irreversible neurological damage can result in lowered IQ, reduced attention span, and hyperactivity. Pregnant women and their fetuses are also at risk from lead poisoning.[29]

§ 3.16   —Lead: Evaluation

A complete survey must be conducted by a qualified consultant, to determine whether a lead hazard exists. A comprehensive survey should consist of sampling all painted surfaces on the interior and exterior of a building. A single paint chip or a single composite sample of several areas in a building will not yield an accurate measure of the hazard nor identify the affected areas. Assessment of lead solder requires analysis of water collected from the suspect system. Should lead be identified in the water, further analysis of the piping and solder may be necessary to determine the source of the lead.

There are three analytical methods for the determination of lead-based paint from surface sampling. Listed in descending order of accuracy, the analytical methods are: atomic absorption spectrometry (AAS), inductively coupled plasma spectrometry (ICP), and x-ray fluorescence (XRF). Of these techniques, the most widely used is XRF. Given the sensitivity of XRF and the amount of variability between readings, the technician performing the analysis must have a keen understanding of the equipment limitations

---

[24] Chisolm, *supra* note 17.

[25] Thomas and Blackfan, *Recurrent Meningitis Due to Lead in a Child of Five Years*, 8 A.J. Dis. Child. 377–80.

[26] Chisolm, *supra* note 17.

[27] *Manual Planned by NIBS*, 73 A. Paint & Coatings J. 18 (Sept. 12, 1988).

[28] Center for Environmental Health, Maryland Dept. of the Environment, Lead Paint Hazard Fact Sheet #1.

[29] *Id.*

and must strictly adhere to the analytical methodology. The laboratory performing the analysis should be fully evaluated for its competence in conducting the analysis procedures. The results of surface sample analysis are expressed as milligrams per centimeter squared (mg/cm^2) or as percent weight (wt%). (See **Appendix 3D** for the advantages and disadvantages of each technique.)

§ 3.17   —Lead: Standards

Given the widespread presence of lead, the fact that no "safe" level is known to exist, and the complexity of the abatement and testing process, one might assume that the regulations addressing this hazard are enormous in volume. However, the only federal regulations that address lead exposures are aimed at general industry and do not apply to building occupants nor to workers in the construction trade (the two groups facing the largest potential exposure).

The federal standard used for determining abatable paint on interior and exterior surfaces is 1 mg/cm^2 or 0.5 wt% for other collection techniques.[30] Air samples are not considered appropriate indicators for preliminary risk assessments, but they can be used in the determination of acceptable levels for reoccupancy following abatement. The only accurate method for determining actual lead exposure in humans is through a specific lead-level analysis of the blood. (See **Appendix 3E.**)

§ 3.18   —Lead: Remedial Alternatives

After a survey and a hazard assessment have been completed, a remedial action for each source or potential source of lead contamination should be selected. The control alternatives used for lead are virtually identical to those of asbestos. Currently, no federal regulations apply to lead abatement; however, some states have established lead removal regulations. Replacement, encapsulation, and removal are the methods most frequently used.

Replacement entails the removal of old piping systems that have been identified as contributing to lead contamination, and the substitution of piping made of safer materials; and/or the stripping and safe recoating of painted surfaces. Encapsulation consists of the application of a sealer over all lead surfaces. This response action is not a permanent solution but is a reasonable alternative for large surfaces that are in good condition or are not easily removable (for example, walls and floors). Removal, the only

---

[30] Lead-Based Paint Hazard Elimination; Final Rule, 24 C.F.R. pt. 35 ff.

permanent solution for elimination of a lead hazard, is the most costly and potentially the most hazardous.

The removal of lead-based paint is accomplished by a variety of appliances and techniques. Among them are chemical stripping, electric heat guns, caustic strippers, HEPA (high-efficiency particulate air) filtered sanders, and blasting. No single tool or method works best on all surfaces; each should be considered separately or in varied combinations that best suit the structure that is being deleaded. Factors such as the thickness of the application, the number of layers, and the condition of the substrate must be considered. Like asbestos, lead removal, if improperly performed, can result in significant exposure for a building's occupants. The *minimal* engineering controls involved in a proper removal will include: containment of the work area, decontamination facilities, respiratory protection, protective clothing, and clearance testing. The clearance criterion[31] generally adopted by the relevant industries and by several states requires a thorough visual inspection followed by each or a combination of the following: XRF readings, wipe samples, settled dust samples, and airborne samples. The level set for wipe samples is 200 micrograms per square foot ($\mu g/ft^2$) for flooring, 500 $\mu g/ft^2$ for window sills, and 800 $\mu g/ft^2$ for window wells and all bioavailable lead.[32]

§ 3.19   —Lead: Summary

Only through the initiative of the Department of Housing and Urban Development (HUD) has interim guidance documentation[33] for the hazard identification and abatement of lead-based paint been issued. Although HUD's documentation addresses only public and Indian housing, it should serve as a minimum standard of care for this problem.

Until additional regulations governing lead are established, if the paint or water tested in a building indicates the presence of lead, the only definitive way to determine lead exposure is by blood testing. The blood lead levels of each building occupant might be tested, but this measure is usually not warranted. Even when lead is present in a structure, it is possible that occupants are not breathing or ingesting detectable amounts.

If water samples indicate the presence of significant amounts of lead, and lead solder or piping is identified as the source, then remedial action should be taken under the advice of a knowledgeable consultant.

---

[31] U.S. Dept. of Housing and Urban Development (HUD), Lead-Based Paint: Interim Guidelines for Hazard Identification and Abatement in Public and Indian Housing, Apr. 1990.

[32] Center for Environmental Health, Maryland Dept. of the Environment, Lead Paint Hazard Fact Sheet #7 at 2.

[33] HUD, *supra* note 31.

If the paint inside a building is determined to be lead-based, owners should not act in haste. Given the lack of regulations and the extreme complexity of proper removal techniques, owners should proceed with remediation cautiously and only under the advice of a knowledgeable consultant. If the painted surfaces are not significantly damaged, the best remediation may be to do nothing.

§ 3.20   Radon: Generally

Of all the hazards identified as existing in buildings, none has stirred greater emotion among the American public or attracted more media attention than radon. With radon given names like "the silent killer" and others, coined by the media, it is no surprise that the concerns generated over this hazard are strong. The primary target of radon is that most sacred of places, the home.

The industry that has grown out of this fear has been a marketing phenomenon; neighborhood grocery stores, department stores, and pharmacies now sell inexpensive radon detectors for home owners' use. There are many misconceptions and myths about radon, but its hazards are very real. Some estimates attribute as many as 20,000 deaths each year in the United States to radon exposure.

In a time when most Americans are aware of the hazards attributed to radiation and limit their annual exposures, the reality is that we live in a world environment of background radiation. Nuclear testing conducted in the 1950s can be partially blamed, but by far the single most deadly source is a colorless, odorless, and tasteless gas called radon.

§ 3.21   —Radon: Sources and Locations

Radon is one of several radioactive materials produced as a result of the natural decay of uranium, which is found in many granites and other types of bedrock. In the decay process, uranium, a solid, changes into radium, which is transformed into a gas. This gas, called radon, is then able to emerge from the ground and become airborne. In most instances, the gas mixes with the atmosphere and quickly becomes diluted to concentrations generally considered as background. The hazards related to radon are realized, however, when the gas percolates up through soil beneath a building and enters a confined area such as a basement, crawl space, or cellar. Once trapped, radon will begin to accumulate. The volume of radon necessary for a hazard to exist is small; enough radon to contaminate hundreds of buildings would occupy a space no bigger than the head of a pencil eraser.[34]

---

[34] Vara, *A Special Report on Radon,* 14 Country J. 16 (Nov. 1987).

Although radon is heavier than air, it is able to eventually work its way up through cracks in flooring and various openings to reach higher levels of a building. Air movements, pressure differentials, and the natural stacking effect found in many buildings aid in this upward flow. As the gas moves, depending on the circulation patterns and tightness of the structure, it will slowly be diluted and dissipate (but far more slowly than in outside air). For this reason, radon levels are typically highest in the lowest reaches of a building and decrease in each higher level.

Surveys conducted in this country have demonstrated that radon is a problem in areas of every state but is of particular concern in a few regions.[35] The best documented and most publicized radon "hot spot" lies atop a geologic formation called the Reading Prong, which extends from Pennsylvania across New Jersey and up through New York and Connecticut. Buildings in this area have been known to have radon concentrations 600-fold above generally acceptable levels.[36] Additionally, the phosphate regions of Florida and the uranium plateau regions of Colorado, Utah, New Mexico, North Dakota, and Minnesota have been identified as high-risk areas.[37] Other exposures occur in areas where well water contains high concentrations of radon, which is released during periods of usage. This hazard has been found in Ohio, Illinois, and New England. Radon was long recognized as a hazard in uranium mines, but its emergence as a hazard in buildings was discovered quite by accident. An engineer working at the Philadelphia Electric Company's Limerick nuclear plant repeatedly set off the radiation monitors when he arrived to work.[38] An investigation ensued and revealed that the employee's home in Boyertown, Pennsylvania, had a radon level 16 times higher than the OSHA level permitted in uranium mines in the United States. It is now estimated that a million homes may contain radon levels that exceed the current EPA guidelines.

§ 3.22   —Radon: Health Effects

The only health effect currently attributed to radon exposure is increased risk of contracting lung cancer. (See **Appendix 3F**.) The EPA and other scientific groups estimate that about 20,000 lung cancer deaths each year may be due to radon.[39] These cancers, however, are not the direct result of the inhalation of radon gas; rather, they are caused by the highly charged

---

[35] Moeller, *How to Control Radon Gas,* 72 Consumers Res. 20 (Feb. 1989).

[36] Vara, *supra* note 34

[37] Moeller, *supra* note 35.

[38] Treffer, *Radon Gas May Seep into Your Liability,* 53 Real Estate Appr. & Analyst 21 (Spring 1987).

[39] EPA, Radon Measurements in Schools, An Interim Report, Pub. No. 520/1-89-010, Mar. 1989.

byproducts of its decay, which attach to dust called alpha particulates. Radon, an inert gas, will not react chemically with the lungs when inhaled and is thus harmlessly exhaled. However, the alpha particles released from radon are solids, and, when respirated, will readily deposit in the lungs. The energy released from these particles may damage the surrounding tissue and lead to the formation of cancerous cells. Through long-term studies of uranium miners, it has been conclusively documented that the risk of cancer rises as the concentration and duration of exposure increase. For this reason, a quantitative measurement is necessary for an accurate risk assessment of radon.

§ 3.23 —Radon: Evaluation and Standards

For a comparison to EPA standards, the common unit for expressing radon gas measured directly is picocuries per liter per year (pCi/l). A picocurie represents a quantity of radon in which there are slightly over 2 atoms decaying each minute. Currently, the EPA recommends that remedial action be taken if radon concentrations exceed 4 pCi/l.[40]

The standard unit applied to measuring radon decay products (the actual culprit of disease) is called a working level (WL). This name originated in the mining industry, where WL was the permissible limit of exposure at any one time.[41] For purposes of converting units from one scale to the other, 200 pCi/l are equivalent to 1 WL. A measurement of 1 pCi/l is generally considered below average for an occupied space in a typical building.

Depending on the construction and air-flow patterns in a building, the process of evaluating the presence of radon is usually quite simple. Although there are commercial firms that perform radon testing, it is one of the few sampling techniques, which, if carefully implemented, can be successfully accomplished by a building owner. The two most popular types of radon detectors are charcoal and alphatrack. The charcoal variety typically consists of a canister or bag filled with activated charcoal that absorbs radon gas as it is emitted from the soil. Though inexpensive and reasonably accurate, the major drawback with this type of test is that results are indicative of only a short period of time (usually 3 to 5 days). At that time, the detector reaches an equilibrium point at which it releases as much radon as it absorbs. Radon levels indicated by short-duration samples have little correlation with the average levels measured over the period of a year. With the charcoal detector, numerous variables may affect results—variations in

---

[40] EPA, A Citizen Guide to Radon: What Is It and What to Do About It (OPA-86-004, Aug. 1986).

[41] Evans, *Engineer's Guide to the Elementary Behavior of Radon Daughters,* 17 Health Physics 229 (1969).

barometric pressure, dilution rates based on the opening or closing of vents and windows, and seasonal changes. Placement of this type of detector is also crucial. Studies have shown that levels can vary over time by as much as a factor of 10.[42]

For most applications, a far superior detector is the alphatrack. The major advantage of this detector is that it can be set out for a number of months and will yield a more representative reading of the average annual emission level. In addition, this type of detector measures the actual release of alpha particles by recording the marks left on a disk as the particles impact it. These impressions are rendered visible by a chemical treatment of the disk and then counted by a microscopic technique. When using either charcoal or alphatrack detectors, it is a good idea to set out several, both in lower areas of initial radon penetration and at higher levels in a building.

Another sampling technique that may be used in certain aspects of an evaluation involves collection grab samples. This technique employs the use of a radon continuous working level monitor (CWLM). Air is pulled through this instrument at a predetermined flow rate and analyzed. Samples are usually collected over a period of 5 to 10 minutes. Given the short sampling time, the results are usually available in less than an hour but should be interpreted with caution. Unlike other measurement techniques, the results of grab samples are greatly influenced by the conditions existing in the building for the 8 to 12 hours just prior to sampling.

Two particularly useful applications for this technique are as a diagnostic tool to help pinpoint routes of entry, and for locations where elevated levels are believed to exist and a quick confirmation is needed. It should be noted, however, that the EPA does not recommend, or consider reliable, radon tests of less than 6 hours.[43]

If the results of samples collected from a building exceed the EPA standard of 4 pCi/l, then response actions should be considered after careful review of the initial data and only under the advice of an experienced consultant. It is prudent to ensure that proper sampling methods were used, that placement was correct, that the duration and number of samples were sufficient, and that the proper analysis was performed. Depending on the level indicated, it might be wise to retest before acting.

§ 3.24   —Radon: Remedial Alternatives

In general, there are three radon remediation approaches: *ventilation*, which relies on reduction of radon through dilution; *infiltration prevention*, which involves the sealing of entry points to a building, and *suction*,

---

[42] Vara, *supra* note 34.

[43] EPA, *A Citizen's Guide to Radon* (Aug. 1986).

which expels radon by depressurizing the soil to release the gas and then venting it away. The specific measures needed to remediate a particular situation will depend on the severity of the hazard, the building construction, and the soil type. Where radon levels are moderate, ventilation will often work well, requiring little more than leaving a vent open or installing a small fan to increase the flow of outside air. This approach generally works best when combined with infiltration prevention; however, both should be used cautiously because any drop in the indoor air pressure will tend to draw the radon up and into the building. Where serious radon contamination is present, the suction approach is usually the most effective but is always the most costly. A state radiation protection department or regional EPA office should be able to provide a more detailed description of these methods as well as a list of contractors qualified to undertake them in a particular area.

Each of the remediation methods described relies on the reduction of radon gas prior to its entering occupied spaces. When radon is inside occupied spaces, its hazards are considerably greater and therefore must also be addressed in a remediation plan. A recent Harvard University study on the control of radon gas presented data that suggest alpha particles in occupied spaces are most effectively reduced through a combination of air circulation (typically by ceiling fan) and a positive ion generator. A preliminary test of this system has shown working level reductions approaching 95 percent.[44]

Research is thus beginning to provide substantial evidence that, in the very near future, buildings with all but the highest of radon concentrations can be significantly remedied through similar methods at substantially less cost and complexity than are required by means available today.

§ 3.25   Polychlorinated Biphenyls (PCBs): Generally

Polychlorinated biphenyls (PCBs) were first manufactured in 1929. Composed primarily of hydrogen, carbon, and chlorine, they were very cheap to make, remained chemically inert, and did not conduct electricity or burn—seemingly, the ideal industrial chemical. For 35 years, they were widely used in products as diverse as inks and transformer fluids. Their primary use or concern to building owners is in the form of askarel (a dielectric fluid comprised of 40 to 80 percent PCB and trichlorobenzene) found in transformers, capacitors, switching gear, and related electrical equipment. So widespread are these applications that it is rare for a commercial or industrial building constructed between the 1930s and the 1970s not to contain numerous sources of PCBs. In 1968, public and

---

[44] Moeller, *supra* note 35.

scientific opinion regarding the chemical changed dramatically when 2,000 people in Japan ate Yusho rice oil that was contaminated by PCBs. Although none died, the victims suffered from a severe skin rash called chloracne and later manifested a variety of problems including reproductive and neurological disorders, liver damage, and respiratory problems. Subsequent media coverage was extensive; photographs of the victims appeared in *LIFE* Magazine. Public opinion became fearful, and PCBs quickly gained a bad reputation and became a symbol of the industrial pollutants affecting the environment.

§ 3.26   —PCBs: Regulations

Research prompted by this incident revealed that, through the careless dumping of tens of thousands of tons of PCBs into the environment worldwide, the chemical was everywhere. With a half-life of 200 years, it accumulates (predominantly in the fat cells of animals) as it moves up the food chain. Reports of highway spills and its discovery in an ever growing number of foods and animals (from seals in the far reaches of the Arctic to the breast milk of expectant mothers worldwide) fueled support for regulation of this toxin. In 1976, through the Toxic Substances Control Act (TSCA), the United States responded by banning all "open" uses of PCBs (in sealants, inks, oils, and carbonless copy paper) and restricting their use to only "closed" electrical equipment.[45]

§ 3.27   —PCBs: Health Effects

Ironically, only in the past few years have scientists discovered that it was not PCBs that poisoned the Yusho rice oil.[46] Following two fires in the early 1980s, one in a state office building in Binghamton, New York, and the other near One Market Square in San Francisco, California, a connection was conclusively made between PCBs and furans, their much more toxic by-product. An investigation subsequent to the fires, combined with new measuring techniques, enabled scientists to learn that PCBs present in the buildings did not burn but, when heated, they released toxic furans. Apparently, heating the Yusho rice oil had produced the same toxic effect.[47]

PCBs enter the body through ingestion, primarily, of contaminated foods (fish, in particular).[48] The PCB molecules attach themselves to the fatty

---

[45] Toxic Substances Control Act, 40 C.F.R. 370 (1976).

[46] Ohlendorf-Moffat, PCBs: *Should You Worry?* Chatelaine 56 (Apr. 1990).

[47] Kump, *Eliminating PCBs on Campus,* 60 A. School & University 257 (Mar. 1988).

[48] Ohlendorf-Moffat, *supra* note 46.

tissue around organs. Some researchers believe PCBs may be cancer-producing, but this has not been proven conclusively. So far, the only health effect directly linked to PCBs is chloracne. Debate regarding whether PCBs can enter the body via skin absorption is still unresolved.[49]

Studies have shown that workers with years of PCB exposure have blood levels of up to 1,000 parts per billion (ppb),[50] far higher than the highest level measured (300 ppb) in some of the Yusho victims; yet, because the PCBs the workers handled were virtually free of furans, they suffered only mild (if any) acne. As a group, their rates of cancer and death were found to be no higher than the general population, whose typical blood levels do not exceed 5 to 10 ppb.

As mentioned, the most serious threat posed by PCBs is associated with fire and the incomplete combustion by-product of furans. A fire may envelop a PCB-filled transformer in only a small area of a building, but, because of air circulation patterns and the natural stacking effect, exposure to occupants and contamination of the entire structure may result. The 1981 state office building fire in Binghamton, New York, is an example. The cleanup cost ran over $20 million, and the building is still unoccupied as of this writing. Acting on this knowledge, the EPA issued the Fire Hazard Rule[51] in 1985. It required, among other things, that by October 1, 1990, all PCB transformers in or near commercial buildings (dependent on their classification and application) were to be remediated.

§ 3.28   —PCBs: Evaluation and Remedial Alternatives

The task of surveying buildings for the location of transformers and the process of conducting hazard and remediation assessment are, like the other hazards addressed in this chapter, best left to experts. The EPA allows basically three options for PCB remediation: (1) complete removal and replacement, (2) retrofill, or (3) installation of fault protection devices.[52] Selection of a particular option or combination of options should address the type of transformer (see **Appendix 3G** for the EPA's three classifications), the location, and the condition or risk associated with each.

All of the options are expensive, because each mandates the use of precautionary measures and requires access to transformers, many of which are hidden behind walls or housed in difficult-to-reach areas. Removal and replacement, usually considered the most desirable option, is certainly the

---

[49] Hedberg, *Hazardous Waste: The Plain Facts*, 80 Buildings 64 (Nov. 1986).

[50] Ohlendorf-Moffat, *supra* note 46.

[51] EPA Fire Hazard Rule, 1985.

[52] *Id.*

most expensive. Full access, careful dismantling of the transformer, and disposal of both the fluid and the contaminated unit are required.

Although removal carries the distinct advantage of elimination of the hazard, this option may, in the long run, still carry considerable liability. The courts have recently upheld that the ownership of a hazardous material is not relinquished upon disposal (even at an EPA-approved landfill), and transportation of PCBs is one of the highest-risk areas for potential leaks or spills. Somewhat less expensive, at least initially, retrofill involves the draining of the PCB-containing askarel fluid and its replacement with a nontoxic coolant (the EPA recommends silicones, non-PCB askarels, or high-temperature hydrocarbons). This option is the most economic for smaller units (usually under 500 gallons); typically, it can be accomplished with minimal disruption. The major disadvantage is that the reduction in risk is proportional to the amount of PCBs left in the transformer (it is impossible to drain them completely). The presence of this residual PCB fluid may require periodic inspection, to verify that the level remains below EPA-prescribed limits. The third option, installation of protective devices, may be the least expensive, depending on the cost of the device, because handling of the transformer fluid is not required. However, the risk due to fire and accidental spill, although reduced, remains a potential hazard and a constant variable to address in future renovations.

§ 3.29   —PCBs: Summary

The choices for remediation are not always clear, but building owners can take actions that will help in making effective business decisions. The development of a facility risk-reduction program addressing the presence of PCBs is one such action. Similar programs should address, at a minimum:

1. Survey of the facility to determine the presence of PCBs, their condition, and the occurrence of any spills;
2. Necessary maintenance of equipment;
3. Assessment of the containment potential of the PCBs found;
4. Availability of appropriate safety equipment for emergencies;
5. Necessary training;
6. Labeling of equipment and registration of transformers.

A good source for this level of expertise is often local power companies; in many facilities, they actually own most of the existing PCB-filled equipment. Given their knowledge and experience in servicing PCB-contaminated equipment, they can be helpful in the remediation process by performing power system studies. These types of studies can provide valuable information when considering the variables of deceased KVA ratings, transformer life expectancy, and the probability of failure. Most power companies are also able to provide a list of contractors in the area who can perform the remedial actions selected.

The EPA's deadline for action by building owners (October 1, 1990) has passed. A building owner now faces fines relating to noncompliance as well as the potentially greater cost associated with remediation of a spill or contamination of an entire building.

§ 3.30   Formaldehyde: Generally

Formaldehyde (HCHO) is a colorless, pungent gas produced by the catalytic oxidation of methyl alcohol. It is sold commercially in an aqueous solution called formalin, formal, or morbicid. Formaldehyde is often identified as a hazardous material in building investigations because of its widespread use in building construction materials and furnishings. It is among the top 25 bulk chemicals produced annually in this country.[53]

§ 3.31   —Formaldehyde: Sources

Formaldehyde has long been used in the industrial setting as a fungicide, germicide, and disinfectant additive. The use of formaldehyde in the manufacture of building materials, textiles, and furniture, however, has led to its prevalence in the indoor environment. Urea-formaldehyde foam insulation (UFFI), a building insulation used in the early 1970s, was intentionally introduced into the wall cavities of a building. Nine types of UFFI were commercially available. These products have been shown to release significant amounts of formaldehyde after 16 months. The subsequent "off-gassing" of formaldehyde into buildings was determined to be a significant source of irritation. One study showed that average formaldehyde levels in UFFI houses in the United States generally peak shortly after installation, drop to 0.1 part per million (ppm) after one year, and slowly decline toward background levels in subsequent years. (Typically, formaldehyde is measured in units of parts formaldehyde per million parts of air.) Other significant sources of formaldehyde include: particle board, plywood, wood paneling, textiles, resins, latex, dyes, and inks. The temperature, relative humidity, moisture content of building components, and operation of the air-conditioning system can affect the release and clearance of formaldehyde gas. An increase in formaldehyde may occur with the onset of fall

---

[53] Samet, Marbury, and Spengler, *Respiratory Effects of Indoor Air Pollution,* 79 J. Allergy & Clinical Immunol. 685–700 (1987).

weather: the start-up of the heating system may evaporate formaldehyde-laden moisture from gypsum walls. The chance of releasing formaldehyde from the wall cavities is increased if the walls are unpainted, cracked, or water-damaged.

§ 3.32 —Formaldehyde: Health Effects

Formaldehyde has been determined to cause severe irritation to the mucous membranes of the respiratory tract and eyes. The primary route of exposure is from inhalation of the gas, but repeated exposure to the liquid may cause dermatitis. Other reported symptoms include cough, respiratory distress, skin irritation, nausea, headache, dizziness, and drowsiness. These symptoms may range from mild to severe, depending on the concentration of formaldehyde and the individual's sensitivity.

Formaldehyde has also been determined by several agencies to be a suspected human carcinogen. The International Agency for Research on Cancer (IARC) and the American Conference of Governmental Industrial Hygienists (ACGIH) Threshold Limit Value (TLV) Committee have designated formaldehyde as a 2A and A2 carcinogen, respectively. The EPA has also classified formaldehyde as a probable human carcinogen.[54] These designations mean that formaldehyde is suspected of inducing cancer in humans, because of human epidemiological evidence or demonstration of carcinogenesis in one or more animal species.

§ 3.33 —Formaldehyde: Identification and Evaluation

Formaldehyde concentrations may be determined through a variety of active and passive sampling methodologies. Liquid sorbent badges containing sodium bisulfite and water may be used to collect formaldehyde over time by controlled diffusion through a diffusion barrier at a predetermined rate. Analysis of formaldehyde concentration can then be determined through a colorimetric technique that can detect formaldehyde in the 0.02 to 2 ppm range. Instantaneous samples of formaldehyde can be collected using calorimetric detector tubes, which change color in the presence of formaldehyde. The determination of a time-weighted average formaldehyde concentration is performed using a battery-operated sampling pump and impinger. Air is bubbled through the impinger solution and formaldehyde concentration is determined using gas chromatography. Most of these

---

[54] Cox, *Formaldehyde Risk Assessed,* ASHRAE J (July 1987) at 17.

techniques were developed to evaluate personal exposure to formaldehyde in the industrial setting. (See **Appendix 3H.**) Some individuals have been found to be sensitive to formaldehyde at a level several orders of magnitude below current exposure limits.

§ 3.34   —Formaldehyde: Standards

The current OSHA permissible exposure limit (PEL) and ACGIH threshold limit value (TLV) for formaldehyde is 1 ppm as an 8-hour time-weighted average. The OSHA and ACGIH short-term exposure limit (STEL) is 2 ppm. The NIOSH recommended exposure limit (REL) and ceiling limits are 0.016 ppm and 0.1 ppm, respectively. As discussed previously, these standards were developed primarily for industrial uses and exposures to formaldehyde. Concentrations of formaldehyde found in the indoor environment may be well below these values and yet may still be associated with health-related complaints.

§ 3.35   —Formaldehyde: Remedial Actions

Currently, no federal regulations govern the remediation of formaldehyde. The approaches generally used to avoid problems caused by formaldehyde are (1) avoid the use of UFFI, particle board, plywood, or other products known to contain formaldehyde; (2) allow formaldehyde-containing products to "age" for a period of time in a building, prior to occupancy by personnel; (3) increase ventilation in areas where formaldehyde-containing products are used.

Aside from avoiding products that contain formaldehyde, which may be difficult to do when remodeling or installing new furnishings, the only effective remedial action appears to be: allow the off-gassing to take place with minimal impact on a building population. This can be accomplished either by allowing the new materials to age for several weeks before occupancy, or by increasing the ventilation rate so that formaldehyde concentrations will not build up in an occupied area. There is no guarantee that either of these techniques will avoid potential problems with formaldehyde, if a sensitive individual occupies the space.

Appendix 3A   U.S. Environmental Protection Agency Regional Offices

Region 1: Connecticut, Maine, Massachusetts, New Hampshire, Rhode Island, and Vermont

Damien Houlihan
U.S. Environmental Protection Agency
JFK Federal Building
Boston, MA 02203
(617) 565-3265
FTS: 835-3265

Region 2: New York, New Jersey, Puerto Rico, Virgin Islands, and Canal Zone

Robert Fitzpatrick
Air and Waste Management Division
U.S.Environmental Protection Agency
26 Federal Plaza
New York, NY 10278
(212) 264-6770
FTS: 264-6770

Region 3: Delaware, District of Columbia, Maryland, Pennsylvania, Virginia, and West Virginia

Carol Febbo
Air Management Division
U.S. Environmental Protection Agency
841 Chestnut Street
Philadelphia, PA 19107
(215) 597-9325
FTS: 597-9325

Region 4: Alabama, Florida, Georgia, Kentucky, Mississippi, North Carolina, South Carolina, and Tennessee

Brian Beals
Air, Pesticides and Toxics Management Division
U.S. Environmental Protection Agency
345 Courtland Street N.E.
Atlanta, GA 30365
(404) 347-2904
FTS: 257-2904

Region 5: Illinois, Indiana, Minnesota, Michigan, Ohio, and Wisconsin

Bruce Varner
Air and Radiation Division
U.S. Environmental Protection Agency
230 South Dearborn Street
Chicago, IL 60604
(312) 886-6793
FTS: 886-6793

Region 6: Arkansas, Louisiana, New Mexico, Oklahoma, and Texas

Martin Brittain
Air, Pesticides and Toxics Division
U.S. Environmental Protection Agency
1445 Ross Avenue
Dallas, TX 75202
(214) 655-7229
FTS: 255-7229

Region 7: Iowa, Kansas, Missouri, and Nebraska

JoAnn Heiman
Air & Toxics Management Division
U.S. Environmental Protection Agency
726 Minnesota Avenue
Kansas City, KS 66101
(913) 236-2896
FTS: 757-2896

Region 8: Colorado, Montana, North Dakota, South Dakota, Utah, and
Wyoming

Cindy Cody
Air and Toxics Management Division
U.S. Environmental Protection Agency
999 18th Street, Suite 500
Denver, CO 80202
(303) 293-1767
FTS: 564-1767

Region 9: Arizona, California, Hawaii, Nevada, Guam, American Samoa, Trust
Territory of the Pacific

Janet Crawford
Air Management Division
U.S. Environmental Protection Agency
215 Fremont Street
San Francisco, CA 94105
(415) 974-7633
FTS: 454-7633

Region 10: Alaska, Idaho, Oregon, and Washington

Armina Nolan
Air & Toxics Management Division
U.S. Environmental Protection Agency
1200 Sixth Avenue
Seattle, WA 98101
(206) 442-1757
FTS: 399-1757

Appendix 3B   EPA Asbestos Ban and Phase-Down Rule Timetable

Stage 1. Effective dates:
  Ban of manufacture* 8/90
  Ban of Distribution 8/92
  Materials: Flooring felt, pipeline wrap, vinyl asbestos floor tile, roofing felt, asbestos clothing, asbestos cement sheets

Stage 2. Effective dates:
  Ban of manufacture* 8/93
  Ban of Distribution 8/94
  Materials: Gasket components, Dutch facings, friction products, automatic transmission components, other automotive components and brake pads, certain types of brake linings

Stage 3. Effective dates:
  Ban of manufacture* 8/96
  Ban of Distribution 8/97
  Materials: Asbestos/cement pipe, corrugated paper, millboard, commercial paper, rollboard, asbestos/cement shingles

Note: The EPA estimates that this Rule will affect approximately 95 percent of all commercially available asbestos-containing products used in the United States.

* Ban includes the manufacture, import and processing of the specified products.

Appendix 3C   Common Asbestos-Containing Materials in Buildings

Surfacing materials:

- Fireproofing
- Acoustical plaster
- Decorative plaster
- Textured wall and ceiling surfaces

Thermal system insulation (TSI):

- Equipment insulation (boilers, water tanks, compressors, air handling equipment, etc.)
- Pipe insulation
- Pipe joint, valve, fitting, and elbow insulation
- Breeching insulation
- Duct insulation

Miscellaneous materials:

- Vinyl asbestos floor tile (VAT)
- Linoleum

- Transite board
- Ceiling tile
- Vibration-dampening cloth HVAC duct systems
- Joint compound

Note: This list represents only the most common forms of asbestos-containing materials found in buildings and in no way should be considered exhaustive, given that over 3,000 were known to have been manufactured.

Appendix 3D Comparison of Advantages and Disadvantages of Analysis Methods for Lead-Base Paint

Methods	Advantages	Disadvantages
Paint scrapings by atomic absorption spectrometry (AAS) or inductively coupled plasma spectrometry (ICP)	1. Analyzed in laboratory 2. Results usually very accurate 3. Expensive to analyze in lab 4. Quantitative results can be "watered down" by many paint layers 5. Destructive to surface	1. Lab needs time to complete sampling process 2. 30 to 70 samples must be taken
Portable XRF spectrometer	1. Performed on site 2. Nondestructive to surface 3. Results available quickly 4. Some surface destruction necessary if results are to be accurate	1. Equipment is expensive 2. Requires trained operators 3. Will not read on all surfaces
Sodium sulfide	1. Quick, on-site results 2. Potential use as screening tool 3. Interference from other metals	1. Some surface destruction necessary 2. Not quantitative

Appendix 3E Blood Lead Level— Standards for Intervention

1. CDC Recommended blood lead level for clinical intervention for children: 25 µg/dl (will be lowered to 10 to 15 µg/dl by late 1990, early 1991)

2. OSHA   Industry standard for removal from the workplace: 50 µg/dl; must be
           below 40 µg/dl before returning
3. HUD   Guidelines for removal from the workplace: 30 µg/dl

CDC = Center for Disease Control.
OSHA = Occupational Safety and Health Administration.
HUD = U.S. Department of Housing and Urban Development.

Appendix 3F   Radon Risk Evaluation Chart

Annual Radon Level	If a Community of 100 People Were Exposed to This Level:	This Risk of Dying from Lung Cancer Compares to:
100 pCi/L	About 35 people in the community may die from Radon.	Having 2000 chest x-rays each year
40 pCi/L	About 17 people in the community may die from Radon.	Smoking 2 packs of cigarettes eacy day
20 pCi/L	About 9 people in the community may die from Radon.	Smoking 1 pack of cigarettes eacy day
10 pCi/L	About 5 people in the community may die from Radon.	Having 500 chest x-rays each year
4 pCi/L	About 2 people in the community may die from Radon.	Smoking half a pack of cigarettes each day
2 pCi/L	About 1 person in the community may die from Radon.	Having 100 chest x-rays each year

Levels as high as 3500 pCi/L have been found in some homes.
The average Radon level outdoors is around .2 pCi/L or less.

The risks shown in this chart are for the general population, including men and
women of all ages as well as smokers and non-smokers. Children may be at higher
risk.

Appendix 3G   EPA Transformer Classifications

1. PCB transformers having 500 or more parts per million (ppm) of PCBs
2. PCB-contaminated transformers containing at least 50 ppm of PCBs but less
   than 500 ppm
3. Non-PCB transformers having less than 50 ppm of PCBs

Appendix 3H   Comparison of Common
Methodologies for Detection of Formaldehyde

Sampling Technique	Range of Sensitivity	Comments
Detector tubes	0.5 ppm	Not recommended for indoor air
Dynamic sampling—impingers	.25 to .1 ppm	
Passive monitors	.1 to .01 ppm	Good for long-term exposure
Continuous Monitors—Dosimeter	.5 to .02 ppm	

CHAPTER 4

SICK BUILDING SYNDROME

Hal Finkelstein
Vice President of Technical Services
Empire Testing & Balancing, Inc.

§ 4.1   Defining Sick Building Syndrome

§ 4.2   Identifying Sick Building Syndrome Complaints

§ 4.3   Performing a Background Assessment

§ 4.4   Building Reviews

§ 4.5   Complaint Documentation

§ 4.6   Interpreting the Data Collected: Guidelines

§ 4.7   —Proper Sampling Procedures

§ 4.8   —Interpretation of Results

§ 4.9   —Chemical Inventory

§ 4.10   —Contaminant Sources

§ 4.11   Quantitative Analysis

§ 4.12   Expert Selection

§ 4.13   The Role of an Expert Before Trial

§ 4.14   —Educating the Client

§ 4.15   —Analyzing and Testing

§ 4.16   —Interrogatories

§ 4.17   —Depositions

§ 4.18   —Budgets

§ 4.19   —Checklist for Expert's Report

§ 4.20   Experts' Fees

§ 4.21   Conclusion

APPENDIXES

4A   Expert Witness Referral Groups

4B   Project Time Account

4C   Agreement and Rate Schedule

§ 4.1 Defining Sick Building Syndrome

Acceptable interior air quality in today's environmentally concerned society means different things to different people. Pinpointing the actual causes and definitions of bad interior air quality can often be extremely difficult. In certain installations, the determination of the cause of bad interior air quality has been a time-consuming investigation, with numerous tests carried out on the building and its air, equipment, and interior furnishings.

What is acceptable interior air quality? What *should* it be for office buildings, hospitals, industrial complexes, schools, and other facilities where individuals spend a great deal of their time indoors? It has been estimated by government sources that 85 percent of our lives is spent indoors—that is, within the confines of a type of building—as compared to 15 percent spent outdoors. We should have been concerned about interior air quality long before the advent of the numerous asbestos lawsuits that continue to be entered on court calendars. The discovery that asbestos within buildings was causing severe health problems among occupants seems to have awakened society to the possibility that we could be harmed in the very shelters where we felt most secure.

In areas subject to severe pollution alerts and similar ambient air quality problems, we once sheltered ourselves within the confines of air-conditioned buildings, believing that their modern systems would keep us safe from the pollutants that would otherwise cause severe harm. In retrospect, it now appears that we may have been no safer indoors than we would have been outdoors in the heart of any pollution alert. We may even have been more severely harmed indoors, because of the increase of pollutant concentrations that can occur in a closed environment and the way in which one pollutant can make us sensitive to others.

In addition to the actual pollutants that might be contained in the air supply to our interior spaces and the pollutants within the interior spaces themselves, one has to define where the actual pollutant level is occurring. For example, the area of most danger, where the presence of pollutants could severely harm an individual, is within the "breathing zone." In different buildings, the breathing zone can occur at different levels. In an office building, the breathing zone is an area measured from a couple of inches above a desktop to about five feet above the finished floor. In hospitals, variations occur within different areas. The breathing zone receives the majority of remedial concern relative to pollutants. If a building has a 30-foot ceiling, there will be minimal concern regarding pollutant accumulation in this area, as long as the ventilation system and the air movement provided within the occupied spaces do not allow pollutants to enter the breathing zone established for this building. In residential buildings, not only does the breathing zone vary, but the type and intensity of the pollutants can vary from room to room.

It may sound simple to make allowances for variations, but today's building designs make it anything but simple. For example, in many large buildings, the air-conditioning return system (the system that recirculates the air for filtering, cooling, and heating) is the system to which attention is least paid. The primary factor for designing any air-conditioning system within a facility or any ventilating system in a nonhazardous area is comfort. Designers are more concerned with the supply of air to the "comfort zone" than they are with the return of this air to the air-conditioning systems.

Many of today's new buildings utilize return plenums: ceiling tiles are perforated with pinholes to enable air from the space to enter the plenum and thereby return to the air-conditioning equipment. Although this method is economical and is quite satisfactory for providing comfort, it is not an efficient method for proper removal of interior space pollutants from particular areas.

The incoming air supply to an air-conditioning system is carefully adjusted and balanced to ensure that the exact quantity of air required is provided to a particular space. The air that enters the return plenum through the perforated tiles is not and cannot be adjusted. Consequently, the air returned from floor areas throughout a large facility can have extreme variations.

In many instances, an improper overall exchange of air helps pollutant buildup within an interior space. For example, building designers' concerns are: Does the air supply to a space create the proper temperature differentials between floor and ceiling? Is the air movement low enough at the comfort zone so as not to create drafts? Are the temperature and humidity of the air supplied to the space kept at just the proper temperature so that they do not create a sense of discomfort?

Various controls and thermostats regulate either the temperature of the supply air or, in newer buildings, the air supply quantity entering the space, which can be regulated to create proper interior comfort. Not enough thought is given to how air movement within a space relates to pollutant concentrations. The key question is: With which pollutant should engineers be concerned? The problem is compounded in hospitals, where infectious diseases and bacteriological contagion can originate from operating rooms, patients' rooms, and other sensitive areas.

Which pollutant should receive primary attention? In specific areas of hospitals and industrial complexes, a particular hazardous pollutant might be easily identified. However, in an occupancy such as an office building, an apartment complex, or a single-family home, isolating one pollutant and requiring designers and builders to concentrate on it as the pollutant of greatest concern is neither easy nor wise. Yet, given some concern about all pollutant concentrations, which concentration levels do we adhere to as being "safe" and which levels reliably signify a sick building syndrome problem?

Studies have identified the pollutants that should most concern building managers and employers who wish to ensure the establishment of proper interior air quality in facilities such as office buildings, hospitals, and schools. Bacteria, carbon dioxide, carbon monoxide, aldehydes, fibers such as asbestos, fiberglass, and other dusts all can contribute to the development of interior air problems. Vapors off-gassing from construction materials such as particle board, plywood, carpeting, and foam padding also must be evaluated.

§ 4.2   Identifying Sick Building Syndrome Complaints

Sick building syndrome sometimes identifies itself via complaints originating from employees. These complaints may include dizziness, nausea, burning eyes, sore throat, headache, tearing eyes, increased respiratory problems, and, in some instances, more serious respiratory illnesses. In hospitals, interior air quality problems can manifest themselves in an increase in infection rates, patient melancholy, apparent hypertension in patients, respiratory complications, and many other apparent medical implications. In single-family homes, people have reported nosebleeds, sore throats, headaches, and dizziness.

When it is apparent that something is wrong, the investigative procedure should begin to determine:

1.   Are complaints truly being caused by interior air pollution?
2.   How can the source be identified?
3.   Who is at fault?
4.   What corrections can be made?
5.   Who is responsible for making the corrections?

Little federal or state guidance has been given regarding the standards that should be utilized to determine what sources constitute an interior air quality problem. For some of the more publicized pollutants such as asbestos, radon, and urea–formaldehyde products, there are recommended standards.[1] In a few cases, there are some OSHA and EPA maximum limitations.[2] However, for many of the other pollutants that appear to generate the sick building syndrome, there is no federal or state guidance as to what concentration will cause the complaints. Many facility owners are open to

---

[1] Note, NIOSH Pocket Guide to Chemical Hazards, 1987, at 70.
[2] *Id.*

liability if they continue to ignore how their occupants are affected by the interior air quality.

As an example, the OSHA maximum recommended level for carbon dioxide is 5,000 parts per million (ppm).[3] However, from research and from literature, engineers know that levels substantially lower can result in interior air quality complaints.[4] Carbon dioxide levels of 1,500 ppm or less can generate extreme interior air quality problems. In some facilities, depending on the level of other pollutants, carbon dioxide levels of 1,500 ppm or less can generate feelings of discomfort, headaches, and burning eyes in a certain percentage of even the healthiest individuals. Hospitals must concern themselves with even lower pollutant levels because patients already suffering from other illnesses may be more sensitive to pollutants' effects.

When building occupants experience signs of sick building syndrome, indications of potential future litigation also begin to manifest themselves. These signs normally unfold as follows:

1. Employees complain in mass to managers or union representatives.
2. Large groups of employees send joint memoranda to senior management concerning ailments.
3. Building tenants continually notify building owners that their profit structure, cash flow, and/or the production of their employees are affected by sick building syndrome ailments.
4. Large quantities of correspondence go back and forth concerning alleged interior air quality problems.

Successful litigation depends, more and more, on the quality and expertise of the technical experts utilized and on the development of reliable and accurate information as to whether there is an interior air quality problem. In many cases, a consultant should be called in at the first sign of a sick building syndrome situation.

Success in winning an interior air quality lawsuit is tied to the everyday steps taken before a lawsuit materializes. A building owner–client should be asked the following questions:

1. Did you keep up with the latest health care and environmental concerns and alerts, as they affect your facility?
2. What steps did you take to ensure that your personnel or service contractors were not creating interior air quality problems, while printing, cleaning, exterminating, or performing general building repairs?

[3] Id.

[4] American Society of Heating, Refrigerating and Air Conditioning Engineers (ASHRAE), *Ventilation for Acceptable Indoor Air Quality,* Standard 62-1989 (1989).

3. Were your HVAC systems checked by independent experts whose evaluations were unbiased as to the systems' condition and as to any interior air quality problems various areas were experiencing?

4. Have you acted in a responsible manner on recommendations made by your outside experts?

5. Did you keep the personnel affected by the sick building syndrome problem apprised of the steps you were taking?

6. Did you allow your consultant to have access, for interview purposes, to the individuals experiencing sick building syndrome symptoms?

7. Has your consultant been allowed to evaluate the sick building syndrome situation during different times of the day and different days of the week, to get the broadest possible sampling of building activities?

Responses to these concerns can determine the outcome of an interior air quality lawsuit, should one be filed.

As pointed out earlier, federal or state regulations do not specify the maximum acceptable concentrations for all interior pollutants identified with sick building syndrome in commercial, residential, or institutional buildings. Two pollutants that have specified levels and are often involved in major lawsuits are carbon monoxide and carbon dioxide. The existence of these pollutants at elevated levels, singularly and with other airborne pollutants, frequently forms the basis for litigation concerning office buildings, hospitals, and other types of nonindustrial public assembly facilities.

OSHA's present exposure limit for *carbon dioxide* in the workplace is 5,000 ppm.[5] However, much of the research on the physiological effects of carbon dioxide has been done to establish safe limits for extremely healthy submarine crews and astronauts.[6] Applying such limits to the occupants of office buildings and, especially, of hospitals is not in itself totally reasonable. The type of building in which the different maximum carbon dioxide values have been determined and their specific cause are significant factors.

Sick building syndrome can occur in facilities that have carbon dioxide levels as low as 1,000 ppm, depending on other pollutants that might be present. NASA's research has shown that prolonged exposure at concentrations between 5,000 and 30,000 ppm had to occur before biochemical changes, which may be considered as mild physiological strain, begin.[7] In reality, mild physiological strain and discomfort can be experienced by occupants of buildings at values far below 5,000 ppm. Some government

---

[5] *Supra* note 1.

[6] Noyes Data Corp. Indoor Air Quality Control Techniques (1987).

[7] *See generally* National Aeronautics and Space Administration (NASA), The Bioastronautics Data Book (1973).

officials are attempting to enact laws that might define what carbon dioxide exposure values can create interior health problems.

For example, the State of New Jersey has developed a draft of proposed Indoor Air Standards that will first apply to buildings where public employees work.[8] Although the standards deal mostly with the operation and design of heating, ventilating, and air-conditioning (HVAC) systems (setting standards for outside air, indoor temperatures, humidity, and other controlled parameters), they will attempt to set a maximum interior carbon dioxide level at about 850 ppm.

Senator George Mitchell (D.-Maine) has introduced S. 455, which attempts to control all indoor air pollution[9] by passing control of *all* indoor air pollutants, not just radon, to the EPA, which would be required to set standards for all potential indoor air pollutants.

Additionally, ASHRAE recently released indoor air quality standard 62-1989, which, among other changes, sets a maximum recommended carbon dioxide guideline at 1,000 ppm and develops guidelines for adequate interior ventilation.[10]

The procedures utilized to evaluate levels of carbon dioxide and other interior pollutants are critical in collecting data that (1) can aid in detecting the cause of a problem and (2) are reliable enough to support any litigation that is attempting to prove a problem with interior air or to disprove that such a situation exists.

Carbon monoxide is a pollutant that is sometimes used as a tag gas—a gas normally present when sick building syndrome is suspected, especially in urban areas. Knowledge that they are breathing even the smallest amount of carbon monoxide always generates a great deal of anxiety among the occupants of a facility. Unlike most other interior pollutants, carbon monoxide is identified with death. It is difficult for many occupants to understand and to accept a situation in which by working in a particular facility, they may be breathing even the smallest amount of carbon monoxide, possibly generated by traffic patterns or a nearby parking garage.

Because the affinity of hemoglobin for carbon monoxide is more than 200 times that of oxygen, the absorption of carbon monoxide reduces the oxygen-carrying capacity of blood and thereby produces death or critical illness. Whenever there is a suspicion that carbon monoxide is being inhaled in large quantities, the standard air tests can be supplemented by blood tests, to indicate an occupant's level of carbon monoxide exposure.

What is happening in the vicinity of a building can sometimes determine what occurs within the building. An indoor parking garage on the premises can cause high carbon monoxide levels within the building;

---

[8] Standards for Indoor Air Quality, N.J. Admin. Code § 12:100-14 (1987, revised 1989).

[9] See § **1.32**.

[10] ASHRAE, *supra* note 4.

carbon monoxide levels in parking garages can run as high as 100 ppm. Elevated carbon monoxide levels throughout a facility may result from close proximity to the garage, depending on the design of applicable ventilation systems.

An 8-hour average level of 9 ppm of carbon monoxide is a recommended maximum level, and 35 ppm is the recommended 1-hour average recommended exposure. However, individuals who are already ill, such as hospital patients, can experience adverse effects at values much lower than 35 ppm during a 1-hour exposure.[11]

An entire combination of chemicals may have to be evaluated, to ensure that one chemical is not sensitizing an occupant to others in the combination. Individuals will react to combinations of pollutants in many different ways.

As many as 50 to 60 pollutants can reveal themselves as playing a part in causing sick building syndrome complaints. NIOSH has found that approximately 50 percent of all interior air quality complaint problems are directly traceable to the HVAC systems, and 35 percent of all problems are traceable to pollutants in the air.[12]

The best procedure for specifically pinpointing the cause of sick building syndrome is a multiphase remediation similar to that utilized by NIOSH and expanded on by many environmental consultants. **Sections 4.3** through **4.5** outline an acceptable procedure for approaching the investigation of a sick building syndrome problem in an orderly and professional manner. Subsequent sections of the chapter offer guidelines for interpreting the data collected and selecting a qualified expert on indoor pollution.

§ 4.3   Performing a Background Assessment

The purpose of a background assessment is to obtain as much information on the building as is possible—date of occupancy, material type, ventilation system, previous investigations into air quality problems, recent renovations, and so on. To establish a trend of events at the building, all available information should be obtained about the kinds of problems employees have been experiencing and the period of time involved. Much of this information can be collected by using or adapting the questionnaire shown in **Appendix 4B**, section 2. Having such information on hand prior to any site investigations allows development of more effective strategies.

---

[11] EPA, National Primary and Secondary Ambient Air Quality Standards, 40 C.F.R. 50.

[12] NIOSH, Indoor Air Quality Investigations in Office Buildings, Pub. No. PB87-174397 (1987).

§ 4.4 Building Reviews

Building reviews are normally carried out in three separate phases: walk-through, occupant interviews, and environmental documentation.

The *walk-through* phase is needed to obtain information not previously received and to gain first-hand information on the building's design and floor plan. A comprehensive evaluation of the ventilation system is important, to thoroughly characterize the building with respect to potential sources of contaminants.

Occupant interviews, performed as part of the overall building review, are required to better understand the building occupancy and to evaluate the type of complaint being initiated. Occupant interviews are important in determining the magnitude of the sick building syndrome problem, especially if the problem is general in nature and widespread throughout the building. (See **Appendix 4B**, section 2, for recommended questions.) An attempt should be made to isolate the problem and the particular section of the building or group of employees in which the problem is most evident.

Environmental documentation of actual building areas is used to confirm or deny problem source possibilities that may have been identified from the background assessment, the walk-through phase, and/or the occupant interview portions of the building review. During the building review, direct indicating detectors can be utilized to check tag gases. These detectors are excellent for screening purposes because they provide immediate results. The most common instruments utilized for tag gas checks are: detector tubes for carbon dioxide and carbon monoxide, psychrometers for measuring temperature and humidity, and smoke bottles containing titanium tetrachloride, for air movement evaluations. However, NIOSH warns that standard industrial hygiene techniques for measuring chemicals may be inconclusive because most contaminants that are monitored are usually present at concentrations far below those known to cause health-related problems in industry.[13]

Other limiting factors in understanding the true meaning of environmental measurements occur among the criteria available for comparison of findings. The criteria in OSHA's permissible exposure limit (PEL), the ACGIH's threshold limit value (TLV), and NIOSH's recommended exposure limit (REL) are most commonly used to assess exposure of workers in factories. For this reason, these guidelines may not be equally valid for workers in an office setting, who are not used to working under the types of environmental stresses endured by manufacturing workers. Office workers judge the basic work environment as it relates to comfort. Many pollutant exposures that affect comfort are much lower than those that affect health, which are covered in the standards listed above.

---

[13] *Id.*

§ 4.5   Complaint Documentation

To gain an idea of the magnitude and distribution of existing problems in occupied buildings, one must utilize a properly prepared questionnaire or interview. A review of the questionnaire will profile the types of complaints that must be dealt with and will pinpoint the areas of the building experiencing most of the problems and any factors of weather, time, occupancy, or activity that may affect the problem (see **Appendix 4B**).

As data from the questionnaire are reviewed, an idea of who has experienced health complaints and who has not will begin to emerge, along with a clearer idea of what symptoms are being experienced. The questionnaire may be evaluated utilizing various statistical comparison procedures. At this point, it may be helpful to place individuals into categories: those who definitely have health complaints, those who definitely do not, and those who are vaguely in between the two extremes. This exercise will at least yield numbers of personnel, to help determine the extent of the problem. At this time it may be helpful to have an occupational health physician review the health complaints. A bar chart or other graphic display of how the complaints are distributed in the building can be helpful in representing the questionnaire results.

§ 4.6   Interpreting the Data Collected: Guidelines

Carbon Dioxide Levels

A normal constituent of exhaled breath is carbon dioxide. If monitored properly, it can indicate whether adequate fresh outdoor air is being supplied to a building or office *within the occupants' breathing zone*. Outdoor ambient concentrations of carbon dioxide are usually 250–350 ppm, million, but this value could be higher in polluted urban areas.[14] Usually, the carbon dioxide level is higher inside than outside, even in buildings with few complaints about indoor air quality. NIOSH indicates that if indoor carbon dioxide concentrations are more than three to four times the outside level, there could be a problem with inadequate ventilation, and complaints such as headaches, fatigue, and eye and throat irritations may be prevalent.[15]

The carbon dioxide concentration itself is not responsible for the complaints. However, a high concentration of carbon dioxide may indicate that the levels of other contaminants in the building may also be increased and could be responsible for occupant complaints. Here, evaluation of ventilation effectiveness—the mixing of factors occurring at the occupants' breathing level—is essential.

---

[14] *Id.*

[15] *Id.*

Carbon Monoxide Levels

Carbon monoxide, like carbon dioxide, is usually used as a tag gas—a pollutant that, by its existence and concentration, is a fast indicator of other problems that may be occurring within a facility. In urban areas, it is not uncommon to find 2–3 ppm of carbon monoxide within a facility. If carbon monoxide levels (1) begin to exceed this reading, (2) compare poorly to outside levels, or (3) vary throughout the facility, further evaluation should be done.

Formaldehyde Levels

Formaldehyde is emitted from building materials such as plywood, wallboard, wallpaper, and carpeting. It is not a tag gas as are carbon monoxide and carbon dioxide, but research has shown it causes sick building syndrome symptoms. Because levels down to 0.1 ppm are fairly simple to test for, this test should be included as part of any building assessment, especially since a buildup of formaldehyde can result from poor ventilation.

Temperature Levels

ASHRAE guidelines are intended to achieve, in a given environment, thermal conditions in which at least 80 percent of the persons visiting that environment are "comfortable." As an example of a guideline, ASHRAE Standard 55-1981 recommends the following building environment for occupancy by sedentary or slightly active persons during the summer season, when the relative humidity is at 50 percent: the operating temperature to achieve thermal acceptability (the comfort zone) should be 73° to 79° F.[16] If the operating temperature is outside this range (at either end-point), then more than 20 percent of healthy people visiting the area are likely to experience some degree of discomfort.

Humidity Levels

ASHRAE Standard 55-1981 also relates comfort to relative humidity.[17] The comfort zone ASHRAE considers to be both comfortable and healthful lies between 73° and 77° F (23° and 25° C) *and* 20 to 60 percent relative humidity. ASHRAE's recommended design conditions are: an effective temperature and dry-bulb temperature of 76° F (24.5° C), a relative humidity of 40 percent, and an air circulation rate of less than 45 feet per minute. Effective

---

[16] ASHRAE, Thermal Environmental Conditions for Human Occupancy, Standard 55-1981.

[17] ASHRAE, *supra* note 4.

temperature is an index of relative comfort determined by successive comparisons of individuals to different combinations of temperature, humidity, and air movement. Relative humidity levels below 40 percent are associated with increased discomfort and drying of the mucous membranes.

Provision of Adequate Amounts of Outside Air

ASHRAE Standard 62-1989 recommends ventilation guidelines for a wide variety of commercial, institutional, and industrial facilities, including office buildings.

§ 4.7   —Proper Sampling Procedures

Sampling performed by a qualified consultant should take place early in the morning. Samples should be taken in all parts of the building that are cause for concern and in outdoor areas. During the day, the consultant will revisit and collect additional representative samples from all sampling locations. The frequency of sampling, to be determined by the consultant, will depend on the variety and duration of activities.

To round out the monitoring, temperature, humidity, and air flow at vents and return air grills should be checked at various times and places throughout the day. For buildings utilizing variable air volume systems, air flows should be measured at both minimum and maximum settings. It is not uncommon for buildings to suffer shortages of air when building variable air volume boxes have their minimums set too low. A minimum setting of the gauge on the variable air volume box may put insufficient air into the building space.

§ 4.8   —Interpretation of Results

Decisions to take further action are normally based on findings during previous assessments. The following general description explains the meanings associated with different test results.

1. When carbon dioxide readings inside a facility are close to outdoor readings and remain fairly steady as the day progresses, outdoor ventilation could be sufficient, if not excessive. Temperature, humidity, and the balance of the ventilating systems should be investigated. If complaints persist, other pollutants will have to be researched.
2. When carbon dioxide readings inside a facility are higher than outdoor readings, insufficient ventilation is probably the cause. The operation of the HVAC systems, especially the operation and minimum air settings of variable air volume boxes, should be evaluated.

Determining the cause of sick building syndrome problems is not simple. The following examples demonstrate two very different sick building syndrome situations.

1. Occupants reported persistent flu-like illness in an office building in which a government agency was a tenant. A walk-through inspection of the building was performed. After a definition of the alleged illness had been established, a questionnaire was distributed to define the distribution of complaints. Air sampling for bacteria and fungi as well as for other possible contaminants was performed. Bulk samples of dust from the HVAC system, and carpet, ceiling, and water samples were analyzed for predominant microorganisms. Nasal swabs for isolation of *amoebae* were also obtained. Sera were drawn from occupants and from controls, for precipitin testing. Spirometry was performed before and after employees were exposed to the air in the building during a workshift. Single-breath carbon monoxide-diffusing capacity was also measured.

On the basis of the questionnaire, it was postulated that affected persons experienced ongoing respiratory exposure to an unidentified antigen associated with water leaks and that this antigen caused the symptoms, which included headaches, myalgias, chills, chest tightness, fever, and nausea. Complaining occupants had lower single-breath carbon monoxide-diffusing capacity than controls, indicating the presence of some type of lung disease.

From these investigations, it was determined that a health hazard caused by the accumulation of water-damaged building materials existed in various building areas. A hypersensitivity pneumonitis-like syndrome is often associated with water leaks and is not normally associated with HVAC systems.

Concluding that these sick building syndrome situations were created by water leaks and associated water damage to building materials and furnishings, experts made the following recommendations were made:

- Discard all water-damaged carpeting, padding, and related materials.
- Discard the ceiling panels where water had leaked; clean the outside surface of the pipes from which the leaks originated; clean or discard any accessory water trays for the ceiling drains.
- Scrub the floor with bleach and let it dry completely.
- Clean all the wall partitions and upholstered furniture with a vacuum incorporating a high-efficiency particulate air (HEPA) filter.
- Vacuum all office materials that need to be reused.

2. In an example of the effect of other pollutants in combination with carbon dioxide, a laboratory facility that utilizes several toxic materials was receiving complaints from occupants basically spanning the entire realm of sick building syndrome symptoms. Testing confirmed that exposures to acetone, 2-Hepatone, carbon tetrachloride, benzene, toluene, epichlorohydrin, carbon disulfide, ether, and acetonitrile were all within the allowable

OSHA limits. However, continued exposure to these compounds under poor ventilation was creating symptoms and work-related problems for the employees. Testing and visual observations revealed that poor housekeeping practices in several of the labs were resulting in spills of the chemicals, and chemical jars were being left open when they should have been properly sealed.

Additionally, there were inadequate exhausts in the laboratory hoods and poor room ventilation overall. Many of the laboratories that were utilizing the toxic materials were found to be under positive pressure; vapors not properly exhausted by the hoods were being exhausted into surrounding corridors and offices, thereby exposing other employees who were not directly working with the materials.

The major exhaust stacks that discharged the ventilation effluent were found to be too short for the height of the building. This building was two stories, yet the ventilation exhaust stacks were only approximately four feet above the roof area, thereby not allowing enough dilution of the vapors being exhausted by the hoods. Additionally, because of various air currents around the building, some of these vapors were infiltrating back into the building through windows and doors.

Traditionally, ventilation exhaust stacks in low buildings should be approximately 1½ to 2 times the building height, to ensure that the effluent being discharged is properly diluted within the air flow around the building before any of that air flow is sucked back into the building interior. Major recommendations at this particular facility were to improve housekeeping, increase the height of the exhaust stack, properly balance out the laboratory ventilation systems, and set the proper positive and negative pressure relationships among the different room areas.

§ 4.9   —Chemical Inventory

As the above examples indicate, it is important to properly evaluate the chemicals that may be utilized in a facility. The chemicals must be cataloged and cross-checked against their suspected environmental effects, as indicated in the hazardous material data sheets provided by the manufacturer. Chemicals, if not directly utilized, can enter the building by the use of solvents, cleansers, pesticides, paints, adhesives, and similar materials.

§ 4.10   —Contaminant Sources

Additional sources of contaminants must be evaluated by reviewing the data sheets presented by the manufacturers. Items related to copy machines and blueprint machines should be given particular attention.

§ 4.11   Quantitative Analysis

If the tasks related to qualitative analysis are completed and reveal enough suspect items, it may not be necessary to proceed with quantitative analysis. If quantitative analysis is undertaken, various categories of pollutants should be evaluated. Some of the basic areas that must be evaluated are described here.

Pesticide Analysis

A detailed list of the chemicals utilized for pesticides in a particular facility would be revealed during a chemical inventory. The pesticide components in **Table 4–1** could be associated with buildings experiencing sick building syndrome and, individually or in combination, all could be considered potential problem sources.

Organic Solvent Vapors

A definitive list to determine specific organic solvents utilized can be put together after a chemical inventory is completed. Organic solvent vapors represent one of the most ubiquitous types of contaminant found in residential buildings. Our homes are virtually warehouses of organic chemical contaminants, introduced via cleaning compounds, polishes, waxes, and drain cleaners. After a good housecleaning, especially in a new, tightly constructed home, more organic vapors are in the air that would ever be in a normal office environment.

For an office building or a facility where extensive graphics are not produced, the organic vapor compounds in **Table 4–2** are most common.

Table 4–1

Specific Insecticides, Pesticides, and Polychlorinated Biphenyls

Arochlor 1016	BHC—gamma
Arochlor 1221	Chlorphyrifos
Arochlor 1232	DDD—P P'
Arochlor 1242	DDE—P P'
Arochlor 1248	Dieldrin
Arochlor 1254	Endosulfan I
Arochlor 1260	Endosulfan II
Arochlor 1262	Endrin
BHC—alpha	Heptachlor
BHC—beta	Heptachlorepoxide

Table 4–2

Specific Organic Solvents

Acetone	Hexane
Acetonitnrite	Isopropanol
Benzene	Isopropyl Alcohol
N-Butyl acetate	Methanol
N-Butyl alcohol	Methyl ethyl ketone
Butyl Cellosolve	Methyl Isobutyl Ketone
Carbon tetrachloride	Methylene chloride
Cellosolve Acetate	Monochloro Benzene
Chloroform	Perchloroethylene
Cyclohexane	Secondary butyl alcohol
Cyclohexanene	Tetrachloroethylene
Cyclohexanone	Tetrahydrofuran
Ethanol	Toluene
Ethylene Dichloride	1,1,1 Trichloroethane

Depending on the results of a chemical inventory, tests for all or some should be conducted.

Trace Metals

Trace metals are not usually found in an office type environment but should not be ruled out as a possible contaminant. Sometimes, these metals enter via dust brought in from outside. They work their way into the environment through the wind, are then picked up from the soil, and enter the building through normal infiltration. If surrounding soil at one time or another had been contaminated with these metals, very small particles can contaminate a building. Screening for the metals in **Table 4–3** should be part of most evaluations.

Table 4–3
Trace Metals

aluminum	cobalt	molybdenum	tellurium
antimony	copper	nickel	thallium
arsenic	iron	phosphorous	titanium
barium	lanthanum	platinum	vanadium
beryllium	lead	selenium	yttrium
cadmium	lithium	silver	zinc
calcium	magnesium	sodium	zirconium
chromium	manganese	strontium	

Nicotine

If smoking is allowed to any great extent in an existing occupied facility, a nicotine screening should be considered, to measure the concentrations of nicotine in the air. In some facilities, nicotine has been found at stagnant breathing-level air spaces even though ventilation appears to be adequate. Adequate ventilation but very poor movement of room air can leave stagnant air at the breathing level and allow nicotine to build up from either side-stream emissions or direct emissions.

Particulants and Fibers

In any building where renovation work is being performed, an air sampling program for particulants must be considered, to help determine the exposure of the building occupants to materials such as plaster, sand, silica, wood dust, and other related building materials.

Microorganisms

A building can have many areas and conduits where microorganisms can multiply and spread throughout a facility, causing work-related illnesses such as hypersensitivity pneumonitis, allergies, humidifier fever, and other related illnesses caused by bacteria, fungi, protozoans, and other complex microorganisms. These microorganisms might be introduced into the atmosphere as a result of growths taking place in stagnant water, in cooling-coil condensate pans, in damp, rotting ceiling tiles and roofing material subject to roof leakage, or in deteriorating and decaying carpeting or wallboard damaged in recent or past floods and other water invasions.

Spirometry Testing

If a sick building syndrome outbreak is severe and hypersensitivity pneumonitis is suspected, it can be useful to recommend spirometry testing of a certain percentage of the occupant population. All spirometer results should be analyzed by a qualified pulmonary specialist. Additionally, spirometer results can be analyzed via modem by the Mayo Pulmonary Services or a similar service recommended by an expert.

Miscellaneous Tests

Other tests that are useful in evaluating sick building syndrome, depending on the use and location of the facility, include:

- Radiation
- VDT (video display terminal) radiation
- Lighting
- Glare

Additional Tests

For occupied buildings that have persistent and difficult problems, the following additional tests should be performed:

- *Butyric acid*—a human bioeffluent with an odor recognition threshold of .001 ppm.
- *Pyridine and furfural testing*—volatile, odorous components of environmental tobacco smoke. Pyridine has an odor recognition threshold of .02 ppm and an occupational TLV of 5 ppm. Furfural has an odor recognition threshold of .002 ppm and a TLV of 2 ppm.
- *Toluene*—a component of many products utilized in offices. Its odor recognition threshold is 2 ppm and its TLV is 100 ppm. Measurements of toluene help in judging the efficiency of "bake outs"—attempts to remove gases in building materials by elevating the temperature in the building through use of the building's heating system.

§ 4.12   Expert Selection

When attempting to solve sick building syndrome and hazardous substance problems, it is always beneficial for the building owner and operator to utilize, upon discovery of a problem, an expert who has specific sick building syndrome experience. When selecting an expert, criteria are not only the experience the individual has demonstrated in being able to properly track down the causes of sick building syndrome, but the expert's credentials and potential for being a proper representative as an expert witness during a trial, should litigation ensue.

There are numerous expert referral organizations; three are listed in **Appendix 4A.** These sources can provide names, résumés, and pertinent information relative to the experts' background and experience. Referral firms advertise in legal periodicals, often in the classified litigation section. An expert's résumé should be reviewed carefully, to determine the number of cases worked on that were similar to the situation at hand. Above all, the expert must demonstrate, verbally and through credentials, a true understanding of the sick building syndrome situation. Has the expert developed orderly and logical procedures for tracking down the cause of a problem? Will these procedures facilitate the collection of data and develop logical procedures that will have a strong impact at a trial, should one occur?

Too many so-called experts attempt to utilize the shotgun approach in locating the causes of sick building syndrome. These experts spread out their resources in many different directions; they perform many small tasks rather than concentrating on comprehensive testing and good investigative approaches. Understandably, when a sick building syndrome situation occurs, a great deal of anxiety is aroused in the occupants and the owners and managers of the facility. Tracking down the causes of many sick building syndrome situations is not a simple task and does not occur readily. Testing for some pollutants, such as bacteria and fungi, takes many days or even weeks. While experts are performing their function, they are normally under a great deal of pressure to produce results. In response to this pressure, novices or the uninformed begin to delete tests and neglect to follow the proper sequence of logical formulated approaches.

An expert who reacts this way is inexperienced and will fail to pinpoint the cause of long-term sick building syndrome because valuable data and information that can be utilized will be overlooked. A competent expert, therefore, should be able to demonstrate the implementation of formal and logical approaches to the correction of sick building syndrome situations.

§ 4.13   The Role of an Expert Before Trial

§ 4.14   —Educating the Client

In all situations, it is the job of the expert to educate both the owner/manager of a facility and his or her attorney as to the potential causes of complaints and the procedures that will be utilized to resolve the problems. An expert should approach this process utilizing simplified procedures. BEWARE of any expert who insists that procedures can only be explained in highly technical language that laypersons cannot understand. An expert who cannot clarify matters for a client will never be able to properly explain them to a judge or jury so that they understand what he is trying to prove.

§ 4.15   —Analyzing and Testing

In analysis and testing, the expert utilizes his or her formal training and experience in tracking down a sick building syndrome problem. At this point, the expert can be expected to communicate, via some type of written proposal, a formal procedure targeted at solving the problem. The formalized procedure would normally involve testing. For a large facility, testing might involve sophisticated investigation of the HVAC systems, including tests of air flows, temperature, humidity, airborne impurities, ongoing filtration, and all relevant functions.

Testing might also involve elaborate chemical tests, industrial hygiene tests, and specialized tracking of any chemicals or related items that could be causing the problem. During the testing phase, a proper systematic procedure helps toward realizing what to exclude and what to include from the various investigative procedures available.

§ 4.16 —Interrogatories

In a highly technical case, interrogatories should consist of very probing questions that draw out the other side's pertinent information regarding who, what, and when, in the situation being litigated. When attorneys utilize prepared standardized questions, two and three sets of interrogatory questions are eventually issued; one set alone is not comprehensive enough to cover all applicable situations. The expert should be utilized to help the attorney prepare properly probing interrogatory questions. An attorney who has significant experience in such lawsuits and might utilize interrogatory questions that have previously been of help, should still solicit the aid of the expert in preparing questions that will be specifically applicable to the case's situation. The expert will develop questions that are targeted to specific areas, such as personnel, work tasks performed by personnel, building equipment, and how the equipment has been operated. The combination of the expert, who seeks to stress specifics of a technical nature, and the attorney, who concentrates on legalities, often produces a comprehensive set of interrogatories.

§ 4.17 —Depositions

Depositions taken by counsel from individuals who will be testifying in the case for the other side are actually pretrial testimony. The attorney must attempt to find gaps in the credibility of the witnesses and/or information relative to the case that was not previously discovered in any other areas of discovery. It is important, therefore, that the expert help in preparing deposition questions that will generate the information that both the attorney and expert need to extract during the deposition process.

Closer to trial, the expert should begin to participate in preparing graphic presentations or other type of materials for trial. If these materials are relative to the work performed by the expert, then the expert should assist in preparing them. The expert would normally produce reports, maps, charts, graphs, video tape, pictures, and all items that are specific and necessary to explain the expert's findings. Computer simulations of pollutant exposure over various periods of time might be included. The expert and the attorney should work together on preparing case strategy. The expert must have a good perspective on what the other side's expert is preparing and on what course of action should be taken technically, to counteract any damaging technical testimony that may be presented by the other side during trial.

Once a decision to proceed with litigation or to settle a claim has been made, one must have a budget as to what amount should be spent, relative to pursuing the litigation process. Sick building syndrome litigations are highly complicated and not inexpensive; an expert's time will be highly valued. Yet, placing an unrealistic budget on the work the expert should perform could easily sabotage a case.

§ 4.18 —Budgets

It is often very difficult for an expert to define a budget when evaluating a complicated technical case. Real-world situations, however, do not normally provide an expert with a blank check. Counsel should solicit a worst-case-scenario budget from the expert, as difficult as that estimate might be, to permit an evaluation of the necessary amount of money to be spent on a particular item.

Along with the worst-case-scenario budget, the expert should provide either an oral or written breakdown of exactly what areas will be examined. It may be difficult to indicate details and specifics; many of these will depend on and change relative to findings as the expert proceeds. An expert who has experience in these matters can give at least a general outline of areas that will be evaluated.

§ 4.19 —Checklist for Expert's Report

From the general breakdown and the budget, an owner and his or her attorney can determine whether the detail the expert plans to evaluate is sufficient or too comprehensive for the problem situation. This area can be hazardous to the success of a case, if insufficient detail is evaluated.

A decision must be made as to what detail should be required from the expert. The tasks the expert may have to perform before arriving at an opinion and developing reports are as follows:

- Any necessary tests;
- Visitation to the area, and if so, how often;
- Interviews of occupants;
- Compilation and distribution of questionnaires to occupants;
- Review and comparison of test results;
- Research to evaluate pertinent information appearing in professional literature.

§ 4.20   Experts' Fees

What will be an expert's fee for help rendered in facilitating a successful settlement or litigation outcome? An entire book could be written about this subject; there are as many ideas as to what an expert's time is worth as there are experts and clients. Hourly rates for experts do not vary too drastically. They normally range from $150 to $400 an hour, depending on the case, its complications, and other related aspects.

However, on highly complicated technical cases, such as environmental litigations, the hourly rate of the expert is not the only cost that is involved. Normally, the expert selected by the owner/client and attorney would not be an individual practitioner, but a member of a firm that has been successful in the area pertaining to the litigation. Therefore, hourly rates can vary with the specialty and with the resources the expert firm will utilize to evaluate a particular situation.

An engineering firm, for example, might designate a partner or principal to be its prime expert witness, but data collection, testing, and other kinds of research will be done by other engineers within the firm. The principal's hourly rate for the work performed might be in the $150–$400 range, but the actual hourly fee for services of other engineers working on the situation could be in the $60–$100 range. In all cases, the lead expert witness— the principal or individual hired initially—should oversee all work being done on the case by the expert firm. First-hand knowledge of the work being done by assisting engineers, direct supervision of all work, and, at all times, awareness of the quality of the work being performed can be demanded by the client/owner.

As the expert proceeds to work on the case, it is important that all invoices submitted be backed up with a detailed synopsis of the work performed. A sample of one type of synopsis form is given in **Appendix 4B**. This form requires the expert to indicate all of the pertinent information, which can then be evaluated by the owner and counsel to ascertain the direction the expert is heading in. All of the expert's invoices should be related to the original agreement and rate schedule. (See the sample in **Appendix 4C**.)

If an evaluation of the material presented on the synopsis form indicates that the expert appears to be deviating from areas of desired concentration, it is a simple and painless task to discuss this deviation with the expert before the next month's tasks are performed. In this way, both the owner and the expert can keep on top of the work that is being done, rather than find out many months down the road that particular tasks were or were not performed or included in the budgeted package.

These forms play another very important role. If a litigation involves a separate trial to determine damages and compensation for the time and expenses of experts is being sought, a detailed record from the expert will easily justify the expenses as to what work was performed and when, and how long that work took the expert to actually perform. The forms will jog the expert's memory when, perhaps several months or years later, testimony must be given as to the work actually performed, and objections to the expert's fees are raised in cross-examination by attorneys for the other side.

Often, after an expert is hired and submits a worst-case-scenario budget, questions arise as to how accurate the budget is and what type of deviations from the budget can be expected. Even when putting together a general budget, the expert has no firm idea as to what evidence might be revealed as the case progresses, what additional studies, research, or testing might then be required, or what information presented by the adversary's experts will have to be evaluated.

From experience, it appears that deviations of 25 to 30 percent from a worst-case-scenario budget can be expected. In most cases, the expert's budget does not include time that will be spent during a trial.

Many individuals attempt to correlate an expert's total fee to a percentage of the damages obtained via either settlement or the litigation process. This procedure is extremely difficult and, in most cases, useless for arriving at a guideline for evaluating the reasonableness of an expert's fee. For example, in certain environmental litigations, the expert's total fee might be somewhere in the neighborhood of 2 to 5 percent of the total damages being claimed. However, in other highly involved environmental and technical litigations, an expert's fees could very easily climb to between 5 and 15 percent of the damages being claimed. If a personal injury is involved, then the amount of damages cannot be estimated because there is no gauge for how much work might be involved by the expert.

It is not recommended, therefore, that an owner or counsel should attempt, in any way, to judge the reasonableness of an expert's budget or total fee as a percentage of the estimated damages being claimed or the estimated damages that eventually will be claimed. The expert's fee should be judged strictly according to the services rendered; how well, how precisely, and how professionally those services were presented; and how useful they were to the attorney. In this writer's opinion, experts should not be hired on a contingency basis. This arrangement immediately introduces credibility problems for the expert because, to a judge and jury, the expert may appear to have a direct monetary interest in the outcome of the trial.

§ 4.21   Conclusion

Identification and mitigation of sick building syndrome problems are not easy tasks. The majority of the symptoms, procedures, and tests that can be utilized to track down this widespread but unusual phenomenon have been discussed, but any building can have an unlimited number of variables that affect the sensitivity of different occupants to different chemicals or fibers in the air.

A common guide, utilized in the past to ascertain whether complaints originating from occupants signal the onset of sick building syndrome, is: if approximately 20 to 30 percent of the occupants are continuously complaining, this could be an indication that sick building syndrome is spreading throughout the facility. However, experience shows that such an off-the-cuff estimation is not a reasonable guide to whether a space or facility is experiencing sick building syndrome. For example, if an occupied space has ten occupants, three of whom are continuously complaining of symptoms that could be related to sick building syndrome, this ratio in and of itself is not necessarily indicative that the space is suffering from interior air quality problems. On the other hand, if a building contains 1,000 occupants and 300 or more are continually complaining of symptoms that are indicative of sick building syndrome, then this condition is obviously more alarming.

In many parts of the United States, seasonal characteristics play an important part in attempting to interpret occupant complaints. In the previously mentioned space occupied by ten individuals, if three people continually complain of symptoms that could be related to colds, flu, other types of viruses, or sick building syndrome, an owner would be apt to consider cold symptoms the culprit rather than sick building syndrome. In a small space occupied by ten people, it is extremely easy for viruses to spread in their usual manner, with no connection to interior air quality defects. On the other hand, if the complaints in the small space were originating during summer months, an owner might suspect that condensate from the air-conditioning coils is accumulating, lying stagnant in the condensate pans, and breeding fungi and molds. The first suspect might be the air-conditioning equipment and interior air quality problems.

These factors should point out that investigation of a sick building syndrome situation, if it is to be done in a credible manner, should be performed by individuals who are experienced experts in this field and who are as well versed in industrial hygiene matters as they are in ventilation and HVAC systems. The organizations listed in **Appendix 4A** can help in locating experienced experts.

Although investigating and litigating a sick building syndrome situation are extremely complicated, an expert should never be allowed to experiment or explore independently, without proper guidance from counsel. To do so will cause excessive fees, credibility problems, and bad will among the owner, the attorney, and the expert. The expert's work should be guided by the needs of the attorney, who remains in charge of the case. The expert is hired to fulfill the needs of the attorney, not to generate work or fees. In highly involved technical cases, few individuals may understand specifically the work that the expert would like to explore. It is doubly important for the expert to be able to explain the intended work in simple terms so that the attorney can ascertain whether the work done is necessary.

The attorney should be willing to listen to the expert and respect the expert's experience as to what might work toward providing credible technical backup for particular problems within the case. Good experts are always leery and uneasy when a case has too many loose ends and when they feel that technical matters need to be ironed out and answers developed. Whenever an expert notifies an owner and/or an attorney that (1) because of budgetary or other restrictions on the projected work, or (2) because a case has an extraordinary amount of unfinished technical matters, he or she fears for the outcome, it would be important for the owner and/or attorney to reconsider their direction. Good, solid preparation is crucial for ensuring a good outcome.

Appendix 4A Expert Witness Referral Groups

Expert Resources, Inc.
4617 North Prospect Road
Peoria Heights, IL 61614

Expert Witness Network
1608 New Hampshire Avenue, N.W.
Washington, DC 20009-2512

Technical Advisory Service for Attorneys
428 Pennsylvania Avenue
Fort Washington, PA 19039

Appendix 4B　Project Time Account

Project:　ABC v. DEF
Client:　JOE, MOE AND JANE
Contact:　TED MOE　　　　　( )　(PHONE)
　　　　　　　　　　　　　　　( )　(FAX)

DATE	INDIVIDUAL	WORK PERFORMED	HOURS

Section 1. Indoor Air Quality Problem Checklist

1. Ascertain from individuals the symptoms they are experiencing. Symptoms to look for are as follows: headache, dry mouth, dizziness, weakness in the knees, eye irritation, hoarseness, fever, burning sensation in eyes, nose, ears, or throat (specifically throat irritation or constant nasal congestion), coughing, skin irritation, other types of symptoms.

2. Determine from individuals how often and at what specific times during the year the symptoms occur.

3. Determine whether symptoms disappear and/or improve when individuals leave the building. If they improve, determine how long it takes for the symptoms to improve.

4. Determine whether individuals are bothered by cigarette smoke and/or whether they smoke. If so, how often do they smoke?

5. Determine whether any areas close to the areas experiencing the interior air quality problem are used for the following purposes: storage of vehicles, garbage storage, animal experiments, cigarette smoking, copying equipment, chemical storage, storage of machinery and tools, or woodworking or other types of maintenance work.

6. Determine whether any remodeling and/or new construction has taken place—specifically, whether any of the following activities have been performed:

   Exterminating
   Painting
   Wallpapering
   Installation of carpeting
   Cleansing of any type.

7. Examine the area carefully, to identify any water damage or stains indicated by:

   Mold growth
   Dirt around diffusers or ceiling tiles
   Dirt around or in air ducts.

8. Make a list of equipment, materials, and supplies utilized in the affected area or surrounding areas.

9. Make a list of any newly acquired furniture, accessories, or protective coating devices, including rugs, drapes, curtains, and other types of decorative materials.

10. Determine the specific activities that are performed in the general area of the problems.

11. Determine whether any unusual events have occurred, such as pipe breaks, roof leaks, floods, or any other similar type of problem.

12. Ascertain whether the building or area in question is served by one HVAC system or several zoned HVAC systems.

13. Determine the minimum setting for each variable air volume box that is in use.

14. Determine the type of heating used for the building (electricity, gas, or oil). If a fossil fuel is used, inspect the boiler installation, breaching, and other related areas.

15. Determine the type of cooling utilized and the temperatures and humidities normal to various areas.

16. Determine the type of filtering system utilized and how efficiently the filtering system works.

17. Ascertain whether any kitchens are utilized. If so, determine how the kitchens are ventilated and how makeup air is provided.

18. Check all outdoor air dampers on air-handling units, to determine whether outdoor air dampers are closed or are allowed to operate in accordance with the original design.

19. Check condensate pans in air-handling units, to determine whether they are draining properly or give evidence of mold or other fungi buildup; determine whether condensate water is being allowed to become stagnant.

Section 2. Individual Questionnaire

1. Were you admitted to a hospital during the past year?

2. Did you make an office visit to a physician during the past year?

3. Did you work in this building for the entire past year?

4. During the past three months, on what floors did you work? What is your evaluation of the temperature range on the floors where you worked? Please give a detailed response for each floor.

5. How would you describe the humidity level on the floors where you worked? Please give a detailed response.

6. Do you have any comments about the working conditions in the building in general? About the areas where you worked?

7. During the past year, was your work area smokeless, smokey, or very smokey?

8. What is the title of your job or work detail?

9. On a regular basis, do you operate a video display terminal?

10. How many hours a day would you say you operate a video display terminal?

11. Do you operate a copy machine? If yes, how many hours a day would you say you operate the copy machine?

12. Do you regularly use chemicals as part of your work? If yes, please indicate the names of the chemicals.

13. When you use the chemicals, are they within a fume hood?

14. If the chemicals you use are within a fume hood, is the fume hood ventilated to the outside?

15. If you use chemicals and you do not use a fume hood, where do you use the chemicals?

16. If you use chemicals and you do not use a fume hood, how far from your face would you say the surface of the chemical is?

17. Why are you specifically using these chemicals?
18. Do you ever notice a stuffy odor in your work area?
19. When does any stuffy odor normally occur?
20. Has your work area or a nearby area been redecorated lately?
21. If redecorating has been done, what type of redecorating was performed?
22. How long ago was the redecorating completed?
23. Briefly and in general terms, what does your typical day consist of?
24. Do you routinely feel exhausted or unusually tired?
25. Do you have frequent headaches? If yes, explain the type and duration of your headaches.
26. Were you sick to your stomach lately?
27. Did you throw up recently at work?
28. Did you feel dizzy or faint at work?
29. Did you feel short of breath?
30. Did you feel a tightness or pain in your chest?
31. Were your eyes, nose, or mouth dry or burning?
32. Do your eyes tear excessively or unusually?
33. Are you often aware of any strange odors that you cannot identify?
34. Do you experience any unusual tastes?
35. Do you have more than normal skin itching?
36. Do you have a skin rash?
37. Do you have any other abnormal symptoms or illnesses?
38. How would you describe your general health over your lifetime, prior to this year?
39. Have you ever had surgery? If yes, describe any surgery you had over the past five years.
40. Have you ever had a heart attack?
41. Have you ever taken any heart medication?
42. Have you had high blood pressure?
43. Are you presently taking high blood pressure medication?
44. Do you have diabetes?
45. Have you ever had seizures or epilepsy?
46. Have you ever been told that you have chronic bronchitis or emphysema?
47. Have you ever been told that you have asthma?
48. Do you wheeze or get short of breath during certain seasons of the year?
49. Have you ever had a cough that lasted longer than three months?

50. Have you ever had hives (itching welts on the skin)?
51. Before this year, have you ever had a skin problem or rash that lasted for more than three weeks?
52. Have you ever had hay fever, sore throat, or itching eyes and nose? If yes, at what seasons do these normally occur?
53. Are you bothered by cigarette smoke in the air?
54. Have you smoked cigarettes over the past two years? If yes, describe how much you smoke.
55. Do you smoke cigars or pipes? If yes, describe how much you smoke.
56. How old are you now?
57. How many persons, excluding yourself, smoke in your household?
58. How long does it take you to get to work?
59. How do you get to work?
60. List the people with whom you commonly come into contact during the course of the workday.
61. List the people with whom you normally take your lunch break.
62. On the whole, how well do the people in your section get along with one another?
63. If you had a complaint about your job, your working conditions, or the area where you work, whom would you talk to?

Appendix 4C   Agreement and Rate Schedule

A. **Identification:**
Client:
Matter: Your File   Our File

B. Hourly billing rates:

Category	Title Example	Billing Rate
* I	Corporate Principal	
II	Senior Engineer	
III	Engineer	
IV	Technician	
V	Draftsperson	
VI	Engineering Aid	
VII	Administrative Assistant	
** VIII	Clerical Assistant	

* Sam Smith, P.E., Mechanical Engineer and Principal, with 30 years' experience in these matters, is assigned to this project at this time. No other Category I personnel

will be utilized unless we discuss this item with you and receive your prior approval. Personnel from all other categories will be assigned as needed, at the discretion of Mr. Smith, in order to ensure a high-quality work product. Work not directly performed by Mr. Smith will be under his immediate and direct supervision; in addition, he will maintain direct and first-hand knowledge of all work being performed for this task.

** This Category is paid extra for overtime, if required. Should overtime be authorized by you, we will bill it at 1.5 times the Category VIII base billing rate.

C. Standard charges: We charge for our time in minimum units of ¼ hour.

D. Travel cost and expenses:

Mileage: .30/mile

Plane fare and auto rentals (when required): Payment required in advance.

Hotel, meals, and miscellaneous expenses: Payment for estimated costs required in advance.

E. Out-of-pocket expenses: Billed at our cost plus 20 percent.

F. Lab fees and similar items: Billed at our cost plus 20 percent.

G. We understand that we are being retained by you, the client, and as such you will be responsible for our payments. Our payments are due within 30 days of our invoice date. Payments to us will not depend on the flow of payments from others to you, nor do our payments depend on the outcome of any legal matter, negotiation, settlement, or any other contingency.

H. Hourly rates apply to preparation, testing, investigations, all depositions, testimony, and all other applicable tasks.

I. Where traveling is involved, rates apply portal to portal.

J. Where waiting time is involved (such as giving testimony, depositions, etc.), such waiting time is figured as regular billable hours.

K. For testimony, depositions, and tasks that occur more than 150 miles from our home office, our minimum billable unit is 8 hrs/individual per day.

L. IMPORTANT NOTE: BY ACTING AS YOUR TECHNICAL CONSULTANT ON THIS OR ANY OTHER MATTER, AND BY PROVIDING EXPERT TESTIMONY, GIVING DEPOSITIONS, AND OTHER CONSULTING FOR YOU OR ON YOUR BEHALF AT YOUR REQUEST, WE ARE IN NO WAY PROMISING OR GUARANTEEING THE OUTCOME OF SAID MATTERS.

M. Subject to change: The rates on this schedule are subject to change on 30 days' written notice.

CHAPTER 5

PLAINTIFFS AND DEFENDANTS

§ 5.1   Introduction

§ 5.2   Class Actions

§ 5.3   States, Municipalities, and Schools

§ 5.4   Manufacturers

§ 5.5   Commercial Building Owners

§ 5.6   —CERCLA Liability

§ 5.7   —Landlords

§ 5.8   —Tenants

§ 5.9   Sellers of Property

§ 5.10   Buyers

§ 5.11   Homeowners

§ 5.12   Real Estate Brokers

§ 5.13   Developers as Defendants

§ 5.14   Corporate Shareholders, Officers, Directors, and Managers as Defendants

§ 5.15   —Corporate Dissolution

§ 5.16   Successors-in-Interest

§ 5.17   Subsidiary Corporations and Piercing the Corporate Veil

§ 5.18   Lenders

§ 5.19   Appraisers

§ 5.20   Property Managers

§ 5.21   Employers

§ 5.22   Employees

§ 5.23   Contractors

§ 5.24   Consultants, Architects, Engineers, and Designers

§ 5.25   Attorneys

§ 5.1   Introduction

This chapter focuses on the possible categories of parties that may become plaintiffs and defendants in lawsuits involving hazardous substances and toxic torts. Property damage and cost recovery claims are emphasized, but discussion also touches on personal injury lawsuits.

Parties that may legitimately claim damages because of hazardous substances include: building and home owners; federal, state, and local governments; municipalities; commercial and residential tenants; lenders; prior building owners; and employees.

Under different circumstances, most of the categories of plaintiffs can wind up as defendants as well. Defendants in hazardous substance lawsuits may also include: product manufacturers; installers; contractors; employers; prior building owners; real estate brokers; architects, contractors, and various consultants; successor corporations; officers, directors, and shareholders of corporations; and lenders.

As of July 1990, there had been only 27 or 28 verdicts nationwide in the 10 years since the first asbestos property damage lawsuit was filed. Of these, 14 or 15 were won by defendants.[1] Far more cases are pending trial or have been settled out of court and are not reported in case books. It is not unusual for an out-of-court settlement agreement in such a case to include a provision prohibiting publicity about the case. This may explain why there are seemingly so few lawsuits.

This chapter discusses in general terms the nature of the liability defendants are exposed to and the kinds of arguments that are made by plaintiffs in such lawsuits. A subsequent chapter will discuss the legal theories that are used in these lawsuits.

§ 5.2   Class Actions

Because asbestos and other hazardous substances affect so many groups and individuals at the same time, many personal injury and property damage lawsuits are brought in the form of class actions.

In order for a class to be certified, questions that are common to the class must be decided and must predominate over questions affecting only individual members.[2] The common issues are decided first; then the individual issues are resolved. If the determination of damages would require only mechanical application of a formula to the plaintiffs, the courts are more likely to find that individual issues do not predominate. For example,

---

[1] Asbestos Abatement Report, July 9, 1990, at 1.

[2] Fed. R. Civ. P. 23(b)(3).

assume that 100 employees were exposed to hazardous substances at work, and injuries and causation were established. If the only issue was how much each plaintiff in the class was to receive, a class would be more likely to be allowed. However, if damage issues require individual proof and separate trials, a class is less likely to be certified.[3]

Damages in building cases are rarely mechanical. Because the courts examine the condition of a particular product in the building, classes are not often certified. Courts will also look at whether abatement was done in the building and whether some of the expenses being claimed are really renovation expenses. In personal injury cases, each individual has a different personal and medical history, which may affect the outcome of the case.

The decisions in this area are evenly divided on the issue of certification.[4] The courts have not allowed mandatory classes.[5]

A plaintiff must have an individual claim before he or she can represent a class.[6] If a product containing asbestos is involved, the plaintiff must be able to identify the product as having been produced by the defendant. This is the most difficult part in these cases.

The plaintiff must be an adequate representative of the class. If the plaintiff is subject to a unique defense that would separate him or her from the class, the plaintiff may not be a proper representative.[7]

Class actions tend to involve complex procedural questions such as: Is there a viable claim under state law? Which state's statute of limitations applies? Which state's statute of repose applies?[8]

---

[3] Windham v. American Brands, Inc., 565 F.2d 59, 66 (4th Cir. 1977), *cert. denied,* 435 U.S. 968 (1978).

[4] Cleveland Board of Education v. Armstrong World Industries, 476 N.E.2d 397 (Ct. Common Pleas, Cuyahoga Co., Ohio 1985) (certification of class of elementary and secondary schools denied); Sisters of St. Mary v. AAER Sprayed Insulation, No. 85-CV-5952 (Cir. Ct., Dane Co., Wis. Dec. 12, 1987), *aff'd,* 151 Wis.2d 708, 445 (N.W.2d 723 (Wis. App. 1989) (certification of nationwide class of hospitals denied); *In re* Asbestos School Litigation, 104 F.R.D. 422 (E.D. Pa. 1984), 107 F.R.D. 215 (E.D. Pa. 1985), *aff'd in part, rev'd in part,* 789 F.2d 996 (3d Cir. 1986), *cert. denied,* 479 U.S. 852 (1986) (certification of nationwide class of schools upheld); City of Detroit v. The Celotex Corp., No. 84-429634 NP (Mich. Cir. Ct., Wayne Co. Feb. 1, 1988) (certification of class of Michigan schools upheld); Kirbyville Independent School District v. National Gypsum, No. 12,391 (Tex. Dist. Ct., Jasper Co., 1989), *aff'd,* 770 S.W.2d 621 (Tex. App. 1989) (certification of Texas schools upheld).

[5] *In re* Asbestos School Litigation, *supra* note 4; *In re* Temple, 851 F.2d 1269 (11th Cir. 1988) (mandamus issued to vacate mandatory class); Waldron v. Raymark, 124 F.R.D. 235 (N.D. Ga. 1989).

[6] Sosna v. Iowa, 419 U.S. 393, 403 (1975).

[7] Weinstein v. Americal Biomaterials Corp., 123 F.R.D. 442 (S.D.N.Y. 1988).

[8] *In re* Asbestos School Litigation, *supra* note 4.

Because there are many kinds of asbestos-containing products, they cannot all be lumped together in one class action.[9] The condition of a particular product in the building may also be a factor.[10]

The U.S. Supreme Court declined to take original jurisdiction over an asbestos property damage lawsuit brought by 29 states against 26 former manufacturers of asbestos building materials.[11]

The City of Philadelphia and its housing authority has filed a class action against lead paint makers for the cost of abatement, education, and liability involving lead paint in building interiors.[12] The action, filed on behalf of every U.S. city with a population over 100,000, claims that paint makers continued to manufacture and promote lead paint long after they were aware of the health hazards involved and even when they knew there were better alternatives. The suit alleges negligent product design, negligent failure to warn of the dangers of lead paint, strict product liability, breach of warranties, fraud, and misrepresentation.

In a group of 64 cases stemming from exposure to asbestos at the Brooklyn Navy Yard, verdicts yielded awards totaling $30.6 million. They were part of Phase 1 cases: more than 90 percent of plaintiffs' exposure was alleged to have taken place at the Navy Yard.[13]

Justice Freedman, a state judge with roughly 180 Phase 1 cases, has handled her group differently. She designated 35 sample cases and is using a procedure known as "reverse bifurcation": the jury assesses damages first, then proceeds to findings on liability.[14] Damages totaling $90 million have been awarded to 35 plaintiffs.

As the number of lawsuits and class actions involving environmental issues increases, more innovative methods can be expected to develop, to deal with the volume of cases.

---

[9] Giden v. Johns-Manville Sales Corp., 761 F.2d 1129, 1145 (5th Cir. 1985); Hardy v. Johns-Manville Sales Corp., 681 F.2d 334, 346–48 (5th Cir. 1982); Mullen v. Armstrong World Industries, Inc., 200 Cal. App. 3d 250, 256, 246 Cal. Rptr. 32 (1988).

[10] The 3250 Wilshire Boulevard Building v. W.R. Grace & Co. (1989 U.S. Dist. LEXIS 17287) (C.D. Cal. 1989), aff'd, 915 F.2d 1355 (9th Cir. 1990); Cleveland Board of Education v. Armstrong World Industries, 476 N.E.2d at 404.

[11] Alabama v. W.R. Grace & Co., 109 L. Ed. 494, 110 S. Ct. 2164 (1990) (1990 U.S. Dist. LEXIS 2482).

[12] Philadelphia v. Lead Industries Association Inc., No. 90-7064-JG (D.C.E. Pa., Nov. 5, 1990). See Engineering News Record, Dec. 3, 1990, at 70.

[13] In re Joint Eastern and Southern District of New York Asbestos Litigation (Jan. 23, 1991), N.Y.L.J., Jan. 26, 1991, at 1, col. 6.

[14] Id. at 2, col. 3.

§ 5.3   States, Municipalities, and Schools

States, school districts, and municipalities have led the way as plaintiffs against asbestos manufacturers and other defendants in property damage lawsuits. Although there is no statutory duty of abatement that confers a private right of action on the school districts, they may still sue under common-law tort and breach of contract theories.[15]

Under contract theories, they may claim losses due to breaches of implied warranties of merchantability[16] or fitness for a particular purpose.[17] However, the Uniform Commercial Code's notice requirements[18] and four-year statute of limitations usually bar the schools' suits on these theories. Under tort theories, claims have been based on negligence and strict product liability claims, alleging losses for property damage caused by "contamination" of buildings by asbestos.

Schools have been able to overcome statute of limitation problems by taking advantage of the "discovery rule," which tolls the statute of limitations until the time the plaintiff actually learned, or through the exercise of reasonable diligence should have learned, of the cause of action against the defendant.

One hurdle the schools have had to overcome as plaintiffs was establishing that they could recover for economic loss without showing actual property damage or personal injury. They used the theory of strict liability in tort to do this. (For a detailed discussion, see **Chapter 7**.) They focused on the argument that, because the product was hazardous, they were exposed to an unreasonable risk of injury to their person and property.[19] This is a departure from the typical product liability case, which focuses on the quality of the product and its suitability for the purpose for which it was intended.

In *School District of City of Independence, Missouri v. U.S. Gypsum Company*,[20] the plaintiff school district brought suit against the manufacturer of a ceiling plaster that contained asbestos. The plaintiff sought to

---

[15] Federal and state government recovery of cleanup costs for hazardous substances under CERCLA is discussed in **ch. 1**.

[16] U.C.C. § 2-314 (1978).

[17] U.C.C. § 2-315 (1978).

[18] U.C.C. § 2-607(3)(a) (1978).

[19] Board of Education of City of Chicago v. A, C and S, Inc., 525 N.E.2d 950, 954 (Ill. App. 1988), *aff'd in part, rev'd in part,* 131 Ill. 2d 428, 546 N.E.2d 580 (1989). *See* Adams-Arapahoe School Dist. No. 28-J v. Celotex Corp., 637 F. Supp. 1207 (D. Colo. 1986); City of Greenville v. W.R. Grace & Co., 827 F.2d 975 (4th Cir. 1987), *reh'g denied,* 840 F.2d 219 (4th Cir. 1988).

[20] 750 S.W.2d 442 (Mo. App. 1988).

recover, on the basis of strict products liability, for the costs of removing the plaster and certain asbestos-contaminated furnishings from seven of its school buildings.

The plaintiff alleged that the plaster was in a defective condition and was unreasonably dangerous at the time the defendant sold and installed it. According to the plaintiff, the plaster was defective because it released asbestos into the atmosphere of the buildings, contaminated the buildings and their furnishings, and thereby exposed occupants of the buildings to a continuing health hazard. The plaintiff also alleged strict liability for failure to warn of the plaster's danger.

In addition to its strict liability claims for actual damages, the plaintiff sought punitive damages on the theory that the defendant knew of the defect and the danger of its product at the time of sale and that the defendant thereby showed complete indifference to, or a conscious disregard for, the safety of others.

The jury awarded $650,000 in actual damages and $400,000 in punitive damages to the plaintiff. The trial court granted the defendant's motion for judgment notwithstanding the verdict as to the punitive damages award, but sustained the award of actual damages. Both parties appealed. The Missouri Court of Appeals affirmed.

The appellate court noted that, as a matter of policy, Missouri law already permitted a finding of liability under *Restatement (Second) of Torts* § 402A, when a dangerously defective product caused personal injury. The court believed that it was also appropriate, under some circumstances, for asbestos manufacturers to be strictly liable for property damage caused by their products. The court stated:

> It is reasonable that Missouri should extend tort liability to a manufacturer whose product threatens a substantial and unreasonable risk of harm by releasing toxic substances into the environment, thereby causing damage to the property owner who has placed the harmful product in his building.[21]

Furthermore, the court noted that asbestos-related diseases may not develop until decades after exposure, and stated that the plaintiff should not be prevented from asserting an action in strict liability merely because none of the occupants of its property had yet developed disease.[22]

In its defense, the defendant manufacturer contended that there had been no proof of tortious injury to any property other than the defective product itself and that, as a consequence, the plaintiff's cause of action, if any, sought recovery for pure economic loss and was founded in warranty rather than in tort. The court rejected this defense, even while acknowledging that

---

[21] *Id.* at 457.

[22] *Id.*

a higher court, in an earlier case, had once denied recovery in tort where the only damage was to the product sold.

In distinguishing the earlier case from the present one, the court noted that the plaintiff school district in the present case did claim damage to property other than the defective product. It claimed that several school buildings, and the contents of those buildings, had been contaminated by asbestos fibers released from the product. In this fashion, the court was able to permit the recovery of asbestos abatement costs in tort, while preserving the general principle that a plaintiff cannot recover in tort for purely economic loss.

Thus, the courts have allowed an expansion of the theory by finding that the loss was not solely economic, but extended to hazardous products.[23] One court stated:

> . . . the incorporation of the asbestos physically altered the buildings in a manner which makes the buildings harmful to their occupants, and . . . the physical damage to the property may be measured by the cost of repairing the buildings to make them safe.[24]

The court in *City of Greenville v. W.R. Grace & Company* reasoned that this type of risk was not normally allocated by agreement between the parties to a contract. As a result, the Circuit Court was willing to extend tort liability to a manufacturer whose product threatens a substantial and unreasonable risk of harm by releasing toxic substances into the environment, thereby causing damage to a property owner who has installed the harmful product in a building.[25]

Schools have led the way in opening up other legal theories for use in this area, such as fraudulent misrepresentation. They have claimed in their lawsuits that manufacturers knew or ought to have known that the products installed were not safe. They have alleged a conspiracy to deprive the schools of data and information necessary to make knowledgeable decisions about purchasing products. The courts have found that fraud may include a breach of duty by silence.[26]

Courts have allowed compensatory damages for the cost of removal, as well as punitive damages, in certain states where the facts have justified the allowance.[27] In one case, the court awarded damages to a city that had a

---

[23] Board of Education of City of Chicago v. A, C and S, Inc., *supra* note 19, 525 N.E.2d at 956.

[24] *Id.* at 956.

[25] City of Greenville v. W.R. Grace & Co., 827 F.2d 975, 978 (4th Cir. 1987), *reh'g denied,* 840 F.2d 219 (4th Cir. 1988).

[26] *Id.* 827 F.2d at 961.

[27] *Id.*

12-year removal plan, even though the work could theoretically be completed sooner.[28]

Another court allowed an indemnity and restitution action by the City of New York and its Board of Education against asbestos manufacturers and installers, based on an alleged breach of duty where the city had removed asbestos. A party seeking indemnity must have already performed the defendant's duty. The city had a common-law duty to protect the health, safety, and welfare of schoolchildren and a statutory duty under the New York Education Law to inspect for asbestos hazards, prepare annual inspection reports, and develop plans for correcting hazardous asbestos conditions. The law implies a contract to reimburse in cases of unjust enrichment.[29]

In *State of New York v. Shore Realty Corporation*,[30] the state sought to recover response costs and injunctive relief to require the defendant to clean up its hazardous waste site. The court found that a state could not avail itself of injunctive relief under CERCLA § 107, because the federal government has that right exclusively.[31] However, injunctive relief was allowed on the state's nuisance claim.

In an unusual move, 29 states sued 26 asbestos companies in the U.S. Supreme Court for the cost of reducing asbestos hazards in public buildings. The states claimed that the defendants had the responsibility to provide products that were safe for their intended uses or to warn the states of the danger posed by their products.[32] As noted above, the Supreme Court refused to hear the case.

The state of Maryland lost a 7-year legal battle to recover $17 million in asbestos property damage claims involving 28 state-owned buildings. The jury found in favor of the three defendant companies that had made asbestos materials that were installed in the buildings. In addition, the court ordered the state to pay the defendants' legal costs, which may be as much as $6 million. This was the first asbestos property damage suit filed by a state and the first of its kind to go to trial.[33]

---

[28] *Id.* at 983.

[29] City of New York v. Keene Corp., 132 Misc. 2d 745, 505 N.Y.S.2d 782 (1986), *aff'd*, 129 N.Y.S.2d 1019, 513 N.Y.S.2d 1004 (1st Dept. 1987).

[30] 759 F.2d 1032 (2d Cir. 1985).

[31] *Id.* at 1049–51.

[32] N.Y. Times, Jan. 31, 1990. The states include: Alabama, Arizona, Arkansas, California, Connecticut, Delaware, Florida, Illinois, Indiana, Iowa, Louisiana, Maine, Missouri, Montana, Nebraska, New Hampshire, New York, North Carolina, North Dakota, Ohio, Oklahoma, Rhode Island, South Dakota, Tennessee, Texas, Utah, Vermont, Washington, and Wyoming. See note 11, *supra*.

[33] Maryland v. Keene Corp., No. 110-8600 (Md. Cir. Ct. Feb. 15, 1991); Asbestos Abatement Report, Feb. 18, 1991, at 1.

The state's claim was grounded in strict liability, negligence, and negligent misrepresentation. The jury ruled in favor of the defendants on the defenses of contributory negligence and assumption of risk by the state.

Defense attorneys argued that 30 to 40 years ago, when the buildings were constructed, there was little indication that asbestos was a cancer-causing material. In addition, the state knew just as much, if not more, about the hazards of asbestos as did the defendant companies.

In what may be the largest asbestos property lawsuit to be tried to date, the City of Boston and its school system sued several asbestos manufacturing companies. The city claimed damages for the removal of asbestos-containing products from the City Hall, libraries, and schools.[34] The jury, in returning a defense verdict, found that in some of the buildings the products did not belong to the defendants; where they did, they were not dangerous.

§ 5.4 Manufacturers

Manufacturers tend to be defendants in lawsuits involving hazardous substances, particularly asbestos. However, they may be plaintiffs in third-party actions against other defendants/manufacturers where product identification is an issue or for contribution and indemnification.

Manufacturers of defective products may be liable to a user or consumer of such a product.[35] A product is "defective" if it is "unreasonably dangerous" to the ultimate user or consumer.[36] The determination of whether a product is unreasonably dangerous or is not reasonably safe is based on balancing whether the utility of the product outweighs the magnitude of the danger.[37]

The manufacturer is held to have the knowledge and skill of an expert and is presumed to be aware of scientific discoveries and advances.[38] A seller may be liable to the ultimate consumer or user for its failure to give adequate warnings.[39] The manufacturer has a duty to warn of foreseeable dangers, such as the inhalation of asbestos dust by insulation workers.[40]

Manufacturers include asbestos manufacturers, furniture manufacturers, and manufacturers of other buildings materials. For example, manufacturers of large fireplaces or solar heating systems that use radon-emitting

---

[34] Boston v. U.S. Gypsum Co., No. CA 8254 (Super. Ct., Suffolk Co., Mass. 1991).

[35] Restatement (Second) of Torts § 402A (1977).

[36] Borel v. Fibreboard Paper Products Corp., 493 F.2d 1076, 1087 (5th Cir. 1973).

[37] Id. at 1087.

[38] Id.

[39] Id. at 1091.

[40] Id. at 1093.

rock to store heat would be included. In the area of sick building syndrome, manufacturers of heating, air-conditioning, and ventilation (HVAC) equipment, and of carpeting, may be held liable.

However, a major difficulty for plaintiffs in lawsuits against manufacturers, particularly where an asbestos product was installed many years ago, has been product identification. (This is discussed in § 7.8.) The problem gets more difficult as the years pass since the building's construction. The original specifications may not be available, or evidence of the exact products used may become unverifiable.

§ 5.5   Commercial Building Owners

Building owners are subject to a substantial amount of potential litigation pertaining to hazardous substances. They can be liable as landlords, sellers of property, and employers. Although the laws do not currently mandate that building owners remove nonfriable, undamaged asbestos and remedy the presence of the hazardous substance or even inspect for it, proposed legislation certainly shows a trend in that direction.

As is discussed in **Chapter 2**, both New York City and Chicago have proposed bills pending that would require building owners, both commercial and residential, to remove asbestos and bear the full cost associated with such removal. As a result of these trends, we can expect to see an increase in the number of lawsuits against building owners for removal and abatement costs, as well as for personal injury.

In the absence of such statutes, owners can still be liable to a variety of plaintiffs whose claims are based on common-law, landlord/tenant, and tort theories. In addition, many possible lawsuits have not been attempted yet or have been started and quietly settled.

A commercial building owner who sells a building has a duty to disclose to a purchaser the presence of asbestos that is in a dangerous condition. The failure to notify can be fraud,[41] even where the property is being sold "as is."[42] The same duty to disclose the presence of asbestos has been found for private residences.[43]

Other hazardous substances commonly found in buildings include PCBs used as hydraulic fluids and dielectric fluids for capacitors and transformers; solvents such as trichloroethylene and trichloroethane, used to clean and degrease metals; and petroleum in underground storage tanks.

It is also possible that a contract of sale or even a lease can be rescinded where neither party knew of the presence of the hazardous substance at the

---

[41] 195 Broadway Co. v. 195 Broadway Corp. (Sup. Ct. N.Y. Co.), N.Y.L.J., Apr. 15, 1988, at 15.

[42] *Id.*

[43] Kinsey v. Jones., Civ. 87-2959 (JM) (E.D.N.Y. Jan. 30, 1989).

time the deal was closed.[44] This is based on the common-law contract principle of mutual mistake. Such a set of facts is rare in this age of due diligence and environmental audits.

Because courts are expanding the liability of building owners in the environmental area, the owners have continuing liability for contamination even after a sale is consummated.[45]

Owners of buildings also have an obligation to protect business invitees who visit their premises. They have a duty to disclose known dangers, as well as dangers discoverable through the exercise of reasonable care. Failure to do so may be "passive concealment."[46]

Interpretations of workers' compensation laws are being expanded by courts; some employees who have hazardous substance claims may now pursue their employers directly.[47] However, this is not always allowed.[48] Thus, there is the growing possibility is that employees may attempt to sue building owners who are not their employers.

Often, commercial building owners either renovate tenants' space or pay for part of tenants' "build out." In New York City, friable asbestos must be removed or encapsulated before a building permit will be issued.[49] This requirement may create an obligation on the part of the building owner to remove the asbestos or at least pay for part of the cost of its removal. An owner or operator of an institutional, commercial, or industrial structure (including an apartment building with more than four dwelling units) who removes asbestos as part of a renovation or demolition project must meet EPA notification, removal, transportation, and disposal requirements. However, depending on the amount removed, only notification may be required.[50]

Commercial lessees usually are required by lease to maintain the property in a safe condition and the landlord is usually not responsible for defective conditions, but the lessor is still liable for personal injuries caused by undisclosed dangerous conditions he or she knows about.[51]

The American Society of Heating, Refrigerating, and Air Conditioning Engineers (ASHRAE) publishes standards for substances such as asbestos

---

[44] Garb-Ko v. Lansing-Lewis Services, Inc., 423 N.W.2d 355 (Mich. App. 1988), *appeal denied,* 431 Mich. 874 (1988).

[45] *Id.* 423 N.W.2d at 358.

[46] Restatement (Second) of Torts §§ 360, 361 (1976); Restatement (Second) of Property §§ 17.3, 17.4 (1976); Lumber Village Inc. v. Siegler, 135 Mich. App. 685, 699–700 (1984).

[47] Johns-Manville Products Corp. v. Contra Costa Superior Court, 612 P.2d 948 (Cal. 1980).

[48] Kofron v. Amoco Chemicals Corp., 441 A.2d 226 (Del. 1982), *aff'd sub nom.* Mergenthaler v. Asbestos Corp. of America, 480 A.2d 647 (Del. Sup. 1984).

[49] See **Ch. 2.**

[50] 40 C.F.R. § 61.141.

[51] Restatement (Second) of Torts § 358 (1965).

and formaldehyde in buildings. (See **Chapter 3**.) Although adherence to these standards is voluntary, some might argue that building owners have a duty to increase ventilation in their buildings, if necessary, to comply with these standards. Liability may arise from sick building syndrome that has its origin in poor maintenance of the HVAC system.

A building owner may be liable for the release of asbestos when a building is demolished. One building owner was found liable for violation of the Clean Air Act even though he had given the demolition contractor the right to the proceeds from any salvageable material. The court would not allow the owner to "contract away" his duty to ensure that asbestos was disposed of in accordance with regulatory procedures.[52]

§ 5.6　—CERCLA Liability

Building owners and operators may be liable for cleanup costs under CERCLA. Damages may include the cost of governmental investigation and penalties. The buildings covered by CERCLA are typically found on large industrial sites with surrounding acreage, rather than in cities, but this is not always the case.

A building owner who is a potentially responsible party (PRP) under CERCLA can avoid liability under the Act's defenses by proving that due care was exercised, precautions were taken against foreseeable acts, and the release or threatened release was caused by an act of God, an act of war, or an act or omission of a third party other than an employee or agent of the defendant, or one whose act or omission occurs in connection with a contractual relationship with the defendant, such as a purchase agreement or lease.[53]

Under SARA, a building owner can claim a defense to liability if:

1. The owner acquired the property after the hazardous substance had been disposed of or placed thereon;
2. The owner did not know that the property was contaminated;
3. The owner had no reason to know that the property was contaminated.

To establish that there was no reason to know, the owner must show that it had "undertaken, at the time of acquisition, all appropriate inquiry into the previous ownership and users of the property consistent with good commercial or customary practice in an effort to minimize liability."[54]

---

[52] United States v. Geppert Brothers, Inc., 638 F. Supp. 996 (E.D. Pa. 1986).
[53] 42 U.S.C. § 9607(b).
[54] 42 U.S.C. § 9601(85)(B).

The court can take into account "any specialized knowledge or experience on the part of the defendant, the relationship of the purchase price to the value of the property if uncontaminated, commonly known or reasonably ascertainable information about the property, the obviousness of the presence or likely presence of contamination on the property, and the ability to detect such contamination by appropriate inspection."[55]

§ 5.7 —Landlords

At common law, unless a tenant has generated the hazardous substance or the lease provides otherwise, the landlord is generally responsible for any cleanup necessary to comply with laws and ordinances. There is no general rule requiring landlords to disclose the presence of asbestos or other hazardous substances *per se* to tenants. However, as discussed in this section, landlords are obligated to disclose concealed dangerous conditions that are unknown to the lessee.

As a matter of policy, being candid with tenants is probably best because it eliminates or at least minimizes future claims by tenants of failure to warn. Even where leases shift maintenance responsibilities to tenants, landlords are still liable for common portions of their buildings, which remain under their control, and for injuries caused by dangerous conditions in these areas.[56]

Under the *Restatement (Second) of Property:*

A landlord who transfers the possession of the leased property in a condition which he realizes, or should realize, will involve unreasonable risk of physical harm to others outside the leased property, is subject to the same liability for physical harm subsequently caused to them by the condition as though he had remained in possession.[57]

In addition,

A lessor of land is subject to liability for a nuisance caused by an activity carried on upon the land while the lease continues and the lessor continues as owner, if the lessor would be liable if he had carried on the activity himself, and

(a) At the time of the lease the lessor consents to the activity or knows or has reason to know that it will be carried on, and

---

[55] *Id.*

[56] Cappaert v. Junker, 413 So. 2d 378 (Miss. 1982).

[57] § 18.1 (1977). *See also* Restatement (Second) of Property §§ 17.3, 17.4 (1977); Restatement (Second) of Torts §§ 360, 361 (1976); 49 Am. Jur. 2d Landlord and Tenant §§ 761, 805 (1970).

(b) He then knows or should know that it will necessarily involve or is already causing the nuisance.[58]

A landlord is generally not liable for injuries resulting from a dangerous condition that arises on the premises *after* the tenant takes possession or that existed when the tenant took possession.[59] However, the landlord is liable for personal injury caused by a dangerous condition of which the landlord knew or should have known,[60] and which the tenant could not be expected to discover from a reasonable inspection of the premises.[61] This liability would apply to situations where contaminants are emanating from portions of the building that are in the lessor's control, such as asbestos in basements and heating ducts, radon from soil beneath the building, or bacteria in ductwork and air-conditioning systems.

To put it another way, even if a landlord can be charged with knowledge, the landlord will not be liable for dangerous conditions in areas not within its control, except in two situations:

1. The defects are hidden or latent, the landlord knows of them, the tenant either does not know of them or would not be aware of them after a reasonable inspection of the property, and the landlord does not make the tenant aware of them;[62]
2. The defect may not even be latent, but the premises will be used for a purpose that involves the admission of the public, such as a retail store.[63] This is called the "public use exception," and in such a case the defect need not be latent.[64]

The general rule would also not apply if the landlord has covenanted in the lease to keep the premises in good repair.[65] A landlord who has no duty to repair but voluntarily does so may be liable for personal injury caused by a dangerous condition resulting from the landlord's own negligent repair of

---

[58] Restatement (Second) of Torts § 837(1) (1979).

[59] Restatement (Second) of Torts §§ 355–56, 358 (1965).

[60] Cruz v. Drezek, 175 Conn. 230, 397 A.2d 1335 (1978) (landlord must know or be chargeable with knowledge of existing or defective condition); McCrorey v. Heilpern, 170 Conn. 220, 265 A.2d 1057 (1976); Young v. Garawacki, 380 Mass. 162, 402 N.E.2d 1045 (1980); Harrill v. Sinclair Refining Co., 225 N.C. 421, 35 S.E.2d 240 (1945); Restatement (Second) of Property §§ 17.1–.4, 17.3 comment c (1976).

[61] Restatement (Second) of Torts § 358(1) (1965).

[62] Ferber v. Orange Blossom Centers, Inc., 388 So. 2d 1074 (Fla. Dist. Ct. App. 1980); Dunson v. Friedlander Realty, 369 So. 2d 792 (Ala. 1979).

[63] Ostermeier v. Victorian House, Inc., 121 A.2d 611, 503 N.Y.S.2d 645 (2d Dept. 1986).

[64] *Id.*

[65] Ferber v. Orange Blossom Centers, Inc., 388 So. 2d 1074 (Fla. Dist. Ct. App. 1980); *see also* Restatement (Second) of Torts §§ 357, 360, and 362 (1965).

the premises.[66] The landlord may be liable to the tenant and even to third parties, if, for example, remodeling stirs up asbestos. There may also be grounds in such a situation for a private nuisance suit.

Asbestos may be regarded as a continuing latent defect, even if the tenant knows of its presence. Its unique qualities distinguish it from the usual latent defect. Even nonfriable asbestos may be a "continuing latent defect," despite disclosure of its presence to the tenant,[67] because it is hazardous only when its fibers become airborne.

If a landlord permitted the installation of asbestos in the belief that such installation was acceptable and subsequently learned of the harmful effects and risks of asbestos, the landlord might be able to discharge its liability under the Restatement, in these circumstances, by disclosing the existence of the defect. Disclosure before the lease is signed would be best.

On the basis of the rules discussed above, a landlord would be strongly advised, upon becoming aware of the presence or deterioration of asbestos, to issue a notice to all tenants and perhaps even to disclose or make available to the tenants the results of any survey taken. By disclosing the presence of asbestos, the landlord may be able to shift the risk to the tenant.

Whether a landlord should reasonably know of a dangerous condition may depend on other factors. For example, a landlord has a greater duty to know of a dangerous condition in an area within its control than in areas that are not within its control. A landlord who has specifically agreed to make repairs is generally only liable after the tenant has notified the landlord of the problem.[68]

A landlord is liable only for injuries that are reasonably foreseeable. For example, in some cases dealing with liability for lead paint, courts have held that the landlord was not liable on the basis that the risk of harm to the tenant was not foreseeable.[69]

The defense that a risk was not known or discoverable is frequently described as the "state-of-the-art defense." It has been used extensively by manufacturers of asbestos and has more recently been used as a defense by other parties. Landlords and architects may claim that when asbestos was installed in their buildings, the state of the art was such that it was considered a safe and acceptable building product.

In commercial buildings, generally the lessor is responsible for permanent repairs if the improvement: is substantial, will survive the term of the lease, will substantially benefit the lessor, and is not required by the tenant.

---

[66] Dunson v. Friedlander Realty, 369 So. 2d 792 (Ala. 1979); Restatement (Second) of Torts § 358 (1976); Restatement (Second) of Property § 17.1 comment h (1976).

[67] Restatement (Second) of Torts § 358 (1976); Restatement (Second) of Property § 17.1 comment h (1976).

[68] 49 Am. Jur. 2d Landlord and Tenant § 838 (1970).

[69] Dunson v. Friedlander Realty, 369 So. 2d 792 (Ala. 1979).

Landlords are not usually obligated to make repairs within the premises itself.[70]

Landlords must use reasonable care to keep the common areas in good condition. This responsibility extends to defects discovered or coming into existence after the lease commences.[71] This is true even if the cost of the repairs is significant and was unforeseen when the lease was executed.

However, this obligation may shift to a tenant who covenanted in the lease to comply with all laws, orders, and ordinances at his or her own expense. Because of the health risks and significant expense created by asbestos, courts are reluctant to impose the cost of removal on tenants unless they explicitly assume the cost in their lease.

Because improvements or alternations may be made during the lease term when there are no specific provisions in the lease allocating responsibility, certain factors should be considered by the parties—and probably would also be examined by the court—in deciding who should pay cleanup costs:

1. Is the work structural?
2. Will the work survive the lease term and inure to the primary benefit of the landlord?
3. Is the work required by the particular use of the tenants?
4. Is the cost substantial?
5. Was the event necessitating the work within the contemplation of the parties when the lease was signed?[72]

Tenants have many arguments in favor of the landlord's payment of these expenses. Asbestos abatement costs are extremely high; the work was probably not contemplated when the lease was signed; most abatement work is structural, because it is integrated with the building's core and components; and the landlord will be the ultimate beneficiary of the work.

A landlord will most likely be responsible for removal or abatement of hazardous substances *unless* the tenant has covenanted to make repairs *or* the removal or abatement has been necessitated by the tenant in some way.[73] Even a tenant who covenants to make repairs is often liable only for

---

[70] 49 Am. Jur. 2d Landlord and Tenant § 774 (1970).

[71] *Id.* §§ 230, 922 (1970).

[72] Glazerman, *Asbestos in Commercial Buildings: An Analysis of Obligations and Responsibilities of Landlords and Tenants,* 22 Real Prop., Prob. & Tr. J. 661 (1987). Baca v. Walgreen Co., 6 Kan. App. 2d 505, 630 P.2d 1185 (1981); *aff'd in part, rev'd in part,* 230 Kan. 443, 638 P.2d 898, *cert. denied,* 459 U.S. 859 (1982); SKD Enterprises Inc. v. L&M Offset, Inc., 65 Misc. 2d 612, 318 N.Y.S.2d 539 (1971); 1 American Law of Property § 3.80 (1952).

[73] 1 American Law of Property § 3.80 (1952).

"ordinary" repairs.[74] However, if the tenant has agreed to make alterations or repairs necessary to comply with laws and ordinances, the tenant may be liable even for extraordinary repairs.

Landlords may wish to take responsibility for hazardous waste abatement, regardless of the terms of the lease or their own legal responsibility. They will want to control: what abatement action is required; who does it; receipt of all regulatory approvals; proper completion of the work; receipt of all necessary certifications, especially regarding disposal of the hazardous products; hiring of a qualified and licensed contractor; verification of the contractor's necessary bonding; and insurance. Proposed regulations in some states have suggested the landlord's total involvement.

Landlords have considerable incentive to be involved in the abatement process and to see that it is done properly. They are still liable to tradespeople, employees, and people who use the building, and are accountable for NESHAP violations. The EPA has taken the position that building owners are ultimately responsible for asbestos-related problems in their buildings.[75]

Contractors may inadvertently release asbestos when they remove wires, work on a hung ceiling, or move partitions without knowing ACM is present. Landlords should have strict rules for controlling alterations and repairs by tenants, and should require prior notification and approval. Landlords may also insist on being indemnified by tenants in leases or in work authorization agreements before any abatement work is approved.

When negotiating a lease, the parties will have to resolve a wide range of issues. Who will bear the cost of inspections, air testing, and removal? Who will be responsible for maintenance programs? Will the landlord indemnify the tenant for personal injury, property damage, consequential damages, and business interruption expenses? Will there by any rent reduction or termination of the lease, if the asbestos or other hazardous substance is not abated or the abatement is disruptive? Can any insurance be purchased to cover the risk and, if so, who will pay the premiums? Landlords may still be able to negotiate leases that require a tenant to accept the premises "as is," but there should be an assurance in the lease (from the tenant's point of view), that the space will be in compliance with all applicable hazardous substance laws and regulations.

Because a landlord largely loses control of rented property during the term of a lease but remains a PRP under CERCLA, he or she may want to have an environmental survey conducted both before and after the lease term, to ensure that the tenant did not generate any hazardous substances. Tenants may create hazardous substances or conditions by disturbing existing asbestos in the course of alterations or repairs. Doctors, dry cleaners, and printing companies, for example, may store, use, or dispose of hazardous

---

[74] *Id.;* Mayfair Merchandise Co. v. Wayne, 415 F.2d 23, 25 (2d Cir. 1969).

[75] EPA, "Guidance for Controlling Asbestos-Containing Materials in Buildings, § 2.1-1.

substances on the premises. Landlords should have tenants covenant that they will not create or allow to be created any hazardous substance problem on the property and will indemnify the landlord for any costs or damages.

Because tenants can potentially also be liable under CERCLA, they may want indemnification from the landlord for any costs or damages incurred due to hazardous substances in the building *before* they moved in or for which they had no responsibility in creating.

Despite the enormous threat of litigation concerning asbestos and all the press, there have been surprisingly few tried cases, especially in the area of a commercial landlord's liability for abatement to a tenant. Yet, in a case of first impression, a New York court ruled that the owner of a commercial building that housed a parking garage had to remove asbestos from the building.[76]

The building had been constructed in 1963. Its structural steel members were coated with an asbestos-containing substance, which at the time had been approved as a fireproofing material for the protection of steel-frame structures. The landlord sought to require the tenant to correct the condition pursuant to the lease clause requiring the tenant to comply with all laws and orders with respect to the tenant's use and occupancy of the premises.

The court examined the New York City Building Code,[77] which requires the owner to be responsible for the safe maintenance of the building.

The lease required the tenant to keep the interior of the demised premises in good repair, and the landlord agreed to make all exterior structural repairs, as long as they were not due to damage by the tenant.

The court found that the asbestos was not a condition requiring "repair" in the normal sense of that word and did not come within the purview of the repair clause in the lease. The repair clause "does not entail the assumption of any responsibility for an inherent characteristic of a material employed in the original construction of the premises . . . ."[78] The court was not persuaded by the landlord's claim that activities of the tenant may have disturbed the asbestos. Also, the regulations that mandate removal were enacted subsequent to the date of the lease. This case will no doubt be cited as a precedent in many cases to come.

§ 5.8 —Tenants

Tenants do not seem to have been as litigious as one might expect in the area of property damage due to asbestos and other hazardous substances.

---

[76] Wolf v. 2539 Realty Associates, 161 App. Div. 2d 11, 560 N.Y.S.2d 24 (1st Dept. 1990).

[77] N.Y.C. Admin. Code, art. 6, § 27-128.

[78] *Id.*

The lack of claims is probably attributable in part to the expense of litigation and in part to the landlord's desire to avoid adverse publicity. Even if many such suits are being brought across the country, settlements are probably being arranged quietly before trial, and the cases are not appearing in the courts' reported cases. Although tenants are usually plaintiffs, they can also be defendants vis-à-vis subtenants and employees.

A tenant, as an occupant of a building, may become an "operator" for purposes of liability under CERCLA. This status would be most likely to occur in an industrial building. When an industrial tenant subleases a property, the tenant is a landlord and functions like the owner.[79] As an operator, a tenant can be liable for its own acts and for disposals of hazardous substances that occur during its operation of the building. The tenant's liability can be coextensive with that of the owner.[80] For example, there may be a leaky underground storage tank in a part of the facility that is not used by the tenant. The tenant may still be deemed an "operator." The tenant would then argue that it is not an operator of those portions of the facility which it did not use or even know about.

There is also the possibility of joint and several liability for the owner of the building and the tenant, under various state statutes.[81] In addition, the courts may imply a right of contribution.[82]

Such a tenant may try to avail itself of an "innocent tenant" defense by claiming that it had leased the premises after placement of the hazardous substance and did not know and had no reason to know that the property was contaminated.

A party may not shift its governmental liability to another party by way of agreement or otherwise, but individual parties may enter into indemnification agreements.[83] Lease agreements may be used by tenants to allocate risk and responsibility and provide for indemnification. However, the interpretation of such clauses often leads to litigation.

A tenant who is concerned about such issues might try to negotiate a provision requiring the landlord to indemnify the tenant for any costs or damages incurred due to hazardous substances that were placed in the building by others and for which the tenant had no responsibility.

The landlord might also be required to represent in the lease that no hazardous substance has been used, stored, treated, or disposed of on the

---

[79] United States v. South Carolina Recycling & Disposal, Inc., 653 F. Supp. 984, 1003 (D.S.C. 1986).

[80] National Wood Preservers, Inc. v. Pennsylvania Department of Environmental Resources, 489 Pa. 221, 414 A.2d 37, *appeal dismissed,* 449 U.S. 803 (1980).

[81] Pa. Stat. Ann., tit. 35, § 691.316 (Purdon 1977); N.J. Stat. Ann. §§ 58:10-23.11 et seq., 13:1K-6 et seq. (West 1987).

[82] Cartel Capital Corp. v. Fireco of New Jersey, 81 N.J. 548, 566 (1980).

[83] Caldwell v. Gurley Refining Co., 755 N.2d 645 (8th Cir. 1985).

property, and that the property is in compliance with all applicable laws, statutes, and regulations, including environmental, health, and safety statutes. The landlord might want to add to such a provision that the representation is "to the best of the landlord's knowledge."

When such cases are litigated, the courts will look at the terms of the lease and the surrounding circumstances, to determine the intention of the parties. Indemnification obligations may also arise by implication based on equity or implied contracts.[84] So far, this has not occurred in the environmental area.

Unfortunately, most leases drafted before 1980 (and many drafted since then) did not specifically allocate responsibility for environmental issues. It is recommended that this responsibility be negotiated before signing a lease, to ensure that litigation concerning the cost of abatement will not occur later.

There are several typical clauses in a lease which a landlord may look at to place environmental compliance and liability on a tenant. Tenants usually agree in leases that they shall not "suffer any waste" to the demised premises and that they shall "comply with all federal, state, county, and municipal laws, ordinances and regulations applicable."

The interpretation of these clauses will depend on the intent of the parties.[85] For example, in *Herald Square Realty Company v. Saks & Company*,[86] although the tenant had an obligation under the lease to comply with laws, it was not obligated to make structural changes required by a revision of the building laws that occurred after the lease was executed. This verdict would be analogous to a long-term lease situation where more stringent asbestos removal laws are passed during the lease term. Should the tenant be required to comply, even though this change was not contemplated by the parties when the lease was signed?

In another interesting case, a commercial tenant sought written permission from its landlord to make renovations.[87] The lease clause provided that such repairs or improvements had to be of equal quality to the original condition of the premises. The landlord gave its consent, but conditioned it upon the tenant's paying the cost of the asbestos removal that would become necessary by virtue of the renovation.

The court read a "standard of reasonableness" into the issue of consent and found that the landlord is usually responsible for making capital improvements or repairs as opposed to repairs or modifications essentially

---

[84] General Electric Co. v. Cuban American Nickel Co., 396 F.2d 89 (5th Cir. 1968).

[85] *See* Glenn R. Sewell Sheet Metal, Inc. v. Loverde, 70 Ca. 2d 666, 451 P.2d 721, 726 (1969).

[86] 215 N.Y. 427, 109 N.E. 545 (1915).

[87] Sun Insurance Services, Inc. v. 260 Peachtree Street, Inc., 192 Ga. App. 482, 385 S.E.2d 127 (1989).

beneficial to the lessee. Where improvements of a structural nature are necessary and the improvements are outside the contemplation of the parties, it is more equitable to require the landlord to make them. The removal of asbestos enhances the value of the building, whereas the renovations enhance the efficiency of the tenant's business.

A tenant may argue that "anti-waste" clauses are intended to apply to abatement of nuisances and compliance with laws pertaining to the structure of the premises, and not to environmental issues.

Before entering into a lease, the tenant may wish to seek from the landlord certain express representations and warranties concerning existing conditions, such as a warranty that the premises are free from hazardous substances or that the landlord will maintain the asbestos to prevent any dangerous release of fibers. Certain portions of the facility or building may be specifically excluded from the description of the leased premises, such as areas that contain electrical transformers or underground storage tanks or similar areas that the tenant will not be using.

The lessor or lessee may require the other to provide a survey on environmental conditions before the lease is signed and then describe in the lease how any problematic conditions will be remedied. Depending on the parties' relative bargaining power, they will either share the cost or the landlord will pay for it.

At common law, a tenant who damages a building during renovation can be liable for waste and for the reduction in value of the building or the cost of renovation.[88] Tenants who undertake abatement actions should be aware of the risks to them if anything goes wrong—for example, if asbestos is released. They may incur liability to the landlord, as well as to other tenants.

A landlord may want the tenant to covenant that it will not create or allow to be created any hazardous substance problem on the property. This protects the landlord if the tenant disturbs asbestos in the course of alterations or repairs to the premises. Such a clause would also include an obligation by the tenant to indemnify the landlord for any costs or damages caused by the tenant in connection with hazardous substances.

Because a cleanup might require the closure of all or part of a building or retail space for a period of time, a tenant may want the right to terminate a lease if the closure lasts beyond a reasonable period of time. An alternative might be a partial or total abatement of rent during the cleanup period.

Tenants in buildings containing hazardous substances may look to the covenant of quiet enjoyment if such conditions interfere with their leasehold. Residential tenants can use the warranty of habitability.[89] Generally, there is no implied warranty of fitness or of habitability in the commercial context. If tenants cease paying rent due to the presence of friable asbestos

---

[88] Restatement (Second) of Property § 12.2, comment i (1976).

[89] N.Y. Real Prop. L. § 235-b.

or other hazardous substances, this may be a defense to a nonpayment proceeding by the landlord. However, it must be borne in mind that the mere presence of asbestos in a building does not justify the nonpayment of rent.

One commercial tenant that refused to pay its rent for more than 4 years because of the presence of asbestos wound up settling a lawsuit with the landlord by paying $475,000 in unpaid back rent and other fees.[90] Apparently, there was some evidence that the tenant was aware of the asbestos *before* the lease commenced.

The possibility of negligent work is lessened somewhat in states where alteration or repair work that may disturb asbestos must be handled by specially licensed professionals.[91]

The same principles should apply to restricting the subletting of the premises and the alteration activities of the subtenant.

Clear lease language can be particularly important in states such as New Jersey and Connecticut, which have statutory provisions on compliance with certain requirements upon termination of the leasehold. No matter how the risk is allocated during or after the lease term, there should be an indemnification, hold harmless, and defense provision in the lease.

If there is a possibility that the landlord will make alterations or repairs that may disturb asbestos, the tenant may want to be indemnified from any liability for damages caused by hazardous substances or conditions created by the landlord or by other tenants during the lease term. Any indemnity clauses should be drafted to survive the lease term; lawsuits may occur many years after the lease ends. This is another argument for having an environmental audit conducted at the end of the lease term. All of these factors must be taken into account before entering into a lease, in order to minimize risk and liability.

§ 5.9   Sellers of Property

Sellers of contaminated property may be sued for failure to disclose the presence of asbestos and other hazardous substances in the building and may continue to face liability even after they sell the property and even if it is sold "as is." They can be liable under CERCLA and under common-law theories. This liability may be expanded as a result of warranties, representations, and indemnification provisions made in sales contracts.

A jury found Prudential Insurance Company liable for $22 million for failing to disclose to a buyer prior to purchase that there was asbestos

---

[90] ARZ Acres, Inc. v. Satellite Business Systems (Ct. Common Pleas, Cuyahoga Co., Ohio), No. 106,608 (settled July 13, 1990); *see* Abestos Abatement Report, Aug. 6, 1990, at 3.

[91] N.Y. Lab. Law §§ 901, 902 (McKinney Supp. 1988); N.J. Stat. Ann. § 34:5A-32 et seq. (West 1988); Md. Envtl. Code Ann. § 6-401 et seq. (1987).

fireproofing in an office building.[92] The award included actual damages of over $6 million, punitive damages of $14.3 million, and attorney fees.

The building was constructed in 1972 with Monokote, an asbestos-containing, sprayed-on, fireproofing material applied on steel structural members and in return air ducts.

Prudential had been abating asbestos in its other buildings in 1980 and 1981 and had brought suits against several former manufacturers of asbestos.

The jury found that Prudential's conduct was committed with conscious indifference to the rights of the plaintiff, with gross negligence, and with actual awareness that such conduct was wrongful. However, they did not believe that Prudential's conduct was committed with knowledge that it was wrongful.

Depending on what types of problems arise after the closing, there may be claims by a purchaser for negligent misrepresentation, fraud, and even deceptive trade practices.[93]

Buyers may seek money damages or try to set aside the purchase because the asbestos or other hazardous condition was latent or hidden, or because there was no meaningful opportunity to inspect. Courts are more inclined to find a viable claim if the seller actually *knew* that asbestos was present and failed to disclose it.

Handling the sale properly from an environmental point of view may be important later on, if the seller wishes to invoke the "innocent purchaser" defense in those instances where CERCLA applies.

A seller may have an affirmative duty to determine whether asbestos or other hazardous substances are present. A seller's failure to discover whether asbestos or other hazardous substances are present, and to advise the buyer, may warrant punitive damages, even when the buyer is a sophisticated corporation that could afford to inspect the premises.[94] A contract of sale would probably not be set aside if the buyer had *notice* that asbestos was present in the building.[95]

Thus, it is recommended that the buyer and seller discuss allocation of the cost of any environmental audits and any work that must be done as a result, and incorporate their agreement into the contract of sale. The buyer should obtain copies of all inspections and surveys done in the building prior to the sale.

---

[92] Jefferson Associates Ltd. v. Prudential Insurance Co. of America, No. 441, 712 (Texas Dist. Ct., Travis Co., 126th Jud. Dist. May 23, 1990); Asbestos Abatement Report, July 23, 1990.

[93] Restatement (Second) of Torts § 552 (1977); *see also* Cook Consultants, Inc. v. Larson, 700 S.W.2d 231 (Tex. App. 1985); Clearwater Forest Industries, Inc. v. United States, 650 F.2d 233 (Ct. Cl. 1981).

[94] 195 Broadway Co. v. 195 Broadway Corp. (Sup. Ct. N.Y. Co.) N.Y.L.J., Apr. 15, 1988.

[95] Elkhart Community School Corp. v. Mills, 546 N.E.2d 854 (Ct. App. Ind. 1989).

The seller will want to try to minimize the number and extent of warranties and representations that will have to be made about issues such as existing environmental conditions and renewability of permits for industrial buildings. The contract of sale should have provisions requiring cooperation between the buyer and seller in the event of litigation, especially by a third party, because the buyer (particularly a buyer of a commercial building) may employ many of the potential witnesses and may have much of the documentation needed to support a lawsuit. A provision allocating expenses for litigation may also be included.

There is no rule requiring owners of a building in which abatement has occurred to disclose to the buyer that an abatement program has been undertaken and completed. However, it is probably prudent to advise the buyer of the abatement and to provide proof of compliance. The seller may then represent in the contract of sale that the work was done by a certified contractor and supervised by a certified consultant.

§ 5.10   Buyers

Traditionally, in the absence of specific warranties and representations, buyers of property had little recourse for problems that came to light after the closing. *Caveat emptor* (buyer beware) was the operative principle. Environmental law has changed that to a large degree.

For example, in the past, liability for violations for off-site disposal did not follow the transfer of assets of the corporation that caused the violation. Now, the purchase of the stock of a corporation may carry prior fines and penalties along with it.[96] Administrative orders and consent decrees may be binding on successors and assigns. Under CERCLA, new owners of buildings may be jointly and severally liable with prior owners.[97] Facilities subject to hazardous waste permit requirements under the Resources Conservation and Recovery Act (RCRA) may have cleanup responsibility as a condition to taking over permits. There may also be superliens on the property.[98]

Because cleanup liability can well exceed the value of the property, buyers must be careful to identify all potential environmental liability for past activities and seek indemnification, hold harmless, and defense provisions from the seller for conditions existing prior to closing.

---

[96] Oner II v. EPA, 597 F.2d 184 (9th Cir. 1979).

[97] State of New York v. Shore Realty Corp., 759 F.2d 1032, 1042 (2d Cir. 1985); United States v. Price, 688 F.2d 204 (3d Cir. 1982), *aff'g* 577 F. Supp. 1055, 1103, 1113–14 (D.N.J. 1981).

[98] N.J. Rev. Stat. § 58:10-23 (11f)(f); N.H. Rev. Stat. Ann. § 147-B:10. The seller may also have notification and cleanup requirements. N.J. Rev. Stat. § 13:1K-9 (1983); Conn. Gen. Stat. § 22a-134a(b)(1986).

Prior to closing, the buyer will want to have the right to an environmental audit. Any problems raised by the audit should be rectified before closing. The buyer may also want the right to terminate the agreement, depending on the nature and extent of the environmental problem.

§ 5.11   Homeowners

Many homeowners are facing a variety of hazardous waste and toxic substance issues and have begun to litigate. Radon and formaldehyde seem to be involved in many of these suits.

In *Brafford v. Susquehanna,* a homeowner sued on a negligence theory for radon exposure.[99] The court denied a motion to dismiss for lack of injury, even though the homeowner was claiming injury for the increased risk of developing cancer. The court found that the damage to the plaintiff's immune system could lead to leukemia.

The prospective purchasers of a single-family home sought specific performance of an agreement with the seller to convey the residence free of any lead paint contamination.[100] The contract of sale included a portion of the Massachusetts lead paint law. The judge found that the sellers and real estate agent should have informed the buyers early in the negotiations that the buyer would be responsible for deleading the premises. Instead, the issue was raised at the closing. The judge ordered the return of the deposit and dismissed the seller's counterclaim for damages.

A homeowner who is also a seller may be liable for intentionally failing to disclose the presence of hazardous substances, such as formaldehyde.[101] This information is considered to be material information in making a decision, and liability exists to the same extent as if there had been an affirmative statement that the condition did not exist. This may be true even though the seller had no reason to know of the presence of the formaldehyde.

In one case, the purchasers sued the sellers of a single-family home when they discovered after closing that the walls were made of asbestos board and not masonite as had been stated by the sellers during a preclosing inspection.[102] The plaintiff/purchaser claimed fraud because of a willful failure to disclose the latent hazardous condition. The defendant/seller sought rescission on the grounds of "mutual mistake of facts." The court dismissed the counterclaim because the plaintiffs could not be put back into *status*

---

[99] 586 F. Supp. (D. Colo. 1984).

[100] Samuels v. Brooks, 519 N.E.2d 605 (Mass. App. Ct. 1988).

[101] Roberts v. Estate of Barbagallo, 531 A.2d 1125, 1131–32 (Pa. Super. 1987).

[102] Kinsey v. Jones, Civ. 87-2959 (JM) (E.D.N.Y. Jan. 30, 1989).

quo after they had done extensive alterations and the defendants did not allege any injury as a result of the mutual mistake.

In South Carolina, the courts have held that a manufacturer or assembler has a duty to test and inspect the components incorporated into its product.[103] The definition of "product" has been expanded to include the sale of a house.[104] Thus, the sale of a defective house may result in strict liability of the seller. Because South Carolina has applied the doctrine of strict liability to sales–service hybrid transactions, the contractor and subcontractor who installed the asbestos may also potentially be liable.

Homeowners can best protect themselves by having in their contracts of sale provisions that address hazardous substance issues and survive the closing. Depending on the location of the house and other facts and circumstances, an environmental audit may be a wise investment prior to closing. The parties can negotiate the allocation of expenses and whether the agreement will terminate if any hazardous substances are found.

§ 5.12   Real Estate Brokers

In the not too distant past, *caveat emptor* protected realtors from liability for innocent misrepresentation and latent defects. Today, a real estate brokerage firm or individual broker can be liable to a purchaser (1) for intentional, innocent,[105] or negligent misrepresentation of the condition of a property,[106] (2) for the failure to disclose the presence of contamination from hazardous substances, such as banned urea formaldehyde foam insulation, prior to execution of a contract of sale, and (3) for simple negligence for the breach of an affirmative duty to make a reasonable investigation of the property for material defects and to disclose any defects found to prospective buyers. This is a departure from the traditional liability which a broker usually only had to a seller.

Brokers may be liable if they knew or should have known that the property was contaminated and did not disclose its true condition. For example, if a realtor allegedly knew or should have known of a high radon danger and sold the building without adequate warnings or protection from gas contamination, litigation may result. The purchaser will claim that the realtor failed to discharge the duty of discovery and disclosure to the buyer of the presence of elevated radon levels.[107] A breach of duty may occur by the

---

[103] Baughman v. General Motors Corp., 780 F.2d 1131 (4th Cir. 1986).

[104] Lane v. Trenholm Bldg. Co., 267 S.C. 497, 501, 229 S.E.2d 728, 730 (1976).

[105] Restatement (Second) of Torts § 552C(1) (1977).

[106] Rosenblum Inc. v. Adler, 93 N.J. 324, 461 A.2d 138 (1983).

[107] Holman, Realty Industry on Edge Amid Developing Liability Trends, Indoor Pollution Law Report No. 2, July 1987.

failure to exercise the care of a reasonable, prudent, professional realtor, and misrepresentation may be actionable even if it was made innocently.

There may be fraud if the broker has knowledge of environmental problems on the property that are material, he or she deliberately misrepresents or fails to disclose them, there is a defect but it is not the type of problem that would have been discoverable by the purchaser in conducting a reasonable investigation of the property, the purchaser relies on the representation or lack of disclosure and is damaged.[108]

There may also be allegations of fraud if the broker has made an affirmative representation of fact concerning the property which is false. This claim is difficult to prove. A plaintiff must prove not only the falsity of the representation and the reliance on it, but also that the broker *knew* the statement was untrue and made it with the *intent* to deceive the purchaser.

The broker may have an affirmative duty to reasonably investigate, discover, and disclose to a purchaser any "red flags" that indicate latent defects and to make no misrepresentations with respect to known or discoverable defects.[109] Nonfulfillment of the duty may be negligence, even when there is no direct contact between the purchaser and the broker prior to the sale.[110]

Only three states thus far have found that brokers have this duty to investigate and disclose.[111]

In *Easton v. Strassburger,* the plaintiff-purchaser sued the real estate listing broker, among others, when massive earth movement on the property shortly after purchase significantly reduced the property's value.[112] Evidence showed that the prior owners, the Strassburgers, had affirmatively concealed from the buyers and agents that there had been two previous slides over the preceding three years. Despite the affirmative concealment by the sellers, the real estate listing broker was held liable because his casual visual inspection did not constitute a reasonable and competent inspection

---

[108] Environmental Protection Dept. v. Ventron Corp., 182 N.J. Super. 210, 440 A.2d 455, *aff'd as modified,* 94 N.J. 473, 468 A.2d 150 (1983).

[109] Easton v. Strassburger, 152 Cal. App. 3d 90, 102, 199 Cal. Rptr. 383, 390 (1984). The California legislature limited the holding of this case to residential property. Cal. Civ. Code § 2079 (West Supp. 1987); Gouveia v. Citicorp Person-to-Person Financial Center, Inc., 101 N.M. 572, 686 P.2d 262, 266 (Ct. App. 1984); Sector v. Knight, 716 P.2d 790, 795 (Utah 1986). *Cf.* Holder v. Haskett, 283 S.C. 247, 321 S.E.2d 192 (Ct. App. 1984) (real estate agent may be liable under implied warranty of habitability theory if party to contract).

As a result of *Easton,* the California legislature codified the broker's duty to the prospective purchaser of residential property. Cal. Civ. Code § 2079 (West Supp. 1989).

[110] *See* Treece and Clawson, *The Real Estate Broker's Duty to Investigate,* For the Defense, May 1988, at 11.

[111] *See* Environmental Protection Dept. v. Ventron Corp., *supra* note 108.

[112] Easton v. Strassburger, 152 Cal. App. 3d at 96, 199 Cal. Rptr. at 385.

of the property. The court held that the broker had a duty to diligently investigate and uncover reasonably discoverable defects.[113]

The *Easton* court based its decision on a number of factors. The court reasoned that the seller's broker is most often in the best position to obtain and provide reliable information on the property.[114] Most buyers justifiably rely on brokers and believe that the brokers are working for them. The court also cited the Code of Ethics of the National Association of Realtors, which includes the provision that a broker must not only "avoid . . . concealment of pertinent facts," but "has an affirmative obligation to discover adverse factors that a reasonably competent and diligent investigation would disclose."[115]

The broker was found negligent for failing to independently investigate a residential property for structural defects. The court stated:

> A real estate broker is a licensed person or entity who holds himself out to the public as having particular skills and knowledge in the real estate field. He is under a duty to disclose facts materially affecting the value or desirability of the property that are known to him or which through reasonable diligence should be known to him.[116]

This liability can come about through negligent misrepresentation or traditional negligence, which uses community standards.[117]

If a broker's representation to a buyer regarding a material fact turns out to be false, the broker may be held liable to the buyer even if the representation was made innocently and in good faith after exercising due diligence. This is called "innocent misrepresentation."[118]

At least half of the states that have considered liability of real estate brokers under the theory of innocent misrepresentation or negligence have rejected it, maintaining that *caveat emptor* still protects brokers.[119]

Some courts have eliminated the requirement of proving negligence and hold that the innocent misrepresentation cause of action found in *Restatement (Second) of Torts* § 552(c) is sufficient. This section provides for strict

---

[113] *Id.* 152 Cal. App. 3d at 103, 199 Cal. Rptr. at 391.

[114] *Id.* 152 Cal. App. 3d at 100, 199 Cal. Rptr. at 388.

[115] *Id.* 152 Cal. App. 3d at 101, 199 Cal. Rptr. at 389. *See also* National Association of Realtors (NAR) Code of Ethics, art. 1 (1974). The Code also requires being informed on laws and regulations affecting real estate.

[116] NAR Code of Ethics, art. 1 (1974).

[117] George Ball Pacific, 117 Cal. App. 3d 248, 172 Cal. Rptr. 597 (1981).

[118] Restatement (Second) of Torts § 552C(1) (1977).

[119] These states include, *inter alia,* Alabama, Florida, Georgia, Illinois, Kansas, Michigan, Nevada, New Hampshire, and Vermont. Guilfoy, *Home Not-So-Sweet Home: Real Estate Broker Liability in the Sale of Previously Contaminated Residential Property: Has Broker Liability Gone Too Far?* 21 Rutgers L.J. 111 (1989).

liability for misrepresentations without requiring proof of intentional deception or negligence.[120] Not all courts subscribe to this theory.[121]

Consumer protection statutes may make innocent misrepresentations actionable without any proof of intentional deception or negligence.[122]

The theories of negligent and innocent misrepresentation have three elements in common. Both require (1) a misrepresentation of a material fact, (2) made by the defendant to induce the plaintiff to act or not to act, and (3) it must be justifiably relied on by the plaintiff.[123] Under negligent misrepresentation, there is an additional requirement: the maker of the statement must have failed to exercise reasonable skill and care in obtaining and communicating the information.[124] Innocent misrepresentation is a form of strict liability in that the speaker's care, or lack of it, is of no import.

Under the theory of negligent misrepresentation, the buyer's own negligence would probably serve as a defense for the broker. However, the theory of innocent misrepresentation provides no such defense to the broker.[125]

There is some authority for allowing the broker to rely on information provided by the seller concerning the property.[126] However, other jurisdictions have held that the broker has a duty to make reasonable efforts to confirm or refute such information.[127] Thus, it is advisable for a broker to not blindly rely on information provided by the seller but to make an effort to independently verify such information. The broker should avoid making statements about the condition of the property or its potential uses. A wise broker will recommend that an environmental audit be done by one of the parties. Any representations made to a purchaser should not be represented as being based on the broker's own knowledge. Brokers may wish to have disclaimer clauses concerning the presence of any toxic substances, in addition to "as is" clauses.

A realty agent was found to have no duty to disclose the presence of urea formaldehyde insulation to home buyers, where the sellers knew of the presence of the insulation and failed to disclose it. The court found that the agent was entitled to rely on the sellers' representation that they knew of

---

[120] Bevins v. Ballard, 655 P.2d 757, 761–63 (Alaska 1982).

[121] Hoffman v. Connall, 108 Wash. 2d. 69, 736 P.2d 242, 244–45 (1987).

[122] *See* Consumer Protection Act, Tex. Bus. and Com. Code § 17.41 et seq., which gives a purchaser a cause of action for misrepresentation and only requires proof that a representation was made, was untrue, and produced actual damages.

[123] Restatement (Second) of Torts § 552 (negligent misrepresentation) and § 552C(1) (innocent misrepresentation) (1977).

[124] *Id.* § 552.

[125] *See, e.g.,* Bevins v. Ballard, 655 P.2d 757 (Alaska 1982).

[126] Lyons v. Christ Episcopal Church, 71 Ill. App. 3d, 257, 389 N.E.2d 623, 625 (Ill. App. Ct. 1979).

[127] Tenant v. Lawton, 26 Wash. App. 701, 415 P.2d 1305, 1309–10 (Wash. Ct. App. 1980).

no material structural defects affecting the sale. There was nothing to alert the realtor to the possibility that the statements in the listing agreement were false.[128]

The broker can also be liable for its sales representative, even if he or she is an independent contractor, because a principal is liable for its agent's fraud in order to ensure protection of third parties.[129]

Furthermore, when someone is induced to enter into a transaction by untrue material misrepresentations by an agent with authority, the person who has been deceived may elect to rescind the transaction or sue for damages.[130] Any disclosures made by a broker should be done in writing. A broker representing a seller should obtain the seller's approval of the form and substance of a disclosure prior to its delivery to the buyer.

The broker may want to disclaim liability or obtain an indemnification provision in the brokerage agreement and in correspondence with prospective purchasers. Any indemnification agreement with the seller should provide that the seller will indemnify the broker for all liabilities, including those imposed by virtue of the broker's negligence, to the extent allowed by law.

A broker who represents a prospective buyer can try to include a provision in the contract eliminating any obligation to independently investigate the property for environmental problems and can make it clear that the buyer is not relying on the broker to perform such an investigation.

§ 5.13   Developers as Defendants

Builder-vendors impliedly warrant that the houses they construct will be of reasonable workmanship and habitability. An increasing number of jurisdictions have applied the doctrine of implied warranty of habitability to the sale of new homes.[131]

If a new home has toxic problems, in a state such as New Jersey, the purchaser can look to the builder-vendor for damages based on strict liability.[132] However, if the home is purchased used, the purchaser must show fault on the part of either the broker or the seller.[133]

---

[128] Brock v. Tarrant, 57 Wash. App. 562, 789 P.2d 112 (1990).

[129] Roberts v. Estate of Barbagallo, 531 A.2d at 1132.

[130] *Id.* at 1132.

[131] McDonald v. Mianecki, 79 N.J. 275, 398 A.2d 1283 (1978).

[132] Patitucci v. Drelich, 153 N.J. 177, 379 A.2d 297 (Law Div. 1977).

[133] Santiago v. E.W. Bliss Div., Gulf & Western Mfg. Co., 201 N.J. Super. 205, 492 A.2d 1089 (App. Div. 1985).

A developer was found liable when a house's well water was not potable.[134] Damages included out-of-pocket expenses, compensation for deterioration in quality of living, and reduction in fair market value of the home attributable to the defect.[135]

A developer and asbestos manufacturers were sued by a shopping mall for costs of renovation, damage to the tenants' property, and losses incurred when the local Health Department ordered the mall closed because of asbestos.[136]

There may be other claims, for example, that a developer knew or should have known of the danger from radon and still constructed a house or sold a building without adequate warnings or protection from contamination.

If a product cannot be made safe, the manufacturer must provide adequate warnings. Not many jurisdictions consider a building a product subject to strict products liability, but this theory has been used for mass-produced buildings.[137] In New Jersey, it has been extended to other buildings.[138] However, because this theory is based on a product, it can be used only against the manufacturer of the product (the builder-vendor) and not, for example, against the contractor.

§ 5.14 Corporate Shareholders, Officers, Directors, and Managers as Defendants

Traditionally, shareholders have not been held liable for damages unless they ignore corporate formalities. A corporation is a legal entity and has an existence separate and apart from the people who compose it.[139] The corporate veil is only pierced if a shareholder acts in a manner inconsistent with the status of a shareholder. Even then, the activity must be egregious.

This concept holds true for claims that involve hazardous substances and fall outside of CERCLA.

However, under traditional agency concepts, "[a]n agent who does an act otherwise a tort is not relieved from liability by the fact that he acted at the command of the principal or on account of the principal . . . ."[140]

---

[134] *Id.*

[135] *Id.* 492 A.2d at 1286.

[136] Jefferson Associates Ltd. v. Prudential Ins. Co., No. 441, 712 (Texas Dist. Ct. 1989); Mealeys Asbestos Report, Jan. 20, 1989, at 17.

[137] Kriegler v. Eichler Homes, 269 Cal. App. 2d 224, 74 Cal. Rptr. 749 (1969).

[138] McDonald v. Mianecki, 79 N.J. 275, 398 A.2d 1283 (1979).

[139] Kirvo Indus. Supply Co. v. Nat'l Distillers & Chem. Corp., 483 F.2d 1098, 1102 (5th Cir. 1973), *reh'g denied,* 490 F.2d 916 (5th Cir. 1974).

[140] Restatement (Second) of Agency § 343 (1958). *See also* Wallace, *Liability of Corporations and Corporate Officers, Directors, and Shareholders Under Superfund;*

Thus, illegal acts by corporate agents acting within the scope of their authority will give rise to liability on the part of their corporate principals. Even when directors and shareholders have actively participated in illegal acts in their respective corporate roles, they can be found liable without piercing the corporate veil.

To pierce the corporate veil, there must be evidence that: (1) the corporation and the shareholder had such a unity of interest and ownership that they were not distinct entities,[141] or (2) it would be inequitable not to disregard the corporate form. In order to show (1), there must be a failure to follow corporate formalities—a commingling of corporate and personal accounts or a failure to maintain adequate records.[142] (For more detailed discussion, see § 5.17.)

However, since CERCLA was enacted, the traditional approach to liability has been modified. Generally, corporate directors are not personally liable for torts committed by the corporation or its officers, *unless* they participate in, manage, or have knowledge amounting to acquiescence *or* their negligence in the management or supervision of corporate affairs causes or contributes to the injury.[143] CERCLA allows the government to impose liability on individual responsible parties regardless of the corporate form.

These individuals may be exposed to liability under CERCLA as "operators" because of their knowledge of or ability to control or prevent environmental problems.[144] The extent of participation by officers or directors in the operation of a corporation's facility determines whether they are "operators."[145] However, courts are still generally reluctant to pierce the corporate veil and hold former shareholders derivatively liable for wrongful corporate conduct in the environmental area.[146]

Persons who participate in the wrongful conduct of a corporation under CERCLA § 107(a)(3) by arranging for the disposal of hazardous substances may be liable individually. They may also be liable under RCRA

Should Corporate and Agency Law Concepts Apply?, J. Corp. L., Summer 1989, at 839.

[141] Lakota Girl Scouts Club, Inc. v. Havey Fund-Raising Management, Inc., 519 F.2d 634, 638 (8th Cir. 1975).

[142] Henn and Alexander, Laws of Corporations 144–47, 344–47 (3d ed. 1983).

[143] Bischofshausen, Vasbinder and Luckie v. D. W. Jaquays Mining and Equipment Contractors Co., 145 Ariz. 204, 700 P.2d 902 (1985). The liability of corporations that are shareholders in subsidiaries of a parent corporation is discussed in § 5.17.

[144] State of New York v. Shore Realty Corp., 759 F.2d 1032, 1052 (2d Cir. 1985).

[145] Riverside Market Dev. Corp. v. International Bldg. Products, Inc. No. CIV-A-88-5317 (E.D. La. May 23, 1990) (LEXIS 6375 Envrn library).

[146] United States v. Northeastern Pharmaceutical and Chemical Co., 579 F. Supp. 823 (W.D. Mo. 1984), *aff'd in part and rev'd in part,* 810 F.2d 726, 742–43 (8th Cir. 1986) (hereinafter, "NEPACCO").

for contributing to the disposal of hazardous waste that may pose an imminent and substantial endangerment to health or the environment. Liability hinges on controlling and managing corporate operations generally, rather than on specific, active participation in tortious activities.

In the leading case, (*NEPACCO*), an officer, Lee, was found liable who was present on the site and personally arranged for the disposal.[147] Although the court spoke of "authority to control," Michaels, the president and majority shareholder, was found liable under RCRA, not under CERCLA, because he contributed to pollution. Other courts have used the *NEPACCO* case as standing for the principle that anyone with "authority to control" any other entity specified in CERCLA § 107(a) can be vicariously liable for the latter's acts.

In *State of New York v. Shore Realty Corporation,*[148] Leo Grande, the sole officer and shareholder of the corporation, was held personally liable for his individual conduct.

The courts look at whether the shareholder, officer, or employee actively participated in the management or day-to-day operations of the facility, and whether the individual had the capacity or power to control the operations or decision making. Having the power to make such decisions may be enough. The courts also examine whether the individual profited from the activity that caused the hazardous waste problem. Sharing corporate profits may satisfy this requirement.

In *Michigan v. ARCO Industries, Inc.,*[149] the court outlined criteria for determining individual liability. They included: distribution of power within the corporation, scope of the individual's authority, personal percentage of corporate ownership, evidence of responsibility for hazardous waste disposal, and any affirmative attempts made to prevent pollution. The judge stated that he was not in favor of imposing personal liability on defendants solely because of their corporate positions.[150]

Shareholder owner and operator liability differs from generator or transporter liability because of the security interest exception, which specifically limits the definition of "owner or operator" to those who participate in management or hold more than mere "indicia of ownership primarily to protect [a] security interest."[151] There is also the innocent purchaser defense, which exempts owners who do not in any way cause or contribute to a hazardous waste release.

---

[147] *Id.*

[148] 759 F.2d 1032 (2d Cir. 1985).

[149] 723 F. Supp. 1214 (W.D. Mich., 1989); 721 F. Supp. 873 (W.D. Mich. 1989). *See also* Kelly v. Thomas Solvent Co., 727 F. Supp. 1554 (W.D. Mich 1989); 1990 U.S. Dist. LEXIS 12585 (W.D. Mich. 1990).

[150] Michigan v. ARCO Industries, Inc., 723 F. Supp. at 1216.

[151] 42 U.S.C.A. § 9601(20(A).

Shareholders are not liable as generators or transporters unless they transport or arrange for the transportation of hazardous waste.[152] If the shareholder is an officer, director, or key employee and supervises or has the responsibility to supervise the disposal or transportation of hazardous wastes, then the shareholder may also be liable under CERCLA.

Directors or officers, however, can be liable if they arrange for transportation of hazardous waste or improperly manage the hazardous waste site, even though they may not directly arrange for waste disposal or actually manage the site. Directors are held to a duty of care; shareholders are not.[153]

A corporate officer-shareholder of the purchaser and the purchasing corporation were found liable for the cleanup of a disposal site contaminated by PCBs, benzene, and other chemicals, despite the fact that the purchaser had knowledge of the contamination and had been advised of the cleanup costs.[154]

In most of the CERCLA cases in which shareholders were found liable, the corporations were small, closely held corporations with few directors.[155]

In *United States v. Mottolo,* the district court granted the government's motion for summary judgment, finding that, among other parties, Richard Mottolo, the sole shareholder of the company that operated the facility, was liable as both an owner and an operator under CERCLA.[156] In 1964, Mottolo had purchased the property on which the dumpsite was located. In 1973, he purchased a company that, from 1975 onward, hauled hazardous waste and disposed of it on the Mottolo property under Mottolo's sole proprietorship. In 1980, Mottolo incorporated the company for the admitted purpose of avoiding personal liability for the company's hazardous waste operations.[157]

The court found Mottolo personally liable under CERCLA, basing its decision on at least three distinct theories. First, Mottolo was liable as the owner of the property at the time of the hazardous waste disposal activities

---

[152] NEPACCO, *supra* note 146.

[153] Henn and Alexander, *supra* note 142, at 547, 622.

[154] NEPACCO, *supra* note 146.

[155] NEPACCO, *supra* note 146, at 848–49 (president was the only director); State of New York v. Shore Realty Corp., 759 F.2d 1032 (2d Cir. 1985) (defendant was the sole shareholder and director of Shore); United States v. Mottolo, 605 F. Supp. 898 (D.N.H. 1985) (sole director); United States v. Mirabile, 15 Envtl. L. Rep. (Envtl. L. Inst.) 20,992 (E.D. Pa. 1985) (shareholder is also sole director); United States v. Conservation Chem. Co., 619 F. Supp. 162 (W.D. Mo. 1985) (three shareholder/directors); United States v. Ward, 618 F. Supp. 884 (D.N.C. 1985) (Ward and son joint directors).

[156] 695 F. Supp. 615 (D.N.H. 1988).

[157] *Id.* at 624.

at issue.[158] Second, Mottolo was liable as an operator because he had been the sole proprietor of the company at the time of the hazardous waste disposal activities and, "whereas the owner of a sole proprietorship is personally liable for tort liabilities incurred by the proprietorship, . . . Mottolo is also liable as a site operator in his capacity as owner of [the Company]."[159] Finally, Mottolo was liable as a transporter, because he had personally driven truckloads of waste to the site, and possibly also as a generator under § 107(a)(3).[160]

Thus, the court did not apply to the postincorporation activities of Mottolo the sort of control test that the court in *Shore Realty* applied to the activities of Leo Grande. The court was able to reach the same result by looking at Mottolo's preincorporation relationship with his company and applying the common-law rule that attributes such control to sole proprietors. It appears likely from the way the court presented the facts that, had the company been incorporated from the outset, the court would still have imposed operator liability on Mottolo.

Thus, as in the parent corporation context, the test for operator liability for individual shareholders appears to turn on the level of control of operations at the facility. With closely held corporations, this analysis boils down to whether the individual in question was "in charge" of the facility.[161] In most such cases, the individual was directly and personally involved in the hazardous waste operations at the facility, and this conclusion is not difficult to reach. There is no need to weigh numerous factors that are only marginally related to hazardous waste activities, such as accounting and fiscal relationships, as is done in the analysis of parent corporations. The tests for liability of parent corporations and for liability of individual majority stockholders seem very similar.

When a corporation sells or transfers substantially all of its assets, it may liquidate and dissolve itself by paying all of its creditors and distributing the remaining assets to the shareholders. However, because claims for environmental liability may not become apparent until after liquidation or dissolution, shareholders may still be subject to lawsuits following dissolution of the corporation. This possibility is discussed in § 5.15.

One theory that can be asserted against the corporation, its shareholders, and its directors, is the common-law "trust fund" theory, which states that the assets distributed to the shareholders are deemed to be a trust fund against corporate creditors have a priority claim; however, the claim is limited to the amount of the assets distributed to the shareholder. Directors

---

[158] *Id.* at 623.

[159] *Id.*

[160] *Id.* at 624.

[161] State of New York v. Shore Realty Corp., 759 F.2d at 1052.

may also have a fiduciary duty to creditors and may be personally liable for the entire amount of the distribution.

§ 5.15   —Corporate Dissolution

There is a long history of corporations being able to end their existence through dissolution. At common law, creditors could not recover any debts or obligations owed to them by dissolved corporations. As a result, the "trust fund" theory was developed. This theory recognized the rights of creditors by providing that the assets of a corporation, even though they were distributed to the shareholders upon dissolution, were subject to an equitable charge and were held "in trust" for the benefit of creditors.[162] A shareholder could be held individually liable for corporate debts, but liability was limited to the amount of assets received,[163] although they could then seek contribution from other shareholders.

Many courts have held, however, that survival statutes replace the trust fund theory, precluding recovery from shareholders at the end of the winding-up period as well as from the undistributed assets of the corporation.[164]

To ensure the protection of the rights of creditors, all state legislatures have enacted "survival statutes" that continue the life of the corporation for specified purposes after dissolution.[165] States vary in the length of time during which a corporation may be sued following dissolution. Usually, the time allowance is two to five years, but in some states it extends indefinitely.[166]

Many states use an approach similar to that of the Model Business Corporation Act.[167] Under the Model Act, a person may assert a claim against

---

[162] Mumma v. The Potomac Co., 33 U.S. (8 Pet.) 281 (1834); Curran v. State of Arkansas, 56 U.S. (15 How.) 304, 311 (1853).

[163] Henn and Alexander, *supra* note 142, at 881.

[164] *See, e.g.,* Reconstruction Finance Corp. v. Teter, 117 F.2d 716, 726–27 (7th Cir.), *cert. denied,* 314 U.S. 620 (1941); Hunter v. Fort Worth Capital Corp., 620 S.W.2d 547, 550–51 (Tex. 1981); Blankenship v. Demmler Mfg. Co., 89 Ill. App. 3d 569, 572–74, 411 N.E.2d 1153, 1155–57 (1980); *see also* Gonzales v. Progressive Tool & Die Co., 455 F. Supp. 363, 367–69 (E.D.N.Y. 1978). *But see* Green v. Oilwell, Div. of U.S. Steel Corp., 767 P.2d 1348, 1353–54 (Okla. 1989) (Oklahoma Supreme Court allowed equitable trust fund theory to permit plaintiff to recover from shareholders for a postdissolution claim).

[165] 16 Fletcher, The Law of Private Corporations § 8224 (rev. 1979).

[166] California, Michigan, and New Jersey place no express time limit on the survival of remedies.

[167] Model Bus. Corp. Act § 105 (1971). *See also* Revised Model Business Corporation Act § 14.05 (Supp. 1986).

the corporation within two years after dissolution for any right or claim existing, or any liability incurred prior to such dissolution.[168] The corporate entity is required to continue for an additional period of time so that actions that have not expired by the date of dissolution may be brought.[169]

The corporate dissolution statutes in many states are patterned substantially after § 105 of the Model Business Corporation Act. The relevant portion of the Model Act provides in part:

> The dissolution of a corporation . . . shall not take away or impair any remedy available to or against such corporation, its directors, officers, or shareholders, for any right or claim existing, or any liability incurred, prior to such dissolution if action or other proceeding thereon is commenced within two years after the date of such dissolution.[170]

Some state statutes do not require that claims asserted in the postdissolution period must have accrued before dissolution.[171] In Ohio, upon dissolution, a corporation shall cease to do business, except as necessary to wind up its affairs, but any claim that exists or any action or proceeding pending by or against the corporation or which would have accrued against it may be litigated to judgment.[172]

In California, a dissolved corporation continues to exist only to wind up its affairs, and former shareholders may be sued in the name of the corporation, after dissolution, upon any cause of action held against the corporation prior to dissolution.[173] In Illinois, litigation must be commenced within two years after the date of corporate dissolution.[174]

Because CERCLA applies retroactively, its cause of action applies to corporate activities that may have occurred prior to both passage of the statute and dissolution. In states where this interpretation has been adopted by the courts, corporations that dissolved prior to CERCLA's passage may be able to claim successfully that a CERCLA claim, although based on predissolution activities, arose postdissolution and is barred.

CERCLA was found not to apply to a dissolved corporation where CERCLA was enacted nine years after the dissolution, even though CERCLA is retroactive. The case involved the California dissolution

---

[168] *Id., see* Anderson, *Note—Corporate Life After Death, CERCLA Preemption of State Corporate Dissolution Law,* 88 Mich. L. Rev. 131 (October 1989).

[169] *Id.* § 105 (1971).

[170] *Id.*

[171] Del. Code Ann. tit. 8, § 278; Mass. Gen. Laws Ann., C. 156 B, § 102.

[172] Ohio Rev. Code. Ann. § 1701.88.

[173] Cal. Corp. Code §§ 2010(a) and 2011.

[174] Ill. Rev. Stat. ch. 32, § 157.94 (1977).

statute and the cause of action arose after dissolution.[175] CERCLA was not found to preempt California law determining capacity to be sued.[176]

Because of variations in state winding-up periods, dissolved corporations in some states may remain liable under CERCLA. Corporations in states that have shorter winding-up periods, or have a bar on postdissolution claims, may escape liability based on factors unrelated to their culpability under the statute.

In *NEPACCO,* the defendant corporation was found not dead but "in a state of coma," because it had failed to file a certificate of voluntary dissolution with the state.[177] In another case, a dissolved PCB manufacturer was revived under Massachusetts law to resolve a dispute over the sale of its assets, one month short of the expiration of Massachusetts' three-year winding-up period.[178] In a Virginia case, a corporate defendant, which had dissolved in 1985, could be sued under CERCLA. Virginia maintains unending liability for predissolution claims.[179]

Federal Rule of Civil Procedure 17(b) directs a federal court to apply state corporate law to determine whether a dissolved corporation has the capacity to be sued. Because many state dissolution laws allow a corporation to end its existence (and thus its capacity to be sued) within two years after dissolution, some plaintiffs with otherwise valid claims against dissolved corporations may not be compensated.

§ 5.16 Successors-in-Interest

This group may include lenders, corporations, buyers, developers, lessees, and sublessors. Courts seem to have rejected attempts to expand traditional common-law liability against successor corporations. Under traditional corporate successor liability principles, the purchaser of a corporation's assets does not assume the debts and liabilities of the seller. However, where a sale of stock or a corporate merger occurs, there is usually liability.[180] The corporate entity remains intact and retains its liabilities, despite the change of ownership. The corporation survives as an entity separate and distinct from its shareholders, even if all the stock is purchased by another corporation.[181]

---

[175] Levin Metals Corp. v. Parr-Richmond Terminal Co., 817 F.2d 1448 (9th Cir. 1987).

[176] *Id.* at 1451.

[177] NEPACCO, *supra* note 146, 810 F.2d at 746.

[178] *In re* Acushnet River & New Bedford Harbor Proceedings, 712 F. Supp. 1010 (D. Mass. 1989).

[179] United States v. Moore, 27 Env't Rep. Cas. (BNA) 1976 (E.D. Va. 1988).

[180] Smith Land & Improvement Corp. v. Celotex Corp., 851 F.2d 86 (3d Cir. 1988), *cert. denied,* 109 S. Ct. 837, 102 L. Ed. 2d 969 (1989).

[181] *Id.* 851 F.2d at 91.

Where there is a purchase of assets, there is no liability unless:

1. Liability is expressly or impliedly assumed by the purchaser;[182]
2. There is a *de facto* (i.e. nonstatutory) merger or consolidation of the corporations;[183]
3. The purchaser is merely a continuation of the selling corporation;[184]
4. There is a fraudulent transfer to escape liability.[185]

The rationales for this policy include: the protection of minority shareholders and creditors, the proper assessment of taxes, and the promotion of alienability of corporate assets.[186]

In determining whether a transaction constitutes a *de facto* merger or consolidation exposing the successor to liability, the courts generally consider the following factors:

1. Is there a continuation of the enterprise of the seller corporation (i.e., through a continuity of management, other personnel, physical location, assets, and general business operations)?
2. Is there a continuity of shareholders because the purchasing corporation pays for the acquired assets with shares of its own stock? Because this stock ultimately will be held by the shareholders of the seller corporation, they become a constituent part of the purchasing corporation.
3. Is the seller corporation ceasing its ordinary business operations, liquidating, and dissolving as soon as legally and practically possible?
4. Is the purchasing corporation assuming those liabilities and obligations of the seller ordinarily necessary for the uninterrupted continuation of normal business operations of the seller corporation?[187]

---

[182] Southland Corp. v. Ashland Oil, Inc., 696 F. Supp. 994 (D.N.J. 1988); GRM Industries, Inc. v. Wickes Manufacturing Co., 1990 WL 168176 (W.D. Mich. 1990).

[183] *In re* Acushnet River & New Bedford Harbor Proceedings, 712 F. Supp. 1010 (D. Mass. 1989).

A *de factor* merger is a judicially created concept to protect (1) minority shareholders, (2) creditors' rights, and (3) tort victims' claims. One distinction between an asset transfer and a merger is that a merger encompasses certain rights and liabilities that generally are not included in a sale of assets when the parties are unrelated and adequate consideration is present.

[184] City of Philadelphia v. Stepan Chemical Co., 713 F. Supp. 1491 (E.D. Pa. 1989).

[185] Louisiana Pacific Corp. v. Asarco, Inc., 1989 U.S. Dist. LEXIS 12149 (W.D. Wash. 1989).

[186] Polius v. Clark Equipment Co., 802 F.2d 75, 78 (3d Cir. 1986).

[187] Bud Antle, Inc. v. Eastern Foods, Inc., 758 F.2d 1451, 1457–58 (11th Cir. 1985); *accord,* Philadelphia Electric Co. v. Hercules, Inc., 762 F.2d 303, 311 (3d Cir. 1985), *cert. denied,* 474 U.S. 980 (1985).

Other factors a court may consider in the determination of a *de facto* merger include:

1. Established insubstantiality of continued existence;
2. Brevity of the continuance;
3. Contractual requirements for dissolution;
4. Prohibition of further normal business operations;
5. The character of the predecessor's remaining assets.

Several jurisdictions have adopted two other exceptions—the product-line rule[188] and the continuation-of-the-enterprise doctrine[189]—which broaden the scope of liability beyond the four traditional exceptions. These exceptions are used mostly in products liability cases, to find a successor strictly liable for injuries caused by equipment that a predecessor has manufactured.[190] One lower state court applied the product-line rule to environmental claims.[191]

Another court found it useful to examine the factors used in evaluating successor liability in the labor context. The factors include:

1. Whether the successor company had notice of the charge;
2. The ability of the predecessor to provide relief;
3. Whether there has been a substantial continuity of business operations;
4. Whether the new employer uses the same plant;
5. Whether the new employer uses the same or substantially the same work force;
6. Whether the new employer uses the same or substantially the same supervisory personnel;

---

[188] Jurisdictions that have adopted the product-line rule include the following: California (Ray v. Alad Corp., 19 Cal. 3d 22, 560 P.2d 3, 136 Cal. Rptr. 574 (1977)); New Jersey (Ramirez v. Amsted Indus., Inc., 171 N.J. Super. 261, 408 A.2d 818 (Super. Ct. App. Div. 1979), *aff'd*, 86 N.J. 332, 431 A.2d 811 (1981)); and Pennsylvania (Dawejko v. Jorgensen Steel Co., 290 Pa. Super. 15, 434 A.2d 106 (1980)). *See also* Branch-Roy, *Corporate Successor Liability for Environmental and Toxic Tort Claims—Part II,* Colo. Law., June 1990, p. 1085.

[189] Michigan has adopted the continuation of the enterprise doctrine in Turner v. Bituminous Casualty Co., 397 Mich. 406, 244 N.W.2d 873 (1976).

[190] For example, the court in Dawejko v. Jorgensen Steel Co., 434 A.2d at 107, 112, held the successor corporation liable for plaintiff's injuries caused by a defective product of the predecessor corporation under the product-line exception to the general rule.

[191] *See* Department of Transp. v. PSC Resources, Inc., 175 N.J. Super. 447, 419 A.2d 1151 (Super. Ct. Law Div. 1980) (product-line test invoked to find PSC liable as successor for water pollution attributable to the action of its predecessor).

7. Whether the same jobs exist under substantially the same working conditions;

8. Whether the same machinery, equipment, and methods of production are used;

9. Whether the same product is produced.[192]

The length of time one holds title is not important. A company that purchased a waste disposal site from the trustee-in-bankruptcy of an inactive pollution control company was found liable, even though it transferred title on the same day to several of its officers and representatives, who formed a new company.[193]

A lender was found liable for cleanup costs when it became involved in the management of a facility after it foreclosed on a loan in default, even though the lender quickly assigned its bid for the property to the actual purchasers.[194] (Lenders are discussed in detail in § 5.18.) Similarly, a bank that foreclosed to protect its security interest incurred Superfund liability.[195]

When two corporations merge pursuant to statutory provisions, the surviving company takes on the liabilities of and may use any defenses available to the old company. When there is a merger in which one corporation ceases to exist and the other continues to exist, the latter is liable for the debts of the former, to the extent of the property and assets received.[196]

When there is no statutory merger or consolidation and one company buys all of the assets of another, the successor is usually not saddled with the seller's liability except under certain conditions.[197] CERCLA does not specifically address this issue, leaving it to the courts to decide. The courts have found that the obligation to correct hazardous conditions should be imposed on a successor corporation if it is a responsible party under CERCLA.[198]

One court, in adopting a strict reading of CERCLA, looked at the four categories of PRPs in § 107(a) and found that, because successor corporations were not listed, they were beyond the scope of CERCLA's liability. The court felt that if Congress wanted successor corporations to be liable, the intent should be stated.[199] Even if the case is not appealed, it is likely to be distinguished by other courts.

---

[192] GRM Industries v. Wickes Manufacturing Co., 1990 WL 168176 (W.D. Mich. 1990).

[193] United States v. Carolawn Co., 14 Envtl. L. Rep. (Envtl. L. Inst.) 20,698, 21 Env't Rep. Cas. (BNA) 2124 (D.S.C. 1984).

[194] United States v. Mirabile, 15 Envtl. L. Rep. (Envtl. L. Inst.) 20,992 (E.D. Pa. 1985).

[195] United States v. Maryland Bank and Trust Co., 632 F. Supp. 573 (D. Md. 1986).

[196] Smith Land & Improvement Corp. v. Celotex Corp., *supra* note 180, 851 F.2d at 91.

[197] *Id.*

[198] *Id.* 851 F.2d at 92.

[199] Anspec Co. v. Johnson Control, Inc., 743 F. Supp. 793 (E.D. Mich. 1989), *appeal dismissed on procedural grounds,* 891 F.2d 289 (6th Cir. 1989).

A Michigan court, rejecting that decision as being inconsistent with the remedial purposes of CERCLA, found that successor liability under traditional concepts is consistent with principles of equity and the underlying purposes of CERCLA. To rule otherwise would allow a corporation to avoid CERCLA liability by crafting its corporate reorganization.[200] The legislative history does indicate that Congress intended the courts to consider common law in interpreting CERCLA.[201]

In reaching its decision, the Michigan court expressly rejected the Third Circuit's decision in *Smith Land & Improvement Corporation v. Celotex Corporation,*[202] which said that successor corporations were liable, as intended by Congress, and that their omission from CERCLA's list of liable parties was caused by the speed with which CERCLA was enacted.

§ 5.17 Subsidiary Corporations and Piercing the Corporate Veil

The most fundamental principle of corporate law is that a corporation is a separate entity from its shareholders. Subsidiaries, whether wholly or partially owned by a parent corporation, have a separate legal existence. As such, corporate shareholders are insulated from the liabilities of the corporation.[203] Courts are loathe to pierce the corporate veil unless there has been fraud, or some great injustice has been committed, or the corporation is being used as a means of carrying on business for personal rather than corporate ends.[204]

Under certain circumstances, the courts may pierce the corporate veil when they find that a subsidiary corporation was a "mere instrumentality of the parent corporation."[205] Few cases have considered whether this equitable remedy is available to hold a parent corporation or individual shareholder liable under CERCLA for hazardous waste releases caused by a corporation. Of these cases, fewer than half have granted the remedy.

---

[200] GRM Industries v. Wickes Manufacturing Co., 1990 WL 168176 (W.D. Mich. 1990).

[201] 126 Cong. Rec. H11,787 (daily ed. Dec. 3, 1980) (remarks of Rep. Florio).

[202] *Supra* note 180, 851 F.2d 86 (3d Cir. 1988).

[203] Lyon v. Barrett, 89 N.J. 294, 300, 445 A.2d 1153 (1982). *See Liability of Parent Corporations for Hazardous Substance Releases Under CERCLA,* 24 Aronousky and Fuller, U.S.F.L. Rev. 421 (Spring 1990).

[204] Lyon v. Barrett, 89 N.J. at 300. *See also* State of New York v. Shore Realty Corp., 759 F.2d 1032 (1985). In *Barrett,* the court did not pierce the corporate veil, but was able to hold the officer/shareholder liable for abatement of the environmental problem because a corporate officer who controls corporate conduct and is an active individual participant in that conduct is liable for the torts of the corporation.

[205] Mueller v. Seaboard Commercial Corp., 5 N.J. 28, 34–35, 73 A.2d 905 (1950).

Recently, one court urged piercing the corporate veil whenever public convenience, fairness, or necessity suggests it is appropriate, and stated that CERCLA's goal of placing responsibility on polluters should encourage courts to give less respect to corporate form than in other contexts.[206] However, even if there is corporate dominance, "liability is generally imposed only when the parent has abused the privilege of incorporation by using the subsidiary to perpetrate a fraud or injustice, or otherwise to circumvent the law."[207]

Generally, courts seem more willing to impose liability on corporate shareholders than on individual shareholders. However, *State of Idaho v. Bunker Hill Company*[208] suggests that corporate shareholders may actively participate in the management of a subsidiary and not incur liability, even though individual shareholders cannot escape liability in the same circumstances. This situation may occur when a corporation actively participates in the management of a partially or wholly owned subsidiary and the subsidiary owns or operates a hazardous waste site, arranges for the disposal of hazardous waste, or transports waste to a site.

Parent corporations may be directly liable under CERCLA for hazardous substances released by a subsidiary corporation, if upholding the corporate veil would "frustrate congressional intent."[209] Entities have been found liable as present or former owners or operators of a facility under §§ 9607(a)(1) and 9607(a)(2) of CERCLA. This liability occurred when "the parent so dominated the subsidiary that it had no separate existence but was merely a conduit for the parent."[210] The majority of these opinions also considered additional factors directly relevant to the improper hazardous waste disposal activities at issue in *Bunker Hill*. These cases are discussed later in this section.

A number of courts have extended CERCLA liability to parent corporations of wholly owned subsidiary corporations.[211] CERCLA provides that "any person who at the time of disposal of any hazardous substance owned or operated any facility at which such hazardous substances were disposed of"[212] is liable as a potentially responsible party. "Owner or operator" is

---

[206] United States v. Kayser-Roth Corp., 724 F. Supp. 15 (D.R.I. 1989), *aff'd,* 910 F.2d 24 (1st Cir. 1990).

[207] Environmental Protection Dept. v. Ventron Corp., 468 A.2d at 164.

[208] State of Idaho v. Bunker Hill Co., 635 F. Supp. 665 (D. Idaho 1986).

[209] *Id.*

[210] Environmental Protection Dept. v. Ventron Corp., 468 A.2d at 164.

[211] *See* State of New York v. Shore Realty Corp., 759 F.2d 1032 (2d Cir. 1985); United States v. Mottolo, 695 F. Supp. 615 (D.N.H. 1988); Colorado v. Idarado Mining Co., 18 Envtl. L. Rep. (Envtl. L. Inst.) 20578 (D. Colo. 1987); Vermont v. Staco, Inc., 684 F. Supp. 822 D. Vt. 1988); State of Idaho v. Bunker Hill Co., 635 F. Supp. 665 (D. Idaho 1986).

[212] 42 U.S.C. § 9607(a)(2) (1983); § 107(a)(2).

defined in the statute as "any person owning or operating such facility, and . . . in the case of any facility, title or control of which was converted due to bankruptcy, foreclosure, tax delinquency, abandonment, or similar means to a unit of State or local government, any person who owned, operated, or otherwise controlled activities at such facility immediately beforehand."[213] But the statute exempts any "person, who, without participation in the management of a . . . facility holds indicia of ownership primarily to protect his security interest in the . . . facility."[214]

Courts have made two types of findings in this area:

1. The controlling entity was significantly involved in the environmental affairs of the controlled entity such that it could have prevented the contamination at issue from occurring (or could have mitigated its effects);

2. The controlling entity exercised actual supervision or control over operations at the facility in question.

Most of the legal reasoning in decisions finding parent corporations and individual shareholders liable for hazardous waste releases under CERCLA can be traced back to the *NEPACCO* decision.[215]

The *NEPACCO* court found both Lee and Michaels liable, in their dual capacities as responsible corporate officers and major stockholders in the company, and as both owners and operators within the meaning of the statute.[216] The court adopted two arguments in support of this result. First, the court focused on the statutory language defining "owner or operator" in § 101(2)(A) of CERCLA, which includes "any person owning or operating [a] facility" but excludes "a person, who, without participating in the management of a vessel or facility, holds indicia of ownership primarily to protect his security interest in the vessel or facility." From this provision, the court concluded that "[t]he statute literally reads that a person who owns interest in a facility and is actively participating in its management can be held liable for the disposal of hazardous waste."[217]

Second, the court adopted the Eighth Circuit's reasoning in *Apex Oil Company v. United States* (a 1977 decision that interpreted the Clean Water Act) to define "owner or operator" as the person who "has the capacity to make timely discovery of oil discharges, . . . to direct the activities of per-

---

[213] 42 U.S.C. § 9601(20)(d)(ii) (1983).

[214] 42 U.S.C. § 9601(20(A) (1983).

[215] NEPACCO, 579 F. Supp. 823 (W.D. Mo. 1984), *aff'd in part and rev'd in part,* 810 F.2d 726 (8th Cir. 1986).

[216] 42 U.S.C. § 9607(a)(1).

[217] *NEPACCO, supra.,* 579 F. Supp. at 848.

sons who control the mechanisms causing pollution . . . [and] to prevent and abate damage."[218]

In another recent decision, the court in *Rockwell International Corporation v. IU International Corporation* denied a parent corporation's motion for summary judgment, finding that the parent could be found liable for the activities of a subsidiary that had operated a hazardous waste site.[219] The court adopted the *NEPACCO* district court's analysis of § 101(20)(A) of CERCLA, concluding that owner or operator liability could attach to a person possessing an ownership interest and actively participating in the management and control of the facility.[220] However, the court rejected the *NEPACCO* court's suggestion that the mere capacity to control might be sufficient, concluding that "[m]ere ability to exercise control as a result of the financial relationship of the parties is insufficient for liability to attach. The entity must actually exercise control."[221]

The *Rockwell* court found several factors present in the relationship between parent and subsidiary that indicated actual control of the subject facility and that could warrant a finding of parent liability, including the parent's involvement in the hiring of certain officers of the subsidiary and in the determination of the responsibilities of those officers. The court did not make explicit findings as to the parent's control of the financial affairs of the subsidiary. Rather, focusing on the parent's control of the subsidiary's environmental affairs, it found that the parent approved and monitored compliance with the operational plans of the facility, and that parent company auditors reviewed requests by the subsidiary for purchases of environmental protection equipment and suggested procedural changes that "directly affected the disposal of hazardous substances."[222]

In *Kayser-Roth*,[223] the parent exerted "practical total influence" and control over Stamina Mills' operations, and the court pierced the corporate veil between the parent and subsidiary. The parent made virtually all operational decisions, including those with respect to budgets, fiscal operations, collections of accounts receivable, and executive compensation. Another factor stressed by the court was that Kayser-Roth had directed Stamina to send its legal department notices of any correspondence with governmental agencies concerning environmental matters.

Unlike the Fifth Circuit in the *Joslyn Manufacturing* case, discussed later, the court explained that CERCLA's provisions should be viewed

---

[218] *Id.*

[219] 702 F. Supp. 1384 (N.D. Ill. 1988).

[220] *Id.* at 1390.

[221] *Id.*

[222] *Id.* at 1391.

[223] United States v. Kayser-Roth Corp., 724 F. Supp. 15 (D.R.I. 1989), *aff'd,* 910 F.2d 24 (1st Cir. 1990). Compare with note 230 *infra* and related text discussion.

expansively, so as not to frustrate Congress's purpose in enacting legislation designed to have those responsible for problems caused by the disposal of chemical poisons bear the costs and responsibility for remedying the harmful conditions they had created. The court concluded that CERCLA places no special importance on corporate structure and that the parent company was, in essence, an owner for CERCLA purposes.

Courts may look at such factors as the capitalization at the time of incorporation, whether the subsidiary was created solely for the purpose of acquiring a property containing hazardous substances, and whether the parent company's personnel, officers, and directors were involved in the day-to-day business of the subsidiary.[224] Courts will also examine whether the parent: was familiar with the disposal practices of the subsidiary, could

---

[224] One writer suggests 23 factors courts might consider.
1. Stock ownership.
2. Reliance on parent financing.
3. Overlapping officers, directors.
4. Separate meetings of officers, shareholders.
5. Commonality of businesses (customers, products, facilities, etc.).
6. Favorability of intercompany contracts.
7. Separate books and records.
8. Extent of management influence.
9. Involvement of parent officer in the alleged tort.
10. Type of business of each.
11. Public's perception of separateness.
12. Perception of injured party as to who promisor was.
13. Awareness by the parent of the problem, and parent's ability to control the subsidiary.
14. Parent's influence over promotion, hiring, etc.
15. Observance of basic corporate formalities.
16. Common usage of financial, professional services.
17. Company's public posture . . . a single company?
18. Premature withdrawals by parent (fraudulent conveyance).
19. Severability of subsidiaries.
20. Public policy interest.
21. Who can afford the lawsuit?
22. Lack of apparent business purpose.
23. Materiality of sub[sidiary] to parent.

Hofstedt, *A Framework for Assessing the Parent/Subsidiary Relationship, in Responsibility of the Corporate Parent for Activities of a Subsidiary,* 520 Corp. L. & Prac. 179, 187 (1986). Although this list is not specific to CERCLA actions, it does supply a framework of factors courts may consider in assessing CERCLA liability. However, the list is overlapping and is not comprehensive.

have controlled or prevented the damage, and received profits from the waste-producing activity.[225]

Although state courts follow the traditional approach even in environmental cases and generally protect shareholder status, federal courts are more inclined to pierce the corporate veil to implement environmental policies.[226] One court pierced the corporate veil and concluded that "the Legislature intended that the privilege of incorporation should not, . . . become a device for avoiding statutory liability. A contrary result would permit corporations, merely by creating wholly-owned subsidiaries, to pollute for profit under circumstances when the Legislature intended liability to be imposed."[227]

Courts have used the following criteria for determining a corporation's "corporateness":

1. Business must be conducted on a corporate and not a personal basis; corporate formalities must be observed, including corporate minutes.
2. The enterprise must be established on an adequate financial basis.[228]
3. Separate bank accounts and records must be maintained.
4. Intercorporate loans and other financial transactions will be scrutinized.
5. Subsidiaries should handle their own hiring and firing, sales, planning, scheduling, and operating procedures.
6. The type and frequency of reports required by the parent will be examined.
7. Intercompany pricing may be a factor.
8. Business dealings between subsidiary and parent must be at arm's-length.

A corporation is not liable for the acts of its subsidiary *merely* because it is wholly owned, has the same officers, and is financed by the parent.[229]

However, in one recent case, a court declined to find the parent liable for the subsidiary. The court found that parent companies of offending, wholly owned subsidiaries were not "owners" or "operators" under CERCLA's

---

[225] State of Idaho v. Bunker Hill Co., 635 F. Supp. 665 (D. Idaho 1986).

[226] United States v. Ira Bushey & Sons, Inc., 363 F. Supp. 110 (D.C. Vt. 1973), *aff'd,* 487 F.2d 1393 (2d Cir. 1973), *cert. denied,* 417 U.S. 976 (1974).

[227] *Id.* 363 F. Supp. at 119.

[228] Bischofshausen, Vasbinder and Luckie v. D.W. Jaquays Mining and Equipment Contractors Co., 145 Ariz. 204, 700 P.2d 902 (1985).

[229] *Id.*

definition of "owner or operator."[230] The court stated that if Congress wanted to extend liability to parent corporations, it could do so. As of this writing, this is the only case to hold that, as a matter of law, parent corporations and corporate officers cannot be held liable as owners or operators under CERCLA § 9601(20).

Congress could have broadly defined "owner or operator" to include any person who otherwise controlled activities at such a facility, as it is defined in CERCLA § 9601(20)(A)(iii). However, absent the "or otherwise controlled" language in subsection (ii), the subsection at issue in the case, the court would not imply an intent to impose on parent corporations direct liability for the acts of their subsidiaries.

The court also found that the facts did not support piercing the corporate veil. Looking to the legislative history, the court concluded that there was no indication that Congress intended to alter this basic legal tenet.[231] The court also evaluated factors such as: separate bookkeeping; frequent shareholders' and directors' meetings; separate daily operations; separate property and tax returns; and separate bills and employee benefits.[232]

The type of "control" required to find liability must amount to "total domination of the subservient corporation, to the extent that the subservient corporation manifests no separate corporate interests of its own and functions solely to achieve the purposes of the dominant corporation."[233] Piercing the veil should be limited to situations in which the corporate entity is used as a means to perpetuate fraud or avoid personal liability, and the court did not find either of those situations.

In *State of Idaho v. Bunker Hill Company,* the court, in holding a parent liable for the toxic discharge of a subsidiary, adopted the following standard:

> The owner-operator . . . has the capacity to make timely discovery of oil discharges. The owner-operator has power to direct the activities of persons who control the mechanisms causing the pollution. The owner-operator has the capacity to prevent and abate damage. . . . A more restrictive interpretation would frustrate congressional purpose by exempting from the operation of the Act a large class of persons who are uniquely qualified to assume the burden imposed by it.[234]

A parent corporation may elect to avoid direct CERCLA liability for the waste disposal practices of its subsidiary by attempting to distance itself from the subsidiary. To do so, the parent must both relinquish the reins of

---

[230] Josyln Manufacturing Co. v. T.L. James & Co., 893 F.2d 80, 30 Env't Rep. Cas. (BNA) 1929 (5th Cir. 1990), *reh'g denied,* 1990 U.S. App. LEXIS 6373 (5th Cir. 1990).
[231] *Id.*
[232] *Id.*
[233] *Id.*
[234] 635 F. Supp. at 672.

active control over the daily affairs of the subsidiary and ensure that the structure of the subsidiary will withstand efforts to pierce the corporate veil. The subsidiary, therefore, must be fully capitalized, strictly adhere to an independent corporate form as reflected in state law alter-ego decisions, maintain independent officers and directors, resolve hazardous substance questions without involvement from the parent, and make expenditures relating to hazardous substances without prior parent approval. In addition, the subsidiary must have a legitimate, independent purpose other than shielding the parent from CERCLA liability. Such an approach, however, remains risky regarding potential liability for the parent (and individual controlling shareholder), even assuming that the parent/shareholder receives adequate assurance that the subsidiary has adopted proper hazardous substance and waste disposal procedures.

§ 5.18 Lenders

The CERCLA statute exempts from liability as an owner or operator a person who "without participating in the management of a . . . facility holds indicia of ownership primarily to protect his security interest in the . . . facility."[235] Thus, lenders must be on guard against becoming involved in the management of a facility. They may provide financial assistance in general, and management advice in isolated instances, but if they participate in day-to-day management of the business or facility either before or after the business ceases operations, they may risk incurring CERCLA liability.[236]

A common situation in which lenders may incur CERCLA liability is upon the foreclosure of their mortgage loans. Actual liability will depend up their degree of involvement. The line between acts that constitute "management" and those that constitute "protecting an interest" is not always clear, and varies depending on the court hearing the case.

In *United States v. Mirabile,*[237] two lenders were granted summary judgment because there was no evidence of control of the business by the lenders. One lender had assigned its successful bid at foreclosure to another party. The critical degree of involvement for finding liability is participation in day-to-day operational, production, or waste disposal activities.

Mere financial ability to control waste disposal practices is not sufficient to impose liability.[238] A third lender in this lawsuit, Mellon Bank (East) National Association, was not granted summary judgment because, in addition to providing financial advice, a loan officer visited the site at least

---

[235] 42 U.S.C. § 9607(a)(1).

[236] *Id.*

[237] 15 Envtl. L. Rep. (Envtl. L. Inst.) 20,992 (E.D. Pa. 1985).

[238] *Id.* at 20,995.

once a week, determined the priority in which orders were filled, and insisted on certain manufacturing changes and reassignment of personnel.

The same reasoning was used in *United States v. Nicolet, Inc.,*[239] where the court stated that, before CERCLA liability could be imposed, there would have to be a showing of management and control over the day-to-day operations of the site, including manufacturing and personnel.

A secured creditor in another case was liable for cleanup costs, after the creditor foreclosed on a CERCLA site and then retained its full ownership interest for four years.[240]

In a case of first impression in the federal appellate courts, a lender was alleged to be an "operator" because it had prevented a borrower from disposing of toxic materials, in order to preserve its security.[241] The court found that, because Fleet's involvement as a secured creditor in the financial management of its borrower's facility was broad enough to support an inference that it could, if it so chose, affect hazardous waste disposal decisions, CERCLA liability would be imposed.[242] The court felt that the borrower could have obtained bankruptcy court approval to sell the hazardous materials.

The court stated that liability for cleanup costs would be imposed on a lender that participates in the financial management of a facility "to a degree indicating a capacity to influence the corporation's treatment of hazardous waste."[243] This finding is significant because the *ability* of the lender to affect hazardous waste disposal decisions may create liability, whether or not the lender actually makes those kinds of decisions.[244] In addition, the court found that the secured creditor's intention to merely protect its security interest in the equipment at the facility was immaterial. The actual nature and extent of the creditor's involvement had to be considered in determining the lender's liability.[245]

This case may have major implications for lenders as well as borrowers, because the lender appears to have acted as any prudent lender might in

---

[239] 712 F. Supp. 1193 (E.D. Pa. 1989).

[240] United States v. Maryland Bank & Trust Co., 632 F. Supp. 573 (D. Md. 1986).

[241] United States v. Fleet Factors Corp., 724 F. Supp. 955 (S.D. Ga. 1988), 901 F.2d 1550, *reh'g denied, en banc,* 911 F.2d 742 (11th Cir. 1990); Bergsoe Metal Corp. v. East Asiatic Co., 910 F.2d 668, 672 (9th Cir. 1990) (the court distinguished *Fleet Factors* conclusion that the mere capacity to influence management or operations is sufficient to trigger CERCLA liability). They looked at what the lender actually did, not what rights he had.

[242] United States v. Fleet Factors Corp., 901 F.2d at 1558.

[243] *Id.* at 1557.

[244] It should be noted that the lender did actually make certain decisions concerning the hazardous waste disposal at the facility, and liability against the lender could have been found on that ground alone.

[245] United States v. Fleet Factors Corp., 901 F.2d at 1560.

similar circumstances. It agreed to advance money in exchange for accounts receivable. It obtained a security interest in the company's textile facility, equipment, inventory, and fixtures. When the company filed for bankruptcy, the factoring agreement continued with the approval of the bankruptcy court. Before the foreclosure, Fleet's involvement with the company increased. It established prices for excess inventory, laid off employees, supervised the office administrator, and controlled access to the facility. After foreclosure and the removal of the machinery and equipment, the EPA inspected and found 700 drums of toxic chemicals and 44 truckloads of material containing asbestos.

However, the court said that nothing in its decision should preclude a secured creditor from simply monitoring any aspect of a debtor's business. It also said that a secured creditor can become involved in "occasional and discreet" financial decisions relating to the protection of its security interest without incurring liability.[246] The lender has filed a petition for certiorari with the United States Supreme Court and the present decision may yet be modified or reversed.

The lender's dilemma is that, if they negotiate stringent controls to secure their loans and if they have the right to affect hazardous waste disposal decisions when the loans are in jeopardy, they may be liable for environmental cleanup costs. If they do not have these controls, their loans are not adequately protected.

If a lender is found liable, it may be liable under CERCLA for the entire cleanup costs, even if the cost exceeds the amount of the lender's loan. Lenders must be extremely cautious in how they handle bad loans, even in situations where CERCLA does not apply.

In another case, individual property owners sued lending institutions, residential developers, construction companies, real estate agents, and agencies for environmental cleanup costs for creosote contamination.[247] The cleanup required the demolition of six homes and was apparently caused by the prior owner of the property, who had abandoned the site. The defendants' motions to dismiss were unsuccessful.

Lenders may have a duty to disclose known hazards to buyers. A construction lender who had ostensibly gained knowledge of the presence of asbestos from the original mortgagor was charged with fraudulent concealment for not disclosing the presence of asbestos when it sold the building.[248]

Two bills currently before Congress (House Bill 4494, introduced by Rep. LaFalce, and Senate Bill 2827, introduced by Sen. Garn) may, if

---

[246] *Id.* at 1558.

[247] Tanglewood East Homeowners v. Charles Thomas, Inc., 849 F.2d 1568 (5th Cir. 1988).

[248] La Placita Partners v. Northwestern Mutual Life Ins., et al., No. C88-2824 (N.D. Ohio Aug. 1, 1988). *See also* Bank Western Federal Savings Bank v. Western Office Partners Ltd., No. 86CV13417, slip op. (D.C. Denver Feb. 1989).

passed, reverse the effect of the *Fleet Factors* decision. The House Bill expands the secured creditor exemption significantly and defines many actions lenders can take without losing their exemption. The Senate Bill also expands the exemption, but would allow liability to be imposed if a lender caused the release or threatened release of a hazardous substance or, with actual knowledge, failed to take reasonable action to avoid the release.

Additional legislation or amendments to the House or Senate bills may soon be introduced for the purpose of restating a blanket exemption for secured lenders and further defining the action that will be considered "participation in management." Lenders hope that this legislation will alleviate the uncertainty that has been created by the *Fleet Factors* decision.

The EPA has indicated some opposition to these legislative efforts and is promoting as an alternative an interpretative rule that would establish a "safe harbor" or clear guidelines allowing a lender to foreclose and engage in traditional workout activities without incurring CERCLA liability, provided that the lender acts responsibly with regard to the property and does not contribute to contamination itself.[249]

Under the proposed EPA rule, the interpretation of "innocent landowner" and "secured creditor" may protect a lender from incurring Superfund liability, if it acts in an environmentally responsible manner by requiring environmental audits of collateral prior to making loans. This interpretation more clearly allows most lenders to foreclose on property or conduct loan workouts without triggering Superfund liability.

The rule also directs a lender to exercise "reasonable behavior" when it initially makes loans and, upon foreclosure, when it discovers contamination. The rule states, however, that a private lender is not to profit from the sale of property that has been cleaned up at taxpayer expense.

The Ninth Circuit recently distinguished *Fleet Factors,* declined to adopt its expansive holding, and appeared to reject the *Fleet Factors* conclusion that the mere capacity to influence management or operations is sufficient to trigger CERCLA liability.[250] The court did not focus on what rights the lender had, but on what the lender did. Until the decision is reversed by the Supreme Court or legislation, *Fleet Factors* poses serious problems and risks for lending institutions.

§ 5.19 Appraisers

Appraisers, as well as consultants who advise on the purchase of property, who fail to take contamination into account and make no mention of

---

[249] *EPA Says New Lender Rule Will Be Written to Clarify Activity Triggering Superfund Law,* 5 Toxics L. Rptr. (BNA) 353 (Aug. 8, 1990).

[250] Bergsoe Metal Corp. v. East Asiatic Co., 910 F.2d 668, 672 (9th Cir. 1990).

cleanup costs for hazardous substances, may incur liability if the true value of the property turns out to be less than they had indicated. They can be liable to any party who may be statutorily liable for cleanup costs, to lenders, and also at common law. While the potential for litigation exists, but there are no reported cases in this area.

§ 5.20 Property Managers

Property managers can conceivably incur liability for environmental issues in a number of ways. They may have sole knowledge about hazardous substances in a building, or their management and maintenance of a particular building may create a problem or exacerbate one. For example, a property manager may instruct certified or uncertified building staff to remove asbestos, thus causing further contamination. A poorly maintained HVAC system, improper use of hazardous chemicals or pooling water can result in sick building syndrome.

Property managers are well-advised to obtain indemnification and disclaimers from the landlord or building owner in their management agreements, warranting that all hazards have been identified, and to assign responsibility for dealing with the hazards to qualified companies. If outside companies are hired by a property manager to maintain HVAC systems, for example, then those companies should agree to indemnify the property manager and building owner against any claims that may result. A building manager cannot be relieved of responsibility for personal negligence and omissions.

§ 5.21 Employers

State workers' compensation laws are generally the exclusive remedy of employees against employers for injury or death arising out of and in the course of their employment. However, environmentally related injuries often seem to fall into exceptions to this rule, especially when intentional conduct has been alleged. In addition, if building staff are employed directly by a management firm, there is no workers' compensation bar.

To avoid the workers' compensation bar, an employee may only need to prove that the employer intended to expose the employee to a dangerous substance, not that there was an intent to harm the employee. Employees have been allowed in some states to bypass that restriction, when the aggravation of a disease is allegedly due to the employer's fraudulent concealment of the condition and its cause.[251]

---

[251] Johns-Manville Products Corporation v. Contra Costa Superior Court, 612 P.2d 948 (Cal. 1980).

A Florida court held that an employee could bring a cause of action in tort against an employer, if the employer's actions exhibit a deliberate intent to injure or if the employer engages in conduct that is substantially certain to result in injury or death.[252]

In a California case, the court allowed the plaintiff to assert a claim for intentional infliction of emotional distress where a class of employees was exposed to toxic substances in the manufacturing process.[253] Such alleged conduct may also subject an employer to punitive damages, which can only be recovered in an action at law.[254]

Not all state courts allow such exceptions to be read into their workers' compensation laws. In *Kofron v. Amoco Chemicals Corporation*,[255] the court read Delaware's state statute narrowly, making it exclusive of all other rights and remedies. The court felt that if such a change were to come about, it would have to come from the legislature.

An employer may also fall outside of the workers' compensation laws by acting in a dual capacity, as employer and building owner. The employer could be sued for negligence as a building owner. OSHA standards may require building owners who are also employers to inspect their buildings for ACM, to determine whether there is occupational exposure to it.

In Michigan, for example, nonmanufacturing employers must comply with the state's Right-To-Know-Act, which provides for disclosure to employees of the existence of ACM. The Act requires informing and training of employees who in the normal course of business or in emergencies would be exposed to ACM.[256]

A Michigan case held that an employer is liable for exposing an employee to a known risk that is substantially certain to result in injury to an employee.[257]

Interpretations of workers' compensation laws are being expanded by courts so that employees with hazardous substance claims may in some instances pursue their employers directly.[258] However, this is not always the case,[259] leaving the possibility that these employees may attempt to sue building owners who are not also their employers.

---

[252] Cunningham et al. v. Anchor Hocking Corp., 558 So. 2d 93, *review denied,* 574 So. 2d 139 (Fla. 1990) (1990 Fla. LEXIS 1486).

[253] Barth v. Firestone Tire and Rubber Company, 661 F. Supp. 193 (N.D. Cal. 1987).

[254] *Id.* at 204.

[255] 441 A.2d 226 (Del. 1982), *aff'd sub nom.* Mergenthaler v. Asbestos Corp. of America, 480 A.2d 647 (Del. Sup. 1984).

[256] Mich. Comp. Laws § 408.1014 a(6)(a).

[257] Beauchamp v. Dow Chemical Co., 427 Mich. 1 (1986).

[258] Johns-Manville Products Corp. v. Contra Costa Superior Court, 612 P.2d 948 (Cal. 1980).

[259] Kofron v. Amoco Chemicals Corp., *supra* note 252.

In cities that have nonsmoking laws, an employee might be able to obtain an injunction against an employer to prevent other employees from smoking on the job.

§ 5.22   Employees

A corporate employee is ordinarily not liable individually for actions in the course of employment. However, it is not a defense to an environmental tort or a statutory violation to state that the act was committed while working for the corporation. A corporate employee who illegally dumps hazardous waste can be personally liable for penalties and damages.

Any person "in charge" of a facility can be convicted of failing to report a release of a prohibited amount of hazardous substances to the appropriate federal agency, no matter how low in rank that person is within the company.[260] This rule extends to any person who is responsible for the operation of a facility from which there is a release.[261]

A civilian supervisor of maintenance at Fort Drum was found liable for directing a work crew to dispose of waste cans of paint in an improper manner and for failing to report it.[262] There were also charges under RCRA § 6928(d)(2)(A) and the Clean Water Act.

CERCLA also contains "whistleblowers" protection for employees who are fired for exposing environmental abuses.[263] A person who violates the statute by countermanding a reinstatement order can be required to pay reasonable litigation costs and expenses, including attorney fees.[264]

§ 5.23   Contractors

Removal and abatement contractors face many of the same liability risks as do other types of contractors, but with more financial risk than is usual on smaller projects. If, in the course of their work, they damage property of the tenants in adjacent areas or in the floors below, they may have to pay damages or replace the furniture or equipment. Damages may include contamination from whatever substance is being removed, as well as business interruption. A contractor may face liability to a building owner for business

---

[260] 42 U.S.C. § 9603.

[261] Apex Oil Co. v. United States, 530 F.2d 1291, 1294 (8th Cir.), *cert. denied,* 429 U.S. 827, 97 S. Ct. 84 (1976).

[262] United States v. Carr, 880 F.2d 1550 (2d Cir. 1989).

[263] 42 U.S.C. § 9610.

[264] 42 U.S.C. § 9610(c).

interruption, lost rent, delays, and liquidated damages. There may also be personal injury claims.

Liability may arise when a removal contractor is hired to do some remedial action in a commercial building and the work causes the hazardous substances—for example, asbestos dust—to contaminate other tenants' offices, or areas that were previously decontaminated. The same situation can occur in a home, if an area is to be abated and fibers are spread to clean areas.

Federal remedial action contractors receive some protection under SARA, through federal indemnification; however, there may still be instances in which a removal contractor may become a party to a lawsuit.[265] There may be disagreement over the applicability of the statute, which exempts from coverage any gross negligence or intentional misconduct. If either of those actions is alleged, there may be a problem.

Regular general contractors and subcontractors can become involved in environmental lawsuits through claims that electrical or other building systems they installed were done improperly and permitted the release and venting of toxic substances into the building (especially during a fire), or that work they did caused negligent disturbance of asbestos.[266]

In a case of first impression, the Manhattan federal appeals court found that a military contractor defense cannot be raised to ward off claims that the contractor failed to provide adequate health and safety warnings.[267] The contractor claimed that it should be protected from state tort law claims, despite failing to warn workers of asbestos hazards, because it followed the requirements of its federal contract.

The court said the federal government's requirement that asbestos be used in cement would only protect the contractor from a state tort claim if it was accused of violating a state law banning asbestos use in products. It would not automatically cover the contractor in cases where it was accused of failing to warn.

Generally, absent specific contract provisions, a contractor's obligations end when the structure is completed and the owner has accepted the work.[268] However, HVAC problems and other issues may cause the building owner to sue the contractor directly for breach of contract or for indemnification. When construction materials contain latent defects, some courts hold that the contractor is not liable for injury to the structure caused by the defect.

---

[265] 42 U.S.C. § 9619(c).

[266] Furch v. General Electric Co., 535 N.Y.S.2d 182 (3d Dept. 1988), *appeal dismissed,* 74 N.Y.2d 792, 545 N.Y.S.2d 106 (1989).

[267] Grispo v. Eagle-Picher Industries, Inc., N.Y.L.J., Feb. 22, 1990, at 1, col. 3.

[268] *See* 13 Am. Jur. 2d Building and Construction Contracts § 27 (1964 & Supp. 1988).

Courts also have found that contractors operate under certain implied warranties. Some of the most common implied warranties include the following:

1. Materials supplied will be of good quality;
2. The construction will be done in a workmanlike manner and in accordance with good usage and accepted trade practices;
3. The resulting structure will be merchantable—a structure that passes in the trade without objection;
4. The contractor's services will be fit or suitable for their intended purpose;
5. The resulting building will be in compliance with local building codes and will be suitable for the use for which the structure was intended.

Most states imply at least one of these warranties.[269]

The implied warranty that construction materials will be of good quality and free from latent defects has emerged only recently. Cases between owners and contractors that install ACM in structures might be a forum for further judicial expansion of the implied warranty of quality for construction materials. This implied warranty theory may be the only method of redress for an owner, if the supplier or manufacturer of ACM cannot be reached.

In some states, vendors of new homes implicitly warrant the house as being free from latent defects that would render it uninhabitable, but general contractors who build the homes are not liable for defects because they are not parties to the initial sale of the building.[270]

In an indoor air pollution case, plaintiffs will typically name as a defendant everyone who had anything to do with the building's construction or design—including all contractors who performed installation or construction work; manufacturers; and suppliers and distributors of new building materials. Anyone involved with floor and ceiling tiles, drapes and curtains, carpets and padding, glues and adhesives, ducts and ventilation systems, room dividers and partitions, and insulation can and may be sued. Plaintiffs will claim that defendants knew or should have known that, if the products were installed in an energy-efficient building, people might suffer

[269] See Note, *Implied Warranties in Home Construction: Subsequent Purchasers*, 33 S.C.L. Rev. 33 (1981); *see also* Lane v. Trenholm Bldg. Co., 267 S.C. 497, 229 S.E.2d 728 (1976); Rutledge v. Dodenhoff, 254 S.C. 407, 175 S.E.2d 792 (1970). *Accord,* Hefler v. Wright, 121 Ill. App. 3d 739, 460 N.E.2d 118 (1984); McDonald v. Mianecki, 79 N.J. 275, 398 A.2d 1283 (1978); Air Heaters, Inc. v. Johnson Electric, Inc., 258 N.W.2d 649 (N.D. 1977).

[270] Carolina Winds Owners' Association v. Joe Harden Builder, Inc., 297 S.C. 74, 374 S.E.2d 897 (Ct. App. 1988), *aff'd on rehearing,* No. 25 Davis Adv. Sh. 21 (S.C. Ct. App. Nov. 30, 1988).

injury, and that they failed to warn of the dangers inherent in the products. Negligence in installation or maintenance may also be charged. An EPA administrative law judge ruled that under the Asbestos Hazard Emergency Response Act (AHERA), inspectors, management planners, or any others who conduct asbestos abatement work for schools on a contract basis may be held liable for violating the statute and the EPA's AHERA regulations. This is the first case in which the EPA tried to take action under AHERA against a contractor.[271]

The case involved a consultant who allegedly failed to inspect, sample, and assess material properly in some schools, which were later found to contain asbestos that had to be removed. The consultant also failed to include all required information in an AHERA management plan.

The confusion arose over the lack of a definition in AHERA of a "person" who may be liable. The consultant's motion for an accelerated decision was denied and the case will proceed to trial.

The first sick building syndrome case to go to a jury was settled, but sent out reverberations of lawsuits to come. The judge ruled that if the jury were to find the HVAC system in the building defective, then the designer and contractor of the building could be subject to a strict liability theory of law.[272] This would create potential liability for anyone in the chain, including architects; engineers; designers, manufacturers, and installers of the HVAC system; contractors; and subcontractors.

The case arose when employees began to experience dizziness, nosebleeds, and respiratory problems when toxic fumes drifted to their side of a floor from new carpets, furniture, and paint on the other side of the floor. The corporations involved alleged losses from business interruption and lack of productivity. They claimed that ducts in the HVAC system leaked and interfered with the delivery of the fresh-air supply. The system would not allow more fresh air to be brought in from outside. Although the case was settled, the original contractor on the building may have to pay damages arising from an indemnification clause in his contract with the building owner.

§ 5.24 Consultants, Architects, Engineers, and Designers

Consultants have a considerable amount of potential liability exposure, because a great deal of reliance is placed on their reports and opinions. For

---

[271] *In re* Garvin, EPA Docket No. TSCA-ASB-VIII-90-41, Jan. 15, 1991; Asbestos Abatement Report, Feb. 18, 1991, at 2.

[272] Indoor Pollution News, Jan. 24, 1991, at 1; Call v. Prudential, No. SWC 90913 (Super. Ct. Cal.), settled Oct. 15, 1990.

this reason, they must be careful in evaluating which clients and projects amthey will take on.

A client who retains a consultant must be fully informed of all known risks and uncertainties in the project. A carefully drafted contract is essential, to ensure that no responsibility for anyone else's work is taken. Any involvement with hazardous substances should be made clear in the contract. The contract should include indemnification from the client and contribution for third-party claims for any damages not covered by insurance.

Those who act as consultants for environmental audits before a client purchases property may be faced with lawsuits, if their conclusions prove to be wrong and others rely on them. Claims may include: failure to identify all toxic materials during investigation; failure to discover toxic substances; failure to discover the location of all toxic substances, possibly causing a need for work to be redone; and failure to provide detailed specifications, causing the job to take longer, cost more, and not be completed. Consultants may also be subject to personal injury suits, if an employee or a member of the public is injured by toxic substances that were not supposed to be there.

Architects and engineers may be deemed to warrant that plans and specifications will create a structure reasonably fit for its intended purpose.[273] A typical allegation is that the architect or engineer designed the building to be too airtight with nonopening windows, and that the ventilation system designed was insufficient and pollutants were trapped inside.

Design professionals are not generally held to a strict liability standard for defective products, but in a recent sick building syndrome case, the court said such a standard might be used.[274] However, design professionals can be liable for mistaken or careless approval of defective products when the defect was ascertainable by reasonable investigation.[275] Architects and engineers are required to exercise the ordinary skill and diligence of others in their profession in preparing plans and specifications, and they must guard against defects in materials and construction.[276] Architects and interior designers may be subject to potential litigation based on their specification of certain furnishings, such as chairs or carpets, that emit toxic fumes.

---

[273] Bloomsburg Mills v. Sordoni Construction Co., 401 Pa. 358, 164 A.2d 201 (1960).

[274] See **ch. 1** and note 272 *infra*.

[275] Kerrigan & Stilwell, *How Do I Avoid Liability from Mistakes in Shop Drawings and Defects in Products Described in Brochures, Manufacturer's Specifications and by Samples?*, in Avoiding Liability in Architecture, Design, and Construction 211, 219 (1983).

[276] *See* Montijo v. Swift, 219 Cal. App. 2d 351, 33 Cal. Rptr. 133 (1963); Miller v. De Witt, 37 Ill. 2d 273, 226 N.E.2d 630 (1967).

Absent a special agreement, a design professional does not implicitly warrant that a design will accomplish the desired result.[277] Liability may turn on the extent to which the use of asbestos, for example, was considered an accepted practice by design professionals in the community. Although acceptance of the completed structure by the owner may be considered *prima facie* evidence that the project was completed in a workmanlike manner, it does not constitute a waiver of claims for latent defects caused by deficient or defective plans and workmanship not discoverable by simple inspection.

There have not been many lawsuits against design professionals for environmental issues, but the potential is certainly there. An architect was sued by the wife of a former junior high school student who allegedly died as a result of exposure to friable asbestos many years prior to his illness and death. The federal district court in New York granted summary judgment because the architect could not reasonably have been expected to know the harmful effects of asbestos at the time he provided professional services. He designed the school in 1956 and construction was completed in 1959.[278]

The court accepted the architect's affidavit that the use of asbestos-containing products in the construction of schools was generally accepted practice in the architectural profession in the late 1950s and was not questioned until the mid-1970s. The court took note of the fact that state agencies approved all plans and specifications for school facilities, including the use of sprayed-on asbestos in schools, until 1979. In addition, there was no federal or state safety standard banning or regulating the use of asbestos in buildings until 1973, when the EPA issued a ban on sprayed-on asbestos materials.

Under the standard of care for professional services, the court found that the architect could not reasonably have been expected to know of the deleterious effects of asbestos between 1956 and 1959.[279]

§ 5.25   Attorneys

Attorneys are not generally parties to environmental lawsuits, but they must consider some ethical issues when advising their clients.

---

[277] *See, e.g.,* City of Mounds View v. Walijarvi, 263 N.W.2d 420 (Minn. 1978); Milau Assocs., Inc. v. North Ave. Dev. Corp., 42 N.Y.2d 482, 368 N.E.2d 1247, 398 N.Y.S.2d 882 (1977). *But see* Hill v. Polar Pantries, 219 S.C. 263, 64 S.E.2d 885 (1951) (design professional held to impliedly warrant that structure will be reasonably fit for its intended use); Avent v. Proffitt, 109 S.C. 48, 95 S.E. 132 (1918) (architect liable for failure to discover and condemn defective plastering in house erected under his supervision).

[278] Barnett v. City of Yonkers, et al., 731 F. Supp. 594 (S.D.N.Y. 1990).

[279] *Id.* at 601.

The attorney–client privilege encourages candid client communications. An attorney has an ethical duty to refrain from disclosing client communications, and there is a legal barrier that prevents compelled disclosures. This includes "confidences" and "secrets."[280]

A confidence is information protected by the attorney–client privilege. A secret is other information, gained in the professional relationship, that the client has requested to be held inviolate because the disclosure would be embarrassing or would likely be detrimental to the client.

However, an exception allows attorneys to disclose a client's intention to commit a crime and the necessary information to prevent it.[281]

The disclosure is discretionary and the attorney must believe beyond a reasonable doubt that the crime will occur. The rule pertains only to future crimes, not past ones.

The attorney–client privilege does not protect communications concerning an intended or continuing crime or fraud. Because these communications are for a criminal purpose, the attorney is put in the nonattorney role of a conspirator, and the attorney's independent judgment is removed.[282]

Crimes or frauds that have already been committed are protected by the attorney–client privilege, which allows consultation to establish a defense.

Courts differ on the scope of the crime–fraud exception. Most cases extend the exception only to allegations of serious wrongdoing, crime, and fraud.[283]

If a client tells an attorney that his or her building is contaminated and seeks legal counsel on the client's rights and duties as owner, this is privileged communication, as is a client's telling an attorney that the client has dumped hazardous wastes in the past, has not reported it, and is continuing the dumping. However, if the client is advised about reporting requirements, and tells the attorney of an intent to continue to dump hazardous waste and not report it, this communication is probably discoverable if the dumping and failure to report are illegal. If a client tells an attorney that a building contains toxic substances in dangerous amounts but the client does not intend to disclose this fact to a prospective purchaser, the communication may be discoverable if the failure to disclose would be fraudulent.[284]

---

[280] DR 4-101(B).

[281] DR 4-101(C)(3). *See also* Gergacz, Attorney–Corporate Client Privilege, at 4-1 through 4-22 (1987).

[282] United States v. Ballard, 779 F.2d 287, 292 (5th Cir.), *cert. denied*, 475 U.S. 1109 (1986).

[283] *In re* Grand Jury Proceedings (FMC Corp.), 604 F.2d 798 (3d Cir. 1979); Garner v. Wolfinbarger, 430 F.2d 1093 (5th Cir. 1970), *cert. denied*, 401 U.S. 974 (1971).

[284] The crime–fraud exception applies to civil frauds as well as crimes. Whetstone v. Olson, 46 Wash. App. 308, 732 P.2d 159 (1986).

CHAPTER 6

THEORIES USED IN COST RECOVERY AND OTHER ENVIRONMENTAL LITIGATION

§ 6.1   Introduction: Basis for Liability

§ 6.2   How Courts Handle Claims

§ 6.3   Pendent Jurisdiction

§ 6.4   Types of Damages

§ 6.5   Suits under the Comprehensive Environmental Response, Compensation, and Liability Act (CERCLA)

§ 6.6   —Building Materials Exception

§ 6.7   —New or Useful Product Exception

§ 6.8   Petroleum Exclusion

§ 6.9   Strict Liability

§ 6.10   —Duty to Warn

§ 6.11   —Economic Loss

§ 6.12   Enhanced Risk of Cancer and Impairment of Quality of Life

§ 6.13   Breach of Warranty

§ 6.14   —Covenant of Quiet Enjoyment and Warranty of Habitability

§ 6.15   Indemnification and Restitution

§ 6.16   Fraud

§ 6.17   Negligence

§ 6.18   Breach of Contract

§ 6.19   Securities Law Violations

§ 6.20   Racketeer Influenced and Corrupt Organization Act (RICO) Violations

§ 6.21   Market Share, Conspiracy, and Other Alternate Theories of Liability

§ 6.22   Rescission and "As Is" Clauses

§ 6.23   Public Nuisance

§ 6.24   Private Nuisance

§ 6.25   Injunctions

§ 6.26   Tax Assessment Reduction

§ 6.27   Contribution

§ 6.28   Punitive Damages

§ 6.29   Attorney Fees

§ 6.1   Introduction: Basis for Liability

This chapter examines the various legal theories that are being used to recover claims for property damage and personal injury from hazardous substances in buildings. It explores the traditional legal theories that have been
invoked and some new theories, originating from other areas of the law, that
may be utilized in hazardous substance and toxic tort complaints in the
future.

Currently, most of the theories of liability are traceable to traditional
common-law tort theories such as strict liability, negligence, fraud, misrepresentation, and nuisance. If a product is involved, breach of contract and
breach of express and implied warranties may be applicable.

Hazardous substance litigation is a rapidly evolving area of the law, and
liability seems to be increasing and expanding as a matter of public policy.
Some theories of liability from other areas, such as RICO and conspiracy,
are being used in innovative ways in an attempt to break new ground in
environmental lawsuits. Depending on the facts, violations of the securities
laws may even be involved.

As we will see, the courts have not allowed recovery of costs for asbestos
abatement in buildings under statutes such as CERCLA, but this too may
change in the future if there are legislative amendments. In the absence of
such legislation, reimbursement for abatement costs is being sought under
general common-law theories. There are many other hazardous substances
in buildings for which CERCLA may apply and provide relief. Most complaints that encompass CERCLA claims tend to include common-law theories as well.

Personal injury cases involving hazardous substances are so plentiful that
a book could be written about that subject alone. We will touch on that area
but will focus more on property damage and economic loss.

Parties may create their own liability in contracts of sale or in leases, by
providing for the payment of removal costs and indemnification in the
event that hazardous substances are found.

Environmental lawsuits that contain a variety of theories of liability are
subject to a tremendous number of motions to dismiss and motions for

summary judgment, as defendants attempt to whittle down the number of theories being alleged against them.

One must be aware that favorable verdicts in such lawsuits may be Pyrrhic victories—that is, the battle is won, but the war is lost. Doubtful legal theories or the cost of the litigation can cause the loss. Nevertheless, this area of the law will continue to grow and to stretch the boundaries of traditional liability for the foreseeable future.

§ 6.2 How Courts Handle Claims

Many courts across the country currently have thousands of asbestos claims pending at one time. Most of them involve personal injuries, but an increasing number involve property damages. The backlog stems from the fact that asbestos personal injury and property damage suits are not often allowed to proceed as class actions and must therefore proceed individually or in small groups. In order to handle the massive number of claims, courts have been trying to develop innovative methods to encourage settlement or to allow the cases to be tried more expeditiously.

In Maryland, a plan was proposed to have each defendant in a personal injury suit make a "blind" contribution to an overall settlement fund.[1] This method would eliminate the need to identify which company's product caused particular injuries and how much of the total liability each defendant is responsible for. A special master was appointed by the court to construct the out-of-court settlement. This may become a model for use by other states.

In Louisiana, a federal judge consolidated 3,031 asbestos cases to bring only 11 of the cases to actual trial, with illustrative reference to 30 additional cases. This solution was found to be a violation of the due process laws and it was decided that any adjustment in the handling of claims probably should be left to Congress and the state legislature.[2]

Special masters are common in federal courts, where there are many cases pending and not enough judges to handle the volume. In an unprecedented move, several hundred cases pending in both state and federal courts in New York, concerning asbestos workers exposed to asbestos in the Brooklyn Navy Yard, were given to a special master.[3] The master's task is to set uniform standards for compensating similarly situated groups of plaintiffs and for contribution by defendants.

When two judges sought to consolidate Texas and Ohio asbestos class action cases with a New York case, the consolidation was challenged by the

---

[1] Wall Street J., Apr. 2, 1990, at B5, col. 1.

[2] *In re* Fiberboard Corp., 893 F.2d 706 (5th Cir. 1990).

[3] N.Y.L.J., Jan. 31, 1990, at 1, col. 3.

U.S. Circuit Court of Appeals.[4] A committee of ten federal judges proposed a plan to certify a single national class of plaintiffs to reach a mass settlement of asbestos injury claims. Some attorneys and others have challenged this idea as unconstitutional.

Under the plan, asbestos-containing products would be declared inherently dangerous as a matter of law, if they are capable of producing dust on use, application, or removal. Such products would be declared as having been marketed without adequate warning and therefore as being defective and unreasonably dangerous. Then the courts would only have to determine each defendant's share of liability and damages.[5]

It was reported that, as of January 1, 1990, there were 29,466 asbestos-related personal injury lawsuits pending in federal courts and 60,000 in state courts.[6] There are far fewer property damage cases in these same courts. Thus, many attempts to formulate a method for handling this number of cases have failed or have created additional confusion. Very active attempts to come up with creative solutions to the problem of the backlog continue, but none so far has emerged as a panacea.

Many of the cases seem to settle; the remaining cases generally proceed to trial separately in state and federal courts rather than in a joint trial.

U.S. District Judge Thomas D. Lambros has issued an order proposing that the Manville personal injury trust be turned into a national facility for settling all asbestos cases.[7] The facility would use the combined resources of the Manville trust, other asbestos defendants, and their insurers, and would be supervised by federal and state judges. This is only the latest of many creative solutions proposed to deal with the volume of asbestos cases. In response to these moves, U.S. Chief Justice William Rehnquist appointed a committee of six federal judges to study the complex issues surrounding asbestos litigation and to propose legislative remedies or amendments to the federal court rules.[8]

§ 6.3 Pendent Jurisdiction

Federal courts may exercise pendent jurisdiction in federal CERCLA actions, in order to consider claims arising under state common law or statutory law. This extension of jurisdiction is important because the federal district courts have exclusive jurisdiction over CERCLA cases and many environmental complaints also contain allegations based on common law.

---

[4] *In re* National Asbestos Litigation, Cleveland Div., No. 1-90-CV-11,000, N.L.J. Aug. 20, 1990.

[5] Asbestos Abatement Report, Sept. 3, 1990, at 1.

[6] *Id.* at 7.

[7] Wall St. J., Aug. 8, 1990, at Legal Beat at B10, col. 1.

[8] Asbestos Abatement Report, Oct. 29, 1990, at 2.

One commentator has described the circumstances in which a court may exercise pendent jurisdiction, as follows:

Federal courts have the power to decide a pendent state claim whenever (1) the federal claim is sufficiently substantial to confer subject matter jurisdiction on the court; (2) the pendent and federal claims "derive from a common nucleus of operative fact"; (3) the plaintiff would "ordinarily be expected to try [the claims] in one judicial proceeding"; and (4) Congress has not precluded pendent jurisdiction in its enactment of the statute conferring jurisdiction over the federal claim. The question of whether a court should exercise its discretion to hear pendent claims is based upon promotion of judicial economy, convenience, and fairness to litigants, taking into account (1) the policy of avoiding needless decisions of state law; (2) whether the state claims will substantially predominate; (3) the extent to which the state claim is tied closely to questions of federal policy; and (4) whether other factors, such as the likelihood of jury confusion, justify separating the state and federal claims for trial.[9]

§ 6.4 Types of Damages

Damages claimed for environmental property damage and personal injury may include the following:

1. Costs of repairs, removal, encapsulation, or abatement and disposal of the hazardous substance, and other economic loss[10] (for example, relocation costs and fees for consultants);
2. Costs of testing and inspecting for asbestos and other hazardous substances, establishing a building operation and management plan, and maintaining the building;
3. Diminution in value of the real estate because of the presence of the hazardous substance;[11]
4. Lost business profits and good will, and business interruption for commercial plaintiffs;
5. Moving expenses, if the building is uninhabitable;
6. Loss of leasehold;
7. Lost billable hours, if employees cannot work or are out sick;
8. Loss of new clients because of inability to solicit new business while servicing existing clients;

---

[9] Babich and Hanson, *Injunctive and Declaratory Relief for States Under CERCLA,* 18 Envtl. L. Rep. (Envtl. L. Inst.), 10,216, at 10,218 (1988).

[10] City of New York v. Keene Corp., 132 Misc. 2d 745, 505 N.Y.S.2d 782 (1986), *aff'd,* 129 N.Y.S.2d 1019, 513 N.Y.S.2d 1004 (1st Dept. 1987).

[11] Ayers v. Township of Jackson, 106 N.J. 557, 525 A.2d 287 (1987).

9. Aggravation and discomfort of tenants during abatement;

10. Cancerphobia;[12]

11. Fear of future injury, increased risk of future harm, and medical monitoring costs for staff and exposed plaintiffs;[13]

12. Ecological illness;[14]

13. Property damages;[15]

14. Criminal penalties, including fines;

15. Related administrative and staff costs;

16. Punitive damages;

17. Injunctive relief;

18. Legal costs;

19. Liability of PRPs, under CERCLA, for:

    a. costs to the government of removal or remedial action,

    b. costs of response incurred consistent with the National Contingency Plan (NCP),

    c. damage to national resources,

    d. costs for any health assessments.

§ 6.5   Suits under the Comprehensive Environmental Response, Compensation, and Liability Act (CERCLA)

The intended purpose of the Comprehensive Environmental Response, Compensation, and Liability Act (CERCLA)[16] is to provide remediation and cleanup of sites contaminated by hazardous substances. With the creation of the Superfund, there is a bifurcated scheme: it gives the federal government the tools to respond to the problem sites, and it gives private parties the right to institute civil actions to recover costs from those responsible for creating the problem sites.

---

[12] Wisniewski v. Johns-Manville Corp., 759 F.2d 271 (3d Cir. 1985), aff'd, 812 F.2d 81 (3d Cir. 1987). However, see Mauro v. Raymark Industries, Inc., 116 N.J. 126 (1989), in which the court ruled that a claimant cannot recover damages for the enhanced risk of cancer unless the prospective damages are reasonably probable to occur.

[13] Dartez v. Fiberboard Corp., 765 F.2d 456 (5th Cir. 1985). See also Sterling v. Velsicol Chemical Corp., 855 F.2d 1188 (6th Cir. 1988); Ayers v. Township of Jackson, 106 N.J. 557, 525 A.2d 287 (1987).

[14] Davis, Ecological Illness, Trial, Oct. 1986, at 34.

[15] Trustees of Columbia University v. Mitchell/Giurgola Assoc., 109 A.2d 449, 495 N.Y.S.2d 371 (1985).

[16] 42 U.S.C. §§ 9601–9675.

Under § 9604 of CERCLA, the federal government may bring a response action against:

(1) the owner and operator of a vessel or a facility;

(2) any person who at the time of disposal of any hazardous substance owned or operated any facility at which such hazardous substances were disposed of;

(3) any person who by contract, agreement, or otherwise arranged with a transporter for transport for disposal or treatment, of hazardous substances owned or possessed by such person, by any other party or entity, at any facility or incineration vessel owned or operated by another party or entity and containing such hazardous substances, and

(4) any person who accepts or accepted any hazardous substance for transport to disposal or treatment facilities, incineration vessels or sites selected by such person.[17]

Section 9607 of CERCLA creates a private right of action for innocent parties to attempt to recover the money they have spent on removal or remediation, as follows:

(1) all costs of removal or remedial action incurred by the United States Government or a State or Indian tribe, not inconsistent with the National Contingency Plan; and

(2) any other necessary costs of response incurred by any other person, consistent with the National Contingency Plan.[18]

To state a *prima facie* case under CERCLA for the recovery of cleanup response costs, a plaintiff must prove the following:

(1) that the defendant is within one of four statutory categories of "covered persons" liable for such costs;

(2) that there has been a release or there is a threat of release of a hazardous substance from a facility;

(3) the release or threatened release has caused the plaintiff to incur clean-up and response costs;

(4) that the costs expended were necessary; and

(5) that the response actions taken are consistent with the National Contingency Plan.[19]

---

[17] 42 U.S.C. § 9607(a)(1)–(4); Retirement Community Developers, Inc. v. Merine, 713 F. Supp. 153, 156 (D. Mo. 1989).

[18] Retirement Community Developers, Inc. v. Merine, 713 F. Supp. at 155; State of New York v. Shore Realty Corp., 759 F.2d 1032, 1040 (2d Cir. 1985).

[19] 42 U.S.C. § 9607(a)(4) and (a)(4)(B). Artesian Water Co. v. Government of New Castle County, 659 F. Supp. 1269, 1278 (D. Del. 1987), *aff'd,* 851 F.2d 643 (3d Cir. 1988).

Many lawsuits for environmental damages are brought under CERCLA, but the statute has not provided relief for the widespread problem of recovery of asbestos abatement costs.

§ 6.6 —Building Materials Exception

The Superfund Amendments and Reauthorization Act of 1986 (SARA) added a limitation on response actions to § 9604(a)(3)(B), which prohibits actions in response to releases or threatened releases "from products which are part of the structure of, and result in exposure within, . . . building structures." This has come to be known as the "building materials exception." Thus, although CERCLA applies to a host of hazardous substances in buildings, including asbestos, it does not apply to *in situ* asbestos, which is part of the structure and must be removed.

There have been several lawsuits in which parties have tried to recover asbestos removal costs under CERCLA. None has been successful thus far. In a suit by the purchaser of a building against the prior owner for the cost of removing asbestos in connection with tenant improvements, the defendant argued that the building materials exception in § 9604 not only precluded actions brought by the EPA, but private suits under § 9607 as well. The court agreed, finding it "unlikely" that Congress intended to preclude the federal government from taking certain action while allowing private parties to bring such suits.[20]

In *Retirement Community Developers, Inc. v. Merine,*[21] building renovators brought an action under CERCLA against the prior owner, to recover damages and the cost of removing asbestos materials from the building. The court found that Congress, when it passed the statute in 1980, did not intend that CERCLA should extend to the recovery of costs for removing asbestos installed in the construction of buildings. The court noted that CERCLA applies "primarily to the cleanup of leaking inactive or abandoned sites and to emergency responses to spills."[22] Other courts have agreed.[23]

This ruling has been interpreted by courts to mean that, although the federal courts have found a private cause of action under CERCLA with respect to hazardous waste sites, they have not expanded the application of

---

[20] 3550 Stevens Creek Associates v. Barclays Bank of California, (D.C. N. Calif., No. C87-20672) 1988 (unpublished). This case has been docketed for appeal before the U.S. Court of Appeals for the Ninth Circuit.

[21] 713 F. Supp. 153 (D. Mo. 1989).

[22] 42 U.S.C. § 9607(a).

[23] 3550 Stevens Creek Associates v. Barclays Bank of California, *supra* note 20; Corporation of Mercer University v. National Gypsum Co., 24 Env't Rep. Cas. (BNA) 1953, 1960–61, (M.D. Ga. 1986).

the statute's definition of "hazardous waste site" to the hundreds of thousands of buildings that have been constructed with asbestos materials installed as part of the structure. Thus, private plaintiffs, as well as the federal government, are precluded from using CERCLA to recover the cost of removing building materials containing asbestos because of the "building materials exception."

One court described the situation this way:

> To extend CERCLA's strict liability scheme to all past and present owners of buildings containing asbestos as well as to all persons who manufactured, transported, and installed asbestos products into buildings, would be to shift literally billions of dollars of removal cost liability based on nothing more than an improvident interpretation of a statute that Congress never intended to apply in this context.[24]

In its *amicus* brief in *3550 Stevens Creek Associates v. Barclays Bank of California*,[25] the EPA argued that the building materials exception only applies to federal government response actions under § 9604 and limits only actions of the EPA. The exception does not preclude parties from using CERCLA to recover cleanup costs incurred in the removal of asbestos from buildings in the presence of a release or threatened release into the environment. The EPA argued that to bar private parties from using CERCLA for recovery of cleanup costs incurred from asbestos removal would be contrary to Congress's desire to encourage private response actions in order to preserve the assets of the Superfund.[26]

This issue became so heated that the U.S. Supreme Court was asked on November 6, 1989, to decide whether the Superfund law applies to private lawsuits brought to recover property damage to buildings.[27] The request was denied. Thus, any change in this area will have to be the result of a legislative change in the statute.

The exclusion was broadened in a California case involving a tenant who sued its lessor to recover abatement costs after a fire swept through rented office space in 1989.[28] The fire damaged asbestos-containing building materials and contaminated office equipment, furniture, and files with asbestos dust. The tenant, a California state agency, was forced to evacuate the building and remove the asbestos.

---

[24] First United Methodist Church v. U.S. Gypsum Co., 882 F.2d 862, 869 (4th Cir. 1989), *cert. denied*, 110 S. Ct. 1113, 107 L. Ed. 1020 (1990). *See also* 58 U.S.L.W. 3526 (1990).

[25] *Supra* note 20.

[26] Prudential Insurance Co. of America v. U.S. Gypsum Co., 711 F. Supp. 1244, 1255 (D.C.N.J. 1989); *cert. denied*, 110 S. Ct. 1113, 107 L. Ed. 1020 (1990) (hereinafter, "Prudential").

[27] Indoor Pollution News, Dec. 14, 1989, at 4.

[28] Anthony v. Blech, No. CV-90-4538 AWT (D.C.C. Cal. Mar. 26, 1991); Asbestos Abatement Report, Apr. 29, 1991, at 1.

The court refused to distinguish between asbestos-containing building materials and asbestos waste materials, such as the asbestos dust. The court ruled that asbestos abatement costs are not recoverable under the federal Superfund law, even when the asbestos has fallen from the building structure, no longer serves its intended use, and poses an imminent threat to building occupants.

Nevertheless, many owners and subsequent purchasers of buildings are attempting to stretch the limits of CERCLA to allow them to bring actions against asbestos manufacturers.[29] The ability to use CERCLA would afford them the opportunity to take advantage of the strict liability aspect of the statute, as well as the liberal statute of limitations.[30] Until an appeal succeeds or the law is changed, common-law theories may be utilized to recover the cost of abatement of asbestos and other hazardous substances in those instances where CERCLA does not apply.

§ 6.7   —New or Useful Product Exception

Asbestos-containing materials are "hazardous substances" within CERCLA, but liability does not attach unless a party has taken affirmative action to *dispose* of a hazardous substance, as opposed to conveying it in the form of a useful product.[31]

A building owner brought suit against asbestos manufacturers, designers, and suppliers, seeking reimbursement under CERCLA for the costs of inspection and abatement programs. A defendant manufacturer sought to dismiss the private cost recovery action on the theory that CERCLA § 107 was intended to apply to the "disposal" of hazardous waste and not to the manufacture and sale of useful products.[32] The defendant contended that the asbestos was not discarded material. This defense has come to be called the "new or useful products exception."

The key issue in the case was determining who was a "covered person" who could be liable for the costs of response. Under the statute:

> any person who by contact, agreement or otherwise arranged for disposal or treatment, or arranged with a transporter for transport, . . . disposal,

---

[29] A federal court in southern California dismissed claims for recovery of asbestos costs on the grounds that a viable commercial product installed in a building does not constitute a release or threatened release into the environment as required by the federal statute. Ssangyong/Kearny Mesa Association v. Al Bahr Temple of San Diego, (D.C.S. Calif., No. 89-0836-R), Asbestos Abatement Report, June 25, 1990, at 6.

[30] Six years after the initiation of on-site remedial construction activity. 42 U.S.C. § 9613(g)(2)(B).

[31] *Id.*

[32] Prudential, *supra* note 26.

or . . . treatment of hazardous substances owned or possessed by such person, by any other party or entity, at any facility . . . shall be liable for . . . Any other necessary costs of response incurred by any other person consistent with the national contingency plan.[33]

Liability under § 9607(a)(3) requires proof of four basic elements:

(1) that the person disposed of hazardous substances;

(2) at a facility which contains, at the time of discovery, hazardous substances of the kind of which the entity disposed;

(3) that there is a release or a threatened release of that or any hazardous substance; and

(4) which triggers the incurrence of response costs.[34]

The court examined the term "disposal." According to § 9601(29):

The term "disposal," "hazardous waste," and "treatment" shall have the meaning provided in section 1004 of the Solid Waste Disposal Act [42 U.S.C. § 6903].

Under the Solid Waste Disposal Act, the term "disposal" means the discharge, deposit, injection, dumping, spilling, leaking, or placing of any solid waste or hazardous waste into or on any land or water so that such solid waste or hazardous waste or any constituent thereof may enter the environment or be emitted into the air or discharged into any waters, including ground waters.

In examining the meaning of the term "disposal" it must be noted that:

In the absence of a clearly expressed legislative intention to the contrary the language of the statute itself must ordinarily be regarded as conclusive. . . . Unless exceptional circumstances dictate otherwise, when we find the terms of a statute unambiguous, judicial inquiry is complete.[35]

The court found that there is liability if there has been an affirmative act to *dispose* of a hazardous substance—that is, "in some manner the defendant must have dumped his waste on the site at issue"—as opposed to conveying a useful substance for a useful purpose.[36]

In *Jersey City Redevelopment Authority v. PPG Industries,*[37] the court found that, for liability to attach under CERCLA § 107(a)(3), there must be

---

[33] 42 U.S.C. § 9607(a)(3)(B).

[34] Prudential, *supra* note 26, 711 F. Supp. at 1251; 42 U.S.C. § 9607(a)(3)(B).

[35] Prudential, *supra* note 26, 711 F. Supp. at 1253.

[36] *Id.* at 1253.

[37] 655 F. Supp. 1257, 1260 (D.C.N.J. 1987), *aff'd,* 1988 U.S. App. LEXIS 18998 (3d Cir. 1988); *see also* United States v. A&F Materials Co., 582 F. Supp. 842 (D.C. Ill. 1984).

an affirmative act or "crucial decision" as to how the waste would be disposed of or treated. In that case, the plaintiff had hired a contractor to perform certain excavation work. The contractor used landfill material from another location which turned out to be contaminated with chromium.

The owner and operator of the plant (PPG) that had processed the chromium ore and had sold the property was found not to be a "covered person." The plaintiff had alleged that PPG, by selling the property, had "arranged for" the disposal of the contaminated waste mud at the site.[38] There was no specific transaction concerning the disposal of the hazardous substance. However, there was a triable issue as to whether the purchaser of the property was a covered person.

In *United States v. Westinghouse Electric Corporation,*[39] the court dismissed Westinghouse's CERCLA claim against Monsanto, the seller of polychlorinated biphenyls (PCBs) used by Westinghouse in its manufacture of electric equipment. The court found that the manufacture and sale of useful products containing hazardous substances for their proper and intended purpose did not result in CERCLA liability, because these acts did not constitute a disposal. Monsanto's affirmative act of selling the PCBs was not a statutory disposal because the sale was not made to get rid of the PCBs, but instead to provide a necessary component for Westinghouse's manufacturing process.[40]

§ 6.8 Petroleum Exclusion

A party, including the government, whose property is contaminated with petroleum products or fractions thereof cannot bring an action under CERCLA because of its "petroleum exclusion."[41]

The term hazardous substance cross-references several other environmental statutes, but the exception states:

> The term [hazardous substance] does not include petroleum, including crude oil or any fraction thereof which is not otherwise specifically listed or designated . . . and the term does not include natural gas, natural gas liquids, liquefied natural gas or synthetic gas useable for fuel (or mixture of natural gas and such synthetic gas).[42]

This exception is important for buildings with underground storage tanks.

---

[38] *Id.* 655 F. Supp. at 1260.
[39] 22 Env't Rep. Cas. (BNA) 1230 (D.C. Ind. 1983).
[40] *Id.* at 1233.
[41] 42 U.S.C. § 9601(14).
[42] *Id.*

§ 6.9   Strict Liability

Under the theory of strict liability in tort, a party can be liable to an injured party if he or she engages in an abnormally or unreasonably dangerous activity, even if it is carried on safely and without negligence. Strict liability may also arise from a design defect in a product or from a failure to warn of a hazard. However, there is no cause of action *per se* against a landlord based on strict liability for defects in leased property.[43]

The *Restatement (Second) of Torts* § 519 (1977) has explained strict liability as follows:

(1) One who carries on an abnormally dangerous activity is subject to liability for harm to the person, land or chattels of another resulting from the activity, although he has exercised the utmost care to prevent the harm.

(2) The strict liability is limited to the kind of harm, the possibility of which makes the activity abnormally dangerous.

The *Restatement* also sets forth six factors that are to be used to guide courts in a determination of whether there should be strict liability:

(a) existence of a high degree of risk of some harm to the person, land or chattels of others;

(b) likelihood that the harm that results from it will be great;

(c) inability to eliminate the risk by the exercise of reasonable care;

(d) extent to which the activity is not a matter of common usage;

(e) inappropriateness of the activity to the place where it is carried out; and

(f) extent to which its value to the community is outweighed by its dangerous attributes.[44]

Thus, if a party can successfully prove that the conditions in a building were abnormally dangerous, there may be strict liability against a building owner. Courts have even applied this theory to find liability as between successive landowners.[45]

Furthermore, the party who creates such an abnormally dangerous condition is absolutely liable and cannot avoid responsibility, unless a purchaser or individual *knowingly* accepts that burden (i.e., knows that hazardous substances were present).[46] This liability may hold even where the parties have signed a contract of sale agreeing to purchase the property "as is."[47]

---

[43] Pezzolanella v. Galloway, 132 Misc. 2d 429, 503 N.Y.S.2d 990 (City Ct. 1986).

[44] Restatement (Second) of Torts § 520 (1977).

[45] T&E Industries v. Safety Light Corp., 680 F. Supp. 696 (D.N.J. 1988).

[46] Amland Properties Corp. v. Aluminum Company of America, 711 F. Supp. 784, 802 (D.N.J. 1989).

[47] *Id.* at 803.

§ 6.10 —Duty to Warn

Under the *Restatement (Second) of Torts* § 402A, there may be liability for a product if there is a negligent failure to warn of danger not readily apparent to the user and the responsibility to test the product to be sure it is safe for the public and for the use for which it is intended. There is a duty to warn if a harmful use of the product is reasonably foreseeable to the manufacturer.

A product is defective if it lacks any element necessary to make it safe for its intended use or contains any condition that makes it unsafe for its intended use. Whether a plaintiff's harmful use of a product was reasonably foreseeable to the manufacturer is a question of fact for a jury.[48]

The *Restatement (Second) of Torts* § 402A (1977) provides:

> One who sells any product in a defective condition, unreasonably dangerous to the user or consumer or to his property is subject to liability for physical harm thereby caused to the ultimate user or consumer, or to his property if
>
> > (a) the seller is engaged in the business of selling such a product, and
>
> > (b) it is expected to and does reach the user or consumer without substantial change in the condition in which it is sold.
>
> (2) The rule stated in Subsection (1) applies although
>
> > (a) the seller has exercised all possible care in the preparation and sale of his product, and
>
> > (b) the user or consumer has not bought the product from or entered into any contractual relation with the seller.

To recover under strict liability, a plaintiff must show:

1. The defendant made or sold a product that was unreasonably dangerous to the user;
2. The defendant knew or should have known the product was dangerous;
3. The defendant failed to adequately warn the plaintiff of the product's dangerous properties;
4. The plaintiff suffered damage or injury from the product sold.[49]

Not all courts have accepted strict liability in tort as a separate theory of products liability; it has traditionally been reserved for ultrahazardous activity, such as blasting.

---

[48] Kalik v. Allis-Chalmers Corp., 658 F. Supp. 631, 635 (W.D. Pa. 1987).

[49] Restatement (Second) of Torts § 402A, comments i and j (1977).

In *Johnson v. Murph Metals, Inc.,*[50] the defendant manufacturer of automobile batteries often resold them to recycle the lead. Employees of a lead smelting company alleged that, during the smelting process, they were exposed to harmful lead fumes and lead dust, and they claimed the battery manufacturer was liable for a negligent failure to warn. The court found that this use of the batteries was not reasonably foreseeable. So too, the destruction of a product, such as ductwork,[51] and the dismantling and processing of junk electrical components that released PCBs are not reasonably foreseeable uses of the products.

This theory has been used extensively in asbestos lawsuits. It may also be used in other product liability cases involving products that emit toxic odors or emit hazardous substances when they burn.

§ 6.11   —Economic Loss

Damage from asbestos contamination has been considered by some courts to be an economic loss and thus not recoverable under tort theories of strict liability and property damage. Under general tort theories, a party not in privity of contract may not sue for economic loss, but only for physical injury or property damage. Thus, if injury is purely economic, the plaintiff's recovery would be limited to contract remedies. Manufacturers argue that strict product liability is for defective products that pose hazards to life and health or cause injury to people and property, and thus there should be no liability for economic loss.

Economic loss has been defined as "the diminution in the value of the product because it is inferior in quality and does not work for the general purposes for which it was manufactured and sold."[52] These losses lie solely in contract. Damage from economic loss would include: (1) reduction in value of a particular product, (2) repair to the product itself, (3) replacement, and (4) loss of profits. Damage may also include diminution in the value of the property because of contamination from hazardous substances.[53]

Some jurisdictions have adopted a "lurking danger" approach to get around the economic loss doctrine. Thus, when asbestos becomes friable, the law should encourage the owner to abate this lurking or latent danger and recover the abatement cost from the ultimate tortfeasor. Under this theory, the cause of action can exist without the statute of limitations

---

[50] 562 F. Supp. 246 (N.D. Tex. 1983).

[51] Wingett v. Teledyne Industries, Inc., 479 N.E.2d 51 (Ind. 1985).

[52] City of Manchester v. National Gypsum Co., 637 F. Supp. 646, 650 (D.R.I. 1986).

[53] Crawford v. National Lead Co., 19 Envtl. L. Rep. (Envtl. L. Inst.) 21,174 (S.D. Ohio 1989).

starting to run. Because the public policy is to prevent injury, abatement occurs before the injury and before accrual of the statute of limitations. Manufacturers will argue that the danger was not hidden and that injury had occurred.

Another rationale that may be used in the future to get around the economic loss doctrine is that there are no economic damages if there has been at least one instance of a calamity that could have caused physical injury to persons or property. The building owner might allege that there was a release of dangerous asbestos fibers, which would allow him or her to sue for the cost of abatement.

The majority of courts agree that "economic loss" is prohibited in strict liability actions, but then hold that, because friable asbestos contaminates other surfaces in the building (ceilings, walls, floors, drapes) and air quality, the contamination is a form of physical damage to property and therefore is recoverable.[54] In a New Jersey case, the court found economic losses recoverable under strict product liability. Damages included the costs for removal and replacement of ACM.[55]

As one court stated:

> The asbestos in this case is apparently found in an acoustical ceiling coating. If this coating had failed in its purpose—if it had fallen off, or failed to muffle reverberations—that would have given rise to an action sounding in contract for an economic loss. However, it appears that the coating functioned satisfactorily in its intended role except that, Hebron alleges, it released harmful asbestos fibers into the building, poisoning it and rendering it unfit for use. This is damage to property on which a tort claim can be founded.[56]

Another court pointed out the practical realities that call for such an extension of the theory in today's world:

> . . . it is at best, somewhat artificial to try to characterize the damage plaintiff claims as either one or the other, as either physical damage to its property or economic damage. Such pigeon holes may have been useful when tort and contract suits were less complex, but today in situations where dangers are discovered only after many years and where the harm caused or to be caused comes from allegedly dangerously defective materials which must be removed so as to avoid further dangers, the reasons for such divisions are less clear and the ability to make such distinctions is questionable.[57]

---

[54] Board of Education of City of Chicago v. A, C and S, Inc., 525 N.E.2d 950, 959 (Ill. App. 1988).

[55] Cinnaminson Township Board of Education v. U.S. Gypsum Co., 552 F. Supp. 855 (D.N.J. 1982), *aff'd*, 882 F.2d 510 (3d Cir. 1989).

[56] Hebron Public School District v. U.S. Gypsum Co., 690 F. Supp. 866 (D.C.N.D. 1988).

[57] City of Manchester v. National Gypsum Co., 637 F. Supp. at 649–50.

A court examining property damage claims brought by a school district against the manufacturer of ceiling plaster rejected arguments against economic loss. The court found that, because of its hazardous nature, asbestos damages other property besides the asbestos materials themselves.[58]

In the context of commercial building owners, some litigants have argued that such plaintiffs may not use this theory because of their sophistication, relative equality in economic strength, and ability to bargain over the specifications of the product and to negotiate concerning the risk of loss from defects in asbestos products.

In *Solow v. W.R. Grace & Company,*[59] the court allowed a sophisticated commercial owner to bring such an action against a manufacturer because the product may have been purchased by a subcontractor, and Solow was never aware of where the product came from or what its qualities were, and never had a chance to negotiate or bargain about the product and the risks involved. The court stated:

> The reality is that here the product was allegedly defective and dangerous in a way and to an extent beyond what a purchaser would contemplate and the defect was also latent. A purchaser of such a product would not be inclined to bargain about the qualities of the product nor would the purchaser be apt to consider that there existed some extraordinary risk against which it needed to take extraordinary protective measures.[60]

A federal judge in New York City denied motions for summary judgment and allowed Chase Manhattan Bank to pursue up to $180 million in abatement costs and other damages from a British manufacturer of asbestos products for Chase's 60-story office building.[61] The court rejected arguments that the alleged property damages were mere economic loss not recoverable under tort law.

However, the court in *Pinole Pointe Properties v. Bethlehem Steel Corporation*[62] stated in *dicta* that strict liability would not be applied where the alleged damages were costs of cleanup and diminution in the value of the property, because these were not the types of damages to which strict liability attaches. This case is of interest to those who might argue that they cannot sell their property, lease, or sublease at market value because of the

[58] Kershaw County Board of Education v. U.S. Gypsum Co., No. 23,270 (Sup. Ct. S.C. Sept. 17, 1990); Asbestos Abatement Report, Oct. 15, 1990, at 4.

[59] Solow v. W.R. Grace & Co., 1989 N.Y. Misc. LEXIS 894 (N.Y. Sup. 1989), N.Y.L.J. Aug. 9, 1989, at 17.

[60] *Id.* N.Y.L.J. at 18, col. 2.

[61] Chase Manhattan Bank v. Turner & Newall PLC, No. 87 Civ. 4436 (S.D.N.Y. Mar. 29, 1990); Asbestos Abatement Report, May 28, 1990, at 3.

[62] 596 F. Supp. 283 (N.D. Cal. 1984).

presence of asbestos. However, diminished value was a factor considered in a case involving asbestos contamination of a residence.[63]

In an incident in New York City, in which a steam pipe exploded and spewed asbestos into residential apartments, the diminution in value of the property because of the asbestos was taken into account in the monetary settlement that was reached.[64] This concept may be more widely used in the future.

A minority of jurisdictions have eliminated the economic loss bar to strict liability lawsuits, in instances where plaintiffs have no bargaining power.[65]

This theory may be used in suits against builders of commercial buildings, contractors, subcontractors, and installers of HVAC systems in buildings that now have indoor air problems.[66]

The Pennsylvania Department of Transportation recently sued a manufacturer of vinyl flooring that contained asbestos, after the flooring was improperly removed. The plaintiff claimed the manufacturer was strictly liable for the damages from the use of its product.[67]

§ 6.12   Enhanced Risk of Cancer and Impairment of Quality of Life

Some plaintiffs have filed suits on the theory that they have an enhanced risk of developing cancer as a result of exposure to a toxic substance. The courts have not generally recognized such claims. However, the New Jersey Supreme Court said it would recognize such a claim if the plaintiff could prove to a reasonable degree of medical certainty that the disease will occur.[68] This is considered a significant case because it represents a slowing down of the expansion of liability. The court felt it was in everyone's best interest to conserve limited financial resources.

[63] Smith v. Carpets by Direct Inc., No. 89-CVS-4974 (Super. Ct., Guilford Co., N.C. Feb. 13, 1990).

[64] Real Estate Weekly, Jan. 17, 1990, at 1, col. 3.

[65] Cinnaminson Township Board of Education v. U.S. Gypsum Co., 552 F. Supp. 855 (D.N.J. 1982), aff'd, 882 F.2d 510 (3d Cir. 1989). See also Adams-Arapahoe School District No. 28-J v. Celotex Corp., 637 F. Supp. 1207 (D. Colo. 1986); City of Greenville v. W.R. Grace & Co., 827 F.2d 975 (4th Cir. 1987).

[66] See § 1.13.

[67] Pennsylvania Dept. of Transportation v. Congoleum Corp., Pa. Commw. Ct., No. 45 MD 1990, Feb. 12, 1990; Asbestos Abatement Report, Mar. 19, 1990. The contractor who installed the new flooring was sued for negligence and breach of contract.

[68] Mauro v. Owens-Corning Fiberglass Corp., 116 N.J. 126, 561 A.2d 257 (N.J. Sup. Ct. 1989).

There has also been a successful claim using the novel theory of impairment of the quality of life.[69] Over $5 million was awarded on a claim of deterioration of town residents' quality of life when they were deprived of potable water for 20 months because of contamination of the aquifer by pollutants leaching from the township's landfill. The quality of life damages were considered by the court to be compensation for losses associated with damage to the property.[70]

§ 6.13   Breach of Warranty

Warranties in the environmental area can arise in a number of different situations. There may be express warranties by the manufacturer or seller of a product. There may also be warranties in various contracts for the sale of property or in leases.

This theory is commonly used against asbestos manufacturers and suppliers. However, this type of lawsuit may ultimately be barred because of applicable statutes of limitations: often, these products were installed many years before the individual became ill or the problem arose.

Where there has been a claim for breach of an express warranty, such as in mass advertisements by a manufacturer and labeling to ultimate business users or consumers with whom the manufacturer has no direct contractual relationship, the requirement of privity of contract has been dispensed with.[71] Liability is based on the falsity of the presentation, not on any particular knowledge of the seller.[72]

Breach of warranty may be used by employers who sue companies that are suppliers of products that pollute the workplace. Employees may try to claim that they are third-party beneficiaries of product warranties.

State commercial codes contain implied warranties of merchantability, fitness for the ordinary purposes for which products are used, and fitness for a particular purpose. Because asbestos is inherently dangerous, most asbestos-containing products may be similarly classified. Urea formaldehyde foam, which releases gas into a building, may fall into this category. One plaintiff suffered respiratory injury from the release of irritating fumes emitted from a bathroom cleaner. The plaintiff prevailed in a suit against the manufacturer, because the product was not fit for ordinary use.[73]

---

[69] Ayers v. Township of Jackson, 106 N.J. 557, 525 A.2d 287 (1987).

[70] Id. 525 A.2d at 294.

[71] Solow v. W.R. Grace & Co., 1989 N.Y. Misc. LEXIS 894 (N.Y. Sup. 1989), N.Y.L.J., Aug. 9, 1989, at 17.

[72] State consumer protection and deceptive trade practice laws may also apply.

[73] Shirley v. The Drackett Products Co., 26 Mich. App. 644, 182 N.W.2d 726 (1970).

On claims for breach of an implied warranty when there are only property damages or economic loss, privity has been required by the courts (i.e., a direct sale by each defendant manufacturer to the plaintiff personally or through agents).[74] Having an asbestos product merely wind up in a building is not considered enough.

This theory is also applicable to defective homes. There may be express warranties because home owners are often directly involved in purchasing products for their homes. In such cases, diminution in value is a standard measure of damages. Other damages may include repair costs and incidental and consequential damages.[75] In one case, the third buyers of a house were awarded damages from the builder for formaldehyde odors emanating from the original carpet and padding, which were found to have been in breach of the warranty of habitability.[76]

Commercial tenants and employees are less likely to be involved in purchasing products. They may argue that they are intended third-party beneficiaries, but it is unclear whether implied warranties of habitability apply to commercial property as they do to residential property.

California has recognized an implied warranty of fitness for human habitation in the landlord–tenant relationship. Tenants may sue for injuries caused by unfit housing owned by landlords.[77] Injured employees may sue their employer's landlord. Some states may require a showing that the landlord had knowledge of the condition before awarding judgment for the plaintiffs.[78]

§ 6.14   —Covenant of Quiet Enjoyment and
Warranty of Habitability

When a tenant is unable to continue to occupy leased premises because an action by a landlord obstructs, interferes with, or takes away from the tenant, in a substantial degree, the beneficial use of the leasehold, the tenant may be entitled to damages and relocation. The breach may involve either an express provision in the lease or an implied warranty.[79] For commercial tenants, such a situation would be a breach of the covenant of

---

[74] *Id.*

[75] McDonald v. Mianecki, 398 A.2d 1283, 1286 (N.J. 1978).

[76] Blagg v. Fred Hunt Co., 272 Ark. 185, 612 S.W.2d 321 (1981).

[77] Cal. Civ. Code § 1941; *see also* Minn. Stat. § 504.18(1)(a).

[78] Meyer v. Parkin, 350 N.W.2d 435 (Minn. Ct. App. 1984).

[79] Nallan v. Helmsley-Spear, Inc., 50 N.Y.2d 507, 407 N.E.2d 451, 429 N.Y.S.2d 606 (1980).

quiet enjoyment resulting in constructive eviction.[80] There are usually no implied warranties for commercial property. For residential tenants, the situation would be a breach of the warranty of habitability.

An Indiana appeals court refused to hold a seller of a home liable for breach of an implied warranty of habitability after the purchasers discovered it was insulated with urea formaldehyde and sought rescission. The court found that the seller was not a builder-vendor and could not be liable for breach of an implied warranty of habitability.[81] The seller hired a professional to install insulation and relied on that individual's expertise. He did not know what kind of insulation had been used.

This theory has also been applied to residential dwellings purchased for income-producing purposes, which have never been occupied by the purchasers.[82] The builder is generally in a better position than the homeowner to know whether a house is suitable for habitation and to evaluate and guard against the financial risk posed by the defect.

Constructive eviction may also be claimed when building services are materially disrupted during abatement or when the potential hazard is so great that the tenant is deprived of the use of the premises. The disruption must be so severe as to amount to eviction or ouster. Termination of the lease due to the mere presence of a dangerous substance such as asbestos is not supportable under current law.[83]

There is a trend to extend the implied warranty of habitability to subsequent purchasers of residential dwellings who suffer purely economic loss from latent defects that manifest themselves within a reasonable time, even if there is no privity of contract.[84]

This is a major remedy and is not granted lightly. Thus, when a law firm claimed it was forced to move to escape noxious fumes from a renovation by another tenant, the court did not find a breach of the covenant of quiet enjoyment.[85] However, when a building owner leased a building to a tenant

---

[80] Constructive eviction is defined as "[a]ny disturbance of the tenant's possession by the landlord whereby the premises are rendered unfit or unsuitable for occupancy in whole or in substantial part for the purposes for which they were leased . . . if the tenant so elects . . . [to] surrender his possession." Black's Law Dictionary 284 (5th ed. 1979).

[81] Kaminszky v. Kukuch, 553 N.E.2d 868 (Ind. App. 3d Dist. 1990).

[82] Tusch Enterprises v. Coffin, 740 P.2d 1022 (1987).

[83] *But see, e.g.,* 1 Tiffany, The Law of Real Property § 144 n.18, *citing* Sully v. Schmidt, 147 N.Y. 248, 41 N.E. 514 (1895) (constructive eviction when sewer under premises became a menace to life and health).

[84] Barnes v. Mac Brown & Co., Inc., 264 Ind. 227, 342 N.E.2d 619 (1976); Terlindo v. Neely, 275 S.C. 395, 271 S.E.2d 768 (1980); Hermes v. Staiano, 181 N.J. Super. 424, 437 A.2d 925 (N.J. Super. Ct. Law Div. 1981); Blagg v. Fred Hunt Co., Inc., 272 Ark. 185, 612 S.W.2d 321 (1981).

[85] Endress v. Equitable Life Assurance, No. 81,925, slip. op., Ct. Appeals, Ohio Oct. 29, 1987.

for use as a boarding house and then built a two-story garage next door, the court found constructive eviction. The garage cut off light and air and emitted fumes.[86]

Another court upheld a commercial tenant's suit asserting breaches of the covenant of quiet enjoyment and the warranty of habitability, and seeking rescission based on mutual mistake of fact. The tenant discovered asbestos in the space four years after the lease began.[87] The court dismissed the plaintiff's claims of negligent misrepresentation and fraudulent misrepresentation against the owner and all of the claims against the building manager and the industrial hygiene firms that did the inspection. This case is unusual in that it allowed a claim for breach of the warranty of habitability by a commercial tenant.

One lower court in New York City has allowed a claim for breach of an implied warranty of fitness for use in a commercial building.[88] The nature of the warranty depends on the relationship of the parties, the nature of the tenant's business, and the nature of the commercial premises involved. The court reasoned that the lessee does not ordinarily have as much knowledge of the condition of the premises as the lessor. A small business owner cannot be expected to know whether the plumbing or wiring systems are adequate or conform to local codes. Another court allowed a claim for breach of a covenant of good faith and fair dealing to a tenant who alleged that he had been fraudulently induced to sign a lease.[89]

Breach of these covenants requires the tenant to move.[90] A tenant who is found to have moved unjustifiably may be liable for the balance due on the lease, subject to the landlord's obligation to mitigate damages.[91] If proven, the tenant may be allowed to terminate the lease or reduce the rent. The landlord may also have an affirmative duty to repair and correct a defect. Thus, a tenant suffering from hazardous substances should be armed with thorough lab and environmental consultant's reports before moving out or not paying rent. Appropriate legal counsel is essential, because litigation will almost surely result.

---

[86] Blaustein v. Pincus, 47 Mont. 202, 131 P. 1064 (1913).

[87] Gurman, Jurtis & Black v. Charles E. Smith Mgmt., Inc., *reported* 2 Nat'l J. Asb. Buildings Lit. 10 (July 28, 1989); 40 Associates Inc. v. Katz, 112 Misc. 2d 215, 446 N.Y.S.2d 844 (Civ. Ct. N.Y. City 1981).

[88] 40 Associates Inc. v. Katz, 112 Misc. 2d 215, 446 N.Y.S.2d 844 (Civ. Ct. N.Y. City 1981). Other New York courts have taken a contrary view. Bomze v. Jay Lee Photo Suppliers, Inc., 117 Misc. 2d 957, 460 N.Y.S.2d 862 (1983). *See also* Kachian v. Aronson, 123 Misc. 2d 743, 475 N.Y.S.2d 214 (1984).

[89] ARZ Acres, Inc. v. Satellite Business Systems, No. 106,608, Cuyahoga Co., Ohio.

[90] Schulman v. Vera, 108 Cal. App. 3d 552, 558–63, 166 Cal. Rptr. 620, 623–26 (1980).

[91] Endress v. Equitable Life Assurance, No. 81,925, slip op., Ct. Appeals, Ohio, Oct. 29, 1987.

There may be implied warranties of merchantability and of fitness for a particular purpose under the states' commercial codes, which contain standards for a product's fitness for the use for which it is sold and for its safety, quality, and utility or merchantability. The duty to meet these standards is separate and distinct from the manufacturer's duty to warn and test.

§ 6.15   Indemnification and Restitution

The theory of indemnification allows a party to recover from others the damages he or she is required to pay. The *Restatement of Law, Restitution* states, with respect to indemnity:

> A person who, in whole or in part, has discharged a duty which is owed by him but which as between himself and another should have been discharged by the other, is entitled to indemnity from the other, unless the payor is barred by the wrongful nature of his conduct.[92]

Under this section, parties seeking indemnity have an independent duty to discharge whatever they are seeking indemnification for. In the case of abatement costs, plaintiffs would have to pay for them first before suing to recover their cost.

In *City of New York v. Keene Corporation,*[93] the court allowed the concept of indemnity as stated in the *Restatement of Law* to be used as a theory in a case brought by New York City and its Board of Education to recover asbestos abatement costs from asbestos manufacturers, installers, and others.

The court pointed out that, to recover in indemnity, an owner must allege the source of the owner's duty to rectify the hazardous conditions caused by ACM and the source of the manufacturer's duty to do the same.

> If defendants are ultimately found to have breached a duty under one of the other causes of action asserted, for example, under either the strict liability or negligence causes of action . . . then, the breach of that duty could serve as the basis for an indemnity claim.[94]

The owner's duty to abate can be found in several ways. For example, AHERA requires school districts to respond to the presence of asbestos by conducting surveys, developing response measures, and preparing

---

[92] Restatement of Law, Restitution § 76 (1937).

[93] 132 Misc. 2d 745, 505 N.Y.S.2d 782, 784 (1986); *aff'd,* 129 N.Y.S.2d 1019, 513 N.Y.S.2d 1004 (1st Dept. 1987).

[94] *Id.* 505 N.Y.S.2d at 785. *Contra,* City of Greenville, Tenn. v. Nat'l Gypsum Co., CV 2-83-294, slip op. (decision of magistrate) (E.D. Tenn. Dec. 21, 1983).

management plans. Schools must pay for asbestos-abatement activities that arguably are the obligation of the manufacturer. Schools may also have a common-law as well as a statutory duty to provide a safe and healthy environment for schoolchildren. The court also found that abating an imminently dangerous condition can support a cause of action in indemnity.[95]

Building owners have a common-law duty to eliminate or warn of known hidden dangers. Friable asbestos probably constitutes such a hidden danger. Depending on the use of the building, the owners may also have a common-law duty to act reasonably to discover possible dangerous conditions, even those of which they previously had no knowledge.[96]

An owner who renovates or demolishes a building may be required to abate ACM if a minimum amount will be disturbed during construction or demolition. The right to indemnity or restitution would accrue during renovation or demolition. The damages would be the difference between the cost of asbestos abatement and the demolition or renovation costs that would have been incurred if no asbestos had been present.

An interesting situation is presented when a city at one time required asbestos fireproofing and now requires its removal prior to renovation and demolition activities. Should the city be required to reimburse an owner for asbestos abatement costs? This issue has not been litigated yet.

Section 115 of the *Restatement of Law* states, with respect to restitution:

> A person who has performed the duty of another by supplying things or services, although acting without the other's knowledge or consent, is entitled to restitution from the other if
>
> (a) he acted unofficiously and with intent to charge therefor, and
>
> (b) the things or services supplied were immediately necessary to satisfy the requirements of public decency, health or safety.[97]

Under this section, the party seeking restitution does not have to abate the asbestos before seeking reimbursement.

To be successful in either an indemnification or a restitution suit, a plaintiff must have the following:

1. A viable underlying claim for which the plaintiff is seeking indemnity or restitution, such as strict liability or fraud;
2. Proof of having actually incurred the abatement costs claimed.[98]

---

[95] City of New York v. Keene Corp., 505 N.Y.S.2d at 786.

[96] Prosser and Keaton, On the Law of Torts § 60, at 417 (5th Ed. 1984).

[97] Restatement of Law, Restitution § 115 (1937).

[98] City of New York v. Keene Corp., 505 N.Y.S.2d at 787.

If the manufacturers of a dangerous product do not test for environmental danger, they have a duty to abate the hazard; if they refuse to do so, they must pay for abatement. The courts have granted restitution to the one who performed the duty by finding a *quasi* contract.[99] The elements of this theory are:

1. The manufacturer has negligently or knowingly supplied a material that is unsafe or dangerous for the use for which it was supplied;
2. The user or recipient justifiably relied on the supplier's or manufacturer's care;
3. The condition must constitute a nuisance by threatening danger to the public welfare;
4. The person having the duty must first be requested to perform it, unless considerations of urgency render a prior request unfeasible.[100]

In *United States v. P/B STCO 213, ON 527 979,*[101] the Fifth Circuit held that, because polluters had a cleanup duty, the "avoidance and consequent shifting to another of the cost of performing a duty that one is primarily obligated to perform" is unjust enrichment. The court recognized a quasi-contract enforcing the duty of one party to reimburse another.[102]

The statute of limitations begins to run when the removal is completed and payment can be demanded from the person whose duty the plaintiff performed.[103] The removal of friable asbestos must be done promptly or dismissal of the cause of action may result.[104]

CERCLA expressly preserves the right of private parties to contractually transfer liability to another or release another from liability (i.e., enter into an indemnification agreement). CERCLA provides:

> No indemnification, hold harmless, or similar agreement or conveyance shall be effective to transfer from the owner or operator of any vessel or facility or from any person who may be liable for a release or threat of release under this section. Nothing in this subsection shall bar any agreement to

---

[99] United States v. P/B STCO 213, ON 527 979, 756 F.2d 364 (5th Cir. 1985).

[100] Brandon Township v. Jerome Builders, Inc., 80 Mich. App. 180, 183, 262 N.W.2d 326, 328 (1978).

[101] *Supra* note 99.

[102] *Id.* at 371.

[103] United States v. Boyd, 520 F.2d 642, 644 (6th Cir. 1975), *cert. denied,* 423 U.S. 1050 (1976).

[104] Corporation of Mercer Univ. v. National Gypsum Co., 832 F.2d 1233, Prod. Liab. Rep. (CCH) P 11603 (11th Cir. Ga. 1987), *certified ques. ans.* 258 Ga. 365, 368 S.E.2d 732 (1988), 877 F.2d 35, Prod. Liab. Rep. (CCH) P 12202, *cert. denied,* 110 S. Ct. 408, 107 F.2d 374 (Ga. 1989).

insure, hold harmless, or indemnify a party to such agreement for any liability under this section.[105]

This does not apply to a government-instituted cleanup.

Contracts requiring indemnification must contain express indemnification provisions.[106] Such clauses can be found in leases and contracts of sale. A release from "all claims, demands and causes of action" was held to encompass CERCLA claims without express reference to the statute.[107] However, it would seem prudent to have an express provision mentioning the statute. Causes of action based on breach of a contract's indemnity provision would be governed by the applicable state statute of limitations.[108]

Because these theories are based on equity, they are available only to those who actually incur abatement costs. A party cannot sue in equity to finance an abatement project. A claim may also be barred by laches if the owner delays in taking steps to remedy the hazard.

§ 6.16   Fraud

Fraud can come about through either a fraudulent misrepresentation or a failure to disclose a material fact. The general elements of fraudulent misrepresentation are:

(1) That a representation was made;

(2) concerning a presently existing material fact;

(3) which was false;

(4) which the representor either

  (a) knew to be false, or

  (b) made recklessly, knowing he had insufficient knowledge upon which to base such representation;

(5) for the purpose of inducing the other party to act upon it;

(6) that the other party, acting reasonably and in ignorance of its falsity;

(7) did in fact rely upon it;

(8) and was thereby induced to act;

(9) to his injury and damage.[109]

---

[105] 42 U.S.C. § 9607(e)(1). *See also* Marden Corp. v. C.G.C. Music, Ltd., 600 F. Supp. 1049 (D. Ariz. 1984), *aff'd on other grounds,* 804 F.2d 1454, 1459 (9th Cir. 1986).

[106] The Southland Corp. v. Ashland Oil, Inc., 696 F. Supp. 994, 1002 (D.N.J. 1988).

[107] FMC Corp. v. Northern Pump Co., 668 F. Supp. 1285, 1292 (D. Minn. 1987), *appeal dismissed,* 871 F.2d 1091 (8th Cir. 1988).

[108] The Southland Corp. v. Ashland Oil, Inc., 696 F. Supp. at 1004.

[109] Restatement (Second) of Torts §§ 525–59 (1977).

Nondisclosure may be the basis of a lawsuit when there is a duty to disclose a material fact. A duty is imposed:

(1) where a fiduciary relationship between the parties to a transaction exists;

(2) where information later becomes known to one party that would correct a prior representation made to the other;

(3) where one party to a business transaction learns that a previous misrepresentation made for another purpose is about to induce action by the other;

(4) where one party learns that additional information must be disclosed to prevent a partial disclosure from becoming misleading to the other party; and

(5) where one party knows that the other party to a transaction is about to act under a mistaken assumption of the facts and would reasonably expect the first party to disclose facts to correct such assumption.[110]

For example, a lawsuit can occur when a real estate broker or a landlord fails to disclose the presence of a hazardous substance in property being sold or leased. If the broker represents a seller, there may be a fiduciary duty.[111] There may also be a statutory duty to avoid misleading the purchaser.

Some owners have sued prior building owners for their fraudulent failure to disclose the existence of asbestos prior to sale. The difficulty in maintaining such a suit is the legal requirement that the circumstances of the fraud must be stated in detail. There must also be detrimental reliance by the party to whom the misrepresentations were made.[112] For these reasons, such causes of action often do not survive motions to dismiss or are not successful at trial.

In denying the defendant's motion to dismiss, the court in *195 Broadway Company v. 195 Broadway Corporation*,[113] stated that, considering the allegations that asbestos in the building was a dangerous condition and endangered the health, safety, and welfare of those occupying the building, a duty for the seller-landlord to disclose the presence of asbestos to the tenant may be found. The court left for trial the issues of whether the defendant knew of the existence of the asbestos and whether the plaintiff could have ascertained its presence with reasonable diligence.

Plaintiffs who had been persuaded to purchase pest control services for a termite problem that did not exist were successful when they alleged that

---

[110] *Id.* at § 551.

[111] Hagar v. Mobley, 638 P.2d 127, 137–38 (Wyo. 1981); Tennant v. Lawton, 26 Wash. App. 701, 706, 615 P.2d 1305, 1309 (1980).

[112] Solow v. W.R. Grace & Co., 1989 N.Y. Misc. LEXIS 894 (N.Y. Sup. 1989), N.Y.L.J. Aug. 9, 1989, at 17.

[113] (Sup. Ct. N.Y. Co.), N.Y.L.J., Apr. 15, 1988, 6, col. 3.

the company had used unfair or deceptive means to persuade them to purchase such services, which resulted in chlordane poisoning.[114]

Because the field of environmental law is constantly evolving, many possible lawsuits could be filed based on extensions of the principles upon which earlier cases have been decided. For example, the *195 Broadway* case may serve as the basis for holding a building owner-landlord liable to a tenant for failing to disclose the existence of a dangerous asbestos condition *prior* to the execution of a lease. This principle may be applicable to both commercial and residential tenants.

A federal court has upheld a cause of action grounded in fraud for failure to disclose the presence of asbestos in connection with the purchase of a single-family home.[115]

Fraudulent concealment may be claimed for failure to notify employees of the fact that they have been exposed to hazardous substances. This argument may also be used to bypass the limitations created by workers' compensation laws.[116]

§ 6.17   Negligence

Negligence is the failure to exercise the degree of care that would be exercised by a "reasonable person." A claim of negligence requires: (1) a legal duty; (2) a breach of that duty; (3) actual and proximate causation; and (4) damage.

Negligence in the environmental area can be found in a variety of areas. It is often found in the performance of professional services. An architect may be alleged to have negligently designed a building to be too "tight" (inadequate ventilation does not allow indoor pollutants to escape), or to have specified unsafe products, such as chairs that emit toxic fumes when they burn. More typically, negligence can be found in the manufacture or specification and use of hazardous products or products containing hazardous substances. A contractor renovating a building may be negligent in releasing asbestos. The owner or seller of a building may be liable in negligence for failing to test for indoor pollutants or to reveal results to tenants and purchasers.

Negligence may also be involved in: the selection of asbestos consultants and contractors; the actual removal of asbestos and other hazardous

---

[114] Bardura v. Orkin Exterminating Co., 664 F. Supp. 1218 (N.D. Ill. 1987), *aff'd,* 865 F.2d 816 (7th Cir. 1988).

[115] Kinsey v. Jones, Civ. 87-2959 (JM) (E.D.N.Y. Jan. 30, 1989).

[116] Blankenship v. Cincinnati Milacron Chemicals, 69 Ohio St. 2d 608, 433 N.E.2d 572, *cert. denied,* 459 U.S. 857 (1982); Jones v. VIP Development Co., 15 Ohio St. 3d 90, 472 N.E.2d 1046 (1984); Millison v. E.I. DuPont de Nemours & Co., 94 N.J. 604, 468 A.2d 236 (1983).

substances; the implementation of tests; and a failure to warn tenants and employees.

A violation of a statute, ordinance, or regulation may lead to a rebuttable presumption that there was an absence of due care. Standards of what constitutes "due care" vary from jurisdiction to jurisdiction.

In the context of negligence caused by a product, a plaintiff must show that the product was dangerously defective when it left the defendant's hands and that the defect was the result of the defendant's failure to exercise due care. A manufacturer has a continuing duty to warn of a product's danger. For failure to do so, the manufacturer may be liable in negligence or strict liability.

Failure to act as a reasonable person in the use or handling of a hazardous substance may result in liability for a seller.[117] Although a claim was made for misapplication of a termiticide to a residence, one court found that it was not supported by the evidence.[118] However, the theory may be valid in another case with stronger facts.

Failure of a lessor to exercise reasonable care over its tenant's activities may be the basis for a negligence claim, especially if the tenant is using hazardous substances or renovates in a negligent fashion. A landlord may also be liable in negligence in the selection of a tenant.[119]

One court found that a co-owner of property "had a duty to prevent the improper use of landfill" even though she was not actively involved in its operation.[120]

A Virginia court adopted the *Restatement (Second) of Torts* § 388, which states:

> The manufacturer . . . will be subject to liability when he (a) knows or has reason to know [his product] is or is likely to be dangerous for the use for which it is supplied, and (b) has no reason to believe that those for whose use the [product] is supplied will realize its dangerous condition, and (c) fails to exercise reasonable care to inform them of its dangerous condition or of the facts which make it likely to be dangerous.[121]

The manufacturer's duty to warn is especially important for an inherently dangerous product, such as asbestos.[122] Liability for damage due to

---

[117] Knabe v. National Supply Division of Armco Steel Corp., 592 F.2d 841 (5th Cir. 1979).

[118] Rabb v. Orkin Exterminating Co., Inc., 677 F. Supp. 424 (D.S.C. 1987).

[119] New York v. Monarch Chemicals Inc., 90 A.2d 907, 456 N.Y.S.2d 867 (3d Dept. 1982).

[120] United States v. Price, 523 F. Supp. 1055 (D.N.J. 1981), *aff'd,* 688 F.2d 204 (3d Cir. 1982).

[121] Featherall v. Firestone Tire & Rubber Co., 219 Va. 949, 962, 252 S.E.2d 358 (1979).

[122] Glover v. Johns-Manville Corp., 525 F. Supp. 894 (E.D. Va. 1979), *aff'd in part, vacated in part,* 662 F.2d 225 (4th Cir. 1981); Oman v. Johns-Manville Corp., 764 F.2d 224 (4th Cir. 1985), *cert. denied,* 474 U.S. 970 (1985).

negligence, either by failing to warn or by selling a defective product, attaches when the injury occurs to the property.[123]

There may also be claims for a negligent misrepresentation of the fact that no hazardous condition exists, when in fact it does. If a consultant represents that the premises are safe or free of hazardous substances and they are later found not to be, he or she may be sued. Damages for economic loss are usually sought.[124]

§ 6.18   Breach of Contract

If written representations or warranties are made in contracts for the sale of a property or building or in a lease and certain stated facts are later discovered not to be true, there may be a breach of contract action. If, for example, representations are made that there are no hazardous substances present prior to sale or execution of a lease and this later proves to be untrue, a breach of contract action may lie.[125]

Breach of contract actions may be brought against removal and abatement contractors because of the quality of their work. A court recently awarded breach-of-contract damages to a couple because their home was contaminated when a flooring company improperly removed asbestos-backed flooring.[126]

As with any contract for services, a consultant or design professional who does not fulfill requirements under a contract may be sued for breach of contract.

§ 6.19   Securities Law Violations

Cooperative corporations have become a common form of property ownership. Residents own shares of stock in the corporation. These shares are sold through offering plans. If the presence of asbestos or other hazardous substances is not disclosed in a prospectus prior to sale, an action for securities fraud may lie.[127]

If representations in a stock purchase agreement for any type of corporation are found to be misstatements or there are omissions of material facts, the shareholders may have a private cause of action under § 10(b) of the

---

[123] Stone v. Ethan Allen, Inc., 232 Va. 365, 350 S.E.2d 629 (1986).

[124] Westrom v. Kerr-McGee Chemical Corp., No. 82-C-2034 (N.D. Ill. Oct. 4, 1983).

[125] Clearwater Forest Industries, Inc. v. United States, 650 F.2d 233 (Ct. Cl. 1981).

[126] Smith v. Carpets by Direct Inc., No. 89-CVS-4974 (Super. Ct., Guilford Co., N.C. Feb. 13, 1990); Asbestos Abatement Report, Mar. 5, 1990, at 4.

[127] Securities Exchange Act of 1934 § 10(b), 15 U.S.C. § 78j(b) (1982).

Securities and Exchange Act of 1934 ("the 1934 Act").[128] Liability or potential liability from hazardous waste may be a "material fact" that should have been disclosed prior to the closing of the stock purchase.

Section 10(b) of the 1934 Act makes it unlawful for any person:

> [t]o use or employ, in connection with the purchase or sale of any security registered on a national securities exchange or any security not so registered, any manipulative or deceptive device or contrivance in contravention of such rules and regulations as the Commission may prescribe as necessary or appropriate in the public interest or for the protection of investors.[129]

Pursuant to authority granted by § 10(b), the Securities and Exchange Commission (SEC) promulgated Rule 10b-5, which provides:

> It shall be unlawful for any person, directly or indirectly, by the use of any means or instrumentality of interstate commerce, or of the mails, or of any facility of any national securities exchange,
>
> (a) to employ any device, scheme, or artifice to defraud,
>
> (b) to make any untrue statement of a *material fact* or to omit to state a material fact necessary in order to make the statements made, in the light of the circumstances under which they were made, not misleading, or
>
> (c) to engage in any act, practice, or course of business which operates or would operate as a fraud or deceit upon any person, in connection with the purchase or sale of any security.[130] [Emphasis added.]

It is well-established, although not expressly stated in the statute or regulations, that a violation of Rule 10b-5 gives rise to an implied private cause of action.[131] To prevail on a Rule 10b-5 claim, case law requires that the plaintiff establish the following facts:

1. A purchase or sale of securities occurred;
2. A breach of fiduciary or comparable duty was fraudulent;
3. The fraudulent breach was in the form of a material misrepresentation or omission;
4. This material misrepresentation or omission was in connection with the sale of a security;[132]
5. An instrumentality of interstate commerce was used;

---

[128] *Id.*

[129] 15 U.S.C. § 78j(b).

[130] 17 C.F.R. § 240.10b-5 (1988).

[131] Basic Inc. v. Levinson, 485 U.S. 224, 108 S. Ct. 978, 983 (1988).

[132] TSC Industries, Inc. v. Northway, Inc., 426 U.S. 438, 440, 96 S. Ct. 2126, 2128, 48 L. Ed. 2d 757 (1976).

6. *Scienter* (intent to deceive)[133] on the part of the defendant or a reckless disregard for the truth occurred;[134]

7. Resultant damages are related to the material misstatement or omission;

8. Plaintiff incurred these damages because of reliance on the misstatement or omission.[135]

Plaintiff's reliance must be justifiable. It must be proven that the plaintiff did not disregard a known risk or a risk so obvious that the plaintiff must be taken to have been aware of it and so great as to make it highly probable that harm would follow.[136]

There is a duty of disclosure where a purchaser acquires environmental liability through stock purchases and a stock purchase agreement is drawn.[137] A fact is "material" when "there is a substantial likelihood that a reasonable shareholder would consider it important in deciding how to vote."[138] A plaintiff need only show that there is *substantial likelihood* that a reasonable investor would have viewed the disclosure of the omitted fact as having significantly altered the "total mix" of available information evaluated by the purchase.[139] Liability for environmental cleanup is usually so substantial in terms of dollars that it would probably be deemed material information for making an investment decision.

A false or incomplete statement is not *per se* misleading as to a "material" fact. The false or incomplete statement must first be significant before it can be found to be material. Materiality involves balancing the probability of contingent or speculative events and the magnitude of the impact of the events on the totality of company activities.[140]

The SEC has not promulgated any rules or regulations expressly governing the duty to disclose contingent environmental liability in the sale of stock in a closely held corporation, but has issued an interpretive release

---

[133] Ernst & Ernst v. Hochfelder, 425 U.S. 185, 96 S. Ct. 1375, 47 L. Ed. 2d 668 (1976).

[134] Sundstrand Corp. v. Sun Chemical Corp., 553 F.2d 1033, 1043–45 (7th Cir.), *cert. denied sub nom.* Meers v. Sundstrand Corp., 434 U.S. 875, 98 S. Ct. 224, 54 L. Ed. 2d 155 (1977).

[135] *Id.*

[136] *Id.* 553 F.2d at 1048.

[137] Fishman, *Duty to Disclose Under Rule 10b-5 in Face-to-Face Transactions,* 12 J. Corp. L. 251, 287–93 (1987).

[138] Basic Inc. v. Levinson, 485 U.S. 224, 108 S. Ct. 978 (1988); TSC Industries, Inc. v. Northway, Inc., 426 U.S. 438, 96 S. Ct. 2126, 48 L. Ed. 2d 757 (1976).

[139] Basic Inc. v. Levinson, 485 U.S. at 240.

[140] *Id.*

informing public companies that existing securities laws require disclosure of all material environmental information.[141]

The SEC directed that such information should include but not be limited to: (1) the existence and nature of pending environmental litigation and (2) circumstances in which compliance with environmental laws "may necessitate significant capital outlays, may materially affect the earning power of the business, or cause material changes in the registrant's business done."[142]

In 1973, the SEC issued regulations that expanded the disclosure requirements of companies regarding environmental matters, as follows:

> [D]isclosure shall also be made as to the material effects that compliance with Federal, State and local provisions which have been enacted or adopted regulating the discharge of materials into the environment, or otherwise relating to the protection of the environment, may have upon the capital expenditures, earnings and competitive position of the registrant and its subsidiaries.[143]

An interpretive release issued later by the SEC addressed the issues that public companies are required to disclose:

1. Total estimated expenditures for environmental compliance beyond two years into the future, as contemplated in the regulations as amended in 1976;
2. Particular types of environmental proceedings;
3. Circumstances under which companies must disclose their policies or approaches concerning environmental compliance.

With regard to total estimated expenditures for environmental compliance, the SEC stated that the principle underlying the two-year disclosure was a requirement that companies indicate the material economic effects that environmental compliance would have on the capital expenditures and earnings of a public company.[144]

---

[141] *See* Disclosures Pertaining to Matters Involving the Environment and Civil Rights, Securities Act Release No. 5170 (July 19, 1971), 36 Fed. Reg. 13,989 (1971).

[142] *Id.*

[143] Notice of Adoption of Amendments to Registration and Report Forms to Require Disclosure with Respect to Compliance with Environmental Requirements and Other Matters, Securities Act Release No. 5386 (Apr. 20, 1973), 38 Fed. Reg. 12,100 (1973).

[144] Environmental Disclosure, Securities Act Release No. 6130, Exchange Act Release No. 16224, 18 SEC Docket (CCH) 453 (Sept. 27, 1979). This release was issued partially in response to: *In re* United States Steel Corp., Exchange Act Release No. 16223, 18 SEC Docket (CCH) 497 (Sept. 27, 1979).

A more recent regulation requires publicly held companies that issue securities—such as corporations, master limited partnerships, and trusts—to include nonfinancial environmental information in SEC registration statements and periodic reports filed with the SEC.[145] A security under the regulations has been broadly defined.[146] Material pending legal proceedings must be disclosed, including any proceedings known to be contemplated by governmental authorities.[147]

If a corporation makes statements in a stock purchase agreement, they must be complete and truthful.[148]

Two SEC Interpretive Releases issued on May 18, 1989, require companies to more fully disclose the potential effect of being designated a potentially responsible party under CERCLA.[149] Companies are being forced to disclose CERCLA liability and quantify the risk "to the extent reasonably practicable."

The use of an instrumentality in interstate commerce can be satisfied by use of a telephone; the use of the interstate instrumentality need only be incidental to the transaction.[150]

The defendant must have acted with *scienter* (i.e., intent to deceive, manipulate, or defraud).[151] Some courts have held that recklessness satisfies this requirement.[152] A defendant who was active in company management or who was on the board of directors is more likely to be able to satisfy the *scienter* requirement than is a passive shareholder.

Reliance must be reasonable, considering the facts and circumstances.[153] The plaintiff's knowledge or sophistication may be a factor,[154]

---

[145] Regulation S-K, 17 C.F.R. § 229 (1989).

[146] Hocking v. Dubois, 839 F.2d 560 (9th Cir. 1988), *vacated,* 863 F.2d 654 (1988), *cert. denied,* 110 S. Ct. 1805 (1990). The federal appellate court found that a real estate broker who offered for sale a single condominium unit with an option for a rental pool arrangement was offering a "security" subject to SEC regulation.

[147] 17 C.F.R. § 229.103 (1989).

[148] *In re* United States Steel Corp., Exchange Act Release No. 16223, 18 SEC Docket (CCH) 497, 505 (Sept. 27, 1979).

[149] SEC Interpretive Releases Nos. 33-6835 and 34-26831.

[150] Gower v. Cohn, 643 F.2d 1146, 1151–52 (5th Cir. 1981).

[151] Ernst & Ernst v. Hochfelder, 425 U.S. at 193.

[152] *See, e.g.,* Woods v. Barnett Bank of Fort Lauderdale, 765 F.2d 1004, 1010, *reh'g denied, en banc,* 772 F.2d 918 (11th Cir. 1985); Sharp v. Coopers & Lybrand, 649 F.2d 175, 193 (3d Cir. 1981), *cert. denied,* 455 U.S. 938 (1982); Mansbach v. Prescott, Ball & Turben, 598 F.2d 1017, 1023 (6th Cir. 1979), *called into doubt by* Moncrieff v. Merrill Lynch, Pierce, Fenner & Smith, Inc., 623 F. Supp. 1005 (E.D. Mich. 1985); Sundstrand Corp. v. Sun Chemical Corp., *supra* note 135, 553 F.2d at 1045.

[153] Vervaecke v. Chiles, Heider & Co., 578 F.2d 713, 718 (8th Cir. 1978). *See* St. Louis Union Trust Co. v. Merrill Lynch, Pierce, Fenner & Smith, Inc., 562 F.2d 1040, 1048 (8th Cir. 1977), *cert. denied,* 435 U.S. 925 (1978).

[154] *See* Beck v. Cantor, Fitzgerald & Co., 621 F. Supp. 1547, 1558 (N.D. Ill. 1985).

but reliance is presumed when there is a failure to disclose material facts.[155] This presumption would be true if the stock purchase agreement failed to disclose environmental liabilities. The plaintiff's due diligence in investigating the business would also be important in determining whether there was reliance.

To establish causation, the plaintiff would have to show that the defendant's fraudulent conduct caused the harm suffered by the plaintiff and that nondisclosure of the alleged violations caused the plaintiff to engage in the transaction giving rise to the suit.[156]

A stockholder in a savings and loan company (S&L) filed a class action suit charging that the S&L's stock value had been artificially inflated because management had hidden the costs associated with asbestos problems.[157] The suit followed a verdict against the S&L for over $9 million, won by the purchasers of a Denver office building who claimed that the bank had defrauded them by failing to disclose that the building contained at least 430,000 square feet of asbestos fireproofing. The complaint charged that the bank reported a profit of $5.7 million in 1984 but would have reported a loss of $3.8 million without the sale of the office building. The plaintiff claimed that the officers violated § 10(b) of the Securities Act, Rule 10b-5, and RICO, by filing quarterly and annual reports that failed to disclose the problem.

In another case, a corporation and several of its managing officers were found liable for not disclosing the existence of fines, potential fines, or illegal waste disposal.[158] They allegedly misrepresented or withheld information concerning the company's compliance with environmental regulations and disputes with regulatory authorities, when they issued an annual report and a prospectus. The court found that the fraud on the market theory of recovery is a viable means of proving liability in a Rule 10b-5 action.[159]

§ 6.20 Racketeer Influenced and Corrupt Organization Act (RICO) Violations

Cooperative apartment conversions and syndicated sales of buildings have become quite common. In making these sales, offering plans are often

---

[155] See Shores v. Sklar, 647 F.2d 462, 476 (5th Cir. 1981), cert. denied, 459 U.S. 1102 (1983); Rifkin v. Crow, 574 F.2d 256, 262–63 (5th Cir. 1978).

[156] See, e.g., Harris v. Union Electric Co., 787 F.2d 355, 366 (8th Cir.), cert. denied, 479 U.S. 823 (1986); Schlick v. Penn-Dixie Cement Corp., 507 F.2d 374, 380 (2d Cir. 1974), cert. denied, 421 U.S. 976 (1975).

[157] Steiner v. J. F. Baxter, Civ. 89-809 (D.D.C. 1989).

[158] Grossman v. Waste Management, Inc., 589 F. Supp. 395 (N.D. Ill. 1984).

[159] Id. at 403.

mailed to prospective buyers, describing what is being offered for sale. Should any misrepresentations be made in these offering plans about the presence of asbestos or other hazardous substances in the building, it can be argued that fraud was committed through the mailing of the offering plan or prospectus. A private RICO action may also exist when a defrauded purchaser acquires substantial environmental liabilities through the purchase of stock. This is a powerful tool for a plaintiff, because RICO awards may include treble damages.[160]

RICO[161] makes it unlawful:

. . . for any person employed by or associated with any enterprise engaged in, or the activities of which affect, interstate or foreign commerce, to conduct or participate, directly or indirectly, in the conduct of such enterprise's affairs through a pattern of racketeering activity . . . .[162]

A party filing a RICO complaint must allege that the defendant violated the substantive or criminal RICO statutes.[163] The plaintiff must allege the following:

- A person,
- through the commission of two or more acts;[164]
- constituting a "pattern"
- of "racketeering activity,"
- directly or indirectly invests in, or maintains an interest in, or participates in
- an enterprise,
- the activities of which affect interstate or foreign commerce.

The terms "racketeering activity," "person," "enterprise," and "pattern of racketeering activity" are respectively defined as follows:

(1) "racketeering activity" means . . . any act which is indictable under any of the following provisions of [18 U.S.C.]: . . . section 1341 (relating to mail fraud) . . . ;

* * *

(3) "person" includes any individual or entity capable of holding a legal or beneficial interest in property;

[160] 18 U.S.C. § 1964(c).
[161] Pub. L. No. 91-452, 84 Stat. 941, 18 U.S.C. §§ 1961–68 (1982).
[162] 18 U.S.C. § 1962(c).
[163] 18 U.S.C. § 1962 (1982).
[164] Ray v. Karris, 780 F.2d 636, 644–45 (7th Cir. 1985).

(4) "enterprise" includes any individual, partnership, corporation, association, or other legal entity, and any union or group of individuals associated in fact although not a legal entity;

(5) "pattern of racketeering activity" requires at least two acts of racketeering activity, one of which occurred after the effective date of this chapter and the last of which occurred within ten years (excluding any period of imprisonment) after the commission of a prior act of racketeering activity; . . . .[165]

A private right of action is given to a person injured in his or her business or property by reason of a RICO violation.[166] The plaintiff must prove a violation of criminal RICO before the court will consider civil damages. The plaintiff must then allege injury in his or her business or property by reason of a violation of RICO section 1962.[167] "Any offense involving . . . fraud in the sale of securities" is a predicate offense included in the definition of "racketeering activity."[168] Other predicate offenses include mail fraud and wire fraud.[169]

To establish an offense for mail fraud or wire fraud, a defendant must show:

1. A scheme to defraud;
2. Use of interstate communications, which includes telephone or mail, in furtherance of the scheme to defraud;
3. Culpable participation by the defendant.[170]

The requisite *scienter* is found in the intent to defraud[171] and is the same as that required for securities fraud violations.[172] Each individual use of the mail or wire constitutes a separate offense, even if it is part of one fraudulent scheme.[173]

Failure to adequately disclose contingent environmental liabilities incurred through a stock purchase agreement may create both a Rule 10b-5 and a RICO action.[174]

---

[165] 18 U.S.C. § 1961(1), (3), (4), and (5).

[166] 18 U.S.C. § 1968(c).

[167] 18 U.S.C. § 1964(c).

[168] 18 U.S.C. § 1961 (1982).

[169] *Id.*

[170] 18 U.S.C. §§ 1341, 1343 (1982).

[171] United States v. Klein, 515 F.2d 751, 754 (3d Cir. 1975).

[172] *Id.* at 754.

[173] Kronfeld v. First Jersey Nat'l Bank, 638 F. Supp. 1454, 1472 (C.D.N.J. 1986).

[174] Smith v. Cooper/T. Smith Corp., 846 F.2d 325, *reh'g granted,* 850 F.2d 1086 (5th Cir. 1988).

In *Beauford v. Helmsley*,[175] a tenant who purchased a co-op and several nonpurchaser-tenants sued the real estate partnership sponsoring the co-op conversion, and others, alleging material misrepresentation, including, *inter alia,* concealment of the presence of asbestos in the insulation. The plaintiffs claimed that these frauds artificially inflated the purchase prices of the apartments and alleged that, because the frauds were committed through various mailings of offering plans and amendments thereto, they violated RICO. The trial court found that the complaint sufficiently alleged a pattern of racketeering activity; however, it was later vacated on appeal. Nevertheless, an action may lie upon subsequent appeal or in another, similar case.[176]

A RICO pattern of racketeering activity may be established by proof of two acts of racketeering activity. A pattern may be adequately pleaded without an allegation that the scheme pursuant to which the racketeering acts were performed is an ongoing scheme having no demonstrable ending point.[177] The thousands of mailings in the *Smith* case had the necessary interrelationship to be considered a pattern with the same goal of inflating profits.[178] The court itself noted that its interpretation of RICO would open the door to more such suits.[179]

§ 6.21   Market Share, Conspiracy, and Other Alternate Theories of Liability

There are five theories of liability that plaintiffs or cross-claimants in asbestos property damage and other environmentally related suits may assert, when they are unable to identify the particular manufacturer or supplier of the injury-causing asbestos or product. These five theories are:

1. Concert of action;
2. Market share liability;
3. Alternative liability;
4. Enterprise liability;
5. Risk contribution.

Of these five theories, concert of action[180] is the most commonly used.

---

[175] 865 F.2d 1386 (2d Cir. 1989), *vacated,* 109 S. Ct. 326 (1989).

[176] *Id.* 865 F.2d at 1389.

[177] *Id.* at 1391.

[178] *Id.* at 1392.

[179] *Id.* at 1393.

[180] The concert of action theory has been adopted in the Restatement (Second) of Torts § 876 (1965).

Under the concert of action theory, a plaintiff must prove both a parallel course of conduct among defendant manufacturers and an express or tacit agreement not to test adequately or not to warn of dangers. Proving an agreement among manufacturers is a difficult burden for plaintiffs. Nevertheless, in *In re Related Asbestos Cases,* [181] the court denied the defendant's motion for summary judgment when the plaintiffs were found to have met the requirements for a concert of action claim.

The market share liability theory was set forth clearly for the first time in *Sindell v. Abbott Laboratories,* [182] when the California Supreme court described this theory as an expansion of the alternative liability theory established in *Summers v. Tice.* [183] Although the market share theory has been adopted by very few jurisdictions since *Sindell,* it has been the topic of much discussion. [184] The reason for so much discussion about both alternative and market share liability is that, if either theory is found to apply, a plaintiff must only prove that he or she was exposed to and injured by a product of the type that each defendant produces, but is not required to prove which defendant was responsible for the product that caused the injury.

Under the alternative liability theory, a plaintiff must only show that he or she was injured as a proximate result of one of the defendants' wrongdoing. Under the market share liability theory, all that is needed to shift the burden of causation to the defendants is an injury by a product manufactured by the defendants in an identical method.

Courts that have accepted a market share theory have reasoned that it is an acceptable theory if the plaintiff ultimately would be able to join manufacturers that comprise a substantial market share of the injury-causing products. [185] These same courts have stated that it is reasonable to measure the likelihood that any of the defendants supplied the offending product by determining the percentage each sold in relation to the entire production of all manufacturers.

This theory is attractive for many plaintiffs, but several recent decisions have shown the inapplicability of a market share claim against asbestos manufacturers. First, a plaintiff must be able to present credible evidence that the named defendants represent a "substantial share of the market." [186]

---

[181] 543 F. Supp. 1152, 1159 (N.D. Cal. 1982).

[182] 26 Cal. 3d 588, 610–13, 607 P.2d 924, 936–38, 163 Cal. Rptr. 132 (1980).

[183] 33 Cal. 2d 80, 86, 199 P.2d 1, 4 (1948).

[184] *See* Boydstun and Webber, *Whatever Happened to "Market Share" Liability?,* For the Defense, June 1987, at 14; Boydstun and Webber, *The Narrow Scope of Market Share Liability,* For the Defense, Apr. 1988, at 23; Bates, *California Courts Limit* Sindell *Market Share Liability,* For the Defense, Jan. 1989, at 20.

[185] Sindell v. Abbott Laboratories, 26 Cal. 3d at 613, 607 P.2d at 937, 163 Cal. Rptr. at 145.

[186] Marshall v. Celotex Corp., 651 F. Supp. 389, 393 (E.D. Mich. 1987).

Second, many courts have prohibited use of the theory on public policy grounds, believing that a policy favoring recovery by an innocent plaintiff does not justify abrogation of the defendants' rights to have a causative link between their tortious acts and the plaintiff's injuries. Third, because of the great variety of manufacturing methods and percentages of asbestos content and fiber type, the market share requirement of manufacture by an identical process is lacking.[187] Finally, the prior absence of Johns-Manville, which was probably the largest asbestos supplier in the world, from any litigation has been cited as undercutting the market share requirement of "presence in the action of a substantial share of the appropriate market."[188]

Enterprise liability, a hybrid of the concert of action and alternative liability theories, has been applied to only three products: diethylstilbestrol (DES), blasting caps, and asbestos. Although enterprise liability often is confused with market share liability, the enterprise theory differs in that each manufacturer may be held liable for all injuries the product caused by virtue of adherence to an industry-wide standard of safety.

The enterprise theory was first adopted in the case of *Hall v. E.I. DuPont de Nemours & Co.*[189] DuPont was shown to have adhered to trade standards regarding the manufacture and design of blasting caps, and joint control of risk was shown by industry-wide agreement and cooperation. The plaintiff proved by a preponderance of the evidence that one of the manufacturers had manufactured the injury-causing caps, thus shifting the causation burden of proof to all the defendants.

The enterprise theory as applied to the asbestos industry has been rejected in almost every jurisdiction. Several courts have found plaintiffs unable to show adherence to any industry-wide standard; others have found the theory itself repugnant to traditional tort law notions.[190] Additionally, as with market share, the plaintiff's ability to identify at least one manufacturer whose product caused the injury makes the theory inapplicable.[191] The only court to adopt the enterprise theory in an asbestos case did so by mistake, having actually adopted the market share theory.[192]

The last theory, risk contribution, was first adopted by the Wisconsin Supreme Court in *Collins v. Eli Lilly Company,*[193] another DES case. The only other state that has adopted this theory is California, in *Gard v.*

---

[187] *See In re* Related Asbestos Cases, 543 F. Supp. 1152, 1158 (N.D. Cal. 1982); Goldman v. Johns-Manville Sales Corp., 33 Ohio St. 3d 40, 50, 514 N.E.2d 691, 700 (1987).

[188] Goldman v. Johns-Manville Sales Corp., 33 Ohio St. 3d at 51, 514 N.E.2d at 701.

[189] 345 F. Supp. 353 (E.D.N.Y. 1972).

[190] *See* Thompson v. Johns-Manville Sales Corp., 714 F.2d 581 (5th Cir. 1983), *cert. denied,* 465 U.S. 1102 (1983).

[191] *See* Prelick v. Johns-Manville Corp., 531 F. Supp. 96 (W.D. Pa. 1982).

[192] *See* Hardy v. Johns-Manville Sales Corp., 531 F. Supp. 96 (W.D. Pa. 1982).

[193] 116 Wis. 2d 166, 342 N.W.2d 37, *cert. denied,* 469 U.S. 826 (1984).

Raymark Industries. [194] Under the risk contribution theory, the plaintiff must allege and prove either negligence or strict liability, but may sue only one manufacturer. Once a *prima facie* case has been established, the burden shifts to the defendant to implead other defendants or to prove it did not manufacture the product that caused the injury.

Rules governing the above-mentioned theories are far from being settled and vary greatly from jurisdiction to jurisdiction. Alternative and market share liability theories appear to have become the most popular among asbestos plaintiffs, but courts are reluctant to accept them. Conversely, while the concert of action theory generally is accepted by most courts, it has been applied in only a handful of asbestos cases.

The newest and least tested theory, risk contribution, may work in favor of many property damage plaintiffs. If a court can be persuaded to follow the reasoning of the California court in *Gard,* plaintiffs may be able to seek punitive damages from defendants even when they were following government or industry specifications. Moreover, under *Gard,* the fact that a plaintiff cannot join other potential defendants, because the plaintiff has settled with them or because they are bankrupt, does not preclude the cause of action against the named defendants. Further, it does not preclude shifting the burden of proof to the defendants, once the plaintiff proves exposure to the products of one or more of the defendants. Thus, although risk contribution is a relatively untested theory, it may provide a viable alternative for plaintiffs who cannot meet the requirement of the more common theories or who find themselves in a jurisdiction that has rejected them.

Some plaintiffs have tried to use a conspiracy theory to show that every manufacturer in the industry was involved in keeping quiet about the dangers of asbestos and, therefore, that they can sue all of them. In most states, conspiracy is not a separate tort and such allegations have been dismissed.[195] Conspiracy claims merely increase the number of people who may be liable for a tort.[196]

Even using such a theory, plaintiffs have the difficult task of being able to prove that they purchased the asbestos-containing product from the conspirator, in addition to the other elements of the tort. This theory has not been used successfully in claims involving asbestos in buildings.[197]

---

[194] 185 Cal. App. 3d 583, 229 Cal. Rptr. 861 (Ct. App. 1986).

[195] Solow v. W.R. Grace & Co., 1989 N.Y. Misc. LEXIS 894 (N.Y. Sup. 1989), N.Y.L.J., Aug. 9, 1989, at 17.

[196] *In re* American Reserve Corp., 70 Bankr. 729 (N.D. Ill. 1987); Bulova Watch Co. v. K. Hattori & Co., 508 F. Supp. 1322 (E.D.N.Y. 1981).

[197] School District of Detroit v. Celotex Corp., *reprinted in* 3 Nat'l J. Asb. Buildings Lit. 48 (Mich. Cir. Ct., Wayne Co. Oct. 20, 1989).

Related to conspiracy is the theory of concert of action. This theory alleges that various manufacturers of asbestos acted together, either through an explicit agreement or an implicit one, to withhold information from the public regarding the health risks of asbestos in order to ensure widespread use of asbestos products. This doctrine has been allowed in personal injury cases where the precise identification of a wrongdoer is impossible, but it has not been extended to causes of action for economic loss.

§ 6.22   Rescission and "As Is" Clauses

It is not uncommon for property to be sold pursuant to a contract of sale containing an "as is" clause and for the purchaser to later discover hazardous substances. The question then is: Can an "as is" clause be used to avoid liability for contaminated property?

"As is" clauses are usually interpreted to bar only actions based on breach of warranty. The purpose of such clauses is to "negate the existence of any representations by the seller as to the particular condition, fitness and type of the premises sold. It merely means that the purchaser must take that for which he bargained, reasonable use, wear, tear and natural deterioration are excepted."[198] Claims based on CERCLA are not barred.

In *Garb-Ko v. Lansing-Lewis Services, Inc.,*[199] a seller was successful in rescinding a contract of sale of land containing a gas station and automotive parts store when it was later discovered that the property had leaking underground storage tanks. Neither party was aware of contamination on the property at the time the buy–sell agreement was executed.

A contract may be rescinded because of a mutual mistake of the parties. Rescission is an equitable remedy that is granted only at the discretion of the trial court.

The *Restatement of Contracts* states:

[W]here a mistake of both parties at the same time a contract was made as to a basic assumption on which the contract was made has a material effect on the agreed exchange of performances, the contract is voidable by the adversely affected party unless he bears the risk of mistake under the rule stated in § 154.[200]

The court noted that environmental-protection statutes had altered the common law so that previous owners of sites were liable for contamination and had a continuing liability after the contaminated property was sold.

---

[198] International Clinical Laboratories v. Stevens, 710 F. Supp. 466, 469 (E.D.N.Y. 1989).

[199] 423 N.W.2d 355 (Mich. App. 1988), *appeal denied,* 431 Mich. 874 (1988).

[200] 1 Restatement (Second) of Contracts § 152(1).

Based on these statutes, the court affirmed the trial court's rescission of the buy–sell agreement.[201]

The contract is voidable by the adversely affected party, unless he or she bears the risk of the mistake. However, the purchaser in *Garb-Ko* was not the adversely affected party, so the "as is" clause was not effective. Rather, the sellers, who had the continuing liability for contamination even after the sale, were the adversely affected parties. The court noted that rescission probably would not have been granted if the seller had agreed to indemnify the purchaser for all costs and penalties arising out of any gasoline storage leakage.[202]

"As is" clauses cannot insulate sellers of property from strict liability for abnormally dangerous activities. In *dicta,* one judge stated:

> Even setting aside my doubts that an "as is" contract clause precludes claims other than those based on breach of warranty, . . . , I cannot accept the proposition that a party, ignorant of the presence of an abnormally dangerous condition may be held to have contractually assumed the risk posed by that condition merely by signing an "as is" purchase contract. Under the Restatement and New Jersey law, as noted, strict liability may be avoided only by a knowing agreement to accept the risk of an abnormally hazardous activity, and an "as is" contract, under the circumstances here, does not amount to a knowing agreement.[203]

In one case, a purchaser of a house was allowed to rescind the sale and deed and obtain a refund of the purchase money when her home was discovered to contain urea formaldehyde, a banned substance, and it was found that the real estate broker had misrepresented and concealed its presence.[204]

The *Restatement (Second) of Agency* § 259 provides that, where one is induced to enter into a transaction by untrue material representations made by an agent authorized to conduct preliminary or final negotiations, the person deceived has the right to elect to rescind the transaction.

§ 6.23   Public Nuisance

A public nuisance is an offense against the state and is subject to abatement or prosecution on application of the proper governmental agency.[205]

---

[201] Garb-Ko v. Lansing-Lewis Services, Inc., 423 N.W.2d at 357.

[202] *Id.* at 358.

[203] Amland Properties Corp. v. Aluminum Company of America, 711 F. Supp. 784, 803 n.20 (D.N.J. 1989).

[204] Roberts v. Estate of Barbagallo, 531 A.2d 1125 (Pa. Super 1987).

[205] Restatement (Second) of Torts § 822 (1977). *See also* Sevinsky, *Public Nuisance: A Common-Law Remedy Among the Statutes,* Nat. Resources & Envt., Summer 1990, vol. 5, at 29.

The theory of public nuisance is based on an unreasonable interference with a right common to the general public.[206] To recover damages for such a claim, "one must have suffered harm of a kind different from that suffered by other members of the public exercising the right common to the general public that was the subject of interference."[207]

Although an individual's damages from cleanup costs are a different kind of harm than that suffered by the general public, the harm is not suffered in the exercise of the general public right that was the subject of the interference. The public has a right to a pollution-free environment, but a contaminated manufacturing plant is the cause of pollution, not the result of it.[208] The special harm in *Philadelphia Electric* was only in the exercise of private property rights over a contaminated site.

However, this theory may be used in an action brought by a state on behalf of the public.[209] One court explained the difference between public and private nuisance as follows:

> The former "is an offense against the State and is subject to abatement or prosecution on application of the proper governmental agency" and "consists of conduct or omissions which offend, interfere with or cause damage to the public in the exercise of rights common to all . . . in a manner such as to . . . endanger or injure the property, health, safety or comfort of a considerable number of persons." [citations omitted]. The latter, however, "threatens one person or a relatively few . . . , an essential feature being an interference with the use or enjoyment of land . . . . It is actionable by the individual person or persons whose rights have been disturbed." [citations omitted]. Public and private nuisance bear little relationship to each other. Although some rules apply to both, other rules apply to one but not the other.[210]

In finding liability for public nuisance, the court held the defendant landowner was subject to liability for public or private nuisance upon learning of the nuisance and having reasonable opportunity to abate it. This was found even though other parties had placed chemicals on the site. The defendant was liable for maintenance of the public nuisance irrespective of negligence or fault.[211] The state was not required to prove actual, as opposed to threatened, harm from the nuisance in order to have it abated. The

---

[206] Restatement (Second) of Torts § 821 B(1) (1977).

[207] *Id.* at § 821 C(1).

[208] Philadelphia Electric Co. v. Hercules, Inc., 762 F.2d 303, 306 (3d Cir., 1985), *cert. denied,* 474 U.S. 980 (1985).

[209] State of New York v. Shore Realty Corp., 759 F.2d 1032 (2d Cir. 1985).

[210] *Id.*

[211] *Id.* at 1051.

state could bring such a suit in its capacity as "guardian of the environment."[212] These actions use a strict liability standard.

The release or threat of release of hazardous waste into the environment was found to unreasonably infringe on a public right and was a public nuisance as a matter of law.[213] The court also noted that public nuisance could have been found on two alternative theories:

1. Continuing violations of state statutory provisions governing disposal and possession of hazardous waste, constituting nuisance *per se;*
2. Maintenance of the site, constituting an abnormally dangerous activity.[214]

Although this theory is usually used to obtain injunctive relief, recent cases seem to indicate that it may also be used for recovery of response costs in the same action.[215] Unlike CERCLA response cost liability, this common-law remedy is not limited to response costs consistent with the NCP.

§ 6.24   Private Nuisance

A private nuisance is one that interferes with the use and enjoyment of land. It typically threatens one person or relatively few, and is actionable by the individual or individuals whose rights have been disturbed.[216] Private nuisance has not been held to apply to successor landowners. Rather, it is usually applied in instances of danger to the public or interference with use of adjoining land.[217]

In one case, a purchaser of land who had to pay for cleanup costs sued the seller-successor company for these costs. The purchaser won in the trial court, but the damages and order to abate the nuisance were reversed on appeal.

The court found that a purchaser of real property, using a private nuisance theory, could not recover from a seller for a condition existing on the very land transferred.[218] The court also stated that a private nuisance

---

[212] *Id.*

[213] *Id.*

[214] *Id.* at 1051–52.

[215] *Id.* at 1042–43 n.14.

[216] Restatement (Second) of Torts § 822 (1977).

[217] Amland Properties Corp. v. Aluminum Company of America, 711 F. Supp. 784, 808 (D.N.J. 1989).

[218] Philadelphia Electric Co. v. Hercules, Inc., 762 F.2d at 313.

action could not be maintained, because the theory traditionally applied to conflicts between "neighboring, contemporaneous land uses."[219]

In *State of New York v. Shore Realty Corporation,* the property owner was found liable for public and private nuisance on its property because it *knew* of the nuisance and had a reasonable opportunity to abate it.[220]

Under the *Restatement (Second) of Torts* § 822, private nuisance has traditionally been confined to instances either of one person's property use interfering with another's, or of property use injuring third parties. The *Restatement* relies on a balancing test to determine whether the utility of the conduct creating the private nuisance outweighs the gravity of harm to the plaintiff.[221]

One is subject to liability for a private nuisance if his or her conduct is a legal cause of the invasion of the interest in the private use and enjoyment of land and such invasion is: (1) intentional and unreasonable, (2) negligent or reckless, or (3) actionable under the rules governing liability for abnormally dangerous conditions or activities.[222]

An invasion is intentional when the actor acts for the purpose of causing it or knows that it is resulting or is substantially certain to result from the actor's conduct.[223]

Negligence is one type of conduct that may give rise to a nuisance. If the nuisance has its origin in negligence, the negligence must also be proven.[224] Nuisance may arise from abnormally dangerous or ultrahazardous conduct or conditions.

Nuisance may be created during the process of abatement of a hazardous substance—for example, asbestos dust may contaminate an adjoining office or store. Another nuisance may be caused by the aggravation of tenants during operation and maintenance procedures.

§ 6.25 Injunctions

As was discussed in **Chapter 1**, only the federal government has the right to injunctive relief under CERCLA.[225] Injunctions can be obtained to stop a person's activity or to mandate that a person take a particular action. States and other plaintiffs may seek injunctive relief through the general powers

---

[219] *Id.* at 314.

[220] 759 F.2d 1032 (2d Cir. 1985).

[221] Restatement (Second) of Torts § 826 (1977).

[222] Copart Industries, Inc. v. Con Ed, 41 N.Y.2d 564, 569 (1977).

[223] *Id.* at 569.

[224] *Id.* at 571.

[225] State of New York v. Shore Realty Corp., 759 F.2d at 1049–51.

available to the courts in any type of lawsuit.An amendment to CERCLA may allow states to claim injunctive relief.

> A State may enforce any Federal or State standard, requirement, criteria, or limitation to which the remedial action is required to conform under this chapter in the United States district court for the district in which the facility is located.[226]

This section may be interpreted to give states the right to seek injunctive relief to enforce compliance after a remedial action has begun. It is not clear whether the section allows mandatory injunctive relief requiring a defendant to begin remedial action when it has not been so ordered by the federal government in an action under § 106.[227]

§ 6.26   Tax Assessment Reduction

Some commercial landowners have attempted to bring legal actions seeking to have the assessed value of their municipal realty taxes reduced by the cost of cleaning up hazardous waste and materials. Many more of these challenges can be expected in the future.

In *Inmar Associates, Inc. v. Borough of Carlstadt,*[228] hazardous chemicals that were stored in above-ground tanks, prior to recycling, leaked into the ground. The trial court did not allow a reduction. It found that the mere costliness of cleanup cannot be the basis of exemption from taxation. The contamination was self-imposed, rather than imposed by government.

The court stated:

> It would indeed be incongruous for the Legislature to enact strict liability provisions for clean-up of hazardous wastes as it has done and at the same time intend that a polluter's tax assessment may be reduced because of the contamination.[229]

On appeal, the court found that the challenge to the tax assessor's methodology was sufficient to warrant an independent determination of value by the Tax Court.[230] The court suggested creative methods of determining market value by considering the depreciated cost of correcting the

---

[226] 42 U.S.C. § 9621(e)(2).

[227] Section 106 also gives the states authority to promulgate strict state standards for remedial actions.

[228] 214 N.J. Super. 256, 518 A.2d 1110 (1986), *aff'd in part, rev'd in part,* 112 N.J. 593, 549 A.2d 38 (1988).

[229] *Id.* 518 A.2d at 1115.

[230] *Id.* 549 A.2d at 45.

contamination over time as a deduction from any income stream which can then be capitalized into an indication of value. Another approach would be to take into account the value in use to an owner-occupant.

In an important case in New York City, the Supreme Court held that the city real estate tax assessment levied on a commercial office building failed to adequately take into account the presence of asbestos in the structure, and granted the building owners a refund of more than $21 million.[231]

The building owners had argued that the cumulative market value and the cumulative tax assessment were overestimated. At trial, it was established that the property had significant physical and functional impairment, including the presence of asbestos throughout the building, which decreased its market value. When building repairs were required, some contractors refused to do the work because of the asbestos.

The court found that the city's reliance on hypothetical rents, based on the building's being empty and then fully leased in each tax year at market rates, ignored lease terms and the burden of high taxes on building owners. Increases could only be passed along to tenants if there were tenants in the building. No major tenant would lease space that was laden with asbestos.

In the matter of *Northfil Industry Corporation v. Board of Assessors of the Town of Riverhead,*[232] the Appellate Division concluded that the whole cost of bringing the property involved into compliance with the Suffolk County Sanitary Code should have been deducted from the tax assessments on the property for each year involved. The court's reasoning in *Northfil* was that no willing buyer of the property (a bulk oil storage terminal facility) would purchase it unless it was brought into compliance with the Suffolk County Sanitary Code. Accordingly, the court stated:

> It is reasonable to assume that a knowledgeable buyer who desired but is not compelled to purchase the property would have been unwilling to do so unless either the work necessary to comply with the code was done or there was abatement in the purchase price.[233]

§ 6.27   Contribution

CERCLA allows any party to seek contribution from any other person who is liable under § 9607(a).[234] Contribution claims are governed by federal law. The court may use such equitable factors as it deems appropriate in

---

[231] Bass v. Tax Commission of the City of New York, No. 56969/84 (N.Y. Sup. Ct. Jan. 22, 1991), N.Y.L.J., Jan. 24, 1991, at 25–26.

[232] 143 A.2d at 138 (2d Dept. 1988).

[233] *Id.* at 138.

[234] 42 U.S.C. § 9607(a).

making such allocations.[235] There may also be a right to contribution under state law or pursuant to a contract.

A party that has resolved its liability to the government is not liable for contribution. Private agreements to indemnify or hold harmless are enforceable between the parties, but not against the government.[236]

Contribution may not always work, because defendants may have difficulty locating a sufficient number of additional solvent parties and it is expensive to bring other parties into court.[237]

The court has considerable latitude in determining each party's equitable share. Possible relevant factors include:

> the amount of hazardous substances involved; the degree of toxicity or hazardousness of the materials involved; the degree of involvement by parties in the generation, transportation, treatment, storage, or disposal of the substances; the degree of care exercised by the parties with respect to the substances involved; and the degree of cooperation of the parties with government officials to prevent any harm to public health or the environment.[238]

§ 6.28 Punitive Damages

Punitive damages are damages that are granted to punish particularly egregious behavior, such as where a party has actual knowledge of a defect or hazard and fails to reveal it. Actual damages are a prerequisite for an award of punitive damages.

A New Jersey court described the requirements for recovery of punitive damages as follows:

> To warrant a punitive damage award, the defendant's conduct must have been wantonly reckless or malicious. There must be an intentional wrongdoing in the sense of an "evil-minded act" or an act accompanied by a wanton and willful disregard of the rights of another.[239]

The typical argument made in such lawsuits is that the individual or company who sold the property containing the hazardous substance either

---

[235] 42 U.S.C. § 9613(f)(1).

[236] Smith Land & Improvement Corp. v. Celotex Corp., 851 F.2d 86, 89 (3d Cir. 1988). *See also* Marden Corp. v. C.G.C. Music, Ltd., *supra* note 106, 804 F.2d at 1459. *See also* AM International Inc. v. International Forging Equip., No. C88-2037 (E.D. Ohio June 29, 1990) (LEXIS 9023, ENVRN library).

[237] O'Neil v. Picillo, 883 F.2d 176, 179 (1st Cir. 1989), *cert. denied,* 110 S. Ct. 1115 (1990).

[238] Amoco Oil Co. v. Borden, Inc., 889 F.2d 664, 672 (5th Cir. 1989).

[239] Jersey City Redevelopment Authority v. PPG Industries, *supra* note 37, 655 F. Supp. at 1266.

knew it was present or was reckless in not knowing it was a hazard; therefore, punitive damages should be awarded.

Although these damages are often not allowed in ordinary fraud and deceit actions, they may be granted (1) in an action where the fraud is aimed at the public generally, or (2) where the acts complained of constitute gross, wanton, or willful fraud or other morally culpable conduct.[240]

Punitive damages were awarded to homeowners against particle-board flooring manufacturers after the homeowners were exposed to formaldehyde in the flooring and became ill. The homeowners argued that the manufacturers knew of the danger of particle-board emissions.[241]

These damages are not allowed where the defendant merely should have known of a dangerous defect in a product. A generalized knowledge of the hazard is not sufficient.[242]

A jury awarded $820,750 in compensatory damages and $2.4 million in punitive damages to a Minnesota school district, after determining that a former asbestos products manufacturer had continued to sell its products after it knew of the dangers of asbestos.[243]

The Supreme Court recently held that an award of punitive damages is not barred by the excessive fines clause of the Eighth Amendment to the Constitution. The court reasoned that the amendment's legislative history and purpose relate to criminal matters and to governmental actions involving punishment, not to civil suits between private parties.[244]

However, a District Court judge found that the repeated imposition of punitive damages on a defendant for the same course of conduct is unconstitutional.[245] This decision was later vacated. The case involved a personal injury claim, and the court found that the plaintiff's claim had to be viewed in the context of the thousands of suits pending against the defendants. Another District Court judge found, in another case, that such punitive damages were not barred and that to do so in mass litigation would be arbitrary and impractical.[246]

---

[240] 195 Broadway Co. v. 195 Broadway Corp. (Sup. Ct. N.Y. Co.) N.Y.L.J., Apr. 15, 1988, at 15; Cinnaminson Township Board of Education v. U.S. Gypsum Co., 552 F. Supp. 855 (D.N.J. 1982), aff'd, 882 F.2d 510 (3d Cir. 1989).

[241] Pinkerton v. Georgia Pacific Corp., Mo. Cir. Ct., Clay Cty., No. CV 186-4651 CC (Jan. 8, 1990).

[242] School Dist. of Independence v. U.S. Gypsum Co., 750 S.W.2d 442, 447 (Mo. App. 1988).

[243] Independent School Dist. No. 622 v. Keene Co., Minn. Dist. Ct., No. C5-84-1701, Oct. 5, 1990; Asbestos Abatement Report, Oct. 29, 1990, at 4.

[244] Browning-Ferris Industries of Vermont, Inc. v. Kelco Disposal, Inc., 492 U.S. 257, 109 S. Ct. 2909 (1989).

[245] Juzwin v. Amtorg Trading Corp., 705 F. Supp. 1053 (D.N.J. 1989), vacated, 718 F. Supp. 1233 (D.N.J. 1989).

[246] Leonen v. Johns-Manville Corp., 717 F. Supp. 272 (D.N.J. 1989).

§ 6.29 Attorney Fees

It is well-established that a party cannot recover attorney fees unless they are provided for by contract, court rule, or statute.[247] They may also be awarded to "[o]ne who through the tort of another has been required to act in the protection of his interests by bringing or defending an action against a third person . . . ."[248]

Thus, although a defrauded party may recover legal fees from the tortfeasor that flow from the tort, in most other instances, they are not recoverable.[249] Private litigants in a CERCLA case may not usually recover such costs,[250] but they may be recovered by the government of the United States.[251]

One court stated the general rule that "sound judicial administration is best advanced if litigants bear their own counsel fees."[252] There may also be an award of attorney fees in a successful RICO action.[253]

---

[247] T&E Industries v. Safety Light Corp., 680 F. Supp. at 707.

[248] Restatement (Second) of Torts § 914(2) (1977).

[249] Environmental Protection Dept. v. Ventron Corp., 182 N.J. Super. 210, 440 A.2d 455, *aff'd as modified*, 94 N.J. 473, 468 A.2d 150, 167 (1983).

[250] 42 U.S.C. § 9659.

[251] 42 U.S.C. § 9604(b).

[252] Environmental Protection Dept. v. Ventron Corp., 468 A.2d at 167.

[253] 18 U.S.C. § 1964(c).

CHAPTER 7

DEFENSES TO LIABILITY

§ 7.1   Introduction

§ 7.2   Statute of Limitations

§ 7.3   Privity of Contract

§ 7.4   Bankruptcy

§ 7.5   —Automatic Stay

§ 7.6   —Abandonment

§ 7.7   —Dischargeability

§ 7.8   Product Identification and Causation

§ 7.9   Asbestos Is Not Dangerous

§ 7.10   State-of-the Art Defense

§ 7.11   CERCLA's Third-Party Defense

§ 7.12   SARA's Innocent Landowner or Due Diligence Defense

§ 7.13   —Checklist for Innocent Landowner Defense

§ 7.14   Estoppel

§ 7.15   Assumption of Risk

§ 7.16   Contributory Negligence

§ 7.17   Unclean Hands

§ 7.18   *Caveat Emptor*

§ 7.19   Disclaimers

§ 7.20   Damage Control

§ 7.1   Introduction

This chapter reviews the legal defenses to claims for liability under CERCLA and common-law theories.

The best offense is a good defense. Avoiding environmental liability is an ongoing process that requires constant monitoring of updates in statutes and case law. An operations and maintenance (O&M) plan in a building, an emergency situations manual, and periodic inspections may be needed.

The statutory defense to CERCLA liability requires advance preparation, before there is any thought of a lawsuit. It requires "due diligence" via an environmental audit, before CERCLA can be invoked. Parties dealing with hazardous substances must be aware of their rights and potential liabilities before there is any hint of litigation, so that they can engage in advance planning.

Successful defenses to liability must be put in place well before there is any actual litigation. Legal advice concerning environmental liability is essential before signing a lease or purchasing a building; before contracting with contractors and design professionals; before hiring employees to work around hazardous substances; and in a host of other situations.

§ 7.2   Statute of Limitations

In the area of environmental litigation, a lawsuit is commonly commenced many years after the hazardous substance or product has been disposed of, installed, or introduced into the building. This is generally the situation with lawsuits involving asbestos. Statutes of limitations are intended to encourage prompt resolution of disputes, in order to avoid stale lawsuits. Limitation periods vary from state to state and according to the legal theories that are being used in the complaint. The SARA amendments to the CERCLA statute have their own statute of limitations. Traditional common-law theories have different limitation periods that vary from state to state.

Courts faced with product liability claims that are raised many years after the product was purchased and installed have had to consider when their statutes of limitations should run. For example, the EPA first regulated the spray-on application of asbestos products in building construction in 1973.[1] If one of the typical six-year statutes of limitations had been deemed to run from the time of application of the asbestos product, all suits to recover abatement costs after 1979 would have been untimely, even if the asbestos, for example, was only first discovered by the property owner years later.

Under the "traditional" rule, the statute of limitations begins to run at the time of wrongful exposure,[2] which occurs at the time of the first harmful contact. This rule can be problematic if the plaintiff's illness has a long latency period.

---

[1] 43 Fed. Reg. 26,372 (1978).

[2] Steinhardt v. Johns-Manville Sales Corp., 54 N.Y.2d 1008, 430 N.E.2d 1297 (1981).

Many jurisdictions have therefore adopted the so-called "discovery rule."[3] Under this rule, a cause of action accrues when the asbestos-containing product that caused the damage is discovered or *should have been* discovered,[4] or when the effects of such exposure manifest themselves.[5]

Knowledge that a building contains asbestos is not the same as injury to property. There must be a dangerous condition, such as friable asbestos, for there to be injury. Manufacturers argue that owners should have taken steps to reasonably detect friable asbestos, as part of their duty to keep the building safe for certain users. Other states' statutes of limitations run from the time of last exposure.

The Supreme Court in Virginia looked at the word "injury" in its statute of limitations and found that it meant the date when the plaintiff had suffered an injury as determined by medical evidence.[6] In the Sixth Circuit, the court found that the statute of limitations accrues when the "manifestation of the disease" occurs.[7]

If the applicable statute of limitations has passed, the action may be barred, unless: (1) the state in which the lawsuit is being brought has a revivor statute; or (2) the plaintiff can demonstrate that the defendant has fraudulently concealed the dangers of asbestos. New York's revivor statute has expired as to claims of which plaintiffs were previously aware.

In *City of Manchester v. National Gypsum Company,*[8] the court allowed the plaintiff's action for strict liability claims and breach of warranty, despite a statute of limitations bar, where it argued fraudulent concealment. Even if a statute of limitations bar can be successfully overcome, the plaintiff still has the problem of proving dealings for the purchase and installation of asbestos, and decades may have gone by.

A statute of repose creates an absolute time limit beyond which liability no longer exists and is not tolled for any reason. Economic considerations, rather than fairness to defendants, are its basis.

As is discussed in **Chapter 6**, many plaintiffs are now trying, under CERCLA, to recover costs for the removal of asbestos from buildings. The courts have not accepted this argument so far. If it is eventually allowed, plaintiffs would get the benefits of CERCLA *and* SARA's favorable statute of limitations (discussed below).

---

[3] Strickland v. Johns-Manville Int'l Corp., 461 F. Supp. 215 (S.D. Tex. 1978), *cert. denied,* 456 U.S. 967 (1982).

[4] The University of Vermont and State Agricultural College v. W.R. Grace & Co., 565 A.2d 1354 (Vt. 1989); *see* N.Y. Civ. Prac. L.&R. § 214-c(2).

[5] Borel v. Fibreboard Paper Products Corp., 493 F.2d 1076, 2002 (5th Cir. 1973).

[6] Locke v. Johns-Manville, 221 Va. 951, 275 S.E.2d 900 (1981).

[7] Clutter v. Johns-Manville, 646 F.2d 1151 (6th Cir. 1981).

[8] 637 F. Supp. 646 (D.R.I. 1986).

CERCLA has its own provisions for determining which statute of limitations and date of discovery will apply, as follows:

(a) State Statutes of Limitations for Hazardous Substance Cases
   (1) Exception to State Statutes

In the case of any action brought under State law for personal injury, or property damages, which are caused or contributed to by exposure to any hazardous substance, or pollutant or contaminate, released into the environment from a facility, if the applicable limitations period for such action (as specified in the State statute of limitations or under common law) provides a commencement date which is earlier than the federally required commencement date, such period shall commence at the federally required commencement date in lieu of the date specified in such State statute. . . .

* * *

(b)(4) Federally Required Commencement Date
   (a) In General

Except as provided in subparagraph (B), the term "federally required commencement date" means the date the plaintiff knew (or reasonably should have known) that the personal injury or property damages referred to in subsection (a)(1) were caused or contributed to by the hazardous substance or pollutant or contaminant concerned. . . .

* * *

(i) The terms used in this section shall have the same meanings as when used in subchapter 1 of this chapter.[9]

SARA created a statute of limitations for private cost recovery actions under CERCLA. A claim for recovery of remediation costs under § 9607(a) of CERCLA must be brought within three years of completion of a "removal action" or discovery of natural resources damages, or six years after "initiation of . . . construction of the remedial action."
The statute provides:

An initial action for recovery of the costs referred to in section 9607 of this title must be commenced—

(A) for a removal action, within 3 years after completion of the removal action, except that such cost recovery action must be brought within 6 years after a determination to grant a waiver under section 9604(c)(1)(C) of this title for continued response action; and

(B) for a remedial action, within 6 years after initiation of physical on-site construction of the remedial action, except that, if the remedial action is

---

[9] 42 U.S.C. § 9658. First United Methodist Church v. U.S. Gypsum Co., 882 F.2d 862 (4th Cir. 1989), *cert. denied*, 110 S. Ct. 1113, 107 L. Ed. 1020 (1990). *See also* 58 U.S.L.W. 3526 (1990).

initiated within 3 years after the completion of the removal action, costs incurred in the removal action may be recovered in the cost recovery action brought under this subparagraph.[10]

The distinction between a "removal" and a "remedial" action is not always clear and can overlap. (See **Chapter 1**.) Most removal actions seem to be temporary in nature; remedial actions are more permanent.[11]

Claims for recovery of damages to natural resources must be presented within three years of the discovery of the loss or of the promulgation of final regulations under § 9651(c), whichever is later.[12]

Claims brought for contribution for either response costs or damages must be brought within three years of the date of judgment, administrative order, or judicially approved settlement.[13] Claims based on subrogation rights must be commenced within three years after the date of payment of the claim on which the subrogation rights rest.[14]

Because the statute created a period of limitations where none existed before, the period begins to run, with respect to preexisting claims, on the effective date of the statute, which was October 17, 1986.[15] Under CERCLA, in any action brought under state law for personal injury or property damage that is caused or contributed to by exposure to any hazardous substance, the state statute of limitations will not begin to run until the plaintiff knows or should reasonably have known that such exposure caused or contributed to the injury or damages.[16]

However, because CERCLA does not authorize response cost recovery actions for removal of asbestos from the structure of a building, it cannot preempt a state's repose period.[17]

Some state courts have enacted revival statutes to resurrect time-barred claims for substances such as asbestos, tungsten-carbide, chlordane, and

---

[10] 42 U.S.C. § 9613(g)(2). Almost every court considering the issue has explained that cost recovery actions, brought under Section 107, seek restitution of federal monies spent on cleanup, and thus are considered essentially equitable in nature. Accordingly, all courts considering the issue have held that there is no right to a jury trial in a cost recovery action brought under Section 107. *See, e.g.,* United States v. Dickerson, 640 F. Supp. 448, 453 (D. Md. 1986); United States v. Mottolo, 605 F. Supp. 898, 912–13 (D.N.H. 1985); United States v. Wade, 653 F. Supp. 11, 13 (E.D. Pa. 1984); United States v. Tyson, 22 Env't Rep. Cas. (BNA) 1471, 1472 (E.D. Pa. 1984); United States v. Argent Corp., 21 Env't Rep. Cas. (BNA) 1353, 1354 (D.N.M. 1983).

[11] State of New York v. Shore Realty Corp., 759 A.2d 1032, 1040 (2d Cir. 1985).

[12] 42 U.S.C. § 9613(g)(1).

[13] 42 U.S.C. § 9613(g)(3).

[14] 42 U.S.C. § 9613(g)(4).

[15] T&E Industries v. Safety Light Corp., 680 F. Supp. 696, 704 (D.N.J. 1988).

[16] 42 U.S.C. § 9658.

[17] T&E Industries v. Safety Light Corp., 680 F. Supp. at 704.

polyvinylchloride.[18] The U.S. Court of Appeals upheld a District of Columbia Council law reviving all asbestos property claims pending in court on July 1, 1986, even though the District's 10-year statute of repose had run against them.[19] Georgia and Virginia state courts struck down their revival statutes as being in violation of due process.[20]

In Connecticut, product liability actions involving injury, death, or property damage caused by contact with or exposure to asbestos must be brought within 30 years from the date the claimant last had such contact or exposure.[21]

In North Dakota, an action to recover damages based on injury to property allegedly resulting from the presence of products containing asbestos fibers must be commenced within six years of the date on which the owner of that property knew or should have known of facts giving rise to the cause of action.[22]

§ 7.3   Privity of Contract

A defendant may be able to defend certain actions by claiming that the plaintiff is unable to show that he or she was in privity of contract with the defendant. In suits against manufacturers of asbestos, privity is unlikely to be available because building ownership may have changed several times since the installation of the asbestos. For most theories, privity will not matter; for certain warranty claims, however, it may be essential.

§ 7.4   Bankruptcy

Bankruptcy and environmental laws can clash when polluters attempt to use bankruptcy as a means to avoid paying for the cleanup and disposal of hazardous substances.[23]

CERCLA does not make it clear whether it has priority over the Bankruptcy Code. The Bankruptcy Code allows a debtor to have a "fresh

---

[18] 1986 Sess. Laws, ch. 682, § 4.

[19] Asbestos Abatement Report, Mar. 5, 1990, at 2. New York's revival statute was upheld. Hymowitz v. Eli Lilly and Co., 73 N.Y.2d 487, 541 N.Y.S.2d 941 (Ct. App. N.Y. 1989), *cert. denied,* 110 S. Ct. 350 (1989). A Massachusetts revival statute for property damage claims was upheld. City of Boston v. Keene Corp., 406 Mass. 301, 547 N.E.2d 328 (1989).

[20] Celotex Corp. v. St. John's Hospital, 259 Ga. 108, 376 S.E.2d 880 (Sup. Ct. Ga. 1989), *cert. denied,* 110 S. Ct. 11,358 (1990); Asbestos Abatement Report, Nov. 26, 1990, at 3.

[21] Conn. Gen. Stat. Ann. § 19a-14.

[22] N.D. Cent. Code § 28-01.1.

[23] My thanks to Judge Ray Reynolds Graves, Chief Bankruptcy Judge, United States Bankruptcy Court, Eastern District of Michigan, for his comments on §§ 7.4–7.7.

start"[24] and to avoid liability for noncompliance with environmental laws, even if there is no actual proof of "balance-sheet" insolvency.[25]

Congress attempted to address this inadequacy in SARA by creating a "federal lien" provision, which attaches a type of judgment lien to the guilty party's contaminated assets at the time liability is discovered or cleanup costs are imposed, whichever is later.[26] On a practical level, the lien may not mean much, because the government's interest falls behind prior secured claims on the contaminated property.

Under CERCLA, the current owner and operator of a facility, or any person who owned or operated the facility at the time hazardous substances were disposed of, is liable for any response costs to remedy a release or threatened release. After a party files for bankruptcy, issues may arise as to whether secured lenders are owners or operators of the facility and thus may be liable for response costs.

CERCLA excludes from the definition of "owner or operator" any "person, who, without participating in the management of a vessel or facility, holds indicia of ownership primarily to protect his security interest in the vessel or facility."[27] This exclusion has been interpreted to permit secured creditors to provide financial assistance and general (and even isolated instances of specific) management advice to its debtors without risking CERCLA liability, so long as the secured creditors do not participate in the day-to-day management of the business or facility either before or after the business ceases operation.[28]

Individuals who manage a facility for a debtor-in-possession pursuant to Chapter 11 of the Bankruptcy Code may risk being deemed active managers. They may also not be able to use CERCLA's third-party defense. Under this defense, a person who otherwise falls within one of the classes liable under CERCLA may avoid liability if he or she establishes by a "preponderance of the evidence that the release or threat of release of a hazardous substance and the damages resulting therefrom were caused solely by . . . an act or omission of a third party other than an employee or agent of the defendant . . . ."[29] As active managers of the debtor-in-possession,

---

[24] Bankruptcy Reform Act of 1978, 11 U.S.C. §§ 101–151, 326 (1982), amended by Bankruptcy Amendments and Federal Judgeship Act of 1984, Pub. L. No. 98-353, 98 Stat. 333 (1984).

[25] Morris, *State Enforcement of Environmental Laws Against Bankrupt Entities,* 16 Envtl. L. Rep. (Envtl. L. Inst.) 10,143 (June 1986).

[26] 42 U.S.C. § 9607(1).

[27] 42 U.S.C. § 9607(a)(2).

[28] United States v. Fleet Factors Corp., 724 F. Supp. 955 (S.D. Ga. 1988), 901 F.2d 1550, *reh'g denied, en banc,* 911 F.2d 742 (11th Cir. 1990).

[29] 42 U.S.C. § 9607(b)(3).

these individuals could obtain bankruptcy court approval to sell or properly dispose of hazardous chemicals in the facility after operations ceased.[30]

Unsecured environmental claims are paid *pro rata* from assets remaining after all secured and priority claims are satisfied. Some environmental creditors have sought to persuade the courts that environmental liabilities are not claims,[31] so that they can enforce them in the future against the reorganized entity, or to raise the priority of their claims.[32] Federal and state liens may eliminate some distribution problems, at least for expenses already incurred.

§ 7.5　—Automatic Stay

Bankruptcies involving environmental issues usually are voluntary liquidations under Chapter 7 of the Bankruptcy Code.[33] After a petition in bankruptcy is filed, it causes an "automatic stay" of all legal actions against the debtor and property in the bankruptcy estate.[34] The stay may be lifted in some instances, but only under the bankruptcy court's supervision.[35] The purpose is to prevent dissipation of the debtor's assets before orderly distribution to creditors can be effected.

The trustee acts in a fiduciary capacity to gather the assets and pay creditors' claims. Secured claims are paid before unsecured claims. Environmental cleanup costs are considered unsecured claims.

This stay allows the bankrupt to "catch up" and ensures the creditors that the remaining assets will be equitably distributed. One of the exceptions to the automatic stay provisions allows the government to enforce "nonmonetary judgments against a debtor's estate."[36]

Thus, there is a question as to whether the government can obtain money for cleanup while the responsible party is under the protection of an automatic stay. Also, should a cleanup order against a bankrupt be treated as a money judgment and delayed by the automatic stay provision or fall within the governmental police or regulatory power and be exempt from the stay provisions?

These issues have not been completely resolved. Some courts have found that the exemption of § 362(b)(5) of the Bankruptcy Code, which prohibits the courts from enforcing money judgments against a bankrupt

---

[30] United States v. Fleet Factors, 724 F. Supp. at 962.

[31] *In re* Chateaugay Corp., 112 Bankr. 513 (S.D.N.Y. 1990).

[32] *In re* Peerless Plating Co., 70 Bankr. 943 (Bankr. W.D. Mich. 1987).

[33] 11 U.S.C. §§ 701–766.

[34] 11 U.S.C. § 362(a).

[35] 11 U.S.C. § 362(d)(1).

[36] 11 U.S.C. § 362(b)(5).

party during bankruptcy, applies only to injunctive relief and not to environmental cleanup orders, because they are, in effect, money judgments.[37]

In *Penn Terra Limited v. Department of Environmental Resources,*[38] Pennsylvania enforced a prepetition consent order by securing an injunction that ordered a debtor surface coal mining operation to cease polluting nearby water supplies. However, a suit by the United States to enforce an environmental cleanup order was stayed during bankruptcy.[39]

In *In re Laurinberg Oil Company,* North Carolina obtained a ruling that reasonable and necessary expenses incurred by a debtor waste disposal facility to abate existing environmental violations were to be considered an administrative expense of the debtor's estate.[40]

However, in *Ohio v. Kovacs,* the Supreme Court held that Ohio's prepetition cleanup order was converted into an obligation to pay money and was therefore dischargeable in bankruptcy.[41]

Other courts have looked at environmental cleanup obligations as one of several responsibilities under an injunction. Thus, the fact that a cleanup may involve expense does not transform it into a money judgment.[42]

§ 7.6 —Abandonment

When a debtor files for bankruptcy under Chapter 7, the court appoints a liquidation trustee to manage and dispose of the assets of the bankrupt estate and distribute any proceeds among creditors.

The trustee may abandon property that is worthless or a "burden" to the estate upon notice or motion and hearing.[43] One court found that abandonment would be authorized in certain instances, such as when the environmental law is not reasonably designed to protect the public health and safety or when it is so onerous as to interfere with the bankruptcy adjudication.[44] The court stated in *dictum* that abandonment may occur where

---

[37] *In re* Kovacs, 681 F.2d 454 (6th Cir. 1982), *vacated and remanded on other grounds,* 459 U.S. 1167 (1983); Ohio v. Kovacs, 469 U.S. 274, 15 Envtl. L. Rep. (Envtl. L. Inst.) 20,121 (1985); United States v. Johns-Manville Sales Corp. Civil No. 81-299-D (D.N.H. Nov. 15, 1982).

[38] 733 F.2d 267 (3d Cir. 1984).

[39] United States v. Johns-Manville Sales Corp., 13 Envtl. L. Rep. (Envtl. L. Inst.) 20,310 (D.N.H. Nov. 15, 1982).

[40] 49 Bankr. 652, 654 (Bankr. M.D.N.C. 1984).

[41] 469 U.S. at 284–85.

[42] United States v. Price, 688 F.2d 204 (3d Cir. 1982); Penn Terra Limited v. Department of Environmental Resources, 733 F.2d 267 (3d Cir. 1984).

[43] 11 U.S.C. § 554 (Supp. III 1985).

[44] Midlantic Nat'l Bank v. New Jersey Dept. of Environmental Protection, 474 U.S. 494, 16 Envtl. L. Rep. (Envtl. L. Inst.) 20,278, 106 S. Ct. 755 (1986).

there is environmental cleanup responsibility and the burden of this cost would then fall on the property's prior owner.[45] However, state laws are still binding if they are reasonably designed to protect public health and safety.[46]

If abandonment were permitted, a trustee or debtor could simply abandon property encumbered with enormous financial cleanup obligations and avoid all environmental liability.

In an important case that was affirmed by the Third Circuit,[47] the court found that the Bankruptcy Code could not be used to circumvent all other regulations, especially when the governmental interest is as pervasive as it is for hazardous waste cleanup.[48] Thus, a trustee in bankruptcy may not abandon property where state law protects the public from identifiable hazards. The court characterized this public safety exception as a narrow one, not designed to encompass future violations of state law that may be speculative or indeterminate.[49]

The legislative history of § 554 revealed no express preemption of other state regulations, unless they directly interfered with the equitable principles of the Bankruptcy Code.[50] Thus, the states could require a trustee to clean up the sites before abandoning them.

However, other courts have allowed abandonment so long as the debtor cooperates with the state and takes reasonable steps to prevent further harm from contamination.[51]

Administrative expenses are the first unsecured claims to be paid, but a landlord of property contaminated by a bankrupt tenant has been held not entitled to administrative priority for cleanup costs incurred before and after the bankruptcy petition. The key seems to be that the contamination was caused by conduct *before* the petition was filed.[52]

However, in a Sixth Circuit case, such expenses were allowed when the Tennessee Department of Health and Environment sought expenses for an inspection and chemical sampling program that occurred after the petition

---

[45] Ohio v. Kovacs, 469 U.S. 274, 15 Envtl. L. Rep. (Envtl. L. Inst.) 20,121, 20,123 n.12 (1985).

[46] Midlantic Nat'l Bank v. New Jersey Dept. of Environmental Protection, *supra* note 44.

[47] *In re* Quanta Resources Corp., 739 F.2d 927, 928 (3d Cir. 1984), *aff'd sub nom.* Midlantic Nat'l Bank v. New Jersey Dept. of Environmental Protection, *supra* note 44.

[48] *In re* Quanta Resources Corp., 739 F.2d at 921–22.

[49] Midlantic Nat'l Bank v. New Jersey Dept. of Environmental Protection, 106 S. Ct. at 762.

[50] *In re* Quanta Resources Corp., 739 F.2d at 929.

[51] *See In re* Oklahoma Refining Co., 63 Bankr. 562 (W.D. Okla. 1986); *In re* Franklin Signal Corp., 65 Bankr. 268 (D. Minn. 1986).

[52] *In re* Dant & Russell, Inc., 853 F.2d 700, 18 Envtl. L. Rep. (Envtl. L. Inst.) 21,312 (9th Cir. 1988).

for bankruptcy was filed.[53] Here, the court looked at when the cleanup action took place.

One court declined to issue a declaratory judgment that liability for hazardous waste cleanup costs was discharged in bankruptcy.[54]

Even though a corporation may be bankrupt, its officers, directors, and shareholders may still face potential personal liability for CERCLA cleanup costs.

§ 7.7 —Dischargeability

Among the Bankruptcy Code's primary tools to allow a fresh start are the discharge of claims arising before the filing of the bankruptcy petition and the Code's definition of a claim.[55] A discharge acts as an injunction against the commencement or continuation of any future action against the debtor or debtor's property and serves to void any judgment for personal liability of the debtor with respect to any discharged debt. The scope of a discharge is greater for corporations than for individuals, because the provision excepting certain debts from discharge applies only to individual debtors.[56]

Under § 524 of the Bankruptcy Act, the trustee or debtor can discharge certain prepetition claims and debts during bankruptcy, including judgments for personal liability.[57] If the debt is dischargeable, the claim is unsecured and does not survive bankruptcy; however, the claimant may receive some distribution of funds remaining in the bankrupt estate. As with applications for an automatic stay, there is a question as to whether a cleanup order is a prepetition debt and subject to discharge.

Bankruptcy discharges liability only for claims that arose *before* the bankruptcy petition was filed. A claim, even a contingent claim, arises under the Bankruptcy Code at "the time when the acts giving rise to the alleged liability were performed."[58] In the realm of environmental issues, there is no tort chargeable to the debtor until there is either a release or a threatened release of hazardous waste. The mere existence of a hazardous substance at a site is insufficient to trigger a claim. When a claim for response costs arises after the filing of a petition in bankruptcy, the claim is

---

[53] *In re* Wall Tube & Metal Products Co., 831 F.2d 118, 18 Envtl. L. Rep. (Envtl. L. Inst.) 20,013 (6th Cir. 1987). *See also In re* Peerless Plating Co.; 70 Bankr. 943 (Bankr. W.D. Mich. 1987).

[54] United States v. Whizco, Inc., 841 F.2d 147, 18 Envtl. L. Rep. (Envtl. L. Inst.) 20,571 (6th Cir. 1988).

[55] 11 U.S.C. § 101(A) (1988).

[56] 11 U.S.C. § 523(a) (1988).

[57] 11 U.S.C. § 101 (11).

[58] *In re* Chateaugay Corp., 112 Bankr. 513 (S.D.N.Y. 1990), *rev'd,* 110 S. Ct. 2668, 110 L. Ed. 2d 579 (S.D.N.Y. 1990); 11 U.S.C. § 101(4) (1988).

not discharged, even though response costs were incurred because of conduct prior to filing the petition.[59]

In *United States v. Union Scrap Iron & Metal,*[60] the debtor's liability for cleanup costs under CERCLA was not discharged in bankruptcy, where the EPA did not know the debtor was a potentially responsible party. Thus, even though the environmental harm caused by the debtor occurred prepetition, CERCLA liability was not discharged when the debtor's reorganization plan was confirmed in July 1985, because the federal government knew nothing of the potential liability and had incurred no Superfund costs.

This case did not occur in a superlien state. If it had, the government might have had a lien on the property that would have come ahead of any lender's lien.

Only claims against the debtor can be asserted and ultimately discharged in a bankruptcy proceeding. To effectuate the "fresh start" policy of the Code, Congress defined claims broadly. The Code defines a "claim" as a:

(a) right to payment, whether or not such right is reduced to judgment, liquidated, unliquidated, fixed, contingent, matured, unmatured, disputed, undisputed, legal, equitable, secured, or unsecured; or

(b) right to an equitable remedy for breach of performance if such breach gives rise to a right to payment, whether or not such right to an equitable remedy is reduced to judgment, fixed, contingent, matured, unmatured, disputed, undisputed, secured, or unsecured.[61]

The legislative history indicates clear Congressional intent that the definition of a claim was to encompass all legal obligations of the debtor, and the courts have interpreted the definition broadly.[62]

Until there is such a release or threatened release, there is no prepetition event as to which a postpetition contingent injury can attach. Any subsequent liability for environmental cleanup or remedial action is not dischargeable in bankruptcy.[63]

Where there has been such a prepetition release or threatened release, injunctive relief that provides that a defendant who fails to comply may be liable for the costs of cleanup is dischargeable in bankruptcy; injunctive relief that does not so provide may not be discharged, even if it provides for

---

[59] Jensen v. Bank of America, 114 Bankr. 700 (E.D. Cal. 1990).

[60] Civ. 4-89-40 (D.C. Minn. Dec. 27, 1990).

[61] 11 U.S.C. § 101(4) (1988).

[62] Ohio v. Kovacs, 469 U.S. 274, 279 n.3 (1985); *In re* Robinson, 776 F.2d 30, 34–35 (2d Cir. 1985), *rev'd on other grounds sub nom.* Kelly v. Robinson, 479 U.S. 36 (1986); *In re* Remington Rand Corp., 836 F.2d 825, 826 (3d Cir. 1988).

[63] *Id.*

punitive civil penalties for noncompliance, because the penalties are not an alternative right to compensatory payment.[64]

A debt to the state has been held to be dischargeable, like a cleanup order that is the equivalent of a money judgment.[65] The Supreme Court characterized the cleanup order as an attempt to remedy a statutory violation and thus an assessment of damages that is dischargeable.[66]

SARA closed this gap for situations that fall within the statute: the federal lien attaches to property like a judgment lien. The United States has a lien for "all costs of removal or remedial action incurred by the United States" on all real property that belongs to a liable party.[67] Thus, debts for hazardous waste liability are no longer dischargeable in bankruptcy.[68] However, they are subject to the rights of any prior purchaser's interest, or judgment-holder lien of a security creditor, as perfected under state law. For non-SARA cases, these issues still exist.

§ 7.8   Product Identification and Causation

Although this is not a true defense, problems may arise in proving whether a particular manufacturer's product was the proximate cause of a plaintiff's injury. The proof is especially important when a worker has worked with a variety of asbestos products over the course of a career or when a building has several asbestos-containing products within it.

Because many asbestos products do not have labels on them, identification of the particular manufacturer who produced the asbestos product can often be problematic, and maintaining a lawsuit against a particular party can be very difficult. Eyewitnesses, such as ACM installers, may not be available. There may have to be laboratory analysis, which may not be conclusive. Possibly, the product specified was not what was actually used.

A statute signed by President Reagan may ease this problem by requiring manufacturers to submit to the EPA a list of identifying characteristics of their products during the years of manufacture.[69] In the context of CERCLA actions, various notification requirements may also make identification of parties easier.[70]

Unlike traditional tort cases, where there is an immediate wrong and a resulting injury, in the typical toxic tort claim, the injury or disease may manifest itself many years after exposure or the exposure may be chronic

---

[64] 11 U.S.C. § 524 (1979).

[65] Ohio v. Kovacs, 469 U.S. 274 (1985).

[66] Id. at 278.

[67] 42 U.S.C. § 9607(1).

[68] Id.

[69] Pub. L. No. 100-577, signed Oct. 31, 1988.

[70] See ch. 1.

and occur over many years. This long latency period makes it difficult to show that the defendant's conduct caused his or her injuries and that it was not a result of other ambient toxic substances, diet, life-style, or smoking. Proving causation is one of the biggest hurdles in a toxic tort case.

The plaintiff must prove by a preponderance of the evidence that the defendant's conduct caused his or her injury. The toxic substances that substantially caused the injury must be identified. To do this, the plaintiff must show that the injury was caused not by the multitude of toxic chemicals to which he or she was exposed over the latency period, but by exposure to the toxic substance under the defendant's control or responsibility.

The exposure to the toxic substance must have been for a duration and in a concentration that scientists believe can cause the injury. The plaintiff must also identify the party or parties responsible for the exposure. Legal causation requires that the plaintiff introduce expert testimony on "reasonable medical certainty" that the alleged injury was caused by the defendant's conduct.[71]

The plaintiff may meet the burden of proof by showing that it is more probable than not that a defendant's negligence or product was a substantial factor in causing the plaintiff's injury.[72] The courts have adopted the *Restatement (Second) of Torts* § 431 approach to deciding whether a manufacturer's product was a "substantial factor" in the plaintiff's injury.[73]

Under the *Restatement's* definition of legal cause:

The actor's negligent conduct is a legal cause of harm to another if:

(a) his conduct is a substantial factor in bringing about the harm, and

(b) there is no rule of law relieving the actor from liability because of the manner in which his negligence has resulted in the harm.

Section 433 of the *Restatement* is used in conjunction with § 431 as a guide to determining whether a defendant's product was a "substantial factor" in causing the plaintiff's injury:

The following considerations are in themselves or in combination with one another important in determining whether the actor's conduct is a substantial factor in bringing about harm to another:

[71] Sterling v. Velsicol Chemical Corp., 855 F.2d 1188, 19 Envtl. L. Rep. (Envtl. L. Inst.) 20,404 (6th Cir. 1988); Anderson v. W.R. Grace & Co., 628 F. Supp. 1219, 16 Envtl. L. Rep. (Envtl. L. Inst.) 20,577 (D. Mass. 1986); Hagerty v. L & L Marine Services, Inc., 788 F.2d 315 (5th Cir. 1986), *reconsid. denied, en banc,* 797 F.2d 256 (5th Cir. 1986).

[72] Prosser, Law of Torts § 41 at 240 (3d ed. 1971); Malone, *Ruminations on Cause-in-Fact,* 9 Stan. L. Rev. 60 (1950); Green, *The Casual Relation Issue,* 60 Mich. L. Rev. 543 (1962); Seltzer, *Personal Injury Hazardous Waste Litigation: A Proposal for Tort Reform,* 10 B.C. Envtl. Aff. L. Rev. 797, 811–12 (1982–83); Rosenberg, *The Causal Connection in Mass Exposure Cases: A "Public Law" Vision of the Tort Systems,* 97 Harv. L. Rev. 849 (1984).

[73] Restatement (Second) of Torts § 431 (1965).

(a) the number of other factors which contribute in producing the harm and the extent of the effect which they have in producing it;

(b) whether the actor's conduct has created a force or series of forces which are in continuous and active operation up to the time of the harm, or has created a situation harmless unless acted upon by other forces for which the actor is not responsible;

(c) lapse of time.[74]

In asbestos-related litigation, any exposure to asbestos could satisfy all three requirements. A single exposure to asbestos can give rise to mesothelioma. Repeated exposure to asbestos does not require another action to produce its harmful effects. Finally, the lapse of time has no impact on asbestos-related diseases. The probability of becoming afflicted with such a disease does not decrease from the time of exposure. In fact, the long latency period increases the probability of becoming afflicted with an asbestos-related disease from the time of the initial exposure.

The jury must also consider: the extent to which a particular product produced the harm or injury; whether the defendant's conduct created a series of forces that were continuous up to the time of the harm; and the actual lapse of time itself.[75]

Some plaintiffs who have been unable to identify a specific product or manufacturer may shift the burden of proof to the defendant, who must then prove that it was not responsible for the plaintiff's injury. Each defendant must then prove that it was not responsible for the plaintiff's injury, or risk liability corresponding to its market share at the time of the injury. Where identification of a specific defendant is difficult, some plaintiffs have argued that a manufacturer may be liable for a share corresponding to its market share at the time of the injury.[76]

The market share concept of liability used in DES cases was rejected in *In re Related Asbestos Cases*.[77] The court found that asbestos, unlike DES, is a product with numerous factors that make it difficult to determine market share. DES is an undifferentiated product unlike asbestos which has many types of asbestos products used in different quantities by many manufacturers, and each asbestos product varies in its carcinogenic effect.

An asbestosis victim's $325,000 jury verdict was overturned because the plaintiff failed to prove specifically which asbestos manufacturer's dust he was exposed to and injured by 30 years before.[78]

---

[74] Restatement (Second) of Torts § 433 (1965).

[75] Prosser and Keeton on Torts, at 265–66 (5th Ed. 1984).

[76] Sindell v. Abbott Laboratories, 26 Cal. 3d 588, 607 P.2d 924, *cert. denied,* 449 U.S. 912 (1980); Hardy v. Johns-Manville Sales Corp., 509 F. Supp. 1353 (E.D. Tex. 1981), *rev'd on other grounds,* 681 F.2d 384 (5th Cir. 1982).

[77] 543 F. Supp. 1152 (N.D. Cal. 1982).

[78] Reaves v. Armstrong World Industries Inc., No. 89-2289 (Fla. Dist. Ct. App. Oct. 31, 1990); Asbestos Abatement Report, Nov. 26, 1990, at 6.

§ 7.9 Asbestos Is Not Dangerous

Some manufacturers have tried to argue that asbestos was not itself dangerous until someone else's mistakes or actions caused it to become friable. For
example, fireproofing containing sprayed-on asbestos may become friable
only because of leaks from a defective roof. A manufacturer may try to
claim, for example, that a roofer's defective work caused an otherwise safe
condition to become unsafe and that there was a breach of the roofing
guarantee.

The manufacturer's liability exposure may be reduced by any settlement
or recovery the owner has from other parties such as the roofer. The owner
will have to determine whether other persons' acts or omissions contributed to the hazard.

§ 7.10 State-of-the-Art Defense

Manufacturers frequently defend themselves in lawsuits by arguing that, at
the relevant times, they did not know nor could they have known of the
danger of their products.[79] This has come to be known as the "state-of-the-
art" defense. Defendants assert that "the danger of which they failed to
warn was undiscovered at the time the product was marketed and that it
was undiscoverable given the state of scientific knowledge at that time."[80]

In *Beshada,* an action for wrongful death and personal injury, plaintiffs
claimed to have developed asbestos-related diseases because of exposure to
asbestos products during their employment. Plaintiffs claimed that defendant manufacturers were strictly liable because they failed to warn of
the hazards of asbestos. Defendants asserted the state-of-the-art defense,
alleging that they could not have known that the hazards existed, based on
available scientific evidence at the time of marketing the products.

The Supreme Court of New Jersey was not persuaded. It held that "in
strict liability cases, culpability is irrelevant. The product was unsafe.
That it was unsafe because of the state of technology does not change the
fact that it was unsafe. Strict liability focuses on the product, not the fault
of the manufacturer."[81] Finally, the court decided that imposing liability

[79] *In re* Asbestos Litigation, 829 F.2d 1233, 1235 (3d Cir. 1987), *cert. denied,* 485 U.S. 1029 (1988).

[80] Beshada v. Johns-Manville Products Corp., 90 N.J. 191, 447 A.2d 539, 542 (1982); *see also* Reynolds and Sunahara, *Johnson v. Raybestos-Manhattan, Inc.: The Death of State of the Art Evidence in Strict Products Liability Actions Involving Inherently Dangerous Products,* 11 U. Haw. L. Rev. 143 (1989); Johnson v. Raybestos-Manhattan, Inc., 69 Haw. 287, 740 P.2d 548 (Haw. 1987).

[81] Beshada v. Johns-Manville Products Corp., 90 N.J. at 204, 447 A.2d at 546.

for failing to warn of unknowable dangers furthered the goals and policies of the strict liability doctrine, thus barring the state-of-the-art defense.[82]

Two years later, however, the New Jersey Supreme Court retreated from this position. In *Feldman v. Lederle Laboratories,*[83] the plaintiff suffered tooth discoloration as a result of taking a tetracycline drug as an infant, and premised her strict liability claim on the defendant's failure to warn of such discoloration as a possible side effect. Defendant asserted that this side effect was not known at the time the drug was marketed.

The court noted that the manufacturer would be deemed to know of reliable information generally available or reasonably obtainable in the industry or in the particular field involved. The knowledge must be "reasonably knowable in the sense of actual or constructive knowledge."[84]

"State of the art" can mean different things in different contexts. In design defect cases, the term refers to the technical feasibility of designing a safer product at the time the product is manufactured. In "failure-to-warn" cases, it refers to scientific knowledge of a risk associated with the product at the time the product is manufactured.

In design defect cases, the jurisdictions are split on the admissibility of state-of-the-art evidence. The jurisdictions excluding state-of-the-art evidence hold that such evidence is irrelevant because it relates to the reasonableness of the design selected for manufacture, and the manufacturer's standard of care is not an issue in strict products liability.

For example, in *Flatt v. Johns-Manville Sales Corporation,*[85] the plaintiff brought a products liability action against the manufacturer of cement pipes that contained asbestos, alleging that exposure to the pipes caused the death of the plaintiff's decedent. The court stated that evidence relating to the state of the art at the time of manufacture was relevant only to the issue of due care in the manufacturing process—a negligence concept not at issue in a strict liability action.[86] The Supreme Court of Illinois, in holding that state-of-the-art defense evidence was inadmissible, held the defendant liable and stated:

> To allow a defense to strict liability on the ground that there is no way, either practical or theoretical, for a defendant to ascertain the existence of impurities in his product would be to emasculate the doctrine and in a very real sense would signal a return to a negligence theory.[87]

---

[82] *Id.* 90 N.J. at 207, 447 A.2d at 549.

[83] 97 N.J. 429, 479 A.2d 374 (1984).

[84] *Id.* at 453, 479 A.2d at 387.

[85] 488 F. Supp. 836 (E.D. Tex. 1980).

[86] *Id.* at 841.

[87] *Id.* Many decisions that have excluded state-of-the-art evidence are from Illinois. *See, e.g.,* Ruggeri v. Minnesota Mining & Mfg. Co., 63 Ill. App. 3d 525, 529, 380 N.E.2d 445,

In jurisdictions admitting state-of-the-art evidence in design cases, the courts hold that such evidence serves as a measure of reasonable consumer expectations. In *Bruce v. Martin-Marietta Corporation*,[88] the plaintiffs brought products liability and negligence actions against the manufacturer of an aircraft, to recover for injuries sustained as a result of the alleged uncrashworthiness of the aircraft. The court expressly rejected the Illinois rule, and noted the plaintiffs' failure to show that the ordinary consumer would expect a plane manufactured in 1952 to have the safety features of a plane manufactured in 1970. Having recognized that consumer expectations change as new safety features are developed, the court noted that "state of the art evidence helps to determine the expectation of the ordinary consumer."[89]

When raised by manufacturers, this defense has not been allowed by many courts. The court in *Johnson v. Raybestos-Manhattan, Inc.*[90] rejected this defense because strict liability causes of action are based on the inherently dangerous nature of the product and not the fault of the manufacturer. State-of-the-art evidence is inadmissible to establish whether the seller knew or should have known of the dangerousness of its product. Therefore, a manufacturer can be held liable for injuries from a defective product, even when the manufacturer had no knowledge of danger at the time of production. The defense will also fail if the manufacturer knew of the specific hazard at the time. Plaintiffs often assert fraud claims and allege that the manufacturer knew of the dangers and concealed knowledge of them.

Courts that have rejected this defense have done so as a matter of policy. They believe that the imposition of liability for failure to warn of dangers that were undiscoverable at the time of manufacture will advance the goals and policies sought to be achieved by strict liability rules.[91] These courts feel that manufacturers and distributors of defective products are best able to allocate the costs of injuries and of failures to discover hazards, and that this liability will create an incentive for them to invest more in safety research.[92]

Manufacturers of asbestos were not allowed to use evidence about the state of the art at an earlier time to prove their lack of knowledge of

---

448 (1978); Stanfield v. Medalist Indus., 34 Ill. App. 3d 635, 640–41, 340 N.E.2d 276, 280 (1975); Matthews v. Stewart Warner Corp., 20 Ill. App. 3d 470, 482, 314 N.E.2d 683, 692 (1974); Gelsumino v. E.W. Bliss Co., 10 Ill. App. 3d 604, 608, 295 N.E.2d 110, 112–13 (1973) (state-of-the-art evidence irrelevant to strict liability). Thus, the rule for exclusion of state-of-the-art evidence is sometimes referred to as the Illinois rule.

[88] 544 F.2d 442 (10th Cir. 1976).

[89] *Id.* at 447.

[90] 740 P.2d 548 (Haw. 1987).

[91] Beshada v. Johns-Manville Products Corp., 447 A.2d at 547.

[92] *Id.* at 548.

the product's dangers, in defending against a strict liability failure-to-warn case.[93] The court felt that disallowing the defense would help implement the policies that underlie strict liability in tort.

§ 7.11 CERCLA's Third-Party Defense

CERCLA contains a limited defense for releases due solely to: (1) acts of God, (2) war; and (3) the so-called "third-party" defense, which states:

> (3) an act or omission of a third party other than an employee or agent of the defendant, or than one whose act or omission occurs in connection with a contractual relationship, existing directly or indirectly, with the defendant (except where the sole contractual arrangement arises from a published tariff and acceptance for carriage by a common carrier by rail), if the defendant establishes by a preponderance of the evidence that (a) he exercised due care with respect to the hazardous substance concerned, taking into consideration the characteristics of such hazardous substance, in light of all relevant facts and circumstances, and (b) he took precautions against foreseeable acts or omissions of any such third party and the consequences that could foreseeably result from such acts or omissions; . . . .[94]

Thus, if the act or omission of the third party occurs in connection with an employment, agency, or contractual relationship with the defendant, the relationship would eliminate this defense. There would be a defense to liability if the problem was caused solely by the act or omission of a third party. This gap was closed by SARA, which added a "due diligence" defense.

A successful defense would require a showing that:

1. The defendant was ignorant of the site's contamination, despite the exercise of due care;
2. The third party was solely responsible;
3. There was no contractual relationship with the third party.

§ 7.12 SARA's Innocent Landowner or Due Diligence Defense

SARA clarified CERCLA's third-party defense by defining "contractual relationship" so that truly "innocent" owners and operators would not be

---

[93] Anderson v. Owens-Corning Fiberglass Corp., 217 Cal. App. 3d 772, 266 Cal. Rptr. 204 (2d Dist. 1990), *review granted in part,* 269 Cal. Rptr. 74, 790 P.2d 238 (1990).

[94] 42 U.S.C. § 9607(b)(3). The courts have not yet absolved anyone of liability based on these statutory defenses.

exposed to liability. Mere ownership of a hazardous waste site, without more, is not sufficient grounds for imposing liability. Because leases usually transfer possession, lessees may be liable for hazardous substances on the leased property, unless the "third-party defense" is available. Previously, liability extended to property owners in any kind of contractual relationship with a third party who was responsible for contamination.

Under the amendment:

> The term "contractual relationship," for the purpose of section 107(b)(3), includes, but is not limited to, land contracts, . . . unless the real property on which the facility concerned is located was acquired by the defendant after the disposal or placement of the hazardous substance on, in, or at the facility, and . . . (i) [a]t the time the defendant acquired the facility the defendant did not know and had no reason to know that any hazardous substance which is the subject of the release or threatened release was disposed of on, in, or at the facility.[95]

"Land contract" does not include real property on which a hazardous waste facility is located, if it was acquired after disposal or placement of the hazardous waste in, or on, or at the facility, provided the defendant can prove by a preponderance of the evidence that:

1. At the time of acquisition of the facility, he or she did not know and had no reason to know that any hazardous substance was disposed of on the property, or
2. The owner is a government entity that acquired the facility by escheat, or through any other involuntary transfer or acquisition, or through the exercise of eminent domain authority by purchase or condemnation, or
3. The owner acquired the facility by inheritance or bequest.[96]

Liability can be avoided, and a party can establish having had no "reason to know" that hazardous substances had been disposed of, by showing that, when the property was acquired, the landowner had no knowledge of contamination and had "undertaken, at the time of acquisition, all appropriate inquiry into the previous ownership and uses of the property consistent with good commercial or customary practice in an effort to minimize liability."[97] This includes:

---

[95] 42 U.S.C. § 101(35)(A)(i) (as added by the Superfund Amendment and Reauthorization Act of 1986, Pub. L. No. 99-499, 100 Stat. 1613, 1616 (1986) (hereinafter, "SARA").

[96] 42 U.S.C. § 9601(35)(A).

[97] 42 U.S.C. § 9601(35)(B).

. . . any specialized knowledge or experience on the part of the defendant, the relationship of the purchase price to the value of the property if uncontaminated, commonly known or reasonably ascertainable information about the property, the obviousness of the presence or likely presence of contamination at the property, and the ability to detect such contamination by appropriate inspection.[98]

Information obtained from employees, professional consultants, public information, visual inspection, and a purchase price below market value may defeat the owner-operator's use of this defense.

A successful defense would require the "innocent" owner to show:

1.   The purchase was after the contamination occurred;
2.   The owner did not know or had no reason to know of the contamination;[99]
3.   A reasonable site investigation was undertaken.

Upon discovering the hazardous substance release or potential release caused by the unrelated third party, the landowner must also prove by a preponderance of the evidence that due care was exercised with respect to the hazardous substance concerned, taking into consideration the characteristics of such hazardous substance, in light of all relevant facts and circumstances, and that precautions were taken against foreseeable acts or omissions of any such third party and the consequences that could foreseeably result from such acts or omissions.[100]

CERCLA does not make clear how much investigation of a property is necessary to avoid liability. Specifically, Congress indicated:

> The duty to inquire under this provision shall be judged as of the time of acquisition. Defendants shall be held to a higher standard as public awareness of the hazards associated with hazardous substance releases has grown, as reflected by this Act, the 1980 Act and other Federal and State statutes.
>
> Moreover, good commercial or customary practice with respect to inquiry in an effort to minimize liability shall mean that a reasonable inquiry must have been made in all circumstances in light of best business and land transfer principles.
>
> Those engaged in commercial transactions should, however, be held to a higher standard than those who are engaged in private residential transactions. Similarly, those who acquire property through inheritance or bequest without actual knowledge may rely upon this section if they engage in a reasonable inquiry, but they need not be held to the same standard as those

---

[98] 42 U.S.C. § 9601(35)(A)(i).

[99] 42 U.S.C. § 9601(35)(A).

[100] 42 U.S.C. § 9607(b)(3).

who acquire property as part of a commercial or private transaction, and those who acquire property by inheritance without knowing of the inheritance shall not be liable, if they satisfy the remaining requirements of section 107(b)(3).[101]

This section has not been challenged, and courts are reluctant to grant summary judgment. There is only minimal case law dealing with the third-party defense, and no one has successfully asserted it thus far.[102]

A House Conference Report expresses the view that those engaged in commercial transactions will be held to a higher standard of inquiry than those engaged in residential transactions.[103]

A residential homeowner's due diligence may be satisfied by an inspection done by an engineer. However, more is expected of commercial investors. As businesspeople, they are held to a higher standard and would be expected to perform more elaborate tests and inquire further than homeowners.

§ 7.13   —Checklist for Innocent Landowner Defense[104]

1. On what date was the property purchased?
2. What affirmative steps were taken by the landowner to determine previous ownership and uses of the property?
3. Who was the prior owner (i.e., seller) and what type of business did he or she conduct?
4. What was the condition of the property when it was purchased?
5. How does the purchase price compare with the fair market value?
6. Did the landowner-building owner have any special knowledge of hazardous substances?
7. Did the seller make any representations at the time of sale regarding the use or condition of the property or building?
8. What is the landowner's and his or her employees' general knowledge of the use or condition of the property or building?

---

[101] Joint Explanatory Statement of the Committee of Conference, H.R. Conf. Rep. No. 963, 99th Cong., 2d Sess. 187–88 (1986), *reprinted in* 1986 U.S. Code Cong. & Admin. News 3280–81.

[102] United States v. Mottolo, 695 F. Supp. 615 (D.N.H. 1988); City of Philadelphia v. Stepan Chemical Co., Nos. 81-0851, 83-5493 (E.D. Pa. 1987) (WL, Allfeds database); United States v. Serafini, 1988 U.S. Dist. LEXIS 7361 (M.D. Pa. 1988).

[103] *See* H.R. Rep. No. 962, 99th Cong., 2d Sess. 187 (1986).

[104] This is not intended to be a comprehensive checklist. Rather, it will give the reader an idea of the main areas of inquiry.

9.   What, if anything, did the landowner-building owner know about hazardous substances on the property?

10. What measures did the landowner-building owner take to eliminate possible health risks to individuals and harm to the environment?

11. What type of inspection was done and when?

12. What was considered "good commercial and customary practice" at the time the property or building was purchased?

§ 7.14   Estoppel

Estoppel is a commonly used defense to a fraud claim. One court described the defense as follows:

> [A] party seeking to invoke a doctrine of estoppel must prove by clear, precise, and unequivocal evidence the following elements: (1) A material fact was falsely represented or concealed; (2) A representation or concealment was made with the knowledge of the facts; (3) The party to whom the presentation was made was ignorant of the truth of the matter; (4) The representation was made with the intention that the other party should act upon it; (5) The other party was induced to act upon it; (6) The party claiming estoppel was misled to his injury.[105]

It is essential that the party claiming estoppel be "ignorant of the true state of facts" and have no way to acquire the true facts. Owners of property damaged by asbestos or other hazardous substances may meet this criterion.[106]

Fraud delays the running of the statute of limitations until the fraud is discovered or should have been discovered by due diligence.

§ 7.15   Assumption of Risk

Assumption of the risk is a traditional defense to the imposition of strict liability. Defendants have raised this argument where purchasers of buildings and facilities have chosen not to test for hazardous substances and have assumed the risk that hazardous substances might be present.[107] The plaintiff's ordinary contributory negligence in failing to discover an abnormally

---

[105] Boykins Narrow Fabrics Corp. v. Weldon Roofing & Sheet Metal, Inc., 221 Va. 81, 86, 266 S.E.2d 887, 890 (1980).

[106] *Id.* 221 Va. at 87.

[107] Amland Properties Corp. v. Aluminum Company of America, 711 F. Supp. 784, 802 (D.N.J. 1989).

dangerous activity or to take precautions against it is not a defense to the strict liability of the individual who carries it on.

However, courts have found that this defense can be raised only where a plaintiff has *actual* knowledge of the danger presented by the defective product and knowingly and voluntarily encounters that risk.

One court described this defense as being predicated upon:

> [an] agreement, express or implied, not to hold defendant responsible for the injury-causing act, negligent though it may have been, which resulted from plaintiff's entering into the activity with knowledge of its danger, or under circumstances from which it could be found that he or she should have had such knowledge of it.[108]

§ 7.16   Contributory Negligence

Contributory negligence occurs when a plaintiff fails to exercise the care of a reasonable person for his or her own protection. The plaintiff is held to have the knowledge, understanding, and judgment of an ordinary reasonable person and must exercise due care to discover and understand the defect or danger.[109] Contributory negligence may also occur when there is voluntary and unreasonable conduct in encountering a known risk.[110]

When a manufacturer claimed an insulation worker was contributorily negligent for not wearing a respirator, the court found that the worker had used the product for its intended purpose. The worker's failure to discover a defect in the product or guard against the possibility of its existence is not a defense to strict liability.[111]

§ 7.17   Unclean Hands

The unclean-hands defense is asserted when there is a claim by defendants that the plaintiffs themselves were actively responsible for the release of hazardous substances and therefore cannot maintain an action.

This defense is available in traditional lawsuits and has also been allowed in private response cost recovery actions under CERCLA.[112] However, at

---

[108] United States v. Hooker Chemicals & Plastics Corp., 722 F. Supp. 960 (W.D.N.Y. 1989).

[109] Borel v. Fibreboard Paper Products Corp., 493 F.2d 1076, 1096 (5th Cir. 1973), *cert. denied*, 419 U.S. 869 (1974).

[110] *Id.* 493 F.2d at 1097.

[111] *Id.* at 1099.

[112] Marden Corp. v. C.G.C. Music, Ltd., 600 F. Supp. 1049, 1057–58 (D. Ariz. 1984), *aff'd on other grounds*, 804 F.2d 1454 (9th Cir. 1986); *see also* D'Imperio v. United States, 575 F. Supp. 248, 253 (D.N.J. 1983); Kalik v. Allis-Chalmers Corp., 658 F. Supp. 631, 637 (W.D. Pa. 1987).

least one court refused to allow this defense in a CERCLA case because of its belief that the defense would be contrary to Congressional intent.[113] If this defense were successful, it would fly in the face of the SARA amendments, which allow contribution among polluters.[114]

§ 7.18 *Caveat Emptor*

Caveat emptor (let the buyer beware) has not proved to be a successful defense in environmental litigation. It is not considered by the government to be a defense to a CERCLA suit for cleanup costs, but may have some bearing on the amount of the award.[115] The court may consider the discount in the sale price of a piece of property and the cost of response.

In suits using common-law theories, *caveat emptor* may be applicable, but public policy considerations may play a major role in defeating it.

§ 7.19 Disclaimers

Sellers of commercial property and commercial landlords often disclaim obligations in their contracts of sale or leases. A good example is the obligation to abate asbestos. Limitations on the amount of damages recoverable may also be stated. These are more commonly upheld in the commercial than in the residential arena. Under § 2-719 (1977) of the Uniform Commercial Code, unconscionable limitations on consequential damages for personal injury may be struck down.

§ 7.20 Damage Control

The best way to avoid liability is to make sure that a site is handled properly from the beginning. Surprises and unexpected emergencies will always occur. How they are handled can go a long way toward lessening liability. Emergencies are discussed in detail in **Chapter 12**.

When there is a sudden release of a hazardous or toxic substance, there will naturally be publicity. It is important for the attorney to handle the situation quickly and professionally. The client should be anxious to cooperate in resolving the problem and working with governmental agencies. Key personnel of the client should be briefed on handling questions for the

---

[113] United States v. Conservation Chemical Co., 628 F. Supp. 391, 404–5 (W.D. Mo. 1985), *modified,* 681 F. Supp. 1394 (W.D. Mo. 1988).

[114] Another equitable defense to a CERCLA claim is restitution. *See* Violet v. Picillo, 648 F. Supp. 1283, 1294–95 (D.R.I. 1986).

[115] Smith Land & Improvement Corp. v. Celotex Corp., 851 F.2d 86 (3d Cir. 1988).

media; depending on the size of the client, a public relations firm may also be involved in answering questions.

Investigation of the problem should be started immediately. It may be advisable for the attorney to hire environmental consultants so that the attorney/work product privilege is maintained.

The best strategy is to present to the agency involved a plan explaining how the problem will be addressed—before the agency issues its orders. This tactic may help lessen the damages and extent of litigation.

CHAPTER 8

ENVIRONMENTAL HAZARDS AND THE MARKET VALUE OF REAL PROPERTY

Harindra de Silva, Mark H. Egland,
and Michael F. Koehn*
Analysis Group, Inc., Los Angeles, California

§ 8.1 Introduction
§ 8.2 Market Value of Property—The Appraiser and Economist
§ 8.3 A Framework to Estimate Market Value Reduction
§ 8.4 —A Real Estate Valuation Model
§ 8.5 —Cash Flows
§ 8.6 —Value of Debt
§ 8.7 —Estimating the Change in Market Value
§ 8.8 Regulations and Market Value
§ 8.9 Evaluating the Impact of Asbestos on Market Value
§ 8.10 —Scope of Government Regulations Relating to Asbestos
§ 8.11 —Cost Implications of Regulations
§ 8.12 —Media Response to Asbestos in Buildings
§ 8.13 —Lender and Investor Response
§ 8.14 Building Occupant Response
§ 8.15 —Response to the Presence of Asbestos
§ 8.16 —Response to Abatement Activity
§ 8.17 —Stigma of Abated Building
§ 8.18 Estimation of Impact of Asbestos on Market Value
§ 8.19 Market Value of Residential Property

*The authors wish to thank C. Jaye Berger, Lois Egland, Michael Egland, Martha Espinoza, Lotte Harding, Michael Williams, and Bradley Zanin for their helpful comments.

273

§ 8.20   Actual Market Response—Transaction Prices

§ 8.21   —Impact of Environmental Hazards on Market Value

§ 8.22   Property Taxes and Market Value

§ 8.23   —Filing for Reassessment

§ 8.24   Investing in Buildings Containing Hazardous Materials

§ 8.25   Conclusion

§ 8.1   Introduction

In this chapter, we examine the ways in which environmental hazards can affect the market value of real property. We first identify the critical factors that must be considered in evaluating the possible impact of an environmental hazard on the market value of real property. We incorporate these factors into a model often used to estimate the market value of property. This framework is then used to study the impact of a widely discussed environmental hazard—asbestos—on the market value of real property. Using this approach, we estimate the impact of asbestos on the market value of a hypothetical property. We will discuss more specifically what investors can do to help minimize the risks associated with investing in property that has environmental hazards. Although the analyses in this chapter largely focus on the specific problem of asbestos in buildings, we also discuss how the analyses can be applied more generally to other environmental hazards.

§ 8.2   Market Value of Property—The Appraiser and Economist

The term "market value" has numerous definitions across different disciplines. Generally in this chapter, the term market value is used the same as defined by an economist. In this section, however, we review the term market value from the perspective of both the appraiser and economist, and discuss the relationship between the two.

Both economists and appraisers study market value and the forces that determine the value of real property. A real estate appraiser typically carries out the appraisal process to value a specific property as of a specific date. The appraiser's objective is to conduct field research, collect and analyze relevant market data, and estimate the "value" of the property using various approaches. Traditional market value appraisals play a key role in the financing of nearly all types of real estate. Investors, lenders, developers, and even homeowners often rely heavily on appraisal reports in analyzing a real estate transaction.

"Market value," as we have discussed earlier, is a term of art. According to the American Institute of Real Estate Appraisers (AIREA), the most widely accepted definitions of market value include the following:[1]

1. The highest price in terms of money that a property would bring in a competitive and open market under all conditions requisite to a fair sale, with the buyer and seller each acting prudently and knowledgeably and under the assumption that the price is not affected by undue stimulus.

2. The price at which a willing seller would sell and a willing buyer would buy, neither being under abnormal pressure.

3. The price expected if a reasonable time is allowed to find a purchaser and if both seller and prospective buyer are fully informed.

The common factor that links the appraiser and the economist is that both rely on "knowledgeable" buyers and sellers.

The objective of the appraiser is to estimate the "market value" of the property. The three methods most commonly employed in estimating the market value of real estate are the replacement cost, market or comparable sales, and income approach methods. Each of these three methods has varying degrees of applicability in terms of evaluating the impact of an environmental hazard on market value. The least applicable method used by the appraiser to estimate market value is the replacement cost method. The replacement cost method is used to estimate the expenses associated with construction of a building equivalent to the property in question. Thus, the replacement cost method cannot provide insight in evaluating the effects of environmental hazards on the value of real property.

The comparable sales or market approach is perhaps the most intuitive way to assess the effects of an environmental hazard on the market value of real estate. This approach relies on the comparison of properties that have sold prior to a specific property in question. The sale price, or market value, of properties that have sold in the past is used as a benchmark to compare to the property the appraiser is valuing.

Because market forces of supply and demand register a market-clearing price on all prior transactions, a comparison can be made between the buildings involved in prior transactions and the property in question. The relevant characteristics (e.g., building age, location, size, use, and condition) of these buildings are considered, and a subset of buildings with similar or "comparable" characteristics to the property being appraised is

---

[1] Pyhrr, Cooper, Wofford, Kapplin, and Lapides, Real Estate Investment: Strategy, Analysis, Decisions (1989). According to Pyhrr et al., the 1987 edition of Appraisal of Real Estate (1987) explored the controversy surrounding the issues of market value definition in the appraisal field.

selected. Inferences can be made regarding the value of a building that has not yet been sold by comparing its characteristics to those that have been sold and have therefore registered a market price. The most important feature of this analysis is that the prices and therefore market values used in conducting the analysis are determined by market forces.

Assessing the effects of an environmental hazard on the value of real property using the comparable buildings approach can be illustrated with the following example. Recently, a building owner filed suit (alleging product liability claims) against the manufacturers of a building's asbestos-containing fireproofing for the costs associated with the removal of asbestos-containing material (ACM).[2] As part of these claims, the plaintiff alleged that the market value of a building with ACM was adversely affected. To evaluate this claim, in the ideal "comparable" world, we would want two identical buildings standing side-by-side, one with ACM and one without ACM. Assuming both buildings were sold on the same day, the difference in the sale prices would equal the effect of asbestos on the market value of the building. Unfortunately, a "perfect" comparable sale rarely exists. However, as discussed later in this chapter, it is possible to develop a statistical aggregation of historical transactions both with and without asbestos, to determine whether the presence of asbestos is associated with a reduction in value.[3]

The income or discounted cash flow approach can also be used to evaluate the effects of environmental hazards on the market value of real estate. This is the method most heavily relied on by economists and appraisers to estimate the market value of a property when actual transaction price data are not available or when such data cannot be easily obtained. We develop this approach in the following section.

§ 8.3   A Framework to Estimate
Market Value Reduction

In this section we develop a framework to analyze the potential effect environmental hazards could have on the market value of property. To quantify the impact environmental hazards have on the market value of a property, it is first necessary to determine how the hazard may affect the fundamental characteristics that determine a building's market value.

---

[2] *See, e.g.,* 3250 Wilshire Boulevard Building et al. v. W. R. Grace & Co., (1989 U.S. Dist. LEXIS 17287) (C.D. Cal. 1989), aff'd, 915 F.2d 1355 (9th Cir. 1990).

[3] We complete this analysis in **§ 8.21.**

§ 8.4   —A Real Estate Valuation Model

As discussed earlier, the concept of market value is relatively simple—the expected price within a competitive open market, with all potential buyers and sellers acting prudently and knowledgeably. However, because real estate, unlike a stock or bond, is not an actively traded and homogeneous asset, its market value cannot be readily estimated without relying on some valuation method. One valuation method often used is the discounted earnings or cash flow approach. Discounted cash flow models fall into two categories: the traditional capitalization-based models and present value models.

The traditional capitalization-based models estimate market value by using the net cash flow in a single time period, and then assume that this single-period cash flow is constant in perpetuity. This single-period earnings or net cash flow is then multiplied by a capitalization ("cap") rate to estimate the market value of the property. However, such models do not explicitly consider relative changes in factors such as rents, vacancies, and operating expenses over the period of ownership.[4] As a result, they are not particularly useful in evaluating how an environmental hazard might affect the value of a building. In contrast, the present value based models focus on the expected income flows in each year and are, thus, ideally suited to evaluate the impact of environmental hazards on market value.

To an economist, the market value of a property is the discounted present value of the annual after-tax cash flows accruing to its owner, plus the value of debt underlying the property. This may be represented simply as:

$$MV = VD + \frac{CF_1}{(1+r)^1} + \cdots + \frac{CF_i}{(1+r)^i} + \cdots + \frac{RV}{(1+r)^n}$$

where MV is the market value, VD is the market value of the debt, CF_i is the expected after-tax cash flow in year i, RV is the future or "reversionary" value of the building, and r is the rate of return on comparable investments. We will discuss the important components of this model and the possible impact an environmental hazard may have on these components.

§ 8.5   —Cash Flows

The present value of the expected after-tax cash flows accruing to the building owner is what is commonly referred to as owner's "equity." The expected cash flow accruing to a building owner in a given year is based on expectations regarding the building's occupancy rate (the percentage of

---

[4] Pyhrr et al., *supra* note 1.

the building that is occupied or rented out), the rental rate (the rent per square foot), rentable area, property tax and other taxes, building operating expenses, and financing costs. An actual or expected change in any one of these variables will, thus, affect the estimated market value of a building.

An environmental hazard has the potential to affect any or all of these factors. If building occupants expect the environmental hazard to pose a health risk, there will be a reduced demand for the building. This will manifest itself in terms of lower occupancy rates and/or lower rental rates. If the building owner charges market rents and if occupying the building is widely regarded as a health risk, then the occupancy rate in that particular building will be substantially lower than that of comparable buildings without the perceived health risk. By lowering the rental rate, the building owner may induce some of these potential occupants to rent space in the building. However, this will also result in a reduction in the revenues accruing to the building owner.

One cash flow implication from the presence of an environmental hazard is the cost of removing the hazard and/or managing an ongoing operations and maintenance (O&M) program to deal with the hazard. If the hazard must be removed, in addition to the direct cost of removal, the building owner may incur the potential costs of relocating tenants, redecoration, and the loss of rental income associated with the vacant space undergoing abatement. It should be noted, however, that expenditures on certain items (i.e., redecoration that enhances the building's value) may increase the reversionary value of the property and this may mitigate the total costs incurred when removing the hazard.

In some cases—for example, when an environmentally hazardous material has been buried under the building—removal may be so costly that it is uneconomic. The building owner must then evaluate the present value of the cash flows associated with the alternative courses of actions, such as leaving the material in place and continuing to rent the building or simply demolishing the building.

In addition to the direct expenses associated with a hazard, such as the cost of removal, there may also exist potential future liability. If building occupants do not perceive a particular environmental hazard as a likely health threat, then a building owner may choose to leave it in place. However, in the event that at some point in the future the material is found to have affected the health of the building occupants, the building owner may be the subject of a lawsuit. Thus, even though occupants do not currently perceive a particular hazard as a health threat, it may be preferable for the owner to remove the hazardous material to eliminate a possible future liability. The key factor in the decision to remove the material is the likelihood of a future lawsuit and the resulting liability. If the probability of such an event is low, then the expected future liability will be small.

The liability does not necessarily lie with those who caused the environmental hazard, but may instead lie with those who own and/or operate the environmentally hazardous real estate. This broadening of liability is a product of SARA, commonly referred to as the Superfund law (see **Chapter 1**). These 1986 amendments to CERCLA state that "innocent purchasers" who acquire real estate without any knowledge of hazardous materials and who do not contribute to it may not be held liable. However, the purchasers must be able to demonstrate that they exercised "reasonable inquiry before acquisition" to include all appropriate inquiry into previous ownership and use of the property. In legal terms, this means that the purchaser must have exercised "due diligence" in determining that the property was free of hazardous materials. In practical terms, it means a complete environmental assessment/audit of the property prior to purchase.[5]

The present value of a change in net cash flow associated with the environmental hazard is the net effect of the hazard on the value of the building owner's equity. Building owners can reduce the magnitude of the change in market value by, if possible, delaying the removal activity further into the future. The longer the period before the hazard has an impact on the net cash flow of a building, the smaller its negative effect on the value of the building.

The change or decline in market value is brought about by the change in the net cash flow. If building occupancy is reduced because of an environmental hazard, then the costs associated with operating the building will also decline. Focusing on the change in revenues will result in an overestimate of the decline in market value. For example, a building in which the occupancy rate declines because of asbestos removal activity also benefits from lower operating expenses and possibly lower property taxes.

§ 8.6   —Value of Debt

The market value of debt on a building is equal to the present value of the mortgage payments at the market rate of interest. The market value, in general, will equal the face value of the loan if the owner or borrower was charged a competitive interest rate. Given the competitive nature of the mortgage lending market, this condition will generally hold at the time the mortgage is issued. Over time, however, the value of the mortgage will change, depending on changes in the real rate of interest, changes in inflation, and changes in the value and variability of the cash flows of the underlying asset accruing to the investor. The influence of the first two factors is well-documented elsewhere and their influence is unaffected by the

[5] Mortgage Bankers Association of America, Environmental Hazards: A Real Estate Lender's View (1988).

presence or absence of environmental hazards.[6] Assuming the mortgage debt is nonrecourse, the cash flows and their variability (or riskiness) may be affected by the presence of an environmental hazard. If the loan is recourse, the lender has claims on the other assets of the borrower. In such instances, if the owner has substantial other assets, the probability of default will not be affected by a change in cash flows associated with an environmental hazard.

When the cash flows accruing to a building fall, the funds available for loan repayments fall commensurately. This causes the riskiness of the underlying loan to increase as the probability of default increases (assuming a nonrecourse note). A rise in the riskiness of the loan results in a decline in its current market value. Therefore, a lender who holds a mortgage on property that has reduced cash flow—for reasons associated with local market conditions or the presence of a hazard such as asbestos—would suffer a decline in the market value of the loan. Examples of such declines are mortgages on properties in depressed real estate markets (Dallas, for example) that have dramatically declined in value over the past few years. The precise magnitude of the decline is related to the decrease in the cash flows, the increase in riskiness, the loan-to-value ratio, the time to maturity of the loan, and the correct market rate of interest on the loan.

Changes in the riskiness and amount of a building's cash flow are by far the most important in determining the change in the value of a mortgage loan. Increases in the riskiness of the cash flow and reductions in the cash flow increase the probability of default. However, for mortgages with low loan-to-value ratios, the probability of default is low and their market value will change only modestly unless the cash flows decline substantially.

Thus, in the event that an environmental hazard affects the cash flows underlying a building, the market value of the building will change not only because of the reduction in market value of the equity, but also because of change in the market value of the underlying mortgage. Even if the expected cash flows remain constant, an increase in their riskiness will result in a decrease in the market value of the building because lenders will recognize the increased probability of default. Thus, when building owners or investors evaluate the impact of a particular hazard on the market value of a property, they must consider the attitude and perceptions of lenders in the marketplace regarding a particular environmental hazard.

Given the fact that lenders are usually sophisticated investors engaging in a large number of transactions, individual investors can gain information regarding the possible market impact of a environmental hazard by evaluating the policies of the lender. If it is generally agreed that a particular material poses a health hazard and affects the market value of a building, then most lenders will have a specific policy regarding that material.

---

[6] Fabozzi, The Handbook of Fixed Income Securities (2d ed. 1987).

Lenders have a strong incentive to be aware of the impacts of a particular hazard, and their views will often reflect the prevailing views in the marketplace.

Lenders are starting to require environmental audits of property because of their legal liability under laws like SARA. Lenders' primary concerns are:

1. The risk that a loan may lose priority to a cleanup lien imposed by a governing agency;
2. In the event of a foreclosure, the risk that the lender may end up owning contaminated property and being responsible for its cleanup;
3. The possibility that the value of the property used as collateral on the loan may drop significantly if a hazard is found;
4. The increased probability of a default on the loan as a result of the cost of removing the hazard;
5. The risk that the lenders will be held liable for personal injury suffered by those who became ill from the contaminated land for which they had lent money.[7]

§ 8.7   —Estimating the Change in Market Value

In this section, we identify specific factors that building owners or investors should consider in valuing a building that is known, or suspected, to contain a hazardous material. By focusing on these specific factors, an investor can estimate the decline in market value associated with a particular environmental hazard. In subsequent sections, we analyze the case of asbestos using this approach.

In assessing the impact of an environmental hazard on market value, a building owner must identify: (1) the regulations related to the particular environmental hazard and its presence in buildings, and (2) the nature and extent of future regulations concerning the hazard.

§ 8.8   Regulations and Market Value

Regulations regarding particular environmental hazards may exist at the local, state, and/or federal level. Although such information is usually easily obtainable from the appropriate authority, the nature and scope of future regulations are much harder to determine. Evaluation of the current

---

[7] *Banks and S&Ls Scramble to Set Policies on Loans for Property Containing Asbestos,* L.A. Bus. J. 11 (1989).

legislative activity can give some indication of the potential for future regulation. In addition, a review of the articles in the public press relating to the particular hazard and the legislative response can give some indication of future legislative activity. Government legislation usually follows public awareness regarding a particular problem in the environment. For example, the enactment of government health and safety regulations, followed reports in the press regarding higher death rates traceable to smog and industrial accidents.[8] Reports in the press also often contain information regarding actual instances of the effect of an environmental hazard on the market value of a building in particular areas of the country.

After determining the specific regulations relating to a particular hazard and the manner in which the hazard must be dealt with, the building owner or investor can estimate the hazard's effect on market value. If building occupants do not perceive the environmental hazard as a likely health threat, then the change in cash flows are simply the expected cost of dealing with the hazard in a manner consistent with the regulations and the reduction in the market value of the debt associated with the reduced cash flows. However, the probability of future regulations and their associated costs must be factored into determining the expected cost of dealing with the hazard.

§ 8.9   Evaluating the Impact of Asbestos on Market Value

In this section, we apply the approach outlined above to evaluate the impact of asbestos on the factors that determine the market value of a building. Our findings are then used to evaluate the impact of asbestos on a hypothetical building (§ 8.10). It should be noted, however, that the approach is equally applicable in determining the market value effects of any environmental hazard.

Our analysis proceeds as follows. First, we determine the nature and scope of government regulations pertaining to asbestos in buildings. We then examine the cost implications of the regulations. The possibility of future regulation and current views regarding the possible impact of asbestos are evaluated by surveying the public literature relating to asbestos in buildings. Next, we focus on the views of lenders on the issue of asbestos in buildings. Finally, in § 8.14, we evaluate the response of building occupants to asbestos and the abatement of asbestos.

---

[8] MacAvoy, The Regulated Industries and the Economy (1979).

§ 8.10   —Scope of Government Regulations Relating to Asbestos

In this section, we review the regulations relating to asbestos so that we can evaluate how they might translate into changes in the market value of a property. Both the EPA and OSHA have promulgated regulations to reduce constructions workers' exposure to asbestos during the renovation or demolition of buildings.[9] In addition, several state legislatures have enacted regulations on certification of abatement contractors, and some municipalities have issued construction license requirements that call for the removal of asbestos in all renovation projects. There is considerable controversy regarding the scope of each of these regulations and the degree to which they are enforced.

Significant public policy initiatives related to asbestos in commercial buildings are summarized in **Table 8–1**. Regulations enacted in the 1970s dealt primarily with workers' exposure to asbestos released during the course of building renovation or demolition. In 1976, OSHA reduced its standard for permissible asbestos concentration in the air, but at the same time established more rigorous requirements for protective equipment to be used by asbestos abatement workers. These 1975–1976 regulations appear to be the first to have some potential cost implications for owners of buildings containing asbestos, but they did not determine whether and to what extent asbestos would be removed.

The EPA first published regulations relating to asbestos in schools. In 1979, the EPA published guidelines for encapsulating or removing asbestos in schools. However, not until 1982 did the EPA issue a ruling requiring a plan for actually dealing with friable ACM in schools.[10] The Toxic Substances Control Act, enacted in 1982, set out specific requirements for identification and management of asbestos in schools. Going one step further with the passage of the Asbestos School Hazard Abatement Act in 1984, Congress established loan and grant programs to assist primary and secondary schools, both public and private, in carrying out asbestos abatement. This was followed by the passage by Congress in 1986 of the Asbestos Hazard Emergency Response Act (AHERA), which began another effort to remove hazardous asbestos from school buildings.[11] AHERA again mandated that schools inspect their buildings for asbestos and prepare plans for asbestos abatement. It stated that school districts must hire

---

[9] The EPA adopted regulations under the National Emissions Standards for Hazardous Air Pollutants (NESHAPS) authorized by the Clean Air Act in 1973 and 1975 (38 Fed. Reg. 8826 and 40 Fed. Reg. 48,292 (1975)). OSHA first adopted regulations in 1972; these regulations were modified in 1976 (29 C.F.R. pt. 1910). See **Ch. 1** and **2**.

[10] EPA, *Friable Asbestos Containing Materials in Schools* (1986).

[11] BNA, *Asbestos Abatement: Risks and Responsibilities* (1987).

Table 8–1

ASBESTOS REGULATORY BACKGROUND

1972	EPA and the National Emissions Standards for Hazardous Air Pollutants (NESHAPS) list asbestos as a hazardous pollutant.
	Occupational Safety and Health Administration (OSHA) sets standard for occupational exposure to asbestos at 5 f/cc.
	New York City Council bans the spray application of asbestos.
1973	The EPA adopts asbestos regulations under NESHAPS authorized by the Clean Air Act:
	—Establishes a "no visible emission" standard for milling and manufacturing asbestos products and controls the emission of friable asbestos materials during the demolition of buildings.
	—Prohibits spray application for mist uses of friable materials containing more than 1% asbestos.
1975	EPA regulations are amended to expand the prohibition of the use of asbestos materials for building purposes and to establish standards for controlling the release of fibers during the renovation or demolition of buildings.
1976	OSHA lowers the standard for asbestos exposure to 2 f/cc and establishes mandatory requirements for asbestos abatement workers regarding respiratory and protective equipment, training programs, and medical examinations.
1977	New Haven (CT) enacts a local ordinance prohibiting exposed friable ceilings with any asbestos content in any dwelling.
1978	The EPA/NESHAPS regulations are again modified and codified at 41 C.F.R. app. C, 61.140 et seq. This extends prohibition included in the no-visible-emissions standard to control all types of asbestos emission during demolition.
1979	The EPA publishes "Asbestos Containing Materials in Schools: A Guidance Document" (the "orange book").
1980	Congress enacts the Asbestos School Hazard Detection and Control Act, 20 U.S.C. 3601 et seq.
1981	The Attorney General publishes "The Attorney General's Asbestos Liability Report to the Congress." Concludes that the United States should not file suit against the manufacturers and distributors of asbestos-containing materials, but recommends that state and local governments consider it.
1982	The EPA adopts a rule concerning "Friable Asbestos-Containing Materials in Schools" under the authority of the Toxic Substance Control Act, 15 U.S.C. 2605. The rule requires public and private primary and secondary schools to inspect for asbestos and document findings.
1983	EPA publishes "Guidance for Controlling Friable Asbestos-Containing Materials in Buildings" (the "blue book").

Table 8–1 *(Continued)*

1984	Asbestos School Hazard Abatement Act establishes loan and grant programs to assist primary and secondary schools, both public and private, in conducting asbestos abatement. It also authorizes the EPA to spend $600 million over a seven-year period.
1985	EPA publishes "Guidance for Controlling Asbestos-Containing Materials in Buildings" (the "purple book"), a revision of the blue book.
1986	EPA publishes "Airborne Asbestos Health Assessment Update." This evaluates the risk of asbestos fibers in buildings. Congress passes the Asbestos Hazard Emergency Response Act of 1986 (AHERA): —Mandates that schools inspect buildings for asbestos and prepare a plan for asbestos abatement. —Requires that schools hire only EPA-accredited or state-certified asbestos inspectors, contractors, and laboratories. —Directs the EPA to do a one-year study of the asbestos problem in public and commercial buildings and recommend whether school regulations should be expanded to cover all public and commercial buildings. The federal asbestos regulations are amended and are now codified in C.F.R. 1910.1001. OSHA reduces the "emergency" worker exposure standard from 0.5 f/cc to 0.2 f/cc, and "short-term" standard from 2 f/cc to 0.5 f/cc.
1987	EPA publishes proposed regulations pursuant to AHERA. New York enacts local laws: —No apartment or commercial space can get a building permit for alterations unless it has been inspected for asbestos and (if asbestos is found) an abatement plan is approved. —Property owners must hire certified contractors to remove asbestos.
1988	EPA's Report to Congress recommends that school regulations should not be extended to commercial and public buildings.
1989	EPA draft guidance document on operations and maintenance suggests asbestos may be best left intact if it is in good condition.
1990	EPA publishes "Managing Asbestos In Place," a recommendation for building owners to establish operations and maintenance programs for ACM rather than removal.

Sources: *The Asbestos Abatement Industry,* Alex Brown & Sons, Environmental Services Group (May 8, 1987); *Asbestos Abatement: Risks and Responsibilities,* Bureau of National Affairs, product code 49 BSP-57 (1987); *Asbestos Abatement Rules: The Complete Resource Guide,* Bureau of National Affairs, product code 49 BSP-80 (1988); EPA, *Asbestos-Containing Materials in School Buildings: A Guidance Document* (March 1979); EPA, *Guidance for Controlling Friable Asbestos-Containing Materials in Buildings,* EPA 560/5-84-002 (March 1983); EPA, *Asbestos in Buildings: A National Survey of Asbestos-Containing Friable Materials,* EPA 560/5-84-006 (October 1984); EPA, *Guidance for Controlling Asbestos-Containing Materials in Buildings,* EPA 560/5-85-024 (June 1985); EPA, *EPA Study of Asbestos-Containing Materials in Public Buildings: A Report to Congress* (February 1988).

only EPA-accredited or state-certified asbestos inspectors, contractors, and laboratories.

Importantly, regulatory policy dealing with asbestos in school buildings has not yet been extended to cover commercial or residential buildings. The prevalence of government regulation regarding the presence of asbestos in schools, however, may lead to participants in the real estate market assigning a higher likelihood to the possibility of future regulations. EPA and OSHA regulations regarding the management of ACM during renovation and demolition applied to all buildings, but EPA did not specify a plan for removal. This was supposed to become the domain of state regulations, but, to date, the regulatory initiative for removal has been virtually nonexistent.

Over 75 percent of the regulations passed by different states were enacted over the period from 1985 to 1987.[12] Since 1985, every state has enacted some type of legislation regarding the presence of asbestos in public buildings. The majority of these regulations have related to the licensing and certification of workers involved in asbestos inspection and abatement. None of the 42 states that responded to a survey request of the National Conference of State Legislatures in 1987 had enacted laws requiring removal of asbestos from commercial buildings.[13] Only some large cities, such as New York, have made it mandatory that inspection be done on issuance of a construction permit.[14]

§ 8.11   —Cost Implications of Regulations

The key concern from an investor's standpoint is the increased costs associated with the treatment of ACM. Indeed, OSHA and EPA regulations (passed as early as 1975), which required specific treatment of asbestos during demolition and renovation, presumptively changed procedures used during building refitting, which in turn raised owners' costs. Moreover, the requirement that abatement workers in schools be certified, as enacted at the state level in the mid-1980s, may have reinforced the expectation that regulations would generate cost increases.

These regulations did not mandate the timing of removal, or even removal any time convenient to the owner. Furthermore, the extent to which these regulations actually changed operating procedures or were strictly enforced varied widely.[15] Indeed, to the extent that these regulations had no

---

[12] National Conference of State Legislatures, Denver, CO (1988).

[13] National Conference of State Legislatures, Denver, CO, State Asbestos Programs Related to the Asbestos Hazard Emergency Response Act (Nov. 1987).

[14] Local Laws of the City of New York for the Year 1985, no. 76, sec. C26.

[15] For an analysis of the importance of the observability and enforcement of regulations see Besanko and Spulber, *Observability and Enforcement*, J. L. & Econ. (Fall 1989).

effect on building owners' conduct, either because they were relatively in-
nocuous or were not enforced, they had little or no market effect.

The most recent pronouncement by the EPA regarding asbestos in buildings was released in 1990.[16] In contrast to earlier positions of the EPA, this
pronouncement emphasizes operation and maintenance programs rather
than asbestos removal. This should produce a benefit to owners of buildings with ACM because the likelihood of any regulations regarding the removal of ACM prior to demolition has been substantially reduced. Thus,
the only additional costs to building owners with ACM in their buildings
will be the added expenditures associated with the implementation of the
O&M program.

§ 8.12   —Media Response to Asbestos in Buildings

Evaluation of the media response to a particular environmental hazard enables the building owner to identify trends in future regulatory activity and
to gain information regarding actual instances in which the hazard has in
fact impacted the market value of a building.

For example, if asbestos-related regulation had a significant effect on the
real estate market, both the regulations and the market effects would be
discussed frequently in the public press. A content analysis of articles in the
public press provides an indication of the importance of ACM regulatory
requirements on the value of real property (see **Table 8–2**).[17] To conduct a
content analysis with respect to asbestos, both general press and trade
source articles have been classified into five categories:

1. The adverse health effects of concentrated exposure to asbestos;
2. Findings that the adverse health effects of less concentrated exposure
   to asbestos have been overstated;
3. Regulations involving asbestos in school buildings;
4. Regulations or proposed regulations involving commercial buildings;
5. ACM health hazards and the effects of such hazards on the market
   value of all buildings.[18]

---

[16] EPA, Managing Asbestos in Place: A Building Owner's Guide to Operations and Maintenance Programs for Asbestos-Containing Materials (July 1990).

[17] *See* Levine and Forrence, *Regulatory Capture, Public Interest, and the Public Agenda:
Toward a Synthesis,* 6 J. L., Econ., & Organiz. (1990) for a discussion of regulations and
how they are influenced by media coverage.

[18] The newspapers, periodicals, and industry publications used in this analysis were based
on thorough searches of the following Dialog databases: ABI Inform, Magazine Index,
National Newspaper Index, PTS Prompt, and the Trade and Industry Index.

Table 8–2

Category 1—References to Asbestos in Buildings

Year	(a)	(b)	(c)	(d)	Total	Cumulative Percent
1970					0	0.00
1971					0	0.00
1972					0	0.00
1973					0	0.00
1974					0	0.00
1975	2				2	1.48
1976	2				2	2.96
1977					0	2.96
1978	1				1	3.70
1979	1	1			2	5.19
1980	1				1	5.93
1981					0	5.93
1982	2				2	7.41
1983	3	2	1	1	7	12.59
1984	4	2			6	17.04
1985	4	7			11	25.19
1986	6	2	13	1	22	41.48
1987	3	2	12	1	18	54.81
1988	15	2	21	4	42	85.93
1989	10		7	2	19	100.00
Total	54	18	54	9	135	

Note: Content Category Descriptions

Category 1: (a) Asbestos-related health hazards in buildings
(b) Liabilities associated with asbestos in buildings
(c) Possible effects on market value
(d) Asbestos abatement standards and owner responsibilities

Source: Financial Institutions Survey.

As shown in **Table 8–2**, in the early 1970s, of the few articles that appeared, a majority related to the hazards associated with occupational exposure to asbestos. In the mid-to-late 1970s, several articles discussed possible health risks associated with the presence of asbestos in buildings. The necessity for removal of asbestos in schools received extensive coverage in the early 1980s, although there was only limited indication that any such removal was taking place.

Media attention shifted from ACM in schools to ACM in nonschool buildings during the mid-1980s. However, only during and after 1986 did several articles appear that dealt with the possible market value effect of ACM in a building. At that time, there were a small number of highly publicized instances in which properties with ACM sold at a significant discount.

These instances may very well have been perceived by those in the industry as forerunners of an industry-wide effect whereby costly changes in removal practices would be required in the future. If so, then market values of ACM buildings should have decreased relative to other buildings after the mid-to-late 1980s. However, there does not appear to be a consensus in the trade and industry press regarding a definitive market impact associated with the presence of asbestos or the likelihood of future regulation.

§ 8.13 —Lender and Investor Response

As discussed earlier, a potential investor must be concerned with the attitudes of lenders and other investors regarding the presence of an environmental hazard, because of possible increased financing costs. In addition, because banks, insurance companies, and other informed investors have large financial stakes in real estate, their policies regarding a particular hazard provide information regarding its likely effect. If an environmental hazard has no current or future market value effect, the majority of lenders and other investors will not incur the cost of developing and implementing a formal policy with respect to that hazard.

Given the potential concern with ACM in buildings, lenders and other investors may perceive ACM buildings as having potential future risks associated with liability and/or abatement. When the likelihood is significant that the presence of ACM will impose substantial renovation costs and thereby affect the future cash flows of a building, then investors will spend the money necessary to determine the extent of ACM in buildings. A decrease in cash flow increases the probability of default of a mortgage loan. Thus, the fact that investors in the real estate market differentiate between buildings with ACM and those without ACM is an indicator of perceived future costs effects.

We attempted to determine the extent to which these risks have resulted in changes in investing and lending policies. In order to determine the response of these informed investors, we conducted a survey of investor reactions to information regarding the potential risks associated with ACM in commercial structures. The survey data were collected in 1988, under our supervision, by Opinion Research Corporation (ORC), Princeton, New Jersey. ORC contacted 550 financial institutions nationwide to request their participation in this survey. Of the lenders and investors contacted, 101 agreed to respond. Each survey respondent was first screened to ensure that the individual was knowledgeable about the institution's policies with respect to asbestos. The 101 institutions surveyed included insurance companies, commercial banks, real estate investment trusts, and mortgage companies in 41 states, and represented total investments and loans exceeding $27 billion.

As shown in **Figure 8–1**, approximately half of the institutions surveyed have a specific lending policy in cases where asbestos is present in commercial real estate. The survey data indicate that these institutions began to establish policies regarding buildings with asbestos only after 1986—a date coinciding with the first articles in the trade and industry press regarding the possible market effects of ACM. Of those companies with a policy, only 16 percent had implemented such a policy prior to 1986. During the period from 1986 through 1988, 31 of the 50 companies implemented policies related to asbestos, not counting 11 companies that were unable to identify the precise year in which they had implemented their policy.

The survey also examined the nature of these lending policies regarding the treatment of asbestos. The results indicated that 70% of the companies chose to implement an ACM policy requiring abatement before making an investment or loan. The remainder of the companies that had any policy would not invest at all in buildings containing asbestos. There was no indication that firms with a specific policy regarding ACM were systematically restricted to a particular geographic region of the country.

Half of the institutions did not consider the ACM risk sufficient to warrant a formal policy. Because these companies are informed market participants with substantial financial stakes in the commercial real estate market, it is significant that half of them did not have a formal ACM policy.

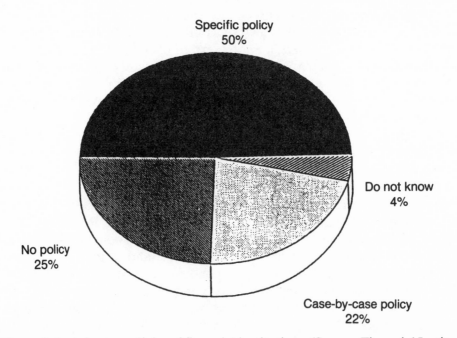

Figure 8–1. Asbestos policies of financial institutions. (Source: Financial Institutions Survey.)

When asked to describe the greatest risk factors associated with ACM in a building, the majority of companies (approximately 40 percent) indicated corporate liability and protection as the primary reasons to implement a special policy in the presence of ACM. There are, however, no regulatory statutes requiring ACM removal in commercial buildings at the federal, state, or local level at the present time. A total of 23 percent of the respondents believed there was a safety hazard, and only 11 percent associated ACM with lower resale values.

There are indications that some investors and lenders differentiate among properties on the basis of the ACM content, but not all companies do so. These results indicate that the presence of ACM in buildings did not have an effect on market value prior to the late 1980s. Even though by 1988 some investors valued investment opportunities consistent with the view that ACM may reduce the market value of property, this behavior was clearly not true for all market participants. Buyers and sellers in the commercial real estate market can still secure financing from banks and insurance companies for properties that contain asbestos. As the percentage of financing companies without a specific policy related to ACM declines, the financing costs associated with an ACM building will increase.[19] Given that the regulatory environment surrounding asbestos in buildings has not changed in the past three years, we would expect that lending policies addressing these issues have not changed substantially either.

§ 8.14   Building Occupant Response

In the prior section, we focused on the potential increased costs associated with the presence of asbestos. In this section, we examine the revenue implications associated with the presence of asbestos. In evaluating the effect of asbestos on revenues, we first examined the response of occupants with respect to (1) asbestos and (2) asbestos abatement activity. Finally, we determined whether occupants attach a lower value to a building that has undergone abatement than they do to one that is intact.

§ 8.15   —Response to the Presence of Asbestos

We begin by studying the rental, vacancy, and lease renewal rates for commercial office buildings in the Los Angeles area. If building occupants (i.e.,

---

[19] A similar survey conducted by Diagnostic Engineering, Inc., in early 1988, showed results consistent to those obtained in this survey. Approximately 50 percent of the companies surveyed had specific policies related to the presence of ACM. A subsequent survey conducted by the same firm revealed that, by late 1988, the percentage of institutions with asbestos-related policies remained virtually unchanged.

lessees) perceive significant health threats from the presence of ACM in buildings, there will be a reduction in the demand for office space in buildings with ACM. Thus, owners of buildings with ACM may lower rents or otherwise provide more favorable lease terms to induce occupants to rent this space. Alternatively, if rents are not reduced, then one would expect to see higher vacancy rates and lower lease renewal rates in buildings that contain asbestos. However, if the perception is that the likelihood of dangerous exposure to asbestos fibers is negligible, then the rental and lease terms of ACM buildings will not differ from those of buildings without ACM.

To test whether building occupants perceived a significant health threat from asbestos in buildings, we gathered data on rental, vacancy, and lease renewal rates for buildings both with and without ACM, located in the mid-Wilshire and downtown areas.[20] We conducted a series of statistical tests aimed at isolating the effects of asbestos on the lease characteristics of buildings with ACM. Using a simple hedonic regression model, we held constant factors that affect lease characteristics, such as building age, vacancy, and location, to determine whether the presence of asbestos had an adverse effect on rents.[21] The results of the analysis showed that buildings with ACM did not rent at rates significantly higher or lower than buildings without ACM.

A similar analysis was conducted to determine whether the presence of ACM in buildings adversely affected vacancy rates and lease renewal rates. If building occupants believed that asbestos can have adverse health effects, then the vacancy rates of buildings with asbestos would be higher than those without asbestos, and the lease renewal rates would be lower. The statistical tests showed that vacancy rates in buildings that contained ACM did not differ significantly from buildings that were asbestos-free. The analysis also showed that ACM and non-ACM buildings did not differ significantly in their lease renewal rates.

We find that, in general, the occupants of commercial buildings do not perceive a significant health threat from ACM in buildings. There are indications that some tenants may differentiate among properties on the basis of ACM content, but the majority of tenants apparently does not. Most owners of buildings containing ACM in the greater Los Angeles area have not experienced lower vacancies or given more favorable lease terms to tenants.

---

[20] Data were collected for 151 office buildings. The sample of 151 buildings included only commercial properties of 100,000 square feet or greater. Within this sample, 67 of the buildings contained asbestos and 84 did not.

[21] A hedonic regression model is a statistical test that is used to hold constant the factors (age, condition, etc.) that may affect price so that the effect of a particular factor (asbestos, for example), can be isolated and evaluated.

These findings are corroborated by a study conducted by Louis Harris & Associates.[22] This study examined building occupants' responses to "hazards" in the office workplace. When over 1,000 full-time office workers were surveyed across the United States, "eyestrain" topped the list of hazards causing most concern in the office. Only 12 percent of the respondents indicated that exposure to hazardous materials (asbestos, for example) was a "very" or "somewhat serious" problem. Thus, it appears that building occupants across the entire United States did not perceive asbestos as a significant health threat.

§ 8.16   —Response to Abatement Activity

Even if occupants do not perceive ACM in buildings as a health hazard, it is possible that abatement activity may affect the rental conditions in the buildings containing asbestos. In this section, we examine how asbestos removal activity affects rental and vacancy rates. Under federal law, asbestos removal that exceeds 260 linear feet or 160 square feet must be reported to the EPA regional office or the state health or environment office.[23] We gathered data from the EPA on abatement activity in Southern California from 1985 to 1988. We used these data in a series of statistical tests to determine whether abatement activity within a building had an effect on rents and vacancies during 1988. Rental and vacancy rates were modeled as a function of building age, location, and whether abatement activity was taking place. This analysis indicated that buildings undergoing asbestos removal did not rent at rates that were systematically significantly different from buildings without asbestos. In addition, vacancy rates were not significantly higher for buildings undergoing asbestos removal.

Vacancy rates in the downtown Los Angeles and mid-Wilshire areas averaged 14 percent and 17 percent respectively during 1988.[24] With vacancy rates in this range, asbestos removal can be completed without serious disruption of tenants. Removal activity can take place in vacant areas of the building, and tenants can be relocated to the newly abated areas of the building. Thus, under these market conditions, it is not surprising that vacancy rates were not higher in buildings undergoing asbestos abatement activity.

If the building is located in an area with high vacancy rates, then the loss in revenues associated with vacancy of the space from which the hazardous material is being removed may be negligible. This implies that the relative

---

[22] Office Environment Index, 1989 Summary Report. Sponsored by Steelcase Inc. and conducted by Louis Harris & Associates, Inc.

[23] 40 C.F.R. pt. 61, subpart M, (1985).

[24] Grubb & Ellis, Los Angeles Basin Real Estate (1989).

effect, if any, of an environmental hazard on the market value of a building will be lower in areas with a high vacancy rate. In addition, if the removal or abatement activity can be performed over an extended period, by timing the activity to coincide with the turnover of tenants, then the building owner can, in turn, minimize the costs of removal. By timing the removal to coincide with the turnover of tenants, the potential costs associated with the relocation of tenants are eliminated. Because rental space typically undergoes renovation prior to the signing of a new lease, no additional renovation costs are incurred with the removal activity.

§ 8.17 —Stigma of Abated Building

After the asbestos abatement process is complete, there has been some controversy as to whether there is a stigma attached to the newly abated building. Recent studies have asserted that improperly completed abatement activity can result in higher airborne quantities of asbestos during the postabatement period than during the preabatement period.[25] If this is indeed the perception of building occupants, we would expect that buildings that have been entirely abated would experience higher vacancy rates and/ or lower rental rates. Using the data described above on rental rates and vacancy rates in the mid-Wilshire area of Los Angeles, we were able to test this hypothesis. We identified, through EPA records, buildings that had completed asbestos abatement projects. We conducted a series of statistical tests to determine whether buildings that had been completely abated differed in rental and occupancy rates from those buildings without asbestos. We found that asbestos-abated buildings did not differ systematically from asbestos-free buildings. In other words, the marketplace does not attach a "stigma" to those buildings that have undergone a complete abatement program, based on our study.

§ 8.18 Estimation of Impact of
Asbestos on Market Value

In the preceding sections, we have evaluated how asbestos may affect several key factors that determine the market value of a building. In this section, we use these findings and the present value approach outlined earlier to estimate the market value reduction associated with the presence of

---

[25] Mossman et al. *Asbestos: Scientific Developments and Implications for Public Policy,* Science 247, Jan. 19, 1990; Spengler et al., Summary of Symposium on Health Aspects of Exposure to Asbestos in Buildings, Harvard University Energy and Environmental Policy Center (August 1989).

asbestos in a hypothetical commercial building. The calculation presented here is simply meant to illustrate the manner in which the asbestos affects market value. When estimating the market value of an actual building containing asbestos, or any other environmental hazard, building owners or investors must incorporate factors specific to that building into the calculation. In most cases, the precise cost or reduction in value associated with an environmental hazard cannot be accurately determined. However, the range of possible reductions in value and the associated likelihood can often be identified and can enable the building owner or investor to quantify the financial risk associated with the hazard.

The preceding analysis reveals that buildings with asbestos do not have lower rents or lower occupancy than comparable buildings without asbestos. Regulations exist regarding the treatment of asbestos during demolition, but no laws mandate the immediate removal of asbestos. However, there is some likelihood that future regulations may mandate the removal of asbestos. The actual costs associated with asbestos abatement activity are the subject of considerable controversy. Moreover, there is considerable debate regarding not only whether removal is necessary, but also who should pay for the removal of asbestos. This controversy has focused on the manufacturers of asbestos and the building owners.

Building owners have claimed damages associated with the removal of asbestos. This theory of damages associated with the alleged environmental hazard, asbestos, can be evaluated with the use of comparables. Many building owners simply estimate the total costs associated with a complete renovation and asbestos removal project. At the outset, this assumes that the asbestos needs to be removed.[26] If the asbestos must be removed, we can again turn to the comparable building approach to assess the incremental costs associated with the removal of asbestos.

Suppose that we have two identical 20-year-old buildings, one with and one without asbestos. Both buildings require major renovation, to complete in the marketplace. Both building owners must expend resources to complete the renovation project. The building with asbestos, however, will incur an additional incremental expense to complete the removal process. Only the incremental costs attributed solely to the asbestos removal process should be used to determine the costs or "damages" associated with the presence of asbestos. Renovation and abatement activity should be planned around the natural lease turnover of the building so that any relocation costs can be minimized. Thus, the diminution in market value of the property with the environmental hazard is equal to the present value of the incremental costs associated with the asbestos removal.

---

[26] *See Reilly Responds to Critics on Asbestos,* 4 *Asbestos Abatement Report,* 1, June 25, 1990.

It appears that the only real cash flow, and hence market value, implication of asbestos stems from the costs associated with its treatment during renovation and demolition. To ascertain the magnitude of these costs, we can use the present value approach to determine its impact on the market value of a hypothetical building.

To construct our example, we assumed that the average annual rental rate on a building net of operating expenses and taxes was in the $12 to $18 range, which approximated the actual range of rental rates in Los Angeles in 1988. Given the high average vacancy rate in the Los Angeles market (approximately 15 percent[27]), abatement activity could take place with virtually no loss in rental revenue. The only direct costs of abatement were removal costs, estimated to be $20 per square foot.[28] For simplicity, we assumed that the building had no underlying debt.

In such an environment, the key factors determining the magnitude of market value changes associated with asbestos are (1) the length of time prior to the owner's actually removing the material and (2) the possibility that the future removal may be mandated by government regulations. Under current regulations, building owners do not have to incur any additional costs associated with the presence of asbestos. The prudent building owner will implement an operation and maintenance program. We assumed that the cost of maintaining an operation and maintenance program is 10 to 20 cents per square foot per year.[29]

Given the likelihood or probability that regulation will require the building owner to incur additional costs because of the presence of asbestos, we can estimate the corresponding reduction in value. The reduction in value is the present value of the expected abatement cost over the lifetime of the building, which we assumed to be between 5 and 50 years. The market value of the building was further reduced by the costs (in present value terms) of the operation and maintenance program until the hazard is eliminated.

The reduction in market value will vary as a result of changes in interest rates and inflation. Increases in inflation will likely result in higher operation and maintenance costs and higher costs of removal. Higher interest rates result in higher discount rates and, therefore, lower present values.

To evaluate fully the risks associated with a hazard, we must evaluate the effect of the hazard on the market value under different assumptions regarding the probability of regulation, inflation rates, and interest rates. The resulting range distribution of values serves as a quantitative measure of the riskiness or uncertainty associated with the reduction in value. If changes in any one assumption result in only small changes in the market value effect of asbestos, there will exist little risk. We assume that the expected rate of

---

[27] Grubb and Ellis, Survey of Los Angeles Basin Real Estate (1988).

[28] National Econ Corp., 1988.

[29] *See* Croke et al., 1989.

inflation is 5 percent and normally distributed with a standard deviation of 2 percent.[30] The real risk-adjusted discount rate is assumed to be 8 percent, and the nominal rate of interest is assumed to vary with the rate of inflation.

The distribution of possible market value reductions under the assumptions described above can be estimated using Monte Carlo simulation techniques, where we estimate the reduction in value associated with different underlying assumptions.[31] Experiments such as these are designed to sample from probability distributions and are called Monte Carlo because of their resemblance to the games of chance made famous in the Riviera city. By estimating the market value reduction under several thousand alternative scenarios, we can estimate the distribution—or range of possible values and associated probabilities—of the reduction in market value.

The estimated distribution of the percentage reduction in market value associated with different assumptions regarding the probability of regulation is shown in **Figure 8–2**. We estimate the distribution, given that the probability of regulation equals 100 percent (i.e., it is certain that the building owner will be required to remove the asbestos sometime during the lifetime of the building or at demolition), 50 percent, or 25 percent. Estimating market value reductions for different probabilities of regulations, we are able to quantify the impact of changes in expectations on market value, i.e., if the probability of regulations mandating the removal of asbestos increased from 25 percent to 50 percent, the market value of the hypothetical building would decrease by the amount estimated. We also estimate the distribution in the event that the probability lies between 0 and 100 percent, with every possible value being equally likely. In the event that an investor has no information regarding the probability of regulation (i.e., the probability is unknown), every value of the probability is equally likely. If, however, an investor believes that the probability of regulation is 25 percent rather than 50 percent, he or she would use the market value estimate based on the 25 percent probability scenario. This model can estimate market values for all views regarding the likelihood of expenditures associated with a particular environmental hazard. Finally, we present a "worst case" scenario in which we assume that the removal of asbestos is mandated immediately (see **Figure 8–3**).

These estimated reductions in values are nonsymmetrically distributed and are generally small. Large percentage reductions in value appear to be very unlikely (see **Figure 8–2**). Indeed, even when it is certain that

---

[30] The average inflation rate during the period 1960 to 1990 in the United States was 5.06 percent, with a standard deviation of 3.3 percent. These figures were calculated using the inflation series in the Ibbotson Stocks, Bonds, Bills, and Inflation database. We chose a smaller standard deviation (2 percent) to reflect the reduction in the variability of inflation rates over the last few years.

[31] *See* Kmenta, Elements of econometrics (2d ed.), 1986.

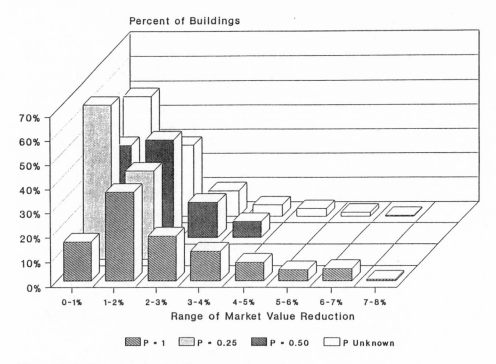

Figure 8–2. Simulated reduction in market value.

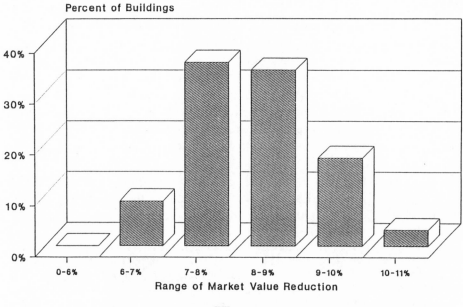

Figure 8–3. Simulated reduction in market-value (based on immediate removal).

regulation will require the building owner to remove the asbestos, the median value of the reduction is around 2 percent, although there exists some likelihood that it could be as much as 7.5 percent. If there is only a 50 percent chance of regulation, then the median value drops to 1.3 percent. If the probability is uncertain—i.e. somewhere between 0 and 1—the median reduction in value is approximately 1 percent, with a maximum decline in market value of approximately 6 percent.

These estimated reductions in value suggest that the effects of asbestos on property values are most likely small for the typical building. Large declines in market values of the order of 5 to 10 percent, while possible, appear unlikely for a building similar to those in downtown Los Angeles during the 1980s. We expect, therefore, that statistical analysis of actual market transactions during the 1980s would reveal that asbestos has little if any systematic effect on the market value of real property. We test this finding in § 8.19. The model in § 8.19 can be used to evaluate the market value of property affected by any environmental hazard, if the revenues and costs can be quantified.

§ 8.19   Market Value of Residential Property

In this section, we discuss the effect of environmental hazards on the market value of residential property. The hazardous materials most often mentioned in relation to the single-family and multifamily housing industry are ACMs, radon, formaldehyde, lead, and underground storage tanks. The framework developed in § 8.3 also can be used to analyze the effect of these environmental hazards on the market value of residential property.

As with commercial property, the market value of residential property is equal to the value of the owners' equity plus the value of debt. In the case of non-income-producing property, the revenue stream is the benefit derived by the occupants. The benefit or pleasure the occupants derive from occupying a residential property is the equivalent of the revenue stream that accrues to the owner of an income-producing property. Although there exist important distinctions in terms of the tax implications of owning versus renting on the cash flow accruing to the owner, the change in market value associated with a nuisance can be analyzed using the same framework. The owners' equity in a residential income-producing property equals the expected cash flows accruing to the owner in a given year, based on the expectations of the property's occupancy rate, rental rate, rentable area, operating expenses, financing costs, and property taxes. The market value of the debt, for both income- and non-income-producing properties, is equal to the present value of the mortgage payments at the market rate of interest. As discussed earlier, environmental hazards have the potential to affect both the market value of the equity and the market value of the debt.

The presence of an environmental hazard in residential property may be perceived as a health risk, thereby reducing demand for the property. This may be manifested in the form of reduced interest on the part of buyers of the property, lower occupancy rates, and/or rental rates. The owner may have to reduce the list price of the property or charge lower-than-market rents to induce potential buyers and renters. The net result is a reduction in sales price or revenues accruing to the property owner. Other direct costs include the actual removal of the hazard or an ongoing O&M program to deal with the hazard.

In the case of ACM in the ceilings of homes, the cost of removal generally ranges from $3 per square foot to $5 per square foot, depending on accessibility and other factors.[32] The cost of encapsulation is approximately two-thirds the cost of removal. Radon problems can usually be mitigated for $200 to $2,000, which is relatively modest in relation to the median price of the home.[33] Nonetheless, radon testing and mitigation can affect the affordability of a residential property, especially for lower-income, first-time home buyers. Lead-based paint can also be removed in a number of ways, including scrapping, chemical removal, heating, or the entire replacement of the area. Contaminated soil and groundwater on a property, as a result of a leaking storage tank or buried chemicals, is an extreme case when the removal may be so costly as to make it uneconomical. In each of these cases, various types of costs are associated with the hazard, all of which affect the owner's equity.

§ 8.20   Actual Market Response—
Transaction Prices

The discounted cash flow models discussed above can be used to estimate the effect of an environmental hazard on market value, but the results obtained using these models are highly dependent on the often subjective inputs to the models. More accurate estimates of the likely effect of a hazard can often be obtained by analysis of actual transaction prices involving buildings containing the hazardous material and comparing these transactions to other transaction prices where no hazardous material was present. When making such comparisons, however, it is important to account for differences in prices caused by factors such as the age and condition of the buildings.

Statistical models are used widely by economists to make such comparisons and to estimate the economic value associated with a particular

---

[32] National Econ Corp., 1989.

[33] *NAR Supports Voluntary Testing and Disclosure of Radon: Flynn Testifies,* PR Newswire, May 16, 1990.

attribute of a building, such as location. These models have also been used to estimate the possible impact of an environmental hazard. The properties of these models have been fully elaborated elsewhere in the economics literature,[34] but briefly, supply and demand determinants yield implicit prices for the different attributes of a building. The market equilibrium condition is represented by two equations, one for demand and another for supply, which are solved simultaneously because both supply and demand are responsive to prices. Here, the supply of real property can be assumed to be price-independent, given that we are concerned with the immediate effects on relative prices for buyers and sellers who learn that there will be additional costs associated with buildings containing asbestos. Therefore, estimation can be limited to a demand equation.

The analysis of the impact of asbestos on the market value of buildings using the approach outlined earlier in this chapter reveals that the impact of asbestos is limited to the costs associated with future removal. We also find that, for the typical building, this market value reduction is likely to be relatively small. In this section, we test the accuracy of this finding by examining the effect of asbestos on the price of buildings involved in actual market transactions.

If ACM does have an effect on the fundamental economic factors underlying a building's value (such as its rental rate and occupancy rate), then its market value will be lower than a comparable building without ACM. The transaction prices of buildings will capitalize the costs of dealing with asbestos. To examine actual market prices, data were collected on 111 commercial real estate transactions in the Los Angeles area over the period 1977 to 1986.[35] Although the study does not include any recent transactions, it is important to note that there have not been any significant regulations that have affected the costs of dealing with ACM in commercial buildings since 1986. Adjustments were made for price variations across buildings, attributable to factors such as building size, age, and physical condition. The presence or absence of asbestos can be viewed as an attribute of a building, and the value associated with this attribute was then estimated using a statistical model.

The price of a building was estimated as a function of building area, lot size, age, condition, location (Los Angeles; Los Angeles County; or Orange County), property use (offices; apartments; or retail stores), a time trend, and a variable for the presence of asbestos. The coefficient on the

---

[34] For example, see Rosen, *Hedonic Prices and Implicit Markets: Product Differentiation in Pure Competition, J. Pol. Econ.* 82 (January 1974).

[35] Price and building attribute data were obtained from an on-line data base maintained by DAMAR Corp., Los Angeles, CA. Information on asbestos was obtained in personal interviews with individuals involved in the transactions. Twenty of the buildings in this sample contained asbestos.

asbestos-related variable was found to be statistically insignificant, i.e., there was no statistically significant difference in prices between buildings with ACM and buildings without ACM over this time period.

§ 8.21   —Impact of Environmental Hazards on Market Value

Environmental hazards, as shown above, can affect the market value of residential property in a number of ways. The homeowner, potential buyer, real estate agent, and lender must also address the current and future regulations related to the particular environmental hazard and the potential liability associated with the hazard, to assess accurately its effect on the market value of the property in question.

Income-producing property can be evaluated in the model we presented in § 8.18. The revenue-per-square-foot generated by commercial property is generally greater than the revenue-per-square-foot generated by residential property. Therefore, an application of this model would result in slightly larger percentage reductions in value, compared to the commercial property example presented in § 8.18.

For a non-income-producing property, the market effect of hazardous materials is the increased operating costs plus the present value of the benefit or pleasure the owner derives from occupying the property. Although the pleasure or utility is often difficult to quantify, it can be estimated from the change in market rent associated with the hazard. The change in market value stems from the change in the utility or value market participants derive from the property and is not dependent on the attitudes or perceptions of the individual owner. Even if an owner attaches a significant decline in value to a residence as a result of discovering a hazard, the owner does not suffer an economic loss unless all market participants view the hazard in a similarly unfavorable manner. In other words, no economic loss is associated with the environmental hazard unless the market discounts the value of the property.

Real estate agents must conduct environmental audits and disclose any findings of environmental hazards.[36] The National Association of Realtors recently distributed a new environmental guide that outlines a real estate agent's responsibilities to search for and disclose hazards. The guide states that agents can be held liable under state and federal laws if they do not inform buyers and sellers about hazardous substances they should have found and reported. The guide also outlines and advises agents on the best way to look for the most common hazards. Many states like California and

---

[36] *Agents Cope with Hazards on Property; Environmental Problems Subject to Full Disclosure,* Washington Post, Nov. 17, 1990.

Maine have passed laws that require sellers to disclose publicly any environmental problems with their property.[37] In Illinois, the Responsible Property Transfer Act, which went into effect on January 1, 1990, requires the seller to make a full environmental disclosure when commercial or industrial property is transferred.[38] Even though the law is aimed at commercial or industrial property, the state has received filings for sales of residential property, vacant lots, and even farmland. These filings are a direct result of people's fear of liability.

In addition to their legal liability under the Superfund law, the Federal National Mortgage Association (FNMA) and the Federal Home Loan Mortgage Corporation (FHLMC) have also established detailed requirements for lenders to practice "due diligence" in environmental audits, which must be met before they will purchase single-family and multifamily residential mortgages on the secondary market. This will most definitely have an effect on mortgages sold to FNMA and FHLMC and an indirect influence on the residential finance industry in general. The Federal Home Loan Bank Board and the U.S. League of Savings Institutions have since issued guidelines for their members to set up programs to evaluate environmental hazards in compliance with the recommendations to minimize their potential liability. This could slow lending dramatically because the members of the League finance more than half of the single-family homes in the country. Lenders will pass on to borrowers the increased costs associated with loans on properties that have environmental hazards. These increased costs may well result in a decline in the market value of properties that are suspected of containing hazardous materials.

§ 8.22 Property Taxes and Market Value

There has been a growing trend among property owners to seek tax relief for properties that have had their value allegedly adversely affected by the presence of an environmental hazard. For example, the New Jersey Supreme Court ruled that hazardous waste cleanup costs can be pertinent to property valuation for tax purposes.[39] The court stated that cleanup costs can be "capitalized and amortized" and that the adjustments in market value will be "left to the competence of the appraisal community." This suggests that any expense associated with an environmental hazard that is applied directly to a property's taxable market value will be spread over time. The cash flow framework presented above is an appropriate method for evaluating the effects of environmental hazards on the market value of

---

[37] *Id.*

[38] *Id.*

[39] Inmar Associates, Inc. v. Borough of Carlstadt, 112 N.J. 593, 549 A.2d 38 (1988).

property. The framework we presented capitalizes the expenses associated with the hazard and values these expenses in the context of the time frame in which they occur.

Most recently, on January 22, 1991, the New York Supreme Court granted the owners of a building containing asbestos a property tax refund of more than $21 million.[40] The court ruled that the real estate taxes levied on One New York Plaza, a 50-story commercial building, "failed to adequately consider the pervasive presence of asbestos in the structure."[41] The building owners argued that the city overestimated the market value of their building and, thus, the taxes levied against the building were overstated as well. Over a cumulative six-year-period, owners of One New York Plaza had paid real estate taxes totaling approximately $65 million. Owners asked the court for a $31 million refund (a 47.7 percent reduction) and received a verdict of $21 million (a 32.3 percent reduction). Because taxes are computed as a percentage of market value, the court has implicitly assumed that the market value of the building had been reduced by 32.3 percent. Building owners have an incentive to claim the largest possible market value reduction so as to cause the greatest reduction in property taxes.

According to the building owners in this case, the market value of the property was affected not only by the presence of asbestos, but also by a design flaw. Almost 70 percent of the costs contributing to the diminution in market value were attributed to the presence of asbestos. Thus, the court implicitly assumed the market value of One New York Plaza has been reduced by approximately 22.6 percent (70 percent of the costs times the 32.3 percent reduction in taxes) because of the presence of asbestos.

In this case, the court decided that abatement was a necessary remedy to "cure" the asbestos problem in the building. If in fact asbestos abatement is the only alternative, then the expenses associated with the abatement activity can be incorporated into the model discussed in § 8.5, and an accurate determination of the diminution in value associated with the hazard can be made. It should be noted that immediate asbestos abatement is *not* the only alternative when dealing with asbestos in buildings. Operations and maintenance programs or delayed abatement methods may be more cost-effective and safe.

The reassessment of property values for tax purposes has been most prevalent in areas of the country where real estate prices have fallen because of the poor economy. Major cities in Texas, for example, have seen dramatic drops in the value of commercial property. Real estate appraisers or economists can be hired to reassess the market value of a property and prepare a report documenting the change in market value.

---

[40] Asbestos Abatement Report, Feb. 18, 1991.

[41] Bass v. Tax Commission of the City of New York, Sup. Ct., N. Y. No. 56969/84, Jan. 22, 1991.

§ 8.23   —Filing for Reassessment

The first step in the process is to file a Tax Rendition Notice to the County Appraisal District stating the reassessed value of the property. Both the cash flow and comparable sale approaches discussed above can be used by the economist or appraiser to determine the value presented in the Tax Rendition Notice. Filing the Notice ensures that the County Appraisal District will send the building owner a statement documenting the current assessed value. The next step is to file a tax protest with the County Appraisal District that will allow the economist or appraiser to meet informally with county appraisers to present documentation of the lower taxable market value. At this point, if a value reduction is not granted, a formal hearing in front of the County Appraisal Board is scheduled.

Specific documentation of comparable sales and cash flow analyses showing a diminution in value (incorporating the effects of the environmental hazard, for example) are presented to the County Appraisal Board by the economist or appraiser representing the building owner. The Board will carefully review all of the factors associated with the environmental hazard that might affect the cash flow of the building. If the Board rules against the building owner, the final step is to file a lawsuit against the local tax authority, such as the One New York Plaza suit discussed above. Although the exact procedure varies from county to county, these are the basic steps to follow when seeking a reduction in market value for the purpose of property tax reassessment.

Some experts have claimed that corporations should include in their financial statements losses in the value of an asset associated with environmental hazards.[42] Environmental audits could potentially lead to the reassessment of property values and the base on which building owners are taxed. This could result in a possible reduction in the tax expenses borne by owners of "contaminated" property, but it could also reduce the asset value held on the balance sheet of those companies with properties that have environmental hazards requiring significant expenses to remedy.

§ 8.24   Investing in Buildings Containing Hazardous Materials

As described above, the presence of an environmentally hazardous material has the potential to decrease the market value of a building by increasing the costs associated with owning the building. Reduced rents, higher

---

[42] *See* MacDowell and D'Angelo, *The Discounted Value of Real Property Resulting from the Presence of Asbestos,* presented to National Association of Corporate Real Estate Executives, annual convention, March 21, 1988.

vacancy rates, higher financing costs, and increased maintenance costs are all examples of the incremental expenses that a building owner may face because of the presence of a hazardous material.

These costs cannot be estimated with certainty. Future government regulations, litigation costs, and changes in the health concerns of occupants are all by their very nature unpredictable. The future cash flows of buildings containing hazardous materials undoubtedly are more uncertain than those of a comparable building without any such hazards. Thus, from the standpoint of a potential investor, the relevant factors are the expected future costs associated with the presence of the hazard and the variability of those future costs.

Because the costs cannot be estimated with certainty, sensitivity analyses must be conducted to value the building under different assumptions. By quantifying the impact of different regulatory requirements and other factors, the likely effect of the hazard on the value of the building can be ascertained.

The increase in the risk associated with investing in a building containing hazardous material can be evaluated based on the range of possible values of the building. The estimated variation in building value associated with the presence of a hazardous material such as asbestos is in the range of 0 to 10 percent (with the largest proportion falling in the range of 0 to 5 percent).[43] This is a relatively small range, given the large fluctuation in the market value of a typical real estate property.[44] Building values fluctuate with changes in the local and regional economy. Thus, the increase in risk associated with the presence of a hazardous material must be viewed in the context of the risks typically assumed by a real estate investor.

By carefully evaluating the economic costs and risks associated with hazardous materials, an investor may be able to earn superior returns. Other studies have found that analysts typically overreact to new information[45] such as changes in the earning potential of a company. This results in the price of an asset changing by a greater amount than a rational investor would expect, given the materiality of the information. There have been no such systematic studies on the real estate market, but careful evaluation of the costs associated with the presence of a hazardous material may provide an investor with an informational advantage regarding the likely market value of a building. In short, the presence or potential

---

[43] Croke, Mensah, Fabian, & Tolley, *Asbestos in Buildings: Effects on Residential and Commercial Real Estate Values,* 11 The Envtl. Prof. 256–63 (1989).

[44] For example, Ibbotson has found that the annual variability of a portfolio of diversified real estate investments is in the region of 15 to 20 percent. See Ibbotson, *A Note on the Variability of Real Estate Returns,* Ibbotson Associates, Chicago (1989).

[45] *See* De Bondt and Thayer, *Do Security Analysts Overreact to Earnings Announcements?,* Fin. Analysts J., June/July 1989 at 33–38.

presence of a hazardous material in a building will, *ceterus paribus,* result in the investor's having to exercise greater care in determining its market value prior to making a purchase.

In the case of asbestos, there have been several instances where the presence of the material has resulted in a large decline in value. Such declines in value, while not systematic, stem primarily from the informational advantage of the buyer over the seller or the ability of the buyer to use the presence of the material as a negotiating tool.

The uncertainty surrounding the proper manner to remedy the problems associated with environmental hazards and the costs of these remedies result in conflicting sets of information being disseminated in the marketplace. The buyer of a building containing an environmental hazard has an incentive to exaggerate the incremental costs associated with the hazard, in order to reduce the purchase price. The seller (building owner), on the other hand, is likely to underestimate the expenses associated with the "proper" way to deal with the hazard. If, however, the property is not involved in a transaction, the building owner may have the incentive to exaggerate the costs associated with an environmental hazard when "pointing the finger" at the party responsible for the hazard.

Thus, we find that, in dealing with environmental hazards, the prudent investor must interpret information regarding the proper remedy and costs associated with hazards within the context in which the information is being presented. With a nonenvironmental hazard issue such as a broken window, there is very little uncertainty regarding the proper remedy and costs, and it is quite easy to quantify the costs and any variability in the costs. In this example, the investor can quickly determine the effects of the broken window with very little effort. With environmental hazards, however, buyers' and sellers' incentives can be varied, and the information regarding the proper remedy and costs may not be entirely accurate.

For example, many asbestos inspection companies also conduct full-scale asbestos abatement projects. It is the interest of these individuals to advise complete removal rather than the implementation of an operations and maintenance program. When dealing with environmental hazards, great care should be taken both when choosing consultants and interpreting information regarding the hazard in the popular press.

§ 8.25   Conclusion

Building owners, lenders, investors, home owners, and all individuals involved with real estate should not respond to environmental hazards with panic, but with concern and commitment to take the best course of action. Gaining an understanding of the regulatory framework and the market reaction to an environmental hazard will minimize any unwarranted discounts in the value of the property. An accurate quantification of the risks associated with any environmental hazard is imperative. Conducting an environmental assessment of a property prior to an acquisition should include not only an engineering report, but also a reliable estimation of the effect of the hazard on financing and cash flow.

In the specific case of ACM discussed above, despite widely published instances of buildings whose values were greatly reduced by the presence of asbestos, the data analyzed in this study suggest that the presence of ACM in buildings has not significantly reduced the net cash flow of buildings that contain asbestos.

Moreover, a real estate investor or building owner who carefully analyzed the potential impact of asbestos would have found that the effect of abatement and operations and maintenance costs, time to removal, and incorporation of the present value of expenses results in modest reductions in the value of a building containing ACM. An informed investor would, thus, not expect a building with ACM to sell at a substantial discount.

Failure to analyze carefully the economic implications of a hazardous substance can often lead to an incorrect assessment of its likely economic effect. Too often the hype surrounding a particular environmental hazard issue such as asbestos in buildings is unwarranted. For example, a professional in the real estate industry (who incidentally would profit from widespread asbestos abatement and will remain anonymous) continually refers to asbestos as the "AIDS of the real estate industry." Real estate professionals who rely on such biased information will be at a disadvantage vis-à-vis those who have conducted in-depth analyses. Only by conducting such analyses themselves, or by hiring an unbiased consultant, can building owners and investors make informed decisions regarding the purchase and sale of properties with environmental hazards.

CHAPTER 9

CONTRACTS OF SALE

§ 9.1   Buyer's and Seller's Considerations

§ 9.2   Landlord's and Tenant's Considerations

§ 9.3   Lender's Considerations

§ 9.1   Buyer's and Seller's Considerations

Purchasers of buildings or homes, who are concerned with potential liability for hazardous substances, are well-advised to include special contract language in their contracts of sale. The clauses will vary, depending on the size of the transaction and the type of building structure involved.

The parties should negotiate who will pay for an environmental audit or how the cost will be divided, if at all. The buyer may have the audit performed and the seller may be allowed to elect whether he or she will actually arrange for the remediation or may terminate the contract.

If the seller does the audit, the buyer may have the option of remediation if the cost of remediation: (1) exceeds a designated dollar amount, (2) takes more than a designated period of time; or (3) involves certain designated hazardous substances. Alternatively, there may be a right to terminate the contract upon notice of the discovery of any hazardous substances or environmental problem following the environmental audit.

Remediation liability may survive the closing. The seller may explicitly agree to retain liability to the purchaser for conditions existing prior to the sale or may agree to share liability with the purchaser. The parties may negotiate a time limit on the assertion of claims and a dollar limit for liability or contribution for cleanup.

The seller may agree to indemnify the purchaser; however, liability to the government, the EPA, or other plaintiffs under CERCLA continues and is joint and several.[1] Nevertheless, indemnification agreements are generally enforceable against private parties.[2]

---

[1] 42 U.S.C. § 9607(e).

[2] See § **6.23.**

Naturally, there is some risk even in proceeding with a sale pursuant to contract with such clause, because indemnification agreements and warranties are often themselves the subject of litigation, and sellers may be difficult to find or insolvent when the need to invoke them arises. Such indemnification clauses should specifically refer to strict liability, to ensure proper interpretation. Indemnification may include having the indemnitor defend the indemnitee against actions brought by regulatory bodies and other third parties. However, pleading rules state that if the allegations in the third party's complaint fall within the coverage of the indemnity agreement, the indemnitor must defend. This is true even if ultimately the third party's claim against the indemnitee fails.

Appropriate subjects for warranties and representations may include one or more of the following items, depending on the type of property being purchased:

1. That the seller and the property are in compliance with all environmental, health, and safety laws, statutes, regulations, and standards. In addition, that no event has occurred which, with the passage of time or the giving of notice or both, would constitute noncompliance with such environmental laws;

2. The condition of the property, such as the presence or absence of specified substances, such as asbestos or radon, and specification of acceptable amounts or levels;

3. Disclosure about the current and prior use, handling, storage, and disposal of any hazardous substance on the property;

4. Disclosure about the disposal of hazardous substances contained in the building;

5. That no hazardous waste or substance was stored, treated, or disposed of in the building and there are no underground storage tanks;

6. That the business on the property has disposed of its waste in accordance with all applicable federal, state, and local statutes, ordinances, and regulations;

7. That the seller has no notice of any pending or threatened claim, action, or proceeding arising out of the condition of the premises or any alleged violation of environmental, health, or safety statutes, ordinances, or regulations;

8. That all governmental permits required to operate the business are in full force and effect and no condition exists which might threaten the validity of such permits;

9. That there are not now and never have been any underground storage tanks or, if there are, they are not leaking and comply with all applicable laws;

10. That there are no agreements, consent orders, decrees, judgments, or other directives issued by a municipal department or agency which relate to the future use of the premises or require any change in the present condition of the premises;

11. That the seller has not received any notice from its insurance carrier or mortgagee as to recommendations made regarding hazardous materials and the seller has not been denied insurance coverage or had any canceled because of hazardous substances in the premises.

The warranties and representations should be drafted to survive the closing, along with the indemnification from a responsible party.

The seller should also covenant that it will not *prior* to closing:

1. Make any change in the present use of the premises;
2. Generate, store, or dispose of hazardous substances on or from the premises nor allow others to do so.

The seller should covenant that, *pending* closing, it will:

1. Comply with all environmental laws;
2. Allow buyer and its agents reasonable access to the premises to ascertain site conditions and for inspection of the premises prior to closing.

Buyers will look at the following areas:

1. Right of inspection before closing;
2. Having an environmental audit which is paid for by the seller;
3. Disclosure by the seller concerning hazardous substances;
4. Warranties and representations;
5. Indemnification from the seller.

Sellers will want to consider:

1. Whether to have ongoing liability from the prior use of hazardous substances;
2. Extent of disclosure to the buyer;
3. Trying to limit the time in which liability may attach and the dollar amount;
4. Indemnification from the buyer for acts occurring after the closing.

Even if the transaction calls for selling the property "as is," the seller's "as is" clause should specifically refer to the condition of the premises with regard to environmental laws and conditions.

§ 9.2   Landlord's and Tenant's Considerations

Whichever way the burden is placed for handling environmental issues, it should certainly be addressed in some fashion in the lease.

Tenants will want landlords to take full responsibility for environmental compliance. Landlords, especially in commercial buildings, will want to try to have the tenant take the responsibility. If the tenant's business—such as a chemical factory or a dry cleaner—involves using hazardous substances, it will be easier for the landlord to make this argument than it might be if a regular office business is being conducted.

Other variables include: the amount of space the tenant will be renting, the term of the lease, and whether any renovation will be done. If the hazardous substance is asbestos and renovation may cause a release that might not otherwise occur, then the landlord may want the tenant to pay the expenses.

Some landlords may want to accept full responsibility to ensure the quality of the work and that it is done in compliance with the laws. In some instances, the landlord may not have a choice: local law or the lease may require the landlord to perform the abatement.

§ 9.3   Lender's Considerations

In evaluating whether to make a loan or give a mortgage, lenders should carefully evaluate their potential borrower's creditworthiness, the value of the collateral, and the effect of potential cleanup costs of hazardous substances and related costs on the borrower's ability to repay the loan. The degree of scrutiny will vary, depending on the type of building involved and the hazardous substances involved. A loan to a borrower in the chemical or metals industry may be riskier than one for an office building.

Currently, it is standard for most banks to require, as a condition to giving mortgage loans, that borrowers submit complete environmental audits covering the property. In some instances, this requirement may assist the lender in the event that it has to assert an "innocent purchaser" defense in a subsequent foreclosure. The results of the audit may cause the lender not to make the loan or may convince the lender that the loan should not be secured by certain portions of the property. Lenders may also require personal guarantees with respect to environmental obligations.

Depending on the kind of business facility or dwelling involved, different types of protection may be required. A loan for a chemical plant may require an extensive environmental audit; a home or store may not.

Lenders should let potential borrowers know early in the relationship that environmental compliance will be a significant issue. The lender should have its own written environmental risk policy. It should give its officers instructions as to the considerations that must be taken into account in every transaction.

Although there are many factors to take into account in determining whether the borrower has met its due diligence, there are no clear guidelines for a lender to determine how it should act with respect to its due diligence. There may be a specific environmental questionnaire to be filled out by borrowers. The questionnaire should require information about the credentials of the individual filling out the form. It will include questions about many of the topics that will later become warranties and representations.

For example, it will inquire about present and past uses of the property and any releases of hazardous substances that may have occurred. Later on, the borrower might be required to represent that there were no uses of the property involving hazardous waste or releases. The existence of any asbestos, underground storage tanks, or transferors should be reported.

Before closing on a loan, lenders should include in their documents provisions requiring:

1. That the mortgagor represent and warrant that it has not used hazardous materials in the premises in a manner that will violate federal, state, or local laws;

2. A representation that, to the best of the mortgagor's knowledge, no prior owner, occupant, or operator of the premises used hazardous materials in a manner that violates federal, state, or local laws;

3. That the mortgagor covenant that it will keep or cause the premises to be kept free of hazardous substances;

4. That the mortgagor covenant that all operators and occupants of the premises will comply with federal, state, and local laws;

5. That the mortgagor defend, indemnify, and hold harmless the mortgagee, its employees, agents, officers, and directors from any claims, fines, damages, and causes of action arising out of hazardous substances in or affecting the premises, such as soil, water, or vegetation.

6. That foreclosure shall not operate as a discharge of the mortgagor's obligation with regard to hazardous materials and that, in the event that the mortgagor delivers a deed in lieu of foreclosure, the mortgagor will deliver the premises to the mortgagee (or its designee) free of any and all hazardous materials;

7. That the agreement be reevaluated if any hazardous substances are discovered prior to closing;

8. Disclosure, investigation, and testing by the mortgagor to determine whether hazardous substances are in the facility or may be the byproduct of any operation at the facility and that all environmental standards are complied with;

9. An engineer's opinion about whether the property may be contaminated;

10. Adequate insurance to cover environmental claims, which names the buyer as an additional insured on the seller's policy;

11. Obtaining opinion letters from counsel and an engineer that there are no liabilities under hazardous waste laws, and that inquiries have been made to appropriate federal, state, and local officers having jurisdiction and there were no known hazardous substance problems or violations;

12. Warranties and representations as to the use of chemical substances in the borrower's operations;

13. An environmental audit by the lender's environmental or engineering consultant;

14. That if the mortgagor does not perform any of its obligations, the mortgagee may perform them and add the expenses to the amount secured by the mortgage.

After making the loan, the lender may require specific periodic assurances in writing as to continuing compliance with environmental laws. Lenders must also consider their conduct and that of their agents and personnel when they are doing a workout on a problem loan or foreclosing so as to avoid CERCLA liability.

There may be additional provisions requiring:

1. Covenants that the building will not be used directly or indirectly for any environmentally hazardous use;

2. A requirement that the lender and seller receive copies of all notices received by the buyer/borrower concerning environmental matters;

3. That any breach by the borrower of any environmentally related provisions will constitute an event of default and allow the lender to accelerate the debt;

4. A covenant from the seller that there have not been and are not now any environmental problems or that any that did exist have been cured;

5. That the lender have access to all records and documents of the borrower relating to hazardous substances used, transported, or deposited on its property;

6. That if there are new or different hazardous substances discovered, the laws pertaining to those will be complied with. Hazardous substances are always being added to the CERCLA list. A property certified as clean today may have a problem in the future.

Lenders may also require continuing audits, which are periodic and unannounced. This requirement allows lenders to be aware of current risk and keeps borrowers on their toes. There may also be preforeclosure audits so that lenders can determine whether abandonment of the security interest may be preferable to purchase.

Lenders may refuse loans where there is a perceived environmental risk. They may also avoid taking a security interest in the property and require the principals to give personal guarantees for the amount of the loan.

If a lender sells a property and fails to disclose the presence of a known hazard, the sale may be voided. Illinois has a statutory disclosure requirement.[3] Noncompliance with New Jersey's Environmental Cleanup Responsibility Act (ECRA) can result in the voiding of the transaction.[4]

When reviewing the financial stability of a mortgagor, it may not be enough to examine the property in question. In Superlien states, it is possible that all property owned by the mortgagor, including that which is the subject of the loan, may be attached to pay for cleanup of other property. A borrower may have property in several states. Lenders should require updates on their borrowers' real estate portfolios, the locations of property, and whether they are in Superlien states. Some lenders require personal indemnification from principals.

Lenders must be aware of proposed legislation and plan for the future. They may require builders to institute construction measures to avoid certain problems such as mitigating infiltration of radon and increasing ventilation capacity to avoid sick building syndrome.

---

[3] Responsible Property Transfer Act of 1988, Pub. L. No. 85-1228, 1988 Ill. Legis. Serv. 2079 (West).

[4] See **ch. 2.**

CHAPTER 10

LIABILITIES INSURANCE FOR HAZARDOUS SUBSTANCES IN BUILDINGS

Henry Nozko, Jr.*
President
United Coastal Insurance Company

§ 10.1   Introduction

§ 10.2   Market Cycle

§ 10.3   Liability and Litigation Issues

§ 10.4   What Types of Coverages Are Needed?

§ 10.5   Building Owner

§ 10.6   —Insurance for Asbestos Left in Place

§ 10.7   Professional Liability

§ 10.8   Environment Impairment Liability Insurance

§ 10.9   Storage and Treatment

§ 10.10   How to Evaluate the Insurer and Its Coverage

§ 10.11   Policy Terms and Conditions

§ 10.12   Claims Made, Sunset Clauses, True Occurrence

§ 10.13   Minimizing Building Owners' Loss Exposure

§ 10.1   Introduction

Business opportunities for environmental cleanup contractors are rapidly increasing in this wide-ranging market. This business is driven in part by public opinion and also is mandated by legislation increasing the cost each year for all forms of contaminate cleanup. Regulations governing remediation are becoming more stringent and more technical, driving up the remediation costs as well.

---

*This chapter was reviewed by Dawn Scanlon and Glynis V. Priester, Environmental Risk Division, Frank B. Hall.

Effective October 1, 1990, PCB transformers that contain 500 ppm of PCBs or greater, and secondary voltages of 480 volts or more, became prohibited in or near commercial buildings. Transformers with lower secondary voltages (less than 480 volts), located in or near commercial buildings, must have enhanced electrical protection from fire. As a result of this new EPA rule, owners and operators of transformers located in or near commercial buildings will need to identify and characterize PCB transformers.

The EPA has also prohibited the use of water treatment systems that use hexavalent chromium compounds in comfort HVAC systems, particularly in cooling towers used at most large commercial and industrial buildings. The prohibition is based on the EPA's conclusion that hexavalent chromium compounds are possible potent human carcinogens. These systems are installed in hospitals, hotels, shopping malls, office buildings, educational facilities, and all types of commercial buildings. The prohibition went into effect on May 18, 1990.

The driving force behind the asbestos problem in all types of buildings is the legal and liability issues connected with the contaminate. Asbestos abatement has reached a far wider spectrum than the initial stages of removal from schools, where EPA regulations require management or removal of asbestos. These and other building contaminates are receiving increasing attention and regulation. The legal and liability issues, in many instances, exceed the regulatory concerns as they apply to commercial, public, and institutional buildings; these issues are becoming the impetus for the growing business of building decontamination and remediation, which is now in excess of $3 billion annually with an aggregate market value in excess of $100 billion.

Liability issues have raised considerable attention to poor indoor air quality (apart from asbestos fibers), which is causing the air in many commercial, industrial, and institutional buildings to be unhealthy. Energy-conserving heating and cooling systems have intensified the health problems in the air systems of buildings, raising bodily injury liability issues among millions of building occupants.

These environment-related issues in connection with buildings and homes have created a huge business opportunity for the construction industry, but at the same time have caused and raised severe insurance availability problems because of the liability associated with these issues. Insurance availability has become a concern for the property owner, architect, engineer, environmental consultant, and remediation contractor, and even for bankers and other lending institutions that mortgage building projects.

§ 10.2 Market Cycle

One of the reasons that insurance is so difficult to find for coverages of environmental exposures in building projects is due to a down cycle in the insurance industry. Insurance companies are highly regulated as to the limits and amounts of insurance they are permitted to sell, which is a function of the financial strength of the insurance company offering a given policy. Generally speaking, insurance companies cannot offer, in any one risk, a policy with a policy limit that exceeds 10 percent of the insurance company's surplus. (The insurance company's surplus is basically the same as its net worth.)

In addition, most insurance departments discourage any insurance company from allowing earned premium to exceed three times the company's surplus. Earned premium is basically the same as sales or revenue. Therefore, if an insurance company has a $100 million surplus, it cannot issue any one policy with a policy limit of greater than $10 million (10 percent of $100 million) and for all the policies sold by that insurance company in one year, the total premium earned should not exceed $300 million (3 times the $100 million surplus).

Therefore, an insurance company is severely restricted in terms of how much insurance it can sell and in terms of how much it can offer to any insured for one policy limit.

These limitations can be modified and increased if the insurance company can negotiate and purchase reinsurance from other insurance companies. In simple terms, the reinsurance contract provides that the policy-issuing insurance company borrow surplus from the reinsurance company, allowing the policy-issuing insurance company to exceed the limitations described above. However, most insurance companies retain a small part of each policy risk and reinsure the balance of the policy risk, which greatly limits the effects of higher limits through the use of reinsurance.

When the insurance industry goes through a cycle of losses, generated either from underwriting losses and/or from losses from investments, the surplus of the company is reduced and the amount of policies sold by the company may, likewise, require reduction. In such a situation, the insurance company resorts to falling back on the traditional lines of insurance, such as automobile insurance, homeowners' insurance, health and accident insurance and workers' compensation, and standard commercial liability lines of coverage, rather than taking on specialty forms of insurance, such as asbestos abatement liability, professional liability, and/or pollution liability, which is less traditional and of greater risk. During a down cycle, the availability of insurance in the high-risk specialty areas is very small, because there is no excess available surplus to venture into these specialty risks. Therefore, whatever insurance there is becomes very costly.

§ 10.3   Liability and Litigation Issues

To complicate the scarce availability of insurance during a down cycle of the insurance industry, most insurance companies avoid asbestos abatement liability and/or contractor pollution liability because of the very complex court interpretations defining coverage issues in these lines. For example, an insurance company must be concerned about potential claims in the future, arising out of operations performed today, especially involving risks with a long latency period for the development of claims, such as asbestos abatement contracting. Likewise, remediation contractors performing hazardous waste remediation cleanup from industrial sites and facilities may be subjected to future claims arising out of the cleanup contractors' remediation efforts that are performed today. Predictability of loss in the asbestos and environmental remediation areas is very difficult for insurance companies to assess.

The courts in the United States today have treated environmental liability issues inconsistently and almost capriciously, and, in some cases, seemingly rely on the theory of "the deep pocket" concerning responsibility of cost of correction. Quite often, the search for the deep pocket ends up on the doorstep of the insurance company, with the courts widely and broadly interpreting insurance contracts to provide coverage where it was not intended by the insurance company at the time of issuing the policy. For example, state Supreme Courts in California,[1] Massachusetts,[2] Minnesota,[3] North Carolina,[4] and Washington[5] have ruled that pollution cleanup costs were insurable as "damages" under the standard commercial general liability (CGL) policy. However, in the state Supreme Courts of Maine[6] and New Hampshire it was ruled that pollution cleanup costs are not "damages" as defined in the CGL policy.

Most CGL policies say that the insurer will "pay on behalf of the insured all sums which the insured shall become legally obligated to pay as damages." Insurers argue that cleaning up facilities or properties with pollution is the cost of doing business rather than "damages" and, therefore, such cleanup is not covered by the policy. Most insurance companies further argue that the standard pollution exclusion eliminates coverage for pollution cleanup, but they have been sidetracked by the courts' favoring policyholders by ruling that the pollution exclusion only bars coverage for pollution that is intentional.

---

[1] AIV Ins. Co. v. Superior Court of Santa Clara County, 799 P.2d 1253, 274 Cal. Rptr. 820 (Cal. 1990).

[2] Hazen Paper Co. v. United States Fidelity and Guaranty Co., 407 Mass. 689, 555 N.E.2d 576 (1990).

[3] Minnesota Mining and Manufacturing Co. v. Travelers Indemnity Co., 457 N.W.2d 175 (Minn. 1990).

[4] C. D. Spangler Construction Co. v. Industrial Crankshaft & Engineering Co., 326 N.C. 133, 388 S.E.2d 557 (1990).

[5] Boeing Co. v. Aetna Casualty and Surety Co., 113 Wash. 2d 869, 784 P.2d 507 (1990).

[6] Patrons Oxford Mutual Insurance Co. v. Marior, 573 A.2d 16 (Me. 1990).

The Sixth Circuit Court of Appeals[7] conversely held that the pollution exclusion bars coverage for pollution that does not occur quickly or abruptly, and the Wisconsin Supreme Court[8] ruled that the pollution exclusion should only apply to bar coverage where there was "intentional" pollution.

These complexities make it extremely difficult for an insurance company to assess what the courts will interpret in the future as to what the policy covered today. For example, on October 6, 1987, the EPA released the "interim guidance on indemnification of Superfund response action contractors under Section 119 of SARA." Generally, the response action contractor is not subject to liability for injuries and damages that result from the release or threatened release of a hazardous substance or pollutant unless the contractor is negligent or grossly negligent, or its conduct constitutes intentional misconduct. Therefore, the contractor would not be responsible for any remediation costs arising out of operations defined as "damages" unless the contractor's conduct was negligent or intentional.

However, the Eleventh Circuit Court, in *United States v. Fleet Factor Corporation*,[9] found that a lender may be liable as an "operator" of its borrower's facility if the lender participates in the financial management of the facility to a degree indicating a "capacity to influence" the facility's treatment of hazardous materials. This is an expansion of liability.

Under the same sort of logic, an environmental consultant today advising and specifying the remediation activities of a facility could be construed by the courts at some future date as an "operator" because, through their consulting services, consultants are participants in the management of the facilities and, therefore, these professionals become responsible for bodily injury or property damage arising out of pollution from the facility. Insurance companies providing professional liability to environmental consultants never intended or anticipated such an exposure. Most insurance companies do not want to play this brand of Russian roulette.

Likewise, many of the regulations offering indemnification to remediation contractors do not preempt or supersede state laws or regulations and, therefore, may not provide such indemnification for contractors working on local or private remediation projects. Further, an insurance company must be concerned as to how the courts will interpret state-of-the-art standards and guidelines used by contractors today and redefined at some later date. For example, could an asbestos abatement contractor be sued for property damage arising out of asbestos abatement because, at some future date, the standards of acceptable clearance become far more stringent than

---

[7] United States Fidelity and Guaranty Co. v. Star Fire Coals, Inc., 856 F.2d 31 (6th Cir. 1988).

[8] Just v. Land Reclamation, Ltd., 155 Wis. 2d 737, 456 N.W.2d 570 (1990).

[9] United States v. Fleet Factors Corp., 901 F.2d 1550 (1990).

the standards today, leaving a completed project in some future status of noncompliance, and exposing the contractor and his or her insurance company to potential property damage and bodily injury claims in the future?

The complexity of litigation and court interpretations of government regulations, policy terms and conditions, and advancing technology make it nearly impossible for an insurer to qualify or quantify the exposures the insurer is underwriting concerning asbestos abatement contractors or remediation contractors. With such chaos abounding, it is unlikely that coverages will be easily purchased for the near future. Some insurance companies are developing specialized insuring contracts to deal with these complex environmental issues, and the insurance industry will slowly respond to the needs of environmental contractors.

§ 10.4 What Types of Coverages Are Needed?

Environmental contractors require general liability insurance to include the specific operations undertaken by the company. The typical coverage purchased by environmental contractors is called commercial general liability (CGL). For hazardous remediation contractors, it may be necessary to also purchase a contractor pollution liability (CPL) policy in addition to the CGL policy. Alternatively, the hazardous remediation contractor may be able to purchase a combined CGL/CPL policy that has general liability coverage and pollution liability coverage.

The insuring agreement provides that the insurer will pay "those sums that the insured becomes legally obligated to pay as damages because of 'bodily injury' or 'property damage' to which this insurance applies." The insuring contract provides for the insurer to defend any suit against the insured seeking damages on account of bodily injury or property damage even if the allegations are groundless. The insured must be legally obligated to pay damages and the damages must result from bodily injury or property damage as each term is defined under the definition section of the insuring contract.

The insurance also applies only to "bodily injury" and "property damage" caused by an "occurrence" during the policy period. An "occurrence" means an accident including continuous or repeated exposure to substantially the same general harmful conditions. The property damage and bodily injury must occur during the policy period. Therefore, no coverage is afforded for bodily injury or property damages that occur before or after the policy period, even if the claim was made against the insured during the policy period. But the insuring contract covers bodily injury or property damage for which the third party makes a claim against the insured after the policy period ends, provided that the bodily injury or property damage occurred during the policy period.

There is a distinction between "claims made" policies and "occurrence" policies that separate the timing for the reporting of an occurrence in order for coverage to occur (this is more fully explained later). The insurer promises to pay on behalf of the "insured," and the insured is identified by and named on the policy. The insurer's duty to settle or defend a claim ceases after the applicable limit of the company's liability has been exhausted by payment of judgments or any settlements up to the policy amount.

Generally speaking, all operations of the insured are covered by the CGL policy and all occurrences at the insured's premises are covered by the CGL policy, but all insuring contracts have exclusions that should be carefully reviewed.

Asbestos abatement contractors and hazardous remediation contractors purchasing general liability insurance will quite often find specialized forms that may differ from the generally accepted standard forms used by the industry. Most commercial general liability policies provide the following exclusions:

1. Contractual liability—this eliminates coverage for liability assumed by the insured under any contract or agreement unless the contract agreement is incidental.

2. Auto—in general, most forms of commercial general liability exclude coverage for liability arising out of the ownership, maintenance, use, loading, or unloading of automobiles, watercraft, or aircraft.

3. Pollution—most CGL policies exclude "bodily injury" or "property damage" arising out of the actual or alleged discharge, dispersal, release, or escape of pollutants. Many CGL policies exclude asbestos as well as pollutants that are generally defined as contaminants, including smoke, vapors, soot, fumes, acids, alkalis, and toxic chemicals, liquids, or gases.

4. War risks—most CGL policies exclude "bodily injury" or "property damage" due to war or any act or condition incident to a war, including civil war, insurrection, rebellion, or revolution.

5. Liquor liability—most CGL policies exclude liability because of the violation of any statute, ordinance, or regulation pertaining to the sale, gift, distribution, or use of any alcoholic beverage or by reason of the selling, serving, or giving of any alcoholic beverage to a minor or to a person under the influence of alcohol, which causes or contributes to the intoxication of any person.

6. Employee exclusions—most CGL policies have exclusions intended to eliminate coverages for liability arising out of injury to the insured's employees. Such coverage is usually found under a separate policy of workers' compensation.

7. Care, custody, or control—most CGL policies exclude "property damage" to property that is in the care, custody, or control of the insured, or property that is owned, occupied, or rented by the insured, or property used by the insured, or property where the insured is exercising physical control. Such coverages are generally purchased under a separate property insurance policy.

8. Failure to perform—although a CGL policy provides coverage for loss of use to tangible property that has not been physically injured or destroyed, but whose access has been blocked by an occurrence, coverage is not provided if the occurrence is a delay or lack of performance by or on behalf of the named insured of any contract or agreement, or if there is a failure of the named insured's products or work performed by or on behalf of the named insured to meet the level of performance, quality, fitness, or durability warranted or represented by the named insured.

9. Explosion, collapse, underground hazards—this exclusion, known as "XCU," eliminates property damage within any of three hazards defined in the policy relating to the explosion hazard, the collapse hazard, and the underground hazard.

Generally speaking, it is the intent of the CGL policy to insure the contractor against a loss to person or property while performing the contractor's operations. Great caution should be exercised, however, by asbestos abatement contractors and hazardous remediation contractors, because claims arising out of asbestos or pollution exposures usually will not be covered. The asbestos removal contractor and the remediation contractor should pay careful attention to the pollution exclusions to be sure that persons and properties are covered, even though the contractor is removing asbestos and/or removing some other pollutant or hazardous material from a building. It may be necessary for the contractor to purchase a separate contractor pollution liability policy to close this coverage gap. The CPL policy is discussed in greater detail later.

§ 10.5 Building Owner

The building owner can secure liability coverage by requesting the contractor to name the building owner as an additional insured to the contractor's CGL policy. This could provide third-party liability coverage to persons and property arising out of the operations of the contractor but may not cover first-party damage to the facility owner where the contractor is performing its work, even though the owner is named on the contractor's policy.

Because the contractor's policy excludes premises under its care, custody, and control, the building owner, by becoming an additional named insured, may not have the benefit of property damage insurance for the facility because that facility is owned by and is under the care, custody, and control of the owner who is additionally named. Therefore, an owner should pay careful attention and carefully consider the request to be an additional insured.

By being an additional insured, the owner receives coverage relating to third-party liability claims by, for example, an individual in the building who may have been exposed to contaminated fibers while asbestos removal activities were in progress; however, the building owner may lose coverage for property damage to his or her premises caused by the contractor, because the building owner becomes an insured and loses coverage under the care, custody, and control exclusion.

Some insurance companies will provide a separate general liability policy to the building owner which includes first-party property damage and liability arising out of asbestos and/or pollution conditions. However, such insurance is very difficult to find and very expensive. The owner can request a separate owners' and contractors' protective liability policy for the separate protection of the owner and purchased by the contractor, in connection with the project undertaken by the contractor. Therefore, the owner can either require the contractor to have the owner added to the contractor's general liability insurance as an additional insured or the owner can require the contractor to purchase an owners' and contractors' protective liability policy in the name of the owner.

In the first instance, the owner, as an additional insured, will share the single-policy limit of insurance with the contractor, even when both the owner and the contractor are sued for one incident. In the owners' and contractors' protective liability policy, the property owner is the named insured and does not share the policy limit. The insurance company promises to pay damages that the owner becomes legally obligated to pay because of bodily injury or property damage arising out of operations performed for the owner by the contractor at the specified and designated project location named in the policy.

The owner can also request that the contractor name the owner's environmental consultant or architect as an additional insured on the commercial general liability policy, but careful consideration should be given prior to such request. First, the one-policy limit is then shared by three separate entities. If all three entities are sued for the same occurrence, the amount of coverage to each insured party is greatly diminished. Second, the commercial general liability policy purchased by the contractor does not provide professional liability and/or coverage for errors and omissions arising out of the consultant's services in connection with the asbestos and/or hazardous remediation project. Such coverage is provided only when a separate professional liability errors and omissions policy is purchased by the consultant, engineer, or architect performing services to the owner.

Many professionals providing asbestos consulting services and/or environmental remediation services to building owners do not have errors and omissions insurance covering their consulting services and only have general liability policies, which have a professional exclusion. Naming a professional to the contractor's general liability policy serves no purpose and does not provide any additional coverage relating to errors and omission.

Therefore, the building owner has no protection or recourse if the contractor incorrectly performs work caused by following errors in the specifications prepared by the consultant or engineer. In such a case, the building owner is at risk. Therefore, the building owner should always require any professional consultant, engineer, architect, hygienist, or environmental professional to demonstrate that he or she has professional liability insurance specifically covering the services being provided to the owner.

§ 10.6 —Insurance for Asbestos Left in Place[10]

"Asbestos in place" insurance offers property owners and managers protection from liabilities associated with asbestos that is not yet removed from buildings. Asbestos might be left in place, or its removal delayed, because of budget and/or scheduling problems, a need to avoid tenant interruptions, or the presence of asbestos that is difficult or impossible to remove.

Asbestos in place insurance covers:

1. Bodily injury to third parties (such as tenants) arising out of an exposure to asbestos;
2. Property damage to third parties resulting from an asbestos release;
3. Business interruption/loss of use expenses to third parties as a result of an asbestos release;
4. Liability from releases caused by subcontractors who do not have asbestos liability coverage themselves (such as electricians, plumbers, HVAC contractors);
5. Defense costs for suits filed by third parties claiming long-term exposure to asbestos in place in an insured location, or a sudden and accidental asbestos release. Coverage includes suits filed by employees of subcontractors.

Because asbestos-related diseases most often appear 20 to 30 years after exposure to asbestos fibers, to be of any real value, the insurance must be

---

[10] This subsection was written by Eric Group, Inc., Englewood, Colorado.

occurrence-form. Occurrence-form coverage protects against third-party claims for bodily injury and property damage, regardless of when the claims are made.

The availability of this type of insurance gives property owners and managers flexibility in developing short- and long-term strategies for maintaining and abating asbestos. Insurance for asbestos in place fills the gap in owners' general liability policies, which typically exclude asbestos-related losses and liabilities.

There may be some economic advantages to delaying abatement. For example, property owners can coordinate asbestos removal with normal tenant turnover to optimize company cash flow. Buying and selling also are simplified because the insurance can be transferred to qualified new owners. In addition, financing is facilitated because lenders can be listed as additional insureds on the policies.

Asbestos in place policies are priced based on facility type, amount of asbestos in the building, fiber levels in the air, and the total square footage exposed to asbestos.

Commercial Property Liability Insurance

Commercial property liability insurance protects property purchasers from liabilities associated with legally mandated cleanup of contamination that was present, but undetected, at the time the property was purchased.

This type of insurance became available from a very limited number of companies in mid-1991. Coverage is limited to contamination that was present prior to purchase of the property, but discovered after the purchase of the insurance. Liabilities must result from specific federal or state statutes named in the policies. Coverage generally includes:

1. Liabilities for remediation to the insured's and third-party property that becomes necessary due to undetected, but preexisting property contamination;
2. Costs associated with remedial investigation and feasibility studies for the contaminated property;
3. Defense costs resulting from the liability named in the statutes.

From the mid-1980s through 1990, approximately 4,000 sites per year were added to the Superfund site list. This means that an average of more than 10 new Superfund sites were being discovered each day of the year. As a result of this situation, commercial property owners throughout the country were exposed to financial risks like never before.

Federal and state environmental laws such as CERCLA and SARA and the Resource Conservation and Recovery Act (RCRA) hold commercial real estate owners strictly liable for environmental contamination on their properties. Strict liability means a current property owner can be held liable for part or all of the cleanup costs, whether or not the owner caused or contributed to the contamination.

To reduce the chances of purchasing a property that may fall under a federal or state cleanup mandate, most potential purchasers insist on a preacquisition site assessment (Phase I audit) prior to finalization of the purchase.

But, because Phase I site assessments can fail to detect contamination such as abandoned underground storage tanks, dioxin, and chemical dumps, this is still no guarantee that a property is contamination-free and that an owner will not be held liable for cleanup should contamination be detected. A Phase II site assessment, which includes expensive additional testing of air, water, and soil, also cannot guarantee that the property is free of contamination. Costs associated with a Phase II audit are generally higher than insurance rates on that same property.

A purchaser therefore remains at risk for government- or court mandated-remediation, regardless of attempts to verify that a property is environmentally "clean." Even more distressing is the fact that cleanup and defense costs often total more than the property's market value.

A preacquisition site assessment, performed by an engineering firm that is approved by the insurance company, is required prior to issuing a policy. If contamination is detected on specific portions of the property, those areas can be excluded while noncontaminated areas may still be considered insurable.

Coverage limits, deductibles, and terms vary from policy to policy and should be analyzed carefully prior to making a decision on which policy is best for an individual property owner.

§ 10.7 Professional Liability

In a professional liability policy, the insurance company will pay, on behalf of the insured, all sums that the insured becomes legally obligated to pay as damages, and all expenses (more fully defined as loss) because of named risks, which include negligence, error, or mistake in rendering, or omission in failing to render, professional services alleged to arise or actually arising out of those services provided by the insured that are specifically designated and defined in the policy.

This insurance relates to damages arising out of professional negligence, error, or mistake in rendering, or an omission in failing to render, professional services. Professional liability does not, in contrast to the commercial general liability policy, cover damages arising out of "bodily injury" or "property damage," but rather the damages arising out of the insured's failure to use due care in the degree of skill expected of a person in a particular profession.

This form of liability insurance is not restricted to an "occurrence," which is caused by an accident, as in the CGL form. A professional may perform a service in exact accordance with his or her intentions, but the diagnosis may turn out to be faulty and result in liability.

Generally, if a contractor performs an asbestos abatement project in exact accordance with the contract documents prepared by the consultant and, at the end of the remediation, contamination remains in the facility by virtue of the specified procedure or by virtue of the consultant's omitting a certain designated area or procedure, and a third party is exposed to the contaminate at conclusion of the project, generally the owner and professional are more at risk than the contractor. The owner could then call upon the professional liability insurance provided by the consultant to respond to any damages suffered by the third party and arising out of the nonperformance or incompleteness of the remediation project.

§ 10.8   Environmental Impairment Liability Insurance

Generally, environmental impairment liability insurance is purchased in combination with and/or in addition to commercial general liability. Many commercial general liability policies available today can include bodily injury or property damage arising out of asbestos abatement operations, in addition to any other bodily injury or property damage caused by the contractor.

Very few insurance companies will provide contractor pollution liability insurance in one combined policy form that includes pollution general liability for those contractors performing hazardous remediation. Most contractor pollution liability policies provide for the insurer to pay on behalf of the insured those losses that the insured became legally obligated to pay as a result of claims arising out of "pollution conditions" and out of the performance of the contractor's operations.

The pollution conditions that the policy insures against are defined as the discharge, dispersal, release, or escape of smoke, vapors, fumes, acids, alkalis, toxic chemicals, liquids or gases, waste materials, or other irritants or pollutants into or upon land, the atmosphere, or any water course or body of water, which results in bodily injury or property damage. In essence, the contractor pollution liability insurance provides the coverage that is eliminated by the pollution exclusion in the commercial general liability policy.

No contractor performing any hazardous remediation activities should operate without contractor pollution liability insurance, because the standard CGL policy form excludes most of everything that the environmental contractor does. Concerning asbestos removal operations, one must look to the policy exclusions in either the CGL form or the contractor pollution liability form to ascertain whether asbestos removal is insured.

For example, the contract pollution liability policy may cover remediation of hazardous pollutants but may have an asbestos exclusion and, therefore, not provide for asbestos abatement. Likewise, the CGL policy may have an exclusion for both asbestos and hazardous remediation operations, or the CGL policy may provide for asbestos abatement operations while excluding hazardous remediation of other pollutants. The exclusion section of each policy must be carefully examined to be sure that the contractor's operations are covered.

Contractor pollution liability policies can provide coverage for both hazardous remediation and asbestos abatement, but the insured may need a special asbestos endorsement. The two biggest concerns facing a contractor purchasing such insurance is that many of the liability insurance policies that are available for asbestos abatement or hazardous remediation activities either do not fully cover the operations contemplated by the contractor or that the company or entity offering the liability insurance policy is not sufficiently capitalized and may not be around when it comes time to pay claims in the future.

§ 10.9   Storage and Treatment

In addition to asbestos, indoor air quality, radon, and PCB building contamination, there are hundreds of thousands of buildings and facilities in the United States that generate, handle, store, treat, or dispose of hazardous substances, and very few of these facilities have insurance to cover pollution risks. The Resource Conservation and Recovery Act (RCRA) sets forth the regulations and standards for the disposal of hazardous waste and regulates the permitting of disposal facilities, including the requirement that these facilities comply with financial responsibility requirements relating to capability for paying damages that might arise from the operations of the storage or treatment facilities. Therefore, facilities operating under RCRA requirements must purchase liability insurance that covers damages arising from their storage and treatment operations or post liquid collateral in the amount of the required policy limit, to substitute for the insurance policy.

In such instances, the insurance company agrees to pay on behalf of the insured all sums which the insured shall become legally obligated to pay as damages because of bodily injury or property damage caused by a sudden accidental occurrence arising from operations conducted at the designated facility concerning hazardous waste storage and/or treatment specifically identified in the policy.

Generally, first-party property damage and liability is excluded for coverage, therefore, excluding property owned, occupied, or rented by the insured. Such first-party insurance is very expensive to purchase and difficult to find because the operations insured relate to an ongoing risk concerning pollution liability.

Owners who deal with facilities that in any way store or treat hazardous materials need to purchase storage and treatment liability insurance by law, or provide a guaranteed self-insurance capability that can respond to potential pollution liability claims. There are approximately 4,000 storage and treatment facilities in the United States seeking pollution liability insurance to protect the facility operator and also to comply with RCRA requirements. Some of these facilities have land disposal operations including surface impoundments and landfills which, under RCRA, are required to have gradual pollution coverage in addition to sudden accidental coverage.

§ 10.10 How to Evaluate the Insurer and Its Coverage

Very few insurance companies are offering asbestos liability and pollution liability insurance. As previously mentioned, court interpretations of insurance contract language and the wide-ranging exposures concerning pollution liability have kept most insurance companies from stepping up to the table. As court interpretations continue to demonstrate ambiguity and conflicting trends in the application of regulations and of policy terms, availability of coverage could get even worse.

Risk retention groups, offshore captives, and onshore captives (such as insured-owned insurers approved usually in one state, such as Vermont, that insure only risks of the insured) are the most prominent forms of coverage available today. Generally, these groups are undercapitalized in proportion to the risks assumed, and they provide the contractor, building owner, or facility operator little true transfer of risk. Premiums paid to such groups or associations for the most part are a waste of money.

However, a few domestic, licensed, legitimate insurance companies provide both asbestos liability insurance and pollution liability insurance to qualified contractors, building owners, and facility operators. This writer estimates that, during calendar year 1990, approximately $200 million was written in connection with asbestos abatement and/or pollution liability insurance out of the insurance industry's approximate $175 billion in written premiums.

Today, several national insurance companies are actively marketing asbestos abatement insurance and pollution liability insurance. An additional ten insurance companies actively market asbestos abatement liability insurance. Trade associations and other financial groups are developing risk retention groups to provide pollution liability insurance.

Risk retention groups were initiated by the Product Liability Risk Retention Act of 1981; the Risk Retention Amendments of 1986 enabled companies, self-insurance associations, or corporations to provide insurance to cover their company membership when such coverage is scarce or unavailable from the insurance industry. Because retention groups and risk pools are not regulated to the degree that licensed and/or approved insurance companies are, seeking coverage from such groups, in this writer's opinion, is unadvisable or should be considered as a last resort and only in the event that the insured cannot find proper coverage from a domestic, licensed, or approved liability insurer.

The easiest way to seek an appropriate insurer for asbestos or pollution exposures is to engage the services of a reputable, qualified, and knowledgeable insurance broker familiar with asbestos and pollution exposures. Most of the major insurance brokers and agents, such as Marsh & McLennan, Johnson & Higgins, Frank B. Hall, Sedgwick James, and others will only deal with insurance companies that meet financial guideline tests set forth by the insurance agent or broker.

Most of the major insurance agents and brokers, and many regional and smaller reputable insurance agencies and brokers, will only deal with insurance companies that meet prescribed minimum financial standards that will ensure the ability to pay claims. For example, Marsh & McLennan, Sedgwick James, Johnson & Higgins, and Frank B. Hall have internal departments that monitor the financial affairs of insurance companies, and these large agencies and brokerage firms maintain an approved list of acceptable insurers with whom agents in the organization can place risks.

Because of the professional liability exposure, most major agencies perform a thorough due diligence evaluation of insurance companies prior to being placed on the agents' approved list and before the insurance company is recommended by the agent or broker. In addition to a major insurance agency's recommendation, one can refer to A. M. Best insurance reports, which are published annually and analyze the financial affairs of each and every insurance company licensed and approved to do business in the 50 states. No insurance company should be utilized by a potential insured unless that insurance company has an A. M. Best rating of B or better.

§ 10.11 Policy Terms and Conditions

After an insurance provider has been selected by a potential insured, the insuring contract must be carefully examined by the insured's agent and/or broker and by the insured. Most policies issued for asbestos and/or pollution exposures have many complicated endorsements that redefine coverage. Therefore, policy price is by no means an indicator for selection of the provider of insurance, because coverage differs widely from company to company. For example, in many cases, property owners ask to be named as additional insureds to the contractor's asbestos abatement or contractor pollution liability policy.

Most of these policies have an exclusion for bodily injury to an employee of the insured arising out of or in the course of employment by the insured or for any obligation of the insured to indemnify another because of damages arising out of such injury. This means that the CGL or CPL insurance provided does not cover bodily injury to an employee working for the insured. Likewise, most of these insurance policies exclude liability assumed by the insured under any contract or agreement except an incidental contract.

When a contractor signs a construction contract with a building owner, indemnification provisions contained in the contract are usually not insured under the typical asbestos abatement or pollution liability policy. Generally, most construction contracts provide that the contractor indemnify the owner from any liability relating to operations of the insured. This indemnification is generally uninsured in the typical asbestos and pollution policy forms. Therefore, if an insured's employee gets injured at the owner's building, that employee may file suit against the building owner in connection with the injury.

The building owner will then look to the contractor through the indemnification clause demanding a defense and indemnification for any damages paid. However, the insurance policy issued to the contractor excludes any liability assumed under a contract and excludes any bodily injury to any employee of the insured arising out of his or her employment. Therefore, if the employee has damages awarded against the owner, the owner in turn, through the indemnification clause in the construction contract, demands that the contractor reimburse the owner for all defense costs, judgment expenses, and losses relating to the injured employee. The contractor then picks up the tab for the owner and has no recourse against the insurer.

For the contractor, the loss is uninsured; yet the contractor must pay such loss to the building owner. Some insurance companies will amend these exclusions and provide contractual liability coverage. Because of the cumbersome protective equipment and difficult working conditions in asbestos-contaminated work areas, it is not uncommon for employees of contractors to get injured in the course of their work activities.

A contractor performing in excess of $10 million of annual abatement activities should expect at least 10 to 15 such contractual liability claims during the course of a year, with such claims potentially amounting to millions of dollars. Without contractual liability coverage, a contractor is signing a death warrant by entering into construction contracts that have broad hold harmless clauses. Yet, contractors, on a regular basis, sign such contracts without any insurance coverage.

A policy that provides contractual liability coverage for an asbestos liability contractor is probably worth two to three times the premium of a policy that does not provide such coverage, because of the very high exposure in the number of incidences relating to this risk. Another exclusion that contractors should be mindful of when reviewing insurance policies is the exclusion pertaining to independent contractors.

Asbestos abatement contractors and remediation contractors quite often subcontract certain aspects of their contractual responsibilities to subcontractors, such as the transportation of removed asbestos and/or the transportation of hazardous materials or even portions of a construction contract that are better handled by the expertise of a specialist. Such specialties may include reinsulation of fireproofing and pipe insulation, or reinstallation of electrical lighting and/or of HVAC systems, including temperature controls, which are often disrupted during asbestos abatement operations.

The contractor is legally liable for the operations of the subcontractors and, therefore, is exposed to claims arising out of bodily injury or property damage as a result of the operations of the contractor's subcontractors. Many of the subcontractors may not have adequate insurance or may have insurance with exclusions, such as described above, leaving the contractor exposed if the subcontractor's insurance does not respond because of financial inadequacy or because of wide-ranging exclusions.

Coverage is then provided by the contractor's insurer, unless the contractor's policy does not exclude independent contractors. Because subcontracting is in the normal course of a contractor's operations in both hazardous remediation and asbestos abatement, exclusions for independent contractors should be avoided. All exclusions in the insuring contract should be carefully reviewed by both the insured and the insurance agent or broker, and discussed prior to acceptance of the policy form.

§ 10.12 Claims Made, Sunset Clauses,
True Occurrence

The occurrence form of coverage provides coverage for bodily injury or property damage that occurs during the policy period. If someone is injured by the named insured's operations today, the policy in effect today will respond to the loss whether the claim is made against the insured during the policy period or at some later date.

In contrast, the claims-made form covers an occurrence during the policy period and *only* when the claim is made against the insurer *during the policy period.* If someone is injured during the policy period but does not make a claim against the insured until after the policy period has expired, the claim is not covered. If the policy is renewed, the claim can be reported under the next policy year, but only in the event of policy renewal. The bodily injury must have occurred during the policy period or after the retroactive date stated on the Declarations' page of the policy.

In claims relating to injury resulting from prolonged and elapsed exposure to dangerous materials or substances such as asbestos, if the claim is made at the time of a manifestation occurring long after the claims-made policy has expired, the policy will not respond. Therefore, with a claims-made form, the insurer will know, by the end of the policy period or any extension of the policy period, the amount of all claims that may be payable under that policy. There will be no need to calculate or reserve for any unreported claims.

Under the occurrence policy, courts have held that bodily injury that occurred over a long period of time, between the time of exposure and the time of manifestation may be covered by every occurrence policy in effect during the years of exposure and may be including those policies in effect during the time of the development of the manifestation. Under the occurrence form, coverage of the claim may be made years after the initial exposure and long after the expiration of the policy period.

Under the occurrence form of coverage, there is no termination date as to when a claim must be reported to be covered by the policy. There is a huge difference between the occurrence policy and the claims-made policy form. Some occurrence policies have what is known as a sunset clause, which states that a claim can be reported at any time after the policy period, but no later than, for example, 10 years from the expiration date of the policy. Such insurance is not true occurrence.

A true occurrence form allows the claim to be reported at any time after the expiration date of the policy period and still be covered. True occurrence coverage is available for asbestos abatement contractors; however, pollution liability insurance is only available in today's market through a claims-made form. If a hazardous remediation contractor continues to renew claims-made coverage with the same insurer, purchasing subsequent year policies, the contractor extends the reporting period, allowing, for example, a third-year renewal policy to cover claims reported in the third year relating to occurrences that took place during the first policy year.

If a remediation contractor needs or desires to switch from one insurer to another, the contractor should try to have the new insurance company go back and pick up occurrences relating to prior-years' operations of the insured for claims reported during the current policy period. This is known as a retroactive policy period and avoids any lapse of coverage under the claims-made form. Retroactive dates are expensive and often unobtainable. In all cases, the insurer will limit the period of time available for such retroactive date.

§ 10.13   Minimizing Building Owners'
Loss Exposure

Building owners can minimize their exposure to loss by selecting contractors that pay for and provide adequate insurance coverage from qualified insurers with national recognition and financial approval, as categorized by A. M. Best and/or as categorized by major insurance agencies or brokers. Such insurance is generally more expensive than insurance from risk retention groups, offshore captives, or insurance companies that do not have approval status of A. M. Best and/or the major insurance agencies and brokers. For example, a $3 million policy limit that provides coverage for hazardous remediation and/or asbestos abatement can range from as low as $75,000 to as high as $600,000, depending on the type of insurance and the quality of insurance purchased by the contractor.

Those contractors who purchase qualified insurance carry the added cost of such insurance in their construction estimates and, therefore, generally provide the building owner with a higher proposal for the asbestos or hazardous material remediation. The owner is foolish to save dollars by purchasing inferior insurance when he or she is risking millions of dollars in potential loss exposure sometime during or after the remediation project has been performed.

To adequately protect oneself, the building owner should consult with a major insurance agency, broker, insurance consultant, or expert knowledgeable in environmental matters when writing insurance specifications, to be sure that certain coverages are provided, proper limits are listed, and certain exclusions are avoided.

Preparation of insurance specifications by environmental consultants, which is done in many instances, is wrong, in my opinion. Professional consultants do not understand the intricacies of insuring contracts and should not be preparing insurance specifications that they do not understand and usually copy from specifications of other projects or prior projects. Secondly, professional consultants typically try to force back-door coverage by having themselves named under the contractor's policy, giving the illusion to the owner that the professional consultant is insured through the contractor's policy, which is incorrect.

The owner should prepare contract specifications that call for separate policies to be provided by the contractor, with specific requests for certain endorsements and the elimination of certain exclusions; the contract specifications should also require that professional liability be provided by the environmental consultant to cover his or her consulting services relating to the project. This is the best method for minimizing the owner's loss exposure.

Terms and conditions of insuring policies sometimes can be negotiated with insurance companies; however, renegotiated terms almost always result in higher premiums. Approximately, 30 to 40 percent of all policies issued by insurance carriers have specially negotiated terms and conditions relating to the specific policy issued. Such negotiations include varying levels of deductible, territorial coverage; redefinition of operations insured; higher limit endorsements; additional insured endorsements; and a multitude of other terms and conditions that modify the insuring contract.

Environmental liability insurance is a highly specialized product which is best understood by those few insurers who specialize in providing such coverage. An owner and contractor will have the most success in dealing with those insurers that have the technical and underwriting expertise to understand the nuances of operations insured and the need to tailor policy terms and conditions from one contractor to the next, from one building owner to the next, and from one facility operator to the next.

CHAPTER 11

ENVIRONMENTAL AUDITS, MANAGEMENT PLANS, AND CONTRACTS

§ 11.1   **Generally**

§ 11.2   **Checklist for Environmental Audit**

§ 11.3   **What to Look For in a Consultant**

§ 11.4   **What Is Involved in an Audit**

§ 11.5   **Contracts with Environmental Consultants**

§ 11.6   **Recordkeeping**

§ 11.7   **Locating an Attorney**

§ 11.8   **Anatomy of an Asbestos Survey in a Commercial Building or Retail Complex**

§ 11.9   **Operations and Maintenance (O&M) Plans**

§ 11.10   **—EPA O&M Guidelines**

§ 11.11   **Areas to Discuss with Consultant**

§ 11.1   Generally

An environmental audit is an investigation of the extent to which a property or building is contaminated and an assessment of the related risk of liability. It is generally conducted prior to the sale of a building or property. It may also occur before a long-term lease is signed or when a business is sold. A mini version may be done prior to the sale of a house.

Although audits are not required by statute, they are useful in a number of ways, including: allocating liability between a buyer and seller if there are environmental problems; establishing the condition of the property at a point in time and as a yardstick for the future; determining the purchase price of the property and the terms of sale; establishing whether representations and warranties are applicable; and establishing the right to a defense under SARA and nonliability for cleanup costs after title passes. Audits can also turn up violations and environmental compliance problems that may affect the sale.

A seller may want such an audit in order to be able to make representations and warranties in a purchase agreement or to understand the cost implications of an indemnification provision. Such a report may also establish a baseline against which to measure future environmental problems caused by the buyer.

A buyer may want such a report to identify the potential liabilities it is being asked to assume or to determine potential capital costs to maintain compliance with applicable laws and regulations.

Audits are usually conducted by prospective buyers. Depending on the results, an audit may be used by a buyer to terminate the deal.

In addition, parties to a Superfund cleanup may be eligible for a *de minimis* settlement[1] if they establish that:

1. Both the amount of the hazardous substances the party contributed to the facility and the hazardous effects of the substances are minimal in comparison to the other hazardous substances at the facility, or
2. That when the party owned the property, he or she did not conduct or permit the generation, transportation, storage, treatment, or disposal of any hazardous substance at the facility, and
3. He or she did not contribute to the release or threat of release of a hazardous substance.

In such cases, an audit may serve as a baseline for establishing the *absence* of liability of the seller.

If the seller conducts an audit and contamination is found, it must be reported to the EPA and/or state agencies. Any persons in charge of a facility, as soon as they have knowledge of a release or threatened release of a hazardous substance in a reportable quantity (generally 1 pound) must immediately notify the National Response Center.[2] State laws may also require notification.[3]

Since the SARA defense is available only to a buyer who establishes that, at the time of acquisition of the property, the buyer did not know or have reason to know of contamination, the audit must take place *before* the buyer decides to purchase.[4]

In order for the buyer to demonstrate that he or she did not know or have reason to know of contamination, the buyer must have exercised "due diligence" through an environmental audit. Due diligence is defined as "all appropriate inquiry into the previous ownership and uses of the property

[1] 42 U.S.C. § 9622.
[2] *Id.* § 9603(a).
[3] See **Ch. 2.**
[4] 42 U.S.C. § 9601(35)(B).

consistent with good commercial or customary practices in an effort to minimize liability."[5] When interpreting this clause, the courts must take into account:

1. Any specialized knowledge or experience of the buyer;
2. The relationship of the purchase price to the value of the property if it were not contaminated;
3. Commonly known or reasonably ascertainable information about the property;
4. The obviousness of the presence of contaminants on the property;
5. The ability to detect contamination by appropriate inspection.[6]

Information may come from a variety of sources, including the records of the federal, state, and local agencies responsible for monitoring and enforcing these laws. Records may include: permit files; enforcement actions and monitoring reports from former and current owners; SEC filings; building plans and specifications. There should also be a title search showing the chain of title over a number of years.

Requests for information are first made to the EPA and state and local regulatory agencies concerning any past or present problems with compliance with environmental laws. If past problems are revealed, the files are examined in detail. If the facility or building is known to have had hazardous substances used or stored in it, the regulatory files should be investigated, even if there are no compliance problems.

All files at the building that could relate to environmental matters should be examined to ascertain the nature of and risks of contamination of the property with hazardous substances. These may include corporate correspondence files and purchasing and accounts receivable records.

Federal and state court files should be reviewed to ascertain whether environmental problems were involved in any lawsuits to which the building owners were a party.

Interviews should be conducted of past and present facility and building owners, plant or building managers, employees, and other persons with knowledge of the building and waste management practices.

The potential buyer, possibly the buyer's attorney, and an environmental consultant must inspect the building or facility. A physical inspection would include observable indications of potential liability, such as leaking pipes or ducts, boilers that may have asbestos wrapping, discoloration, and the existence of underground storage tanks. Air samples may be taken by the environmental consultant.

---

[5] *Id.*

[6] *Id.*

The environmental consultant used for this inspection must be experienced in performing these audits, in order to maximize the results. For example, knowledge of an agency's internal filing system and methods may mean the difference between finding and not finding valuable information. Violations or records may not be listed by property, but rather by an individual or business name. Interviewing agency personnel may also be helpful.

Because the audit may later become evidence, it requires the participation of an attorney if it will be claimed as confidential under the attorney-client or work-product priviledges. Preparation of the report may be done by an attorney, with factual data being supplied by the environmental consultant, or the attorney may just oversee the preparation of the report. Much of the information in the report is not protected by the attorney-client privilege or the attorney work product doctrine. However, legal opinions and conclusions of the attorney, if communicated to the buyer in confidence, are protected under the attorney–client privilege.

Lenders conduct such audits not only as a means of avoiding CERCLA liability, but in order to assess the value of their security before accepting it as collateral. This may also be done later on, when the lender is deciding whether to foreclose on a potentially contaminated property. If the audit does not reveal any contamination, the lender may be able to utilize SARA's innocent purchaser defense.[7]

§ 11.2   Checklist for Environmental Audit

Areas for investigation by a potential purchaser of a building may include:

1. A physical inspection of the property, including photographs;
2. An examination of public documents such as court records, government agency permits, and enforcement files;
3. Review of SEC filings and administrative proceedings involving environmental matters;
4. Testing of air or bulk samples;
5. Determining whether the seller has owned any other properties which were the subject of environmental cleanups;
6. Determining the chain of title of prior owners and the prior use of the building or facility;
7. Determining whether there are any underground storage tanks and, if so, their condition and history of testing;
8. Obtaining copies of any earlier environmental audits or assessments;

---

[7] A lender may also require a borrower to personally guarantee loans where the value of the property may be affected by CERCLA or other toxic liability.

9. Reviewing the owner's correspondence with federal, state, and local environmental authorities, including any litigation or enforcement files;

10. Determining whether the current owner has any environmental permits from the local, state, or federal governments;

11. Determining whether the building has ever been the subject of any environmental investigation by the federal, state, or local government;

12. Determining whether the property on which the building is located is on the EPA's National Priorities List or Emergency and Remedial Response Information System;

13. Determining whether adjacent property has ever been on the EPA's National Priorities List or Emergency and Remedial Response Information System;

14. Determining what types of commercial enterprises have been operating on the property and on adjacent property or in adjacent buildings;

15. Checking local newspaper records;

16. Interviewing employees of current and prior owners and operators; neighbors and tenants, if any; and maintenance personnel;

17. Examining tax records and local building department records;

18. Reviewing applicable indoor air quality or hazardous substance legislation;

19. Reviewing recent judicial decisions;

20. Determining whether any state statutes or OSHA standards are being violated or have been violated in the past;

21. Inspecting ventilation and air-conditioning systems, ducts, and humidifiers;

22. Testing for radon and other substances.

Expenses incurred in connection with these items should be allocated.

§ 11.3 What to Look For in a Consultant

1. Checking references is essential, to be sure that the consultant has done similar work satisfactorily for other clients. For example, a consultant may only have experience working in school buildings, which are unoccupied during the abatement process. Abatement in an occupied high-rise office building or shopping center may call for different expertise. Thus, it is helpful if the consultant has worked on comparable projects.

2. The consultant should not have any conflicts of interest such as an interest in any abatement contracting firms that may bid on the work or in any testing laboratories or equipment suppliers.

3. No precise number of prior years of experience is required, but three to five years should be a minimum.

4. The background of staff is important because each may have different areas of expertise to contribute and a project may have special needs.

5. Staff should be good at recordkeeping and should submit copies of everything pertaining to the project.

6. Staff should demonstrate a high ethical track record.

7. If the staff are going to work with an attorney, they should have prior experience working with a team. The team may include attorneys; insurance agents; a consulting or engineering firm; representatives of the owner, management, unions, tenants, and other interested parties; a medical advisor; and the abatement contractor. Developers and owners of numerous buildings may want to continue working with the same team on other audits, to ensure consistency of approach on all buildings.

8. Some consulting firms have in-house laboratories; others need to employ a laboratory.

9. Sometimes, public relations skills are required. There may be questions raised by the media which need to be responded to. If this skill is needed, ensure that the firm has such skills or else recognize that there may be a need to retain a public relations consultant.

10. Experience in dealing with tenants, employees, and unions may be needed.

11. The consultant should have the ability to provide a complete environmental management program. In the case of asbestos, abatement may be required. There will need to be future monitoring and laboratory services. Records of all these procedures will be required. An operations and maintenance (O&M) plan may be required, as well as employee training for people working around hazardous substances.

12. Reports should be individualized rather than produced in canned language on a word processor.

13. The consultant should be financially stable and adequately staffed.

14. The consultant should be adequately insured with both comprehensive general and professional liability insurance from a company with an A+ or better rating.

15. A broad range of services may be required. The consultant should have the ability to provide services from the initial inspection through management planning, preparation of specifications, and project monitoring. Not all firms test for all types of hazardous substances.

16. The firm's training should include EPA-accredited courses for workers, job supervisors, investigators, and management planners who will be dealing with asbestos. It should be licensed under the applicable

regulations for the state, city, or municipality where the work will be performed, if it is asbestos-related.

§ 11.4   What Is Involved in an Audit

An environmental audit is usually done in phases. There may be up to three phases. Phase I involves a general site survey, historical property evaluations, and regulatory agency records check. It may propose areas for more in-depth study or raise problems with the building. There may also be interviews with employees.

The scope and complexity of a Phase I investigation will vary, depending on the type of building involved. A manufacturing facility will require a more extensive review than an office building, a store, or a home. It must be adequate to disclose necessary information. An office building may contain asbestos or transformers with PCBs. A store may have an underground gasoline storage tank.

Consultants who are knowledgeable about these issues will determine the scope of the investigation.

Phase I investigation consists of two parts: information review, and inspection of the site.

The extent and availability of information will vary, depending on the present and past uses of the building. It may include:

1. Prior ownership and uses of the property;
2. Materials used or stored at the site;
3. Waste treatment processes;
4. Wastes generated (past and present) and their disposition;
5. Permits and other regulatory requirements applicable to the property and conditions affecting transferability;
6. Compliance with permit requirements, enforcement history, past and/or outstanding violations and their status or disposition, and regulatory investigations;
7. Compliance with recordkeeping, monitoring, and reporting requirements;
8. Upcoming changes to permits or other regulatory conditions applicable to the facility;
9. Complaints, oil spills, chemical releases, and similar incidents;
10. Presence and condition of underground storage tanks and the contents of such tanks;
11. Information about building components (e.g., presence and condition of materials containing asbestos, contents of transformers, and capacitors that may contain polychlorinated biphenyls (PCBs));

12. Past or current practices or operations that may warrant close scrutiny as possible sources of contamination (e.g., fueling areas, machine shops, vehicle maintenance facilities, chemical storage, abandoned buildings, waste disposal areas, and uncontrolled access routes that may have resulted in unauthorized dumping);

13. Evidence that may indicate contamination or factors affecting the future development of the property (examples include areas of disturbed or discolored soil or flooring, evidence of debris, construction rubble or other waste materials on the surface, blighted vegetation, filled-in or highly eroded areas, streams, marshes, ponds, or other bodies of water);

14. Status of the site with regard to programs for protection of historic resources, endangered species, scenic rivers, and the like.

Title and tax records will disclose information about prior ownership and uses of the property. State agency records will offer information about past violations or complaints, investigations, and permits. Federal records will indicate whether there are any liens under CERCLA, enforcement actions, or investigations for environmental violations.

A Phase I investigation cannot establish the absence of contamination. It can only provide information to assist in determining whether future investigation is necessary. Phase II involves a detailed site survey, including historical area land-use evaluation. If the building is on a large property, Phase II may include sampling of soil, water, and building materials and components. There will also be a check of regulatory agencies' records. It will include tank testing, asbestos and air sampling, wipe samples of equipment, and analysis of materials stored or disposed of at a facility. It is far more expensive and time-consuming than a Phase I investigation. It may not be necessary unless the nature of the site, the building, or the Phase I investigation indicates otherwise. Phase II will certainly involve the consultant and the party's attorney. The nature and extent of the problem may be defined in this phase.

Phase II will require having a consultant design a study and perform sampling and analyses. If this is being done for a real estate closing, the contract should allow for any delays necessitated by the investigation. There should also be an allocation of the cost of the study in the contract of sale, in case the parties decide not to proceed with the closing.

Phase III may or may not be required. It may include similar tests to Phases I and II. This is the phase in which a remediation and implementation plan is developed based on information gleaned in Phases I and II.

Although the emphasis in this book is on buildings, it is impossible to look at buildings and ignore the surrounding property for possible sources of hazardous substances. Some conditions that may require further investigation include:

1. Depressions or mounds;
2. Odors;
3. Septic tanks and leach fields;
4. Evidence of caverns or shafts;
5. Damaged vegetation;
6. Presence of debris or trash;
7. Underground storage tanks;
8. Transformers or generators;
9. Pesticides.

Inside the building, some things to look at include:

1. HVAC systems;
2. Boiler and compactor rooms;
3. Insulation around piping;
4. Known asbestos or asbestos-containing materials and other known hazardous building materials;
5. Stored chemicals;
6. Waste disposal systems;
7. Electrical transformers;
8. Evidence of seepage, pooling, and stains;
9. Ceiling tiles;
10. Presence of lead;
11. Contaminated water;
12. Indoor air quality;
13. Utilities.

Historical evaluation includes the review of current and past site operations. Interviews may be taken of facility managers, superintendents, employees, and local residents. A title search will be done to uncover prior ownership and uses of the property. If the building is a larger site, there may be aerial photographs and geological testing of large areas where contamination may filter into a building.

The various federal, state, and local regulations will need to be examined in relation to the transaction.

Typical cost ranges are:

Phase I: $2,500 to $3,500
Phase II: $3,500 to $25,000
Phase III: $25,000 and up.

These ranges will vary, depending on the size of the property, whether there are multiple sites, and where the work is being done. Costs will also vary, depending on the type and level of testing.

The language of the report should be discussed with legal counsel to avoid unduly alarming lenders. A consultant's report for a seller may indicate conditions that can lead to violations and civil and criminal penalties. Consultants do not have a duty to disclose findings unless they are life-threatening problems. However, the owner or operator of the facility may have a duty to disclose the findings.

§ 11.5   Contracts with Environmental Consultants

Consulting firms come in many sizes, from sole practitioners to large firms. A consultant must be carefully interviewed before a selection is made. If the consulting firm has a number of people, it should be clear who will be in charge and how work will be delegated.

There is no standard form for such a contract, but there are certain issues and terms that should appear in every agreement and the agreement should be signed by both parties. The consultants will usually furnish a contract. Clients should not hesitate to negotiate any unacceptable terms.

It is important to establish the scope of the consultant's work, because their services may vary from a survey to an environmental audit to supervising or monitoring an abatement project. If the scope is limited, provisions should be made in the agreement for determining what will be construed as additional services and how they will be paid for.

The firm chosen should be able to act quickly and meet deadlines. Reports should be well-written and understandable. They should be written for the specific project and not in prepackaged language. If costs must be quantified, it is important to know whether the consultant selected is able to do that. There should be a monthly work plan and a projected budget. Time may be an important consideration if the sale of a building is imminent. If so, the consultant should be required to state how long the project will take.

§ 11.6   Recordkeeping

Proper recordkeeping is essential in the event that there is a violation or litigation. The records should be safely stored and retained for at least 30 years. Records include:

1.   The asbestos or other hazardous substance assessment study;
2.   Laboratory analysis of samples;

3. Contracts and contract documents for any consulting or abatement work;
4. Bid proposals;
5. Contractor's submissions;
6. Copies of notifications to agencies, as required by law;
7. Daily construction logs;
8. Daily air monitoring logs;
9. Certificate of final visual inspection;
10. Clearance certificates;
11. Hazardous waste manifests;
12. Respirator fit testing;
13. Training records;
14. Medical examination records;
15. O&M report;
16. Key correspondence.

§ 11.7 Locating an Attorney

As with other consultants, it is important to have an attorney who knows this highly specialized area of the law. Specialists can be located through the various legal referral services of local bar associations, industry organizations, and trade publications, and by referral from other attorneys, consultants, and colleagues.

Even within the environmental specialty, attorneys will have different focuses. Some work a lot in cities, with building owners; others work in suburban or rural areas, with large industrial sites.

The law in this area is constantly changing, and legal counsel should be immersed in this area enough to be aware of all the recent cases and legislation.

§ 11.8 Anatomy of an Asbestos Survey in a Commercial Building or Retail Complex

The first step before dealing with an asbestos or other hazardous substance problem is determining whether one exists. Building owners who suspect they may have asbestos or other hazardous substances in their building will need to hire an environmental consulting and engineering firm to conduct a survey. Because asbestos fireproofing was banned in the mid-1970s, buildings built before that date are most likely to have asbestos.

To solicit proposals, it is wise to develop some criteria for the work that is to be done, so that proposals can be compared fairly. This might conclude how, how many, and when samples will be taken, and the format for the consultant's final report.

Once a firm has been selected, a contract will be signed. The contract will usually be prepared by the consultant, but changes and additions can always be made.

The survey can vary from a preliminary inspection to a simple identification of the likelihood of ACM, or to a full survey that verifies the presence of friable and nonfriable ACM and indicates the location, type, and condition; recommendations on remedial action; and the cost of implementing such actions. Building records will be checked for the presence of such things as asbestos-containing surfacing materials, pipe and boiler insulation, and dropped ceilings. All ACM identified in building records will be located and documented.

Most likely, tenants will be given notice of the scheduling and occurrence of the survey. It is best to do this in writing. The letter should explain why the survey is being done. Building owners may require tenants to sign an acknowledgment of receipt of the letter.

In very large buildings or shopping malls, there may even be one or more meetings with tenants to explain what will be done in the survey and to answer any questions.

The inspectors first usually examine the space for suspicious materials such as ceiling tiles, pipe insulation, and surfacing materials used for fireproofing, soundproofing, or decoration, which might contain asbestos materials.

Depending on the site of the building, a schedule will have to be made of how many inspectors there will be and how much square footage each will cover per day.

If suspicious materials are spotted, the inspectors will take bulk samples back for analysis in a laboratory. If the samples show more than 1 percent asbestos, the building contains ACM.

Access to offices and stores will need to be coordinated. Building managers, tenants, and project managers will all work together.

If any hazardous conditions are encountered in the course of the survey, a plan should be in place for isolating the area and engaging a contractor quickly to do the cleanup or encapsulation immediately.

§ 11.9 Operations and Maintenance (O&M) Plans

For those who believe that removal of asbestos is more dangerous than leaving it in place, assuming it is nonfriable and there is no applicable law mandating removal, O&M plans are a viable alternative. The program is usually put together by a team including the property manager, an asbestos consultant (usually a certified industrial hygienist), a qualified abatement contractor, and the building owner's legal counsel.

It should be done in a way that satisfies the owner's common-law and statutory duties and avoids claims by tenants.

An O&M plan should include: recommendations for removal or enclosure of damaged or crumbly ACM; recommendations for repair or encapsulation of less damaged ACM and restriction of access to areas with damaged ACM until the response action has been implemented; maintenance and notification procedures; and tenant notification. There may be a program of phased work for leased space as it becomes available, and there may be training sessions for building supervisors and employees, to ensure that they implement the program.

Part of this plan usually involves notification to the tenants. This is a prudent thing to do because there may be an implied duty to warn building occupants and the presence of asbestos may be construed as a latent defect for which the owner is liable.

There should be a list of emergency telephone numbers available in the event of a sudden accident. This list should include telephone numbers for the removal companies' supervisor, an asbestos removal contractor, asbestos counsel, and an environmental consultant. A release might occur during: renovation or demolition; ordinary maintenance operations; asbestos removal; or in the transportation and removal of asbestos.

Records should be kept of:

1. All surveys;
2. O&M plans;
3. Copies of the consultant's and contractor's certifications and licenses;
4. Any response action taken;
5. The names of people involved and their certifications and licenses;
6. The name, address, telephone number, and license of the disposal transporter;
7. The contracts with the consultants and contractors.
8. The disposal site manifest;
9. The asbestos supervisor's daily notes and records;
10. Copies of air test results.

If removal is done in tenant space, there should be records of the tenant's and employees' names, addresses, ages (if possible), and smoking habits, and of the location and extent of the ACM and the pre-removal fiber count.

All of the asbestos in the building should be located and its type and condition determined. There should also be air monitoring to determine a baseline. Finally, there should be a written report showing the location of the ACM and recommending action.

To avoid sick building syndrome, it is recommended that building owners have environmental consultants examine HVAC systems for operation levels, filters, and contamination sources. Periodic monitoring will help avoid problems. Design professionals should require suppliers of building materials to provide information on emissions. Owners should make sure that there is easy access for testing and balancing of the system.

A training program should be established for custodial and maintenance personnel who come in contact with or work near the ACM. Equipment may need to be purchased for cleaning the building. Wet cleaning and high-efficiency particulate air (HEPA) vacuum techniques will be used.

There should be a plan for periodic reinspection of all ACM for damage and follow-up air monitoring at least twice a year. The plan should be established for dealing with any alterations and repairs that may involve the asbestos.

There will have to be a recordkeeping program. The program should establish whether the asbestos will be removed quickly or in a phased plan as tenant space turns over, or whether asbestos will be removed as problems arise.

Because building owners may still be liable for any violations of applicable regulations by a tenant's contractor, the owner may want to have his or her own industrial hygienist monitor the project. In addition, the building owner's liability continues even after the waste is removed from the building and turned over to a licensed hauler. For this reason, it would be prudent for the owner to receive copies of all project documents, such as notification of applicable governmental agencies, air-monitoring results, waste manifest information, contracts and specifications, and the hauler's insurance. The owner may want to verify that the landfill site is an approved site for asbestos disposal and that the ACM removed from the building was deposited in the landfill and not illegally dumped elsewhere.

The plan should consist of the following:

1. Identification
    a. Conduct preliminary air monitoring and bulk samples.
    b. Perform building-wide survey identifying location and type of ACM.
    c. Present result of survey in written report, recommending actions to be taken.
2. Notification
    a. Prepare and distribute appropriate notification of location of ACM to tenants and building personnel.

  b. Conduct training and education seminars for custodial and maintenance workers.

 3. Periodic Cleaning

  a. Vacuum all carpets, curtains, and horizontal surfaces throughout the building with HEPA vacuum cleaners.

  b. Mop and clean all uncarpeted floors, shelves, and other horizontal surfaces.

  c. Repeat cleaning procedures periodically.

 4. Periodic Reinspection

  a. Conduct air monitoring at least semiannually.

  b. Periodically inspect all ACM materials for damage.

  c. Take remedial measures necessitated by changes in condition.

 5. Limited Abatement

  a. When necessary, perform asbestos abatement to (i) facilitate installation of telephone, electrical, and computer lines and (ii) repair damaged ACM or ACM that will be disturbed by minor repairs or improvements.

  b. Perform air sampling during the course of work.

  c. Perform clearance air monitoring.

  d. Arrange for lawful transport and disposal of ACM.

  e. Furnish required notices, waste manifests, and governmental approvals.

  f. Maintain and provide complete records of air sampling, work performed, and procedures followed.

 6. Evaluation of HVAC

  a. Inspect and evaluate HVAC system for operating and filtration efficiency.

  b. Recommend improvements to system through cleaning, adjustment, repair, and filtration devices.

§ 11.10   —EPA O&M Guidelines

In an effort to lessen the unnecessary removal of asbestos from buildings, the EPA has released guidelines aimed at encouraging building owners to establish O&M programs for asbestos-containing materials. The guidelines are to ensure that day-to-day management of the building is carried out in a manner that minimizes the release of asbestos fibers into the air.

 According to the EPA, such a program should include: inspection and testing of building materials; notification to building workers and occupants of potential asbestos hazards; proper work practices in handling asbestos materials; recordkeeping; training of custodial and maintenance workers; and other steps. The new guidelines also suggest that a management program might call for the removal of some asbestos materials that are badly damaged or difficult to maintain.[8] They also acknowledge that an effective O&M program can be expensive and may approach the cost of removal.

According the the EPA guidelines, each building owner should:

1. Appoint an Asbestos Program Manager in charge of dealing with all asbestos-related activities in the building;
2. Inspect the building, take bulk samples of suspect materials to determine whether they contain asbestos, establish an inventory of asbestos materials, and assess the condition and potential for disturbance of the materials;
3. Develop and implement an O&M program;
4. Select and implement more aggressive abatement actions, including removal, where necessary.

A successful O&M program should include seven elements, according to the EPA. These elements are:

1. Notice to building service workers and other occupants about the location of asbestos materials and how to avoid disturbing them;
2. Regular surveillance to detect any changes in the condition of asbestos materials identified during the inspection;
3. A work-permit system to control repair, installation, and maintenance activities that might disturb asbestos;
4. Proper work practices to avoid exposure during work that involves asbestos materials;
5. Recordkeeping to document all asbestos-related activities;
6. Medical and respiratory protection for workers who come in contact with asbestos materials;
7. Training of the Asbestos Program Manager and custodial and maintenance staff.[9]

The EPA guidelines provide only general descriptions of proper work practices and training needed to conduct a good O&M program. The EPA is working with the National Institute of Building Science (NIBS) to write a detailed technical guide to proper O&M practices.

---

[8] Asbestos Abatement Report, Sept. 17, 1990, at 2.
[9] *Id.* at 3.

§ 11.11   Areas to Discuss with Consultant

An initial determination must be an made as to the type and level of audit desired. The consultant should be able to give some direction on this. Proposals that seem to be a "bargain" should be avoided. By the same token, it is unrealistic to expect a consultant to assume liability greater than his or her final invoice.

There must be an agreement on a fee for the consultant. Sometimes a cap or ceiling on fees should be established, especially if an hourly rate is being used, so that approval is required before work continues. Consultants can provide supervision varying from full-time to periodic inspections; thus the cost will vary. There should be a clear understanding of how much time the consultant will spend at the site.

Consultants frequently ask to be indemnified from third-party liability for property damage and personal injury resulting from a site investigation.

The consultant may ask to be indemnified for removal work by the contractor. Similarly, the owner may wish to be indemnified by the consultant. The consultant should furnish evidence of appropriate insurance.

Consultants may review documents, interview corporate managers, and investigate the site. They may be required to sign a confidentiality agreement and to return documents furnished to them by the building owner, upon completion of their work.

A decision should be made as to whether counsel will accompany the consultant on site visits. Counsel's presence may help to explain the context to employees and to limit the investigation to material issues. It also increases the likelihood of being able to claim a legal privilege for interviews.

The consultant may give brief initial oral reports. Written reports may not be privileged and may be subject to discovery. The agreement should state what type of report, if any, is required. Often, lead counsel retains the consultant to preserve privileged communications. Some attorneys put a provision in the contract with an engineering consultant stating that the consultant is being retained to assist the attorney in rendering legal advice to the client. If so, the documents prepared by the engineer should be marked privileged and reviewed by the attorney before being transmitted as a final product.

There should be a termination clause. If the consultant is terminated and is being paid at an hourly rate, generally he or she will only be paid to the date of termination. All work prepared by the consultant should be given to the client. If there are any limitations on this practice, they should be clearly spelled out.

CHAPTER 12

EMERGENCY SITUATIONS

Brent Kynoch

President

Asbestos Abatement Services, Inc.

§ 12.1   Introduction

§ 12.2   Prior Planning

§ 12.3   Establishment of an Operations and Maintenance (O&M) Plan

§ 12.4   —Survey

§ 12.5   —Training

§ 12.6   —Notification

§ 12.7   —Labeling

§ 12.8   —O&M Manual

§ 12.9   Name an Environmental Coordinator

§ 12.10   Emergency Procedures Manual

§ 12.11   —Asbestos Emergency Checklist

§ 12.12   Phone Tree and Emergency Contacts

§ 12.13   When an Accident Occurs

§ 12.14   Execution of Plan

§ 12.15   Locating the Problem

§ 12.16   Isolating the Area

§ 12.17   Cleanup of Environmental Contamination

§ 12.18   Notifications

§ 12.19   —Regulatory Notification

§ 12.20   —Occupants' Notification

§ 12.21   —Neighbors'/Public Notification

§ 12.22   —Insurance Companies' Notification

§ 12.23   —Attorneys' Notification

§ 12.24   —Others

§ 12.25   Handling Regulatory Agencies

§ 12.26   —Making Contact

§ 12.27   —Acknowledging Possible Violations

§ 12.28   —Establishing Ongoing Communications for Remediation Efforts

§ 12.29   —Working within "Intent" of Regulations

§ 12.30   —Agreeing on Objectives

§ 12.31   Handling Public Relations/Media

§ 12.32   —Developing Message Points

§ 12.33   —Selecting a Spokesperson

§ 12.34   —Honesty

§ 12.35   Conclusion

§ 12.1   Introduction

Emergencies occur in our lives, and that is something that we all come to live with. Webster defines emergency as "an unforeseen combination of circumstances or the resulting state that calls for immediate action." In fact, the words "unforeseen combination of circumstances" mean that "emergency situations" can be a rather subjective term. Persons who are prepared for the unforeseen combinations of circumstances that are certain to occur in their lives may not refer to some of these situations as being emergencies. As this chapter will show, the key to success in handling and treating an emergency situation is good prior planning. This planning involves, first, working to "see" these unforeseen combinations of circumstances that call for immediate action and, second, putting the foundation and systems in place to allow immediate action in a defined, methodical manner when such events occur.

Emergency situations involving hazardous substances are certainly no different from other types of emergencies. Hazardous substances can be released through unforeseen combinations of circumstances at any time. Thus, a building or site owner should have a plan in place for handling emergency situations before they occur.

Planning will ensure that emergencies are dealt with quickly and effectively and with the least disruption possible. Specific containment or cleanup procedures will vary according to the type of substance involved. However, the organization and approach are the same for all environmental emergencies.

The building owner's emergency plan should first recognize that circumstances will occur that call for immediate action and then list all steps, procedures, and methods that will be followed to bring the event under control. Additionally, any emergency plan should contain contingencies for handling the expected adverse publicity that will surround any release of contaminants into the environment. Through the establishment of specific emergency procedures, an emergency situation can often be quickly down-graded into a well-managed, orchestrated series of events.

§ 12.2   Prior Planning

Prior planning is essential to the success of any environmental manager. Planning is done by building managers and the building owner. Through proper prior planning, emergency situations can be confronted as though they are expected, intended events, and can be handled in an expeditious fashion.

Planning is done in two general ways. It should be designed (1) to antici-pate any and all combinations of events and circumstances that may lead to a state of emergency; and (2) to lay out procedures and practices in the event of an emergency.

Environmental contaminants should be managed in place, with an eye toward what could happen to release these contaminants to the environment in an uncontrolled, excessive fashion. Further, because emergency situa-tions will still undoubtedly occur, the planning of specific emergency proce-dures will serve to eliminate any additional, unnecessary hazardous expo-sure beyond the event giving rise to the emergency. For example, the owner of an oil storage tank farm should anticipate and plan for the following types of environmental emergencies:

- A major oil spill at the tank truck loading station;
- A tank rupture resulting in a major spill at the tank;
- A fire or explosion at the tank truck loading station;
- A fire or explosion at or involving one of the tanks;
- A loss of electrical power alone or associated with another emergency which incapacitates pumps and loading and transfer stations as well as certain emergency systems;
- Contamination of the underground water table from a leak or spill of oil;
- If the tank is close to a roadway, railroad, or airport, an accident caused by a vehicle, train, or airplane, which may be a high possibility;
- Earthquakes or other natural disasters like tornadoes or hurricanes, to which the area may be prone.

The owner of a commercial office building should anticipate and plan for these types of environmental emergencies:

- A water leak (roof leak or pipe rupture) that causes asbestos to delami-nate from structural members or the ceiling;

- An electrical fire in the transformer room, involving PCBs (polychlorinated biphenyls) (PCBs when burned produce dioxin and polychlorinated dibenzofurans (PCDF), a highly toxic compound);
- A steam pipe explosion causing widespread asbestos contamination;
- An unexpectedly high incidence of sickness, disease, or even death among office workers, caused by indoor air quality problems (e.g., carbon monoxide, legionella, and bacteria);
- A building fire that causes widespread asbestos fiber release from both the fire and firefighting techniques;
- An underground storage tank leak;
- Water table contamination caused by a toxic chemical spill on an adjacent property;
- Lead poisoning of the building's drinking water supply, caused by deterioration of lead solder joints in the building's water supply lines.

§ 12.3   Establishment of an Operations and Maintenance (O&M) Plan

The first step in implementing a plan to handle emergencies is the establishment of an operations and maintenance (O&M) plan. The O&M plan is adopted and implemented in facilities and buildings where there is a presence of a hazardous substance and the building owner chooses to maintain the substance in place.

Asbestos is an example of a hazardous substance that can be maintained in place, and an asbestos O&M plan is recognized by the EPA as an acceptable temporary alternative to removal. In fact, the EPA has published a guidance document for building owners who wish to manage asbestos in place.[1]

Another example of a hazardous substance that can be managed in place is PCBs. Federal law requires that PCB-containing equipment must be properly labeled, visually inspected every 3 months, and registered with the local fire department.[2]

The O&M plan consists of several key elements including: (1) a thorough survey, (2) training, (3) notification, (4) labeling, and (5) the creation of a site-specific O&M manual.

---

[1] EPA, Managing Asbestos in Place—A Building Owner's Guide to Operations and Maintenance Programs for Asbestos Containing Materials, No. 20T-2003 (July 1990).

[2] See 40 C.F.R. § 761 and 47 Fed. Reg. 37,342 (Aug. 25, 1982).

§ 12.4 —Survey

The O&M plan begins with a thorough survey of the facility or building. The survey will locate the potential contaminant form (i.e., asbestos, PCBs, hydrocarbons, pesticides, heavy metals) and will note its condition.

This information can be catalogued in the form of a written report or electronically through the use of a computerized data base. A proper and thorough survey or environmental audit is essential to the success of any O&M plan.

When the survey locates potential environmental contaminants and notes their condition, the O&M plan will set in place a defined system for dealing with these contaminants over a specific period of time. The survey should be a rigorous, exhaustive search for all potentially hazardous materials. It must be orderly in its progression and thorough in its coverage, and the results of the survey must be reported in an understandable, usable manner.

The environmental survey or audit should be conducted by a team of individuals well-trained in performing surveys of a similar nature. For this reason, most companies will generally look to outside consultants to perform the actual survey and to assist in the development and implementation of an O&M program. The outside consultants utilized should be environmental engineers or industrial hygienists with specific, documented experience in performing environmental surveys and designing O&M and remediation programs.

The environmental survey or audit consists of several elements that together form the basis for a successful O&M program. An environmental audit can take many forms and levels of detail, depending on the purpose for conducting the audit. For establishing an O&M program, the audit must identify all hazardous substances, assess the current condition and potential for release, and identify their location and quantity.

The survey team begins the environmental survey with a thorough record search and review of all accumulated records pertaining to the specific property and the surrounding area.

Typical sources of information for the record search include: original building plans and specifications, county tax records, aerial photographs, property title searches, regulatory agency files (permits, citations), the EPA's CERCLIS data base (which contains 30,000 abandoned sites in the United States),[3] the National Priority List (NPL), Facility Index System (FINDS), Resource Conservation and Recovery Act (RCRA), and notification lists.

---

[3] Cahill and Kane, Environmental Audits (6th ed.), at XIII 6-7 (1989).

The team should collect all original building plans and specifications from the building or facility to be surveyed. These plans and specifications will provide the team with evidence of potential hazardous substances that may be faced during the actual on-site survey.

Original plans routinely give evidence of asbestos-containing materials used in a facility construction, the location of underground and aboveground storage tanks, the location and type of electrical transformers that may contain PCBs, and other pertinent information that allows for better planning of the on-site survey and ensures less chance for errors or omissions during the survey.

Once the environmental survey team arrives on-site, interviews are conducted with superintendents, shop supervisors, maintenance managers, or any persons with complete knowledge of the building or facility, its operations, construction, and past problems. These interviews are perhaps the single most important part of a thorough environmental survey or audit.[4] Through the interview, the auditor can determine what, if any, procedures are currently in place for hazardous substances, what emergency procedures exist, and what the general attitude is in the facility regarding hazardous substances and their control and remediation.

During the walk-through of the building or facility, the environmental survey team should collect samples of suspect hazardous substances (e.g., asbestos, water, PCBs, and lead-based paint) for later laboratory analysis and should make an assessment of the current condition of each hazardous substance or material and an assessment of the potential for uncontrolled, excessive release of these substances, which might create an emergency condition. The assessment of the hazardous substances forms the basis for continuing an O&M plan. The O&M plan should include periodic reassessments that are compared over time to note any deterioration in the condition or disposition of the hazardous substance.

Lastly, the environmental survey team should prepare location drawings that show quantities of all hazardous materials or substances. These location drawings are an important component of both the O&M plan and the emergency procedures manual. During an emergency, the location plan forms the "battlefield diagram" for approaching and addressing the emergency situation. With the diagram, the environmental coordinator can know exactly how to effectively isolate an area to prevent further contamination.

Larger companies may possess the necessary expertise in-house to complete the survey and design the O&M plan without hiring consultants. These firms may wish to hire an outside consultant to complete a third-party review of the survey report and results and to review the final O&M plan. In either case, the involvement of an independent, third-party consultant is important as a quality control measure.

---

[4] *Id.* at IX-13.

This quality control effort is necessary for two reasons:

1. Environmental laws are so wide-ranging and change so rapidly that an expert, outside consultant is necessary to ensure that the company remains in compliance with applicable environmental laws at all times.

2. Because compliance with environmental laws can be burdensome and extremely expensive for a company, the engagement of an outside consultant will show due diligence on the part of the company in identifying and controlling all potential environmental contaminants. Using only in-house personnel to identify environmental contaminants and design remediation programs may appear to be a conflict of interest and self-serving in nature.

The extent of the involvement of an environmental consultant will vary, based on the needs of the company or environmental manager.

The environmental survey report is the foundation for the development of an O&M program, emergency response procedures, and an eventual remediation program. For this reason, the environmental survey report should be a thorough, working document that will assist the building owner in achieving and maintaining compliance with any and all environmental laws.

The environmental survey report should include a discussion of the survey process, an overview of the facility or site surveyed, and a presentation of the findings of the survey, including analytical results of any samples analyzed and the existing conditions noted during the survey, and recommendations for corrective actions. It should also contain copies of or make specific reference to any laws governing hazardous substances located at the facility. The inclusion of these laws is important because it forms a basis for the development of an O&M plan and emergency response plan.

§ 12.5   —Training

After the survey is complete, the environmental manager, and possibly other occupants of the facility or building, must receive O&M training. Training can be provided by the outside consultant retained to conduct the initial survey, or may be provided by one of the publicly available environmental training providers. In either case, it is important that the training cover the basics of hazardous substances involved at the facility, as well as specific training in the methods of control that will be employed at this particular facility.

General, basic training requirements include regulations relating to hazardous substances located at the facility, health effects associated with exposure to these substances, and general maintenance and remediation techniques. The specific training provided will include hands-on measures and other field exercises involving the staff who must work most closely with the hazardous substances as part of any O&M program.

When dealing with asbestos, for example, training for the O&M program will involve classroom and hands-on instruction. Classroom instruction is provided for custodial and maintenance employees or others who are generally likely to come into inadvertent contact with asbestos-containing materials or other hazardous substances, or for persons who have a need to understand the O&M program for asbestos.

The classroom training for an asbestos O&M program includes discussion of the hazards associated with inhalation of asbestos fibers and information on the location and conditions of asbestos-containing materials in the facility, based on the results of the survey. The training concludes with procedures that might be utilized in any emergency situation involving asbestos so as to minimize the potential impact of asbestos exposure.

In the case of asbestos, further hands-on training will be required for maintenance employees who might be required to actually disturb asbestos-containing materials. This training involves dealing with asbestos-containing materials in the performance of their normal occupational duties. For example, the maintenance engineer may be required to replace a leaky valve that is wrapped with asbestos-containing insulation. This O&M training will outfit the maintenance engineer with the proper procedures for safely and effectively removing the asbestos-containing insulation prior to repairing the leaky valve. In some states, this maintenance engineer may be required to pass an examination and receive a certificate before disturbing asbestos.

The building owner may have to purchase some specialized equipment, in order to facilitate the successful operation of an O&M plan. For some hazardous substances requiring special certifications and licensing for handling, the building owner may not purchase specialized equipment required for the O&M plan without first obtaining the necessary licenses and/or certifications. The applicable laws in each state or local community must be checked prior to initiating the O&M plan, to ensure that all elements are in compliance with the existing regulations.

For an asbestos O&M plan, a HEPA-filtered vacuum cleaner, specialized "glove-bag" removal devices, respiratory equipment, and other personal protective gear must be purchased for the persons implementing the O&M plan. Without this specialized equipment, the O&M plan remains just a written document and never becomes implemented to the extent necessary to control the further deterioration or accidental release of asbestos. The training of the maintenance staff, during the hands-on portion, must include the utilization of this specialized equipment. The maintenance staff that will utilize the equipment should participate in simulated exercises using each piece of equipment as it might be used during performance of actual duties or during an actual emergency situation.

§ 12.6   —Notification

Notification is an important part of any O&M plan. This fact has been noted by the EPA in the establishment of worker right-to-know laws.[5]

Building owners of a facility where hazardous chemicals are produced, used, or stored must report to the state Emergency Response Commission that they are subject to the right-to-know laws.[6] Further, any releases of these hazardous chemicals must be reported to the Emergency Response Commission unless the release exposes only persons at the site where the facility is located.[7] The specific requirements for notification of an emergency condition involving a release of a hazardous chemical will be discussed later in this chapter.

Any owner of a facility who is required under OSHA to prepare and maintain a material safety data sheet (MSDS) for a hazardous substance must submit to the state Emergency Response Commission, the appropriate local emergency planning committee, and the local fire department a copy of such MSDS.[8] Additionally, the owner must submit a hazardous chemical inventory form to the Emergency Response Commission, the local emergency planning committee, and the local fire department, and must update these forms annually.[9] These annual inventory forms must estimate the maximum amounts of specific chemicals present at any one time during the prior year and specify the locations of these chemicals within the facility.

Under the right-to-know laws, a "hazardous chemical" is defined by reference to a list published in OSHA's hazard communication standard.[10]

Even if an environmental containment does not fall under SARA, all persons in a building or facility should be notified regarding the presence of a hazardous substance if there is a possibility that they may come into contact with or accidentally release these hazardous substances. Notification can occur through dissemination of memoranda or through verbal presentations. The actual wording of the notification or the presentation should be reviewed with both legal counsel and a public relations expert. It is important that this notification meet all of the legal and regulatory

---

[5] 42 U.S.C. § 11001 et seq. (1987).

[6] 42 U.S.C. § 11002(c).

[7] 42 U.S.C. §§ 11002(c), 11004(a) and (b).

[8] 42 U.S.C. § 11021.

[9] 42 U.S.C. § 11022.

[10] 42 U.S.C. § 11021(e).

requirements without creating unnecessary panic or concern among building and facility occupants.

Some environmental contaminants, such as asbestos, do not fall under the notification requirements of SARA. However, in the spirit of the right-to-know laws, the building owner should provide this notification.

If the notification is provided properly and in an open and honest fashion, it probably will not produce panic within the building or facility. Asbestos presents a particularly difficult problem in terms of public relations, because it generally is pervasive in a building, having been applied to structural members and/or ceilings throughout the entire facility. In cases such as these, the building owner may choose to notify all occupants of the building regarding the presence of asbestos to ensure that these occupants do not disturb the ACM, thereby releasing potential hazardous fibers.

If the ACM is located above a suspended ceiling or behind some other type of partition, the owner may choose to notify only those persons who work near the asbestos or whose work would require that they go behind the partition or above the suspended ceiling. This would mean that the owner might choose to notify such persons as telephone technicians, computer technicians, electricians, plumbers, and air-conditioning service people.

§ 12.7 —Labeling

An important part of notification strategy involves labeling of objects or areas that may contain hazardous substances. The labels should be used to identify hazardous materials or substances so that they can be distinguished from nonhazardous materials. As noted earlier, federal law requires labeling of certain hazardous substances, including PCBs, in use in the facility or building. The purpose of labeling is to alert uninformed persons of the presence of a hazardous substance. Labels should be designed to be seen and clearly understood. Many different types of effective labels for hazardous substances are commercially available and can be purchased through safety supply houses.

Additionally, the environmental manager may find it useful to prepare a location drawing of potential environmental contaminants if one was not prepared as part of the environmental survey report. This location drawing will note the presence and relative location of any potential environmental contaminant and is an important part of any planning for possible emergencies.

As noted earlier, the environmental engineer or outside consultant retained to provide the environmental survey should provide a location drawing as part of the survey report. Because this is not typically a part of an environmental survey report, the building owner or environmental manager must specifically request and contract for the preparation of this location drawing. The location drawing is an integral part of any emergency response plan, because it gives a quick and clear indication of the location of various environmental contaminants in graphic form. The location diagram will form a kind of environmental contaminant road map for the building or facility. It is important that this location diagram be kept up-to-date as environmental contaminants are removed or relocated throughout the facility or building.

Labeling of asbestos-containing materials is required under the Asbestos Hazard Emergency Response Act of 1986 (AHERA).[11] This law applies only to primary and secondary schools, but is used as a model for other types of buildings. AHERA states that warning labels must be placed immediately adjacent to any asbestos-containing material, to warn persons of the presence of this material.[12] The provisions of the law follow:

763.95 (a) The local education agency shall attach a warning label immediately adjacent to any friable and non-friable asbestos-containing building material (ACBM) suspected ACBM assumed to be asbestos-containing material (ACM) located in routine maintenance areas (such as boiler rooms) at each school building. This shall include:

1. Friable ACM that was responded to by a means other than removal

2. ACBM for which no response action was carried out

763.95 (b) All labels shall be prominently displayed in readily visible locations and shall remain posted until the ACBM that is labelled is removed.

763.95 (c) The warning label shall read, in print which is readily visible because of large size or bright color, as follows:

CAUTION: ASBESTOS, HAZARDOUS. DO NOT DISTURB
WITHOUT PROPER TRAINING AND EQUIPMENT.[13]

For asbestos-containing pipe insulation in a boiler room or mechanical space, the building owner may find it effective to color-code asbestos-containing insulation to distinguish it from non-asbestos-containing insulation. In many facilities, pipe insulating material is color-coded to denote the particular system with which the piping is associated. In this case, the building owner may choose to add a stripe, in addition to the color-coding, to denote an asbestos-containing insulation. A solid color on a particular piping system might indicate a non-asbestos-containing material. Because there are no laws governing the labeling of asbestos in public and commercial buildings, the building owner or the environmental manager is free to

---

[11] Pub. L. No. 99-519. This law amended TSCA to add a new title: Title II—Asbestos Hazard Emergency Response Act of 1986. Actual regulations were issued October 30, 1987, § 40 C.F.R. 763.99 and app. A, B, and D to subpt. E.

[12] 40 C.F.R. § 763.95.

[13] 40 C.F.R. pt. 763, subpt. E, § 763.95; 52 Fed. Reg. 41,855 (October 30, 1987).

use his or her imagination in providing this labeling. It is, however, important to provide a legend that is clearly visible, to denote what the various colors and stripes signify.

§ 12.8 —O&M Manual

The O&M manual is another essential element of any effective operations and maintenance plan. This manual is a written set of procedures to be followed by maintenance and custodial staff who must work around or with hazardous substances. The O&M manual should be a specific document developed exclusively for the operations and maintenance program.

As discussed earlier, the O&M manual can be developed by an outside consultant with specific expertise in environmental engineering or industrial hygiene, or by experienced in-house staff.

The manual should be placed in a three-ring binder or some similar type of binder, and distributed to all persons involved in the operation of the O&M program. The O&M manual becomes the documentation of the environmental coordinator's diligence in maintaining safe conditions within the facility, should any litigation occur. When a three-ring binder is used, the manual can be easily updated and amended as necessary to keep the plan in compliance with any regulatory requirements.

This documentation may be a very important legal document in the face of an emergency situation that releases any contaminant or hazardous material to the environment. The O&M manual should contain all practices and procedures to be used to ensure the safe in-place management of hazardous substances. The manual should also contain a listing of all forms that are to be used and completed by persons participating in the O&M program.

Lastly, the O&M manual should contain copies of all regulatory standards relating to the hazardous materials to be left in place at the facility and addressed through the implementation of the O&M program.

Figure 12–1 is a sample table of contents for an O&M manual developed for asbestos-containing materials. An O&M plan for other types of hazardous materials would not be significantly different in format. However, the content of the manual and the work practices should be specific to the type of material and the particular building or site as well.

§ 12.9 Name an Environmental Coordinator

Perhaps the most important step in proper prior planning for emergency situations is to name an environmental coordinator for the facility, site, or building. This environmental coordinator is key to the success of any O&M

OPERATIONS AND MAINTENANCE MANUAL

Table of Contents

Overview
  Purpose
  Scope
Facility Description
  Materials Included in Program
  Location Drawings
Implementation of Program
  Inspection and Assessment
  Work Practices and Procedures
    Asbestos Control Techniques
    Materials and Equipment Needed
    Waste Storage and Disposal
    Procedures for Surfacing Materials Spray-Applied or Trowelled-on
  Material
    Plaster Material
  Procedures for Thermal System Insulation
    Repair of Pipe Joint Insulative Compound
    Repair of Material on Boilers and Tanks
    Glovebag Removal
  Procedures for Miscellaneous Materials
    Ceiling Tile: Removal and Replacement
    Floor Tile Removal
    Vibration Isolator Removal
  Notifications and Warnings
  In-house Asbestos Operations & Maintenance
  Staff
  Employee Training
  Medical Surveillance
  Periodic Monitoring (Air and Visual) and Reinspection
  Recordkeeping
Initial Survey and Evaluation Report
  Hazard Assessment
  Sample Results
  Location Drawings of ACM
Appendices
  A. Forms
    1. Periodic Surveillance Report
    2. Worker Medical Surveillance
    3. Operations and Maintenance Activities
    4. Asbestos Work Order
    5. General Work Authorization
    6. Asbestos Abatement Project Notice
    7. Asbestos Disposal Document

Figure 12–1. Sample contents listing for O&M manual.

   8. Assessment Factors Form
   9. Bulk Sampling Record Form
  10. Air Monitoring Record Form
B. Regulatory
   1. NESHAP
   2. OSHA 1910.1001
   3. OSHA 1926.58
   4. OSHA 1910.134
   5. RCRA
   6. CERCLA
   7. Worker Protection Rule
   8. Asbestos in Schools Rule
   9. AHERA
C. Guidance
   Managing Asbestos in Place—EPA 20T-2003
   Guidance for Controlling Asbestos-Containing Materials in
     Buildings—EPA 560/5-35-024

Figure 12-1. *(Continued)*

plan and is therefore absolutely necessary for the successful disposition of any emergency situation.

Generally, the environmental coordinator is chosen from existing staff and given the coordinator function as an extra duty. The environmental coordinator may be the chief engineer of the building or facility or may be the resident manager. Qualifications for the individual to be named environmental coordinator are good organization and leadership skills and a curiosity and enthusiasm for taking on new responsibility. Necessary training regarding the particular environmental hazards to be addressed can be obtained from a variety of sources and is as important as the organizational and leadership skills.

Training for the environmental coordinator can be given by the consultant utilized to provide the environmental survey and develop the O&M plan, or may be obtained from one of several publicly available environmental training courses. The training for the environmental manager should be an executive-style training that discusses the regulations that apply to all of the various hazardous substances located at the building or facility, the health effects associated with exposure to these substances, the legal liabilities involved in maintaining these potential hazardous substances in place, the property transfer requirements when hazardous substances are present at the property, and the insurance exclusions associated with hazardous substances and pollutants.

Some sophisticated or large facilities may find that the position of environmental coordinator is a full-time job. In these cases, management should seek an individual who has an industrial hygiene, safety, and engineering background to fill the position. No specific licensure or certification

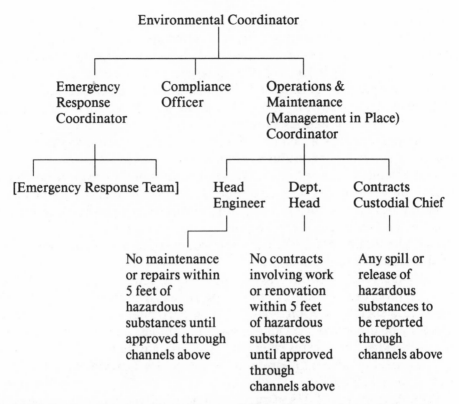

Figure 12-2. Organization chart of responsibilities for hazardous substances.

requirements apply to the environmental coordinator position. The environmental coordinator should be the key for any planning or implementation regarding hazardous substances. He or she must be at the top of any management chart involving hazardous substances and should be notified or consulted anytime an individual's work progress may involve contact with asbestos, PCBs, hydrocarbons, pesticides, or heavy metals. (See **Figure 12-2** for an example of an organization chart.)

The environmental coordinator will be responsible for the establishment of the O&M plan and all emergency procedures, and will establish daily management procedures for working in and around these potential environmental contaminants.

§ 12.10   Emergency Procedures Manual

The environmental coordinator, as part of any O&M plan, should develop a detailed and specific emergency procedures manual. This emergency procedures manual should be distributed to all persons who may be involved in the remediation of any emergency situation. The emergency procedures manual is a set of plans for dealing with accidents quickly, effectively, and decisively when they occur. Because of the specific, unique procedures required to act calmly in the face of an emergency, the emergency procedures manual should be an entirely separate manual from the O&M manual.

As seen in **Figure 12–1**, an O&M plan includes procedures for handling minor emergency situations. However, the emergency procedures section of the O&M manual is a condensed version of the information given in a complete emergency procedures manual.

The emergency procedures manual should contain an introduction, a definition of an emergency condition, a list of contacts if an emergency situation develops, a series of operating forms (developed in checklist format) to be completed when responding to an emergency situation, and specified containment and cleanup procedures for any emergency release of an environmental contaminant.

The emergency procedures manual should detail a containment and cleanup procedure for any hazardous substance. The manual should be divided into specific sections, one for each particular hazardous substance that may be present at the facility, site, or building. The manual must contain a checklist for asbestos emergencies, a separate checklist for PCB emergencies, and the same for hydrocarbons, pesticides, heavy metals, and other hazardous substances.

Prior distribution of this manual to all persons who might be involved in the emergency procedures will ensure that these persons are knowledgeable about the specific and detailed procedures that will be followed to clean up and contain the environmental hazard. Further, the training that occurs as part of the O&M plan provides some training in the handling of emergencies.

Emergency training should be conducted in the form of simulated accidents, rather than just a review of the emergency procedures manual. During the training, the participants are placed in a simulated emergency situation involving a hazardous substance at the facility. The participants should follow the steps outlined in the emergency procedures manual in order to bring the emergency condition under control.

This type of training also provides great help in assessing the quality and workability of the emergency procedures manual. The simulated accident is the best and probably the only way to test the manual's effectiveness.

§ 12.11   —Asbestos Emergency Checklist

As noted above, the operating forms of the manual should be developed in a checklist-type format. The checklist format is much easier and more effective to deal with than a paragraph format, when working in the face of an emergency. The checklist format can be followed from top to bottom or across the page, checking off each item or requirement as it occurs or is fulfilled. **Figure 12–3** shows a sample checklist.

§ 12.12   Phone Tree and Emergency Contacts

Undoubtedly, an important first step in handling an emergency situation involving an environmental contaminant will be the emergency contact or phone tree procedure. The emergency contact procedure should be detailed in the emergency procedures manual and its implementation should be quick and thorough. The emergency contacts procedure is designed to inform all persons who will be involved in the remediation of an emergency situation as quickly as possible.

The emergency contacts procedure should begin with the environmental coordinator. An emergency situation involving a hazardous substance may be noted by a worker but the worker should immediately contact the environmental coordinator, who will begin the emergency telephone contacts or phone tree procedure. **Figure 12–4** shows an outline of a typical phone tree.

As discussed earlier, when an emergency situation involving a hazardous substance occurs, the worker immediately makes contact by phone or in person with the environmental coordinator. The environmental coordinator then begins the emergency contacts or phone tree procedure.

Date: _____   Area (sq. ft.) Involved _____
(for each emergency)

Location: _____   Brief Description: _____
                                                           _____
                                                           _____
                                                           _____

I. Notification (Y, N, or N/A)   Notes:
   Phone Tree Started   ____   _____
   Emergency Response   ____   _____
   Team Contacted   ____   _____
   Regulatory Contacted   ____   _____
   Emergency Contacted   ____   _____
   Legal Contacted   ____   _____
   P.R. Contacted   ____   _____
   Insurance Contacted   ____   _____

Figure 12–3. Sample checklist for asbestos emergency.

Public Notification
    Made   ____

II. Isolating the Area (Y, N, or N/A)
    Traffic Stopped   ____
    Proper Signage   ____
    Critical Barriers
       Established   ____
    Negative Pressure
       Established   ____
    Decontamination
       Established   ____

III. Work Practices (Y, N, or N/A)
    Material Worked Wet   ____
    HEPA Vac Used   ____
    Prompt Bagging of Waste ____
    Water Filtered or Bagged
       (Circle)   ____
    Showers Functioning
       and Used   ____
    Material Not Dropped
       Over 4 feet   ____
    Proper PPE Used   ____
    Type _____

IV. Final Clearance (Y, N, or N/A)
    Wet Wiping/HEPA Vac
       Complete   ____
    Lockdown Encapsulant
       Applied   ____
    Final Air Test Complete   ____
    Critical Barrier Removed ____
    Decon Removed   ____
    Area Reopened   ____

V. Waste (Y, N, or N/A)
    Properly Packaged   ____
    Properly Labeled   ____
    Transported to Landfill   ____
    WSR Received   ____

Name: _____   Signature: _____

Figure 12–3. *(Continued)*

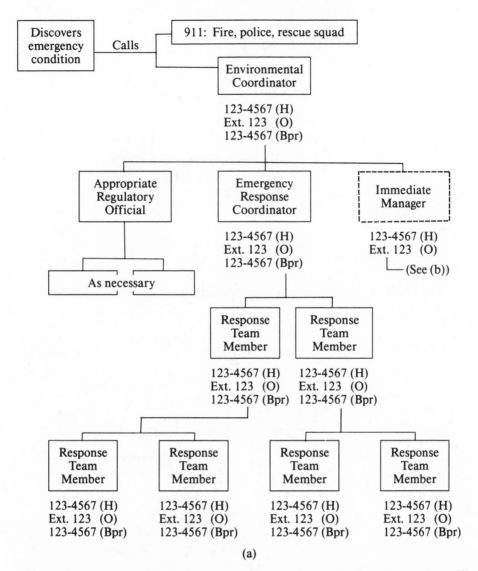

(a)

Figure 12–4. Emergency response phone tree: H = home phone; O = office extension; Bpr = beeper number.

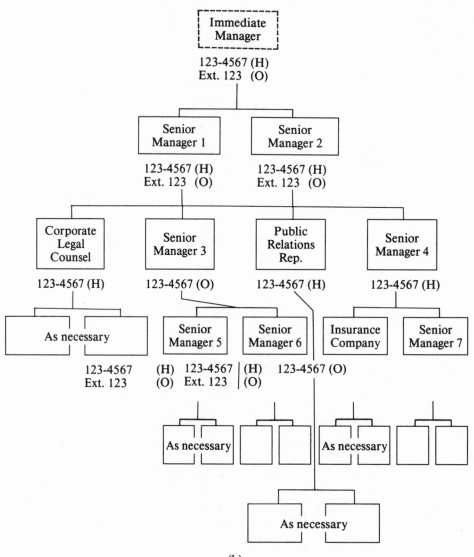

(b)

Figure 12–4. *(Continued)*

The general rule for an effective phone tree is that one person contacts two other persons.

If persons on the phone tree cannot be contacted, the initiator of the phone call must contact the two other persons beneath the unreachable party on the phone tree. For the emergency contacts phone tree to be effective, it is important that all persons involved in the phone tree provide a list of phone numbers or locations where they can be contacted at all times. Many environmental coordinators find that beepers or other paging systems are particularly effective for emergency contact procedures. If an individual included on the emergency contacts phone tree is to be unreachable for any period of time, the environmental coordinator should be informed regarding this absence, and should inform other affected persons on the phone tree.

Regulatory officials, as appropriate, are included as part of the emergency contacts procedure. It is important that, in dealing with any emergency situation, appropriate regulatory officials are contacted as soon as possible.

This contact should be made quickly, for two reasons: (1) the regulatory officials may possess specific expertise that can help in dealing with the emergency situation and, it is hoped, in ensuring its successful remediation; (2) early notification of the regulatory official serves to show that the company or firm is decisively and effectively discharging its duties involving a hazardous substance and may result in some leniency involving citations for violations of environmental regulations.

The emergency contacts or phone tree procedure will also include other persons who will ultimately become involved in the emergency situation. These persons might include: police and fire departments, a rescue squad, attorneys, senior management of the company, public relations experts, and others. Each of these persons will ultimately have a part in the emergency situation. If not involved in actually remedying the emergency condition, these persons will be involved after the emergency in some way. Later in this chapter, the notification of these persons and the roles they will play are discussed in detail.

§ 12.13   When an Accident Occurs

Through proper planning and thorough training, when an accident occurs, the emergency procedures plan will methodically be called into action. The first response in most emergency situations is hysteria. Through the planning and training process, the hysterical response should be kept to a minimum. The environmental coordinator can still expect a general heightened awareness from those people involved with or close to the event giving rise to the emergency; however, through the subsequent implementation of the procedures of the emergency response plan, the event can be rapidly downgraded to a manageable set of priorities and procedures.

§ 12.14   Execution of Plan

The complete and proper execution of the emergency procedures plan is extremely important in the initial stages of any emergency situation. The emergency plan should have been practiced and rehearsed enough times so that execution of the plan is second nature to those persons involved with the emergency.

Emergency preparedness drills and education are essential to the successful execution of the plan. Companies should have emergency training sessions at least once each quarter, to ensure that all employees involved in emergency response plans fully understand their function during an emergency. As soon as the emergency occurs, the environmental coordinator and others must begin execution of the emergency plan to bring the emergency situation under control and to eliminate the possibility of any unnecessary contamination or injury.

As soon as an emergency situation arises, the emergency phone tree procedure goes into effect. This important first step starts every other process and informs all necessary parties of the emergency.

§ 12.15   Locating the Problem

The next step in the execution of the emergency plan is to locate the problem, or the source of the accident. One example of an emergency situation might be a rupture of a water main wrapped with asbestos-containing insulating materials. The rupture of the water main will cause large quantities of asbestos-containing insulation to come off of the water main and to be washed away into the environment. If the water main is buried beneath a street, the water and the asbestos-containing debris will eventually find their way to the street surface.

When the emergency is created by the presence of the asbestos-containing material in the street or in the environment in an uncontrolled fashion, this type of asbestos-containing material can easily become airborne, thereby exposing large numbers of people to dangerously high quantities of asbestos fibers in the air.

In this situation, locating the problem might be particularly difficult. Having been informed of asbestos debris or an apparent water leak, the environmental coordinator for the water supply system and other technicians must set about finding the source of the contamination problem or the rupture in the water main.

Depending on the age and complexity of the water supply system, there are a number of methods for locating or isolating the source of the problem or the rupture in the water main. A change in pressure along the water main will help to locate the problem, or simply tracing water and asbestos-containing materials back to the source may be a simple way of locating the problem. Some water supply systems have sophisticated pressure-monitoring stations which can be used to locate not only ruptures, but small leaks. Other, older systems must be traced using the indicators of asbestos and water.

§ 12.16 Isolating the Area

The third step in the execution of the emergency plan is isolating the area. In the example of a rupture in the water main releasing asbestos-containing insulating materials into the environment, once the problem is located, the area surrounding the problem must be isolated. This means that water flow should be shut off or diverted from the area of the rupture in the water main. This action will be performed by technicians associated with the water supply authority. The surrounding area and areas affected by the asbestos-containing insulating materials that have been washed away should be isolated so that repair and cleanup procedures can begin. Assuming, in this example, that the rupture in the water main occurred beneath the street and water and asbestos-containing debris were washed to the surface of the street and affected an area two blocks away from the actual rupture site, the entire two-block area should be cordoned off by police, fire, and rescue personnel, or by water supply authority personnel, so that people are not unnecessarily exposed to elevated asbestos fiber levels in the air.

The isolation of this area would occur in two distinct stages. The first stage would be isolation of the area immediately adjacent to the rupture of the water main, and the second would be the isolation of the entire two-block area affected by the rupture of the water main.

The area closest to the rupture of the water main is likely to have the greatest degree of asbestos contamination, because the water main was insulated with asbestos-containing materials that were the actual source of the asbestos contamination. Thus, this area will be isolated and in fact might require a complete containment system utilizing negative air and other engineering controls in order to successfully clean or abate any asbestos hazard.

The surrounding two-block area, having also been affected by the release of asbestos-containing materials, is also isolated. However, it is not practical to place a containment around this entire two-block area. Thus, the area should be cordoned off to block passage of pedestrian or vehicular traffic into the area until the asbestos-containing debris can be cleaned up by workers.

§ 12.17   Cleanup of Environmental Contamination

Once the area surrounding the source or cause of the environmental problem has been isolated, then the cleanup procedures can begin. This cleanup should begin as soon as possible after isolation of the area, and should continue at a vigorous pace continually until the affected area has been decontaminated of the hazardous substance. Every environmental emergency has its own set of cleanup procedures and disposal requirements. In the case of the example given, asbestos-containing debris in the two-block area surrounding the rupture in the water main would be collected by properly outfitted and licensed asbestos workers, and placed into asbestos disposal bags. Proper outfitting involves respiratory protective devices and full-body protective clothing. These bags filled with asbestos-containing debris are taken to an EPA-approved landfill and buried in accordance with EPA procedures as asbestos-containing waste. Further, the entire area that may have been affected by the release of asbestos-containing material should be properly cleaned using water and brushes, to ensure that no asbestos fibers remain.

At the site of the rupture in the water main, any dislodged asbestos-containing materials are also removed and disposed of as described above. The asbestos-containing insulation remaining on the water main should be patched and repaired to ensure that no further contamination or release of this asbestos-containing material occurs. Lastly, the entire area should be sufficiently cleaned, to ensure that no asbestos fibers remain that could give rise to a contamination problem.

§ 12.18   Notifications

As the execution of the emergency plan progresses, notifications must also be given as part of this plan. At the same time that the environmental coordinator and other technicians are locating the problem, isolating the area, and beginning cleanup procedures, notifications must be given on several different fronts to ensure that appropriate officials are made aware of the environmental problem and that the general public is not unnecessarily exposed. These notifications should occur as part of the phone tree process. However, completion of the phone tree is not necessary before proceeding with efforts to locate the problem, isolate the area, and begin cleanup procedures.

§ 12.19   —Regulatory Notification

Regulatory officials who have jurisdiction over the particular environmental contaminant or system giving rise to the emergency should be notified promptly. Regulatory officials may have emergency procedures or requirements of their own, as well as significant experience in dealing with emergency problems. For these reasons, regulatory officials should receive one of the first notifications made after the emergency is discovered. More detail will be provided later in this chapter regarding notification, contact, and working with regulatory officials and agencies.

Under the requirements of SARA, owners or operators of a facility where a hazardous chemical listed in SARA is produced, used, or stored must immediately report any releases to the state Emergency Response Commission and others.[14] The provisions of the reporting conditions under SARA are extensive and difficult to understand, so great care should be taken in understanding these requirements and reporting promptly and correctly the release of hazardous substances. The notification of any releases must include the name of the chemical or substance released, an estimate of the quantity of material released, the time of the release, the duration of the release, known anticipated health risks associated with the emergency release, appropriate medical advice for exposed individuals, and proper precautions in response to the release.[15]

It is important that the building owner and the environmental manager comply promptly with the reporting requirements under SARA or any other state or local regulations applying to the release of hazardous substances as a result of an emergency. By involving regulatory officials early and completing the necessary reporting requirements, the building owner will find the regulatory officials to be much more cooperative in correcting the problems created by the emergency. Even regulatory officials realize that sometimes emergencies or accidents occur that are beyond the building owners' control. In these cases, a well-practiced and defined emergency procedures plan involving all of the appropriate notification, isolation, and cleanup steps is the best that anyone can hope for.

§ 12.20   —Occupants' Notification

Occupants of the building or area must also be notified as soon as the emergency occurs. Notification of these occupants is part of isolating the area surrounding the emergency condition. For example, if water treatment chemicals used in the building's mechanical system are accidentally spilled, there may be a need to immediately notify and evacuate occupants of the building until the levels of the released or spilled chemicals can be ascertained and brought within safe limits.

---

[14] 42 U.S.C. §§ 304(a) and (b), 11004(a) and (b); *see also* 40 C.F.R. pt. 300, app. D and E.
[15] SARA, § 304(b)(2), 42 U.S.C. § 11004(b)(2).

In the case of spilled hazardous chemicals in the building, it would be prudent for the building owner and/or the environmental manager to immediately notify and evacuate all occupants of the building, to ensure that no unnecessary exposures that might cause injury or even death are allowed to occur.

Even in the event of a chemical or hazardous material release that would not cause immediate injury, affected occupants should be notified as soon as possible, to ensure that no further release occurs, that exposure is limited, and that isolation of the area may begin to prevent contamination of additional areas of the building or areas outside of the building.

Prompt occupant notification should be a priority, to avoid unnecessary exposures and to keep legal liability problems to a minimum.

§ 12.21   —Neighbors'/Public Notification

Neighboring areas and the general public must always be notified regarding an emergency environmental situation. This notification occurs to ensure that persons who are not presently in the area of contamination caused by this accident do not inadvertently stray into an area affected by this contamination. In the example of a chemical spill in a building, after occupants and those immediately affected are notified of the emergency condition, the general public and neighboring community should be notified, to ensure that persons do not enter the contaminated facility or exaggerate the emergency situation further. The notification of neighbors and the general public can occur in conjunction with isolation of the area, to ensure that additional persons are not unnecessarily exposed to the environmental contaminant release.

§ 12.22   —Insurance Companies' Notification

Insurance companies who might be forced to pay a claim for environmental contamination cleanup or damage must also be notified. As with regulatory officials and agencies, insurance companies may have emergency procedures and practices that can be followed, or may have specific requirements that must be followed in order for insurance to remain in force and in effect. Additionally, the insurance company may have loss control specialists who can become involved with other emergency technicians and coordinators to ensure that damage, loss, and injury are kept to a minimum, and to assist in documenting the damages.

Insurance companies have a great deal at stake in the face of an environmental emergency and should be allowed to bring their expertise into the emergency solution process.

§ 12.23   —Attorneys' Notification

Attorneys for the building or property owner or companies or persons who might be liable for any loss or damage because of the environmental emergency should be notified promptly. Attorneys can work with the emergency management teams to provide proper paperwork and follow-up practices and to ensure that liability concerns are addressed during each step of the emergency response plan.

Attorneys are not generally involved in the emergency itself in terms of locating the problem, isolating the area, and cleaning up the contamination caused by the environmental emergency. However, attorneys should be notified and involved in the management process, to ensure that all documentation of appropriate emergency response is in order, in anticipation of future claims from persons who may have been exposed to environmental contamination. For these reasons, it is vitally important that an attorney specializing in environmental law be retained to review the emergency procedures manual as it is developed.

§ 12.24   —Others

Depending on the type of environmental emergency encountered, a host of other persons might be part of a notification procedure as well. These might include community boards, condominium associations, and hospitals. The emergency procedures manual should discuss in detail which persons, agencies, or groups of people will be involved in a notification process, given each type of environmental emergency that might occur. Additionally, the environmental coordinator who is involved in an emergency situation will find that, by notifying regulatory agencies, occupants, the general public, insurance companies, and attorneys, these persons will have additional insight as to who else should be notified regarding the emergency situation.

§ 12.25   Handling Regulatory Agencies

The regulatory agencies are an important asset in remediating an environmental emergency. However, if proper contact and communication are not established with regulatory authorities or agencies, they may in fact become more of a liability in the total effort than an asset. A regulatory agency's normal role is one of being a "watch dog" over its regulations. However, in the face of an emergency, it is important that the help and expertise of a regulatory agency is enlisted, rather than having an agency in a position to find fault with the decisions and actions of the building owner.

Therefore, working with and handling regulatory agencies is a very important part of the emergency process. Environmental coordinators and those who would be involved in any emergency management team should work and practice their involvement with regulatory officials to ensure that, in the event of an emergency, communications will flow freely with the regulatory agencies having authority over the particular environmental situation. In fact, the regulatory agency should be made aware of the existence of a written emergency plan and the procedures and practices that have gone into emergency preparedness.

This can be done by calling the appropriate regulatory official and scheduling a meeting with the official during a visit to the building or facility to review the plan. This little bit of public relations goes a long way in establishing a solid working relationship. Having made previous contact with regulatory agencies and officials will help immensely when emergency communications become necessary.

Regulatory agencies and officials should never be strangers to any environmental coordinator. Thus, efforts should be made well before the occurrence of an emergency to make contact with and become familiar with appropriate regulatory officials and agencies who might become involved with any environmental emergency.

§ 12.26 —Making Contact

As discussed earlier, the regulatory agency should be one of the first persons contacted in the event of an environmental emergency. This contact should be made promptly. It should be in verbal form, either by phone or in person, and should be made only to the regulatory official who has been the contact point previously, or a higher ranking official at the agency. In fact, the regulatory agency should probably be part of the phone tree so that contact is made promptly.

§ 12.27 —Acknowledging Possible Violations

Once contact is made with the regulatory officials, the extent of the emergency situation involving a hazardous substance should be discussed honestly and completely. The person making contact with the regulatory official should not mention or use the word "violation" but should discuss honestly the extent of the emergency situation. Fault should not be discussed at this time, and should only be discussed after consultation with legal counsel. The party at fault is not important in handling an emergency situation in an expeditious and complete fashion.

In the case of the rupture of a water main releasing asbestos-containing insulation to the environment, the regulatory agency should be informed immediately regarding the cause of the emergency, if it is known, and the extent of the hazardous substances expected. The release of this asbestos-containing material would likely be a violation of the National Emission Standards for Hazardous Air Pollutants (NESHAP). This potential violation should not be discussed with the regulatory official; however, the extent of the emergency must be fully disclosed. Discussions of violations or fault can occur at a later time, through legal counsel, after the emergency is under control.

By informing the regulatory agency of the extent of the problem, the fact that a violation may have occurred is implicit in the discussion. Thus, it is not necessarily important that the regulatory official be told that the emergency situation places the owner or operator in violation; however, the extent of the possible or projected environmental contamination should be communicated completely and honestly.

§ 12.28   —Establishing Ongoing Communications for Remediation Efforts

The regulatory agency is likely to have emergency procedures of its own regarding a particular environmental contamination problem faced during an emergency. In addition, the regulatory agency probably has experience and/or training involving emergencies of the type that may be faced. Thus, the environmental coordinator should work with the regulatory agency to establish ongoing communication during the course of the remediation and cleanup efforts. The regulatory agency may in fact have workers and inspectors who can become involved in the remediation effort to ensure that the extent of the contamination is kept to a minimum.

§ 12.29   —Working within "Intent" of Regulations

Often, an environmental emergency situation will exist where regulations regarding control of this environmental contaminant do not apply to the particular emergency or cleanup situation involved. For instance, cleanup and abatement of asbestos-containing materials are regulated but are generally applied to asbestos-containing materials inside buildings. Thus, cleanup of asbestos-containing materials from a street or from the outside of a building may not be specifically regulated. In these situations, it is important, through contact with the regulatory agencies, to work within the intent of the regulations to clean up the environmental problem.

§ 12.30   —Agreeing on Objectives

In initial meetings with officials of any regulatory agency immediately following the discovery of an emergency situation, objectives of the emergency plan and remediation effort should be discussed and agreement reached among all parties. The first objective is to stop any further release of environmental contaminants that could produce injury or other adverse effects, and to clean up any areas that have been contaminated.

However, there are many steps and subobjectives involved in reaching these global objectives. The steps toward achieving normalcy again must be discussed and agreed upon with the appropriate regulatory agencies.

For example, consider that a high-rise office building containing friable asbestos fireproofing material has suffered a fire on a floor midway up the building. The fire has caused much of the ACM to become dislodged, and smoke has carried the asbestos to other parts of the building. Several floors of the building have clearly evident smoke damage that likely has caused an accompanying severe asbestos contamination problem. On other floors of the building further removed from the site of the fire, the visual indicators of smoke damage are not as acute; however, there is still concern over the spread of asbestos contamination.

As soon as the fire is discovered, an emergency plan goes into effect to notify the fire department, evacuate the building, and extinguish the blaze. Subsequent notifications are made to regulatory officials regarding the potential widespread asbestos contamination. Here are some of the questions that remain and that should be discussed with regulatory officials quickly, in order to reach agreement before proceeding:

- How will the building be checked for possible asbestos contamination—with air sampling or settled dust sampling?

- Because there generally are no regulations for "safe" levels of airborne asbestos or content of asbestos in settled dust, what will be established as a safe reoccupancy level?

- What can be done about valuable and important papers and other business and personal items? Can these materials be decontaminated or must they be discarded? Can some of these items be removed from the building promptly, before overall cleanup efforts begin?

- Where should cleanup efforts begin? Should they start on the most contaminated floors or the least contaminated floors?

- Can some floors be reoccupied while other floors are still being cleaned of contamination?

- How will the cleanup effort be coordinated? Will the responsible regulatory agency be actively involved in overseeing the cleanup, or will the agency expect to see only the results of these efforts?

§ 12.31   Handling Public Relations/Media

Any time an emergency occurs involving a hazardous substance, the event is immediately newsworthy. The extent of its newsworthiness depends only on the relative size of the emergency situation. The goal in handling public relations/media associated with any emergency condition is to avoid making news. The important issue in communications involving emergencies is knowing what to say, how to say it, and when to say it.

As with handling the physical aspects of the emergency situation, in order for crisis communications to be effective, all aspects of handling public relations and the media must be prepared for a great deal in advance. The principal elements of an effective, responsive crisis communication plan are:

- Have a prepared, crisis-management public relations (PR) team available to call on for consultation purposes and implementation.
- Have a well-organized, detailed procedure for obtaining factual, up-to-date information on any potential emergency situation.
- Make a list of appropriate spokespersons.
- Conduct training sessions for members of the crisis-management PR team, and identify specific emergency situations that will apply.
- Prepare a detailed section of the emergency procedures manual that deals with public relations in the event of an emergency.

§ 12.32   —Developing Message Points

Message points are the core of any crisis communication strategy. Emergency situations involving hazardous substances are newsworthy because they involve both of the elements used by the media to define news: controversy and change. An explosion, leak, or release of a hazardous substance is a change. The effects of the hazardous substance on the environment or on the persons exposed to the substance are controversial.

It is important that message points be developed as much as possible in advance of the actual emergency situation. Once the emergency occurs, the message points may be refined to specifically address the situation at hand. Message points should be a few (three or four) key and concise points. Conciseness will ensure that the media clearly understand the public relations message that is being given in relation to the emergency situation.

Further, the message points must be provable assertions. In other words, the message points must be clearly backed up by documentable facts and actual conditions.

For example, if the message point of a communication is that the fire from an explosion is under control and a one-square-mile area around the site of the explosion has been evacuated, then the facts must back up the message point.

Message points also provide a focus for the spokesperson communicating the crisis message. When asked questions regarding the emergency situation, the spokesperson can always find "shelter" in the few, concise message points developed for communication of the emergency situation to the public.

§ 12.33 —Selecting a Spokesperson

Selecting a spokesperson or persons for crisis communications must be done in advance of the emergency situation. A list should be made, in the planning stages, of the appropriate persons to address each specific emergency situation that might occur. Individuals selected as spokespersons for crisis communications should be persuasive, credible, and, above all else, well-prepared. In a few situations, it may be appropriate to use a spokesperson from a public relations firm outside of the company involved in the emergency situation. However, in most cases, crisis communications will be made more effective by selecting an in-house spokesperson and providing appropriate training and planning in advance of the emergency situation. The media will find a spokesperson associated with the company involved in the emergency to be more credible.

§ 12.34 —Honesty

Above all else, it is important in crisis communications involving an emergency situation to be honest. Because message points must be provable assertions, or facts that can be verified by independent third parties, honesty is paramount. Media and public reaction to an emergency situation involving a hazardous substance is likely to be generally negative, no matter how well the execution of an emergency cleanup plan is proceeding. However, the public perception of a company's commitment to rectify an emergency situation quickly and effectively rests upon the honesty, or the perceived honesty, of the spokespersons involved in public relations of the event.

Spokespersons who are not honest, or do not use message points that are provable assertions, will find that public perception can very quickly become negative. Honesty must be practiced with good news or bad news. If a situation is bad, the spokesperson should admit that the situation is bad, but go on to describe the measures being taken to bring the emergency situation under control. One of the key message points that would bring great credibility to the spokesperson and the company is the existence of a well-defined and practiced emergency response plan. If a spokesperson, in the face of an emergency, can report that the company has a detailed emergency response plan and has practiced execution of the plan a number of times, the negative aspects of the communication will be diminished.

§ 12.35 Conclusion

Because emergency situations will undoubtedly occur, it is important that appropriate planning be done prior to an emergency, to ensure that emergency situations can quickly be brought under control. The elements of establishing an emergency response plan and dealing with emergency situations are straightforward, common-sense steps. Emergencies are unforeseen combinations of circumstances that call for action. Through advance planning that results in well-organized, detailed procedures for taking immediate action, emergency situations can quickly be brought under control. Thereafter, the release of any hazardous substance can be treated as a foreseen combination of circumstances with procedures in place to handle each particular type of situation.

The environmental coordinator is the key to the success of any plan for dealing with emergency situations. The environmental coordinator must have the support of top management of the company. Planning for emergencies is an "insurance policy" that no company can afford to be without.

CHAPTER 13

CONTRACTS WITH CONTRACTORS

§ 13.1   Introduction
§ 13.2   Selecting a Contractor
§ 13.3   Site Conditions
§ 13.4   Contract Documents
§ 13.5   Compliance with Laws
§ 13.6   Payment
§ 13.7   Observation of Work
§ 13.8   Title to Waste Materials
§ 13.9   Time
§ 13.10   Subcontractors
§ 13.11   Licenses and Permits
§ 13.12   Final Acceptance
§ 13.13   Standard of Care
§ 13.14   Damages for Delays
§ 13.15   Indemnification
§ 13.16   Confidentiality
§ 13.17   Dispute Resolution
§ 13.18   —Arbitration
§ 13.19   —Mediation
§ 13.20   —Rent-a-Judge
§ 13.21   Insurance and Bonding
§ 13.22   Notification and Recordkeeping
§ 13.23   Applicable State Law

§ 13.1   Introduction

This chapter will discuss some of the more significant provisions in contracts with contractors.

The key to limiting or avoiding liability from an owner's or a removal contractor's viewpoint is to have a good, tight contract. Although the National Insulation and Abatement Association has issued a standard work agreement, there is no one standard form contract which is always used for the removal or abatement of hazardous substances.

There are standard contracts which contain some of the necessary boilerplate language. The American Institute of Architects (AIA) Forms 101 and 201 and the National Institute for Building Sciences (NIBS) Model Guide Specifications for Asbestos Abatement in Buildings provide a useful starting point. In addition, the American Industrial Hygiene Association has published its Recommendations for Asbestos Abatement Projects. Contracts vary from project to project and client to client. Thus, riders are frequently attached to these contracts. As many potentially problematic areas as possible should be discussed and resolved prior to executing such a contract, so that problems are avoided later on.

Many people forget that asbestos removal is a construction project which is performed in accordance with detailed specifications and drawings like any other construction work. If these contract documents are not detailed, there will be extra work, extra charges, and disputes.

The biggest problems seem to arise when the scope of work is not clearly defined and there are open questions about the contractor's entitlement to fees. These are two important areas which should be thoroughly discussed and carefully drafted. If for some reason they cannot be nailed down prior to execution of the contract, the parties should state the basis on which the contractor will be paid if a particular contingency occurs. This is probably a more frequent subject of lawsuits than even the quality of the work.

Bids are usually taken from a number of contractors. The one selected should be not only the lowest bidder, but the lowest "responsible" bidder. This means that the contractor's references have been examined and checked out. The firm has had the required experience on similar projects and has the appropriate licenses. The contractor must also be able to provide the required insurance and bonding, if applicable.

Among other things, the contract should address these issues:

1. The equipment to be used;
2. The training level of the personnel;
3. Site security, safety, and who controls the work area;
4. Recordkeeping;
5. Waste disposal;
6. Cleanliness of the site;
7. Insurance and/or a performance bond.

Because disputes may occur even with the most carefully drafted contract, a dispute resolution mechanism—for example, arbitration—should be included in the contract.

Careful attention to the terms of a contract will lessen the likelihood of litigation over the abatement work.

§ 13.2 Selecting a Contractor

Referrals from consultants, trade associations, state and local agencies, and advertising in trade publications are good sources of names of contractors, as well as attorneys in this area. Anyone who has had similar work done is also a good source. In some commercial buildings, there is a list of approved contractors. It is critical that references be given and that someone call the references to verify what work was actually done by the contractor and how the project turned out.

As with consultants, it may be important that the contractor have experience in doing the particular type of project at hand. Someone who typically does abatement work on houses may not be the right person to do an office building asbestos abatement project or a school. Similarly, a contractor who usually works with asbestos removal may not be the best choice for working with other types of hazardous substances such as lead or mercury.

Good management and financial stability are important, especially if the project may last for a long time. The contractor should have the necessary capital to: provide support and staff for the complexity of the project; avoid cash flow problems; and provide the number of trained workers and supervisors who are properly licensed and certified and the necessary equipment.

They should be very familiar with existing and pending laws pertaining to the substances they will be working with. It is not unusual for a law to change during a project. The contractor should be able to discuss this with a client and to negotiate how it may affect the price. Also, asbestos removal abatement is different from underground storage tank leaks or lead-based paint removal, and involves different laws.

Supervisors must meet OSHA Competent Person requirements for training and handling of nine areas of responsibility.[1] Whether the workers the contractor employs are union or nonunion may be important if the project is in a city office building. Clients may look at their employee training, as well as medical, respiratory protection, and industrial safety programs.

The firm's bonding capacity and insurance limits are important. They should be in amounts suitable for the size of the project and with reputable

---

[1] 29 C.F.R. 1926.58, para. (e)(6).

carriers. The policies should name the building owner as an additional insured.

The firm's policies on documenting its work should be reviewed. Records may have to be maintained for 30 years or longer. The firm should have the capacity to do this and the organization to keep accurate records.

The client should be aware of the contractor's arrangements for waste hauling and disposal and documentation of this. Most owners retain title to hazardous waste and liability. Toxic material should be buried in EPA-licensed landfills.

The client should know who the contractor's project representatives and supervisors are and whether they are likely to be involved for the entire project.

§ 13.3   Site Conditions

The first major issue is to define the condition of the site. This is essential so that if the site should turn out to be different from what was represented, the contractor will have a basis for claiming additional fees or the owner can claim additional fees are not justified. From the owner's perspective, the more evidence there is of access to the site, the less likely it is that a contractor will be able to successfully claim additional fees due to hidden conditions. However, hidden conditions are not unusual if the building is older and the plans and specifications are missing or have not been updated. This may also result in an inadequate survey.

Contractors are generally required to inspect the site and represent that they are familiar with its condition. This places a burden on them for any undiscovered or concealed conditions. Usually they must advise the client of any differing or changed site conditions before the contract is signed. The contractor may want to limit its potential exposure to concealed conditions which are materially different from those a contractor would *reasonably* expect.

If the change is so substantial, it may even call for rescission of the contract. There may also be grounds for a contractor to sue the owner for misrepresentation, if the contractor finds a lot more asbestos insulation, for example, than was indicated in the contract documents and there is no provision for increasing the fee and on what basis.

The contractor should be allowed adequate access to the site. Although the contractor has a duty to inspect the site and find discoverable conditions, "extraordinary means" do not have to be used to make this determination. The contractor should avoid having to inspect subsurface and concealed areas. This lessens an argument that contractors have a duty to perform these inspections and do work that may be materially different from the conditions a contractor would reasonably expect to encounter.

Thus, furniture and equipment should be out of the way and building systems should not interfere with the work.

The contractor may also want to provide that it will not take responsibility for any toxic substances in the building, other than what it has been hired to deal with. In the course of asbestos removal, for example, PCBs, lead, benzene, and other hazardous substances may be present. An asbestos abatement contractor may only want to deal with asbestos. If other substances are found, the contract may have to be amended or another contractor be brought in. This may also be significant because it could void a "no damage for delay" clause. It may mean that the owner's representations in the contract documents were not accurate. The contractor may not be able to proceed with work, which can create other problems.

It is prudent to anticipate and provide a means for payment of work due to concealed conditions, since they are likely to be found. The very nature of asbestos and other hazardous substances is such that it can be found above ceilings, behind walls, and in other concealed areas. It may not have been detected for some reason by the engineer who inspected the premises.

§ 13.4   Contract Documents

The drawings and specifications provided to a contractor are part of the contract documents. They must be detailed to show existing facilities, underground and above-ground obstructions, and details of sections showing how problems should be handled at specific locations. The specifications and plans should comply with and incorporate federal, state, and local requirements. Similarly, the contractor should be able to rely on the accuracy of field measurements it is given. If the drawings and specifications are not sufficiently detailed or contain inaccurate information, there may be fee claims by the contractor for additional work.

Sometimes, specifications call for the contractor to make its own investigation of the site, which might include subsurface areas. This places the burden on the contractor to spend its own funds to hire engineers to inspect and interpret data. A contractor should be careful before signing such a clause.

§ 13.5   Compliance with Laws

Contracts usually require contractors to assume responsibility for familiarity and compliance with all applicable laws and regulations. There are laws on the federal, state, and local levels. Cautious contractors may want to require a list in the contract of the statutes they are responsible for complying with.

Contractors may want to limit their agreements to compliance with *current* laws and rules. Owners will want current rules *and* amendments or changes enacted during the contract period to apply.

§ 13.6 Payment

As with any work done by a contractor, fees to be paid should be clearly spelled out. Because this is an area in which hidden conditions are likely to crop up, parameters for additional fees should be clearly stated. Payment should be linked to the amount of work completed rather than to a period of time. This is usually monitored by the architect, a construction manager, a consultant, or a property manager on behalf of the owner. Applications for payment will be reviewed and approved based on the amount of work completed.

All change orders increasing or decreasing the work should be in writing and signed *before* the work described in them is undertaken. Unfortunately, often work is done without a signed change order and disputes can later arise as to what is owed.

All payments to the contractor should be minus a retained sum, which is held until final completion (i.e., retainage). This is usually 10 to 15 percent of the payment due.

An implied contract was created when a subcontractor gave a price for removal work to a general contractor and the general contractor did not object. The court found that, if the general contractor did not agree, he should have objected and prevented the subcontractor from performing the reinsulation work.[2]

This area is fraught with potential for disputes, unless it is fully negotiated. If more work is discovered than was originally contemplated, disputes may arise as to whether, in fact, it was part of the original contract and thus part of the base contract price or is additional work. This is why careful examination of the site and specifications is so important.

A per-square price can be good for a contractor because it is quantifiable and can be increased if more work is discovered. Most clients prefer a fixed price.

---

[2] Western Insulation Services, Inc. v. Central National Insurance Co. of Omaha, Minn. Ct. App., No. C0-90-162, 9/18/90; Asbestos Abatement Report, Oct. 15, 1990, at 6.

§ 13.7   Observation of Work

Although the contractor will have its own supervisor, it is recommended that a consultant also be retained to supervise, observe, or inspect the work, to ensure compliance with all prescribed work practices and worker protection measures and contract compliance. Some work requires inspections and air testing at least four times a day.

For example, there will be a containment barrier around the entire work area and/or containment bags for wrapped insulation. Workers will wear protective coveralls and respirators. Special facilities will be set up for workers to change and for decontamination. Federal, state, and local laws and regulations must be complied with.

This is also important because owners can be responsible for removal violations.

§ 13.8   Title to Waste Materials

It is common for owners to try to require contractors to take title to demolition materials, construction debris, and salvage. Some contracts attempt to require contractors to take title to asbestos waste. However, many courts will not enforce this. In addition, under CERCLA, the generator of the waste is still always directly liable under CERCLA.

§ 13.9   Time

Owners frequently require that projects be completed within a fixed period of time—months, weeks, or days. This is often accompanied by a provision requiring the contractor to pay so many dollars per day for each day the work is behind schedule. This is called a "liquidated damage" clause. The amount of such damages is supposed to be enough to reasonably compensate the owner, but not so much that it is a penalty. Often, when this is used, there is also a bonus for early completion.

Because this work may cause businesses to be delayed in opening, time may be of the essence in completing such work.

§ 13.10   Subcontractors

Owners should know who is working in their building and clients should know who is working on their project. If a contractor uses subcontractors, the general contractor should advise the owner of who will be working on this project and obtain the owner's prior approval. This helps ensure that subcontractors are licensed and competent. It also eliminates the possibility of one of them filing a mechanic's lien. In addition, if for any reason the general contractor is terminated from the project, it will be easier to make arrangements to have it completed.

§ 13.11   Licenses and Permits

The contractor should provide evidence to verify that all necessary permits, certifications, and licenses are in order, including certification of the investigator, handler, or supervisor for asbestos work and the licensing by the city or state (or both) of the hauler and contractor.

There may be various forms which need to be filed with federal, state, and local governmental agencies. The contract should specify which filings there are and who will be responsible for filing them.

§ 13.12   Final Acceptance

The basis for determining final acceptance should be clearly stated. A good gauge is following a favorable test for the particular substance involved. Similarly, the point at which retainage and final payment is to be released should be clearly stated. This is usually upon final completion of work and inspection.

The work site should be thoroughly cleaned at least twice and should pass a visual test for abatement completion and cleanliness. It should also pass a test for airborne asbestos. Whatever criteria for final acceptance the parties agree on should be stated in the contract.

The contractor should sign a *waiver of lien* so that no mechanic's liens can be filed against the property, and a *general release* to eliminate any possible lawsuits over unpaid fees. This should be done before final payment is issued.

§ 13.13   Standard of Care

Technology in the environmental area is constantly changing and varies from state to state and even among local areas. Therefore, it is advisable to state the standard of care that must be adhered to by the contractor.

Contractors should avoid agreeing to perform according to the highest and best standards. Their services should be performed in accordance with the relevant standard of care in their profession, in the locality in which the services are being performed, and in the time frame in which they were performed. Contractors will want to avoid extensive guarantees or warranties of work; however, some owners may insist on them.

§ 13.14   Damages for Delays

Contracts frequently prohibit contractors from recovering damages for delay, and such provisions are enforceable. Unanticipated, unforeseeable hazards are outside the application of "no damage for delay" clauses. This may also be true if there are misrepresentations in the contract documents. Finally, if the owner "actively interferes" with the contractor's work and thereby delays the work, a "no damage for delay" clause will not be enforced. Failure to provide a site in a condition to proceed with construction may be "active interference," for example, because additional hazardous substances have been discovered. Therefore, these areas should be addressed to avoid such problems.

§ 13.15   Indemnification

Indemnification clauses are probably the most argued-about clauses in these contracts. Often, these clauses are the barrier between reaching an agreement and not reaching one. Owners occasionally agree to indemnify contractors for work done by others. More often than not, owners require contractors to indemnify them. This clause can be invoked long after the contract work has been completed. However, many states have anti-indemnity statutes that prevent an owner from indemnifying a party against its own negligence as being against public policy, although some statutes allow indemnification for the full amount of the damage. Such a requirement may nullify the entire indemnification clause, or even the contract, if it is not permissible.

Typically, a contractor will agree to indemnify the client or owner for damages caused by the contractor's breach of contract or negligence. This can arise when an employee of the contractor is injured and sues the building owner. The building owner will then bring a third-party action against the contractor for indemnification.

Owners may require contractors to indemnify them against loss, damage, and expense relating to the contractor's performance, whether or not it is caused in whole or in part by the owner. The contractor may only want to indemnify the owner from loss, damage, or expense directly caused by the contractor's breach of contract or negligence.

Contractors may have difficulty in agreeing to indemnify owners because their insurance may not cover them and because they may be responsible for acts of the owner which they cannot control. Limiting liability to a specified dollar amount, such as the amount of fees paid to the contractor, may be a viable option, because liability can well exceed the dollar amount of any contract.

Contractors should be careful to review such clauses for provisions requiring them to pay the owner's litigation expenses. They must decide whether this is a business risk they wish to take.

§ 13.16 Confidentiality

Owners should require contractors to keep their work confidential. This should not be a problem for the contractor, as long as there is an exception for any disclosure compelled by law, court order, or subpoena.

§ 13.17 Dispute Resolution

Most disputes are litigated in court; however, there are some alternative methods for resolving disputes. Arbitration and mediation are the principal alternative methods. The parties can also fashion their own parameters for resolving disputes.

§ 13.18 —Arbitration

Arbitration is a viable dispute-resolution option for most types of contracting work, unless the work involves a CERCLA claim. All CERCLA controversies are within the exclusive jurisdiction of the federal courts. Thus, arbitration is usually not compelled when there is a right of action under CERCLA. An arbitration clause may also make it difficult to join all the parties who may be "deep pockets" in a cost recovery lawsuit. However, because asbestos removal in buildings is not covered by CERCLA, this is a viable dispute-resolution mechanism for that type of work.

Arbitration is usually handled through the American Arbitration Association (AAA), a nonprofit organization. There is a special construction forum for hearing such claims. It is commenced by a demand for arbitration and the filing of a fee. The only catch is that the parties must have an arbitration provision in a signed, written contract in order to invoke this process. It is only in rare instances that the parties will agree to do so voluntarily once a dispute has arisen.

Arbitration's main benefit is that decisions are rendered quickly as compared with the court system. Some view this as a disadvantage because it does not allow extensive discovery. Discovery is limited and is determined by the arbitrator at his or her discretion. It may involve no more than an exchange of documents.

Unless a case is unusually large and complex, the hearings will be completed in a matter of weeks and an award will be issued within 30 days after the hearings are closed.

The award is supposed to be paid within 30 days after it is issued. If this procedure is followed, arbitration works beautifully. If it is not, the process of converting the award into a judgment and collecting on it can sometimes be time-consuming and frustrating, as with any court judgment.

It is also not really appealable, except in cases of fraud or abuse. Generally, the courts do not want to interfere with the process because the parties have selected it as a way to resolve their disputes.

§ 13.19 —Mediation

This method of dispute resolution follows the same basic format as an arbitration hearing, but it is nonbinding. If the parties do not like the decision, they can continue to litigate either by arbitration or in the courts.

Mediation can be handled by the AAA or through private organizations, and the parties can negotiate the parameters of how it will be conducted. Generally speaking, once they complete the process the parties wind up agreeing to abide by the mediator's decision and do not pursue other litigation forums, but they do have the option to do so.

§ 13.20 —Rent-a-Judge

This is another variation on mediation. The parties agree to have a retired judge hear their case and render an opinion, which may or may not be binding, depending on what they agree to beforehand.

A variety of methods can be utilized to resolve disputes, if the parties are so inclined. However, they work best when they are agreed to prior to signing a contract and are incorporated therein.

§ 13.21 Insurance and Bonding

These are two important requirements for a project. However, the limits called for are equally important so that otherwise qualified contractors are not turned away.

Clients should carefully examine the certificate of insurance to be certain that it covers the named party with whom they are contracting and insures the type of services being contracted for. General liability insurance listing the owner as an additional insured may be required. A certificate of coverage should be presented prior to commencement of the work. It should be examined to verify whether it is effective and covers the type of work being done.

There may also be payment and performance bonds. Payment bonds ensure that subcontractors are paid for their work so that they do not file mechanic's liens. Performance bonds ensure that the contractor completes the work and that if it does not, the bonding company will step in and see that it occurs.

§ 13.22 Notification and Recordkeeping

Responsibility for notifying EPA and other governmental agencies should be clearly spelled out, even if it is the contractor's legal responsibility.

Clients and contractors will need records showing the work that was done, copies of the notifications, and manifests. The contractor should be required to keep those records and turn them over to the client upon request or at the end of the project.

§ 13.23 Applicable State Law

Because contractors often work in a number of states and the project may be in a state other than the contractor's principal place of business, deciding which state's law will apply and where disputes will be litigated can be important. If a New Jersey based contractor does work in Michigan for a corporation headquartered in New York, it may not be clear whether New York, New Jersey or Michigan law will apply and which state's court will have jurisdiction. This should be spelled out in the contract.

CHAPTER 14

ASBESTOS ABATEMENT AND MANAGEMENT: A CASE STUDY

Laura J. Kuhman
Building Supervisor

§ 14.1   What Is a Facility Manager?

§ 14.2   Facility and Contractor Philosophy

§ 14.3   Certified Asbestos Training

§ 14.4   Identifying the Asbestos Problem

§ 14.5   An Asbestos Removal Project

§ 14.6   Asbestos Handling Policy

§ 14.7   Communication

§ 14.8   Prequalification of Contractors

§ 14.9   Specifications for Contingency Planning

§ 14.10   The Bid Process

§ 14.11   Conclusion of Project

§ 14.1   What Is a Facility Manager?

As a building supervisor for a gas and electric utility company in the western United States, I am a member of the rapidly growing profession of facilities managers. Facilities management, as defined by the International Facility Management Association which is a professional organization headquartered in Houston, is "the practice of coordinating the physical workplace with the people and work of the organization; it integrates the principles of business administration, architecture, and the behavioral and engineering services."

I am responsible for my company's 320,000-square-foot corporate headquarters facility. The facility's insulation and fireproofing have been identified as asbestos-containing material (ACM).

§ 14.2 Facility and Contractor Philosophy

My facility was opened in 1962, and the insulation contractor did a thorough job. The asbestos insulation is used on the pan and beam structure as well as on hot water lines and steam lines. The insulation is in excellent condition except where past maintenance and construction activities disturbed its surface. These activities occurred before an awareness existed of the possible harm to workers' health from breathing or ingesting asbestos fibers.

Today, my crew understands that I require strict adherence to the rule of thumb: "When you deal with an insulation material, if it has not been absolutely identified as a nonasbestos material, treat it as asbestos!"

Our constantly changing regulations have made my facility management role challenging because each new construction, maintenance, and operations job is analyzed for its possible impact on existing asbestos insulation, and proper handling procedures are identified to ensure the safety of my facility's tenants.

It is my job to know what kind of asbestos exists in my facility, where it is located, its condition, and how executive management wants the asbestos dealt with in various situations. This allows for quick decision and minimizes the possibility of lost productivity time for my tenants/employees due to closures of the facility.

Consultants have been able to provide valuable assistance to me in the collection and evaluation of data. They provide specialized skills and knowledge, and they increase the productivity level of our organization when it is challenged with large multiple asbestos projects. Consultants bring with them a wide variety of knowledge and experience, as well as expertise in their individual area of study. Consultants are able to suggest solutions to problems which are based on the accumulation of their past experiences as well as their knowledge of new practices and regulations.

Normally, contractors have a good working knowledge of various regulatory agencies and can suggest the most expeditious communication and approval processes. In addition, in today's economic environment of doing more with fewer staff members, I find one benefit of hiring a consultant for peak work periods is that, at the end of the project, the consultant is not a full-time member of the workforce and is not receiving pay and benefit packages during slow times.

I contract with consultants to give me advice, but as the Facility Manager, I feel I too must have sufficient knowledge to know how to act upon the advice I am given. Because I have done my homework and have acquired a sound, basic working knowledge of asbestos, I feel I am in a good position to identify the expertise required to assist in the development of a corporate philosophy for an asbestos management program.

§ 14.3 Certified Asbestos Training

I recommend that before a Facility Manager initiates an asbestos management program, he or she should attend certified asbestos worker and supervisor classes. Local training classes can be found in the Yellow Pages™ of the telephone directory under Environmental and Ecological Services. The EPA regularly publishes updates in the Federal Register to its "Asbestos-Containing Materials in Schools; EPA Approved Courses and Accredited Laboratories Under the Asbestos Hazard Emergency Response Act."

It is mandatory that the training organization be certified. EPA has defined the requirements for the training classes but has turned over the actual certification to the states.[1]

In Colorado, the certification agency is the Colorado Department of Health, Air Pollution Control Division. The certification and training are consistent with the EPA's Asbestos Hazard Emergency Response Act (AHERA), Colorado Statute 25-7-503, Air Quality Control Commission Regulation 8, and OSHA regulations that pertain to the safety of the workers, workplace, and workers' tools.

The federal government, through the EPA, has stipulated that training must be provided to any employee who is exposed to airborne asbestos in excess of the action level (0.1 fiber per cubic centimeter of air, as an 8-hour time weighted average) for 30 days in any one-year period of time. The regulations are in a constant state of change, and the action level defined above could be altered by the Occupational Safety and Health Act (OSHA) by the time this information is read. The classes will present up-to-date information on asbestos regulations, will explain what asbestos is, will provide training in asbestos management and removal techniques, will describe the health effects of asbestos exposure, and will define the purpose of an active medical surveillance program (the collection of data in a systematic manner on groups of workers exposed to asbestos or other harmful agent).[2] After completing these classes, even an asbestos novice will be able to understand and communicate with experts in the field.

I earned my certification from Hall-Kimbrell Environmental Services. Certification must be renewed annually by attending additional certified classes which bring the attendee up to date on new removal methods and new government regulations.

My company has been extensively involved in asbestos removal and control in our production power plants. Our Production Safety Training organization has established asbestos worker and supervisor classes for our own employees. The classes are certified by the EPA and future employee

---

[1] EPA, Model Accreditation Plan, 40 C.F.R. pt. 763, subpt. E, app. C (Apr. 30, 1987).

[2] OSHA, 29 C.F.R. 1926.58, Construction Standard.

asbestos certification and renewals of existing certifications will be performed by in-house training personnel. As a certified asbestos supervisor,
or competent person ("one who is capable of identifying existing asbestos
hazards in the workplace and who has the authority to take prompt corrective measures to eliminate them"),[3] I gained management support to establish an in-house asbestos removal crew for our office facility in 1986. I kept
the number on the crew small, and each member of the crew earned his or
her own asbestos worker and supervisor certifications.

§ 14.4   Identifying the Asbestos Problem

When routine maintenance and construction jobs caused insulation to be
disturbed or the opening of a ceiling tile revealed insulation on the ceiling
surface, a member of the asbestos crew immediately obtained bulk samples
which were analyzed through independent laboratories.

Careful records were maintained of each sample location on our facility's
structural and mechanical floor plans as well as in an asbestos sampling log
book. My log book was separated into two sections, one for air monitoring
and one for bulk sampling results. The results were filed in the appropriate
section in sequence by date and numbered in sequence. An index was set up
for each section of the log book. By looking at the index, I could identify a
sample by its date, location, sequence number and final results. Samples of
the index log sheets are found in **Figure 14–1**.

Through this procedure, we soon accumulated detailed records which
related individual sample analyses to individual sample points. The analyses identified three types of asbestos in the facility: chrysotile (white or grey
asbestos), amosite (brown asbestos), and crocidolite (blue asbestos).

Our visual inspections revealed the condition of the asbestos. By condition I mean: Is it friable ("any material containing more than one percent
asbestos by weight which when dry, may be crumbled, pulverized, or reduced to powder by hand pressure")?[4] Is it delaminating (splitting into sections or layers)? Is it a significantly damaged hazard (a severely damaged
area that is widespread)? Is it a potential significant hazard (air erosion,
vibration, or accessibility may lead to future damage)?[5] Or is it performing
its job as intended without contaminating the environment?

---

[3] EPA, Worker Protection Rule, 40 C.F.R. pt. 763, subpt. G (Feb. 25, 1987).

[4] EPA, Worker Protection Rule, 40 C.F.R. pt. 763, subpt. G (Feb. 25, 1987).

[5] *Id.*

Page ____

_____   * ASBESTOS CONTROL

* Identify Air Monitoring or Bulk Sampling Results for each index.

Sample Number	Date	Project	Results
_____	_____	_____	_____
_____	_____	_____	_____
_____	_____	_____	_____
_____	_____	_____	_____
_____	_____	_____	_____
_____	_____	_____	_____
_____	_____	_____	_____
_____	_____	_____	_____
_____	_____	_____	_____
_____	_____	_____	_____
_____	_____	_____	_____
_____	_____	_____	_____
_____	_____	_____	_____
_____	_____	_____	_____
_____	_____	_____	_____

Figure 14–1. Log book index, sample sheet.

§ 14.5   An Asbestos Removal Project

During 1989, the drain from our twelfth-floor cafeteria overflowed. The water spread across the parquet floor and seeped through cracks in the concrete and corrugated metal pan to absorb in the chrysotile insulation on the eleventh-floor ceiling.

The leak from the eleventh-floor ceiling was reported to me on a Friday night by security after our employees had left. The supply and return fans were immediately shut down for the space and our in-house industrial hygienist was called to perform air monitoring.

My log book for bulk samples revealed that beams and pans in the area had tested at 5 to 15 percent chrysotile.

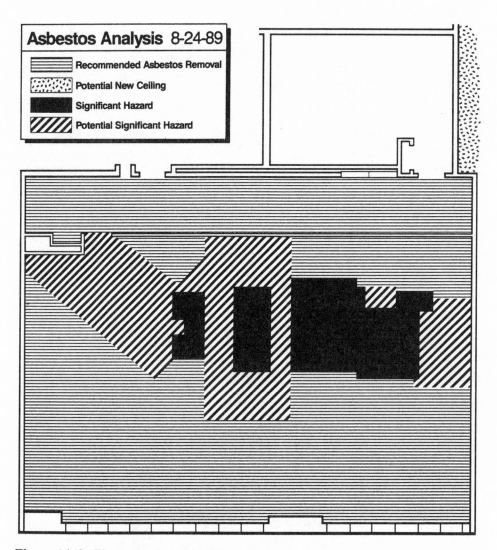

Figure 14–2. Floor-plan "map" of hazardous substance.

An independent laboratory, under contract through our industrial hygienist, was notified that air analyses would be required Sunday morning for a report by Sunday night.

A visual inspection by me along with members of the asbestos crew determined the cause of the leak.

Before the employees were scheduled to return to the work space Monday morning, air monitoring results determined that there was no airborne asbestos and the environment was safe.

Because of my past air monitoring records, I was able to make comparisons of the current analyses with past analyses and be assured that there was no change in background air monitoring results.

To determine the condition of the asbestos and to recommend a course of action for handling the asbestos soaked by the water, a visual inspection was performed by my in-house asbestos crew and me to determine the cause of the leak and the extent of the damage. The information obtained from the inspection was transferred to or "mapped" on an architectural floor plan. I used color codes to identify "significant hazard" locations (red) where asbestos was delaminating from the pan and "potential significant hazards" (yellow) where possible leaks along the drain line which ran through the eleventh-floor ceiling could cause future delamination. **Figure 14–2** represents the final map in black and white with the various areas identified with different symbols.

I took pictures of unusual structural details which would be difficult to construct asbestos removal enclosures around and of building systems which would have to remain intact through an asbestos removal project (i.e., life safety system for fire protection). I maintained a log of each location from which a photograph was taken and I numbered the photographs and identified their location on an eleventh-floor structural plan.

Armed with the knowledge gained through the asbestos inspection and mapping process, I was prepared to recommend an asbestos handling procedure to management which was in harmony with my asbestos policy for the facility.

§ 14.6 Asbestos Handling Policy

I had several objectives when I developed the asbestos handling policy for my facility. Because the asbestos insulation is not friable, I wanted to minimize the disturbance of it. The corporate strategy plan was to relocate the headquarters, and a decision had not been made on how to dispose of my facility. Until a decision was made, I wanted to minimize asbestos handling costs.

Through the use of a simple decision grid/flowchart, management and I came to the same policy decisions. We demanded compliance with existing regulations and we demanded a safe environment for our facility tenants. Answers to fundamental questions, which led in the flowchart to alternate questions and ultimately to action items, were consistent with existing government regulations and handling procedures and formed the basis of our decisions. **Figure 14–3** depicts the index from my decision grid and **Figure 14–4** depicts the flowchart. Because this asbestos decision grid/flowchart was available for use by my management, I had the understanding and concurrence of my management for my decisions relating to the eleventh-floor asbestos project.

I demanded compliance with existing regulations, and I demanded a safe environment for my facility's tenants. I led my management to the same

DECISION GRID
Asbestos Abatement Program
Headquarters Office Building

INDEX

Decision Grid 1
General Building Information (Section 1) 2
Respond to Immediate Needs Only (Section 2) 3
Respond to 1989–1990 Needs Only (Section 2) 3
Respond to 1991 and Beyond Needs for a Secured Building
   (Section 3) 5
Respond to 1991 and Beyond Needs for a Public Access Building
   (Section 4) 7

NOTE:
This recommended decision grid is based
on the information available on
October 12, 1989

Prepared by: Laura J. Kuhman

Figure 14–3. Index for decision grid.

policy conclusions through the use of a simple decision grid/flowchart. I asked simple "yes" and "no" questions, which led in the flow chart to alternate questions and ultimately to action items.

§ 14.7   Communication

As a Facility Manager I am one of the people responsible for the safety of employees, tenants, the public, and the environment. The core of my asbestos management program is communication.

Employees on the eleventh floor were kept informed about the safety of their work environment. This helped to avoid panic. In addition, "Worker Right to Know"[6] legislation clearly requires open, frank communications with facility employees about potential hazards in the workplace just as "Community Right To Know"[7] legislation demands that members of the community be made aware of potential environmental hazards originating from a facility.

I assured the employees that the air they breathed was in compliance with OSHA, state, and local standards and that air monitoring would

---

[6] OSHA, Hazard Communication Standard, 29 C.F.R. 1910.1200 and 1910.20.

[7] Superfund Amendments and Reauthorization Act of 1986, 42 U.S.C. §§ 9601–9675 (Supp. IV 1986). Pub. L. No. 99-499, 100 Stat. 1613 (1986).

October 12, 1989

DECISION GRID

Asbestos Abatement Program
Headquarters Office Building

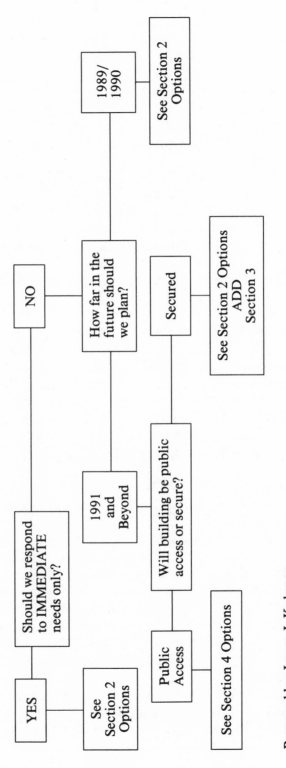

Prepared by: Laura J. Kuhman
This decision grid is based on the information I have available as of this date.

Figure 14–4. Flow chart for decision grid.

continue at weekly intervals. I made the air-monitoring records from our in-house industrial hygienist available to concerned employees.

I explained that approximately 2,000 square feet of asbestos had been identified for removal from the 19,000-square-foot floor. This square footage was identified through the mapping process discussed earlier and was reviewed with regulatory agency personnel for concurrence. I assured management and my tenants that the removal project would be scheduled and planned to minimize impact on their daily operations. A 4-day Thanksgiving weekend was rapidly approaching, and that became my target date for removal.

My biggest concerns were: (1) Could the job be planned so that actual removal could occur while our employees enjoyed their 4-day Thanksgiving holiday? (2) How could I make the achievement of this schedule as important to the removal contractor as it was to me? (3) How could contingency planning guarantee the reopening of the facility on Monday morning even if something went wrong on the eleventh floor?

Before I wrote the specifications and before I initiated communications with my prequalified contractors, I formulated potential answers to the aforementioned questions and talked to our corporation's attorneys, the local regulatory agency personnel, and asbestos removal experts from our Production Division, to obtain their ideas and concurrence with my plans. My contingency plan included the following.

1. The construction of two barriers was indicated. The outer barrier would be constructed the weekend previous to the Thanksgiving holiday and would isolate the inner 2,000-square-foot asbestos removal barrier. I wanted it to be airtight, so the contractor could work during the evening hours before and after the actual removal and it would serve three purposes:

1. Isolation of construction dust;
2. Isolation of contamination if the contractor should have the unexpected occur;
3. Isolation of the reinsulation dust after the removal.

2. A bonus/penalty clause was included in the contract. If the removal was concluded so that the final 24-hour air-monitoring results could be received by 6:00 A.M. Monday morning, and were within regulated limitations, my company would pay a 10 percent bonus. If the contractor did not get the air-monitoring results to me by the deadline, the contractor's payment would be reduced by 10 percent during each 24-hour period the monitoring was late.

3. If the unexpected had occurred and contamination had extended outside the inner removal barrier, my asbestos crew was prepared to isolate the eleventh floor from the remainder of the facility so all employees, excluding those who normally worked on the eleventh floor, could return to

work on Monday morning. Our plan included the isolation of all supply and return fan air plenums, the isolation of all elevator doors and the isolation of stairwells from functioning building air systems. In addition, workspace in alternate locations had been identified for key personnel so that the organization's primary business functions could continue. Had this contingency plan been implemented, the extensive damage to our fan air plenums would have required time-consuming costly repairs, but the entire facility would not have been closed. We estimated that the isolation of the eleventh floor with a 12-person in-house crew would take 6 hours to implement.

§ 14.8   Prequalification of Contractors

Communication with contractors is also important. My contractor selection process was relatively easy, because I had a list of prequalified contractors from which to select. Early in the planning for the corporation's asbestos management program, a communication tool was prepared by our company's Production Division to prequalify contractors by documenting the minimum asbestos handling standards our corporation would accept.

The procedures manual that resulted from this process identified the facilities to which the standards applied and clearly stated our objectives: to comply with federal, state, and local regulations on asbestos; to prevent exposure of employees to asbestos fibers above regulated limits; and to comply with environmental regulations.

All of the standards stated in our prequalification manual were stricter than or equivalent to the federal, state, and local regulations on asbestos. The prequalification manual for contractors also serves as a guideline to all employees who deal with asbestos in our company. It ensures that procedures are consistently enforced throughout the corporation.

Our Production Safety Department personnel were the first individuals in our company to be certified for asbestos removal. Today, our production safety trainers are certified to instruct in-house asbestos workers and supervisors, and these trainers maintain our prequalification manual.

Our manual includes standards for: exposure limits (a company's requirements may be stricter than OSHA regulations but not more lenient); medical examinations for individuals working with asbestos containing materials; notification of regulatory agencies for various situations including removal of more than 50 linear feet on pipes, 32 square feet on other surfaces or more than one 55-gallon barrel per individual job; guidelines for communicating asbestos hazards in controlled access areas or regulated areas; enclosures for dust control, removal and packaging methods; work practices including tools, removal techniques, ventilation; cleanup and disposal procedures; handling of sealed bags, barrel requirements, acceptable dump sites, and recordkeeping; personal protective equipment; inspection intervals and acceptable results; air sample and bulk sample monitoring; reinsulation (nonasbestos products); and local fire-code testing requirements for the insulation application. I have a section of the manual with specifications which apply only to my facility. I state reinsulation and testing requirements that may comply with the local fire codes, and I have a color code for the reinsulation process.

Color coding during the reinsulation process creates an easily recognized visual communication record for the future. Encapsulation over asbestos is red ("stop"); reinsulation of non-asbestos insulation is green ("go"). Color codes should be stated in the standards manual and should be applied consistently.

The standards manual was distributed to contractors interested in bidding on future jobs. After their review of the manual, contractors were asked to sign a statement that they understood the minimum standards demanded and would meet those standards if contracted to perform work in our facility.

In addition, those contractors who were prequalified were asked to sign an "open-ended service agreement." This agreement contains all the general contract language that pertains to future jobs on which the contractor may be a successful bidder, but it does not guarantee work to the contractor.

The "open-ended service agreement" concept was suggested by our attorneys as a method to have prequalified asbestos removal contractors under contract and to allow a speedy bid process in case of an asbestos emergency.

Our company will not allow an outside contractor on-site without a signed contract agreement on file in our Documents Department.

I found the advantages of preparing an "open-ended service agreement" were many:

1. Our "agreement" contained all general contract language without committing me to use the contractor's services. Rather, it stated the terms under which work would be performed if the contractor were the successful bidder and selected to perform asbestos removal work in the future.

2. The "agreement" allowed me to bid unexpected asbestos handling jobs such as our eleventh floor quickly and to act without the delay of contract preparation in an emergency.

3. The "agreement" does not contain a termination date but rather states that specifications for individual jobs, including work schedules, will be stated in work authorization or purchase orders prepared for individual jobs and referencing the signed "open-ended service agreement."

4. The "agreement" does not state dollar amounts for work but does outline that compensation for individual jobs shall be based on accepted bid limits stated in the work authorization, after work is completed to

my satisfaction in accordance with the specifications and, lastly, when the work has passed final regulatory agency inspection.

§ 14.9   Specifications for Contingency Planning

After I identified the eleventh-floor asbestos removal job, I wrote detailed specifications for performing the work. Below is a brief description of each of the sections that made up my specifications.

General Overview of Work—This section provided a detailed description of the job: its location, size, the type of asbestos and its condition. I included a reference guide to ensure the contractor had a good understanding of the unusual structural problems from which asbestos had to be removed or around which the enclosure had to be built. I also enclosed a floor plan, color-coded with the visual inspection information, and a set of photographs referenced on the floor plan.

Water and Electrical Requirements—Water and electricity are essential elements to successful asbestos removal. I carefully defined what was available at the project site and described what could be made available through minimal modification of existing systems.

If water and electrical power available at the site are not sufficient to meet contractor equipment power and removal procedure needs, then the contractor will have to identify and plan for the deficiencies before the project begins, and those plans and costs need to be included in the contractor's bid.

If these essentials are not discussed prior to awarding a job, deficiencies can necessitate additional cost for unforeseen work. During the pre-bid meeting, show the contractors the building systems and the source of electricity and water for the project.

Asbestos Removal and Disposal Procedures—Reference your standards manual with the stated minimal requirements for working in your facility. If an unusual requirement exists due to the project's location or size, state it here. If your company requires the use of a specific disposal site, indicate the site's name and location.

A Facility Manager should identify one or more alternate locations for accumulating the full waste drums on-site. These locations should be viewed during a pre-bid meeting. Alternate sites will allow the contractor to select a location most efficient for the removal enclosure layout.

Reference your standards manual with the stated minimal requirements for recordkeeping. Records should be maintained by the contractor and by the Facility Manager or Hazardous Waste Coordinator on-site. Records include, but are not limited to: copies of medical certification for each worker; EPA certification for each supervisor; all air-monitoring and bulk-monitoring analyses; a list of all personal safety equipment and manufacturers; a list of all compressors, HEPA filters, and other equipment and manufacturers; and signed manifests for transportation and disposal of the asbestos.

Remember Federal regulations require that all hoses, couplings, and other components that make up the personal safety or removal equipment be of the same manufacturer. The on-site supervisor and company are liable if regulatory inspectors find these regulations are not complied with during the removal project.[8]

Reinsulation Requirements and Testing in Accordance With Local Fire Codes—The assumption here is that the asbestos removed provided a fire barrier within the facility. Obviously, this is not true in every removal job. The Facility Manager should either state the manufacturer's name, and type for reinsulation, or should require the contractor to submit manufacturer's specification information and material safety data specifications for non-asbestos reinsulation products. I referenced my color code specifications here from the standards manual.

If the insulation provides a one- or two-hour fire barrier, then local fire codes should be reviewed to determine what tests may be required for the fire department and building department to sign-off on the project.

Performing these reapplication tests prior to the addition of a ceiling is the easiest way to proceed. My local fire codes require a manufacturer specification sheet and random core drills and depth test results be submitted to the local fire department to ensure that the manufacturer specifications were met for the required fire barrier. The requirements should be defined in the specifications, so the costs for the tests are included in the contractor's bid.

Special Enclosure Construction Demands for Unique Conditions of the Project—During the pre-bid meeting, all contractors should be given an opportunity to view the site and structural concerns should be referenced in the overview section. A statement of how these unique structural concerns will be addressed by the contractor during the barrier construction and the actual asbestos removal process should be a requirement of the bid process. I requested that detailed construction drawings be submitted with the bid package on my project. On my eleventh-floor job, the contractor was asked to provide an enclosure with a double barrier.

My contingency plan included the specification of an inner removal enclosure barrier, with an outer barrier to contain any contamination if the unexpected should occur. It allowed me to maintain the occupancy level on the eleventh floor of my facility while isolating the inner 2,000-square-foot removal barrier.

The outer barrier also assisted in my communication program with employees. A viewing window was left in the barrier so employees could monitor the activities inside the enclosure and ask questions about the activities which they did not understand.

The outer barrier wall had to be fitted to the asbestos insulation on the pan prior to the construction of the inner barrier and it was not removed until after the reinsulation process was concluded and passed fire code inspection requirements. The barrier was removed during unoccupied hours

---

[8] OSHA, 29 C.F.R. 1926.58, Construction Standard.

and the removal procedure was air-monitored. Each contractor was required to submit an engineered plan on how the construction of these barriers would be carried out to ensure the asbestos would not be disturbed and that there was minimal impact on the productivity of my tenants.

My contingency plan did cause the cost of this project to escalate to $50 a square foot (in 1989) but, by comparison, closing the eleventh floor of my facility for one 8-hour shift would have cost more in lost labor than the entire asbestos removal project.

Work Schedule Constraints—If there are any time constraints associated with the project, they should be clearly stated in this section. I addressed issues such as: the time frame in which the job had to be completed; the time periods and days during which contractor employees could be on-site, and the specific hours during which waste and construction debris could be moved through the facility.

Details Pertaining to Payment Schedules, Additional Work and Bonus/ Penalty Clauses—State how payment will be made and under what conditions payment will be authorized. I stated that a lump sum payment including bonus if earned, would be made within 30 days of my receipt of both the final 24-hour air-monitoring analyses and the final regulatory inspection of the project. I stipulated that air monitoring had to be within the most stringent regulatory limits.

If the time frame for completing the work is restrictive, then penalty and bonus clauses may be appropriate. One should not be used without the other. Completion of all final inspections prior to a given date and time could result in a bonus for the contractor. The delay in completion of final inspections beyond a specific day and time can result in a penalty for every 24-hour delay. The penalty can be a reduced payment for the job.

A pre-bid meeting and detailed specifications should eliminate any change order requests from the contractor. It should be clearly stated in the contract that change orders must be preauthorized, especially if a change in payment will result.

Insurance—Where asbestos is concerned, ignorance of a dangerous situation will not reduce a corporation's or the Facility Manager's financial liability if someone is hurt or contamination of the environment results from the mishandling of the asbestos removal project.

Because of the long-term liability associated with asbestos removal, I would strongly urge all Facility Managers to check into the various insurances available before specifying the insurance obligations of their selected contractor.

The Facility Manager should consider the risks involved in their abatement work and explore the different types of liability insurance available: all risk liability; bonds; general liability, etc. A company's insurance department or insurer should also be consulted.[9]

---

[9] Ylvisake, *Is There Liability After Removal?,* Buildings, Mar. 1988, at 67–68.

Termination Clause—The "open-ended service agreement" did not include a termination clause. It simply allowed easy access to the contractor through a contractual agreement which defined minimal requirements for work performance. Thus, a termination clause should be included in the work authorization which references the specifications for a specified project. I included a verbal communication clause followed by written confirmation through registered mail to terminate the agreement if I was not satisfied with the contractor's performance, if specifications were not being met, or if time frames were not adhered to.

Other Language—Any changes to the "open-ended service agreement" language, either more stringent or more lenient, should be stated here. Examples of such topics may be restroom and lunch room facility locations, access limitations, security access or exit requirements, personnel dress requirements, or areas identified as off-limits to contractor personnel.

In my contract, I specified the location of the restrooms and the lunch room which would be available to the contract employees, the security procedures for entering and leaving my facility, the fact that contract employees would not be allowed on floors other than the project floor and lunch room floor, and that contract employees would not be allowed to park personal vehicles on company property. I did not want the liability for any damage to my property from a private vehicle.

Before I sent a letter to invite contractors to bid on the asbestos job, I reviewed my specifications with representatives from the regulatory agencies who would perform the final inspections.

§ 14.10   The Bid Process

After I received management's approval for my specifications, I invited contractors to attend a pre-bid meeting. The pre-bid meting was scheduled to allow contractors to view the job, to receive their specifications package, and to ask questions about the project.

The contractors were given a specific time for returning their bids. If a contractor did not attend the meeting and did not pick up the specifications package, the contractor was not allowed to bid on the project. If the contractors did not meet the specified deadline for returning their bids, they were disqualified.

The specifications package included a letter that identified the project and the bid process, and clearly stated all the information to be returned with the bid.

The required information included such submittals as a design plan that addressed the special barriers and architectural features identified in the specifications, product lists, material specification sheets, equipment lists, asbestos removal employee names, doctor certificates for each, respirator fitting tests for each, laboratory name for air and bulk sample analyses, subcontractor names, a list of references for similar jobs, and the name of the competent person who would be assigned to the project.

The bids returned to me were all in the same format and could be easily compared. If any portion of the bid process was not completed as specified, the contractor was eliminated from consideration.

Of the five contractors invited to the pre-bid meeting only two properly addressed my double barrier construction concern. The remaining contractors were disqualified because their bid packages did not include the construction drawings required for a complete bid package.

During the bid process, I interviewed the competent person who would be assigned to complete the project and who would report directly to me on an agreed-upon schedule. I interviewed extensively because I needed to be confident of the abilities of the competent person representing me and the corporation. I needed to be able to trust the recommendations for decisions made by this individual.

§ 14.11   Conclusion of Project

My asbestos removal project was successful and completed without change orders because I selected a contractor workforce through a vigorous prequalification and bid process. My crew and I performed quality control during the actual project. I ensured that all specifications were met. I defined the circumstances under which the project would be considered complete and for which payment would be made.

As importantly, I maintained open lines of communication with the company's employees, the contractor, and the regulatory agencies: all knew that I was available at all times. My office staff was knowledgeable and answered all questions and addressed all concerns promptly.

ENVIRONMENTAL
STATUTES

Statute	Code Citation	Regulations
Asbestos Hazard Emergency Response Act (AHERA)	20 U.S.C. §§ 3601–3611	
Clean Air Act	42 U.S.C. §§ 7401–7671q	14 C.F.R. § 1216 19 C.F.R. § 12 23 C.F.R. §§ 450, 770, 771 29 C.F.R. § 24 40 C.F.R. §§ 2, 22, 23, 35, 45–87, 600, 1500–1508 45 C.F.R. § 640 49 C.F.R. § 613, 623
Comprehensive Environmental Response, Compensation, and Liability Act; Superfund Amendments and Reauthorization Act of 1986 (SARA)	42 U.S.C. §§ 9601–9675	33 C.F.R. §§ 1, 153 40 C.F.R. §§ 300–310 42 C.F.R. §§ 65, 90 43 C.F.R. § 11
Federal Hazardous Substances Act	15 U.S.C. §§ 1261–1277	16 C.F.R. §§ 1009, 1010, 1015, 1019, 1031, 1061, 1500–1512, 1702
Hazardous Materials Transportation Act	49 U.S.C. §§ 1801–1819	14 C.F.R. § 13 32 C.F.R. § 619 46 C.F.R. §§ 28, 150, 154 49 C.F.R. §§ 171–179, 209, 385, 386
Occupational Safety and Health Administration Act (OSHA)	29 U.S.C. §§ 651–678	29 C.F.R. §§ 1901–1928, 1975–1978, 1990 30 C.F.R. § 11 34 C.F.R. § 75 40 C.F.R. § 311 42 C.F.R. §§ 85–87

Statute	*Code Citation*	*Regulations*
Safe Drinking Water Act (SDWA)	42 U.S.C. §§ 201, 300f, 300g–300g-6, 300h–300h-7, 300i–300i-1, 300j–300j-11, 300j-21–300j-26	21 C.F.R. §§ 10, 12–16 29 C.F.R. §§ 1, 5, 24 40 C.F.R. §§ 2, 22–25, 35, 45, 46, 135, 141–149
Soil and Water Resources Conservation Act of 1977 (SWRCA)	16 U.S.C. §§ 2001–2009	18 C.F.R. § 290
Solid Waste Disposal Act (SWDA)	42 U.S.C. §§ 6901–6922k	40 C.F.R. §§ 1, 2, 5, 22–24, 30–35, 40–46, 90, 124, 125, 144–148, 233, 244–281
Toxic Substances Control Act (TSCA)	15 U.S.C. §§ 2601–2629, 2641–2656, 2661–2671	19 C.F.R. § 12 29 C.F.R. § 24 40 C.F.R. §§ 2, 22, 24, 30–34, 700–799
Water Pollution Prevention and Control Act	33 U.S.C. §§ 1251–1377, 1381–1387	7 C.F.R. § 634 9 C.F.R. §§ 307–320, 381 19 C.F.R. § 4 29 C.F.R. §§ 1, 5, 24 33 C.F.R. §§ 25, 130, 131, 151–156, 159, 209, 221, 300, 320–328 40 C.F.R. §§ 2, 6, 15, 22–34, 40, 45, 46, 100–145, 233, 270, 271, 300, 302, 400–471, 501 46 C.F.R. § 91 47 C.F.R. § 471

TABLE OF CASES

Case	Book §
Acushnet River & New Bedford Harbor Proceedings, *In re,* 712 F. Supp. 1010 (D. Mass. 1989)	§§ 5.15, 5.16
Adams-Arapahoe School Dist. No. 28-J v. Celotex Corp., 637 F. Supp. 1207 (D. Colo. 1986)	§§ 5.3, 6.11
Air Heaters, Inc. v. Johnson Electric, Inc., 258 N.W.2d 649 (N.D. 1977)	§ 5.23
AIV Ins. Co. v. Superior Court of Santa Clara County, 799 P.2d 1253, 274 Cal. Rptr. 820 (Cal. 1990)	§ 10.3
Alabama v. W.R. Grace & Co., 109 L. Ed. 494, 110 S. Ct. 2164 (1990)	§ 5.2
AM International Inc. v. International Forging Equip., No. C88-2037 (E.D. Ohio June 29, 1990)	§ 6.27
American Reserve Corp., *In re,* 70 Bankr. 729 (N.D. Ill. 1987)	§ 6.21
Amland Properties Corp. v. Aluminium Company of America, 711 F. Supp. 784 (D.N.J. 1989)	§§ 1.11, 1.12, 1.14, 6.9, 6.22, 6.24, 7.15
Amoco Oil Co. v. Borden, Inc., 889 F.2d 664 (5th Cir. 1989)	§ 6.27
Anderson v. Owens-Corning Fiberglass Corp., 217 Cal. App. 3d 772, 266 Cal. Rptr. 204 (2d Dist. 1990), *review granted in part,* 269 Cal. Rptr. 74, 790 P.2d 238 (1990)	§ 7.10
Anderson v. W.R. Grace & Co., 628 F. Supp. 1219, 16 Envtl. L. Rep. (Envtl. L. Inst.) 20,577 (D. Mass. 1986)	§ 7.8
Anspec Co. v. Johnson Control, Inc., 743 F. Supp. 793 (E.D. Mich. 1989), *appeal dismissed on procedural grounds,* 891 F.2d 289 (6th Cir. 1989)	§ 5.16
Anthony v. Blech, No. CV-90-4538 AWT (D.C.C. Cal. Mar. 26, 1991)	§ 6.6
Apex Oil Co. v. United States, 530 F.2d 1291 (8th Cir.), *cert. denied,* 429 U.S. 827, 97 S. Ct. 84 (1976)	§§ 5.17, 5.22
Artesian Water Co. v. Government of New Castle County, 659 F. Supp. 1269 (D. Del. 1987), *aff'd,* 851 F.2d 643 (3d Cir. 1988)	§ 6.5
ARZ Acres, Inc. v. Satellite Business Systems (Ct. Common Pleas, Cuyahoga Co., Ohio), No. 106,608, (settled July 13, 1990)	§§ 5.8, 6.14
Asbestos Litigation, *In re,* 829 F.2d 1233 (3d Cir. 1987), *cert. denied,* 485 U.S. 1029 (1988)	§ 7.10
Asbestos School Litigation, *In re,* 104 F.R.D. 422 (E.D. Pa. 1984), 107 F.R.D. 215 (E.D. Pa. 1985), *aff'd in part, rev'd in part,* 789 F.2d 996 (3d Cir. 1986), *cert. denied,* 479 U.S. 852 (1986)	§ 5.2

424   **TABLE**

Case	*Book §*
Associated Industries of Massachusetts v. Snow, 717 F. Supp. 951 (D. Mass. 1989), *aff'd in part, rev'd in part,* 898 F.2d 274 (1st Cir. 1990)	§ 2.12
Avent v. Proffitt, 109 S.C. 48, 95 S.E. 132 (1918)	§ 5.24
Ayers v. Township of Jackson, 106 N.J. 557, 525 A.2d 287 (1987)	§§ 6.4, 6.12
Baca v. Walgreen Co., 6 Kan. App. 2d 505, 630 P.2d 1185 (1981), *aff'd in part, rev'd in part,* 230 Kan. 443, 638 P.2d 898, *cert. denied,* 459 U.S. 859 (1982)	§ 5.7
Bank Western Federal Savings Bank v. Western Office Partners Ltd., No. 86CV13417, slip op. (D.C. Denver Feb. 1989)	§ 5.18
Bardura v. Orkin Exterminating Co., 664 F. Supp. 1218 (N.D. Ill. 1987), *aff'd,* 865 F.2d 816 (7th Cir. 1988)	§ 6.16
Barnes v. Mac Brown & Co., Inc., 264 Ind. 227, 342 N.E.2d 619 (1976)	§ 6.14
Barnett v. City of Yonkers, et al., 731 F. Supp. 594 (S.D.N.Y. 1990)	§ 5.24
Barth v. Firestone Fire and Rubber Company, 661 F. Supp. 193 (N.D. Cal. 1987)	§ 5.21
Basic v. Levinson, 485 U.S. 224, 108 S. Ct. 978 (1988)	§ 6.19
Bass v. Tax Commission of the City of New York, No. 56969/84 (N.Y. Sup. Ct. Jan. 22, 1991)	§ 6.26
Baughman v. General Motors Corp., 780 F.2d 1131 (4th Cir. 1986)	§ 5.11
BCW Associates Ltd. v. Occidental Chemical Corp., 1988 U.S. Dist. LEXIS 11, 275 (E.D. Pa. Sept. 29, 1988)	§§ 1.11, 1.12
Beauchamp v. Dow Chemical Co., 427 Mich. 1 (1986)	§ 5.21
Beck v. Cantor, Fitzgerald & Co., 621 F. Supp. 1547 (N.D. Ill. 1985)	§ 6.19
Bergsoe Metal Corp. v. East Asiatic Co., 910 F.2d 668 (9th Cir. 1990)	§ 5.18
Beshada v. Johns-Manville Products Corp., 90 N.J. 191, 447 A.2d 539 (1982)	§ 7.10
Bevins v. Ballard, 655 P.2d 757 (Alaska 1982)	§ 5.12
Bischofshausen, Vasbinder and Luckie v. D.W. Jaquays Mining and Equipment Contractors Co., 145 Ariz. 204, 700 P.2d 902 (1985)	§§ 5.14, 5.17
Blagg v. Fred Hunt Co., 272 Ark. 185, 612 S.W.2d 321 (1981)	§§ 6.13, 6.14
Blankenship v. Cincinnati Milacron Chemicals, 69 Ohio St. 2d 608, 433 N.E.2d 572, *cert. denied,* 459 U.S. 857 (1982)	§ 6.16
Blankenship v. Demmler Mfg. Co., 89 Ill. App. 3d 569, 411 N.E.2d 1153 (1980)	§ 5.15
Blaustein v. Pincus, 47 Mont. 202, 131 P. 1064 (1913)	§ 6.14
Bloomsburg Mills v. Sordoni Construction Co., 401 Pa. 358, 164 A.2d 201 (1960)	§ 5.24

Case	*Book §*
Board of Education of City of Chicago v. A, C and S, Inc., 525 N.E.2d 950 (Ill. App. 1988), *aff'd in part, rev'd in part,* 131 Ill. 2d 428, 546 N.E.2d 580 (1989)	§§ 5.3, 6.11
Boeing Co. v. Aetna Casualty and Surety Co, 113 Wash. 2d 869, 784 P.2d 507 (1990)	§ 10.3
Bomze v. Jay Lee Photo Suppliers, Inc., 117 Misc. 2d 957, 460 N.Y.S.2d 862 (1983)	§ 6.14
Borel v. Fiberboard Paper Products Corp., 493 F.2d 1076 (5th Cir. 1973), *cert. denied,* 419 U.S. 869 (1974)	§§ 5.4, 7.2, 7.16
Boston v. U.S. Gypsum Co., No. CA 8254 (Super. Ct., Suffolk Co., Mass. 1991)	§ 5.3
Boston, City of v. Keene Corp., 406 Mass. 301, 547 N.E.2d 328 (1989)	§ 7.2
Boykins Narrow Fabrics Corp. v. Weldon Roffing & Sheet Metal, Inc., 221 Va. 81, 266 S.E.2d 887 (1980)	§ 7.14
Brafford v. Susquehanna, 586 F. Supp. (D. Colo. 1984)	§ 5.11
Brandon Township v. Jerome Builders, Inc., 80 Mich. App. 180, 262 N.W.2d 326 (1978)	§ 6.15
Brock v. Tarrant, 57 Wash. App. 562, 789 P.2d 112 (1990)	§ 5.12
Browning-Ferris Industries of Vermont, Inc. v. Kelco Disposal, Inc., 492 U.S. 257, 109 S. Ct. 2909 (1989)	§ 6.28
Bruce v. Martin-Marietta Corporation, 544 F.2d 442 (10th Cir. 1976)	§ 7.10
Bud Antle, Inc. v. Eastern Foods, Inc. 758 F.2d 1451 (11th Cir. 1985)	§ 5.16
Bulk Distribution Centers, Inc. v. Monsanto Co., 589 F. Supp. 1437 (S.D. Fla. 1984)	§ 1.18
Bulova Watch Co. v. K. Hattori & Co., 508 F. Supp. 1322 (E.D.N.Y. 1981)	§ 6.21
C. Greene Equipment Corp. v. Electron Corp., 697 F. Supp. 983 (N.D. Ill. 1988)	§ 1.11
C.D. Spangler Construction Co. v. Industrial Crankshaft & Engineering Co., 326 N.C. 133, 388 S.E.2d 557 (1990)	§ 10.3
Caldwell v. Gurley Refining Co., 755 N.2d 645 (8th Cir. 1985)	§ 5.8
Call v. Prudential, No. SWC 90913 (Super. Ct. Cal.)	§ 5.23
Cappaert v. Junker, 413 So. 2d 378 (Miss. 1982)	§ 5.7
Carolina Winds Owners' Association v. Joe Harden Builder, Inc., 297 S.C. 74, 374 S.E.2d 897 (Ct. App. 1988), *aff'd on rehearing,* No. 25 Davis Adv. Sh. 21 (S.C. Ct. App. Nov. 30, 1988)	§ 5.23
Cartel Capital Corp. v. Fireco of New Jersey, 81 N.J. 548 (1980)	§ 5.8
Celotex Corp. v. St. John's Hospital, 259 Ga. 108, 376 S.E.2d 880 (Sup. Ct. Ga. 1989), *cert. denied,* 110 S. Ct. 11,358 (1990)	§ 7.2

Case	*Book §*
Chase Manhattan Bank v. Turner & Newall PLC, No. 87 Civ. 4436 (S.D.N.Y. Mar. 29, 1990)	§ 6.11
Chateuagay Corp., *In re,* 112 Bankr. 513 (S.D.N.Y. 1990), *rev'd* 110 S. Ct. 2668, 110 L. Ed. 2d 579 (S.D.N.Y. 1990)	§§ 7.4, 7.7
Clearwater Forest Industries, Inc. v. United States, 650 F.2d 233 (Ct. Cl. 1981)	§§ 5.9, 6.18
Cleveland Board of Education v. Armstrong World Industries, 476 N.E.2d 397 (Ct. Common Pleas, Cuyahoga Co., Ohio 1985)	§ 5.2
Clutter v. Johns-Manville, 646 F.2d 1151 (6th Cir. 1981)	§ 7.2
Collins v. Eli Lilly Company, 116 Wis. 2d 166, 342 N.W.2d 37, *cert. denied,* 469 U.S. 826 (1984)	§ 6.21
Colorado v. Idarado Mining Co., 18 Envtl. L. Rep. (Envtl. L. Inst.) 20578 (D. Colo. 1987)	§ 5.17
Cook Consultants, Inc. v. Larson, 700 S.W.2d 231 (Tex. App. 1985)	§ 5.9
Copart Industries, Inc. v. Con Ed, 41 N.Y.2d 564 (1977)	§ 6.24
Corporation of Mercer Univ. v. National Gypsum Co., 832 F.2d 1233, Prod. Liab. Rep. (CCH) P 11603 (11th Cir. Ga. 1987), *certified ques. ans.* 258 Ga. 365, 368 S.E.2d 732 (1988), 877 F.2d 35, Prod. Liab. Rep. (CCH) P 12202, *cert. denied,* 110 S. Ct. 408, 107 F.2d 374 (Ga. 1989)	§ 6.15
Council for Owner Occupied Housing v. Abrams, Matter of, 125 A.2d 10, 511 N.Y.S.2d 966 (3d Dept. 1987)	§ 2.7
Crawford v. National Lead Co., 19 Envtl. L. Rep. (Envtl. L. Inst.) 21,174 (S.D. Ohio 1989)	§ 6.11
Cinnaminson Township Board of Education v. U.S. Gypsum Co., 552 F. Supp. 855 (D.N.J. 1982), *aff'd,* 882 F.2d 510 (3d Cir. 1989)	§§ 6.11, 6.28
Cruz v. Drezek, 175 Conn. 230, 397 A.2d 1335 (1978)	§ 5.7
Cunningham et al. v. Anchor Hocking Corp., 558 So. 2d 93, *review denied,* 574 So. 2d 139 (Fla. 1990)	§ 5.21
Curran v. State of Arkansas, 56 U.S. (15 How.) 304 (1853)	§ 5.15
D'Imperio v. United States, 575 F. Supp. 248 (D.N.J. 1983)	§ 7.17
Dant & Russell, Inc., *In re,* 853 F.2d 700, 18 Envtl. L. Rep. (Envtl. L. Inst.) 21,312 (9th Cir. 1988)	§ 7.6
Dartez v. Fiberboard Corp., 765 F.2d 456 (5th Cir. 1985)	§ 6.4
Dawejko v. Jorgensen Steel Co., 290 Pa. Super. 15, 434 A.2d 106 (1980)	§ 5.16
Department of Environmental Protection v. Exxon Corp., 151 N.J. Super. 464, 376 A.2d 1339 (Ch. Div. 1977)	§ 1.2
Department of Transp. v. PSC Resources, Inc., 175 N.J. Super. 447, 419 A.2d 1151 (Super. Ct. Law Div. 1980)	§ 5.16

Case	*Book §*
Detroit, City of v. The Celotex Corp., No. 84-429634 NP (Mich. Cir. Ct., Wayne Co. Feb. 1, 1988)	§ 5.2
Dunson v. Friedlander Realty, 369 So. 2d 792 (Ala. 1979)	§ 5.7
Easton v. Strassburger, 152 Cal. App. 3d 199 Cal. Rptr. 385 (1984)	§ 5.12
Edward Hines Lumber Co. v. Vulcan Materials Co., 685 F. Supp. 651 (N.D. Ill. 1988), *aff'd,* 861 F.2d 155 (7th Cir. 1988)	§ 1.11
Elkhart Community School Corp. v. Mills, 546 N.E.2d 854 (Ct. App. Ind. 1989)	§ 5.9
Emhart Industries, Inc. v. Duracell Int'l., Inc., 665 F. Supp. 549 (M.D. Tenn. 1987)	§ 1.11
Endress v. Equitable Life Assurance, No. 81,925 slip. op., Ct. Appeals, Ohio Oct. 29, 1987	§ 6.14
Environmental Protection Dept. v. Ventron Corp., 182 N.J. Super. 210, 440 A.2d 455, *aff'd as modified,* 94 N.J. 473, 468 A.2d 150 (1983)	§§ 5.12, 5.17, 6.29
Ernst & Ernst v. Hochfelder, 425 U.S. 185, 96 S. Ct. 1375, 47 L. Ed. 2d 668 (1976)	§ 6.19
Fagan v. Axelrod, 550 N.Y.S.2d 552 (Sup. Ct. 1990)	§ 2.15
Featherall v. Firestone Tire & Rubber Co., 219 Va. 949, 252 S.E.2d 358 (1979)	§ 6.17
Feldman v. Lederle Laboratories, 97 N.J. 429, 479 A.2d 374 (1984)	§ 7.10
Ferber v. Orange Blossom Centers, Inc., 388 So. 2d 1074 (Fla. Dist. Ct. App. 1980)	§ 5.7
Fiberboard Corp, *In re,* 893 F.2d 706 (5th Cir. 1990)	§ 6.2
First United Methodist Church v. U.S. Gypsum Co., 882 F.2d 862 (4th Cir. 1989), *cert. denied,* 110 S. Ct. 1113, 107 L. Ed. 1020 (1990)	§§ 6.6, 7.2
Flatt v. Johns-Manville Sales Corporation, 488 F. Supp. 836 (E.D. Tex. 1980)	§§ 5.18, 7.10
40 Associates Inc. v. Katz, 112 Misc. 2d 215, 446 N.Y.S.2d 844 (Civ. Ct. N.Y. City 1981)	§ 6.14
Franklin Signal Corp., *In re,* 65 Bankr. 268 (D. Minn. 1986)	§ 7.6
Furch v. General Electric Co., 535 N.Y.S.2d 182 (3d Dept. 1988), *appeal dismissed,* 74 N.Y.2d 792, 545 N.Y.S.2d 106 (1989)	§ 5.23
Garb-Ko v. Lansing-Lewis Services, Inc., 423 N.W.2d 355 (Mich. App. 1988), *appeal denied,* 431 Mich. 874 (1988)	§§ 5.5, 6.22
Gard v. Raymark Industries, 185 Cal. App. 3d 583, 229 Cal. Rptr. 861 (Ct. App. 1986)	§ 6.21
Garner v. Wolfinbarger, 430 F.2d 1093 (5th Cir. 1970), *cert. denied,* 401 U.S. 974 (1971)	§ 5.25

Case	*Book §*
Garvin, *In re,* EPA Docket No. TSCA-ASB-VIII-90-41, Jan. 15, 1991	§ 5.23
Gelsumino v. E.W. Bliss Co., 10 Ill. App. 3d 604, 295 N.E.2d 110 (1973)	§ 7.10
General Electric Co. v. Cuban American Nickel Co., 396 F.2d 89 (5th Cir. 1968)	§ 5.8
George Ball Pacific, 117 Cal. App. 3d 248, 172 Cal. Rptr. 597 (1981)	§ 5.12
Giden v. Johns-Manville Sales Corp., 761 F.2d 1129 (5th Cir. 1985)	§ 5.2
Glenn R. Sewell Sheet Metal, Inc. v. Loverde, 70 Cal. 2d 666, 451 P.2d 721 (1969)	§ 5.8
Glover v. Johns-Manville Corp., 525 F. Supp. 894 (E.D. Va. 1979), *aff'd in part, vacated in part,* 662 F.2d 225 (4th Cir. 1981)	§ 6.17
Goldman v. Johns-Manville Sales Corp., 33 Ohio St. 3d 40, 514 N.E.2d 691 (1987)	§ 6.21
Gonzales v. Progressive Tool & Die Co., 455 F. Supp. 363 (E.D.N.Y. 1978)	§ 5.15
Gouveia v. Citicorp Person-to-Person Financial Center, Inc., 101 N.M. 572, 686 P.2d 262 (Ct. App. 1984)	§ 5.12
Gower v. Cohn, 643 F.2d 1146 (5th Cir. 1981)	§ 6.19
Grand Jury Proceedings (FMC Corp.), *In re,* 604 F.2d 798 (3d Cir. 1979)	§ 5.25
Green v. Oilwell, Div. of U.S. Steel Corp., 767 P.2d 1348 (Okla. 1989)	§ 5.15
Greenville, Tenn., City of v. Nat'l Gypsum Co., *Contra,* CV 2-83-294, slip op. (decision of magistrate) (E.D. Tenn. Dec. 21, 1983)	§ 6.15
Greenville, City of v. W.R. Grace & Co., 827 F.2d 975 (4th Cir. 1987), *reh'g denied,* 840 F.2d 219 (4th Cir. 1988)	§ 5.3
Grispo v. Eagle-Picher Industries, Inc., N.Y.L.J., Feb. 22, 1990	§ 5.23
GRM Industries, Inc. v. Wickes Manufacturing Co., 1990 WL 168176 (W.D. Mich. 1990)	§ 5.16
Grossman v. Waste Management, Inc., 589 F. Supp. 395 (N.D. Ill. 1984)	§ 6.19
Gurman, Jurtis & Black v. Charles E. Smith Mgmt., Inc., *reported* 2 Nat'l J. Asb. Buildings Lit. 10 (July 28, 1989)	§ 6.14
Hagar v. Mobley, 638 P.2d 127 (Wyo. 1981)	§ 6.16
Hagerty v. L & L Marine Services, Inc., 788 F.2d 315 (5th Cir. 1986), *reconsid. denied, en banc,* 797 F.2d 256 (5th Cir. 1968)	§ 7.8
Hall v. E.I. DuPont de Nemours & Co., 345 F. Supp. 353 (E.D.N.Y. 1972)	§ 6.21
Hardy v. Johns-Manville Sales Corp., 509 F. Supp. 1353 (E.D. Tex. 1981), *rev'd on other grounds,* 681 F.2d 384 (5th Cir. 1982)	§ 7.8

Case	Book §
Hardy v. Johns-Manville Sales Corp., 531 F. Supp. 96 (W.D. Pa. 1982)	§ 6.21
Hardy v. Johns-Manville Sales Corp., 681 F.2d 334 (5th Cir. 1982)	§ 5.2
Harrill v. Sinclair Refining Co., 225 N.C. 421, 35 S.E.2d 240 (1945)	§ 5.7
Harris v. Union Electric Co., 787 F.2d 355 (8th Cir.), *cert. denied,* 479 U.S. 823 (1986)	§ 6.19
Hazen Paper Co. v. United States Fidelity and Guaranty Co., 407 Mass. 689, 555 N.E.2d 576 (1990)	§ 10.3
Hebron Public School District v. U.S. Gypsum Co., 690 F. Supp. 866 (D.C.N.D. 1988)	§ 6.11
Hefler v. Wright, *Accord,* 121 Ill. App. 3d 739, 460 N.E.2d 118 (1984)	§ 5.23
Herald Square Realty Company v. Saks & Company, 215 N.Y. 427, 109 N.E. 545 (1915)	§ 5.8
Hill v. Polar Pantries, 219 S.C. 263, 64 S.E.2d 885 (1951)	§ 5.24
Hocking v. Dubois, 839 F.2d 560 (9th Cir. 1988) *vacated,* 863 F.2d 654 (1988) *cert. denied,* 110 S. Ct. 1805 (1990)	§ 6.19
Hoffman v. Connall, 108 Wash. 2d 69, 736 P.2d 242 (1987)	§ 5.12
Holder v. Haskett, 283 S.C. 247, 321 S.E.2d 192 (Ct. App. 1984)	§ 5.12
Hermes v. Staiano, 181 N.J. Super. 424, 437 A.2d 925 (N.J. Super. Ct. Law Div. 1981)	§ 6.14
Hunter v. Fort Worth Capital Corp., 620 S.W.2d 547 (Tex. 1981)	§ 5.15
Hymowitz v. Eli Lilly and Co., 73 N.Y.2d 487, 541 N.Y.S.2d 941 (Ct. App. N.Y. 1989) *cert. denied,* 110 S. Ct. 350 (1989)	§ 7.2
Idaho v. Howmet Turbine Component Co., 814 F.2d 1376 (9th Cir. 1987) *aff'd,* 882 F.2d 392 (9th Cir. 1989)	§ 1.7
Idaho, State of v. Bunker Hill Co., 635 F. Supp. 665 (D. Idaho 1986)	§ 5.17
Independent School Dist. No. 622 v. Keene Co., Minn. Dist. Ct., No. C5-84-1701, Oct. 5, 1990	§ 6.28
Inmar Associates, Inc. v. Borough of Carlstadt, 214 N.J. Super. 256, 518 A.2d 1110 (1986) *aff'd in part, rev'd in part,* 112 N.J. 593, 549 A.2d 38 (1988)	§ 6.26
International Clinical Laboratories v. Stevens, 710 F. Supp. 466 (E.D.N.Y. 1989)	§ 6.22
Jefferson Associates Ltd. v. Prudential Insurance Co. of America, No. 441 (Texas Dist. Ct., Travis Co., 126th Jud. Dist. May 23, 1990)	§§ 5.9, 5.13
Jensen v. Bank of America, 114 Bankr. 700 (E.D. Cal. 1990)	§ 7.7
Jersey City Redevelopment Authority v. PPG Industries, 655 F. Supp. 1257 (D.C.N.J. 1987) *aff'd,* 1988 U.S. App. LEXIS 18,998 (3d Cir. 1988)	§§ 1.11, 6.7, 6.28

Case	*Book §*
Johns-Manville Products Corporation v. Contra Costa Superior Court, 612 P.2d 948 (Cal. 1980)	§§ 5.15, 5.21
Johnson v. Raybestos-Manhattan, Inc., 69 Haw. 287, 740 P.2d 548 (Haw. 1987)	§ 7.10
Joint Eastern and Southern District of New York Asbestos Litigation, *In re* (Jan. 23, 1991)	§ 5.2
Jones v. VIP Development Co., 15 Ohio St. 3d 90, 472 N.E.2d 1046 (1984)	§ 6.16
Joslyn Manufacturing Co. v. T.L. James & Co., 893 F.2d 80, 30 Env't Rep. Cas. (BNA) 1929 (5th Cir. 1990) *reh'g denied,* 1990 U.S. App. LEXIS 6373 (5th Cir. 1990)	§ 5.17
Just v. Land Reclamation, Ltd., 155 Wis. 2d 737, 456 N.W.2d 570 (1990)	§ 10.3
Juzwin v. Amtorg Trading Corp., 705 F. Supp. 1053 (D.N.J. 1989) *vacated,* 718 F. Supp. 1233 (D.N.J. 1989)	§ 6.28
Kachian v. Aronson, 123 Misc. 2d 743, 475 N.Y.S.2d 214 (1984)	§ 6.14
Kalik v. Allis-Chalmers Corp., 658 F. Supp. 631 (W.D. Pa. 1987)	§§ 6.10, 7.17
Kaminszky v. Kukuch, 553, N.E.2d 868 (Ind. App. 3d Dist. 1990)	§ 6.14
Kaufman v. City of New York, 891 F.2d 446 (2d Cir. 1989) *cert. denied,* 110 S. Ct. 2561 (1990)	§ 2.6
Kelly v. Robinson, 479 U.S. 36 (1986)	§ 7.7
Kelly v. Thomas Solvent Co., 727 F. Supp. 1554 (W.D. Mich. 1989)	§ 5.14
Kershaw County Board of Education v. U.S. Gypsum Co., No. 23,270 (Sup. Ct. S.C. Sept. 17, 1990)	§ 6.11
Kinsey v. Jones, Civ. 87-2959 (JM) (E.D.N.Y. Jan. 30, 1989)	§§ 5.5, 5.11, 6.16
Kirbyville Independent School District v. National Gypsum, No. 12,391 (Tex. Dist. Ct., Jasper Co., 1989) *aff'd,* 770 S.W.2d 621 (Tex. App. 1989)	§ 5.2
Kirvo Indus. Supply Co. v. Nat'l Distillers & Chem. Corp., 483 F.2d 1098 (5th Cir. 1973) *reh'g denied,* 490 F.2d 916 (5th Cir. 1974)	§ 5.14
Knabe v. National Supply Division of Armco Steel Corp., 592 F.2d 841 (5th Cir. 1979)	§ 6.17
Kofron v. Amoco Chemicals Corp., 441 A.2d 226 (Del. 1982) *aff'd sub nom.*	§§ 5.5, 5.21
Kovacs, *In re,* 681 F.2d 454 (6th Cir. 1982) *vacated and remanded on other grounds,* 459 U.S. 1167 (1983)	§ 7.5
Kriegler v. Eichler Homes, 269 Cal. App. 2d 224, 74 Cal. Rptr. 749 (1969)	§ 5.13
Kronfeld v. First Jersey Nat'l Bank, 638 F. Supp. 1454 (C.D.N.J. 1986)	§ 6.20

Case	*Book §*
La Placita Partners v. Northwestern Mutual Life Ins., et al., No. C88-2824 (N.D. Ohio Aug. 1, 1988)	§ 5.18
Lakota Girl Scouts Club, Inc. v. Havey Fund-Raising Mangement, Inc., 519 F.2d 634 (8th Cir. 1975)	§ 5.14
Lancaster v. Tennessee, 831 F.2d 118 (6th Cir. 1987)	§ 1.19
Lane v. Trenholm Bldg. Co., 267 S.C. 497, 229 S.E.2d 728 (1976)	§§ 5.11, 5.23
Laurinberg Oil Company, *In re,* 49 Bankr. 652 (Bankr. M.D.N.C. 1984)	§ 7.5
Leonen v. Johns-Manville Corp. 717 F. Supp. 272 (D.N.J. 1989)	§ 6.28
Levin Metals Corp. v. Parr-Richmond Terminal Co., 817 F.2d 1448 (9th Cir. 1987)	§ 5.15
Locke v. Johns-Manville, 221 Va. 951, 275 S.E.2d 900 (1981)	§ 7.2
Louisiana Pacific Corp. v. Asarco, Inc., 1989 U.S. Dist. LEXIS 12149 (W.D. Wash. 1989)	§ 5.16
Lumber Village Inc. v. Siegler, 135 Mich. App. 685 (1984)	§ 5.5
Lyon v. Barrett, 89 N.J. 294, 445 A.2d 1153 (1982)	§ 5.17
Lyons v. Christ Episcopal Church, 71 Ill. App. 3d, 257, 389 N.E.2d 623 (Ill. App. Ct. 1979)	§ 5.12
Manchester, City of v. National Gypsum Co., 637 F. Supp. 646 (D.R.I. 1986)	§§ 6.11, 7.2
Mansbach v. Prescott, Ball & Turben, 598 F.2d 1017 (6th Cir. 1979)	§ 6.19
Marden Corp. v. C.G.C. Music, Ltd., 600 F. Supp. 1049 (D. Ariz. 1984) *aff'd on other grounds,* 804 F.2d 1454 (9th Cir. 1986)	§§ 6.15, 6.27, 7.17
Marshall v. Celotex Corp. 651 F. Supp. 389 (E.D. Mich. 1987)	§ 6.21
Maryland v. Keene Corp., No. 110-8600 (Md. Cir. Ct. Feb. 15, 1991)	§ 5.3
Matthews v. Stewart Warner Corp., 20 Ill. App. 3d 470 314 N.E.2d 683 (1974)	§ 7.10
Mauro v. Raymark Industries, Inc., 116 N.J. 126 (1989)	§ 6.4
Mauro v. Owens-Corning Fiberglass Corp., 116 N.J. 126, 561 A.2d 257 (N.J. Sup. Ct. 1989)	§ 6.12
Mayfair Merchandise Co. v. Wayne, 415 F.2d 23 (2d Cir. 1969)	§ 5.7
McCrorey v. Heilpern, 170 Conn. 220, 265 A.2d 1057 (1976)	§ 5.7
McDonald v. Mianecki, 79 N.J. 275, 398 A.2d 1283 (1978)	§§ 5.13, 5.23, 6.13
Mercer University v. National Gypsum Co., 24 Env't Rep. Cas. (BNA) 1953 (M.D. Ga. 1986)	§ 6.6
Mergenthaler v. Asbestos Corp. of America, 480 A.2d 647 (Del. Sup. 1984)	§§ 5.5, 5.21
Meyer v. Parkin, 350 N.W.2d 435 (Minn. Ct. App. 1984)	§ 6.13

Case	*Book §*
Michigan v. ARCO Industries, Inc., 723 F. Supp. 1216 (W.D. Mich., 1989)	§ 5.14
Midlantic Nat'l Bank v. New Jersey Dept. of Environmental Protection, 474 U.S. 494, 16 Envtl. L. Rep. (Envtl. L. Inst.) 20,278, 106 S. Ct. 755 (1986)	§ 7.6
Midlantic National Bank v. New Jersey Department of Environmental Protection, 474 U.S. 494 (1986)	§ 1.19
Milau Assocs., Inc. v. North Ave. Dev. Corp., 42 N.Y.2d 482, 368 N.E.2d 1247, 398 N.Y.S.2d 882 (1977)	§ 5.24
Miller v. De Witt, 37 Ill.2d 273, 226 N.E.2d 630 (1967)	§ 5.24
Millison v. E.I. DuPont de Nemours & Co., 94 N.J. 604, 468 A.2d 236 (1983)	§ 6.16
Minnesota Mining and Manufacturing Co. v. Travelers Indemnity Co., 457 N.W.2d 175 (Minn. 1990)	§ 10.3
Mola Dev. Corp. v. United, 22 Env't Rep. Cas. (BNA) 1443 (C.D. Cal. 1985)	§ 1.18
Moncrieff v. Merrill Lynch, Pierce, Fenner & Smith, Inc., 623 F. Supp. 1005 (E.D. Mich. 1985)	§ 6.19
Montijo v. Swift, 219 Cal. App. 2d 351, 33 Cal. Rptr. 133 (1963)	§ 5.24
Mounds View, City of v. Walijarvi, 263 N.W.2d 420 (Minn. 1978)	§ 5.24
Mueller v. Seaboard Commercial Corp., 5 N.J. 28, 73 A.2d 905 (1950)	§ 5.17
Mullen v. Armstrong World Industries, Inc., 200 Cal. App. 3d 250 Cal. Rptr. 32 (1988)	§ 5.2
Mumma v. The Potomac Co., 33 U.S. (8 Pet.) 281 (1834)	§ 5.15
Nallan v. Helmsley-Spear, Inc., 50 N.Y.2d 507, 407 N.E.2d 451, 429 N.Y.S.2d 606 (1980)	§ 6.14
National Asbestos Litigation, Cleveland Div., *In re,* No. 1-90-CV-11,000, N.L.J. Aug. 20, 1990	§ 6.2
National Wood Preservers, Inc. v. Pennsylvania Department of Environmental Resources, 489 Pa. 221, 414 A.2d 37, *appeal dismissed,* 449 U.S. 803 (1980)	§ 5.8
National-Standard Co. v. Adamkus, 685 F. Supp. 1040 (N.D. Ill. 1988) *aff'd,* 881 F.2d 352 (7th Cir. 1989)	§ 1.12
NEPACCO, 579 F. Supp. 823 (W.D. Mo. 1984) *aff'd in part and rev'd in part,* 810 F.2d 726 (8th Cir. 1986)	§§ 5.14, 5.15, 5.17
New York, City of v. Exxon Corp., N.Y.L.J. Aug. 8, 1990	§ 1.9
New York, City of v. Keene Corp., 132 Misc. 2d 745, 505 N.Y.S.2d 782 (1986) *aff'd,* 129 N.Y.S.2d 1019, 513 N.Y.S.2d 1004 (1st Dept. 1987)	§§ 5.3, 6.4, 6.15
New York v. General Electric Co., 592 F. Supp. 291 (N.D.N.Y. 1984)	§ 1.8
New York v. Monarch Chemicals Inc., 90 A.2d 907, 456 N.Y.S.2d 867 (3d Dept. 1982)	§ 6.17

Case	Book §

New York, State of v. Shore Realty Corp., 759 F.2d 1032 (2d Cir. 1985)

§§ 1.2, 1.4, 1.5, 1.7, 1.12, 5.3, 5.10, 5.14, 5.17, 6.23, 6.24, 6.25, 7.2

O'Neil v. Picillo, 883 F.2d 176 (1st Cir. 1989) *cert. denied,* 110 S. Ct. 1115 (1990)

§§ 1.2, 6.27

Ohio v. Kovacs, 469 U.S. 274, 15 Envtl. L. Rep. (Envtl. L. Inst.) 20,121 (1985)

§§ 1.19, 1.20, 7.5, 7.6, 7.7

Oklahoma Refining Co., *In re,* 63 Bankr. 562 (W.D. Okla. 1986)

§ 7.6

Oman v. Johns-Manville Corp., 764 F.2d 224 (4th Cir. 1985) *cert. denied,* 474 U.S. 970 (1985)

§ 6.17

195 Broadway Co. v. 195 Broadway Corp. (Sup. Ct. N.Y. Co.) N.Y.L.J. April 15, 1988

§§ 5.5, 6.16, 6.28

Oner II v. EPA, 597 F.2d 184 (9th Cir. 1979)

§ 5.10

Ostermeier v. Victorian House, Inc., 121 A.2d 611, 503 N.Y.S.2d 645 (2d Dept. 1986)

§ 5.7

Patitucci v. Drelich, 153 N.J. 177, 379 A.2d 297 (Law Div. 1977)

§ 5.13

Patrons Oxford Mutual Insurance Co. v. Marior, 573 A.2d 16 (Me. 1990)

§ 10.3

Peerless Plating Co., *In re,* 70 Bankr. 943 (Bankr. W.D. Mich. 1987)

§§ 7.4, 7.6

Penn Terra Limited v. Department of Environmental Resources, 733 F.2d 267 (3d Cir. 1984)

§ 7.5

Pennsylvania Dept. of Transportation v. Congoleum Corp., Pa. Commw. Ct., No. 45 MD 1990, Feb. 12, 1990

§ 6.11

Pezzolanella v. Galloway, 132 Misc. 2d 429, 503 N.Y.S.2d 990 (City Ct. 1986)

§ 6.9

Philadelphia, City of v. Stepan Chemical Co., 713 F. Supp. 1491 (E.D. Pa. 1989)

§ 5.16

Philadelphia, City of v. Stepan Chemical Co., Nos. 81-0851, 83-5493 (E.D. Pa. 1987)

§ 7.12

Philadelphia v. Lead Industries Association Inc., No. 90-7064-JG (D.C.E. Pa., Nov. 5, 1990)

§ 5.2

Philadelphia Electric Co. v. Hercules, Inc., 762 F.2d 303 (3d Cir. 1985) *cert. denied,* 474 U.S. 980 (1985)

§§ 5.16, 6.23, 6.24

Piccolini v. Samon's Wrecking, 686 F. Supp. 1063 (M.D. Pa. 1988)

§ 1.14

Pinkerton v. Georgia Pacific Corp., Mo. Cir. Ct., Clay Cty., No. CV 186-4651 CC (Jan. 8, 1990)

§ 6.28

Pinole Pointe Properties v. Bethlehem Steel Corporation, 596 F. Supp. 283 (N.D. Cal. 1984)

§ 6.11

Polius v. Clark Equipment Co., 802 F.2d 75 (3d Cir. 1986)

§ 5.16

Case	*Book §*
Prelick v. Johns-Manville Corp., 531 F. Supp. 96 (W.D. Pa. 1982)	§ 6.21
Prudential Insurance Co. of America v. U.S. Gypsum Co., 711 F. Supp. 1244 (D.C.N.J. 1989) *cert. denied,* 110 S. Ct. 1113, 107 L. Ed. 1020 (1990)	§§ 1.1, 6.6, 6.7
Quanta Resources Corp., *In re,* 739 F.2d 927 (3d Cir. 1984) *aff'd sub nom.*	§ 7.6
Rabb v. Orkin Exterminating Co., Inc., 677 F. Supp. 424 (D.S.C. 1987)	§ 6.17
Ramirez v. Amsted Indus., Inc., 171 N.J. Super. 261, 408 A.2d 818 (Super. Ct. App. Div. 1979) *aff'd,* 86 N.J. 332 A.2d 811 (1981)	§ 5.16
Ray v. Alad Corp., 19 Cal. 3d 22, 560 P.2d 3, 136 Cal. Rptr. 574 (1977)	§ 5.16
Ray v. Karris, 780 F.2d 636 (7th Cir. 1985)	§ 6.20
Reaves v. Armstrong World Industries Inc., No. 89-2289 (Fla. Dist. Ct. App. Oct. 31, 1990)	§ 7.8
Reconstruction Finance Corp. v. Teter, 117 F.2d 716 (7th Cir.) *cert. denied,* 314 U.S. 620 (1941)	§ 5.15
Related Asbestos Cases, *In re,* 543 F. Supp. 1152 (N.D. Cal. 1982)	§§ 6.21, 7.8
Remington Rand Corp., *In re,* 836 F.2d 825 (3d Cir. 1988)	§ 7.7
Retirement Community Developers, Inc. v. Merine, 713 F. Supp. 153 (D. Md. 1989)	§§ 1.2, 1.6, 1.15, 6.5, 6.6
Rifkin v. Crow, 574 F.2d 256 (5th Cir. 1978)	§ 6.19
Riverside Market Dev. Corp. v. International Bldg. Products, Inc., No. CIV-A-88-5317 (E.D. La. May 23, 1990)	§ 5.14
Roberts v. Estate of Barbagallo, 531 A.2d 1125 (Pa. Super. 1987)	§§ 5.11, 5.12, 6.22
Robinson, *In re,* 776 F.2d 30 (2d Cir. 1985) *rev'd on other grounds sub nom.*	§ 7.7
Rockwell International Corporation v. IU International Corporation, 702 F. Supp. 1384 (N.D. Ill. 1988)	§ 5.17
Rosenblum, Inc. v. Adler, 93 N.J. 324, 461 A.2d 138 (1983)	§ 5.12
Ruggeri v. Minnesota Mining & Mfg. Co., 63 Ill. App. 3d 525, 380 N.E. 2d 445 (1978)	§ 7.10
Rutledge v. Dodenhoff, 254 S.C. 407, 175 S.E.2d 792 (1970)	§ 5.23
Safe Buildings Alliance v. EPA, 846 F.2d 79 (D.C. Cir. 1988) *cert. denied,* 488 U.S. 942 (1988)	§ 1.20
St. Louis Union Trust Co. v. Merrill Lynch, Pierce, Fenner & Smith, Inc., 562 F.2d 1040 (8th Cir. 1977) *cert. denied,* 435 U.S. 925 (1978)	§ 6.19

CASES

Case	*Book §*
Samuels v. Brooks, 519 N.E.2d 605 (Mass. App. Ct. 1988)	§ 5.11
Santiago v. E.W. Bliss Div., Gulf & Western Mfg. Co., 201 N.J. Super. 205, 492 A.2d 1089 (App. Div. 1985)	§ 5.13
Schlick v. Penn-Dixie Cement Corp., 507 F.2d 374 (2d Cir. 1974) *cert. denied,* 421 U.S. 976 (1975)	§ 6.19
School District of City of Independence, Missouri v. U.S. Gypsum Co., 750 S.W.2d 442 (Mo. App. 1988)	§§ 5.3, 6.28
School District of Detroit v. Celotex Corp., *reprinted in* 3 Nat'l J. Asb. Buildings Lit. 48 (Mich. Cir. Ct., Wayne Co. Oct. 20, 1989)	§ 6.21
Schulman v. Vera, 108 Cal. App. 3d 552, 166 Cal. Rptr. 620 (1980)	§ 6.14
Sector v. Knight, 716 P.2d 790 (Utah 1986)	§ 5.12
Sharp v. Coopers & Lybrand, 649 F.2d 175 (3d Cir. 1981) *cert. denied,* 455 U.S. 938 (1982)	§ 6.19
Shirley v. The Drackett Products Co., 26 Mich. App. 644, 182 N.W.2d 726 (1970)	§ 6.13
Shores v. Sklar, 647 F.2d 462 (5th Cir. 1981) *cert. denied,* 459 U.S. 1102 (1983)	§ 6.19
Sindell v. Abbott Laboratories, 26 Cal. 3d 588, 607 P.2d 924, *cert. denied,* 449 U.S. 912 (1980)	§§ 6.21, 7.8
Sisters of St. Mary v. AAER Sprayed Insulation, No. 85-CV-5952 (Cir. Ct., Dane Co., Wis. Dec. 12, 1987) *aff'd,* 151 Wis. 2d 708 (N.W.2d 723) (Wis. App. 1989)	§ 5.2
SKD Enterprises Inc. v. L&M Offset, Inc., 65 Misc. 2d 612, 318 N.Y.S.2d 539 (1971)	§ 5.7
Smith v. Carpets by Direct Inc., No. 89-CVS-4974 (Super. Ct., Guilford Co., N.C. Feb. 13, 1990)	§§ 6.11, 6.18
Smith v. Cooper/T. Smith Corp., 846 F.2d 325, *reh'g granted,* 850 F.2d 1086 (5th Cir. 1988)	§ 6.20
Smith Land & Improvement Corp. v. Celotex Corp., 851 F.2d 86 (3d Cir. 1988) *cert. denied,* 199 S. Ct. 837, 102 L. Ed. 2d 969 (1989)	§§ 5.16, 6.27, 7.18
Solow v. W.R. Grace & Co., 1989 N.Y. Misc. LEXIS 894 (N.Y. Sup. 1989) N.Y.L.J. Aug. 9, 1989	§§ 6.11, 6.13, 6.16, 6.21
Sosna v. Iowa, 419 U.S. 393 (1975)	§ 5.2
Southland Corp. v. Ashland Oil, Inc., 696 F. Supp. 994 (D.N.J. 1988)	§§ 5.16, 6.15
Ssangyong/Kearny Mesa Association v. Al Bahr Temple of San Diego (D.C.S. Calif., No. 89-0836-R)	§ 6.6
Stanfield v. Medalist Indus., 34 Ill. App. 3d 635, 340 N.E.2d 276 (1975)	§ 7.10
Steiner v. J.F. Baxter, Civ. 89-809 (D.D.C. 1989)	§ 6.19
Steinhardt v. Johns-Manville Sales Corp., 54 N.Y.2d 1008, 430 N.E.2d 1297 (1981)	§ 7.2
Sterling v. Velsicol Chemical Corp. 855 F.2d 1188, 19 Envtl. L. Rep. (Envtl. L. Inst.) 20,404 (6th Cir. 1988)	§§ 6.4, 7.8

Case	*Book §*
Stone v. Ethan Allen, Inc., 232 Va. 365, 350 S.E.2d 629 (1986)	§ 6.17
Strickland v. Johns-Manville Int'l Corp., 461 F. Supp. 215 (S.D. Tex. 1978), *cert. denied,* 456 U.S. 967 (1982)	§ 7.2
Sully v. Schmidt, 147 N.Y. 248, 41 N.E. 514 (1895)	§ 6.14
Summers v. Tice, 33 Cal. 2d 80, 199 P.2d 1 (1948)	§ 6.21
Sun Insurance Services, Inc. v. 260 Peachtree Street, Inc. 192 Ga. App. 482, 385 S.E.2d 127 (1989)	§ 5.8
Sundstrand Corp. v. Sun Chemical Corp., 553 F.2d 1033 (7th Cir.)	§ 6.19
T&E Industries v. Safety Light Corp., 680 F. Supp. 696 (D.N.J. 1988)	§§ 1.8, 1.14, 1.16, 6.9, 6.29, 7.25
Tanglewood East Homeowners v. Charles Thomas Inc., 849 F.2d 1568 (5th Cir. 1988)	§ 5.18
Temple, *In re,* 851 F.2d 1269 (11th Cir. 1988)	§ 5.2
Tenant v. Lawton, 26 Wash. App. 701, 415 P.2d 1305 (Wash. Ct. App. 1980)	§§ 5.12, 6.16
Tennessee Coal, Iron & Railroad Co. v. Hortiline (sic) 244 Ala. 116, 11 So. 2d 833 (1943)	§ 1.2
Terlindo v. Neely, 275 S.C. 395, 271 S.E.2d 768 (1980)	§ 6.14
The 3250 Wilshire Boulevard Building v. W.R. Grace & Co. (1989 U.S. Dist. LEXIS 17287) (C.D. Cal. 1989), *aff'd,* 915 F.2d 1355 (9th Cir. 1990)	§ 5.2
The University of Vermont and State Agricultural College v. W.R. Grace & Co., 565 A.2d 1354 (Vt. 1989)	§ 7.2
Thompson v. Johns-Manville Sales Corp., 714 F.2d 581 (5th Cir. 1983) *cert. denied,* 465 U.S. 1102 (1983)	§ 6.21
3250 Wilshire Blvd. Building et al. v. W.R. Grace & Co.	§ 8.2
3550 Stevens Creek Associates v. Barclays Bank of California (D.C. N. Calif., No. C87-20672) 1988	§ 6.6
Trustees of Columbia University v. Mitchell/Giurgola Assoc., 109 A.2d 449, 495 N.Y.S.2d 371 (1985)	§ 6.4
TSC Industries, Inc. v. Northway, Inc., 426 U.S. 438, 96 S. Ct. 2126, 48 L. Ed. 2d 757 (1976)	§ 6.19
Tusch Enterprises v. Coffin, 740 P.2d 1022 (1987)	§ 6.14
United States v. A&F Materials Co., 582 F. Supp. 842 (D.C. Ill. 1984)	§ 6.7
United States v. Aceto Agricultural Chemicals Corp., 872 F.2d 1373 (8th Cir. 1989)	§ 1.21
United States v. Allied Chemical Corp., 587 F. Supp. 1205 (N.D. Cal. 1984)	§ 1.18
United States v. Argent Corp., 21 Env't Rep. Cas. (BNA) 1353 (D.N.M.) 1984	§§ 1.7, 7.2
United States v. Ballard, 779 F.2d 287 (5th Cir.) *cert. denied,* 475 U.S. 1109 (1986)	§ 5.25

Case	*Book §*
United States v. Bliss, 667 F. Supp. 1298 (E.D. Mo. 1987)	§ 1.8
United States v. Boyd, 520 F.2d 642 (6th Cir. 1975) *cert. denied,* 423 U.S. 1050 (1976)	§ 6.15
United States v. Carolawn Co., 14 Envtl. L. Rep. (Envtl. L. Inst.) 20,698, 21 Env't Rep. Cas. (BNA) 2125 (D.S.C. 1984)	§§ 1.7, 1.9, 5.16
United States v. Carr, 880 F.2d 1550 (2d Cir. 1989)	§§ 1.26, 5.22
United States v. Cauffman, 21 Envtl. L. Rep. (Envtl. L. Inst.) 2167 (C.D. Col. 1984)	§ 1.7
United States v. Charles George Trucking Co., 624 F. Supp. 1185 (D. Mass. 1986) *aff'd,* 823 F.2d 685 (1st Cir. 1987)	§ 1.26
United States v. Chem-Dyne Corp., 572 F. Supp. 802 (S.D. Ohio 1983)	§ 1.2
United States v. Conservation Chemical Co., 619 F. Supp. 162 (W.D. Mo. 1985)	§§ 1.8, 5.14
United States v. Conservation Chemical Co., 628 F. Supp. 391 (W.D. Mo. 1985), *modified,* 681 F. Supp. 1394 (W.D. Mo. 1988)	§ 7.17
United States v. Dickerson, 640 F. Supp. 448 (D. Md. 1986)	§ 7.2
United States v. Fiber Free Co., No. A-89-0624 (D.W. Va. 1990)	§ 1.23
United States v. Fleet Factors Corp., 724 F. Supp. 955 (S.D. Ga. 1988) 901 F.2d 1550, *reh'g denied, en banc,* 911 F.2d 742 (11th Cir. 1990)	§§ 1.8, 5.18, 7.4, 10.3
United States v. Geppert Brothers, 638 F. Supp. 996 (E.D. Pa. 1986)	§§ 1.23, 5.5
United States v. Hooker Chemicals & Plastics Corp., 722 F. Supp. 960 (W.D.N.Y. 1989)	§ 7.15
United States v. Ira Bushey & Sons, Inc., 363 F. Supp. 110 (D.C. Vt. 1973) *aff'd,* 487 F.2d 1393 (2d Cir. 1973) *cert. denied,* 417 U.S. 976 (1974)	§ 5.17
United States v. Johns-Manville Sales Corp., 13 Envtl. L. Rep. (Envtl. L. Inst.) 20,310 (D.N.H. Nov. 15, 1982)	§ 7.5
United States v. Kayser-Roth Corp., 724 F. Supp. 15 (D.R.I. 1989) *aff'd,* 910 F.2d 24 (1st Cir. 1990)	§ 5.17
United States v. Klein, 515 F.2d 751 (3d Cir. 1975)	§ 6.20
United States v. Long, 687 F. Supp. 343 (S.D. Ohio 1987)	§ 1.12
United States v. Maryland Bank & Trust Co., 632 F. Supp. 573 (D. Md. 1986)	§§ 1.7, 5.16, 5.18
United States v. Metate Asbestos Corp., 584 F. Supp. 1143 (D. Ariz. 1984)	§ 1.8
United States v. Mirabile, 15 Envtl. L. Rep. (Envtl. L. Inst.) 20,992 (E.D. Pa. 1985)	§§ 5.14, 5.16, 5.18
United States v. Mirabile, 23 Env't Rep. Cas. (BNA) 1511 (E.D. Pa. 1985)	§ 1.7
United States v. Monsanto Co., 858 F.2d 160 (4th Cir. 1988) *cert. denied,* 109 S. Ct. 3156 (1989)	§ 1.6

Case	*Book §*
United States v. Moore, 27 Env't Rep. Cas. (BNA) 1976 (E.D. Va. 1988)	§ 5.15
United States v. Mottolo, 605 F. Supp. 898 (D.N.H. 1985)	§§ 5.14, 5.17, 7.2
United States v. Mottolo, 695 F. Supp. 615 (D.N.H. 1988)	§ 7.12
United States v. Nicolet, Inc., 712 F. Supp. 1193 (E.D. Pa. 1989)	§ 5.18
United States v. Northeastern Pharmaceutical and Chemical Co., Inc., 597 F. Supp. 823 (W.D. Mo. 1984) *aff'd in part, rev'd in part and remanded,* 810 F.2d 726 (8th Cir. 1986) *cert. denied,* 484 U.S. 848 (1987)	§§ 1.4, 1.6, 1.7, 1.21
United States v. Northernaire Plating Co., 670 F. Supp. 742 (W.D. Mich. 1987) *aff'd,* 889 F.2d 1497 (6th Cir. 1989) *cert. denied,* 110 S. Ct. 1527 (1990)	§ 1.12
United States v. P/B STCO 213, ON 527 979, 756 F.2d 364 (5th Cir. 1985)	§ 6.15
United States v. Price, 523 F. Supp. 1055, *aff'd,* 688 F.2d 204 (3d Cir. 1982) *aff'g* 577 F. Supp. 1055 (D.N.J. 1981)	§§ 5.10, 6.17, 7.5
United States v. Protex Industries, 874 F.2d 740 (10th Cir. 1989)	§ 1.27
United States v. Serafini, 1988 U.S. Dist. LEXIS 7361 (M.D. Pa. 1988)	§ 7.12
United States v. South Carolina Recycl. & Disp., Inc., 653 F. Supp. 984 (D.S.C. 1984) *aff'd in part, vacated in part, sub nom.*	§§ 1.6, 5.8
United States v. Stringfellow, 661 F. Supp. 1053 (C.D. Cal. 1987)	§ 1.4
United States v. Tyson, 22 Env't Rep. Cas. (BNA) 1471 (E.D. Pa. 1984)	§ 7.2
United States v. Union Scrap Iron & Metal, Civ. 4-89-40 (D.C. Minn. Dec. 27, 1990)	§ 7.7
United States v. Wade, 577 F. Supp. 1326 (E.D. Pa. 1983)	§ 1.2
United States v. Wade, 653 F. Supp. 11 (E.D. Pa. 1984)	§ 7.2
United States v. Ward, 618 F. Supp. 884 (E.D.N.C. 1985)	§§ 1.8, 5.14
United States v. Whizco, Inc., 841 F.2d 147, 18 Envtl. L. Rep. (Envtl. L. Inst.) 20,571 (6th Cir. 1988)	§ 7.6
United States Fidelity and Guaranty Co. v. Star Fire Coals, Inc., 856 F.2d 31 (6th Cir. 1988)	§ 10.3
United States Steel Corp., *In re,* Exchange Act Release No. 16223, 18 SEC Docket (CCH) 497 (Sept. 27, 1979)	§ 6.19
Vermont v. Staco, Inc., 684 F. Supp. 822 (D. Vt. 1988)	§§ 1.21, 5.17
Vervaecke v. Chiles, Heider & Co., 578 F.2d 713 (8th Cir. 1978)	§ 6.19
Violet v. Picillo, 648 F. Supp. 1283 (D.R.I. 1986)	§ 7.17
Waldron v. Raymark, 124 F.R.D. 235 (N.D. Ga. 1989)	§ 5.2
Wall Tube & Metal Products Co., 831 F.2d 118, 18 Envtl. L. Rep. (Envtl. L. Inst.) 20,013 (6th Cir. 1987)	§§ 1.19, 1.20, 7.6

Case	Book §
Weinstein v. American Biomaterials Corp., 123 F.R.D. 442 (S.D.N.Y. 1988)	§ 5.2
Western Insulation Services, Inc. v. Central National Insurance Co. of Omaha, Minn. Ct. App., No. C0-90-162, 9/18/90	§ 13.6
Westrom v. Kerr-McGee Chemical Corp., No. 82-C-2034 (N.D. Ill., Oct. 4, 1983)	§ 6.17
Whetstone v. Olson, 46 Wash. App. 308, 732 P.2d 159 (1986)	§ 5.25
Wickland Oil Terminals v. Asarco, Inc., 792 F.2d 887 (9th Cir. 1986)	§ 1.4
Windham v. American Brands, Inc., 565 F.2d 59 (4th Cir. 1977) *cert. denied,* 435 U.S. 968 (1978)	§ 5.2
Wingett v. Teledyne Industries, Inc., 479 N.E.2d 51 (Ind. 1985)	§ 6.10
Wisniewski v. Johns-Manville Corp., 759 F.2d 271 (3d Cir. 1985) *aff'd,* 812 F.2d 81 (3d Cir. 1987)	§ 6.4
Wolf v. 2539 Realty Associates, 161 App. Div. 2d 11, 560 N.Y.S.2d 24 (1st Dept. 1990)	§ 5.7
Woods v. Barnett Bank of Fort Lauderdale, 765 F.2d 1004, *reh'g denied, en banc,* 772 F.2d 918 (11th Cir. 1985)	§ 6.19
Young v. Garawicki, 380 Mass. 162, 404 N.E.2d 1045 (1980)	§ 5.7

INDEX

AIR CONDITIONING SYSTEMS
Dangers of § 4.2
AMERICAN CONFERENCE OF
GOVERNMENTAL INDUSTRIAL
HYGENISTS (ACGIH)
Research and §§ 3.32, 4.4
AMERICAN SOCIETY OF
HEATING, REFRIGERATING
AND AIR-CONDITIONING
ENGINEERS (ASHRAE)
Standards of §§ 1.35, 4.2, 4.6, 5.5
ASBESTOS
Abatement. See ASBESTOS
ABATEMENT
Building occupant and § 8.14
Danger of § 7.9
Disclosure of §§ 6.15, 6.16
Emergency checklist § 12.11
Emission prevention § 1.23
Evaluation and analysis § 3.10
Generally §§ 3.7, 3.13
Health effects § 3.9
Identification of § 14.4
Impact of §§ 8.9, 8.18, 8.20
Investor response to § 8.13
Insurance and § 10.6
Lender response to § 8.13
Mandatory inspection for § 2.6
Market value § 8.9
Materials containing, Appendix 3C
Media response to § 8.12
Permissible exposure limit § 3.12
Regulations regarding §§ 3.12,
8.10
Remedial alternatives § 3.11
Response to presence of §§ 8.13,
8.14, 8.15
Survey of § 11.8
Uses of § 3.8
ASBESTOS ABATEMENT
Air testing and § 1.20
Case study § 14.1–14.11
Cost recovery and § 1.12

ASBESTOS ABATEMENT
(Continued)
Facility manager and § 14.1
Requirements of § 6.15
Response to § 8.16
Statute violation and § 5.23
Stigma of § 8.17
ASBESTOS BAN AND PHASE OUT
RULE
Generally § 3.8
ASBESTOS HAZARD EMERGENCY
RESPONSE ACT (AHERA)
Asbestos contractor's certification
§§ 2.10, 14.3
Generally §§ 1.20, 8.10
Labeling of materials § 12.7
Training/certification requirements
§ 14.3
Violations and § 5.23. See also
ASBESTOS ABATEMENT
"AS IS" CLAUSE
Significance of § 6.22
ATOMIC ABSORPTION
SPECTROMETRY (AAS)
Use of § 3.16
ATTORNEYS
Client communication § 5.25
Environmental specialists § 11.7
Fees § 6.29
Notification of emergency § 12.23

BANKRUPTCY
Abandonment § 7.6
Automatic stay § 7.5
Dischargeability § 7.7
Generally § 7.4
BREACH OF CONTRACT
Generally § 6.18
BREACH OF WARRANTY
Generally §§ 6.13, 6.22
See also COVENANT OF QUIET
ENJOYMENT, WARRANTY OF
HABITABILITY

BUILDING MATERIALS
EXCEPTIONS
Generally § 6.6

CANCER
Risk of § 6.12
CARBON DIOXIDE
Levels §§ 4.2, 4.6
CARBON MONOXIDE
Generally § 4.3
Levels of § 4.6
CAVEAT EMPTOR
Principle of §§ 5.10, 7.18
CLEAN AIR ACT
Generally § 1.23
COMMUNICATION
Significance of §§ 14.7, 14.8,
14.9
COMPREHENSIVE
ENVIRONMENTAL RESPONSE,
COMPENSATION AND
LIABILITY ACT OF 1990
(CERCLA)
Amendments and § 1.2
Claim elements § 1.5
Contribution claims § 6.27
Corporations and §§ 5.15, 5.17
Cost recovery §§ 1.4, 1.19, 5.18, 6.5,
7.2
De minimus settlements § 1.17
Defendants § 1.6
"Disposal" defined § 1.11
Exceptions §§ 1.15, 6.6, 6.7
Exclusions § 6.8
"Facility" defined § 1.8
Generally §§ 1.1, 1.3, 8.5
Hazardous substances list § 1.9
History of § 1.2
Injunctive relief §§ 1.16, 5.3,
6.25
Lawsuits under §§ 6.5, 6.6
Liability of §§ 1.10, 5.6, 5.7, 5.8,
5.9, 5.14, 6.6, 6.7, 9.3
Notification requirements §§ 1.18,
1.33
"Owner/operator" defined § 1.7
Penalty provisions § 1.26
"Release" defined § 1.12
Remedial actions § 1.14
Removal actions § 1.14
Response action and §§ 1.14, 1.15
Third-party defense § 7.11

CONSULTANT(S)
Discussion issues § 11.11
Hazardous substances and § 3.3
Hiring of § 3.3
Lead survey § 3.16
Liability of §§ 5.19, 5.24
Selection of § 11.3
CONTRACTOR(S)
Communication with § 14.8
Contracts with § 13.1
Insurance and §§ 10.4, 13.21
Liability of § 5.23
Prequalification of § 14.8
Remedial actions and § 3.29
Selection of § 13.2
Standards of care § 13.13
State laws and § 13.23
Title to waste material § 13.8
Training certification and licensing
§§ 2.10, 14.3
See also CONTRACTS WITH
CONTRACTORS
CONTRACTS WITH
CONTRACTORS
Compliance with laws § 13.5
Confidentiality § 13.16
Damages for delays § 13.15
Dispute resolution. See DISPUTE
RESOLUTION
Documents § 13.4
Final acceptance § 13.12
Generally § 13.1
Indemnification § 13.15
Insurance/bonding § 13.21
Licenses/permits § 13.11
Notification § 13.22
Observation of work § 13.7
Payment § 13.6
Recordkeeping § 13.22
Site conditions § 13.3
Standard of care § 13.13
State laws § 13.23
Subcontractors § 13.10
Time and § 13.9
Title to waste materials § 13.8
CONTRACTS OF SALE
Buyer's considerations § 9.1
Landlord's considerations
§ 9.2
Lender's consideration § 9.3
Seller's considerations § 9.1
Tenant's considerations § 9.2

CO-OPERATIVE/CONDOMINIUM
APARTMENTS
remediation and § 2.7
CORPORATIONS
Damage responsibility § 5.14
Dissolution of § 5.15
Subsidiaries § 5.17
Violations of § 6.19
COURT CLAIMS
Generally § 6.2
COVENANT OF QUIET
ENJOYMENT
Generally § 6.14
CRIME-FRAUD EXCEPTION
Generally § 5.25

DAMAGES
Types of § 6.4
DEPARTMENT OF HOUSING AND
URBAN DEVELOPMENT (HUD)
Standards of § 3.19
DES PLANCHES, TANQUEREL § 3.15
DEVELOPERS
Implied warranty of habitability
§§ 5.13, 6.14
DISPUTE RESOLUTION
Arbitration § 13.18
Mediation § 13.19
Rent-a-judge § 13.20
DUTY TO WARN
Generally § 6.10

ECONOMIC LOSS
Significance of § 6.11
EMERGENCIES
Accident occurrence § 12.13
Asbestos checklist § 12.11
Cleanup of environmental
contamination § 12.17
Environmental coordinator §§ 12.9,
12.25
Generally §§ 12.1, 12.35
Insurance companies and § 12.22
Isolating the area § 12.16
Locating problem/source § 12.15
Notifications §§ 12.6, 12.18
Operations and maintenance plan.
See OPERATIONS AND
MAINTENANCE PROGRAMS
Phone tree and contacts § 12.12
Plan execution § 12.14
Procedural manuals § 12.10

EMERGENCIES *(Continued)*
Prior planning § 12.2
Public relations/media. See PUBLIC
RELATIONS/MEDIA AND
EMERGENCIES
Regulatory agencies and. See
REGULATORY AGENCIES
EMERGENCY PLANNING AND
COMMUNITY RIGHT-TO-KNOW
ACT (EPCRA)
Generally §§ 1.26, 1.33
ENVIRONMENTAL AUDITS
Attorneys and § 11.7
Checklist for § 11.2
Consultant selection §§ 11.3, 11.5
Contracts and § 11.5
Generally §§ 8.6, 8.21, 11.1
Process of § 11.4
Recordkeeping § 11.6
ENVIRONMENTAL CLEANUP
RESPONSIBILITY ACT (ECRA)
Generally § 2.2
ENVIRONMENTAL COORDINATOR
Role of §§ 12.9, 12.24, 12.25
ENVIRONMENTAL PROTECTION
AGENCY (EPA)
Asbestos and §§ 1.20, 3.8, 3.10, 5.7,
8.10, 14.3
Authority of § 1.3
Building materials exception and
§ 6.6
Formaldehyde and § 3.32
Guidelines of § 11.10
Lead and § 3.15
Liability to §§ 1.6, 9.1
Notification requirements §§ 1.18,
1.26, 1.33
Polychlorinated biphenyls (PCBs) and
§ 3.28
Proposed legislation and §§ 1.35, 4.2,
5.18
Radon and §§ 3.21, 3.23
Regional offices § 3.2, Appendix 3A
Regulations and §§ 1.22, 1.23, 1.24,
1.34, 3.11, 3.12, 3.27
Right of access to property § 1.12
Role of § 1.13
Sick building syndrome and § 4.2
Standards §§ 3.5, 3.6, 3.23
Training and § 14.3
Transformers and § 10.1
Water treatment systems and § 10.1

ESTOPPEL
Generally § 7.14

FACILITY MANAGEMENT
Role of §§ 14.1, 14.2, 14.7
FEDERAL HOME LOAN
MORTGAGE CORPORATION
(FHLMC) § 8.21
FEDERAL NATIONAL MORTGAGE
ASSOCIATION (FNMA) § 8.21
FEDERAL STATUTES
Federal penalty provisions §§ 1.25,
1.30
Generally § 1.1
Proposed legislation § 1.32
State cost recovery § 1.4
State/local penalty provisions
§ 1.31
See also specific legislation
FIRE HAZARD RULE
Generally § 3.27
FORMALDEHYDE
Evaluation of § 3.33
Generally § 3.30
Health effects § 3.32
Identification of § 3.33
Levels of § 4.6
Remedial actions § 3.35
Sources of § 3.31
Standards § 3.34
FRAUD
Defined § 6.16
Estoppel and § 7.14

HAZARDOUS SUBSTANCES
Analysis of § 3.5
Consultants and § 3.3
Generally § 3.1
Identification of § 3.4
Sampling methodology § 3.5
Standard comparisons § 3.6
See also specific substances

INDEMNIFICATION
Generally § 6.15
INDOOR AIR POLLUTION
Cases involving § 5.23
Effect of § 1.35
INDOOR AIR QUALITY ACT
Generally §§ 1.32, 1.35
INDOOR AIR STANDARDS
New Jersey § 4.2

INDUCTIVELY COUPLED PLASMA
SPECTROSCOPY
Use of § 3.16
INJUNCTIONS
Described § 6.25
INNOCENT LANDOWNER
DEFENSE
Checklist for § 7.13
Generally § 7.12
INSURANCE
Building owner and § 10.5
Claims made § 10.12
Commercial general liability (CGL)
policy §§ 10.3, 10.4, 10.7
Commercial property and § 10.6
Contractor pollution liability policy
(CPL) § 10.4
Environmental impairment § 10.8
Evaluation of § 10.10
Generally § 10.2
Litigation issues § 10.3
Loss exposure minimization § 10.13
Market cycle § 10.2
Notification requirements of § 12.22
Policy terms and conditions § 10.11
Professional liability and § 10.7
Storage and treatment issues § 10.9
Sunset clauses § 10.12
True occurrence § 10.12
Types of coverage § 10.4
INTERNATIONAL AGENCY FOR
RESEARCH ON CANCER (IARC)
Research by § 3.32

LAWSUITS
Class actions § 5.2
Defendants/plaintiffs §§ 5.1, 5.3, 5.4,
5.8
See also specific liable parties
LEAD
Blood level Appendix 3E
Evaluation § 3.16
Generally §§ 3.14, 3.19
Health effects § 3.15
Paint and Appendix 3D
Remedial alternatives § 3.18
Standards § 3.17
LEGAL DEFENSES
Asbestos and § 7.9
Assumption of risk § 7.15
Bankruptcy §§ 7.4, 7.5, 7.6, 7.7
Contributory negligence § 7.16

LEGAL DEFENSES *(Continued)*
Damage control § 7.20
Disclaimers § 7.18
Due diligence § 7.12
Estoppel § 7.14
Generally § 7.1
Innocent landowner § 7.12
Privity of contract §§ 6.11, 7.3
Product identification and causation
§ 7.8
State-of-the-art § 7.10
Statute of limitations § 7.2
Third-parties § 7.11
Unclean hands § 7.17
LIABILITY THEORIES AND
Appraisers § 5.19
Architects § 5.24
Basis of liability § 6.1
Buyers § 5.10
Commercial building owners §§ 5.5,
10.5
Consultants §§ 5.19, 5.24
Contractors §§ 5.23, 10.4
Designers § 5.24
Employees § 5.22
Employers § 5.21
Engineers § 5.24
Generally § 6.21
Homeowners § 5.11
Landlords §§ 5.7, 6.16
Lenders § 5.18
Property managers § 5.20
Real estate brokers §§ 5.12, 6.16
Sellers of property § 5.9
Successors-in-interest § 5.16
Tenants § 5.8
MARKET VALUE OF PROPERTY
Appraiser § 8.2
Asbestos abatement and §§ 8.16, 8.17
Asbestos impact §§ 8.9, 8.18, 8.20
Building occupant and § 8.14
Buildings containing hazardous
material § 8.24
Cash flow §§ 8.5, 8.6
Change estimation § 8.7
Debt value § 8.6
Economist § 8.2
Generally §§ 8.1, 8.25
Investor and § 8.13
Lender and § 8.13
Property taxes § 8.22
Reduction estimation § 8.3

MARKET VALUE OF PROPERTY
(Continued)
Regulations and §§ 8.8, 8.10, 8.11
Residential property §§ 8.19, 8.21
Transaction prices § 8.20
Valuation model § 8.4
MICROORGANISMS
Dangers of § 4.11
**MINNESOTA ENVIRONMENTAL
RESPONSE AND LIABILITY ACT
(MERLA)**
Generally § 2.3
**MONTE CARLO SIMULATION
TECHNIQUES**
Generally § 8.18
**NATIONAL CONTINGENCY PLAN
(NCP)**
Cost recovery and § 1.4
Generally § 1.13
Response action and §§ 1.2, 1.14, 1.15
**NATIONAL EMISSION STANDARDS
FOR HAZARDOUS AIR
POLLUTANTS (NESHAP)**
Asbestos removal § 3.11
Generally § 1.23
Penalty provisions § 1.28
Violations of § 5.7
**NATIONAL INSTITUTE FOR
OCCUPATIONAL SAFETY AND
HEALTH (NIOSH)**
Research by §§ 4.3, 4.4
NEGLIGENCE
Generally §§ 6.17, 6.24
**NEW/USEFUL PRODUCT
EXCEPTIONS**
Generally § 6.7
NICOTINE
Danger of § 4.11
NOTIFICATIONS
Attorneys and § 12.23
Environmental coordinator and
§ 12.24
Insurance companies and § 12.22
Neighbors/public § 12.21
Occupants and § 12.20
Regulatory §§ 1.18, 1.33, 12.6, 12.19

**OCCUPATIONAL SAFETY AND
HEALTH ADMINISTRATION ACT
(OSHA)**
Asbestos exposure § 3.12
Asbestos removal § 3.11

OCCUPATIONAL SAFETY AND
  HEALTH ADMINISTRATION ACT
  (OSHA) *(Continued)*
  Carbon dioxide level § 4.2
  Cost implications of regulations
    § 8.11
  Generally §§ 1.24, 8.10
  Hazardous Communications
    Standard (HAZCOM) § 1.24
  Notification requirements § 12.6
OPERATIONS AND MAINTENANCE
  PROGRAMS
  Cash flow and § 8.5
  Cost implications §§ 8.11, 8.22
  Defined § 3.11
  Establishment of § 12.3
  Generally §§ 11.9, 12.3
  Guidelines § 11.10
  Labeling § 12.7
  Manual § 12.8
  Notification § 12.6
  Success of § 12.9
  Survey § 12.4
  Training for §§ 12.5, 14.3
ORGANIC SOLVENT VAPORS
  Dangers of § 4.11

PARTICULANTS/FIBERS
  Dangers of § 4.11
PENDENT JURISDICTION
  Generally § 6.3
PESTICIDES
  Analysis § 4.11
PETROLEUM EXCLUSION
  Generally § 6.8
PHASE CONTRAST MICROSCOPY
  (PCM)
  Use of § 3.12
POLYCHLORINATED BIPHENYLS
  (PCBS)
  Evaluation § 3.28
  Generally §§ 3.25, 3.29
  Health effects § 3.27
  Regulations regarding § 3.26
  Remedial alternatives § 3.28
  Transformer classifications
    Appendix 3G
"POTENTIALLY RESPONSIBLE
  PARTIES" (PRP)
  Defined § 1.6
  Identification of § 1.6

"POTENTIALLY RESPONSIBLE
  PARTIES" (PRP) *(Continued)*
  Liability and §§ 1.4, 1.10
  Notification of § 1.4
PRIVATE NUISANCE
  Defined § 6.24
PROPERTY TAXES
  Property value and § 8.22
  Reassessment § 8.23
PUBLIC NUISANCE
  Defined § 6.23
PUBLIC RELATIONS/MEDIA AND
  EMERGENCIES
  Handling of § 12.31
  Honesty § 12.34
  Message point development § 12.32
  Spokesperson selection § 12.33
PUNITIVE DAMAGES
  Recovery of § 6.28

QUALITY OF LIFE
  Significance of § 6.12

RACKETEER INFLUENCED AND
  CORRUPT ORGANIZATION ACT
  (RICO)
  Violations of § 6.20
RADON
  Evaluation § 3.23
  Generally § 3.20
  Health effects § 3.22
  Remedial alternatives § 3.24
  Risk evaluation chart Appendix 3F
  Sources/locations of § 3.21
  Standards § 3.23
  Working level (WL) § 3.23
READING PRONG
  Described § 3.21
REGULATORY AGENCIES
  Communication and remediation
    § 12.28
  Contacting § 12.26
  Handling of § 12.25
  Objectives agreement § 12.30
  Possible violations acknowledgment
    § 12.27
  Role of § 12.25
  Working with "intent" of regulations
    § 12.29
RESCISSION
  Described § 6.22

RESOURCE CONSERVATION AND
RECOVERY ACT (RCRA)
  Generally §§ 1.21, 10.9
  Penalty provisions § 1.27
RESPONSIBLE PROPERTY
TRANSFER ACT
  Generally § 8.21
RESTITUTION
  Generally § 6.15

SECURITIES AND EXCHANGE ACT
OF 1934
  Generally § 6.19
SECURITIES LAW
  Violations § 6.19
SICK BUILDING SYNDROME
  Background assessment § 4.3
  Building reviews § 4.4
  Causes of § 1.35
  Chemical inventory § 4.9
  Complaint documentation § 4.5
  Complaint identification § 4.2
  Contaminant sources § 4.10
  Definition of § 4.1
  Expert selection. See SICK
    BUILDING SYNDROME
    EXPERTS, Selection of
  Generally § 4.21
  Interpretation of data collection and
    results §§ 4.6, 4.8
  Liability and § 5.24
  Project time account, Appendix 4B
  Quantitative analysis § 4.11
  Referral groups Appendix 4A
  Sampling procedures § 4.7
SICK BUILDING SYNDROME
EXPERTS
  Agreement/rate schedule sample
    Appendix 4C
  Analysis § 4.15
  Budgeting § 4.18
  Client education § 4.14
  Depositions § 4.17
  Fees § 4.20
  Interrogatories § 4.16
  Report checklist § 4.19
  Role of § 4.13
  Selection of § 4.12
  Testing § 4.15
SOLID WASTE DISPOSAL ACT
  Generally § 1.11

SPILL COMPENSATION AND
CONTROL ACT
  Generally § 2.2
SPIROMETRY TESTING
  Use of § 4.11
STATE/LOCAL STATUTES
  Generally § 2.1
  Mandatory inspections § 2.6
  California §§ 2.8, 2.15
  Colorado § 2.14
  Massachusetts § 2.12
  Minnesota § 2.3
  New Jersey § 2.2
  New York §§ 2.11, 2.15
  Pennsylvania § 2.9
  Virginia §§ 2.4, 2.13
  Washington, D.C. §§ 2.5, 2.15
STRICT LIABILITY
  Duty to warn § 6.10
  Economic loss § 6.11
  Generally § 6.9
SUPERFUND AMENDMENTS AND
REAUTHORIZATION ACT OF
1986 (SARA)
  Audits and § 8.21
  Building materials exception § 6.6
  De minimus settlements and §§ 1.2,
    11.1
  Due diligence § 7.12
  Generally §§ 1.2, 6.5, 8.5, 8.6
  Innocent landowner defense
    § 7.12
  Notification requirements
    § 12.6
  Protection under § 5.23
  Response actions §§ 6.5, 6.6
  "Response authorities," 1.15
  Statute of limitations § 7.2
SUPERLIENS
  Effect of § 1.19

TAX ASSESSMENT
  Reduction and § 6.26
TEMPERATURE AND HUMIDITY
  Significance of § 4.6
TOBACCO SMOKE
  Legislation and § 2.15
TOXIC SUBSTANCES CONTROL
ACT (TSCA)
  Generally § 1.22
  Notification requirements § 1.33

TOXIC SUBSTANCES CONTROL
  ACT (TSCA) *(Continued)*
    Penalty provisions § 1.29
    Polychlorinated Biphenyls (PCBs)
      and § 3.26
TRACE METALS
  Dangers of § 4.11

UNDERGROUND STORAGE TANKS
  (UST)
    Generally § 1.34

U.S. ENVIRONMENTAL
  PROTECTION AGENCY. See
  ENVIRONMENTAL PROTECTION
  AGENCY (EPA)

WARRANTY OF HABITABILITY
  Defined §§ 5.13, 6.14

X-RAY FLUORESCENCE (XRF)
  Use of § 3.16